PRINCIPLES OF CONFLICT ECONOMICS

Conflict economics contributes to an understanding of violent conflict and peace in two important ways. First, it applies economic concepts and models to help one understand diverse conflict activities such as war, terrorism, genocide, and peace. Second, it treats appropriation as a fundamental economic activity, joining production and exchange as a means of wealth acquisition. Drawing upon more than a half century of scholarship, the book presents important data trends, theoretical models, and empirical results on economic aspects of violent conflicts and peacebuilding efforts worldwide. Although much work in the field is abstract, the book is made accessible to a broad audience of students, scholars, and policymakers from various disciplines by relying on historical data, relatively simple graphs, and intuitive narratives. In exploring the interdependence of economics and conflict, the book presents current perspectives on conflict and peace in novel ways and offers new insights into economic aspects of violence.

Charles H. Anderton received his PhD in economics from Cornell University. He is Professor of economics at the College of the Holy Cross (Worcester, Massachusetts). His course offerings include the economics of war and peace, topics in conflict economics, and genocide: perspectives from the social sciences. Anderton's research on conflict and peace has appeared in journals such as *Economic Inquiry, Journal of Economic Behavior and Organization, International Studies Quarterly, Journal of Conflict Resolution*, and *Journal of Genocide Research*, as well as in the *Handbook of Defense Economics, Volumes I and II*. He co-edited (with Jurgen Brauer), *Economic Aspects of Genocides, Other Mass Atrocities, and Their Prevention* (2016).

John R. Carter received his PhD in economics from Cornell University. He is Professor Emeritus at the College of the Holy Cross (Worcester, Massachusetts). While at Holy Cross, Carter taught a wide range of courses including public choice and political economy, experimental microeconomics, and research methodology. In 1993, Carter received the Holy Cross Distinguished Teaching Award. His research on conflict and peace has appeared in numerous journals and books including *Defence and Peace Economics, Economic Inquiry, Journal of Economic Behavior and Organization*, as well as in the *Handbook of Defense Economics, Volume II*.

Principles of Conflict Economics

The Political Economy of War, Terrorism, Genocide, and Peace

CHARLES H. ANDERTON

College of the Holy Cross

JOHN R. CARTER

College of the Holy Cross

CAMBRIDGE
UNIVERSITY PRESS

CAMBRIDGE
UNIVERSITY PRESS

University Printing House, Cambridge CB2 8BS, United Kingdom

One Liberty Plaza, 20th Floor, New York, NY 10006, USA

477 Williamstown Road, Port Melbourne, VIC 3207, Australia

314–321, 3rd Floor, Plot 3, Splendor Forum, Jasola District Centre,
New Delhi – 110025, India

79 Anson Road, #06–04/06, Singapore 079906

Cambridge University Press is part of the University of Cambridge.

It furthers the University's mission by disseminating knowledge in the pursuit of
education, learning, and research at the highest international levels of excellence.

www.cambridge.org
Information on this title: www.cambridge.org/9781107184206
DOI: 10.1017/9781316875506

First published 2009
Second edition 2019

Printed in the United Kingdom by TJ International Ltd. Padstow Cornwall

A catalogue record for this publication is available from the British Library.

Library of Congress Cataloging-in-Publication Data
Names: Anderton, Charles H., author. | Carter, John R. (John Randall), 1948– author.
Title: Principles of conflict economics : the political economy of war, terrorism, genocide,
and peace / Charles H. Anderton, College of the Holy Cross, John R. Carter, College of the
Holy Cross.
Description: Cambridge, United Kingdom ; New York, NY : Cambridge University Press,
2019. | Includes bibliographical references and index.
Identifiers: LCCN 2018042535 | ISBN 9781107184206 (hardback)
Subjects: LCSH: War – Economic aspects. | Ethnic conflict – Economic aspects. |
Terrorism – Economic aspects. | Peace – Economic aspects.
Classification: LCC HB195 .A549 2019 | DDC 330–dc23
LC record available at https://lccn.loc.gov/2018042535

ISBN 978-1-107-18420-6 Hardback
ISBN 978-1-316-63539-1 Paperback

To our families

Contents

Figures

Tables

Preface and Acknowledgments

Now the earth was corrupt in God's sight and was full of violence.

Genesis 6:11

Throughout history, violent conflict has been a conspicuous aspect of the human experience. In recent decades, terrorism, civil strife, nation-state warfare, genocide, and the proliferation of weapons of mass destruction have dominated the headlines. At first blush it might appear that economics has little to say about such realms of conflict. After all, most economics textbooks restrict their attention to the behavior of consumers, producers, and governments operating peacefully in secure environments. Fortunately, however, the field of conflict economics can contribute greatly to an understanding of conflict and peace in two important ways. First, conflict economics applies the concepts, principles, and methods of economics to the study of diverse conflict and peace activities. Second, conflict economics treats the coercive appropriation of goods and resources as a fundamental economic activity, revealing how conflict both shapes and is shaped by the traditional economic activities of production and trade.

This book provides the reader with an accessible overview of the basic principles and major themes of conflict economics. Following an introduction to the field in Chapter 1, Chapters 2 through 8 survey many of the economic concepts and methods applied in subsequent chapters. These chapters provide numerous applications to conflict and peace topics and will be useful to readers who either have no formal training in economics or would like to review economic principles with a focus on conflict and peace. Chapters 9 through 17 explore major topics in conflict economics including the geography and technology of conflict; the bargaining theory of war and peace; conflict between states; civil war; terrorism; genocide and other mass atrocities; arms rivalry, proliferation, and arms control; alliance behavior; and peace.

These chapters provide a balanced mix of applications, theoretical models, and empirical content. Bibliographic notes are provided at the ends of chapters to help readers who want to pursue topics in greater depth. Five appendixes are also available: a brief primer on weapons technologies, a formal bargaining model of war and peace, matrix algebra methods for solving network models with Excel, an overview of conflict and peace datasets, and a primer on regression analysis.

The book's chapters can be combined in various ways to focus on historically important topics in conflict economics and peace research more generally. For example, following the introductory chapter and coverage of standard production, supply and demand, rational choice, and game theory tools (Chapters 2–5), one could emphasize economic aspects of interstate conflict by including the geography and technology of conflict, the bargaining theory of war and peace, and conflict between states (Chapters 9–11). If one wished to focus upon civil wars, terrorism, or genocide, the same chapters could be followed but with civil wars (Chapter 12), terrorism (Chapter 13), or genocides and other mass atrocities (Chapter 14) substituting for interstate conflict (Chapter 11). A similar approach could be followed if one wished to emphasize security economics in the form of arms rivalry, proliferation, and arms control (Chapter 15) and security alliances (Chapter 16). Across all of these possibilities, one could selectively include new perspectives on conflict and peace available in behavioral economics and the economics of identity (Chapter 6), network economics (Chapter 7), and the integration of conflict and trade at the core of economic analysis (Chapter 8). Moreover, peace (Chapter 17) serves as a valuable capstone to any of these modules.

Given our training and background, the book concentrates on economic aspects of conflict and peace. While we incorporate contributions from various disciplines, especially political science, psychology, and sociology, we defer to specialists in other fields to convey those contributions more thoroughly. Our emphasis on economic aspects of conflict and peace can be valuable to both economists and non-economists. For economists, the book shows numerous ways in which economic methods can be applied to conflict and peace issues. Moreover, the book's treatment of appropriative conflict as a fundamental category of economic activity will help economists reduce the gap that now exists between textbook models of peaceful production and exchange and real economies subject to potential or actual violence. The book should also appeal to those with backgrounds in fields other than economics. Non-economists are naturally drawn to incorporate economic variables in their studies of conflict and peace, and our book offers accessible coverage of such variables from the perspective of the economist. Also, many models and methods central to conflict economics (for example, rational choice theory, game theory, and econometrics) are of growing importance in disciplines other than economics.

Much of the academic work in conflict economics is theoretical and abstract, but we take steps to increase the accessibility of the text. In addition to the overview of economic fundamentals in Chapters 2 through 8, the book contains extensive coverage of conflict and peace data, intuitive narratives, relatively simple algebra and graphs, and summaries of empirical evidence on conflict and peace phenomena. The book should be useful to scholars, policy-makers, and practitioners from a variety of disciplines and backgrounds, including economics, political science, international relations, social psychology, peace studies, military sciences, and public policy. It should likewise be suitable in undergraduate or beginning level graduate courses on the economics of war and peace at universities and military service schools and in training programs on violence prevention, conflict management, postconflict reconstruction, and peacebuilding in government agencies and nonprofit organizations.

The social science literature on conflict is massive. Hence, we are selective in the topics covered, theories emphasized, empirical articles reviewed, and bibliographic notes provided. Most of the empirical articles that we review are selected because they are relatively recent and highlight the importance of economic variables in the analysis of conflict and peace. Thus, we do not necessarily choose seminal empirical studies for review, nor do our summaries of results necessarily reflect ongoing empirical controversies within topic areas. Finally, although the book covers issues pertinent to many contemporary conflicts such as Afghanistan and Syria, we do not attempt to focus the book on current events and policy debates. Instead, our goal is to emphasize principles of conflict economics that will be as useful in exploring conflicts and peaceful outcomes yet to emerge as they are in studying historical and contemporary events.

Over the years, many scholars have shaped our thinking about conflict economics and encouraged our attempts to contribute to the field. We regret that we can mention only a few, but they include Jurgen Brauer, Keith Hartley, Jack Hirshleifer, Michael Intriligator, Walter Isard, and Todd Sandler. We also wish to acknowledge our former students, especially those in experimental microeconomics, economics of war and peace, and topics in conflict economics, from the Department of Economics and Accounting at the College of the Holy Cross. Their questions and comments have contributed greatly to our understanding of pedagogy in general and conflict economics in particular.

We are indebted to Karen Maloney at Cambridge University Press for her steadfast support and advice over the course of the project and to Rachel Blaifeder for her outstanding production work; to several anonymous reviewers for valuable comments on various drafts; to Roxane Anderton for help with citations; to Holy Cross for timely research leaves; and to Katherine Kiel for a generous letter of support. We also benefitted from the insightful comments of Atin Basuchoudhary, Liam Clegg, Patrick Franco, Edward Ryan, and Shikha Silwal on chapter drafts, and from the support and encouragement of our colleagues in the Department of Economics and Accounting at Holy Cross. We also wish to recognize the extraordinary support we received from our friend and colleague, Jurgen Brauer, who read numerous drafts of work in progress and provided many valuable comments. Finally, we are especially grateful to our wives Roxane Anderton and Gloria Carter for their love and understanding, without which this book would not have been possible.

PART I

Introduction

Nature, Scope, and Interdependencies
of Conflict and Economics

For many people in many places, violent or potentially violent conflict is part of the human experience. Headline stories of terrorism, civil strife, nation-state hostilities, genocide, refugee flows, and proliferation of weapons of mass destruction document the prevalence of conflict as a distressing fact of life. Less dramatic indications of conflict include deadbolt locks, gated residential communities, electronic security systems, identity theft, and handgun sales, to name a few. At first blush, it might appear that economics has little if anything to say about life's harsher side. Economics textbooks typically restrict their attention to the peaceful behavior of consumers, producers, and governments in the marketplace. Thus, it might seem that potential and actual violence over resources, goods, political power, and ideology lie outside the domain of economics. But this is a misperception, as is demonstrated by the well-established yet often ignored field of conflict economics.

1.1 What Is Conflict Economics?

Conflict economics has two defining characteristics. First, it maintains that the concepts, principles, and methods of economics can be fruitfully applied to the study of violent conflicts and their prevention. Thus, diverse phenomena like war, terrorism, genocide, and peace are analyzed and understood as outcomes of purposeful choices responsive to changes in underlying incentives. As just one example, economics explains how consumers shift purchases from one good (say orange juice) toward another (say grape juice) when the price of one rises relative to the other. Similar economic forces are at work in many conflict settings: when one type of weapon is constrained by arms control, another type is substituted; when political targets are hardened, terrorists turn to less costly civilian targets; and when genocide perpetrators find a village protected by peacekeeping troops, they turn to unprotected villages to destroy civilians.

But conflict economics is more than the application of economics to conflict and peace. It also involves a reconstruction of the core of economic theory to take account of conflict. Conflict of the sort considered in this book ultimately involves intended or realized appropriation, where the term "appropriation" refers to a taking that rests on force or the threat of force. As its second defining characteristic, conflict economics treats appropriation as a fundamental economic activity, joining production and exchange as a means of acquiring wealth. Traditional economic models assume that economic behavior is peaceful. Yet in real economies, conflicts over goods and resources abound. Conflict economics seeks to close this gap between theory and reality. Thus, a range of appropriative activities has been modeled including resource conflicts, piracy, cyber insecurity, and extortion. These models reveal how conflict both shapes and is shaped by the traditional economic activities of production and exchange.

For the purposes of this book, we define conflict economics as, first, the study of violent or potentially violent conflicts, violence prevention, and peacebuilding using the concepts, principles, and methods of economics and, second, the development of economic models of appropriation and its interaction with production and exchange activities. By including the qualifier that conflict on some level be violent or potentially violent, the definition intentionally excludes analysis of ordinary market competition and, more tentatively, activities like litigation and rent seeking. Clearly included by the definition is the study of what might be called macro conflicts, comprising interstate hostilities (for example, war between states), intrastate conflict (for example, civil war, domestic terrorism), extrastate hostilities between states and external nonstate actors (for example, colonial wars, international terrorism), nonstate conflicts among nonstate actors (for example, drug cartel wars, wars between ethnic groups), and genocides and mass killings in which relatively defenseless civilians are purposely targeted for destruction by states or nonstate groups. Also included is the study of micro conflicts, meaning conflict among private persons and organizations (for example, human trafficking, gang warfare, cybercrime). Finally, the definition encompasses a variety of actors that promote nonviolent approaches to conflicts and foster peaceful outcomes among potential or actual disputants. In the next section, we begin to document empirically the enormity of conflict in the human experience, as well as efforts to promote peace.

1.2 A Look at Conflict and Peace Large and Small

Macro Conflicts: Wars, Terrorism, and Mass Atrocities

Figure 1.1 shows the frequency of interstate, intrastate, extrastate, and nonstate war onsets from 1820 to 2017. War onsets are wars initiated during the time periods indicated. Figure 1.1 shows that there were 663 war onsets of all types in the world from 1820 to 2017. About half the wars were intrastate (348), followed by extrastate (153), interstate (95), and nonstate (67). Figure 1.1 also shows that, over the past six decades, intrastate wars have become more frequent relative to earlier decades, while extrastate wars have diminished significantly.

Figure 1.2 depicts the worldwide frequency of international and domestic terrorist incidents combined for the period 1970 to 2016. Domestic terrorism "is perpetrated within the boundaries of a given nation by nationals from that nation," while international terrorism involves "the interests and/or nationals of more than one country" (LaFree, Dugan, Fogg, and Scott 2006, pp. 5 and 22). Figure 1.2 suggests two observations. First, there was a general increase in the number of terrorist incidents from the 1970s into the early 1990s. Second, terrorist incidents around the globe exploded in the second decade of the twenty-first century reaching the unprecedented level of 16,840 attacks in 2014 (an average of 46 attacks per day).

Wars and terrorism are disturbing enough, but imagine powerful destructive forces of states or nonstate groups directed to the purposeful elimination of large numbers of civilians. Genocide is the intentional destruction of a specifically identified people-group, in whole or in part. Genocide is sometimes distinguished from mass killing where, for the latter, perpetrators do not intend to eliminate the group or those targeted for elimination cannot be clearly identified as part of a specific group (Waller 2007, p. 14). We use the term "mass atrocity" to encompass genocides, mass killings, and other forms of intentional large-scale destruction of civilians. Figure 1.3 shows the stock (or number per year) of state-perpetrated mass atrocities in which at least 1,000 civilians were killed since 1900 (measured on the left axis). Also shown is the number of "low-level" attacks against civilians (fatalities per attack as "low" as five) since 1995 by states and nonstate actors such as rebels and militia groups (measured on the right

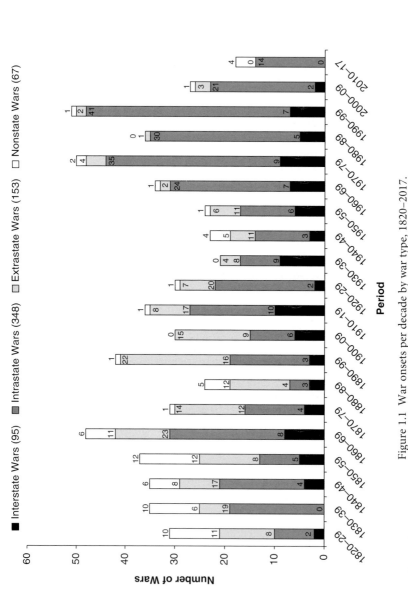

Figure 1.1 War onsets per decade by war type, 1820–2017.

Note: Correlates of War (COW), Uppsala Conflict Data Program (UCDP), and International Peace Research Institute, Oslo (PRIO) definitions of interstate, extrastate, and civil war (a form of intrastate war) are similar. Definitions and categorizations of wars between nonstate actors differ across COW and UCDP/PRIO.

Sources: Sarkees and Wayman (2010) for 1820–2007 COW data; Uppsala Conflict Data Program (2017); and Gleditsch, Wallenstein, Eriksson, et al. (2002) for 2008–17 data.

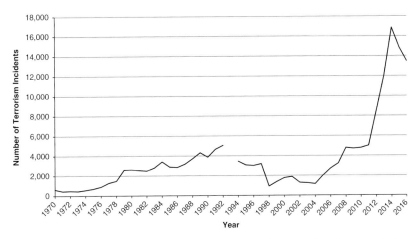

Figure 1.2 International and domestic terrorist incidents combined, 1970–2016.
Note: Data for 1993 are missing.
Source: Global Terrorism Database (2017).

axis). Following the destruction of Jews and other people-groups during the Holocaust (1933–45), many scholars and policymakers said "never again"; Figure 1.3 and the more extensive data presented in Chapter 14 reveal that humanity has fallen gravely short of achieving that goal.

Although scholars distinguish interstate, intrastate, extrastate, and non-state conflict, as well as war, terrorism, and mass atrocity, some conflicts fit multiple categories. For example, according to Mabon (2016), about 60 factions have been involved in the 2010s Syrian civil conflict, with many fighting each other as well as the Syrian government. Moreover, many external actors tapped into various factions to bring their own influence to the conflict including nonstate actors such as the Islamic State of Iraq and Syria (ISIS) and Hezbollah, and states such as Iran, Russia, Saudi Arabia, Turkey, and the USA. Indeed, the various conflicts encompassing the Syrian case are so multiactored and multifaceted that virtually all of the macro conflict types (wars of various types, terrorism, mass atrocities) relevant to conflict economics have been on horrific display.

Micro Conflicts: Human Trafficking, Gang Warfare, and Cybercrime

Human trafficking, gang warfare, and cybercrime are but a few examples of appropriation possibilities at work in modern economies at the micro

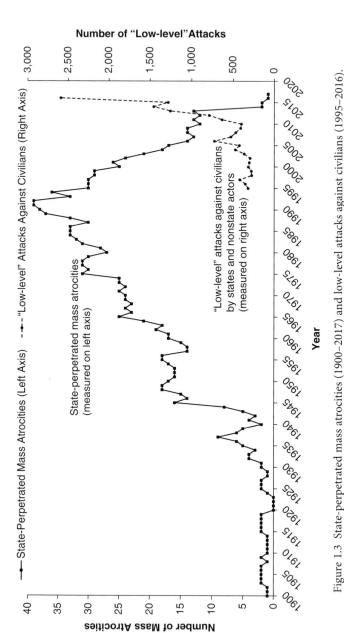

Figure 1.3 State-perpetrated mass atrocities (1900–2017) and low-level attacks against civilians (1995–2016).

Sources: Easterly, Gatti, and Kurlat (2006), Ulfelder and Valentino (2008), Marshall, Gurr, and Harff (2017), and Ulfelder (2017) for mass atrocity data. Schrodt and Ulfelder (2016) for data on low-level attacks against civilians.

level, that is, among private persons and organizations. Human trafficking is "a worldwide form of exploitation in which men, women, and children are bought, sold, and held against their will in slave-like conditions" (United States Government Accountability Office 2006, p. 1). According to the United States Department of Homeland Security (2017), "human trafficking generates many billions of dollars of profit per year, second only to drug trafficking as the most profitable form of transnational crime." Estimates of the number of people held captive in slavery worldwide range from 20.9 million (End Slavery Now 2017) to 45.8 million (Freedom United 2017).

The US Department of Justice (USDOJ) characterizes a gang as an "association of three or more individuals . . . whose members collectively identify themselves by adopting a group identity . . . [and] engage in criminal activity and . . . violence or intimidation to further its criminal objectives" (National Gang Intelligence Center 2015, p. 4). There are currently some 33,000 gangs operating in the USA and tens of thousands of gangs operating in other countries (Federal Bureau of Investigation 2017, Hazen and Rodgers 2014). Along with "identity benefits" accruing to people who join gangs, gangs seek profits from criminal activities such as drug trafficking, human trafficking, and financial crimes (National Gang Intelligence Center 2015). The USDOJ's definition of gang is intended to exclude international organized crime groups, but some gangs operate in more than one country, conduct activities in conjunction with crime syndicates, and evolve over time into organized crime groups (Smith, Rush, and Burton 2013).

Table 1.1 summarizes characteristics of selected gangs and organized crime groups. Most operate in more than one country, and a few function in ten or more. Although the activities of most gangs and organized crime groups do not usually appear in social science datasets on war or mass atrocity, the harms they perpetrate are often characterized as war or atrocity by those living through the violence. For example, an Independent Lens documentary states that in "South Central Los Angeles, more than 15,000 people have died in a four-decade civil war between two of America's most notorious street gangs: the Crips and the Bloods" (Public Broadcasting Service 2017a). According to Insight Crime (2017), the criminal activities of MS-13 (Mara Salvatrucha) "have helped make the Northern Triangle – Guatemala, El Salvador, and Honduras – the most violent place in the world that is not at war." Furthermore, data provided by the Mexican government show that more than 160,000 Mexicans were victims of homicide between 2007 and 2014, with many

Table 1.1 *Selected gangs and organized crime groups.*

Gang or Crime Group	Country, City of Origin	Selected Countries of Operation	Selected Criminal Activities
Bloods	USA, Los Angeles	Canada, USA	Drug trafficking, robbery, murder, prostitution
Crips	USA, Los Angeles	USA	Drug trafficking, robbery, murder, prostitution
MS-13 (Mara Salvatrucha)	USA, Los Angeles	Canada, El Salvador, Guatemala, Honduras, Mexico, USA	Drug trafficking, human trafficking, extortion
Hammerskins	USA, Dallas	Australia, Canada, France, Germany, Hungary, Italy, Portugal, Spain, Sweden, Switzerland, USA	Harassment, beatings, murder, vandalism
14K Triad	China, Guangzhou	Australia, Belgium, Canada, China, France, Malaysia, Philippines, Thailand, UK, USA	Human trafficking, identity theft, money laundering, extortion, prostitution
Asociación Ñeta	Puerto Rico, Rio Piedras	Puerto Rico, Spain, USA	Drug trafficking, murder, rape, extortion
Sinaloa Cartel	Mexico, Culiacán	Argentina, Brazil, Chile, Colombia, El Salvador, Guatemala, Honduras, Mexico, Nicaragua, Panama, Peru, Philippines, USA	Drug trafficking, murder, kidnapping, money laundering
Los Zetas Cartel	Mexico	Colombia, Costa Rica, Guatemala, El Salvador, Honduras, Mexico, Nicaragua, Panama, Peru, USA	Drug trafficking, human trafficking, arms trafficking, assassination, murder, money laundering
Yakuza	Japan	Japan, USA	Drug trafficking, human trafficking, arms trafficking, extortion

Table 1.2 *Identity theft in the USA, 2008–17.*

Year	Number of Identity Theft Victims (in millions)	Amount Stolen (in billions of USA $)
2008	12.5	28.9
2009	13.9	31.4
2010	10.2	19.9
2011	11.6	18.0
2012	12.6	20.9
2013	13.1	18.0
2014	12.7	16.0
2015	13.1	15.3
2016	15.4	16.0
2017	16.7	16.8

Source: Javelin Strategy & Research (2018).

deaths caused by Mexican drug cartels (Public Broadcasting Service 2017b). These examples serve as a reminder that "micro conflict" does not mean small-scale conflict, but conflict among private persons and organizations, which can be quite large indeed.

Cybercrime involves the use of computer technologies to conduct illegal activities including computer theft of proprietary business or government information, credit card numbers, and personal identities. Table 1.2 focuses upon identity theft in the USA from 2008 to 2017. The second column shows that the number of identity theft victims in the USA was more than 10 million for each year of the series. Shown in column 3 is the amount stolen by identity thieves. Although Table 1.2 focuses on one type of cyberattack as a form of micro conflict, we will see in later chapters that cyberattack and defense technologies are growing in importance in macro conflicts involving states and nonstate groups.

Peace Efforts Large and Small

Numerous governments, intergovernmental organizations (IGOs), international nongovernmental organizations (INGOs), and local nongovernmental organizations (NGOs) allocate resources to promote peace in the world. Table 1.3 shows the number of worldwide multilateral peace

Table 1.3 *Multilateral peace missions by intergovernmental organizations,*
2007–16.

Year	No. of Missions, United Nations	No. of Missions, Regional Organizations	No. of Missions, Ad Hoc Coalitions	No. of Deployed Personnel Across All IGO Missions
2007	22	33	6	169,467
2008	23	31	6	187,586
2009	21	27	6	219,278
2010	20	26	6	262,842
2011	20	26	6	262,129
2012	20	27	6	233,642
2013	21	28	8	201,232
2014	22	30	10	162,052
2015	20	31	10	162,703
2016	22	33	6	169,467

Source: Stockholm International Peace Research Institute (various years).

missions conducted by IGOs from 2007 to 2016. Column 2 shows the number of such missions conducted by the United Nations, while column 3 does the same for regional organizations such as the African Union, European Union, and Organization of Security and Cooperation in Europe. Column 4 shows the number of missions conducted by ad hoc coalitions. Finally, column 5 shows the number of personnel (that is, military troops, police, civilian staff) deployed by these missions. There was a substantial surge in the number of deployed personnel for peace missions from 2007 to 2010, followed by an equally dramatic decline from 2011 to 2014. The primary reason for the large swings in personnel was the reinforcement of and subsequent drawdown of personnel associated with the North Atlantic Treaty Organization's (NATO) International Security Assistance Force (ISAF) in Afghanistan.

Even as IGOs have come to pay greater attention in recent years to local conditions where they operate, peacekeeping efforts by large multilateral organizations tend to have a top-down or macro perspective on conflict prevention and postconflict peacebuilding because much of their work is channeled through national leaders and governments of host states (see, for example, Marriage 2016 and Myerson 2016). Meanwhile, many NGOs and INGOs allocate resources to promote peace in numerous locales

Table 1.4 *Selected NGOs and INGOs promoting peace in Afghanistan, Iraq, and Syria, 2017.*

Organization	Type	Summary of Organization's Work
Afghanistan		
Afghan Development Association	Local NGO	Provides peacebuilding and conflict resolution projects
Cooperation for Peace and Unity	Local NGO	Fosters sustainable cultures of peace through peacebuilding and peace education programs
Concordis International	INGO	Increases public participation in political processes and supports civil society peacebuilding
War Child	INGO	Supports children who have suffered in conflict
WomanKind Worldwide	INGO	Helps integrate women into social and political processes
Iraq		
Center for Peace and Conflict Resolution	Local NGO	The only degree program [at University of Duhok] in Iraq dedicated to the emerging theory and practice of peacebuilding
Muslim Peacemaker Teams	Local NGO	Uses nonviolent methods to support communities struggling with violence
Danish Refugee Council	INGO	Fosters protection and durable solutions for displaced populations
International Center for Transitional Justice	INGO	Advises Iraqis on accountability and justice options
Islamic Relief	INGO	Provides emergency support to people affected by conflict
Syria		
Badael Foundation	Local NGO	Strengthens civil society groups and NGOs that promote nonviolence
Project Amal ou Salam	Local NGO	Empowers Syria's children to rebuild their country and work for peace
Carter Center	INGO	Promotes conflict resolution, democracy, disease prevention, and mental healthcare
Catholic Relief Services	INGO	Assists displaced people by providing shelter, clean water, food, hygiene, medicine, and education
Centre for Humanitarian Dialogue	INGO	Mediation organization engaged in a political dialogue initiative to address circumstances in Syria

Note: Some of the summaries of each organization's work are quoted from Peace Direct (2017a).
Source: Peace Direct (2017a).

around the globe, which is often bottom-up or micro-oriented peace work. Table 1.4 is a selection of such organizations operating in Afghanistan, Iraq, and Syria in 2017. The organizations in Table 1.4, though small in number, represent a variety of efforts to promote peace and development including peacebuilding, conflict resolution, advancement of the rights of women and children, support for people affected by conflict, and strengthening of civil society. Consider also that the organizations in Table 1.4 represent a small sample of NGOs and INGOs operating in the three countries. According to Peace Direct (2017a), the total number of NGOs and INGOs operating in each of the three countries in 2017 was: Afghanistan (50), Iraq (37), and Syria (more than 800).

The conflicts, predatory appropriations and associated defense efforts, and peace activities shown in Figures 1.1–1.3 and Tables 1.1–1.4 represent the primary subject matter in conflict economics. In the chapters that follow, we delve deeply into the economic aspects of many of these forms of conflict and their prevention, while also paying attention to important noneconomic considerations.

1.3 Conflict and Peace over Time and Geographic Space

Conflict and Peace Life Cycle

Many of the conflicts studied in this book pass through phases as shown by Lund's (1996) life-cycle diagram in Figure 1.4.* The conflict in question may be interstate, intrastate, extrastate, nonstate, or genocidal. The bell-shaped curve represents the course of a prototypical conflict as hostility rises and falls over time. The vertical axis marks levels of peace and conflict beginning with durable peace and rising successively to stable peace, unstable peace, crisis, and war. Around the outside of the curve are terms used for third-party interventions at various stages of a conflict. The "P series" (preventive diplomacy, peacemaking, and so on) is typically used in discussions associated with the United Nations, while the "C series" (conflict prevention, conflict management, and so on) is used in the scholarly literature (Lund 1996, p. 385). The arrows along the curve show that violence can be prevented, escalate, or recur.

---

* Parts of this subsection are adapted from Charles H. Anderton and John R. Carter's article "A Survey of Peace Economics," published in *Handbook of Defense Economics, Volume 2* edited by Todd Sandler and Keith Hartley, pp. 1211–58, Copyright © Elsevier 2007. We gratefully acknowledge Elsevier's permission to republish material from the article.

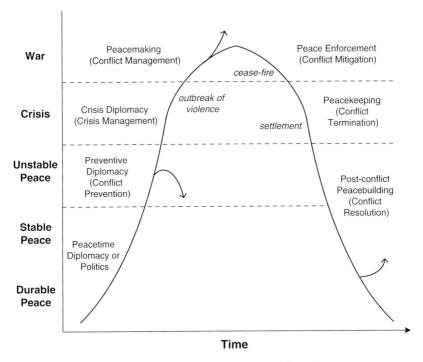

Figure 1.4 Lund's conflict and peace life cycle.
Source: Adapted from Lund (1996).

In numerous places in this book we focus on the upper portion of the conflict and peace cycle corresponding to the outbreak and then termination of violence. Moving initially upward along the curve, we would like to know risk factors for the onset of violent conflicts. Moving down the curve to the right, we are interested in elements that contribute to cessation of hostilities. In other parts of the book we focus on the lower left and lower right portions of the conflict cycle corresponding to conflict prevention and postconflict peacebuilding, respectively. Just as we are interested in factors that lead to the onset of violent conflicts, we would also like to know how peace processes begin before and during hostilities and what factors allow peace to "win out" over violence. Moreover, as noted earlier, states and regions can be involved in conflicts at the same time with each operating on its own portion of the conflict cycle. Multiple conflicts lead to waves of conflict cycles following their respective paths, but also intermingling with one another in ways that can create dynamic instabilities and long-lasting conflict.

The "Danger Zone" for Violent Conflicts in Global Society

In recent decades, violent conflicts across the globe have tended to cluster in geographic space. Barnett (2004) offers a simplified dichotomy of the world into "functioning core" and "nonintegrating gap" states. Functioning core states generally have well-developed political and economic systems and are integrated with the rest of the world though trade, technology, and international organizations. Nonintegrating gap states, however, tend to have nondemocratic political systems, under-performing economies, colonial legacies, and weak integration with the rest of the world. According to Barnett, most of the gap states in the world are located in Central and South America, Africa, the Middle East, and Asian states in the 10/40 window (that is, between 10 and 40 degrees north of the equator). There are obviously exceptions to this characterization (for example, Botswana is quite healthy economically and politically), but Barnett's point is that a preponderance of the world's violent conflicts (for example, about 80–5 percent of wars), peacekeeping efforts (for example, about 85–90 percent of IGO peace missions), sources of refugees and internally displaced persons (more than 90 percent), and bases for international terrorist organizations are located in gap states.

A great challenge for gap states is that they can become ensnared in "conflict and poverty traps" in which economic underdevelopment and political weakness elevate the risk of violent conflict and violent conflict keeps individuals and states economically underdeveloped and politically weak (Collier 2007). Furthermore, peace efforts to break out of conflict and poverty traps are especially challenging because they require sustained and coordinated progress across numerous domains (for example, economic, political, military, social, legal, local, and regional) and actors (for example, families; communities; local, regional, and national leaders; mediators; NGOs, INGOs, and IGOs; and representatives from other states).

1.4 Methodologies of Conflict Economics

Interdependencies between Conflict and Economics

Conflict and economics combine naturally in six distinct ways that we draw on throughout the book. The six key interdependencies are summarized by the numbered boxes in Figure 1.5, while the lower boxes provide additional information.

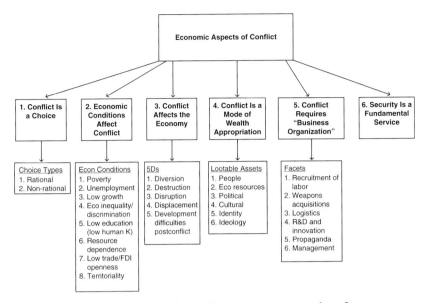

Figure 1.5 Interdependencies between economics and conflict.

Conflict Is a Choice

The first box in Figure 1.5 indicates that conflict is a choice. Economics is defined as the study of choices that people make under conditions of scarcity. Because conflict involves choices among various violent and nonviolent alternatives, the concepts, principles, and models of economics apply directly to conflict and peace activities. The subsidiary box shows that choices can arise from rational (narrowly defined cost/benefit calculations) and nonrational motives (for example, psychological and social elements).

Economic Conditions Affect Conflict

Box 2 in Figure 1.5 indicates that economic conditions affect conflict. As will be documented later in the book, empirical studies have found that economic conditions such as poverty, high unemployment, low growth, concentrations of natural resources (for example, oil, precious metals, diamonds), and low trade openness can affect the risk and seriousness of violent conflicts. On the flip side, economic conditions going the other way (for example, low poverty and strong growth) are often found to be correlated with peace.

Conflict Affects the Economy

The third box in Figure 1.5 states that conflict affects the economy. The subsidiary box indicates that the economic effects occur through five major channels, which we call the "5 Ds." "Diversion of resources" is the allocation of labor, capital, and natural resources to produce weapons and recruit and train soldiers. Violence leads to the "destruction of people and property" including people killed and injured and damage to buildings, roads, and land. "Disruption of economic activities" involves conflict's alteration and often diminishment of economic processes including trade, investment in physical and human capital, economic growth, regional and local markets, and household work. The movement of people within and across nations (that is, refugees and internally displaced persons or IDPs) owing to conflict can be thought of as a form of disruption. Given the economic significance of and trauma to people on the move, we break out such disruption into its own category: "displacement." Finally, "development difficulties after conflict" represent the immense challenges of reconstructing a postwar or postgenocide society. The next two figures and two tables provide some sense of the nature and magnitude of the economic costs of conflict as represented by the "Ds."

Figure 1.6 shows real (inflation-adjusted) military expenditures for several nations in selected years in the 1990s, 2000s, and 2010s. Military expenditures serve as a proxy for the direct diversion of resources associated with potential or actual conflict. The years 1992 and 1997 reflect conditions following the end of both the Cold War rivalry between the USA and the USSR in 1989 and the 1990/91 Gulf War. The decline in real military spending for the USA and Russia from 1992 to 1997 is consistent with a hoped for "peace dividend" following the Cold War. The years 2002, 2007, 2012, and 2017 follow major conflict events including the September 11, 2001 terrorist attacks in the USA, the USA-led coalition wars against Iraq (2003–11) and Afghanistan (2001–14), the 2010s Syrian conflict, and the rise of ISIS in the Middle East. The substantial increases in real military spending by the USA and Russia since 1997 imply that the peace dividend period was short-lived. Figure 1.6 also shows dramatic increases in real military spending for China, India, and Iran since 1992. The increases for China and India partly reflect tensions in South Asia such as maritime resource disputes, but also the striking increases in economic growth for the two nations, especially China (Furuoka, Oishi, and Karim 2016; Ali and Dimitraki 2014). Keeping in mind that China's real military spending data are divided by ten for 2007, 2012, and 2017, real military spending increased from $27.2 billion in 1992 to $228.2 billion in 2017

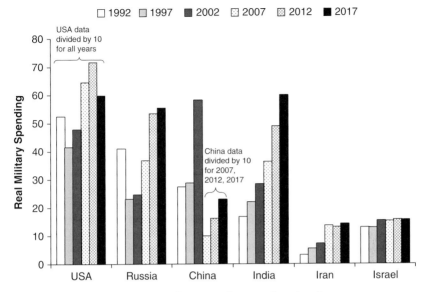

Figure 1.6 Real military spending in selected nations.
Note: In billions of USA dollars at constant 2016 prices and exchange rates.
Source: Stockholm International Peace Research Institute (2018).

(about an eight-fold increase) during a period in which China's real GDP grew about nine-fold (World Bank 2018). Meanwhile, India's real military spending grew almost four-fold and Iran's almost five-fold from 1992 to 2017. Finally, over the same period, Israel's real military spending grew about 20 percent.

Estimates of the destruction of human and physical assets for selected states involved in World War II are presented in Table 1.5. The table shows the destruction of human lives as a percent of the working age population and the destruction of physical assets as a percent of national wealth (or industry fixed assets for Germany and Italy). Human destruction ranged from 1 percent for the UK and USA to as high as 19 percent for the USSR. Physical asset destruction ranged from zero percent for the USA to 25 percent for the USSR and Japan.

Figure 1.7 shows the USA's real merchandise trade (exports plus imports) with Germany and Japan before, during, and after World War II. Notice how trade is driven to zero or near zero during the war and rebounds with the restoration of peace. Figure 1.7 is but one example of how conflict disrupts economic activity, in this case trade.

Table 1.5 *Destruction of human and physical assets during World War II.*

Country	Percent of human assets destroyed	Percent of physical assets destroyed
United Kingdom	1.0	5.0
USA	1.0	0.0
Soviet Union	18.5	25.0
Germany	9.0	17.0
Italy	1.0	10.0
Japan	6.0	25.0

Source: Harrison (2000, p. 37).

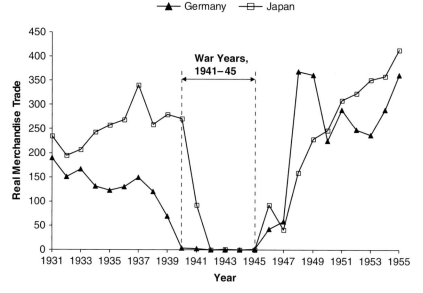

Figure 1.7 USA's real merchandise trade with Germany and Japan.
Notes: In millions of USA dollars at 1913 prices. Data for Germany from 1952 through 1955 are for West Germany only.
Source: Anderton and Carter (2003, pp. 302–3).

Another important cost of conflict is the displacement of people in the form of refugees and internally displaced persons (IDPs). Refugees are "people who are outside their countries because of a well-founded fear of persecution based on their race, religion, nationality, political opinion or

Table 1.6 *Number of refugees and IDPs at the beginning of 2017 for selected nations (in millions).*

Country	No. of Refugees	No. of IDPs	Total (Refugees+ IDPs)	Refugees+IDPs as Percent of Population
Afghanistan	2.50	1.80	4.3	12.4
Central African Rep.	0.49	0.41	0.9	19.6
Colombia	0.31	7.41	7.7	15.9
Iraq	0.32	3.60	3.9	10.5
Somalia	1.01	1.56	2.6	18.0
South Sudan	1.44	1.85	3.3	26.9
Sudan	0.65	2.23	2.9	7.3
Syria	5.52	6.33	11.9	64.3
Ukraine	0.24	1.80	2.0	4.5
Yemen	0.02	2.03	2.0	7.4

Sources: United Nations High Commissioner for Refugees (2017, pp. 12–16) and World Bank (2018).

membership in a particular social group, and who cannot or do not want to return home" (United Nations High Commissioner for Refugees 2006a, p. 6). IDPs are "civilians, mostly women and children, who have been forced to abandon their homes because of conflict or persecution" but continue to reside in their own countries (United Nations High Commissioner for Refugees 2006b, pp. 5–6). Displaced populations can arise for different reasons, but violent conflict constitutes a major cause. Table 1.6 shows the number of refugees and IDPs at the beginning of 2017 for ten countries as well as the percentage of each country's population in flight as refugees and IDPs. Note that Syria had close to 12 million of its people (64.3 percent of its population) on the run as refugees and IDPs in 2017.

The costs associated with serious conflicts typically lead to substantial development difficulties after conflict. In postconflict societies, return to local, regional, and national economic stability and growth requires reestablishing security for individuals and families (for example, protection from violence, food and water security, access to shelter and healthcare); rebuilding infrastructure (for example, roads, bridges, power plants); reviving community social bonds, education, and markets; restoring and perhaps revamping legal and political institutions both locally and nationally; and repairing international linkages (for example, diplomacy, trade, foreign investment, aid). Such reconstitution is immensely challenging for three major reasons. First, numerous actors with a variety of interests will have a stake in how a postconflict society moves forward including families, businesses, and communities; local, regional, and national political, religious, and cultural leaders; local and international aid organizations; foreign states; and former combatants and contesting groups. Second, numerous organizations (private and governmental) will bring their own programs to bear in how the society moves forward. Such efforts can work at cross purposes and pay too little attention to local actors on how to reconstitute society (Myerson 2016). Third, reconstitution efforts can inadvertently entrench the interests of powerful elites within postconflict societies, including former combatants (Marriage 2016). When such entrenchment occurs, the risk of conflict recurrence is high.

Conflict Is a Mode of Wealth Appropriation

Box 4 in Figure 1.5 indicates that conflict is a mode of wealth appropriation. The additional box shows a selection of "lootable assets," that is, assets that can be appropriated by state and nonstate actors through force. As we will see in later chapters, most interstate and civil wars involve contestation over territory (for example, land, borders, maritime areas, islands) or other resources (for example, oil, diamonds, precious metals, timber) in which some agents seek to enrich themselves through threatened or actual violence. Moreover, in virtually all genocides an in-group seeks to enrich itself at the expense of one or more out-groups. Hence, victims of genocide often have their assets (for example, homes, land, and valuables) including their own personhoods looted by perpetrators (that is, they are enslaved, raped, and/or killed). Although some of the items over which people fight are physical (for example, land, oil, and islands), it is important to recognize that violent conflicts in human affairs can arise over disputes related to nonphysical items such as identity and ideology (Boulding 1962, ch. 14).

Conflict Requires "Business Organization"

The fifth box in Figure 1.5 indicates that conflict perpetration requires "business organization." When a state or nonstate group initiates or threatens violence, whether for offensive or defensive reasons, it becomes a violence-producing (or threatening) organization. As such, it must operate according to certain business principles to be viable. If it fails to do so, it will cease to exist; that is, it will "go out of business." For example, suppose leaders from an aggrieved ethnic group form a rebel organization to contest the state government with threatened or actual violence. Much like for-profit or nonprofit organizations just starting out, the rebel organization will need to have a revenue stream to cover its costs of operation including costs of recruiting, training, and feeding soldiers and support personnel; costs of weapons and materiel for waging war; costs associated with information and intelligence; and logistical costs (for example, creation of supply lines and communications systems).

Security of People and Property Is a Fundamental Service
The sixth box in Figure 1.5 points to security as a fundamental service for an economy to provide. Individuals acquire many goods and services (for example, food, clothing, clean water, healthcare, and entertainment), but there is one particularly important service that people desire but that virtually all economics textbooks ignore: security. Nineteenth-century political economist Nassau Senior ([1836] 1965, p. 75) characterized security as "the most important of all services." If security of people and property do not exist in a society, many other economic processes will be stunted in their developments (for example, markets, investments in future technologies, economic growth). On the flip side, when people and property are secure, peaceful economic discourse typically ensues. Standard economics textbooks simply assert that security and peace exist; the models and theories built upon such assertions are well-behaved, but often unrealistic. This book, in contrast, assumes that economic actors must allocate resources to create security and peace; they cannot simply be taken for granted.

Rationality and Equilibrium

Like other scholarly disciplines, economics is distinguished by its analytical concepts and organizing principles. Analytical concepts are just terms that categorize and refer to abstract aspects of the phenomena studied. Examples already encountered here include production, trade, and poverty. Organizing principles are the systematic and general means by which the analytical pieces are brought together to yield explanations and predictions. Paramount in economics are the organizing principles of rationality and equilibrium. Actors are assumed to be rational, meaning that they have consistent preferences and choose the best from a set of feasible alternatives available to them. The choices in turn are assumed to adjust and combine in ways that yield equilibrium outcomes. An equilibrium is a coordination among the actors' choices so that no single actor has an incentive to change its choice. For example, a market is said to be in equilibrium when the quantity that consumers want to buy just balances the quantity that producers want to sell at the current price.

The rationality assumption has been subject to criticism, sometimes from within economics but more often from the other social sciences. Here we are content to make two points. First, in this book we often assume that groups (including nations) behave as if they have well-defined preferences. We believe this assumption is useful in many cases, but it is not without problems as documented in economics, political science, psychology, and sociology. Second, the assumption of rationality by itself says nothing about either the origin or the content of preferences. The formation of preferences of violence-producing individuals and organizations is an important question studied by a variety of disciplines including economics. For example, the field of behavioral economics builds upon insights into human decision-making from economics and psychology to explain why individuals' preferences can deviate from those assumed in standard rational choice theory. A second field that has offered important refinements to standard rational choice theory is identity economics, which builds upon insights into human decision-making from economics and sociology. In this book we will often take the preferences of individuals and organizations as given, which is a common approach in economic analysis. At other times, however, we will explore how preferences can change in conflict and peace settings, sometimes quickly and with dramatic consequences.

Quantitative Methods

Economics, like other social sciences, requires interplay between theory and observation, or in practice, between models and empirical tests. The models tend to be mathematical, because the organizing principles of rationality and equilibrium are themselves mathematical. Rationality is formalized as a constrained optimization problem, whereby an actor maximizes an objective (for example, territory controlled) subject to one or more constraints. Equilibrium is a solution to a set of simultaneous equations. Fortunately, the logic of models can often be conveyed verbally together with relatively straightforward algebra and graphs. Because the outcomes of conflict or peace depend on the choices of multiple actors, there arises strategic interdependence, meaning that the best choice for one actor depends on the choices of others. To allow for this interdependence, conflict models are often constructed using the principles of game theory and networking theory. Again, the basics of game theory and networking theory can be presented with relatively modest demands in mathematics.

Conflict models are tested empirically using standard methods of statistical inference. The sources of data for various forms of conflict have grown rapidly in this age of information. Large panels of cross-country data over time now permit scholars to conduct epidemiological studies, wherein the risks of interstate, intrastate, extrastate, nonstate, and mass atrocity conflicts are estimated based on socioeconomic and geopolitical variables, much like studies in medicine estimate risk factors for cancer and other diseases. Most of the data used in studies of conflict are naturally occurring, meaning that they result from historical events and are collected and disseminated by various organizations. With the growth of game theoretic models of conflict, data are also being generated with increasing frequency using experimental methods in controlled laboratory settings.

Multidisciplinary Nature of Conflict Economics

Conflict activities generally have important political, psychological, and sociological aspects, not to mention significant historical and cultural roots. The central purpose of conflict economics is to better understand the "economic" nature, causes, and consequences of conflict and violence prevention. But conflict economics is informed by other disciplines. At numerous places in this book we draw on literature from political science, psychology, sociology, and history. Furthermore, at times we bring a "political economy" perspective to the study of conflict and peace. There is no agreed upon definition of political economy but, when applied to conflict and peace, we view it as a diagnostic lens for analyzing the political, security, economic, historical, and cultural factors that shape the interests, incentives, and constraints of various actors and stakeholders involved in potential or actual violent conflict (Wennmann 2011, p. 9).

1.5 Organization of the Book

This book is a gateway into conflict economics for economists and non-economists alike. We have defined conflict economics as the economic analysis of violent or potentially violent conflicts, violence prevention, and peacebuilding together with the development of models of appropriation. The remainder of the book is organized in accordance with this definition.

Part I (Chapter 1) is this chapter's overview of the nature, scope, and interdependencies of conflict and economics, which permeate the book.

Part II (Chapters 2–8) provides grounding in crucial concepts and models for the economic analysis of conflict and peace, which are contextualized with numerous historical and contemporary applications. Chapters 2 through 5, respectively, provide grounding in standard economics principles of production, demand and supply, rational choice, and game theory, which are used throughout the book. Chapter 6 highlights how concepts from behavioral economics and identity economics can be integrated with standard economics principles to shed novel insights into why violence occurs and how it can be prevented. Chapter 7 turns to a relatively new area of economic analysis, namely, network economics, with applications to conflict and peace. Chapter 8 is an advanced chapter that integrates conflict into a standard economic model of production and trade. The chapter echoes a theme that can be heard in nineteenth-century political economy and, more recently, in the work of Hirshleifer (1994, 1995): actual and potential conflict over goods and resources is a fundamental dimension of economic activity which should be integrated with production and trade in economic theory.

Part III (Chapters 9–14) focuses on economic aspects of war, terrorism, and genocide including why violence is chosen, economic factors that elevate the risk of violence, how violence can be prevented, and economic consequences of hostilities. Chapter 9 emphasizes geographical and technological aspects of war and peace in the context of territorial contestation. Chapter 10 presents the bargaining theory of war and peace, which has been used by scholars to derive various causes of war and sources of peace. Chapter 11 focuses on conflict between states (for example, interstate wars), while Chapter 12 does the same for civil war. Chapters 13 and 14 then provide economic analysis of terrorism and genocide, respectively.

Part IV (Chapters 15–17) analyzes economic aspects of the creation of security and peace between and within states. Chapter 15 focuses on arms rivalry, proliferation, and arms control, including continuing tensions in the world over the proliferation of nuclear weapons. Chapter 16 analyzes security alliances between and within states, while Chapter 17 focuses on economic aspects of peace. At the end of each chapter we include bibliographic notes whereby the interested student, scholar, policymaker, or practitioner can explore the field in more depth. The book also provides five appendixes. Appendix A offers a brief primer on weapons technologies. Appendix B presents a formal bargaining model of war and peace. Appendix C provides matrix algebra methods for solving network models with Excel. Appendix D offers datasets on conflict and peace. Appendix E offers a brief overview of regression methods.

1.6 Bibliographic Notes

Insightful perspectives on the economics of war and peace were developed by well-known economists in the eighteenth, nineteenth, and early twentieth centuries (see Goodwin 1991, Brauer 2003, 2017a, and Ikeda and Rosselli 2017 for overviews). The widespread application of formal economic models to the study of conflict and peace began largely during the Cold War, when attention was drawn to various aspects of international conflict. The resulting scholarship was variously called defense economics, military economics, security economics, conflict economics, defense and peace economics, and peace economics (Caruso 2010, Brauer and Caruso 2013, Brauer 2017a). Richardson (1960a, 1960b), Schelling and Halperin (1961), Boulding (1962), and Isard (1969) provided classic works in peace economics, as did Hitch and McKean (1960) and Peck and Scherer (1962) in defense economics. Also important were Schelling (1960, 1966) on strategic behavior and game theory, Olson and Zeckhauser (1966) and Sandler and Cauley (1975) on alliance behavior, McGuire (1965) and Intriligator (1975) on arms rivalry, and Benoit (1973) on military expenditures and economic growth. Defense and peace economics then expanded to include such topics as civil wars, peacekeeping, arms trade, proliferation of weapons of mass destruction, terrorism, economic interdependence and conflict, appropriation and defense of wealth, and mass atrocities. Key contributions in these and other topic areas are available in the edited volumes of Hartley and Sandler (1995, 2001), Sandler and

Table 1.7 *Selected journals that focus on economic aspects of conflict and peace.*

Conflict, Security and Development	*Journal of International Relations and Development*
Defence and Peace Economics	*Journal of Peacebuilding & Development*
The Economics of Peace and Security Journal	*Peace, Conflict and Development: An Interdisciplinary Journal*
International Journal of Development and Conflict	*Peace Economics, Peace Science and Public Policy*
International Journal of Peace Economics and Peace Science	*Stability: International Journal of Security & Development*

Hartley (2003, 2007), Braddon and Hartley (2011), Coyne and Mathers (2011), Garfinkel and Skaperdas (2012), Justino, Brück, and Verwimp (2013), and Anderton and Brauer (2016a).

Many other valuable contributions can be found in journals that publish quantitative research on war and peace from a variety of disciplinary perspectives (for example, *Conflict Management and Peace Science, Journal of Conflict Resolution, Journal of Peace Research*). Valuable articles can also be found in specialty journals that focus on the economic analysis of conflict and peace and/or intersections between conflict, peace, security, and development; see Table 1.7.

PART II

Key Concepts and Models for the Economic Analysis of Conflict and Peace

2

Production Possibilities and Economic Growth

Modern economies are highly complex. In the USA in 2016, for example, 159.2 million workers combined their labor with $56.7 trillion worth of physical capital to produce $18.6 trillion worth of finished goods and services. In this chapter we explain selected aspects of the economics of production such as the production function, production possibilities, opportunity cost, efficiency, comparative advantage, and gains from trade. We then apply these principles to understand better the economic costs of conflict, the effects of military spending on economic growth, the depressed state of North Korea's militarized economy, the economic benefits of Costa Rica's demilitarization, and the effects of insecurity on a refugee family's economy.

2.1 Production Possibilities Model

Production Function

Assume an economy produces two goods: military (M) and civilian (C). Military goods include tanks, fighter aircraft, and the like, while civilian goods encompass food, clothing, shelter, and so on. In economics, military goods are often called "guns," while civilian goods are called "butter." Production of guns and butter requires inputs such as labor (L) and capital (K), where the latter refers to physical assets like buildings and machines. A production function specifies the maximum amount of a good that can be produced with any given combination of inputs under the current state of technology. Technology is the scientific and organizational knowledge available to transform inputs into outputs. Production functions for M and C can be summarized algebraically as:

$$M = f(L_M, K_M) \qquad (2.1)$$

$$C = g(L_C, K_C), \qquad (2.2)$$

where L_M and K_M are labor and capital inputs in military production and L_C and K_C are the same for civilian production.

Equations (2.1) and (2.2) represent production functions in general functional form, but economists often work with specific functional forms. The most famous specific production function in economics is the Cobb-Douglas function, which for M and C can be written:

$$M = AL_M^\alpha K_M^\beta \qquad (2.3)$$

$$C = \tilde{A}L_C^a K_C^b. \qquad (2.4)$$

In equations (2.3) and (2.4), the A and $\tilde{A}$ terms are positive constants representing the state of technology in the production of military and civilian goods. The positive parameters α, β, a, and b capture the productive capability of the inputs. The parameters for production functions often can be estimated statistically using historical data, but for our purposes a numerical example is sufficient to understand the functions. Suppose $A = 50$, $\alpha = 0.5$, and $\beta = 0.5$ in equation (2.3). If labor and capital inputs are $L_M = 100$ hours and $K_M = 9$ units, then military output would be $M = 50(100)^{0.5}(9)^{0.5} = 1,500$ units.

Two well-known production concepts are marginal product and returns to scale. Marginal product is the change in output that occurs when one unit of a given input is added, holding other inputs constant. In mathematical terms, it is the partial derivative of output with respect to the given input. For example, using the Cobb-Douglas production function for military goods, the marginal product of labor is $\partial M/\partial L_M = \alpha AL_M^{\alpha-1}K_M^\beta$. Given parameter values $A = 50$, $\alpha = 0.5$, and $\beta = 0.5$ and the input values $L_M = 100$ and $K_M = 9$, the marginal product of labor in the military industry is $MP_{L_M} = 7.5$. This means that if labor input is increased by one hour (holding capital fixed), military output will rise by 7.5 units. According to the law of diminishing returns, as the amount of an input increases (holding the other input fixed), after some point its marginal productivity will diminish. For example, if L_M is raised to 144 and K_M held fixed at 9, the marginal product of labor in the military industry diminishes from 7.5 to 6.25 units. This means that even though the total output is now larger, the addition to the output is now smaller. Now consider increasing both inputs at the same time. For example, suppose both inputs are doubled, so that output becomes $M = 50(200)^{0.5}(18)^{0.5} =$ 3,000 units. Doubling both inputs causes output to exactly double, which is known as constant returns to scale. For the Cobb-Douglas production function, constant returns to scale exists when $\alpha + \beta = 1$. If $\alpha + \beta > 1$, doubling inputs causes output to more than double, which is known as increasing returns to scale. If $\alpha + \beta < 1$, doubling inputs causes output to less than double, which is called decreasing returns to scale.

Production Possibilities Frontier

In economics, the fundamental fact of nature is scarcity, whereby individuals, groups, and nations have limited resources and technology to produce goods and services to meet peoples' virtually unlimited wants. Assume the labor and capital employed in the military and civilian sectors equal the total labor and capital available to the economy, L and K:

$$L = L_M + L_C \tag{2.5}$$

$$K = K_M + K_C. \tag{2.6}$$

The scarcity of labor and capital is reflected in equations (2.5) and (2.6). The technological limits to production of goods for given input combinations are implied by the production functions (2.3) and (2.4). Scarcity of inputs and technological limitations in production imply a production possibilities frontier (PPF) such as shown in Figure 2.1. Points on or within the PPF constitute the attainable region, which includes all combinations of guns (M) and butter (C) that are possible to produce within an economy at a given point in time.

The PPF in Figure 2.1 depicts the fundamental notion of scarcity in two ways. First, all combinations of guns and butter above the PPF lie in the unattainable region, meaning they cannot be produced given available resources and technology. Second, the slope of the PPF is negative, meaning there exists a production tradeoff between the two goods. At any point on the PPF, say point A, the only way to obtain more guns (moving to point B, say) is to give up some butter. When production is on the frontier, gaining more of one good requires giving up or forgoing some of the other good. This tradeoff is captured by the concept of opportunity cost. In Figure 2.1, the opportunity cost of an increase in guns from m^1 to m^2 is the $c^1 - c^2$ units of butter given up. Note that the PPF in Figure 2.1 is bowed out. This indicates that the opportunity cost of a good will increase

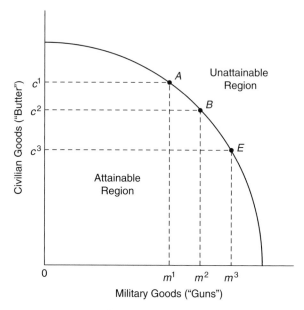

Figure 2.1 Production possibilities frontier (PPF).

as more of the good is acquired. For example, in moving from point *B* to point *E*, even more units of butter must be given up for an equal increment of guns than when moving from point *A* to point *B*. Economists believe that PPFs are often bowed out because the resources shifted from one good to another tend not to be equally adaptable in the two sectors.

As depicted by the PPF, many alternative production points exist; hence, choice is inescapable. Among the thousands of goods and services that might be produced in a modern economy, decisions must somehow be made about what quantities of which goods will be produced, what input combinations will be used, where the goods will be produced, how the goods will be distributed, and how all these decisions will be coordinated as technology, resources, and peoples' preferences change over time. Different nations have different economic systems for addressing these issues. In many countries in the Americas and Europe, there is substantial private property ownership and reliance on markets (supply and demand) to coordinate economic activity. In North Korea, most property is not privately owned, and economic activity is directed by state central planning. Other economies have some important limitations to private property yet a significant role for markets (for example, China).

Figure 2.1 can also be used to understand the concepts of productive and allocative efficiency. Productive efficiency occurs when inputs are fully employed, so equations (2.5) and (2.6) hold, and maximum output is produced from those inputs based on available technology, so equations (2.3) and (2.4) hold. When productive efficiency is achieved, the economy operates at some point on the PPF. If the economy fails to employ all resources fully and productively, then it operates at a point inside the PPF, which is called productive inefficiency. Allocative efficiency, also known as Pareto efficiency, occurs when it is not possible to improve one individual's or group's well-being without hurting another's. For example, suppose the economy is operating at point *B* in Figure 2.1, which is productively efficient. Now assume the movement from point *B* to point *A* makes everyone better off, but any further move from point *A* will leave at least one person worse off. This would imply that *B* is productively efficient but not allocatively efficient, whereas *A* is both productively and allocatively efficient.

Specialization and Trade in the Production Possibilities Model

We, the authors of this book, produce teaching and research services, and maybe a few vegetables from gardening, but we consume hundreds of other products. Our case is typical of workers in modern economies who specialize in the production of one or a few items and then trade their specialized output (with money facilitating exchange) for the goods they consume. Specialized production and trade are fundamental aspects of economic life, not only for individuals but also for nations.

In Figure 2.2 we depict specialized production and trade using the production possibilities model. Recall that along a PPF there exists a tradeoff between one good and another. This tradeoff is internal to the country; that is, within the country's own production possibilities, it can trade off one good for another as reflected in the slope of its PPF. But there is another possibility available to the country; it can trade some of its output with another country. This is an external exchange possibility. In Figure 2.2 we draw a curved line, known as an indifference curve, tangent to the PPF. We will discuss indifference curves in more detail in Chapter 4, but for now it is sufficient to say that points along any given indifference curve generate a fixed level of well-being or utility, and the higher the indifference curve, the greater the well-being or utility. In Figure 2.2, if the nation produces goods only for itself and does not trade, the highest attainable indifference curve is the one tangent to the

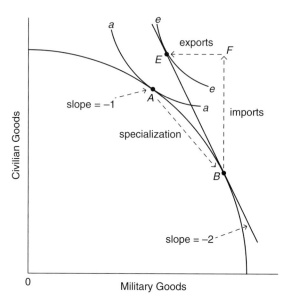

Figure 2.2 Specialized production and trade.

PPF (labeled *aa*), say at point *A*. Point *A* is known as an autarky optimum, because it is where the country would produce to maximize its material well-being in the absence of any external trade. Assume the opportunity cost of military goods in the neighborhood of point *A* equals –1, meaning that production of an additional unit of *M* would cost one unit of *C* forgone. But suppose prices on world markets are such that one unit of *M* could exchange for *two* units of *C*. This external terms-of-trade is represented by the line with slope –2 drawn tangent to the PPF at point *B*. With external trade, the country can achieve a higher indifference curve and therefore a higher level of well-being by following an "economic two-step." First, it specializes more in the production of *M* by moving its production point from *A* to *B*. Second, it trades away some *M* in return for some *C*, arriving at a final consumption point *E* on higher indifference curve *ee*. The distance *FE* represents the country's exports of *M*, while *BF* represents its imports of *C*.

Figure 2.2 shows that specialized production and trade allow the country to consume more goods and services than it could produce in isolation. At consumption point *E*, the country is consuming a bundle of goods that lies outside the PPF. Although *E* is an unattainable production point, it is not an unattainable consumption point because of the opportunity presented by external trade. When specializing in a product (good *M* in this case) that is more valued on world markets relative to the opportunity cost of producing it in isolation, the country is operating according to what is known as its comparative advantage. Such specialization increases the value of the country's production and, through trade, allows the country to reach a higher indifference curve. The increase in the indifference curve from *aa* to *ee* is a graphical representation of the gains from trade.

Economic Growth in the Production Possibilities Model

Over time, most economies experience an increase in the amount of goods and services produced as more labor and capital and better technology become available. This is known as economic growth. For example, since the early 1940s, a growing proportion and number of women have entered the work force in the USA, contributing to its post-World War II growth in gross domestic product (GDP). In some countries, women are discouraged from paid employment, which tends to depress GDP growth. When new resources or technology become available, the PPF moves outward, causing some previously unattainable production points to become attainable. The PPF does not necessarily shift out equally along the two axes. If resources or technological developments are biased in favor of, say good *C*, the PPF would shift out more along the *C* axis than the *M* axis. The PPF can also shift in, which constitutes negative economic growth. For example, natural disasters such as Hurricane Katrina in 2005, the 2011 Japanese earthquake and tsunami, and the 2013 typhoon in the Philippines destroyed lives and capital stock, causing the PPFs for the regional economies in the devastated areas to shift inward.

2.2 Applications

Economic Costs of Conflict

Chapter 1 noted that violent conflict involves economic costs of five sorts: diversion of resources to the military, destruction of goods and resources, disruption of economic activities, displacement of people in the form of refugees and internally displaced persons (IDPs), and development difficulties after conflict. Figure 2.3 illustrates such costs in the production possibilities model. Conflict typically leads to an increase in military production as a proportion of overall production. In panel (a), the increase in military relative to civilian goods causes the production point in the

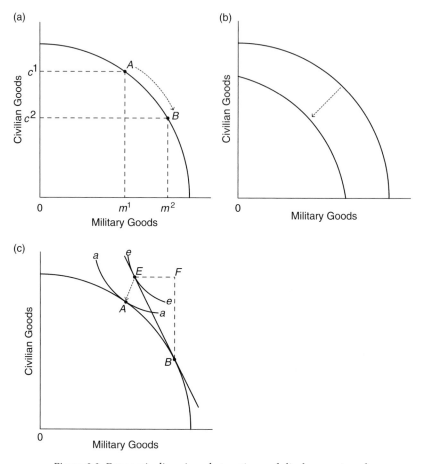

Figure 2.3 Economic diversion, destruction and displacement, and
disruption from violent conflict.
(a) Diversion
(b) Destruction and Displacement
(c) Disruption

economy to move from say *A* to *B*. In this case, the increase in "guns"
from m^1 to m^2 occurs at the expense of "butter," which declines from c^1 to
c^2. In panel (b), the destruction of goods, capital, and people through
violent conflict and the displacement of people from their economies of
residence cause production possibilities to shrink, reflected by the inward
shift of the PPF. In this example, violent conflict leads to negative economic growth. In panel (c), disruption of trade by conflict leads to
a decline in material well-being. Initially, the country produces at point

B, exports *FE* units of guns, imports *BF* units of butter, and reaches indifference curve *ee* at consumption point *E*. Assume now that trade ceases with conflict. This causes the country to operate in autarky at point *A*, with reduced consumption of each good and a lower level of utility shown by indifference curve *aa*. All three panels suggest development difficulties postconflict. Specifically, it is challenging to ratchet back the expanded military spending that occurs with war; replace people killed and infrastructure destroyed; reintegrate returning refugees and IDPs into their homes and communities; and reconstitute local, regional, and international trading relationships.

Military Spending and Economic Growth

There are multiple channels by which military spending can impact a nation's economic growth. Figure 2.4 considers three major channels: (a) crowding out, (b) crowding in, and (c) growth spinoffs. In panel (a), assume the preponderance of a nation's investment goods (that is, new machines and factories) is embodied in civilian goods *C*. If the nation operates at point *A*, it will have a relatively large amount of investment goods this year leading to a relatively large capital stock next year and a correspondingly higher PPF. If instead the nation operates at point *B*, it will have a relatively small amount of investment goods this year, leading to a relatively small capital stock next year and a correspondingly lower PPF. Thus, when more military goods are chosen (point *B* rather than point *A*), it crowds out or dampens capital accumulation, leading to diminished growth. In panel (b), assume the nation initially operates at inefficient point *I*, perhaps because the country is experiencing a recession with underutilized labor and capital. In this case, increased military spending can stimulate economic activity, moving production from *I* to *I'*, for example. The increase in military goods production raises the incomes of workers and owners in the military sector. These income earners will spend some of their increased income on civilian goods, causing civilian goods production to rise from *I'* to *E* via a multiplier effect. This stimulation of civilian production is called crowding in. Panel (c) looks like panel (a) except the arrow from point *B* out to the PPF is now longer than the arrow from point *A*. Suppose greater military spending leads to what are called growth spinoffs, such as increases in education and advances in technology. If this is the case, the diversion of resources to military goods when moving from *A* to *B* can cause the future PPF to be further out than otherwise.

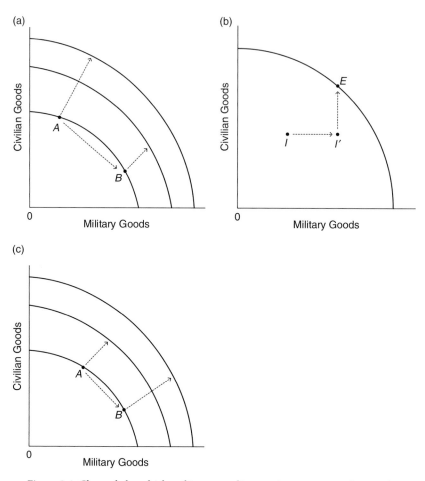

Figure 2.4 Channels by which military spending can impact economic growth.
(a) Crowding out
(b) Crowding in
(c) Growth spin-offs

Following the end of the Cold War in 1989, the military spending/ economic growth relationship was of particular interest because it was thought that military spending would fall throughout the world. Many scholars expected a "peace dividend" in the form of greater economic growth, based on the view that military spending dampens growth as shown in panel (a). Other scholars warned that cuts in military spending could have a recessionary impact or dampen technological development as suggested by panels (b) and (c). Of course, the multiple channels by which military spending can affect growth are not mutually exclusive. For example, consistent with panel (b), it is possible that cuts in real USA military spending from 1989 to 1991 contributed to the recession of 1990–1. On the other hand, consistent with panel (a), the resources freed up from cuts in military spending may have been partly responsible for the rapid growth experienced by the USA in the later 1990s.

Benoit's (1973) study of the effects of military spending on economic growth was path-breaking because it was one of the first to apply statistical methods to the topic, stimulated a vast literature, and led to (for Benoit at least) unexpected results. Based on a sample of 44 developing countries for the 1950–65 period, Benoit (1973, p. xix) concluded that the more that countries "spent on defense, in relation to the size of their economies, the faster they grew—and vice versa." Benoit believed that the mechanism for the growth stimulation from military spending was an educational spinoff. The countries in Benoit's sample were developing and many tended to have mediocre educational opportunities. The military sectors of many of these countries, however, had good education programs. Hence, many who enrolled in the military had opportunities to build their education (human capital) beyond what would have otherwise been attainable. When these personnel left the military, they integrated their higher endowments of human capital into the civilian sector leading to positive impacts on growth. Since Benoit's seminal work, statistical studies of the impacts of military spending on growth have employed more sophisticated models and methods, included developed economies in the samples, and considered more channels by which military spending might affect growth. Some of these studies find that greater military spending is correlated with greater growth, while others report that greater military spending has no impact on or hampers growth (see Bibliographic Notes).

North Korea's High Defense Burden

The Korean demilitarized zone (DMZ), established after the Korean War (1950–3), serves as a buffer zone separating North and South Korea. Despite attempts at reconciliation, the borders of the DMZ represent one of the world's most militarized areas, with large numbers of North and South Korean troops, many US troops, and large stocks of prepositioned military equipment ready for use should hostilities break out. The tension on the Korean Peninsula is heightened by North Korea's long-range

Table 2.1 *Economic and military data for North Korea, South Korea,*
and USA, 2016.

	North Korea	South Korea	USA
Economic Variables			
Gross Domestic Product (GDP)	$40.0 billion	$1.97 trillion	$18.95 trillion
GDP per Capita	$1,700	$38,400	$58,600
Military Spending as % of GDP	24.2%	2.3%	3.3%
Armed Forces			
Active Armed Forces	1,190,000	630,000	28,500
Active Paramilitary Forces	189,000	4,500	0
Weapons			
Main Battle Tanks	3,500	2,534	–
Artillery	21,100	11,038	–
Surface-to-Air Missiles	350	206	–
Tactical Submarines	73	23	–
Combat Capable Aircraft	545	567	–

Notes: USA armed forces data are for the Korean peninsula only. North Korean economic
variables are for 2015.
Sources: Central Intelligence Agency (2018) for economic variables, except for North Korea's
military spending as a percent of GDP, which is from World Military Expenditures and Arms
Transfers (2017). International Institute of Strategic Studies (2017) for armed forces and weapons.

missile capabilities and its continuing research into nuclear, biological, and
chemical weapons. Most analysts believe North Korea has at least several
nuclear warheads and they may have as many as 13 to 30 (Albright 2017).
Currently, tensions between North and South Korea may be thawing.
Nevertheless, the future of peace, security, and weapons developments
on the Korean peninsula remain uncertain.

Table 2.1 summarizes economic and military data for North and South
Korea and for the South's ally, the USA. Three observations follow. First,
North Korea's gross domestic product (GDP) in 2015 was about 2.2 per-
cent of South Korea's GDP. On a per person basis, North Korea produced
only $1,700 worth of finished goods and services in 2015, whereas South
Korea created $38,400 (in 2016). These figures are striking because North
Korea's per capita GDP was greater than the South's in the years immedi-
ately after the Korean War (1950–3) (Kim 2003, p. 77). The stagnation of
North Korea's production is all the more shocking given that

approximately 2.5 million of its people starved to death from 1995 to 1997 (Natsios 2001, pp. 212–15). Second, North Korea's defense burden is unusually high. In 2015, it is estimated that North Korea devoted 24.2 percent of its GDP to military spending. To put that figure in perspective, only two other countries in the world had defense burdens exceeding 10 percent in 2015: Oman (14.4 percent) and Saudi Arabia (13.5 percent) (Stockholm International Peace Research Institute 2018a). Despite widespread famine in the 1990s and ongoing problems with food provision, North Korea continues to deploy over one million troops and substantial weaponry. Third, the estimated 189,000 paramilitary forces deployed in North Korea is large compared to the number deployed by the South. Although North Korea fears its external enemies, its leaders also fear internal unrest, as evidenced by the large number of paramilitary forces.

We can use the production possibilities model to explore four elements that have contributed to North Korea's severe economic and humanitarian problems: high defense burden, sclerotic central planning, displacement of people, and paucity of external trade. As shown in Figure 2.4(a), a high defense burden leads to resource diversion along a PPF. If crowding out of capital accumulation outweighs crowding in and growth spinoffs from defense, then a high defense burden will stifle growth and possibly even shift the PPF inward (negative growth). A second source of economic decay in North Korea is communist central planning. When a few leaders attempt to answer for a large society the vastly complex questions of what to produce, who will produce it, and who will receive it, economic stagnation eventually emerges. Central planning tends to stifle movements of labor and capital into new industries and locations, causing an economy to operate at an inefficient point inside the PPF, such as point *I* in Figure 2.4 (b). Moreover, when the distribution of the fruits of new investments is determined by central planners, initiative and innovation can be stunted, causing the PPF to grow more slowly than otherwise. Third, owing to severe repression of human rights, it is estimated that up to 120,000 men, women, and children have been imprisoned in which they are subjected to forced labor, torture, rape, and murder (Griffiths 2016). In addition to the trauma experienced by these victims of atrocity crimes, the displacement of so much of an economy's most potent resource – people – has had a devastating impact on North Korea's growth and development. Fourth, as a somewhat insular economy, North Korea has pursued comparatively little external trade. For example, exports in 2015 as a percentage of GDP were estimated to be 5.9 percent for North Korea as compared to over 40 percent for South Korea (Central Intelligence Agency 2018). As we saw in Figure 2.2, external trade allows a state to consume goods and services beyond what it is able to produce in isolation. To the extent that North Korea pursues little trade, it ends up on an unnecessarily low indifference curve such as *aa* in Figure 2.3(c).

Costa Rica's Demilitarized Economy

At the other end of the defense burden spectrum is Costa Rica, which allocates close to 0 percent of its GDP to military spending. It has not always been this way for Costa Rica. Following a series of military-led coups in the first half of the twentieth century and a civil war in 1948 that claimed 2,000 lives, Costa Rica abolished its military and instituted a police force of 1,500 to uphold security within the nation (Buscone 2017). Over subsequent decades, Costa Rica experienced internal and external threats including a 1949 coup attempt, invasions by Nicaragua in 1948 and 1955, and a Nicaragua/Costa Rica territorial dispute known as the "Google Maps War" (Jacobs 2012, Buscone 2017). Nevertheless, Costa Rica was able to resolve such disputes through diplomacy and the support of the Organization of American States.

Since dissolving its military, Costa Rica has faced security and economic challenges, but it has been able to respond to them without the need to wield a coercive threat. The combination of virtually zero military spending, economic diversification away from heavy reliance on commodities (for example, coffee), the welcoming of external trade opportunities (including tourism), and democracy have created a vastly different destiny for Costa Rica and its people relative to North Korea. From 1950 to 2014, Costa Rica's real GDP per capita increased almost five-fold from $2,826 to $13,463 (Penn World Tables 2017). Currently, Costa Rica's real GDP per capita may be almost eight times greater than North Korea's.

Effects of War on a Family's Economy

The field of family economics treats parents and children as a unit of analysis in which the family is analogous to a small "firm." Some family members specialize in acquiring goods by working in the marketplace (for example, as a shopkeeper or employee in a factory), while others emphasize work within the household such as child and elder care, cooking, and shopping. Children and, sometimes, one or both parents, might also develop their human capital through education. One can imagine several household production functions that capture the items produced by the family, which in turn can be conceptualized by the family's production possibilities frontier. Trading for goods in the marketplace allows the family to take advantage of specialized production and trade opportunities to achieve a higher level of utility than otherwise. In short, Figure 2.2 can apply, not just to a nation, but also to a family.

Not surprisingly, war can devastate a family's economy. Potential and actual violent conflicts cause many people to flee their homes and seek safety in other countries (refugees) or in other locations within the home country (IDPs). For example, as noted in Chapter 1, the brutal civil war in Syria has caused more than half of the country's population to flee their homes. The United Nations High Commissioner for Refugees (2018) provides personal accounts of refugees that fled their homes in Syria, Myanmar, Ethiopia, and numerous other countries experiencing violent conflict. Many of the stories feature a family that has lost its business and household production. The stories of refugee children often highlight lost educational opportunities. In the short term, a refugee family's production and trade possibilities shrink dramatically as it is severed from employment, markets, community networks, and schools. This "triple hit" on the family's economy (losses in production, trade, and educational opportunities) implies a downward shock to the family's production possibilities frontier such as in Figure 2.3(b) and a disruption to trade as represented by Figure 2.3(c). The losses are further magnified when one considers the future implications of disrupted education for the children and the psychological harm from insecurity and disconnection from the family's former community.[1]

2.3 Bibliographic Notes

Graphical presentations of production functions and the production possibilities model are available in economics principles texts (for example, Mankiw 2018), with more advanced treatments in many intermediate microeconomics books (for example, Nicholson and Snyder 2016). For coverage of comparative advantage and the gains from trade in a production possibilities model, see international trade texts (for example,

---

[1] Our analysis focuses only on the short-term impact of insecurity on the family's economy. A refugee family's economic productivity and well-being could improve in the future if the host country has comparatively strong employment and education opportunities.

Krugman, Obstfeld, and Melitz 2018). Virtually all principles and intermediate texts in macroeconomics cover economic growth (for example, Case, Fair, and Oster 2016; Blanchard 2016).

Since Benoit's path-breaking work, empirical literature on military spending and economic growth has proliferated. Some studies report that military spending's impact on economic growth is significantly negative (for example, Dunne and Tian 2015; d'Agostino, Dunne, and Pieroni 2017), significantly positive (for example, Yilgör, Karagöl, and Saygili 2014; Augier, McNab, Guo, and Karber 2017), or zero or mixed (for example, Töngür and Elveren 2016; Aziz and Asadullah 2017). Dozens of empirical studies of relationships between military spending and economic growth are available in the journal *Defence and Peace Economics*.

For studies of North Korea's nuclear weapons developments and related security issues, see Kim and Cohen (2017). For coverage of refugee issues in which economic perspectives receive substantial attention, see Collier and Betts (2017). Refugee and migration studies is a growing interdisciplinary field, see Fiddian-Qasmiyeh, Loescher, Long, and Sigona (2014) and Triandafyllidou (2015).

3

Demand and Supply

The demand and supply model is the most well-known model in economics. The framework is especially useful for understanding how prices and quantities of goods sold are determined in competitive markets such as those for food, clothing, and financial assets. In this chapter we present the principles of demand and supply and then apply the model to several conflict and peace issues including the difficulty of controlling the trade in small arms, how prices and quantities of AK-47 assault rifles are determined in northern and southern Mexico, and the liberal peace hypothesis.

3.1 Demand, Supply, and Market Equilibrium

Demand and Supply

Figure 3.1 depicts demand and supply in a hypothetical market for cereal. The demand curve D shows at any given price the corresponding quantity demanded per week by consumers, holding preferences, incomes, and other prices fixed. The negative slope depicts the law of demand, in which price and quantity demanded are inversely related. When the price per box of cereal is $4.80, for example, the corresponding quantity demanded in the market is shown to be six thousand boxes per week. If the price falls to $3.20, quantity demanded increases to 14 thousand, as consumers direct more of their consumption toward cereal, which now provides a relatively cheaper breakfast. The supply curve S in Figure 3.1 shows at any given price the corresponding quantity supplied by producers, holding technology and input prices fixed. The positive slope depicts the law of supply, according to which price and quantity supplied are directly related. Producers are profit maximizers and thus are willing to supply

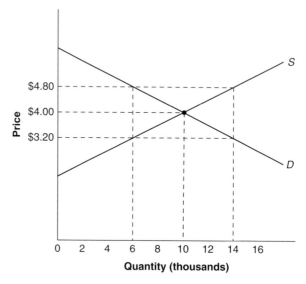

Figure 3.1 Market demand, supply, and equilibrium.

only those units of output that generate profit. In Figure 3.1, for example, if the price per box of cereal is $3.20, producers are willing to supply six thousand but only six thousand boxes of cereal; thus we can infer that boxes of cereal beyond that quantity are too costly to produce at that price. If, however, the price rises to $4.80, some of those costlier units become profitable, causing quantity supplied to increase now to 14 thousand boxes.

It is important to recognize that if one of the other variables in the demand relationship changes, then the entire demand curve will shift its position. For example, if cereal is a normal good and incomes rise, then demand for cereal will increase. This means the demand curve will shift to the right, indicating that at any given price consumers are now willing to buy a larger quantity. Similarly, an increase in the price of a substitute good like eggs will increase the demand for cereal, meaning again that the entire demand curve will shift to the right, as consumers substitute away from relatively more expensive eggs at breakfast. Working in the opposite direction, an increase in the price of a complement good like milk will tend to decrease the demand for cereal, shifting the demand curve to the left, as consumers move away from the consumption of milk used with cereal.

As on the demand side, changes in one of the other variables in the supply relationship will cause the entire supply curve to shift. For example, if a technological improvement lowers costs, then more units of output can be profitably produced; as a result, the supply of cereal will increase, meaning the entire supply curve will shift to the right. Similarly, an increase in the number of producers will increase the supply for cereal, meaning again that the entire supply curve will shift to the right. Working in the opposite direction, if the price of an input like grain increases, then costs will be higher and supply will decrease, meaning the supply curve will shift to the left.

Market Equilibrium

An equilibrium can be thought of as a resting point that occurs when opposing forces are in balance. In the context of a competitive market, it is a price at which the plans of both buyers and sellers can be realized. Given an equilibrium price, consumers are able to buy those quantities they want to consume, and producers are able to sell those quantities they want to produce. Hence, it is a price at which quantity demanded equals quantity supplied in the market.

Figure 3.1 illustrates how the forces of demand and supply tend to generate a market equilibrium. To begin, suppose the price of cereal is $4.80 per box. As shown in Figure 3.1, the quantity supplied is 14 thousand boxes per week, while the quantity demanded is six thousand. This means that of the 14 thousand boxes that producers plan to sell, consumers are willing to buy only six thousand. The surplus of eight thousand boxes that are planned but unsold constitutes an excess supply of cereal. This excess supply signals to producers that the price is too high and creates an incentive for them to decrease the price of cereal. The incentive continues until the price is cut to $4.00 per box. At this price, consumers have increased their quantity demanded to 10 thousand boxes and are able to buy 10 thousand boxes; on the other side, producers have decreased their quantity supplied to 10 thousand boxes and are able to sell 10 thousand boxes. Because the plans of both buyers and sellers are realized, there is no further incentive for change, meaning that $4.00 is the equilibrium price. The same result occurs if the price begins below $4.00. For example, suppose the price is $3.20, so that consumers plan to buy 14 thousand boxes but producers are willing to sell only six thousand boxes. The shortage of eight thousand boxes constitutes an excess demand for cereal and creates an incentive for producers to raise the price. As the price is raised, the quantity supplied increases and the quantity demanded decreases until equilibrium is reached at the price of $4.00.

3.2 Changes in Demand and Supply

The demand and supply model provides a simple but powerful method for explaining and predicting market responses to changes in underlying variables. The method is called comparative-static analysis because it involves the comparison of equilibriums before and after a fundamental change affecting the market. As just one example, suppose the price of grain falls significantly, perhaps because of an unusually large bumper crop. The effect on the market for cereal is depicted in Figure 3.2. Given demand D and supply S, the initial equilibrium is at a price of $4.00 and a corresponding quantity of 10 thousand boxes. If the price of grain drops, then the cost of producing cereal is reduced. This in turn increases the profitability of cereal production, causing producers to increase their supply. In Figure 3.2 this is shown by the rightward shift of the supply curve from S to S'. Because the price of grain has no direct bearing on consumers' demand for cereal, the demand curve remains unchanged at D. This means that with the same demand D but increased supply S', there exists an excess supply at the original price of $4.00. Consequently, producers are led to cut price so as to encourage consumers to increase their quantity of cereal demanded. When the various adjustments are complete, a new equilibrium emerges with a price of $3.20 and quantity of 14 thousand boxes. Thus, the comparative-static analysis shows that the fall

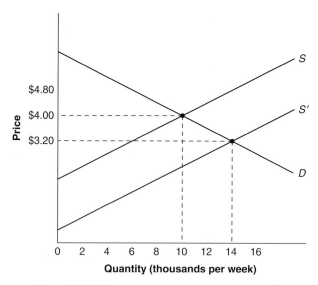

Figure 3.2 Market response to an increase in supply.

in the price of grain will cause the price of cereal to decrease and the quantity of cereal to increase.

Comparative-static analyses proceed similarly for changes involving decreased supply, increased demand, and decreased demand. For example, working in the opposite direction of the previous example, if the price of grain increases, then costs will be higher and supply will decrease, meaning the supply curve will shift to the left. Similarly, a decrease in the number of producers of cereal will decrease the supply for cereal, meaning again that the entire supply curve will shift to the left. On the demand side, if the price of a substitute good like eggs increases, the demand for cereal will increase, meaning that the entire demand curve will shift to the right, as consumers substitute away from relatively more expensive eggs at breakfast. Working in the opposite direction, an increase in the price of a complement good like milk will tend to decrease the demand for cereal, shifting the demand curve to the left, as consumers move away from the consumption of milk used with cereal.

3.3 Applications

Difficulty of Small Arms Control

Weapons in the contemporary international system fall into several categories, one of which is small arms and light weapons (SALW) such as assault rifles and improvised explosive devices (IEDs or "roadside bombs"). Although data on small arms are relatively sparse, scholars generally agree that in recent decades far more people have been killed by small arms than by major conventional weapons and weapons of mass destruction combined. Hence, efforts to control the production and sale of small arms have been growing among nations and intergovernmental and nongovernmental organizations (see Chapter 15 for examples of small arms control organizations and protocols). According to the Small Arms Survey (2017), numerous companies from some 100 countries were involved in some aspects of small arms and light weapons production in recent years. The sizeable number of small arms producers and locales, along with economic incentives in the arms market, make control of small arms difficult.

Figure 3.3 shows a demand and supply model for small arms. The model might apply to the world or to a particular region such as the Middle East or Subsaharan Africa. The arms in question might be small arms broadly conceived or a particular class of weapons such as

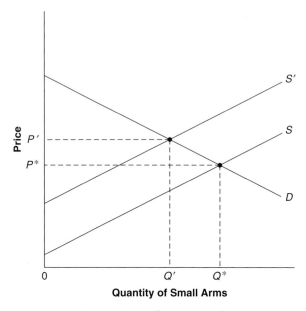

Figure 3.3 Small arms control.

assault rifles. Assume initially that the market is at a long-run equilibrium with price P^* and quantity Q^*, such that arms producers are just able to cover costs and hence earn normal profits on the sale of small arms. Suppose that an arms control agreement places output restraint on some small arms producers, causing supply to decrease from S to S' in Figure 3.3. The result is that the equilibrium price rises to P' and the equilibrium quantity falls to Q'. The supply restraint appears effective, but the new equilibrium is only a short-run outcome. If the underlying cost conditions of arms producers are unchanged, then the higher price P' reflects an above-normal profit opportunity for the production of small arms. Hence, firms restricted by the agreement have an incentive to secretly increase output, unrestricted firms are eager to expand production, and new firms are drawn to enter the small arms business. The result over the long run is that the supply curve will tend to shift back to its original position until the industry is returned to normal profitability again with price P^* and quantity Q^*. The lesson suggested by the model is that small arms restraints that do not increase producers' costs generate powerful economic incentives that tend to diminish the effectiveness of the restraints over time.

Market Conditions and the Price of AK-47 Assault Rifles in Mexico

In Mexico, violent conflicts between drug-trading organizations (DTOs), police, and government troops and among DTOs themselves led to about 23,000 fatalities in 2016 (Roberts 2017). Moreover, from 2004 to 2016, there were more than 18 thousand fatalities of drug cartel members (Uppsala Conflict Data Program 2016). Among the major DTOs that fight among themselves are the Los Zetas cartel, which controls territory in northern, central, and southern parts of Mexico, and the Sinaloa cartel, which primarily operates in the northern and central parts of the country.

As in many other intrastate and nonstate conflicts around the world, SALW are the military equipment of choice for the DTOs, Mexican police, and citizens attempting to protect themselves. AK-47 assault rifles are especially prized by the DTOs owing to their firepower and ease of use. The prices for AK-47s have varied significantly between northern and southern Mexico. In 2011, for example, AK-47s sold in the north for about $1,400 on average while in the south the average price was about $3,000 (Olson 2011). The demand and supply model can be used to analyze the price discrepancy. In panel (a) of Figure 3.4, we posit functions for demand (D) and a supply (S_{North}) for AK-47s with a resulting equilibrium price assumed to be $1,400 and an unspecified equilibrium quantity of q^*. Panel (a) represents market conditions for AK-47s in northern Mexico in 2011. In panel (b) we assume the same demand function D as in panel (a), but we posit a more restricted supply curve S_{South}. The resulting equilibrium price in panel (b) is assumed to be $3,000 with an unspecified equilibrium quantity of q^*. Panel (b) represents market conditions for AK-47s in southern Mexico in 2011. Of course, demand conditions are not likely to be identical in the north and south. We assume they are to focus the analysis on what we believe is the main reason for the price discrepancy: differing supply conditions between north and south. Specifically, the supply of AK-47s and other high-quality small arms illegally trafficked from the USA into northern Mexico was high in the years leading up to 2011. Meanwhile, the supply of such weapons coming into southern Mexico from Central America was comparatively small (Olson 2011, p. 5).

Figure 3.4 is a starting point for analyzing AK-47 price differentials in Mexico. Further exploration would ask: why would those selling AK-47s for $1,400 in northern Mexico not ship them to the south where they could be sold for $3,000? Moving goods from where they have low value to sell

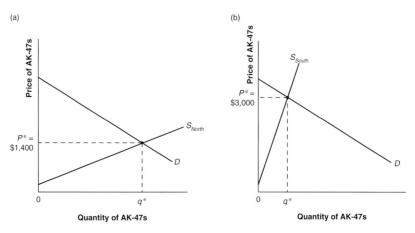

Figure 3.4 Market conditions for AK-47 assault rifles in Mexico.
(a) Northern Mexico
(b) Southern Mexico

them where they are more highly valued is known as arbitrage, which leads toward an equalization of prices for the same good across regions. Two plausible explanations for the lack of arbitrage in AK-47 prices in Mexico are the cost of transporting goods over distance and the many security checkpoints to be negotiated by the arms dealers. For example, in the southern Mexican state of Chiapas, security checkpoints increased by 330 percent from 2011 to 2013 (Ureste 2015). Furthermore, since 2014 there has been an increasing number of "both fixed and mobile [check-points] strewn across southern Mexico" (Arizona Public Media 2015).

Liberal Peace Hypothesis

According to the liberal peace hypothesis, salient trade between two nations makes it less likely they will fight each other, all else equal (Russett and Oneal 2001). Figure 3.5 presents a theoretical rationale for the liberal peace hypothesis based on the demand and supply model. For simplicity, we assume bilateral trade between two nations A and B. In this context, the demand curve D represents nation A's demand for imports from nation B, and the supply curve S represents nation B's supply of exports to nation A. Since A's imports equal B's exports in a two-nation model, we can measure the quantity of trade as a single variable on the horizontal axis. For the hypothetical demand and supply curves in Figure 3.5, trade equilibrium occurs at a price of $150 and a quantity of 100 thousand.

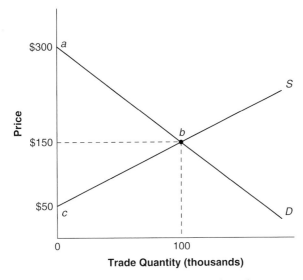

Figure 3.5 Trade and the liberal peace hypothesis.

At this equilibrium, the aggregate gains from trade for *A* and *B* equal the area of triangle *abc*. To understand the gains-from-trade triangle, it is helpful to see that demand and supply curves can be read not only horizontally but also vertically. If read horizontally, the demand curve in Figure 3.5 shows that when the price is $150, nation *A* is willing to import units of trade up to and including the 100 thousandth unit. This means that the highest price *A* is willing to pay for the 100 thousandth unit, and hence *A*'s subjective valuation of that unit, is $150. The same logic implies more generally that the vertical distance up to the demand curve shows *A*'s subjective valuation for any given unit of trade. Similarly, the supply curve shows that at a price of $150, nation *B* is willing to export units of trade up to and including the 100 thousandth unit. This implies that *B*'s cost of producing the 100 thousandth unit, and hence the lowest price at which *B* is willing to sell it, is $150. Thus, the vertical distance up to the supply curve shows *B*'s cost for any given unit of trade.

With these principles in mind, consider the first unit traded between *A* and *B*. Nation *A* values this first unit at very close to $300, as reflected by the vertical intercept of $300 on the demand curve. Yet *A* only has to pay the equilibrium price of $150 to obtain the first unit, thus generating a gain from trade of close to $150 for that unit. On the other side, the cost of the first unit to *B* is very close to $50, as reflected by the vertical intercept of the supply curve. Yet *B* receives $150 when it exports the first unit, thus generating a gain from trade of close to $100 for that unit. Hence, for *A* and *B* together the gains from trade from the first unit traded is equal to $250, the vertical gap between the demand and supply curves. When the gains are computed similarly on all successive units traded, it can be seen that the total of the gains from trade at the equilibrium quantity of 100 thousand is equal to the area of the triangle *abc*. Computing the area of the triangle as one-half base times height, the resulting aggregate gains from trade in Figure 3.5 equal $12.5 million.

These gains provide a plausible explanation of the liberal peace hypothesis. Suppose if war broke out between *A* and *B*, political decisions would lead to the termination of trade between them. In Figure 3.5, trade quantity would go to zero. Unless some or all of this trade could be recovered elsewhere, *A* and *B* would lose gains equal to the trade triangle *abc*. Hence, the gains from trade that would be forgone raise the opportunity cost of war and thereby reduce the likelihood of war between *A* and *B*, all else equal.

3.4 A Taxonomy of Goods: Private, Common Resource, Club, and Public

The demand and supply model is useful for understanding the market allocation of private goods like cereal. In economics terminology, however, not all goods are private. Goods can be classified as to whether they are rival or nonrival, and also whether they are excludable or nonexcludable. A good is rival if one person's consumption of a unit precludes another person's consumption of that same unit, and it is excludable if selected persons can be excluded from its consumption.

As summarized in Table 3.1, these characteristics combine to define four types of goods. (1) A private good is both rival and excludable. Cereal is a typical private good. One person's consumption of cereal necessarily means the same cereal is unavailable to a second person; furthermore, suppliers can exclude those consumers who are not willing to pay the requisite price. (2) A public good is both nonrival and nonexcludable. A good example is an antimissile defense system. If one person enjoys the security of such a system, others in the same location can enjoy identical security at no added cost. Moreover, others cannot be excluded from that security, even if they contribute nothing to its cost. (3) A common resource good is rival but nonexcludable. An example is fish in open waters. When fish are caught by one person, they are not available to be caught by other

Table 3.1 *Taxonomy of goods with examples.*

	Excludable	Nonexcludable
Rival	Private Good (cereal, medicine)	Common-Resource Good (fish in open waters, clean air)
Nonrival	Club Good (proprietary website, satellite radio)	Public Good (anti-missile defense system, FM radio)

persons; other persons, however, cannot be excluded from attempting to catch those same fish. (4) A club good is nonrival but excludable. An example is a proprietary website that provides valuable data to subscribers. Subscribers can enjoy the use of the data simultaneously, but nonsubscribers are denied access. The taxonomy in Table 3.1 assumes that the characteristics of rivalry and excludability are dichotomous, meaning they are either present or absent. It is sometimes useful to assume instead that the characteristics can exist in different degrees. In this case, the goods would vary continuously across the two dimensions of rivalry and excludability.

It is important that the labels in Table 3.1 be correctly understood and applied. Private goods are not equivalent to privately-provided goods, and public goods are not equivalent to publicly-provided goods. Medicine is a private good, yet medicine is sometimes provided by the public sector. Going in the other direction, FM radio broadcasts are public goods, but broadcasts are typically provided by the private sector. Thus, a good's type is determined by its characteristics, not by the sector through which it is provided.

That being said, it is true that private goods generally are more easily allocated through private-sector markets than are public goods. Because private goods are rival, additional consumption requires additional production and hence is costly. Because they are also excludable, additional consumption can be rationed by willingness to pay. Putting the two characteristics together, a private good can be allocated easily and efficiently by demand and supply forces, because consumers can be induced to pay for their own consumption and thereby allow producers to cover their costs. The same cannot be said for public goods. Because public goods are nonrival and nonexcludable, each consumer has the incentive to free ride, that is, to share in the consumption of the public good but not in its cost. In the absence of other institutional arrangements, such as tying radio broadcasts to advertisements, free riding by consumers leaves producers in the private sector with no incentive to supply the good.

Distinctions between private and public goods are important in many areas of conflict economics. A nation's deterrence of external enemies is sometimes modeled as a public good: deterrence is nonrival because one person's security does not preclude other persons from enjoying the same security, and it is nonexcludable because individuals can enjoy the security regardless whether they help cover the cost. In an alliance, two or more nations may find it in their interest to share the burden of defense when military goods used for deterrence purposes are nonrival. Peacekeeping operations can also have public goods characteristics. Establishing peace in a nation experiencing civil war might benefit several surrounding nations at the same time, regardless whether they contribute to the peacekeeping operation. As a last example, consider resources like water and oil deposits that span national borders or ethnic communities. Such transboundary resources are clearly rival in consumption, but they are also nonexcludable because different groups have direct access to the same resource pool. Potentially violent disputes can arise between nations or groups over the division and optimal rate of depletion, due in large part to the nonexcludability of such common resource goods.

3.5 Bibliographic Notes

Textbook presentations of demand and supply and the taxonomy of goods abound (for example, Mankiw 2018; Case, Fair, and Oster 2016). Brauer (2007) reviews data and models on arms production and trade, including an overview of small arms and light weapons. Brauer (2013) applies the demand and supply model to commercial firearms markets in the USA. For analysis of the trade in small arms and light weapons in Mexico, see Small Arms Survey (2013). Chapters 11 and 12 provide additional analyses of the liberal peace hypothesis.

4

Rational Choice Theory

Economic analyses of conflict and peace choices normally rest on the organizing principle of rationality, which pertains to how actors choose purposefully among alternatives. In this chapter we highlight the rationality principle by reviewing the economic model of consumer choice, which has also been called the rational choice model. Along the way, we explore several issues in conflict economics including terrorist targeting choices, a ban on landmines and its impact on a rebel organization's recruitment, and the fungibility of civilian aid into military goods.

4.1 Rational Choice Model

Rational choice theory assumes that an actor has consistent preferences over alternatives and chooses the best alternative available. The actor might be a consumer, producer, politician, insurgent, terrorist, nation, or any number of other entities. Here we sketch a basic consumer choice model, so we assume the actor is a consumer. Suppose the consumer chooses among alternative combinations or baskets of two commodities labeled X (say food) and Y (say entertainment). They operate with a fixed income I per day, which is spent completely on the two commodities at prices P_X and P_Y. The rational choice problem is to choose the most preferred basket that the consumer can afford given its budget. The two basic elements of the problem are then the consumer's preferences and budget constraint, which we can treat separately before combining them to determine the optimal choice.

Preferences

Rational choice assumes that preferences over alternatives are complete and transitive. Completeness means that when comparing any two alternative baskets *a* and *b*, our consumer can determine whether it prefers a to *b*, prefers *b* to *a*, or is indifferent between *a* and *b*. Transitivity means that comparisons of this sort are consistent with one another. For example, given three alternative baskets *a*, *b*, and *c*, if our consumer prefers *a* to *b* and *b* to *c*, then it is assumed the consumer prefers *a* to *c*. Similarly, if the consumer is indifferent between *a* and *b* and between *b* and *c*, then it is indifferent between *a* and *c*. Putting completeness and transitivity together, rationality assumes that our consumer has a subjective ordering over all baskets, with more preferred baskets ranked higher, less preferred baskets ranked lower, and possible ties of indifference along the way. Notice that this rank ordering is independent of our consumer's budget constraint; hence it tells us which baskets the consumer would most like to have without consideration of cost. Analytically, we can represent the rank ordering in two equivalent ways, graphically with indifference curves and algebraically with utility functions.

Indifference Curves

An indifference curve for our consumer is a locus of points representing alternative baskets among which it is indifferent. A full collection of indifference curves is called an indifference map and represents the consumer's complete rank ordering of preferences. Figure 4.1 shows just three of what would be an infinite number of curves in our consumer's indifference map. In drawing the curves we assume that both commodities are strictly goods for our consumer, meaning that more of each is always preferred. In later chapters we consider cases in which one of the commodities, say X, is a bad, so that the consumer prefers to have less of X rather than more.

The figure depicts several properties of indifference curves. First, points on an indifference curve are equally preferred by definition. Thus, for example, baskets *a* (with $X = 1$ and $Y = 4$) and *c* (with $X = 4$ and $Y = 1$) are equally preferred. Second, points on higher indifference curves are more preferred, because the commodities are goods and preferences are transitive. For example, according to these hypothetical indifference curves, basket *f* (with $X = 3$ and $Y = 4$) is preferred to basket *e* (with $X = 4$ and $Y = 2$). Third, although indifference curves can squeeze together or spread apart, they never intersect, because preferences are transitive and hence consistent.

As a fourth property, notice that in Figure 4.1 the indifference curves slope downward. Because both commodities are goods, our consumer is

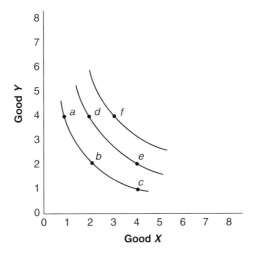

Figure 4.1 Indifference curves for two goods.

willing to substitute between the two goods, that is, to give up some of one good in return for more of the other good. Consider baskets *a*, *b*, and *c*, which all lie on the same indifference curve. Because our consumer would be neither better off nor worse off, it would be just willing to move from basket *a* to basket *b*, that is, to give up 2 units of *Y* for 1 added unit of *X*. Likewise, it would be just willing to move from *a* to *c*, that is, to give up 3 units of Y for 3 added units of *X*. In this manner, we can generate various descriptions of our consumer's willingness to substitute between *X* and *Y*, beginning from basket *a*. We standardize these descriptions by focusing on the slope of the indifference curve at point *a*. Assume that a precise measurement of the slope at *a* shows $\Delta Y / \Delta X = -4/1 = -4$. This then means that beginning from basket *a*, our consumer is just willing to substitute between *X* and *Y* at a rate of 4*Y* per unit of *X*. For convenience, we drop the minus sign and define the marginal rate of substitution (or MRS) between *X* and *Y* at any given point as the absolute value of the slope of the indifference curve at that same point. Because the MRS measures the amount of *Y* that our consumer is just willing to give up per added unit of *X*, we can think of the MRS as a measure of our consumer's subjective value of *X* in terms of *Y*. So, at point *a*, for example, we can say that the consumer's subjective value of a unit of *X* is equivalent to 4*Y*. Notice that the shape of the indifference curve through *a* indicates that the MRS diminishes with rightward movements along the curve. For example, the absolute slope and hence the subjective value of *X* is smaller at point *c* than at point *a*.

Utility Functions

A utility function is a numerical rule that preserves the rank ordering of preferences. In particular, it is a function that assigns higher numbers to more preferred baskets, lower numbers to less preferred baskets, and equal numbers to equally preferred baskets. Thus a utility function can be thought of simply as a rule according to which baskets on higher indifference curves are assigned higher numbers, where these numbers are called utilities. Suppose our consumer has preferences over X and Y as depicted in Figure 4.1. Now consider the following algebraic utility function $U = xy$, which assigns to any basket a utility equal to the product of the respective quantities of goods X and Y. This is an example of what is called a Cobb-Douglas utility function, which has the general form $U = x^{\alpha}y^{\beta}$, with the exponents in this case both equal to one. Is this a valid utility function for our consumer's preferences? That is, does it correctly preserve the consumer's rank ordering over alternative baskets?

In Table 4.1, we show how the utility function assigns numbers to the various baskets labeled in Figure 4.1. Notice that the utilities assigned to baskets a, b, and c are all equal, correctly indicating that the baskets are equally preferred. Likewise, the utilities assigned to baskets d and e are equal, showing that these baskets are equally preferred. Lastly, the utility of 12 assigned to f is greater than the utility of 8 assigned to d and e, which is greater than the utility of 4 assigned to a, b, and c, correctly indicating that baskets on higher indifference curves are more preferred. In this way we can confirm that the utility function $U = xy$ is indeed a valid utility function for our consumer, because it accurately preserves its rank ordering of preferences.

The utility function $U = xy$ correctly represents one set of preferences, in particular those depicted by the indifference map in Figure 4.1. If our

Table 4.1 *Utilities assigned by the*
function $U = xy$.

Basket	Quantities (x,y)	Utility $U = xy$
a	(1,4)	4
b	(2,2)	4
c	(4,1)	4
d	(2,4)	8
e	(4,2)	8
f	(3,4)	12

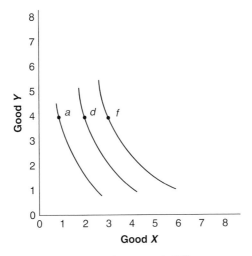

Figure 4.2 Comparatively steeper indifference curves.

consumer had different preferences, they necessarily would be represented by a different utility function. Suppose, for example, that our consumer's preferences change so that in general its subjective valuation of X in terms of Y is now greater. Then its preferences might look like those depicted in Figure 4.2. Notice that the indifference curves through points a, d, and f are now steeper than are the curves through the same three points in Figure 4.1, thus showing higher marginal rates of substitution between X and Y. Because the preferences have changed, so too has the utility function. Our consumer's new preferences are accurately represented by the utility function $U = x^2y$, as the reader can confirm with numerical computations similar to those in Table 4.1. Notice that the exponent on the quantity of good X is now higher, which reflects the higher subjective valuation of X in terms of Y.

Budget Constraint

Our consumer is not free to choose just any basket of X and Y, but rather only those baskets that are affordable given its income I and the market prices P_X and P_Y. Assuming the consumer spends all of its income, the budget constraint is $P_Xx + P_Yy = I$, which in words says that expenditures on X plus expenditures on Y must equal available income. Solving for y, we can write $y = (I/P_Y) - (P_X/P_Y)x$, which when graphed is a straight line. The vertical intercept is I/P_Y, which is the maximum amount of Y that can

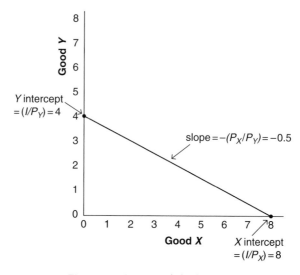

Figure 4.3 Consumer's budget line.

be purchased if all income is spent on Y. The slope is $-(P_X/P_Y)$, which is the negative of the relative price of X in terms of Y. Points on the budget line represent baskets that our consumer is just able to afford.

Suppose, for example, that our consumer has income of $I = \$4$ per day and faces prices of $P_X = \$0.50$ and $P_Y = \$1.00$. The maximum amount of Y that can be purchases is $I/P_Y = \$4/\$1 = 4$, which fixes the vertical intercept of the budget constraint at $4Y$. For the slope, we need the relative price of X, meaning the number of units of Y that our consumer would necessarily forgo if it purchased 1 added unit of X. One unit of X costs $\$0.50$, which could be used alternatively to purchase one-half unit of Y. Thus, the relative price of X is $P_X/P_Y = \$0.50/\$1 = 0.5$ units of Y, so that the slope of the budget constraint is -0.5. In Figure 4.3 we plot the resulting budget line, which shows all of the baskets that our consumer can afford.

Optimal Choice

Our consumer's choice problem is to choose the most preferred basket given their budget. Because preferences can be represented with either an indifference map or a utility function, we can model the problem in either of two ways: as a geometric task of reaching the highest indifference curve along a budget line, or as a calculus exercise of maximizing utility subject to the budget constraint. Here we take the former approach, which combines

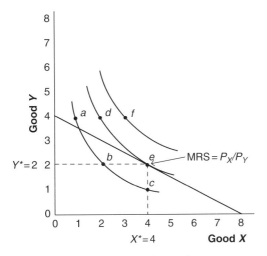

Figure 4.4 Consumption optimum.

our earlier indifference curves from Figure 4.1 and our budget constraint from Figure 4.3. The result is Figure 4.4. Our consumer is free to choose any basket within their budget. Because baskets on higher indifference curves are more preferred, the consumer would choose the basket lying on the highest indifference curve along the budget line. As shown in Figure 4.4, the consumption optimum, X^* and Y^*, occurs at basket e, which consists of $4X$ and $2Y$. Notice that the indifference curve passing through e is just tangent to the budget line. Hence, at the optimum, the MRS (the absolute slope of the indifference curve) is equal to the relative price of X (the absolute slope of the budget line). This means that the amount of Y the consumer is just willing to give up to consume its marginal unit of X is equal to the amount of Y it must give up to purchase that unit of X. At any other point along the budget line, either its subjective value of X would exceed the cost of X in terms of Y, so it would want to buy more X, or the subjective value would be less than the cost, and it would want to buy less X.

4.2 Changes in Parameters

The amounts of X and Y included in the consumption optimum are called the quantities demanded of X and Y, respectively. In the example in Figure 4.4, our consumer's quantities demanded are $4X$ and $2Y$. To extend the analysis without getting into too much detail, we focus now on the quantity demanded of just one of the goods, in particular that

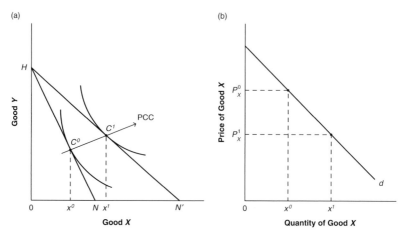

Figure 4.5 Price response and the law of demand.
(a) Price-consumption curve
(b) Individual demand curve

of X. Holding our consumer's preferences constant, if for some reason the price of good X, price of good Y, or the consumer's income changes, so too will its optimum and hence the quantity demanded of X. The systematic relationship between the consumer's quantity demanded of X and the price parameters and income of its budget line is called the consumer's demand function for X. In exploring the demand function, we restrict our attention to how quantity demanded changes when either the price of X or income changes. Also, to simplify, we develop our graphical analysis more generally, without use of explicit numerical values.

Changes in Price and the Individual Demand Curve

We are ready now to consider what happens to quantity demanded of X if the price of X decreases, holding income, the price of Y, and preferences constant. According to the law of demand, we expect price and quantity demanded to move in opposite directions. Thus, we expect quantity demanded to increase when price decreases. Panels (a) and (b) of Figure 4.5 illustrate the law of demand. Assume initially in panel (a) that the price of X is P_X^0, which generates budget line HN, consumption optimum C^0, and quantity demanded x^0. Suppose now that the price of X decreases to P_X^1. The vertical intercept of the budget line remains fixed in panel (a) because neither income nor the price of Y changes. The relative price of X falls, however, causing the absolute slope of the budget line to decrease. Thus, our consumer's budget line rotates outward to *HN'*, resulting in a new optimum C^1. The line that traces out the movement in the consumption optimum is called the price-consumption curve (PCC), which points in the direction of higher utility. In accordance with the law of demand, the decrease in the price of X results in an increase in quantity demanded from x^0 to x^1 in panel (a).

To focus on the relationship between price and quantity demanded, we can draw information from the PCC in panel (a) of Figure 4.5 to construct our consumer's demand curve for X shown in panel (b). From budget line *HN* and optimum C^0 in panel (a), we can take the price P_X^0 and the corresponding quantity demanded x^0, which yields one point on the demand curve in panel (b). Similarly, from *HN'* and optimum C^1 we can take the price P_X^1 and the quantity x^1, which yields a second point on the demand curve. Repeating the process at other optimums in panel (a) (not shown), we can plot our consumer's complete demand curve, which shows the quantity demanded for any given price of X, holding income, the price of Y, and preferences constant. Notice the preceding ceteris paribus clause. If income, the price of Y, or preferences were to change, then the demand curve in panel (b) of Figure 4.5 would change. For example, assuming that good Y is a close substitute for good X (for example, pancakes and waffles are close substitutes for some people), an increase in price of good Y would cause the consumer's entire demand curve in panel (b) to shift to the right, indicating a larger quantity demanded for X at any given price of X.

Changes in Income and the Individual Engel Curve

Now consider what happens to quantity demanded of X if income increases, holding preferences and prices constant. Ordinarily we expect the quantity demanded of a good to increase when income increases. In panel (a) of Figure 4.6 we show our consumer's initial situation with budget line *HN*, consumption optimum C^0, and quantity demanded x^0. When income increases, say from I^0 to I^1, the intercepts of the budget line rise because the maximum amount of each good that the consumer can purchase is now higher. The slope of the budget line is unchanged, however, because the relative price of X is unchanged. Thus, the budget line shifts upward to a new parallel budget line denoted *H'N'*, resulting in a new optimum C^1. The line that traces out the movement in the consumption optimum is called the income-consumption curve (ICC), which like the PCC points in the direction of higher utility. As anticipated, the increase in income results in an increase in quantity demanded from x^0 to x^1. Because

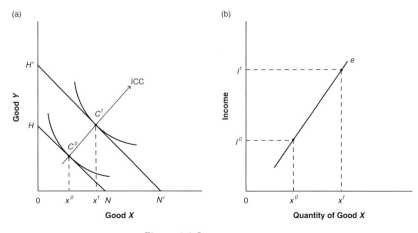

Figure 4.6 Income response.
(a) Income-consumption curve
(b) Individual Engel curve

this is the ordinary case, we say that X is a normal good for our consumer. Some goods, however, can be inferior, meaning that quantity demanded can actually decrease with an increase in income. An example for our consumer might be bus transportation. Over higher ranges of income, it might choose less transportation by bus, perhaps because it could now afford more travel by car. If X was indeed an inferior good, then in panel (a) of Figure 4.6 the new consumption optimum C^1 would lie somewhere to the left of C^0.

To focus on the relationship between income and quantity demanded, we can draw information from the ICC in panel (a) of Figure 4.6 to construct our consumer's Engel curve for X shown in panel (b). For example, from budget line HN (associated with income I^0) and optimum C^0 in panel (a), we can take the income I^0 and the corresponding quantity demanded x^0, which yields one point on the Engel curve in panel (b). Similarly, from $H'N'$ (associated with income I^1) and optimum C^1 we can take the income I^1 and the quantity x^1, which yields a second point on the Engel curve. Repeating the process at other optimums in panel (a) (not shown), we can generate our consumer's complete Engel curve, which shows the quantity demanded for any given income, holding preferences and the prices of X and Y constant. Notice again the preceding ceteris paribus clause. If the prices of X or Y were to change, then the Engel curve in panel (b) would change. For example, if the price of good X were to increase, the entire Engel curve would shift to the left indicating a smaller quantity demanded for X at any given income. Note also that the upward slope of the Engel curve in panel (b) shows that X is, in this case, a normal good.

4.3 Applications

Terrorists' Targeting Choices and the Substitution Principle

The rational choice model can be applied to the choices of terrorist organizations. These choices might pertain to levels of terrorist activity or to specific targets for attack. To understand decisions about terrorist targeting choices, in Figure 4.7 we assume that a terrorist organization allocates a portion of its yearly income, I_t, to attack political targets (*Pol*) (for example, embassy buildings, diplomats) and civilian targets (*Civ*) (for example, tourists; shoppers in the marketplace; worshippers in a church, mosque, or synagogue). Although the distinction between political and civilian targets is not always clear, the distinction can be helpful for under-standing a terrorist organization as a rational entity in its targeting beha-vior. Assume that the average cost or price to the terrorist organization of training and equipping personnel to attack political targets is P_p and P_c is the same for civilian targets. The organization's budget constraint *HN* then satisfies the equation $P_pPol+P_cCiv=I_t$. Preferences over *Pol* and *Civ* are represented by indifference curves in the usual manner. Steeper indiffer-ence curves would indicate a greater willingness to engage in attacks against political targets, while flatter indifference curves would imply a greater taste for civilian targets. The curvature of the indifference curves is also important for understanding terrorist targeting behavior. Specifically, more curvature implies a lower degree of substitutability between *Pol* and *Civ*, while less curvature implies a higher degree of substitutability. The optimum targeting profile occurs at point e in Figure 4.7, with *Pol** in political targets and *Civ** in civilian targets attacked. Notice at the optimum that the marginal rate of substitution between *Pol* and *Civ*, which is the absolute value of the slope of the indifference curve, is just equal to the relative price of political targets P_p/P_c, which is the absolute value of the slope of the budget line.

To understand decisions about terrorist targeting in the rational choice model, consider the high-profile bombings by al Qaeda against US embassies in Kenya and Tanzania on August 7, 1998 and the alleged al Qaeda role in the October 12, 2000 attack against the USA naval vessel, the USS Cole. These targets can be classified as political. After such attacks,

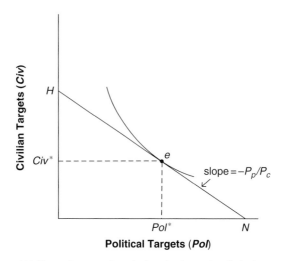

Figure 4.7 Terrorist targeting choices in the rational choice model.

it was not surprising that the USA and other countries implemented measures to better secure or harden such targets such as new barricades at embassy buildings, new travel measures to protect diplomats, and modified security protocols for US military forces when entering foreign ports. In the rational choice model, such policies serve to raise the average cost or price to a terrorist organization of attacking political targets, that is, P_p rises. In panels (a) and (b) of Figure 4.8, we show two possible outcomes of the increase in P_p on a terrorist organization's targeting behavior. In accordance with the law of demand, the terrorist organization responds to the price increase by reducing its attacks against political targets at the new optimum *f*. Driving the response is the substitution principle, whereby the higher price of political targets creates an incentive to substitute away from political targets in favor of civilian targets. What distinguishes the two panels of Figure 4.8 is the strength of this substitution. In panel (a), the substitution effect is assumed to be relatively small, implying limited substitutability between political and civilian targets. As a result, the decrease in political targets is comparatively small. This means that when the limited cutback in political targets is combined with the higher cost per political target, the terrorist organization's expenditures on political targets actually increase. Given their fixed budget, this in turn leads the organization to decrease also their targeting of civilians. Alternatively, in panel (b), the substitution effect is assumed to be relatively large, implying easier substitutability between the two target types. As a consequence, the

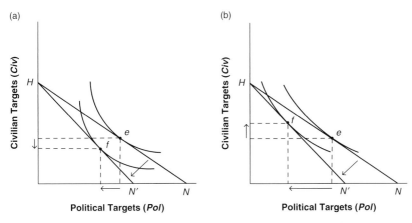

Figure 4.8 Terrorist targeting and the substitution principle.
(a) Small decrease in political targets
(b) Large decrease in political targets

decrease in political targets is comparatively large. However, as an unintended consequence, the terrorist organization actually increases their targeting of civilians. Despite the higher cost per political target, the decrease in the number of political targets is large enough to cause expenditures on those targets to fall. This decrease in expenditures on political targets then frees up income and permits the terrorist organization to finance an increase in civilian targeting. In brief, the substitution principle in Figure 4.8 sets up a dilemma: the more responsive the terrorist organization is to the increased price of political targets, the more likely it is that the hardening of political targets will have the unintended consequence of increased attacks against civilians.

Notice in Figure 4.8 that the indifference curves in panel (b) have relatively little curvature compared to the indifference curves in panel (a). This is no trivial matter. When a terrorist organization's indifference curves over targets have relatively little curvature, it implies that the organization sees the target classes as highly substitutable and thus is quite willing to substitute among the targets. There is some evidence that high target substitutability characterizes some terrorist organizations, including al Qaeda. For example, former al Qaeda leader Osama bin Laden was quoted: "We do not differentiate between those dressed in military uniforms and civilians. They're all targets" (BBC News 1998). The statement implies that al Qaeda's indifference curves over military and civilian targets may be close to or actually linear (perfect substitutes)

(Anderton and Carter 2006, p. 444). Given such preferences, one could predict that the hardening of political targets by the USA and other countries in the late 1990s and early 2000s could lead to unintended consequences for civilians. Terrorist analysts Walter Enders and Todd Sandler reached this very conclusion. Prior to the September 11, 2001 terrorist attacks by al Qaeda, Enders and Sandler (2000, p. 330) cautioned that terrorist substitution possibilities raise the risk to civilians: "If a government responds by tightening security at official sites (for example, embassies and government buildings) as is currently being done by the United States, its civilian targets (for example, hotels, market-places, parks) will become *relatively* less secure and [more] attractive."

Landmines and the Substitution Principle

We have introduced the rationality principle in the context of consumer choice, but as noted earlier, actors in rational choice models can take on a variety of identities. For example, most economic theory assumes that producers, like consumers, are rational. In particular, producers are assumed to minimize cost for any given output or to maximize output for any given cost. The parallels between consumer choice models and producer choice models are abundant and close. To demonstrate just how close they are, we now adapt the terrorist targeting model of Figure 4.8 to the following application dealing with landmines.

The use of landmines in various interstate and civil wars around the world has caused not only severe civilian casualties but also serious economic dislocations, including the abandonment of fertile farmlands due to fear of mines (Merrouche 2008). To control the proliferation of landmines, the Antipersonnel Mine-Ban Convention (also known as the Mine Ban Treaty or the Ottawa Treaty) was entered into force in 1999; it has a current membership of 166 nations. To the extent that the treaty is effective, its direct impact is to reduce the supply of landmines and thus raise the price to nonsignatories.

Assume a rebel organization in a civil war attempts to maximize the amount of territory it controls by allocating a fixed income between two military inputs: landmines and young males armed with assault rifles. To adapt Figure 4.8 to this context, assume now that the items labeled on the X and Y axes are landmines (L) and young males (YM), respectively. The corresponding unit costs or prices for these inputs are P_L and P_{YM}. Given these input prices, the fixed income generates a cost constraint, as shown in either panel of Figure 4.8 by the budget line HN. The final adaptation of Figure 4.8 to our new context is to assume that the indifference curves are isoquants, as they are called in production theory. An isoquant is a locus of points showing alternative input combinations that can be used to produce the same amount of output, in this case territory controlled. Isoquants in many ways are analogous to indifference curves. For example, higher isoquants correspond to larger outputs, and isoquants ordinarily slope downward. The rebel organization is free to choose any combination of inputs within its budget. To maximize territory controlled, it chooses an input combination lying on the highest isoquant along its budget line, as shown by point *e* in either panel of Figure 4.8.

Now suppose that the Mine Ban Treaty is successful in raising the price of mines, which in either panel causes the rebels' budget line to rotate inward to *HN'*. In accordance with the law of demand, and consistent with the aims of the treaty, the rebels respond to the price increase by reducing their use of landmines at the new optimum *f*. Driving the response is the substitution principle, whereby the higher price of landmines creates an incentive to substitute away from mines in favor of young males with assault rifles. In panel (a) of Figure 4.8, the substitution effect is relatively small, implying limited substitutability between landmines and young males. As a result, the decrease in mines is comparatively small. Alternatively, in panel (b) of Figure 4.8, the substitution effect is assumed to be relatively large, implying easier substitutability between landmines and young males. As a consequence, the decrease in mines is comparatively large. However, as an unintended consequence, the rebels in this case increase their use of young males with assault rifles. Once again, Figure 4.8 sets up a dilemma: the more responsive the rebels are to the increased price of mines, the more likely it is that the treaty will have what are perhaps unintended consequences in the increased recruitment of young males.

The substitution principle illustrated in the terrorist targeting and landmine control cases is no small matter in conflict economics. Such effects occur in many domains related to conflict and peace, for example, arms control that restrains weapons system *X* might lead to greater developments of weapons system *Y*, greater protection of rebel territorial strongholds (item *X*) against a government might cause the government to attack the rebels' civilian support structure (item *Y*), and protection of civilians in one town (item *X*) might cause atrocity perpetrators to attack civilians in and unprotected town (item *Y*). Such substitutions are not always nefarious; for example, policymakers promoting peace often implement protocols designed to raise the cost or price of war to induce the parties to substitute peace for war. A formal condition for the "ballooning out" of

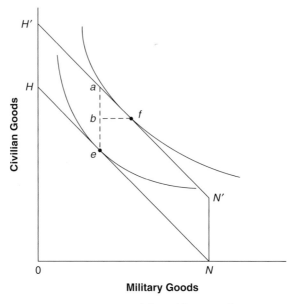

Figure 4.9 Fungibility of foreign aid.

purchases of some other item *Y* (young males in this subsection, civilian targets in the previous subsection) when the price of an initial item *X* rises (landmines in this subsection, political targets in the previous subsection) is available in Anderton and Carter (2005).

Arms and the Fungibility of Civilian Aid

Many governments and nongovernmental organizations provide humanitarian aid to nations suffering from war and its aftermath. One policy challenge is how to prevent aid from inadvertently stimulating the recipient's acquisition of military goods. This is an example of the fungibility problem whereby the aid recipient reduces the allocation of domestic income to the sector receiving aid and increases the allocation of domestic income to one or more other sectors. Here we use the rational choice model to depict an aid recipient's incentive to increase its military goods, even when the aid package is designed to strictly support nonmilitary activities.

Figure 4.9 shows the effects of pure civilian aid on the recipient's allocation of resources between military and civilian goods. Think of the aid as food, clothing, or medical supplies earmarked for nonmilitary purposes. The recipient might be a nation or a nonstate group, while the donor might be an intergovernmental organization like the United Nations, an international nongovernmental organization like the Red Cross or Red Crescent, or a sympathetic foreign government. In the figure, the recipient's consumption optimum without aid occurs at point *e* on budget line *HN*. When the donor supplies *ae* units of civilian goods as aid, the recipient's budget line shifts up by that same vertical distance. The new consumption optimum occurs at point *f* on budget line *H'N'N*. Notice that the aid package, though purely civilian, has served to increase the amount of military goods consumed. In Figure 4.9, the aid package of *ae* units of civilian goods has made it possible for the recipient to reduce its own acquisition of consumer goods by *ab*, thereby freeing up enough income to purchase *bf* additional units of military goods.

4.4 Bibliographic Notes

Textbook presentations of the rational choice model abound; see, for example, Mankiw (2018) and Nicholson and Snyder (2016). For a sampling of the debate surrounding the rationality assumption see in economics, Kahneman (2003) and Gintis (2009), and in political science Brown, Cote, Lynn-Jones, and Miller (2000), Singer (2000), Kaufman (2005), Oppenheimer (2012), and Vahabi (2015). For supportive and critical views of rational choice theory applied to genocide, see Anderton (2014a, pp. 126–32) and Midlarsky (2005, pp. 64–74), respectively.

Feridun (2014) reviews the theoretical and empirical literature on the fungibility of foreign aid. His own empirical analysis finds that aid to North Cyprus is fungible and "results in an increase in non-development military expenditures" (p. 506). Based on a large sample empirical analysis, Kono and Montinola (2013) find that "autocratic recipients have systematically diverted development aid toward military spending" (p. 626). For literature related to terrorism targeting and landmine control, see, respectively, Chapters 13 and 15 and the bibliographic notes therein.

5

Game Theory

A strategic interaction wherein outcomes are systematically determined by the combination of players' actions is called a game. By this definition, poker and baseball are games, as are wars and arms races. Because outcomes in games are jointly determined, players' well-being depends not only on their own decisions but also on the decisions of others. This interdependence can greatly complicate any attempted rational choice by the players. It also makes game theory, the formal study of such strategic interaction, both challenging and fascinating.

5.1 Basic Concepts and the Aggression Game

Elements of the Game

Games consist of certain elements, the specifics of which distinguish the different games. The players may be individuals or groups, including nations. Explicit and/or implicit rules control the feasible actions, order of play, available information, and determination of outcomes. Preferences over outcomes in turn determine players' payoffs or utilities. In basic game theory, players are assumed to have common knowledge of the rationality of all players and of the elements of the game, including payoffs. When these assumptions hold, the game is said to be one of complete information.

To illustrate these elements, consider a simple game that we will refer to as the aggression game. The game involves two players called, generically, *A* and *B*. Player *A* moves first and can either *Aggress* against player *B* or *Refrain*. If *B* is aggressed against, then *B* can either *Retaliate* or *Appease*. Assume *A*'s most preferred outcome occurs when *A*'s aggression is followed

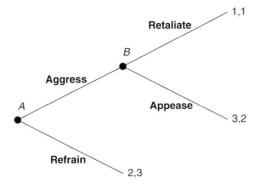

Figure 5.1 Aggression game shown in extensive form.

by *B*'s appeasement; least preferred is aggression met with retaliation; intermediate is the status quo of no aggression. For *B*, retaliation has a formidable cost. Hence, least preferred by *B* is a retaliatory response to aggression; most preferred is the status quo of no aggression; intermediate is a response of appeasement. Because *A* moves prior to *B*, the game is said to be sequential; because the prior move by *A* is known by *B*, the game involves what is called perfect information.

Extensive and Normal Forms

A game can be represented in two ways: the extensive form and the normal form. The preferred representation is largely a matter of convenience. As we will see, the extensive form is typically used when moves are sequential and the normal form is more often used when moves are simultaneous.

Figure 5.1 shows the extensive form for the aggression game. Appearing as a tree diagram, the extensive form gives special attention to the order of play and to the information available to the players. Points at which a player is obliged to make a choice are called decision nodes. Branches leading from the nodes represent the actions or moves available to a player. A play of the game generates a path through the tree diagram leading to a particular outcome and a pair of payoffs, with *A*'s payoff listed first. In Figure 5.1 the payoffs are assumed to be ordinal utilities, so that higher numbers indicate more preferred outcomes.

Game theory analyzes the strategies available to the players in a game. A strategy specifies what action the player will take at each and every point at which the player is obliged to make a move. Hence, a strategy is a complete plan that in principle can be written down in advance and then executed as

Player *B*

		Retaliate	Appease
	Aggress	1,1	3,2
Player *A*			
	Refrain	2,3	2,3

Figure 5.2 Aggression game shown in normal form.

the play of the game unfolds. In the aggression game, the players' strategies are easily identified. Player *A* has two strategies *Aggress* and *Refrain*, and player *B* has two strategies *Retaliate* and *Appease*. Strategies in other games can be more numerous and more complicated. A strategy profile is a listing of strategies, one for each player. In the aggression game there are four strategy pairs (with *A*'s strategy first): (*Aggress,Retaliate*), (*Aggress,Appease*), (*Refrain,Retaliate*), and (*Refrain,Appease*). Because strategies are complete plans, a strategy profile determines a play of the game and hence a path leading to a particular outcome with payoffs. For example, in Figure 5.1 it can be seen that the strategy pair (*Aggress,Retaliate*) results in payoffs equal to 1 for each player. For the strategy pair (*Refrain,Retaliate*), the play of the game both begins and ends with *A*'s move, resulting in payoffs of 2 for *A* and 3 for *B*. Note that *B*'s specified strategy of *Retaliate* means that *B* will retaliate if the game reaches *B*'s decision node, but the strategy profile determines whether that node will actually be reached during the play of the game.

This leads naturally to the second way a game can be represented, namely, by its normal form, which gives emphasis to the available strategies and strategy profiles. As shown in Figure 5.2 for the aggression game, the normal form consists of a payoff matrix corresponding to the various strategy profiles. For example, if *A*'s strategy *Aggress* in the first row is combined with *B*'s strategy *Retaliate* in the first column, then the strategy profile (*Aggress,Retaliate*) is formed, resulting in the payoff pair (1,1) shown in the top left cell of the matrix and derived in the preceding paragraph. Other profiles and payoff pairs are generated similarly.

Solutions and Equilibriums

Given a game set forth in either extensive or normal form, we want to determine how the game will be played. Equivalently, we want to find the solution of the game expressed in the form of a strategy profile. Think of a solution as a way of playing the game that is compelling and hence is believable for the players and predictable by the theorist. Turning to the aggression game, are there any strategy profiles that qualify as a solution? We might attempt to answer the question by trial and error. For starters, could (*Aggress,Retaliate*) be a solution, that is, a compelling and hence believable way to play the game? The answer is no, shown as follows. If *A* believed *B* was going to choose *Retaliate*, then *A*'s optimal strategy or best reply would be *Refrain* rather than *Aggress*, because her payoff would then be 2 compared to a lower payoff of 1 (see Figure 5.2). Hence, *A* would not believe that the game will be played in accordance with the strategy pair (*Aggress,Retaliate*). Similarly, if *B* thought *A* was going to choose *Aggress*, then *B*'s best reply would be *Appease* rather than *Retaliate*, which would return for him a payoff of 2 rather than 1. Hence, *B* also would not believe that the game will be played according to the strategy pair (*Aggress,Retaliate*). In short, (*Aggress,Retaliate*) is not a compelling way to play the game and therefore cannot be a solution to the game. Similar reasoning shows that (*Refrain,Appease*) cannot be a solution.

What emerges from this way of thinking is an important principle: if a strategy profile is a solution, then it must be the case that each player's strategy is a best reply to the strategies of the other players. This in turn leads to the concept of Nash equilibrium, defined as a strategy profile wherein each player's strategy is optimal given the equilibrium strategies of the other players. Equivalently, a Nash equilibrium is a strategy profile wherein no player has an incentive to change its strategy unilaterally. The original principle can now be restated as follows: if a strategy profile is a solution, then it must be a Nash equilibrium.

A consequence of the principle is that the search for a solution can be narrowed to a systematic identification of Nash equilibriums. The method of search follows from the definition of Nash equilibrium. To keep things simple, assume a two-person game represented in normal form. For each strategy of each player, identify the other player's best reply by underlining the highest payoff available to that player. A Nash equilibrium is then a pair of mutual best replies and is identified by a payoff pair in which both payoffs are underlined.

We can illustrate the method with the aggression game, repeated in normal form in Figure 5.3. We begin by finding player *A*'s best replies. Suppose *B* chooses *Retaliate*. Player *A*'s available payoffs appear in the first column of the matrix and equal 1 if they play *Aggress* and 2 if they play *Refrain*. We underline the higher payoff of 2, thereby identifying *A*'s best reply as *Refrain*. Suppose instead that *B* chooses *Appease*. Now *A*'s

Player *B*

		Retaliate	Appease
	Aggress	1,1	<u>3</u>,<u>2</u>
Player *A*			
	Refrain	<u>2</u>,<u>3</u>	<u>2</u>,<u>3</u>

Figure 5.3 Aggression game with Nash equilibriums.

available payoffs appear in the second column and equal 3 if they play *Aggress* and 2 if they play *Refrain*. We underline the higher payoff of 3, thereby indicating *A*'s best reply as *Aggress*. We repeat the exercise to find *B*'s best replies. Suppose *A* chooses *Aggress*. Player *B*'s available payoffs are in the first row and equal 1 if they play *Retaliate* and 2 if they play *Appease*. We underline the higher payoff of 2, showing *B*'s best reply as *Appease*. Suppose instead that *A* chooses *Refrain*. Now *B*'s available payoffs are in the second row and both equal 3 regardless of whether they play *Retaliate* or *Appease*. We underline the equal payoffs of 3, indicating that *Retaliate* and *Appease* are equally best replies for *B*.

Using this method, Nash equilibriums are shown by strategy pairs for which both players' payoffs are underlined in the corresponding payoff pair. As seen in Figure 5.3, the aggression game includes two Nash equilibriums (*Refrain,Retaliate*) and (*Aggress,Appease*). According to the Nash equilibrium principle, if a solution exists, it must be one of these two strategy pairs, but which one? In the case of the aggression game, we can push the analysis farther by either of two solution techniques, called iterated dominance and backward induction.

To understand iterated dominance, we need several definitions and another basic principle. When comparing a player's strategies, we say that one strategy strictly dominates another if the first strategy earns a payoff that is strictly higher regardless of what strategy the other player might choose. Hence, one strategy strictly dominates another if it is "always better." Similarly, we say that one strategy weakly dominates another if the first strategy earns a payoff that is, first, at least as high regardless of what strategy the other player might choose and, second, strictly higher for at least one strategy that the other player might choose. Hence, one strategy weakly dominates another if it is "always at least as good and sometimes better." If a single strategy dominates every other strategy available to a player, then it is called a dominant strategy for that player.

Building on these definitions, the dominance principle states that a rational player will not choose a dominated strategy. When the rationality of the players is common knowledge, the dominance principle can be used to eliminate dominated strategies from consideration in the search for a solution. In some games, a dominant strategy exists for each player, meaning that all other strategies can be eliminated. The game is then said to be solved by strict or weak dominance, and the profile consisting of each player's dominant strategy is called a dominant-strategy equilibrium. The best known example of a game solved by strict dominance is the prisoner's dilemma, which we will take up in Section 5.2. Unfortunately, most games cannot be solved by either strict or weak dominance. Many games, however, do yield a solution by the repeated application of the dominance principle in a technique known as iterated dominance.

Iterated dominance can be used as follows to solve the aggression game in Figure 5.3. Notice that neither of *A*'s strategies initially dominates the other: *A*'s best reply is *Refrain* if *B* chooses *Retaliate*, but it is *Aggress* if *B* chooses *Appease*. On the other hand, *B*'s strategy *Appease* weakly dominates *Retaliate*: *B*'s payoff for *Appease* is the same as for *Retaliate* if *A* chooses *Refrain*, and it is strictly higher if *A* chooses *Aggress*. By the dominance principle, *B* will not choose *Retaliate*, so we can eliminate *Retaliate* from consideration and count on *B* to play *Appease*. But if it is known that *B* will *Appease*, *A*'s *Aggress* now strictly dominates *Refrain*: *A* will earn a payoff of 3 by aggressing but only 2 by refraining. Thus, applying the dominance principle for a second time, *A* will not choose *Refrain*. Successively eliminating the strategies *Retaliate* and *Refrain* leaves the strategy pair (*Aggress,Appease*), which is one of the two Nash equilibriums and what we take to be the solution to the game.

The same solution can be reached by the technique of backward induction also known as rollback. The method is built on the assumption that rational players are forward looking, so that in a sequential game they will choose their moves in anticipation of other players' optimal reactions. Accordingly, a sequential game of perfect information can be solved by determining players' optimal moves from back to front, that is, by beginning with the last move of the game and working backward to the first move. We illustrate the method with the aggression game, repeated in extensive form in Figure 5.4. The last decision point of the game belongs to *B*, who, if given the move, would optimally choose *Appease* for a payoff of 2 rather than *Retaliate* with a payoff of 1. We indicate *B*'s optimal action by darkening the branch for *Appease*. Next we back up to the preceding move (here the first move of the game), which belongs to *A*. If *A* chooses *Aggress*, they can

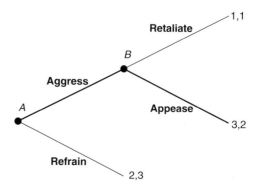

Figure 5.4 Aggression game solved by backward induction.

anticipate that *B* will optimally play *Appease*, thereby returning to *A* a payoff of 3. If *A* chooses *Refrain*, they know the game ends with a payoff of 2 for them. Thus, their optimal choice is *Aggress*, which we indicate by darkening the branch for that action. From the darkened actions we form the players' optimal strategies, yielding the strategy pair (*Aggress,Appease*), which we recognize as one of the two Nash equilibriums and again take as the solution of the game. In formal terms, the solution (*Aggress,Appease*) obtained by backward induction is known as a subgame perfect equilibrium; more intuitively, it is sometimes called a rollback equilibrium (Dixit, Skeath, and Reiley 2015, ch. 3).

A side benefit of the backward induction technique is that it helps expose why the other Nash equilibrium (*Refrain,Retaliate*) does not qualify as a solution to the aggression game. Think of *B*'s equilibrium strategy in this case as a threat made by *B* to retaliate if *A* aggresses against them. If *A* believed the threat, then *A*'s optimal action would be *Refrain*, which explains why (*Refrain,Retaliate*) is a Nash equilibrium. Under the game's assumptions, however, *A* would not find the retaliatory threat to be credible. If *B* threatens to retaliate but *A* aggresses anyway, then as seen already, it is in *B*'s interest to appease, and *A* knows this. Thus, *A* will not believe that *B* will play *Retaliate*, and for that reason (*Refrain,Retaliate*) fails as a solution to the game.

5.2 Prisoner's Dilemma

In this and the following section, we introduce two of the best-known games in game theory, the prisoner's dilemma and chicken. These games are especially useful in conflict economics because they help explain why

Figure 5.5 Prisoner's dilemma game.

tensions between cooperation and conflict are prevalent in social interactions and particularly in international and intrastate relations. They also allow us to illustrate and elaborate on some of the concepts introduced to this point.

Elements of the Game

The prisoner's dilemma is a generic game that arises in many contexts. In the original scenario, two suspects in a crime, say *A* and *B*, are interrogated in separate rooms. If one of them confesses and the other does not, the first gets a light sentence of one year and the other gets a hard 10 years. If both confess, each gets a reduced sentence of five years. If neither confesses, they each get a two-year sentence on a related but lesser crime. The normal form of the game is shown in Figure 5.5. Each prisoner simultaneously chooses *Confess* or *Not Confess*, thus resulting in the four possible jail sentences shown in the matrix.

Dominant Strategies and Nash Equilibrium

The game in Figure 5.5 is solved by strict dominance. Note that *Confess* is a strictly dominant strategy for *A*: if *B* chooses *Not Confess*, then *A*'s best reply is to choose *Confess* to achieve a light sentence of one rather than two years; if *B* chooses *Confess*, *A*'s best reply is again *Confess* to obtain a sentence of five rather than 10 years. By the same logic, *Confess* is also strictly dominant for *B*. Thus the solution is (*Confess*, *Confess*), which is a unique Nash equilibrium. The dilemma in Figure 5.5 is that while it is in the prisoners' collective interest to stay quiet and not confess, self-interest drives them to select their dominant strategies and confess.

To appreciate why this solution is remarkable, we begin with some additional terminology. An outcome is Pareto inefficient if there exists an alternative outcome that would make at least one player better off and no player worse off. If no such alternative exists, then the outcome is said to be Pareto efficient. Now return to Figure 5.5. Instead of both choosing their dominant strategy of *Confess*, if both chose *Not Confess*, they could each achieve a jail term of two years rather than five years. In this way both prisoners could be better off, thus rendering the solution outcome Pareto inefficient. Here we see a tension between cooperation and conflict. The benefits of mutual restraint draw the prisoners toward not confessing, but the lure of an even lower jail term pulls them even more strongly toward confessing. They each end up with a jail term of five years (as given by the Nash equilibrium solution) even though the strategic setting contained an outcome in which they could have each achieved two years in jail.

Application: Arms Rivalry and Arms Control

We now consider the prisoner's dilemma game in the context of an arms rivalry between two countries A and B, where each country perceives that its security is determined by its relative armaments. Each country simultaneously chooses either a *Low* or *High* level of arms, thus resulting in one of four possible outcomes. Unlike the original prisoner's dilemma in Figure 5.5 where lower numbers (jail terms) were preferred, now we assume ordinal payoffs where higher numbers are preferred Assume that a country is best off (ordinal payoff=4) when it has military superiority, with its own arms at a high level and its rival's at a low level. Second best (ordinal payoff=3) is an outcome of military balance of low arms and hence low economic costs. Less desirable is a military balance with high arms and thus high costs (ordinal payoff=2). Worst for a country is a position of military insecurity with low arms facing the rival's higher arms (ordinal payoff=1). Under these assumptions, the arms rivalry generates a prisoner's dilemma game, the normal form for which is shown in Figure 5.6. As in Figure 5.5, the game in Figure 5.6 is solved by strict dominance. *High* is a strictly dominant strategy for A: if B chooses *Low*, then A's best reply is to choose *High* to achieve military superiority; if B chooses *High*, A's best reply is again *High* to reach military parity. By the same logic, *High* is also strictly dominant for B. Thus the solution is (*High,High*), which is a unique Nash equilibrium in Figure 5.6.

Suppose instead of both countries choosing their dominant strategy of *High* in Figure 5.6, they both chose *Low*. Under these circumstances they

	Country *B*	
	Low Armaments	High Armaments
Low Armaments	3,3	1,4
High Armaments	4,1	2,2

Country *A*

Figure 5.6 Arms rivalry as a prisoner's dilemma game.

could still have military parity but at a lower economic cost to each. In this way both countries could be better off, thus rendering the solution outcome Pareto inefficient. Here again we see a tension between cooperation and conflict. The benefits of mutual restraint draw the countries toward low armaments, but the lure of military superiority pulls them even more strongly toward high armaments. Moreover, if the game is played sequentially, backward induction shows that there is no first- or second-mover advantage, and the outcome will still be high armaments by both countries. Hence, whether the decisions are made simultaneously or sequentially, the predicted outcome is Pareto inefficient.

In response to the inefficiency of the prisoner's dilemma outcome, suppose the two rivals enter into an arms control agreement that stipulates mutually low armaments. Their choices would then be to *Cooperate* (by abiding by the agreement with low arms) or to *Defect* (by cheating on the agreement with high arms). A little reflection shows that the rivals would still find themselves in a prisoner's dilemma, each with a dominant strategy to *Defect*. Game theoretic considerations would therefore predict that the agreement would fail.

5.3 Repeated Prisoner's Dilemma

Does game theoretic analysis of the prisoner's dilemma mean there is no prospect for cooperation between the rivals, despite the inefficiency of the outcome? Suppose, for example, in the arms rivalry game the players could add an inspection and verification mechanism to the arms control agreement in an attempt to bind themselves to mutual cooperation. What is to prevent the rivals from attempting to secretly cheat on such a mechanism? The question of the incentive to defect in a prisoner's dilemma game is important and worth addressing more generally because the strategic context of the game is so prevalent in human affairs.

Player *B*

	Cooperate	Defect
Cooperate	R,R	S,T̲
Defect	T̲,S	P̲,P̲

Player *A* (Cooperate / Defect rows)

Figure 5.7 Stage game for repeated prisoner's dilemma game.

The Potential for Mutual Cooperation

Assume two players choose simultaneously between *Cooperate* and *Defect* in a prisoner's dilemma environment. Mutual cooperation promises gains to both, but self-interest favors mutual defection. In the absence of effective external enforcement, does standard game theory offer any reason to believe that cooperation might emerge and be sustained? The answer is yes, if the prisoner's dilemma game is repeated by the players an indefinite or infinite number of times. The basic intuition is that in a repeated game, a player can be punished for defecting by the other player's choosing to defect in one or more subsequent rounds. If that punishment is anticipated and sufficiently costly, then it can be rational to cooperate throughout the repeated game. Without getting too formal, let's sharpen this intuition.

Suppose players *A* and *B* participate in a repeated prisoner's dilemma. Figure 5.7 presents the normal form using more general notation due to Axelrod (1984). In the present context, the figure shows what is known as the stage game, meaning the game that is played in each round of the repeated game. The payoffs in the stage game can be remembered as follows: *T* is the temptation to defect, *R* is the reward for mutual cooperation, *P* is the penalty for mutual defection, and *S* is the sucker's payoff. For the game to qualify as a prisoner's dilemma, assume that $T > R > P > S$. Assume also that the payoffs are cardinal, meaning that their magnitudes as well as rank ordering are meaningful. For simplicity, we can think of the payoffs as denominated in dollars. At the completion of each round, the game continues to the next round with known probability π and terminates with probability $(1-\pi)$. Hence, the length of the game is indefinite but is known by the players to be subject to the laws of probability.

The impetus for cooperation in the repeated game is the threat that a player's defection will be punished. Suppose after a number of rounds of mutual cooperation, *A* defects. How might *B* punish that defection? Player *B* could defect in the next round and then forgive *A* by returning to cooperation in the round after that. More severely, B could defect in each of the next two rounds and then forgive A by returning to cooperation. Extending the logic, it is easy to see that the severest punishment available to B is to defect in every subsequent round and hence never forgive A. The strategy that threatens this severest punishment is called the grim-trigger strategy, or more simply *Unforgiving*: cooperate until the other player defects, and then always defect thereafter. If any strategies exist whereby B can induce A to cooperate, *Unforgiving* must be among them. By the symmetry of the game, the same logic applies to A's inducing B to cooperate. We can now rephrase our earlier question by asking whether the strategy pair (*Unforgiving,Unforgiving*) is a Nash equilibrium. If the answer is yes, then there is reason to believe that cooperation can emerge and be sustained; otherwise, basic game theory must predict that rational players will defect in a repeated game, just as in a one-shot game.

To determine whether (*Unforgiving,Unforgiving*) is a Nash equilibrium, let's focus on A and ask whether *Unforgiving* is a best reply to B's *Unforgiving*. If A plays *Unforgiving* (as does B), then they (like B) never defects and in every round they (like B) receive the reward R for mutual cooperation. Alternatively, suppose A defects in some round t. Because that would elicit B's defection in every subsequent round, A should also defect in every subsequent round to avoid the sucker's payoff S in those rounds. If A defects in round t and every round thereafter, then A will receive the temptation payoff T in round t and the penalty for mutual defection P in every round thereafter. Comparing these payoffs to those they would receive by playing *Unforgiving*, in the single round t they gain $(T–R)$, but in every round thereafter they lose $(R–P)$. If the single period's gain is outweighed by the string of subsequent losses, then defection does not pay, and A's *Unforgiving* is a best reply to B's *Unforgiving*. By symmetry, B's *Unforgiving* is likewise a best reply. Thus, (*Unforgiving, Unforgiving*) is a Nash equilibrium, and the answer to our earlier question is a qualified affirmative: if the string of losses outweighs the gain, then cooperation can emerge and be sustained in the repeated game.

This is an important result because it says that cooperation can be mutually rational in long-term interactions characterized by the prisoner's dilemma incentives. To this result we must add several points, however. First, in the formal mathematics of the preceding argument, the losses in subsequent rounds are systematically discounted because they are realized only if the game continues and because they occur later in time relative to the single-period gain. Holding constant the payoffs T, R, and P, the higher the continuation probability π and the lower the interest rate, the more heavily the future losses are weighted, and hence the greater is the prospect for cooperation. Second, while (*Unforgiving,Unforgiving*) can be a Nash equilibrium, it is by no means a unique equilibrium. For example, it can also be shown that both players' defecting in every round is also a Nash equilibrium, resulting in a decidedly uncooperative Pareto inefficient outcome. Lastly, cooperation can emerge under standard assumptions only if the number of rounds is infinite or indefinite. In a game of known length, there is no incentive to cooperate in the end round and consequently, by backward induction, in any other round. Hence, for a finitely repeated game, mutual defection in all rounds is the predicted outcome.

Tit-for-Tat

A particularly famous strategy for inducing cooperation in a repeated prisoner's dilemma of indefinite or infinite length is *Tit-For-Tat* (*TFT*), whereby a player cooperates in the first round and then matches the other player's preceding move in each round thereafter. Using an argument similar to that noted earlier, it can be shown that (*TFT,TFT*) can be a Nash equilibrium with mutual cooperation in every round. Suppose in an arms rivalry, for example, that two nations *A* and *B* are each playing *TFT* and they have been cooperating over the past several years by each choosing *Low* rather than *High* weapons. Under *TFT*, each player will respond next year with *Low* armaments because each is mimicking its rival's move from the prior year. It would seem that the players, though rivals, can stay on the mutually cooperative path into the indefinite-length future with *Low* armaments persisting in every year.

There is, however, a nagging flaw associated with *TFT*, namely, it is vulnerable to misperceptions. Suppose that *B* perceives that *A* is cheating on the arms control agreement even though this is not the case. In the next round, *B* will retaliate against *A* by choosing *High* armaments because *B* perceived that *A* chose *High* armaments. In the subsequent round, *A* will react under *TFT* to *B*'s choice of *High* armaments by also choosing *High* armaments. If the players' continue to stick with *TFT*, high armament choices by the two sides will echo back and forth from one round to the next until a counter-misperception offsets the original misperception. Misperceptions are quite common in social relations. Even if the probability of misperception in any given round is low, *TFT* will eventually react incorrectly, thereby fostering noncooperation in the relationship. As Dixit and Nalebuff (1991, p. 107) note, even "the slightest possibility of misperceptions results in a complete breakdown in the success of tit-for-tat."

Other Trigger Strategies to Induce Cooperation

The reason *TFT* is vulnerable to misperceptions is that it is too reactive. Specifically, *TFT* is an "eye-for-an-eye" or a one-to-one retaliation strategy: if you cross me by one unit of harm, I will cross you with one unit of harm. The problem with *TFT* is that the perception of a rival's one unit of harm might simply be a misunderstanding; that is, no harm really happened or the rival's action was much less than one unit of harm. Moreover, your one unit of harm in retaliation under *TFT* will cause your rival to retaliate under *TFT* with one unit of real harm in the next round. If, owing to misperception, full reactions and counter-reactions under *TFT* are unleashed, the relationship will degenerate into animosity. Animosities owing to misperceptions happen quite frequently in relations between and within states and even in our personal lives. In games where one adopts a trigger strategy in an ongoing rivalry, the solution to the risk of misperception is to be slow to react and to seek more complete information. Dixit and Nalebuff (1991, p. 113), for example, recommend a trigger strategy in which one forgives when an aggressive act appears to be an exception. In some religious orders, a trigger strategy of never reacting with aggression is cultivated (for example, "turn the other cheek").

5.4 Chicken

Elements of the Game

The generic chicken game can arise in many contexts, but it takes its name from a supposed encounter between two teenage rivals who drive their cars toward each other on a collision course with their friends looking on to see who will swerve first. Here we consider the possible outcomes to the game based upon ordinal payoffs in which 4 is best and 1 is worst. The teenager who swerves first is a "chicken" and loses in the eyes of peers (ordinal payoff=2), while the one who steers straight is the winner (ordinal payoff=4). If both steer straight, they suffer the worst outcome, which is death (ordinal payoff=1); if both swerve, they share the shame, but avoid death (ordinal payoff=3).

Nash Equilibriums

As one might imagine, the game has no satisfactory solution as shown by the normal form in Figure 5.8. Notice that there are two Nash equilibriums

Teenager *B*

		Swerve	Don't Swerve
	Swerve	3,3	2,4
Teenager *A*			
	Don't Swerve	4,2	1,1

Figure 5.8 Chicken game with simultaneous moves.

(*Don't Swerve,Swerve*) and (*Swerve, Don't Swerve*). The solution methods of sections 5.1 and 5.2 do not help distinguish between the two equilibriums; neither player has a dominated strategy, and backward induction is of no use when the moves are simultaneous. Of the two equilibriums, *A* prefers (*Don't Swerve,Swerve*) because it allows her to win the contest, but *B* prefers the second equilibrium (*Swerve, Don't Swerve*) for like reason. The two teenagers thus face a tension between cooperation and conflict. They are pulled together by their shared interest in avoiding death, but pushed apart by their private interest in winning the game and achieving the best outcome. Without something more, like an enforceable prior agreement, the simultaneous-move chicken game admits no compelling way to play the game and hence no solution.

Application: The Peacekeeping Game

In what follows, we recast the chicken game as a strategic interaction between nations *A* and *B* who are to send forces into a hostile territory for peacekeeping purposes. The mission will be most successful if each country sends a military unit with heavy arms. The success of the mission will be modestly reduced if one country sends a military unit with heavy arms and the other contributes a unit with light arms, but the cost savings to the country contributing light rather than heavy arms will be substantial. The mission will be a failure if both send a light arms unit. The nations share in the realized benefits of the mission, but they bear individually their own unit's cost, which by assumption is higher for heavy arms. Each country must decide whether to send a heavy arms or a light arms unit.

Initially assume that *A* and *B* choose their respective deployments simultaneously. The result is a chicken game, the normal form for which is shown with ordinal payoffs in Figure 5.9. As is the case with chicken,

Country *B*

	Heavy Arms	Light Arms
Heavy Arms	3,3	2,<u>4</u>
Light Arms	<u>4</u>,2	1,1

Country *A* (left label spanning Heavy Arms / Light Arms rows)

Figure 5.9 The peacekeeping game with simultaneous moves.

there are two Nash equilibriums (*Light,Heavy*) and (*Heavy,Light*). Of the two equilibriums, country *A* prefers (*Light,Heavy*) because it allows *A* to enjoy the benefits of a modestly successful mission with the low cost of a light arms unit. Unfortunately for the mission, country *B* prefers the second equilibrium (*Heavy,Light*) for like reason. The two nations thus face a tension between cooperation and conflict. They are pulled together by their shared interest in a successful mission, but they are pushed apart by their private interest in a low economic cost. Once again, without something more, the simultaneous-move chicken game provides no compelling solution.

Consider an alternative protocol whereby the game is played sequentially with nation *A* choosing first. Figure 5.10 shows the game's extensive form and its solution by backward induction. In the sequential game, nation *B* has two decision nodes: the upper node is reached if *A* chooses *Heavy*, and the lower is reached if *A* chooses *Light*. If given the move, *B* optimally chooses *Light* at the upper node and *Heavy* at the lower node, as shown by the respective darkened branches. Backing up to *A*'s decision node, if *A* chooses *Heavy*, then *A* can anticipate that *B* will play *Light*, thereby returning a payoff of 2 to *A*. By similar reasoning, if *A* chooses *Light*, *A* can anticipate a higher payoff of 4. Thus *A*'s optimal choice is *Light*, as indicated by its darkened branch. From the three darkened branches, we see that *A*'s optimal strategy is *Light*, and *B*'s optimal strategy is to choose the opposite of *A*'s action. The outcome, therefore, is that *A* deploys a light arms unit with a payoff of 4, and *B* deploys a heavy arms unit with a payoff of 2.

Notice that the tension between cooperation and conflict in Figure 5.10 is resolved in favor of country *A*, which secures its preferred outcome. Hence, the sequential chicken game has a first-mover advantage. By moving first, country *A* is able to exploit its position in such a way that *B*'s own interest leads it to choose the action preferred by *A*. In some

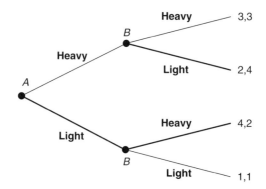

Figure 5.10 The peacekeeping game with sequential moves.

games the advantage goes to the second mover, who is able to exploit information revealed by the other player's prior move. In other games the order of play provides no advantage to either player. For example, recast the prisoner's dilemma game of Figure 5.5 as a game played sequentially rather than simultaneously with *A* choosing first. It would still be in *A*'s interest to choose *Confess* because *A* would know that it would be in *B*'s interest to choose *Confess* in the second move regardless what *A* chose in the first move. Hence, the prisoner's dilemma game has neither a first- nor a second-mover advantage.

5.5 Bibliographic Notes

This chapter offers a brief introduction to game theory, and as such there is much that is not covered including expected utility, mixed strategies, bargaining, incomplete information, and evolutionary games (bargaining and incomplete information will be touched upon in Chapter 10 and evolutionary game theory in Chapter 14). Fortunately, there exist many fine game theory texts that are rigorous and yet accessible including Dixit and Nalebuff (1991); Binmore (2007); and Dixit, Skeath, and Reiley (2015). For a game theory text focused on topics in international relations, see Kydd (2015). Because game theory's early impetus came largely from the Cold War, applications abound in conflict economics. For a single seminal contribution we would cite Schelling's (1960) wide-ranging analysis of rational behavior in situations that mix elements of conflict and common interest. Muggy and Stamm (2014) provide a literature survey on game theory applications in humanitarian operations.

6

Behavioral Economics and the Economics of Identity

In the standard rational choice model (RCM) presented in Chapter 4, decision-makers pursue their objectives by weighing the benefits and costs of possible actions and choosing the best feasible action to maximize utility. When we expanded the decision-making arena to strategically interdependent agents, we entered the realm of game theory (Chapter 5), but we continued to assume that actors behave according to standard rationality principles. In recent decades, however, numerous laboratory experiments at the intersections of economics, psychology, and sociology have discovered that human choices often deviate in systematic ways from the predictions of the standard RCM. Behavioral economics is a field in which economists and psychologists explore deviations from the RCM based primarily on psychological phenomena, while the identity economics field seeks explanations for such departures in social context, which is a domain of sociology. In this chapter we review selected concepts from behavioral economics and identity economics that seem particularly relevant for understanding violent conflict and its prevention.

6.1 Key Concepts in Behavioral Economics

Reference Dependence and Loss Aversion

Suppose in Scenario A you have accumulated $0.9 million in wealth. If your wealth goes up by $100,000, you would then have $1 million and you'd presumably be happier, all else equal. Suppose instead in Scenario B that you have $1.1 million in wealth, which then falls by $100,000 to $1 million, all else equal. In which Scenario would you be happier? Perhaps you would be equally happy in the two scenarios because your wealth is the same ($1 million) in each. But maybe you'd be happier in Scenario A than in Scenario B because your wealth increased in the former and declined in the latter. The prediction that you would be equally happy in the two scenarios is consistent with the standard RCM, which assumes that the absolute amount of a good determines happiness or utility. The prediction that you would be happier in Scenario A than in Scenario B assumes that your happiness from a choice or an event (such as a change in wealth) is governed by the outcome relative to a reference point. Which prediction is accurate? It depends. In contexts in which reference dependence matters a lot for an actor, choices will be strongly affected by possible outcomes relative to a reference point. When reference dependence is weak, absolute returns will matter most.

In many laboratory experiments in behavioral economics, subjects were found to be particularly sensitive to losses (Kahneman 2011, Cartwright 2011). An actor is subject to "loss aversion" when its well-being goes down substantially more than an equivalent gain causes its well-being to go up. The concept of loss aversion is illustrated in Figure 6.1 by the famous S-shaped curve of behavioral economics (Kahneman 2003, p. 1456). The origin is assumed to be the reference point relative to which the actor perceives gains and losses on the right and left portions of the X axis, respectively. Those gains and losses convey positive and negative psychological values, which are measured on the Y axis. The upper portion of the S-curve shows how a gain of $200 is valued by an actor, while the lower part shows the same for a loss of $200. Note that the psychological values associated with a gain of $200 and a loss of $200 are asymmetric. Specifically, the loss in psychological value from a $200 loss ($= -2PV_1$) is two times greater than the gain in psychological value from a $200 gain ($= PV_1$).

Reference dependence and loss aversion can be important for understanding war and peace. To take just one example, suppose a key political leader currently has monopoly control over a nation's government. Suppose the leader is suddenly faced with a strong rebel group that seeks substantially to reduce its power. If the leader has become adapted to a strong hold on power, that is, monopoly control of the government is its reference point, then the rebel uprising represents a serious threat of loss. The standard RCM often predicts that a leader facing a serious loss of power would choose violence to prevent or minimize the loss (Kalyvas 2006, Anderton and Brauer 2016c). Reference dependence and loss aversion imply that the leader could cognitively magnify the value of the loss and be even more prone to choose violence than the standard RCM predicts.

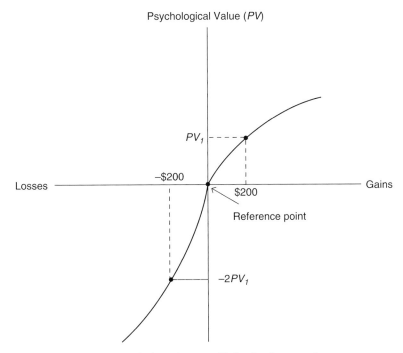

Figure 6.1 S-shaped curve of behavioral economics.
Source: Adapted from Kahneman (2003, p. 1456).

Reference dependence and loss aversion are not necessarily bad news for peace. It depends on the reference point. Suppose the reference point for a society's political system is one in which no individual or group obtains substantial power, which is generally true of democracies. In this case, the "sting" of power loss would be inoculated against by institutional design. In such societies, the risk of serious violence emerging over political control would generally be low because power would be known to be limited and temporary and thus concentrated permanent power would not likely emerge as a reference point.

Endowment Effect

Laboratory experiments have found evidence of an endowment effect, in which people value goods more highly than otherwise when they own or hold those goods (Cartwright 2011, pp. 49–50). For example, imagine you value a coffee mug on a store shelf at $3. Suppose we buy the mug and give it to you and the gift conveys no sentimental value. According to the endowment effect, you will now value the mug more (say at $4) simply because you own it. One explanation for the endowment effect is reference dependence and loss aversion. Specifically, if you do not possess the mug, there is no "mug holding reference point." But if you possess the mug, to now have it taken away is to experience a loss, which you will tend to cognitively magnify according to the principle of loss aversion. As such, you will now value the mug more because it is yours.

Throughout the world, all sorts of economic, political, social, and ideological outcomes have become the endowments of various groups owing to historical and cultural factors. For example, in many societies today and throughout history, one ethnic or religious group can be dominant over others, males can be dominant over females, or certain political or cultural ideologies can become the norm while others are not tolerated. Obviously, contests over territory and other resources can lead to violence as we will see in later chapters, but violence over political, social, and ideological holdings can also be serious owing, in part, to magnified valuations of such holdings implied by the endowment effect.

Framing Effects

The contexts in which people operate can have significant impacts on the choices they make. This will be clear when we consider the effects of social context on choices later in this chapter. Another context that can affect choices is the cognitive frame of a decision-maker. For example, a person might find itself in a negative frame where potential losses are emphasized (you might fail the exam) or in a positive frame where potential gains are highlighted (you might do well on the exam). Experimental research has shown that people often make different choices in equivalent decision-making scenarios depending on how the scenarios are framed.

Consider, for example, the experiment designed by neuroscientists De Martino et al. (2006) as summarized in Table 6.1. The top of the table shows the "gain frame" in which subjects were handed £50 (about $65) and then told they could keep £20 or face a gamble in which they could keep the £50 with probability 40 percent or lose all with probability 60 percent. Note that the sure return of £20 is the same as the expected return of the gamble (that is, 0.4x50 + 0.6x0 = £20). In the "loss frame" shown in the lower half of the table, subjects were handed £50 and told they could lose £30 or face a gamble in which they could keep the £50 with probability 40 percent or lose all with probability 60 percent. In the loss frame, once again, there is

Table 6.1 *Gain and loss frames in De Martino et al. (2006) experiment.*

	Sure Outcome	Gamble
Gain Frame	Keep £20 out of the £50	Keep £50 with probability 0.4 OR Lose all with probability 0.6
Loss Frame	Lose £30 out of the £50	Keep £50 with probability 0.4 OR Lose all with probability 0.6

a sure return of £20 (that is, losing £30 from the £50 is the same as keeping £20), which is the same as the expected return of the gamble (that is, 0.4x50 + 0.6x0 = £20). Hence, the outcomes of the gain and loss frames are identical. Yet, De Martino et al. (2006) find that a significantly greater percentage of subjects chose the gamble in the loss frame than in the gain frame. The standard RCM would predict that there would be no significant difference in the percentage of people choosing the gambles in the two trials because the decision-making situations are essentially identical. One possible explanation for De Martino et al.'s result is loss aversion. In the "loss frame" subjects focus upon loss and magnify its value in a negative direction, thus prompting them to prefer the gamble. In the gain frame, subjects do not associate the sure thing with loss and thus would be more inclined to choose the sure thing.

Framing effects likely matter in many cases for understanding how violent conflicts begin and how they might be brought to an end. Consider, for example, a violent conflict that is underway. Ending the conflict can be framed as a gain to many of the country's citizens. For example, the gain frame would emphasize that by stopping the conflict, resources that are currently diverted to the fighting will be saved, the regular economy can be rebuilt with markets and trade once again flourishing, and soldiers and civilians will no longer be threatened. At the same time, key political leaders might lose power from conflict termination and thus frame it as a loss. A mediator can take account of insights from behavioral economics to develop policy options to help political leaders overcome the loss frame that hinders conflict termination.

Confirmation Bias and the Polarization of Attitude

The standard RCM assumes that people accurately assess new information that comes along. Laboratory experiments, however, find that people are often influenced by confirmation bias in which they interpret new and even ambiguous information as consistent with their prior beliefs (Cartwright 2011, pp. 210–11). For example, in an experiment by Darley and Gross (1983), subjects were asked to assess the learning abilities of a fourth grade child. Half the subjects were led to believe that the child was from a middle-class background; the other half believed she was from a low-class area. Those with a prior belief that the girl was from a middle-class area thought that her future learning would be better relative to those who thought she was from a low-class area. In the experiment, half the subjects were asked to watch an uninformative video about the girl. Those who watched the video had their prior beliefs reinforced even though the video provided no new information of substance. Specifically, those with a prior belief that the girl was middle class believed she would do even better than those with the middle class prior who had not watched the video. Likewise, those with the prior belief that the girl was from a low class area believed she would do even worse than those with the lower class prior who had not watched the video (Cartwright 2011, p. 211).

A danger of confirmation bias is that it can lead to a polarization of attitude, in which, for example, a person's negative attitude toward people of another race, religion, or political party can become magnified with additional and even ambiguous information. As we will see later in this chapter, the Islamic State of Iraq and Syria (ISIS) uses sophisticated media technologies to construct polarized attitudes against out-groups by providing propaganda that "confirms" and then magnifies the latent racism, antireligious sentiment, or political animosity already present in the people that ISIS seeks to recruit. If even neutral additional information can reinforce prior beliefs about a group, the potential for negative information to polarize seems stark. On the positive side, architects of peace can attempt to use information to create or magnify the positive priors of people toward those from other groups.

Psychic Numbing

How might people value the saving of human lives? Experimental evidence on this question is disconcerting. For example, Fetherstonhaugh et al. (1997) found that people were less likely to provide aid that could save 4,500 lives in a large refugee camp (250,000 people) than when the camp was small (11,000 people). In Small, Loewenstein, and Slovic's (2007) experiment, one group of subjects could contribute up to $5 to feed a seven-year-old African girl named Rokia, whose picture was provided.

A second group could likewise donate up to $5, but to help save millions of Africans from a hunger. A third group could contribute $5 to Rokia, but they were also told that millions of Africans could die from hunger. The average donation across the three groups was greatest for the first group (focused only on helping Rokia), significantly lower for the third group (helping Rokia, but made aware of the millions who were vulnerable), and even lower for the second group (focused only on the millions who were vulnerable). Studies like these reveal that people's valuation for saving additional lives tends to diminish the greater the number of people who are at risk of dying. Slovic, Västfjäll, Gregory, and Olson (2016) characterize the diminishing valuation that people attach to ever larger losses of human lives as "psychic numbing."

Psychic numbing has profound implications for the field of conflict economics. For example, it suggests that the more that people are being killed in war or genocide, the less that onlookers may care at the margin about the increasing carnage. Slovic, Västfjäll, Gregory, and Olson (2016) use psychic numbing to partially explain the apparent apathy and lack of action by governments and intergovernmental organizations to genocide (see Chapter 14). In regard to postconflict peacebuilding, practitioners and policymakers need to understand how their appeals for donations and actions can fall victim to psychic numbing and how such appeals should be modified to achieve greater success.

6.2 Reference Dependence and Loss Aversion: A Formal Model

Reference Dependent Utility Function

Suppose a key leader obtains utility from consumption good C and political power or strength S. Owing to political, social, and historical circumstances, assume the leader has become accustomed to holding a substantial level of political strength designated by $\hat{S}$. In other words, $\hat{S}$ is the reference amount of power that governs the leader's perceptions of gains and losses in strength. Suppose the leader is governed by loss aversion. The following reference dependent utility function U^r is consistent with these assumptions:

$$U^r = \begin{array}{l} SC \ \text{if} \ (S - \hat{S}) \geq 0 \\ SC + \lambda(S - \hat{S}) \ \text{if} \ (S - \hat{S}) < 0, \lambda > 0. \end{array} \qquad (6.1)$$

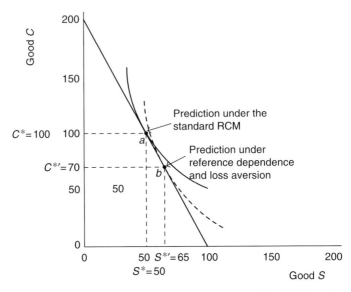

Figure 6.2 Leader's optimal choice under standard model and under reference dependence and loss aversion.

In equation (6.1) the λ parameter governs the degree to which the leader is affected by loss aversion when strength S falls short of reference point strength $\hat{S}$.

Budget Constraint

The leader is not free to choose any amount of S and C, but only those bundles that it can afford. Assuming the leader spends all of its income I and the average costs or unit prices of S and C are P_s and P_c, the budget equation is:

$$I = P_s S + P_c C. \tag{6.2}$$

Optimal Choice

The political leader chooses amounts of S and C to maximize utility in (6.1) subject to the budget constraint in (6.2). Suppose, for example, that the leader's income is $I{=}200$ and the respective average costs or unit prices of S and C are $P_s = 2$ and $P_c = 1$. Figure 6.2 shows the leader's optimal allocation of income to C and S under these assumptions. Two scenarios are shown in the figure. The tangency between the solid indifference curve and the income constraint line (point *a*) depicts the leader's optimal choice when it is not governed by reference dependence and loss aversion. This outcome obtains when the loss aversion parameter is $\lambda = 0$ or there is no reference dependence such that $\hat{S} = 0$. In this case, the optimal choices are $C^* = 100$ and $S^* = 50$, which is the outcome predicted by the standard RCM. The second scenario in Figure 6.2 is the tangency between the dashed indifference curve and the income constraint line (point *b*). Here the leader's utility is governed by the absolute amounts of *C* and *S*, the amount of *S* relative to an assumed reference point of $\hat{S} = 100$, and an assumed loss aversion sensitivity of $\lambda = 60$. The optimal choices under these conditions are $C^{*\prime} = 70$ and $S^{*\prime} = 65$.

Figure 6.2 is remarkable for two reasons. First, the more general model of optimal choice, which includes both absolute and relative returns to an actor, causes the leader's choice to deviate from the prediction of the standard RCM. In short, behavioral phenomena – in this case reference dependence and loss aversion – "twist" the predicted outcome away from what the standard RCM predicts. Second, the new outcome that occurs in this example is not good news for peace. Notice how much the political leader is willing to sacrifice the consumer side of the economy (represented by *C* in the model) in order to hold political strength. The magnified grasp for power in Figure 6.2 ($S^{*\prime} = 65$ rather than $S^* = 50$) and the elevated risk of violence that it may portend, are brought about by reference dependence and loss aversion.

Loss Aversion Sensitivity and the Kahneman-Tversky (KT) Curve

To focus on the relationship between loss aversion sensitivity and political strength demanded, we can draw information from Figure 6.2 to construct our leader's loss aversion curve, which we also call the Kahneman-Tversky or KT curve in honor of two pioneering behavioral economists: Daniel Kahneman and Amos Tversky. The KT curve is the locus of quantities of political strength demanded *S* for various loss sensitivity values λ holding prices and income constant. From optimal choice point *a* in Figure 6.2, the quantity of strength demanded is $S^* = 50$ when loss aversion sensitivity is $\lambda = 0$, which yields one point on the individual's KT curve in Figure 6.3. At loss aversion sensitivity $\lambda = 60$, the corresponding quantity demanded for strength at point *b* in Figure 6.2 is $S^{*\prime} = 65$, which yields a second point on the KT curve in Figure 6.3. An increase in loss aversion sensitivity to,

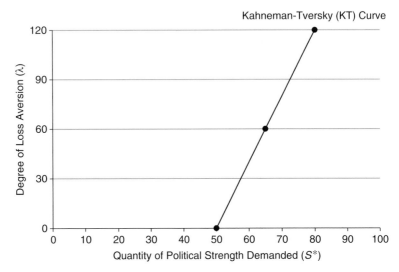

Figure 6.3 The Kahneman-Tversky (KT) curve.

say, $\lambda = 120$ would further steepen the indifference curve in Figure 6.2 and lead to a new quantity demanded for strength of $S^{*\prime\prime} = 80$ (not shown), which yields a third point on the KT curve in Figure 6.3.

Assuming a political leader's demand for political strength is associated with an elevated risk of violent conflict, advocates of peace would like to reduce such demand, which would require a leftward shift of the KT curve in Figure 6.3. This will happen if the leader's income (I) is lower and S is a normal good, the price of S is greater, or the price of C goes down and S and C are substitute goods. Note also that a reduction in loss aversion sensitivity (λ) will reduce the amount of political power demanded by the leader as it moves down the KT curve.

Application: Reference Dependence, Loss Aversion, and Nazi "War Ideology"

Midlarsky (2005, pp. 104–7 and 135–53) applies the concepts of reference dependence and loss aversion to help explain the rise of Nazi war ideology and genocide in the 1930s and early 1940s. Consider Midlarsky's quote of Schweller (1996, p. 99): "[S]tates value what they possess more than what they covet" and "rational states do not seek relative gains so much as to avoid relative losses." The first part of the quote suggest that a state's valuation of assets such as territory will depend mostly on what they are accustomed to possessing, which is their reference point for such holdings. The second part of the quote suggests loss aversion. Midlarsky traces the emergence of extreme Nazi war ideology and genocide heading into World War II (1939–45) to (in part) the extreme losses in territory, power, and resources that Germany experienced following World War I (1914–18). According to Midlarsky (2005, p. 104), the "unacceptability of the defeat of 1918 and its [Germany's] territorial losses . . . was a basis of Nazi ideology."

6.3 Key Concepts in the Economics of Identity

Social Categories, Norms, and Identity Utilities

In 1949, Muzafer and Carolyn Sherif conducted an experiment on inter-group conflict at Robbers Cave State Park in Oklahoma (Sherif et al. 1988). The subjects were two dozen 11- and 12-year-old white boys from lower middle class Protestant backgrounds who did not know each other. When the 24 boys arrived at the park, they interacted in a variety of activities and friendship groupings began to emerge. Sherif et al. then divided the boys into two groups of 12 and separated the groups from each other for a period of time. During this phase of the experiment, called the bonding stage, the boys in each group carried out joint activities such as swimming and baseball. During the bonding stage, each group developed an identity by adopting a group name – the Eagles and the Rattlers – and cultural norms governing acceptable behavior within each group emerged including hierarchies among group members and sanctions for deviant behavior. The next stage of the experiment involved competition in which the two groups played winner-take-all games such as football and tug-of-war. The winners received prizes and the losers received nothing. During the competition stage, verbal aggression and other hostile acts emerged between the groups including fistfights and cabin raiding. At the end of the competition stage, each group had highly negative views of the other group and strongly positive views of its own. Furthermore, the presence of a negatively-viewed outgroup created greater solidarity within the in-group. The final stage of the experiment brought the two groups together to collectively solve problems such as fixing a broken water tank.

Among the lessons culled from the Robbers Cave experiment, we emphasize three. First, once the groups were set against each other in experimentally contrived zero-sum competitions, enmity quickly arose and hardened each group's identity. The conditions for identity formation and rising enmity were rooted in scarcity (that is, zero-sum competitions) rather than racial, religious, political, class, or gender divisions because the boys were essentially homogeneous along these characteristics. It was surprising to see how little manipulation was necessary to set off an "us versus them" dynamic, even among a homogeneous population. Second, peaceful interactions between the groups occurred when positive-sum possibilities were introduced in the experiment. Sheriff et al. concluded that reduced frictions did not occur by simply bringing the groups together, but by focusing each group on superordinate goals that required both groups to act collectively for improvements to occur. Finally, the Robbers Cave experiment points to the importance of social categories, norms, and identities in understanding hostility and peace.

Sociologists emphasize "social categories" and "norms" to explain how people behave. In the Robbers Cave experiment, the social categories in which the boys became aligned were the Eagles and the Rattlers and the norms that emerged were "we're the good guys," "they are the enemy," and "it's okay to harm them." Social categories and norms connect to economics because they affect people's happiness or utility levels, which economics of identity pioneers George Akerlof and Rachel Kranton characterize as "identity utility." All of us are involved in a variety of social categories with associated norms and identity utilities. Social categories are people-groupings that occur based on the choices of individuals (for example, I'm a member of the American Economic Association or the Peace Science Society or this political party) or that are assigned by nature (for example, I'm in this age bracket). Most of the social groups in which we find ourselves have norms that govern how we and others believe we should behave as part of the group. Such behaviors (ours and theirs) relative to norms will affect our (and others') identity utility. For example, if a group of adults was to go trick-or-treating at Halloween, they would likely feel awkward as would those who would be answering the door at their knock.* The discomfort (and thus disutility) that would arise for the actors in this case would occur because of a dissonance between the social category of adulthood and the norm that adults should not do this. If the group knocking at the door was children, however, there would be no disutility emerging for the actors owing to social categories and norms.

---

* Trick-or-treating, associated with Halloween, is a custom practiced on October 31 in many Western parts of the world in which children go door-to-door dressed in costumes to receive candy.

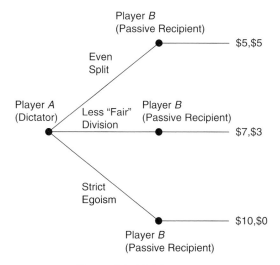

Figure 6.4 Dictator game.

Self-Identity and Motivated Reasoning and Beliefs

In addition to social context, experimental evidence indicates that people care about self-context or self-identity, that is, about how they view themselves in regard to being "good" or moral beings. Consider, for example, the dictator game in Figure 6.4. Player A is the dictator and must choose how much of the $10 to share with anonymous player B. Player B is a passive recipient of whatever player A chooses to do (that is, A is the "dictator"). Many distributions are possible. In the top branch of the game tree we show a "fair" outcome in which A splits the $10 evenly. In the middle branch, a "less fair" distribution is selected in which A receives $7 and B $3. The lower branch's outcome reflects strict egoism in which A keeps the $10 and B receives nothing.

Although a wide range of results are reported in the more than 100 published dictator game experiments (Engel 2011), many reveal that dictators often choose to share some of the money with the passive recipient even though the strict rational choice is to share nothing. Such results are often interpreted as reflecting people's altruism or concern for fairness. Nevertheless, recent experiments suggest that human behavior in contexts involving moral decisions may be more complex than previously realized (Gino, Norton, and Weber 2016). For example, a dictator experiment conducted by Hamman, Loewenstein, and Weber (2010) (hereafter, HLW) casts some doubt on the alleged moral behavior of subjects.

In experimental treatment 1 (called the "Baseline"), HLW had subjects play the classic dictator game in which they decided how much of $10 to keep and how much to give to an anonymous and passive recipient. Across 12 rounds of the Baseline experiment, subjects (dictators) gave an average of $2.19 per round. In another treatment (Called "Agent Choice"), the subjects (dictators) could choose in rounds 9–12 whether to make the allocation decision themselves or whether to recruit an agent to make the allocation decision. About 40 percent of the subjects chose an agent to act on their behalf. The average amount given in rounds 9–12 of the Agent Choice design (by agents and those who acted on their own behalf) was $0.25. According to HLW, when given the opportunity to do so, many experimental subjects would seek an agent that would share the least. Furthermore, experimental subjects who chose agents to act on their behalf were more inclined than treatment 1 subjects to perceive highly unequal distributions as fair. Given the experimental results and based on questionnaires given to principals and agents after the experiment, HLW concluded that principals in the experiment had "positively biased perceptions about their own behavior" and did not "feel responsible for ultimate outcomes" when they delegated responsibility to agents (p. 1843).

Human abilities to rationally arrive at self-serving norms and beliefs are obviously important for understanding violent conflict and peace. As just one example of how people can reinterpret their egoistic (and even abominable) behavior as morally justifiable, Gino, Norton, and Weber (2016, p. 190) offer the following quote from Fritz Sander, a German engineer who worked on designing more efficient incineration equipment for Nazi extermination camps during World War II: "I was a German engineer and key member of the Topf works [a German engineering firm], and I saw it as my duty to apply my specialist knowledge in this way to help Germany win the war, just as an aircraft construction engineer builds airplanes in wartime, which are also connected with the destruction of human beings" (as quoted by Fleming 1993). Furthermore, people have multiple identities. Hence, rulers seeking to conduct violence can "establish a hierarchy of identities so that loyalty to the 'top identity' can be demanded" (Brauer 2017b). A key policy question in social contexts where rulers manipulate identities to achieve nefarious ends is "how do individuals resist having their identities so ordered?" (Brauer 2017b).

Social Contexts and Changes in Preferences

In the standard RCM, the preferences of a decision-maker are assumed to be fixed and rooted in the individual's character or nature. Changes in the person's behavior are then explained, not by changes in preferences, but by changes in constraints such as a change in the price of a good or the individual's income. The fundamental starting point of identity economics, however, is that an individual's tastes and preferences vary with social context (Akerlof and Kranton 2010) as well as with self-serving processing of self-contexts (Gino, Norton, and Weber 2016; Bénabou and Tirole 2016, 2011). This was the case for the boys in the Robbers Cave experiment, for the adults and children in the Halloween example, for the subjects in dictator game experiments, and often for us as well in the many social and self-contexts in which we operate.

6.4 Identity Utility: A Formal Model

Identity Sensitive Utility Function

We now turn to modifications of the standard RCM to account for identity and to explore why identity economics can play an important role in understanding conflict risk and prevention. Assume an individual is in a social context in which it receives identity utility from being part of a group. Suppose, owing to historical and cultural antecedents, the group the person belongs to views people of a particular race or religion with disdain. For example, during the 1930s and 1940s, many people affiliated with the Nazi party in Germany viewed Jews and other people-groups with contempt. Even if some Nazi supporters did not originally have such views, Nazi leaders inculcated norms of disdain for out-groups and they expected those within the party to uphold and even prioritize those norms in what Brauer (2017b) has characterized as the creation of "identity dominance." Hence, identity as a Nazi meant that one should change its valuation of outed groups and not only adopt, but also prioritize, the "party line" of contempt toward them.

Suppose an individual receives utility from consumption good C. In addition, assume the individual, owing to its social categories, norms, and self-serving adjustments in values receives identity-related utility from acts of "meanness" M that it directs toward an out-group. A utility function that captures such notions is:

$$U_i = CM^i, i \geq 0. \tag{6.3}$$

The identity parameter i represents the person's strength of preference for meanness. In the special case in which $i = 0$, the person would obtain no utility or disutility from meanness and would only achieve utility from consumption good C. (When $i < 0$, the individual would gain utility from acts of kindness toward outsiders; see Chapter 14.)

Budget Constraint

Suppose the individual has income, I, which is allocated to purchasing units of C at price P_c and to directing acts of meanness M to the out-group at unit cost P_m. The individual's budget constraint would be:

$$I = P_c C + P_m M. \tag{6.4}$$

Optimal Choice

The individual chooses C and M to maximize utility in (6.3) subject to the budget constraint in (6.4). Suppose, for example, that the individual's income is $I = 1,000$ and the respective unit prices of C and M are $P_c = 1$ and $P_m = 2$. Figure 6.5 shows the individual's optimal allocation of income to C and M under these assumptions. Two scenarios are shown. The intersection of the horizontal indifference curve and the income constraint line (point a) depicts the individual's optimal choice when it is *not* governed by identity utility, that is, when the identity parameter is $i = 0$. In this case, the optimal choices are $C^* = 1,000$ and $M^* = 0$, which is the outcome predicted by the standard RCM. The second scenario in Figure 6.5 is the tangency between the indifference curve and the income constraint line (point b) assuming that the identity parameter is $i = 1$. The optimal choices under these conditions are $C^{*\prime} = 500$ and $M^{*\prime} = 250$.

Identity Sensitivity and the Akerlof-Kranton (AK) Curve

To focus on the relationship between identity sensitivity and quantity of meanness demanded, we draw information from Figure 6.5 to construct our individual's identity curve, which we also call the Akerlof-Kranton or AK curve in honor of two pioneering identity economists: George Akerlof and Rachel Kranton. The AK curve is the locus of quantities of meanness demanded M for various identity sensitivity values i holding prices and income constant. At point a in Figure 6.5, the quantity of meanness is $M^* = 0$ when identity sensitivity is $i = 0$, which yields one point on the individual's AK curve in Figure 6.6. At identity sensitivity $i = 1$, the corresponding quantity for meanness at point b in Figure 6.6 is $M^{*\prime} = 250$, which yields

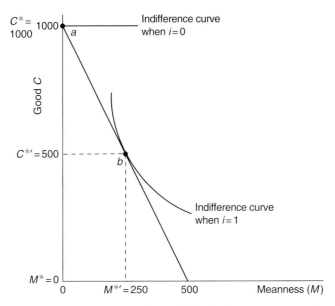

Figure 6.5 Optimal choice in the model with identity-sensitive utility.

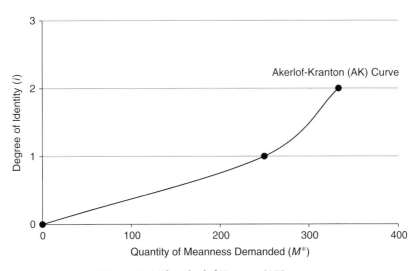

Figure 6.6 The Akerlof-Kranton (AK) curve.

a second point on the AK curve in Figure 6.6. An increase in identity sensitivity to, say, $i = 2$ would further steepen the indifference curve and lead to a new quantity demanded for meanness of $M^{*\prime\prime} = 333.3$ in

Figure 6.5 (not shown), which yields a third point on the AK curve in Figure 6.6.

Those who advocate harm against an outgroup (for example, the Nazis against the Jews) would wish to see greater identity parameters of individuals in society, which would lead to greater amounts of meanness demanded up and along the AK curves of the people in the in-group. The harmers would also welcome rightward shifts of the AK curves of individuals in society, which would occur if the price of meanness fell, the incomes of individuals rose and meanness is a normal good, or the price of consumption goods fell and C and M are complements. The architects of such harms could achieve their aims through various acts including propaganda (raising i values), changing laws that make looting assets of outed people legal (lowering P_m), or providing more income (raising I) for those in the in-group. Those seeking to protect targeted groups would wish for the opposite, which could include countering in-group propaganda (reducing i); providing safe havens, means of escape, or peacekeeping troops to protect potential victims (raising P_m); levying economic sanctions against architects and perpetrators (reducing I); or religious and cultural reformers that promote a "change of heart" so that individuals' identity parameters fall to zero or even become negative.

Application: Identity-Modified Preferences and Lone Wolf Terrorists

Attacks by individuals or small groups of people acting as "lone wolf" or "autonomous cell" terrorists may be increasing in frequency and potency (Kaplan, Lööw, and Malkki 2015; Hamm and Spaaij 2017). Definitions of terrorism in general and lone wolf terrorism in particular are debated; by lone wolf terrorism we mean that an individual (lone wolf) or small group of people (autonomous cell) carries out one or more terrorist actions autonomously, that is, without any command, material support, or logistical assistance from a terrorist organization. Nevertheless, the lone wolf or autonomous cell may be influenced by the ideology of a terrorist organization along with their own ideological motives and beliefs.

The identities and thus preferences of people all around the world can be influenced by ideologies promoted on the internet though Facebook, YouTube, Twitter, chat rooms, the deep web, the dark web, and so on. Suppose an individual becomes influenced by ISIS or al Qaeda propaganda such that it receives utility from identifying with one of these terrorist organizations. Even without logistical support from the terrorist organization, the individual can be ideologically manipulated to carry out a lone wolf attack. In Figure 6.5 from earlier, suppose our individual begins with horizontal indifference curves in which no utility is achieved by directing acts of meanness against those designated as targets by a terrorist organization. In this case, the individual's identity parameter in equation (6.3) is $i = 0$ and no attacks will occur (outcome a in Figure 6.5). Given sufficient ideological and identity priming by an extremist organization, along with the individual's willingness to change its beliefs and to rationalize doing so, the identity parameter can become activated and escalated ($i \gg 0$) such that the person carries out attacks as a lone wolf terrorist (outcome b in Figure 6.5). Of course, many moderates in religious, ethnic, and political communities attempt to alter the preferences of people toward kindness. Hence, a large game is being played in parts of the world between those fostering extremist preferences toward outsiders and those promoting peaceful dispositions. Such contestation over "ideological territory" is a critical dimension of conflict and peace in the world today and will likely remain so for decades to come.

6.5 Bibliographic Notes

For an early application of reference dependence, loss aversion, and framing to international conflict and peace, see Levy (1997). Anderton (2014) surveys principles of behavioral economics for application to mass atrocity. Savage (2016) explores the potential for applying behavioral economics in field surveys in conflict and postconflict environments. Huettel and Kranton (2012) connect identity economics and experimental methods from neuroscience, which they call "identity neuroeconomics," to understand social conflict. Caruso (2016) and Murshed and Tadjoeddin (2016) apply identity economics principles to understand the Holocaust and mass killing in Indonesia (1965–66), respectively. A special issue of the *Journal of Peace Research* (Checkel 2017) provides theoretical and empirical contributions on socialization and violence. There exists a growing number of textbooks on behavioral economics that are rigorous and yet accessible; see, for example Cartwright (2018) and Dhami (2017). In addition to Akerlof and Kranton (2010), see Davis (2010) for a textbook treatment of identity economics. This chapter emphasizes the effects of psychological and social factors on conflict, but conflict can of course impact the psyches and identities of conflict victims and their descendants (see, for example, Lupu and Peisakhin 2017).

7

Network Economics

Social and economic networks saturate our lives. Along with Facebook and texting, there are at least 60 other technology-based platforms by which people link to family, friends, and professional colleagues (Spencer 2017). Moreover, there are numerous groups whose network links would exist even if there were no modern technologies (for example, family members; environmental clubs; worshippers at churches, synagogues, and mosques). The formation and structure of networks can have significant effects on social and economic outcomes. Some examples include who trades with whom in markets, how new technologies spread, how jobs are found, how opinions are formed, whether financial panics spread or stay contained, how peer effects elevate or diminish educational performance, and which nations end up in the core and which in the gap in global economic linkages. Violence-producing organizations also exploit networks to increase efficiency in such activities as narcotics trafficking, terrorist attacks, and insurgency. Meanwhile, governments form networks to contest the networks of such groups.

This chapter provides an overview of the rapidly developing field of network economics. We first review key network concepts and behaviors. Next we present a stylized linear quadratic model to illustrate the dramatic increase in aggregate output that accrues to a violence-producing organization built upon networked rather than isolated individuals. We then use the model to analyze network intervention policies designed to reduce the hostility generated by a violence-producing group. The chapter concludes with applications of network principles to the September 11, 2001 terrorist attacks in the USA.

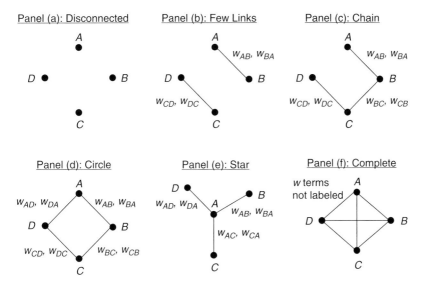

Figure 7.1 Network structures.

7.1 Key Concepts of Network Analysis

Actors and Their Connections

A network is a set of relationships among "nodes," which are also called vertices, players, agents, or actors. Since we focus on human behavior in this book, we usually refer to nodes as actors, which can be individuals or groups, including organizations and nations. Figure 7.1 shows various ways in which four actors might be interconnected, beginning in panel (a) with no interconnections at all. Suppose actors A and B form a texting connection with one another, as do actors C and D. This outcome is shown in panel (b) of Figure 7.1 by a connector line between A and B and between C and D. In network theory, connector lines are referred to as edges, ties, or, the term that we use, "links." For now, ignore the w terms labeled on the links in panels (b)–(e). Panel (c) shows a chain network in which some actors (B and C) are connected to two other actors and some (A and D) are connected to one actor. Panel (d) shows a circle network, also called a "cycle-graph," even though it is not shaped like a circle. In a circle network, each actor is connected to exactly two other actors and there is a "cycle" or walk through the network such that each actor (other than the actor in which the walk begins and ends) is touched only once (Jackson 2008, pp. 23–8). Panel (e) shows a star network in which every link involves a specific actor, in this case A. Finally, panel (f) shows a complete network in which each actor is connected to every other actor. Figure 7.1 represents a small sample of network types that exist in human relations.

Undirected, Directed, and Weighted Links

The links in Figure 7.1(b)–(f) might be undirected or directed. Undirected links are reciprocal, for example, A texts B and B texts A. Suppose B refuses to text A but A continues to text B. This is an example of unrequited texting in which the link is directed (from A to B) and would have an arrow showing the direction of the link (not shown).

Panels (b)–(f) in Figure 7.1 show links between actors, but it is also important to know the value or "weight" of the links (Newman 2010, p. 113). The w labels in Figure 7.1 are parameters reflecting such weights. For example, suppose A receives benefits of 0.2 units from each B text. We are not concerned here with the unit of measure of the benefits (perhaps it is measured in US$), which would depend on the application of the theory. What's important is that A's connection to B results in positive spillovers or externalities to A; that is, B's actions increase A's well-being. In this case, the weight parameter w_{AB} would be 0.2. If B receives the same benefits when receiving texts from A, the weight parameter w_{BA} would also be 0.2. Suppose B does not like receiving texts from A; in such a case the w_{BA} parameter might be -0.2. In this scenario, A's texts to B create negative spillovers or externalities equal to -0.2 for each A text sent to B. Undesired texts are negative externalities to the recipient much like second-hand smoke is to an asthmatic.

Network links are "little highways" by which "substances" are conveyed between the actors analogous to how a wire link between a switch and a lamp conveys the substance we call electricity. "Substances" conveyed along links include information, money, identity reinforcement, peer pressure, prejudice, sympathy, forgiveness, hate, and love. In the special case of a "self-link," an actor can convey motivated reasoning and belief (see Chapter 6) to themselves to drum up the courage to carry out a sacrificial act or to rationalize immoral actions.

Degree, Density, Structural Holes, and Weak Ties

"Degree" of an actor is the number of links that involve that actor. In panel (a) of Figure 7.1, each actor has no links so the degree for each is 0. In panel (b), each actor has one link so the degree for each is 1. In the chain network in panel (c), *B* and *C* each have degree 2 and *A* and *D* each have degree 1. In the star network in panel (e), *A* has degree 3 while *B*, *C*, and *D* each have degree 1. In panel (f), each actor is linked to three others, so each has degree 3. If network links are directed, then the terms "in-degree" and "out-degree" are used to reflect the direction of the links. For example, suppose the star network in panel (e) has information flowing in one direction from actor *A* to the others. Since the information is flowing out from *A*, we would say that *A* has out-degree 3. Since the information is flowing into *B*, *C*, and *D* from one source, each of these would have in-degree 1. It also follows from this example that *A* has in-degree 0 and *B*, *C*, and *D* each have out-degree 0.

The concept of degree applies to an "actor" and is one measure of the actor's network importance. Density, however, focuses upon the level of connectivity in a network and is defined as the number of actual links divided by the number of possible links. Let's assume the links in Figure 7.1 are undirected and the link weights between directly connected actors are the same (for example, $w_{AB} = w_{BA} = w$). For an undirected network, the number of possible links is $n(n-1)/2$ where n is the number of network nodes. Panel (f) in Figure 7.1 is a complete network, so the number of actual links (*AB, AC, AD, BC, BD, CD*) is 6 and the number of possible links is $n(n-1)/2 = 6$, giving a density measure of $6/6 = 1.0$. In panel (a), the number of actual links is zero, leading to a density measure of 0.0. Panels (b)–(e) have density measures, respectively, of 0.33, 0.5, 0.67, and 0.5. Density is important in networks because it "facilitates the transmission of ideas, rumors, and diseases. Other things being equal, the greater the density, the more likely is a network to be considered a cohesive community, a source of social support, and an effective transmitter" of substances (Kadushin 2012, p. 29). This can, of course, be troublesome when, for example, the networked organization seeks to produce harm such as a terrorist organization conducting attacks or a genocidal authority destroying a people-group. On the other hand, if the networked organization is humanitarian, the causes of poverty reduction and peace could be substantially improved.

Related to density is the concept of "structural hole," which is a void in a network and, more particularly, the "absence of connections between groups" (Jackson 2008, p. 70). Consider, for example, the two groups, *AB* and *CD*, in Figure 7.1(b). The lack of connection between the groups represents a structural hole. Suppose some additional actor, say *E*, sets itself up as a conduit between the two groups by linking with *A* and with *C* (not shown). In this case, *E* would fill the structural hole between *AB* and

CD, which in turn would allow the flow of "substances" between the two groups and establish *E* as an important actor in the network.

Actor *E*'s critical role in filling the structural hole in Figure 7.1(b) also relates to the concept of "weak ties" in network theory (Granovetter 1973, 2005). Think of strong ties as friends and weak ties as acquaintances (Easley and Kleinberg 2010, p. 48). In Figure 7.1(b), assume *A* and *B* and *C* and *D* are friends in which many interactions occur per week such as sharing information, emotional support, and so on. Such friendship ties are "strong ties" owing to the many interactions between the friends each week. Assume again that actor *E* sets itself up between *AB* and *CD* by linking with *A* and *C*. Suppose, however, that the *EA* and *EC* pairs are just acquaintances in which few interactions occur per week (maybe just one or two). Given the scarcity of interactions among the acquaintances, the links are weak ties. Granovetter emphasizes that weak ties can be critical in building bridges between groups and fostering the flow of substances that would otherwise not occur. As Granovetter (2005, p. 34) notes: "Because our close friends tend to move in the same circles that we do, the information they receive overlaps considerably with what we already know. Acquaintances, by contrast, know people that we do not and, thus, receive more novel information." Hence, weak ties can be strong (what Granovetter calls the "strength of weak ties") in their impact on network performance (Granovetter 2005, p. 34).

Centrality

"Centrality" focuses on how important an actor is to the network's performance. There is no single measure of centrality because there are many ways to conceptualize the notion of "importance." One measure of actor *i*'s importance is "degree centrality," dc_i, which is the actor's degree divided by $n-1$ where *n* is the number of actors in the network (Jackson 2008, p. 38). An actor's degree centrality ranges from 0 to 1. Degree centrality captures how well networked an actor is in direct connections (Jackson 2008, p. 38). Consider, for example, Figure 7.2 in which *A* has degree 2, there are $n = 7$ actors in the network, and $n - 1 = 6$. It follows that *A*'s degree centrality is $dc_A = 2/6 = 0.33$. Actors *B* and *E* in Figure 7.2 each have degree 3, so they each have degree centrality of $3/6 = 0.5$. The degree centrality score of each actor is labeled in Figure 7.2. Although degree centrality misses how well located an actor is in a network, actors with many connections can still have substantial influence over the flows of substances in the network (Newman 2010, p. 169; Jackson 2008, p. 38).

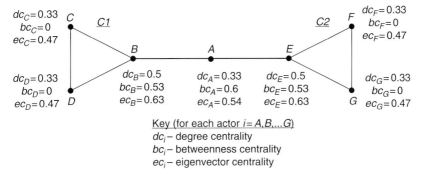

$dc_C=0.33$
$bc_C=0$
$ec_C=0.47$

$dc_D=0.33$
$bc_D=0$
$ec_D=0.47$

$dc_B=0.5$
$bc_B=0.53$
$ec_B=0.63$

$dc_A=0.33$
$bc_A=0.6$
$ec_A=0.54$

$dc_E=0.5$
$bc_E=0.53$
$ec_E=0.63$

$dc_F=0.33$
$bc_F=0$
$ec_F=0.47$

$dc_G=0.33$
$bc_G=0$
$ec_G=0.47$

Key (for each actor $i=A,B,...G$)
dc_i – degree centrality
bc_i – betweenness centrality
ec_i – eigenvector centrality

Figure 7.2 Measures of actors' centralities on a network.

Another measure of an actor's importance is "betweenness centrality," which captures how well located an actor is in a network. A well-located actor can create connections between other actors and foster the flow of substances between actors that would otherwise not exist. In Figure 7.2, *A* is in the "middle of things" and thus well-positioned to influence the flow of substances between actors. Moreover, *A* fills a structural hole between subnetworks *BCD* and *EFG*. Although *A*'s degree centrality is lower than that of some of the actors and higher than none, *A* is clearly vital in brokering connections between the other actors. Betweenness centrality captures *A*'s importance in this regard. To calculate *A*'s betweenness centrality, bc_A, we first determine the shortest paths that exist between any pair of actors other than pairs with *A*. This is done in the first two columns of Table 7.1. The first column shows actor pairs other than those involving *A*. Note that there are 15 such pairs. The second column shows the shortest path on the network between each actor pair. For example, the shortest path from *B* to *F* is to go from *B* to *A* to *E* to *F* rather than *B* to *A* to *E* to *G* to *F*. Hence, in the BF row in Table 7.1 we label the shortest path, *BAEF*, in column 2. Notice in column 2 that some of the shortest paths go through actor *A*. We put a 1 in column 3 when a shortest path involves *A* and 0 otherwise. The total number of "1s" in column 3 is 9, which is the number of shortest paths in Figure 7.2 involving *A*. To calculate *A*'s betweenness centrality we divide the number of shortest paths involving *A* (9) by the number of actor pairs in the network other than those involving *A* (15). This leads to actor *A*'s betweenness centrality score of $9/15 = 0.6$, which is labeled in Figure 7.2 as are the betweenness centralities of the other actors (Jackson 2008, pp. 38–43). Although *A* has comparatively low degree centrality, *A* has the highest betweenness centrality out of

Table 7.1 *Calculation of actor A's betweenness centrality based on Figure 7.2.*

(1) Actor Pairs from Figure 7.2	(2) Actor Pair's Shortest Path	(3) Does Actor Pair's Shortest Path Involve Actor A? (Yes=1, No=0)
BC	BC	0
BD	BD	0
BE	BAE	1
BF	BAEF	1
BG	BAEG	1
CD	CD	0
CE	CBAE	1
CF	CBAEF	1
CG	CBAEG	1
DE	DBAE	1
DF	DBAEF	1
DG	DBAEG	1
EF	EF	0
EG	EG	0
FG	FG	0

Number of shortest paths involving actor A: 9.

Note: Divide the number of shortest paths involving A (9) by the number of actor pairs in column 1 (15) to obtain A's betweenness centrality score of 9/15=0.6.

the seven actors in the network. This aligns with intuition because A lies between many other actors in the network and serves as a bridge over the structural hole between subnetworks *BCD* and *EFG*.

Another class of centrality measures deals with the "prestige" of an actor's connections, that is, how well-connected an actor is to others who are well-connected. One such prestige measure is "eigenvector centrality," which is not simple to calculate (see Jackson 2008, p. 41). Jackson (2008, p. 43), however, provides eigenvector centrality scores for the actors in the Figure 7.2 network, which are labeled in the figure. Notice that A scores highest in betweenness centrality, but scores lower than B and E in eigenvector centrality. This makes sense intuitively. Actor A lies between many other actors in the network and fills a crucial brokerage role in closing the structural hole between *BCD* and *EFG*. At the same time, B and E are connected to A, who is important, but they are also well-connected in their respective circle networks *C1* and *C2*, which *A* is not. As such, *B* and *E* score higher than *A* on eigenvector centrality because they are better connected than *A* to others who themselves are connected.

7.2 Behavioral Outcomes on Networks

Hubs, Spokes, and Clusters

Links can increase the output of networks by enhancing the flow of substances across nodes. Hence, there are incentives for organizations to increase the number of links. At the same time, links can be costly to form and maintain so it is advantageous to economize on them. For example, links between computers within or across subsidiaries of an organization require information technology resources to establish and support. Similarly, airlines need to have staff and equipment in place for each of the cities that it serves, which obviously entails costs. Given the benefits and costs of links, we would expect many human endeavors to display some links but not a maximum number. This is indeed what is often observed. For example, many businesses develop a variant of the "hubs and spokes" and "hubs and clusters" approach to distribute goods or resources.

Consider, for example, FedEx's major distribution points for packages in the USA in Figure 7.3. Theoretically, FedEx could establish transportation links between each pair of cities shown in the figure (and between pairs not shown), but the costs would be exorbitant. Instead, FedEx establishes hubs, which are nodes (locations in the FedEx case) that connect between many other nodes (Maoz 2011, p. 385). An obvious hub in Figure 7.3 is Memphis, but each city in Figure 7.3 can be viewed as a hub with surrounding nodes. For example, we use the dotted patterns around Atlanta, Minneapolis-St. Paul, and Phoenix to represent the many actors that receive or send FedEx packages through the respective hub. Figure 7.3 shows a hub-and-spoke pattern in which packages flow from and to hubs along spokes or links connecting to numerous customers (nodes). What is amazing about hub-and-spoke networks is that anybody in the network can reach anybody else in the network in a surprisingly small number of links or hops. For example, Sally in Atlanta can send a package to Bob in Phoenix in only four hops (from Sally's FedEx store in Atlanta to the Atlanta hub, to Memphis, to Phoenix, to delivery to Bob in his locale). If we changed the destination of Sally's package to a person in Seoul, South Korea, only five hops would be required. The ability of anybody in the

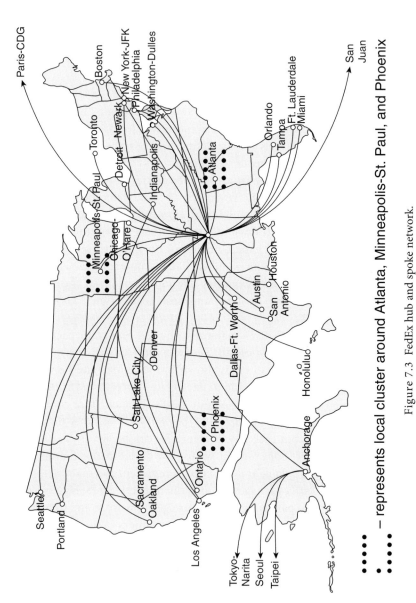

Figure 7.3 FedEx hub and spoke network.

Source: Adapted from Bowen (2012, p. 428). Used with permission.

•••••
••••• – represents local cluster around Atlanta, Minneapolis-St. Paul, and Phoenix

world to reach anybody else in the world covered by the FedEx network in so few steps is remarkable and points to the power of hubs and spokes to "deliver the goods." It is not surprising therefore that hubs and spokes appear in many other forms of human activity including transportation networks (airlines, railways, buses), electric power grids, cell phone towers and customers, and financial systems (between hub banks and their affiliates).

The hubs-and-spokes network is similar to the hubs-and-clusters network in that hubs connect between many other nodes in the network. Clusters, however, are nodes that are connected to one another as well as to a hub. An example of a hub-and-cluster network would be a company with headquarters in Paris, France connected to a set of interconnected plants in China and, perhaps, other sets of interconnected plants in other countries. Recently, General Motors (GM) turned its Lake Orion manufacturing plant (north of Detroit) into a hub-and-cluster assembly line. The actors in the plant are not people, but robots (about 800 of them). In what Vanian (2016) calls "an impressive display of coordination," GM connected the robots to each other and to a hub (called a "mother brain" by Vanian) based upon cloud computing technology.

Small Worlds

Many of us have had the experience of speaking with a stranger far from home, only to find out that we had a common acquaintance, upon which one of us would say, "It's a small world." The oft-experienced "small world phenomenon" reflects the reality that the average number of links from most people in the world to almost anybody else in the world is quite small. More formally, a "small world" is a network with many nodes (large network) in which there is a small number of shortest path links between any two nodes in the network. As noted in Figure 7.3, the shortest path on the FedEx network between a person in Atlanta, USA and someone in Seoul, South Korea is only five links. FedEx has certainly made the world a "smaller place" as has the Internet. In Adamic's (1999) study of connectivity of 153,127 web sites in the 1990s, there was a path by which one could move from one site to another for 85.4 percent of the websites, and the average shortest path from one site to another was only 3.1 hops (Jackson 2008, p. 58).

The small world phenomenon has been popularized by the phrase, "six degrees of separation," which is the name of a play written by John Guare that premiered in 1990. The notion behind "six degrees of separation" is that just about everybody in the world is connected to just about everybody else in the world through six or fewer links. Toward the end of Guare's play, a character reflects on the meaning of six degrees of separation:

> I read somewhere that everybody on this planet is separated by only six other people. Six degrees of separation. Between us and everybody else on this planet. The president of the United States. A gondolier in Venice. Fill in the names . . . I am bound to everyone on this planet by a trail of six people. It's a profound thought . . . (quoted from Wikipedia 2017).

It's a small world after all.

Contagions

We use the terms "contagion," "diffusion," and "cascade" synonymously to represent the spread of substances across networks, which can be harmful (for example, hateful ideologies) or helpful (for example, humanitarian fundraising). To fix the idea of contagion more concretely, consider the following thought experiment about the emergence and spread of rioting due to Granovetter (1978). Suppose there are 100 individuals in a city who would consider joining a riot if others joined in. Assume each of the 100 has a specific "riot preference" as follows. Person 1 will riot regardless of what the other 99 do because 1 is quite angry. Person 2 is pretty angry also, but not quite as much as person 1. Person 2 will riot if at least one other person riots. Since person 1 will riot no matter what, we can count on person 2 joining the riot network. Person 3, meanwhile, will join if at least two others participate. Since persons 1 and 2 are in, person 3 will join too. We can carry this sequence of thinking out to the 100th person. The result will be a network of 100 rioters – a "major riot" – which will likely lead to substantial damage. Moreover, given the magnitude of the riot, it could inspire other riots to break out in other cities across the country. The riot example displays the contagion of joining the rioting network. Since person 1 is in, person 2 joins, and subsequent "joinings" then spread to other individuals via a domino or bandwagon effect. The social outcome spreads from a minor riot (just a few people) to a major riot as joining the riot builds up steam.

But suppose person 2 caught a cold and did not show up. What would the network outcome be then? Since person 2 did not join, person 3 would not join (recall that person 3 needed two others to join to be willing to participate). It then follows that person 4 will not join; in fact, nobody other than person 1 will join the riot if person 2 does not show up. What the news organizations will report the next day is not that a major riot emerged in the city or that rioting spread to other cities. Rather, the report will merely say that some vandal threw bricks through the courthouse windows and was hauled off by the police (Granovetter 1978, p. 1425). The riot example is remarkable because it shows how a major difference in a social outcome (vandal breaking windows or a major riot) can be determined by a virtually trivial change in an underlying condition (person 2 caught a cold). Hence, one cannot necessarily infer a macro outcome from the underlying micro dispositions of individuals. The "meso-level" of the network structure that resides between individuals and aggregate outcomes can have a dramatic impact on whether and how micro conditions translate into macro outcomes.

Thresholds and Tipping Points

The riot case is an example of a dynamic process on a network whereby the number or ratio of actors taking an action at time t affects the number or ratio taking that action in the next period at time $t+1$ and so on into future time periods. Suppose, for example, that 5 percent of actors at a party begin to ingest narcotics at 9 pm. Perhaps peer pressure leads to 10 percent ingesting narcotics by 10 pm, 15 percent by 11 pm, and so on. Just as participating in the riot spreads through the population, so can the use of narcotics at a party. As a matter of fact, all kinds of "substances" can diffuse through networks of people. Some examples include rumors, fake news, disease, propaganda, ideological camaraderie, and material support for a city devastated by a natural disaster. Moreover, when a critical mass of individuals in a population is, say, infected with a harmful ideology, the population can be at the "threshold" of a dramatically new state of being. When the population transitions from the old state (for example, few people holding a harmful ideology) to a significantly new state (many people adopting or not resisting a harmful ideology) we say that the network has undergone a "tipping point" from one state to another.

To fix ideas on threshold and tipping point, consider Figure 7.4, which depicts an S-shaped diffusion curve of some substance or behavior on a network (Granovetter 1978, pp. 1425–8; Jackson 2008, pp. 298–304). Suppose, for example, the substance potentially transmitted on the network is "negative stereotype" of people from a racial, religious, or political group. Actors in the network who choose action 1 adopt the negative stereotype, while those selecting action 0 refuse to adopt the stereotype. The X-axis shows the ratio of the population adopting the stereotype r^t at

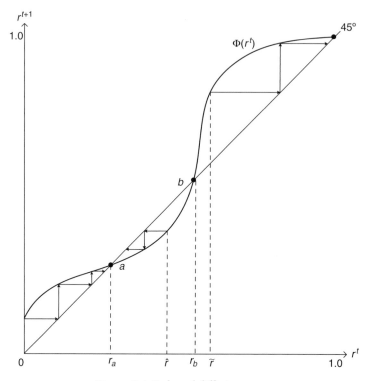

Figure 7.4 S-shaped diffusion curve.

time t, while the Y-axis shows the ratio of the population adopting the stereotype r^{t+1} at time $t + 1$. The figure shows a 45° line and an adoption curve, $\Phi(r^t)$, in which $r^{t+1} = \Phi(r^t)$. Note that the adoption curve shows the ratio of the networked population adopting the stereotype at time $t +1$ based upon the ratio that adopted the stereotype at time t. Many forms of the adoption curve are possible depending on the underlying network structure upon which it is based. We provide a stylized example in Figure 7.4 that demonstrates several important features. First, the adoption curve has a positive intercept on the Y-axis. This implies that even if the ratio of stereotype adopters in period 1 is zero, there will be a positive ratio of stereotype adopters in period $t + 1$. This is analogous to the riot example in which person 1 would riot even if no others would initially. Second, starting from the intercept of the adoption curve, a dynamic process unfolds over the next several periods in which a greater ratio of people adopts the stereotype as shown by the arrows in the figure. Eventually an equilibrium is reached at point a in which r_a proportion of the people on the network adopt the stereotype. Notice that if the ratio of adopters temporarily rose to $\hat{r}$ in the figure, the ratio would fall back over time to the adoption rate r_a at point a as shown by the arrows. Third, extreme stereotyping emerges if the initial ratio of stereotype adopters is high, that is, it falls to the right of r_b, such as $\tilde{r}$. Now the adoption curve implies, as shown by the arrows beyond point b, that an ever growing ratio of the population adopts the stereotype until adoption diffuses through the whole network leading to $r = 1$ at some future time period. In Figure 7.4, r_b is a threshold or tipping point. The initial subset of the population holding to the stereotype will do so for many reasons including the social, cultural, and historical contexts in which they were raised and live. If these elements combine to make the initial r sufficiently high (that is, $r > r_b$), the diffusion process will lie beyond a key threshold and tip into a dynamic whereby more and more people adopt the stereotype over time until eventually the whole society adopts the stereotype.

S-shaped adoption curves have been applied in a variety of contexts including the spread of information, technologies, diseases, financial panics, social norms, and opinions. When the S-shaped curve is applied to the spread of harms such as hurtful ideologies, one can ask: what would make the adoption curve shift down? If the adoption curve shifts down enough, it will lie below the 45° line everywhere and the rate of adoption will be zero. This non-harmful outcome will emerge in the model when there is little benefit and high cost from adopting harmful actions relative to not doing so. For networked actors, when there are low positive externalities being conveyed across network links among those adopting harmful positions, and many actors experience negative externalities from the harmful actions of networked peers, the adoption curve will also shift down. One might also consider ways in which links might be broken between those perpetrating harm and those who would be influenced to join the perpetrators through peer effects. Such policies will cause the adoption curve to lose its force and cease to serve as an effective diffuser of harm.

7.3 Linear Quadratic Model of Conflict and Peace

As noted in Chapter 1, about a dozen states and 60 nonstate groups have been involved in the fighting at some point in the 2010s Syrian civil war. To these groups we can add families, businesses, and communities that have been displaced by violence. Furthermore, more than 800 inter- and nongovernmental organizations are attempting to foster peace among the combatants or provide assistance to the conflict's victims (Peace Direct 2017b). The many linkages, formal and informal, allied and enemy, temporary and permanent, that exist among the multitude of actors who have a stake in the conflict represent an extraordinarily complex network of dynamic relationships. Network analysis can help one understand how actions of such interconnected agents reinforce one another and diffuse through networks and, in settings of potential or actual violence, what third parties might do to pacify violence-producing networks. Toward that end, we present a stylized linear quadratic model of a networked group that is producing violence against civilians. We then analyze the "optimal" amount of violence generated by the group's network as well as pacification policies by a third party seeking to reduce the group's hostility.

Key Elements of the Linear Quadratic Model

Own Benefits and Costs

Assume A undertakes violent actions x_A against civilians in a nation undergoing civil war. Actor A could be the leader of a subgroup of rebels who themselves are part of a larger rebel movement encompassing many other leaders B, C, D, and so forth. Alternatively, A might be the leader of a militia group sponsored by a state government, which is carrying out civilian atrocities. As we will see in Chapter 14, intentional harm against civilians can be driven by many motives including manipulations of civilians to gain strategic or tactical advantages in war and the desire to eliminate a people-group as such (that is, genocide).

Assume A receives benefits equal to ax_A when undertaking actions x_A, which might be, for example, the number of attacks against civilians. The parameter a reflects the marginal benefit of A's actions; that is, for every unit increase in x_A, A's benefits increase by the amount a. Actions generally entail costs. Assume that the cost of A's actions equals $(b/2)x_A^2$, where the greater is the parameter b, the greater is the cost of A's actions. Notice that A's benefit function is linear, but its cost function is squared (that is, quadratic); hence the model is called the linear quadratic model (LQM). It turns out that the marginal cost of A's actions is equal to bx_A. Hence, unlike marginal benefits which are constant (equal to a), marginal cost increase with A's actions. To maximize its net benefits (benefits minus costs), A chooses a level of action in which marginal benefit (a) equals marginal cost (bx_A), leading to A's optimal action of $x_A^* = (a/b)$. For example, if $a = 2$ and $b = 1$, A's optimal choice would be $x_A^* = 2$.

Network Benefits
A's optimal action of $x_A^* = (a/b) = 2$ results when *A* acts alone, that is, when *A* is not connected to colleagues who might provide network benefits. Suppose now that *A* and *B* are on the same side and they interconnect such that their link creates positive spillover benefits or synergies from sharing information, resources, camaraderie, and other "substances." Assume that *A*'s net benefit function π_A with spillover benefits is:

$$\pi_A = ax_A - (b/2)x_A^2 + w_{AB}\, x_A\, x_B, \tag{7.1}$$

where w_{AB} is the spillover benefit parameter for *A* based on the synergy that arises from the *A/B* interaction, $x_A x_B$. The synergy created by the *A/B* link causes *A*'s marginal benefit function to become $MB_A = a + w_{AB}x_B$. *A*'s optimal action correspondingly rises to $x_A^* = (a + w_{AB}x_B)/b$. For example, if $a=2$, $b=1$, $w_{AB}=0.2$, and $x_B=2$, *A*'s optimal choice would be $x_A^* = 2.4$.

Equilibrium Actions on the Network
To simplify, assume *A* and *B* have the same parameter values for benefits (*a*), costs (*b*), and spillover benefits ($w_{AB} = w_{BA} = w$), and that spillover benefits are not too large relative to costs ($w < b$). It follows that *A*'s reaction function (that is, how much x_A it will choose as a function of x_B) and *B*'s reaction function (how much x_B it will choose as a function of x_A), respectively, are:

$$x_A = \frac{a}{b} + \frac{w}{b}x_B \tag{7.2a}$$

$$x_B = \frac{a}{b} + \frac{w}{b}x_A. \tag{7.2b}$$

The simultaneous solution of equations (7.2a) and (7.2b) gives the optimal amount of action for each actor *i* (*i* = A,B):

$$x_i^* = \frac{a}{b - w}. \tag{7.3}$$

For example, if $a = 2$, $b = 1$, and $w = 0.2$, the optimal action of each actor *i* is $x_i^* = 2.5$, for an aggregate output of 2x2.5 = 5. Note that if there are no network benefits ($w=0$), equation (7.3) implies that each actor's optimal action would be $x_i^* = 2$ for an aggregate output of 4. Clearly, network synergies "amp up" the aggregate output of the interconnected actors, in this example from 4 to 5 units.

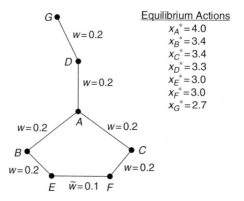

Figure 7.5 Network with application of the linear quadratic model.

What if instead of 2 there are 3 or 4 or 1,000 networked actors? Moreover, what if the actors are not completely linked, there are structural holes on the network, some links convey substances in one direction (directed) rather than both (undirected), or spillover benefits are not symmetric? The beauty of the LQM is that the reaction functions will be linear regardless of the number of actors and the nature of their links. This in turn implies that methods of matrix algebra can be used to solve the network model (assuming an equilibrium exists) for a vast array of network possibilities. Consider, for example, the network in Figure 7.5 in which A is linked to B, C, and D according to weight parameter $w = 0.2$. Links also exist between B and E, C and F, and D and G, each with $w = 0.2$. There is also a link between E and F with link weight $\tilde{w} = 0.1$, which is assumed to be different than the others to demonstrate that a variety of link weights can be easily accommodated in the LQM. Assuming each actor's own benefit and costs parameters are $a = 2$ and $b = 1$, we label in Figure 7.5 the equilibrium amount of optimal action for each actor on the network. The methods for deriving the equilibrium are available in Appendix C.1. Note that the aggregate output of the network of $X = 22.8$ is far greater than what it would be ($X = 14$) if the seven individuals chose their actions alone (un-networked). This is a disturbing result given that our context is one in which the network is harming civilians. It is important, then, to consider how third-party interventions for peace might alter the networks of violence-producing groups.

Interventions for Peace

The Key Player Policy

We saw earlier in this chapter various measures of the importance or centrality of network actors. We now consider another critical way of assessing an actor's importance. Given that the actors in Figure 7.5 are delivering harm to civilians, suppose we can remove only one player from the network. Which player's removal would degrade the network's aggregate performance the most? The player so identified is called the Key Player Negative (or KP-Neg) and the removal of such a player is called the Key Player Policy (or KPP) (Ballester, Calvó-Armengol, and Zenou 2006; Zenou 2016). KPP should be a critical issue in conflict economics because policymakers often wish to optimally degrade harmful groups such as organizations that traffic human beings, state militias or insurgent groups that harm civilians, and terrorist organizations that threaten civilian and political targets. It's pretty clear in Figure 7.5 that removal of player A will degrade the performance of the network the most. This is confirmed in Table 7.2, which shows the effects on the network's aggregate output from the removal of each actor one at time. As the table shows, aggregate network performance falls from 22.8 to 15.1 when A is removed, which is the largest decline in the table (−7.1). Hence, A is the KP-Neg in Figure 7.5.

Changes in Benefit, Cost, and Link Parameters

Assuming a third party does not remove a key player or any other actors from a network, it can still affect the outcome by modifying the benefit,

Table 7.2 *Determination of Key Player Negative in Figure 7.5.*

Player Removed from Network	Aggregate Output in Baseline Model	Aggregate Output after Player Removed	Change in Output after Player Removed
A	22.8	15.7	−7.1
B	22.8	17.5	−5.3
C	22.8	17.5	−5.3
D	22.8	17.7	−5.1
E	22.8	18.6	−4.2
F	22.8	18.6	−4.2
G	22.8	19.4	−3.4

Table 7.3 *Changes in benefit, cost, and link parameters in Figure 7.5.*

(1) Row	(2) a	(3) b	(4) w	(5) $\tilde{w}$	(6) Aggregate Output (X)
1 (baseline)	2	1	0.2	0.1	22.8
2	1.5	1	0.2	0.1	17.1
3	2	1.5	0.2	0.1	12.5
4	2	1	0.1	0.05	17.3
5	1.5	1.5	0.1	0.05	8.0

cost, and link weight parameters in the network. This, of course, boils down to changing the incentives of the actors through "carrots and sticks." Moreover, changing the parameters in the model is one more example (of many) in this book of comparative statics in which the analyst determines the impact of a parameter change on the equilibrium outcome, all else equal. Let's do that now using the model of Figure 7.5 under the assumption that each of the networked actors remains in play.

Table 7.3 shows a series of comparative static analyses of the network model of Figure 7.5. Row 1 shows the "baseline" in which the benefit, cost, and link parameters are $a = 2$, $b = 1$, $w = 0.2$, and $\tilde{w} = 0.1$ in columns 2–5. As shown in column 6 of row 1, aggregate civilian atrocity actions in the baseline case is $X = 22.8$. Row 2 shows the effect of reducing the benefit parameter from atrocity actions from $a = 2$ to $a = 1.5$, all else equal. This parameter might fall, for example, if religious leaders or other conscientious objectors strenuously communicated their objections to civilian atrocities. The outcome in column 6 of row 2 shows a decline in aggregate actions from $X = 22.8$ to $X = 17.1$. Row 3 shows, relative to the baseline in row 1, the effects of increasing the cost parameter from $b = 1$ to $b = 1.5$, all else equal. This parameter might rise, for example, if an arms embargo, threat of litigation, or other sanction was placed against the atrocity-perpetrating organization, thus making it more costly to carry out atrocities. As shown in column 6 of Table 7.3, aggregate output falls from $X = 22.8$ in the baseline to $X = 12.5$. Row 4 shows, relative to the baseline, the effects of reducing the positive synergies between the networked actors from $w = 0.2$ and $\tilde{w} = 0.1$ to $w = 0.1$ and $\tilde{w} = 0.05$, all else equal. Such synergies might fall, for example, if the "hate radio" that was fostering atrocity-perpetrating camaraderie among networked actors was jammed or countered by alternative messages over the airwaves. As shown in column 6 of row 4, aggregate output falls from $X = 22.8$ to $X = 17.3$. Finally, row 5 shows the effect of changing all parameters in an atrocity-preventing direction. When $a = 1.5$, $b = 1.5$, $w = 0.1$, and $\tilde{w} = 0.05$, aggregate output falls to $X = 8.0$.

Contested Networks

Another form of intervention occurs when a third party brings its own network into contestation with the violence-producing organization's network. There are at least two (not necessarily mutually exclusive) ways in which contesting networks can be modeled in the LQM. One is to consider how actors from the violence-producing organization and those from the third party impose negative externalities upon one another when their actions interact. For example, building upon A's payoff function from equation (7.1), suppose actor H from the third-party links itself in contestation with A such that H's actions diminish A's well-being. To reflect this, we could modify equation (7.1) to be:

$$\pi_A = ax_A - (b/2)x_A^2 + w_{AB}x_Ax_B + w_{AH}x_Ax_H, \tag{7.4}$$

where $w_{AH} < 0$ reflects the negative effect of H's helping actions for vulnerable civilians x_H on A's payoff. In a full development of such a model (which we do not do), a third party contesting network could be brought to bear against the atrocity perpetrating network in Figure 7.5. Various actor linkage assumptions within and across the networks could be modeled in which both positive and negative externalities are conceptualized in actor payoff functions. In the LQM, the reaction functions of each actor would be linear and equilibrium outcomes, key player analyses, and comparative statics results could be derived using the matrix algebra methods summarized in Appendix C.1.

A second approach to modeling contesting networks is to assume that each network produces an aggregate output. Such outputs can be conceptualized as the "weapons" in the contest between the networks in which the outcome of the struggle would be modeled by a contest success function (CSF). For example, aggregate output of the baseline case of the atrocity network in Figure 7.5 is $X = 22.8$. Suppose a third party brought $Y = 34.2$ units to contest the atrocity-perpetrating network. A ratio-form CSF would be $p = Y/(X+Y) = 34.2/(22.8+32.2) = 0.6$ where p is the proportion of the vulnerable population that survives the atrocity network's assault or the probability that any given vulnerable civilian survives. In this example, 60 percent of the vulnerable civilian population would survive, but 0 percent would survive if there was no third-party help ($Y = 0$). The CSF on networks approach can be further refined by assuming that the competing networks allocate their efforts to particular locales of contestation in which each locale has its own CSF and the leaders of each network are strategic in their decision-making.

7.4 Application: September 11, 2001 Terrorist Attacks in the USA

Krebs (2002) mapped the central portion of the covert network of al Qaeda terrorists that carried out the September 11, 2001 (hereafter 9/11) attacks in the USA. As information about the 9/11 tragedies unfolded in fall 2001, Krebs faced three challenges that accompany analysis of criminal networks: first, incompleteness – the analyst will inevitably miss nodes and links that are part of the network given the covert nature of criminal activities; second, fuzzy boundaries – there will be incomplete information about who to include and exclude from the network; and, third, dynamic structure – the actors and their links are always in flux (Krebs 2002, p. 2). After going through various updates as news became available, Krebs created a map of connections between the 19 al Qaeda hijackers as shown in Figure 7.6. The figure shows the names of the hijackers, the links between them, and the subnetworks of terrorists assigned to each hijacked plane. Also labeled is the degree (number of links) for each actor.

Krebs offers several observations about the 9/11 attacks based on network analysis, two of which we emphasize. First, the network had relatively few links and many of the actors were quite distant from one another (the network was "sparse"). Recall that network density is the number of actual network links divided by the number of possible links $n(n-1)/2$, where n is the number of network nodes. The number of actual links in Figure 7.6 is 27 among $19(18)/2 = 171$ possible links, so the network's density is $17/171 = 0.16$, which is quite low. Moreover, the shortest paths between some of the actor pairs in Figure 7.6 are quite long. For example, the shortest path between Satam Suqami and Majed Moqed is 9 hops. Second, the 9/11 conspirators made judicious use of temporary links to accomplish certain tasks; such links would then go dormant to reduce the risk of detection. Krebs (2002, p. 4) emphasizes that features of a criminal network such as low density, long shortest paths, and temporary links are purposeful: "A strategy for keeping cell members distant from each other, and from other cells, minimizes damage to the network if a cell member is captured or otherwise compromised." Krebs (2002, p. 4) cites a video-recording in which former al Qaeda leader Osama bin Laden describes the intentionality of network sparseness: "Those who were trained to fly didn't know the

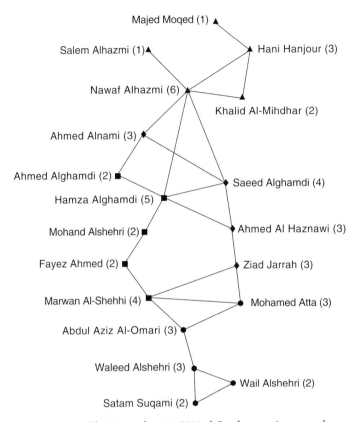

● Flight AA #11 – Crashed into WTC North
■ Flight UA #175 – Crashed into WTC South
♦ Flight UA #93 – Crashed in Pennsylvania
▲ Flight AA #77 – Crashed into Pentagon

Figure 7.6 The September 11, 2001 al Qaeda terrorist network.
Note: Each actor's degree shown in parentheses.
Source: Adapted from Krebs (2002). Used with permission.

others. One group of people did not know the other group." Krebs' analysis of the 9/11 network reveals a fundamental tradeoff that terrorist (and other criminal) organizations face. On the one hand, a network with many highly connected actors can enhance the feasibility of logistically complex attacks; on the other hand, a dense network with many actors lowers the security of the organization by making it vulnerable to government infiltration (Enders and Jindapon 2010, p. 264).

Not surprisingly, the 9/11 attacks and subsequent attacks by al Qaeda (for example, the July 7, 2005 London public transit bombings) fostered substantial increases in counterterrorism efforts by the USA, UK, and other threatened nations. There is debate in the literature about the degree to which al Qaeda has been degraded by counterterrorism (see Byman 2017 for a range of views). One thing that is certain is that al Qaeda's network structure has undergone substantial changes since 9/11 owing, in part, to counterterrorism efforts, the deaths of Osama bin Laden and other key al Qaeda leaders, and the rise of ISIS as a competitor to al Qaeda for recruits and influence (Barber 2015; Byman 2017; Ouellet, Bouchard, and Hart 2017). In the few years prior to 9/11, many analysts viewed al Qaeda as a hierarchical organization with a clear central leader (Osama bin laden) from whom inspiration and directives flowed. Following the 9/11 attacks (in the 2001–5 period), other extremist groups clamoured to affiliate with al Qaeda such that a hub-and-spoke network formed with al Qaeda as the hub (Barber 2015, p. 16). During this period, some of the affiliate groups began to connect to one another such that the structure moved toward a hub-and-cluster network. After 2005, concentrated counterterrorism efforts directed against al Qaeda and the decisions of some affiliates to go their own way diminished al Qaeda's centrality in its network. According to Barber (2015), al Qaeda's betweenness and eigenvector centrality scores first rose after 9/11 and then fell dramatically. By 2013, al Qaeda's betweenness and eigenvector centralities were not even in the top three within its network (Barber 2015, p. 20).

7.5 Bibliographic Notes

Rigorous and comprehensive textbook treatments of network analysis include Jackson (2008), Easley and Kleinberg (2010), Newman (2010), and Scott (2017). Bramoullé, Galeotti, and Rogers' (2016) edited volume provides intuitive and wide-ranging literature reviews and comprehensive surveys of network concepts and models by pioneers in the field. Also valuable are the literature surveys of Jackson and Zenou (2015) and Proskurnikov and Tempo (2017). Jackson and Zenou (2013) compile an extensive volume of key articles in the economic analysis of social networks. Maoz (2011), Acemoglu, Malekian, and Ozdaglar (2016), Dziubinski, Goyal, and Vigier (2016), and the special issues of *Conflict Management and Peace Science* (Maoz 2012) and *Journal of Peace Research* (Dorussen, Gartzke, and Westerwinter 2016) provide literature surveys and analyses of network aspects of crime, conflict, and insecurity. On the use of dark networks by clandestine groups, see Gerdes (2015) and Cunningham, Everton, and Murphy (2016). König, Rohner, Thoenig, and Zilibotti (2017) develop a rich network model of the actions and reactions of dozens of armed groups involved in conflict in the Democratic Republic of the Congo (DRC). Their empirical analysis for the period 1998–2010 reveals that the optimal way to reduce violence is not necessarily to reduce the actions of the most violent players; network effects can lead to counter-intuitive outcomes. They also find that foreign armies are among the most conflict-causing players in the DRC. Hausken and Ncube (2017) model the triggering and spread of revolutions based upon (among other drivers) Granovetter-like contagion mechanisms. They apply the model to the spread of Arab Spring revolutions in Tunisia and other countries in the Middle East and North Africa in the 2010s.

8

Conflict Success Functions and the Theory
of Appropriation Possibilities

Standard economics textbooks treat individuals and groups (including nations) as enriching themselves through specialized production and trade. These are presented as peaceful activities because the resources used and the goods produced and traded are implicitly assumed to be secure from appropriation. In many parts of the world, however, conflicts over resources and goods abound. While the first seven chapters of this book drew upon standard and new economics concepts and models for analyzing conflict and peace, this chapter adds a new premise, namely, that appropriation stands coequal with production and trade as a fundamental category of economic activity. The chapter begins with an overview of the conflict success function, which is a fundamental element of the theory of appropriation possibilities. Next, we present a model of conflict over a resource, which is then integrated with an Edgeworth box model of production and trade. The integrated model shows how standard economic variables can be dramatically affected by appropriation possibilities. The analysis also reveals that conflict models that exclude trade possibilities and trade models that exclude conflict possibilities are but special cases of a more general economic model in which production, trade, and appropriation are integrated. The integration of production, trade, and conflict in economic theory is analytically challenging, so this is may be the most difficult chapter in the book.

8.1 Conflict Success Functions

A central building block for introducing appropriation possibilities into mainstream economic models is the conflict success function (CSF) (Hirshleifer 1995, Garfinkel and Skaperdas 2007, Jia and Skaperdas

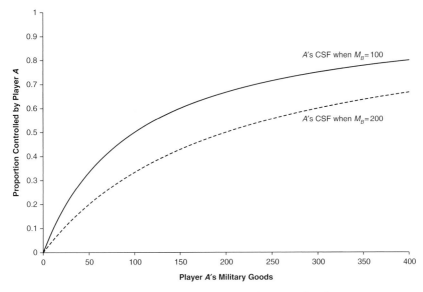

Figure 8.1 Ratio form conflict success functions for player A.

2012). A CSF specifies how players' weapons or fighting efforts combine to determine the distribution of a contested resource or good. Suppose, for example, that players A and B employ M_A and M_B units of military goods to determine the holdings of a resource such as land, oil, or water. Let p_A be A's conflict success in the resource dispute, with p_B the same for B. Conflict success might be measured by the proportion of the disputed resource controlled by a player or by the probability that a player controls the entire resource in a winner-take-all contest. The technology relating the military inputs M_A and M_B and the success outputs p_A and p_B is summarized by the CSF.

There are various functional forms that the CSF might take. We use the following ratio form CSF in which the conflict successes of A and B are:

$$p_A = \frac{(M_A)}{(M_A) + (ZM_B)} \text{ and } p_B = \frac{(ZM_B)}{(M_A) + (ZM_B)}, Z > 0. \qquad (8.1)$$

Parameter Z represents the relative effectiveness of B's military goods. For example, if one unit of B's military goods is as effective in generating conflict success as two units of A's military goods (perhaps owing to superior training in B), then Z would be 2. Figure 8.1 illustrates the ratio form CSF for player A when $Z = 1$, with A's military goods M_A measured horizontally and conflict success p_A vertically. Assume first that B's military goods are fixed at $M_B = 100$, which results in the solid curve in the figure. As seen, A's conflict success rises at a diminishing rate as M_A increases from zero along the horizontal axis. When A's military goods reach $M_A = 100$, A's conflict success p_A equals 0.5; for values of M_A above 100, A's conflict success is greater than 0.5. Suppose now that player B's military goods rise to $M_B = 200$. This causes A's conflict success function to rotate downward, as shown by the dashed curve in Figure 8.1. In this case, A does not reach a conflict success of 0.5 until M_A is 200.

8.2 A Model of Appropriation Possibilities

Economists have incorporated conflict over resources and goods into models of economic activity. A common theme linking the models is that appropriation possibilities divert resources away from alternative economic activities such as production or consumption. Some models also consider the destruction of assets and disruption of economic activities. Another theme linking economic models of conflict is the use of a CSF whereby appropriative outcomes are determined by competing military goods and conflict technology. We illustrate these themes by presenting a variation of a conflict model due to Skaperdas (2006, pp. 664–6).

Basic Model of Resource Conflict

Model Setup
Suppose players A and B dispute control of a fixed resource $\tilde{R}$. The players also have respective holdings of secure and undisputed resources, R_A and R_B. A and B divert M_A and M_B units of their respective secure resources to produce military goods, which can be used to fight over the disputed resource. For simplicity, assume each unit of resources diverted to conflict generates one unit of military goods. Assume that fighting between A and B destroys a fixed proportion δ of the disputed resource, where $0 < \delta < 1$. Hence, $\tilde{R}(1 - \delta)$ is the amount of the disputed resource that would remain following a fight. Assuming a ratio CSF from (8.1), the net resources NR_A and NR_B controlled by the players if fighting occurs are:

$$NR_A = (R_A - M_A) + \left(\frac{M_A}{M_A + ZM_B}\right)\tilde{R}(1 - \delta) \qquad (8.2a)$$

$$NR_B = (R_B - M_B) + \left(\frac{ZM_B}{M_A + ZM_B}\right)\tilde{R}(1 - \delta). \qquad (8.2b)$$

Equations (8.2a) and (8.2b) show that each player's net resources is equal to the secure resource holding minus the diversion of resources to military goods plus the portion of the remaining disputed resource claimed in the fight. We assume that the CSF determines the share of $\tilde{R}(1 - \delta)$ seized, so that equations (8.2a) and (8.2b) show the net resources controlled by A and B with certainty. If we assume alternatively that the CSF determines the probability of capturing the resource in a winner-take-all contest, then NR_A and NR_B equal expected net resources of A and B.

Optimization Problem, Reaction Functions, and Equilibrium

Initially we focus on player A's optimization problem, with B's being analogous. Player A's objective is to choose M_A to maximize its net resources. The tradeoff that A faces in (8.2a) is that, for any given M_B, more M_A will increase A's share of the remaining disputed resource $\tilde{R}(1 - \delta)$, but it will also divert additional resources away from A's secure resource holding. Player A's optimization gives rise to A's reaction function, which shows the level of military goods that A will choose given alternative levels of military goods for B. Mathematically, A's reaction function is derived by differentiating equation (8.2a) with respect to M_A, setting the derivative to zero, and then solving for M_A. B's reaction function is derived similarly using equation (8.2b). Assuming each player's optimal resource diversion to military goods is less than its secure resource holding, the respective reaction functions of A and B are:

$$M_A = \sqrt{ZM_B\tilde{R}(1 - \delta)} - ZM_B \qquad (8.3a)$$

$$M_B = \frac{1}{Z}\left(\sqrt{ZM_A\tilde{R}(1 - \delta)} - M_A\right). \qquad (8.3b)$$

Solving the two reaction functions simultaneously yields the equilibrium military goods:

$$M_A^* = M_B^* = \frac{Z\tilde{R}(1 - \delta)}{(1 + Z)^2}. \qquad (8.4)$$

Equation (8.4) shows that the players' equilibrium military goods depend positively on the amount of the disputed resource $\tilde{R}$, positively (negatively) on the relative effectiveness of B's military goods for $Z < 1$ (for $Z > 1$), and negatively on the destructiveness of war δ. Substituting M_A^* and M_B^* into the CSF and multiplying by $\tilde{R}(1 - \delta)$ gives the amounts of the remaining disputed resource seized in a fight:

$$D_A^* = \frac{\tilde{R}(1 - \delta)}{1 + Z} \tag{8.5a}$$

$$D_B^* = \frac{Z\tilde{R}(1 - \delta)}{1 + Z}. \tag{8.5b}$$

Similarly, substituting M_A^* and M_B^* back into equations (8.2a) and (8.2b), gives the final net resources controlled by the players in equilibrium after a fight:

$$NR_A^* = R_A + \frac{\tilde{R}(1 - \delta)}{(1 + Z)^2} \tag{8.6a}$$

$$NR_B^* = R_B + \frac{Z^2\tilde{R}(1 - \delta)}{(1 + Z)^2}. \tag{8.6b}$$

Numerical Example

As a numerical example, suppose the amount of the disputed resource is $\tilde{R} = 200$, the secure resource holdings of A and B are $R_A = R_B = 100$, the relative military effectiveness parameter is $Z = 1$, and the destructiveness of conflict is $\delta = 0.2$. Based on equation (8.4), each player diverts 40 units of secure resources to military goods. If they fight over the disputed resource, 20 percent of the disputed resource is destroyed, leaving 160 resource units. Based on the CSF, the players' military capabilities imply that each claims 50 percent of the remaining disputed resource, or 80 resource units each. Net resources controlled by each player in equilibrium is then 140 units, made up of the 60 units of secure resources not diverted to military goods plus 80 units of the remaining disputed resource seized. This result is consistent with the equilibrium net resource values implied by equations (8.6a) and (8.6b). Table 8.1 summarizes the numerical example of the resource conflict model.

Table 8.1 *Numerical example of resource conflict model.*

Parameters	
Secure Resource Holding of A	$R_A = 100$
Secure Resource Holding of B	$R_B = 100$
Amount of Disputed Resource	$\tilde{R} = 200$
Relative Military Effectiveness of B	$Z = 1$
Destructiveness of Conflict	$\delta = 0.2$
Equilibrium Values of the Variables	
Military Goods of A and B	$M_A^* = M_B^* = 40$
Remaining Disputed Resources Controlled by A and B	$D_A^* = D_A^* = 80$
Final Net Resources Controlled by A and B	$NR_A^* = NR_A^* = 140$

Settlement Opportunities in the Resource Conflict Model

To this point we have assumed that the players fight to determine control of the disputed resource. Given the destructiveness of conflict, however, each player can potentially gain from nonviolent settlement of the dispute. This is shown in Figure 8.2 using a linear model together with the parameters and equilibrium values of the resource conflict example in Table 8.1.

The horizontal axis in Figure 8.2 measures A's net resources expected from fighting or settlement and the vertical axis does the same for B. If A and B fight, the net resources controlled by each player is 140 units, as shown by point E in the figure and the last row of Table 8.1. If fighting is avoided, however, $\delta\tilde{R} = 40$ units of the disputed resource will not be destroyed, which is a surplus available to the players from peaceful settlement. Assume for simplicity that under peace the players distribute the disputed resource according to what Garfinkel and Skaperdas (2007, p. 674) call the "split-the-surplus rule of division." Under this division rule, the surplus from peaceful settlement $\delta\tilde{R}$ is split evenly, while the remaining disputed resource $(1 - \delta)\tilde{R}$ is divided according to the players' military stocks and the conflict success function in equation (8.1). Given the split-the-surplus division rule, each player's diversion of resources to military goods is the same whether they fight or settle (Skaperdas 2006, pp. 665–6). Based on Table 8.1 and the split-the-surplus division rule, each player will divert 40 units of secure resources to military goods under war or peace, but if war is avoided $\delta\tilde{R} = 40$ units

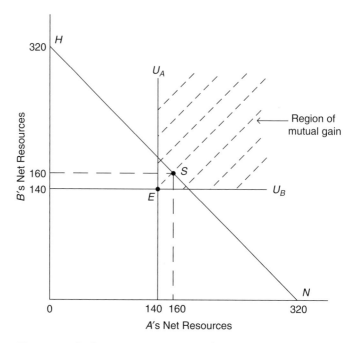

Figure 8.2 Settlement opportunities in the resource conflict model.

of the disputed resource will not be destroyed. Hence, under peaceful settlement, 320 resource units will be available to the players, made up of 100 units of secure resources for each player, 200 units of disputed resources, less each player's diversion of 40 units of secure resources to military goods. Since 320 resource units are potentially available to the players' under peace, the settlement opportunity line *HN* in Figure 8.2 has intercept values of 320.

Players are assumed to be strict egoists as indicated by their respective indifference curves U_A and U_B passing through point E. Since the settlement opportunity line intersects the region of mutual gain, the model predicts peaceful settlement over violence. Given that the players are fully informed, equally capable ($M_A^* = M_B^* = 40$ and $Z = 1$), and adopt the split-the-surplus division rule, the players are predicted to reach a peaceful settlement whereby each obtains 160 units of net resources as shown by point S in Figure 8.2.

8.3 Appropriation Possibilities in a Production/ Exchange Economy

Virtually all textbook models of economic activity assume that resources and goods are secure from appropriation. Given perfectly secure property, an ideal economy emerges wherein costs from conflict are absent and specialized production and trade generate increases in consumption opportunities relative to autarky. In what follows we present a model of production and trade to illustrate how that ideal economy is dramatically reshaped by appropriation possibilities.

Specialized Production and Trade under Secure Property

Production Possibilities and Autarky Equilibrium
We begin with the resource conflict model summarized in Table 8.1, where the amount of the disputed resource is $\tilde{R}=200$ and the secure resource holdings of A and B are $R_A = R_B = 100$. Assume now that the entire disputed resource is split evenly between A and B and that all resource holdings and goods produced are perfectly secure. The secure resource holdings of A and B are now $R_A = R_B = 200$. Given the assumption of perfect security, there is no incentive to produce military goods because there is no ability to take property from others and thus no need to defend. Hence, the full amount of the players' resources ($R_A = R_B = 200$) is available for producing goods.

Assume the players use their resources to produce two goods X and Y. The production of each good is based on a production technology that specifies the number of units of resources required to produce one unit of a good. For example, let $a_X = 1$ and $a_Y = 2$ be player A's unit resource requirements. These coefficients imply that A needs one unit of resources to produce one unit of good X and two units of resources to produce one unit of good Y. Hence, if A allocated all 200 units of its resources to produce good X, it could produce 200 units of X. Alternatively, if A allocated all 200 units of resources to produce good Y, it could produce 100 units of Y. Of course, A might choose to produce some combination of both X and Y. For example, if A allocated half of its resources to the production of each good, it could produce $X_A = 100$ and $Y_A = 50$. For simplicity, assume player B's unit resource requirements are the reverse of A's, namely, $b_X = 2$ and $b_Y = 1$. Player B could allocate all 200 units of its resources to produce good X (giving $X_B = 100$) or good Y (giving $Y_B = 200$), or it might divide its resources between the two goods to produce, say, $X_B =$

50 and $Y_B = 100$. In general, A's production possibilities are governed by the constraint equation $R_A = a_X X_A + a_Y Y_A$ and B's by $R_B = b_X X_B + b_Y Y_B$. Given the parameter values, A's production possibility frontier (PPF) is shown by the straight line in panel (a) of Figure 8.3, while B's is shown in panel (b).

The PPFs in Figure 8.3 show possible production points for players A and B, but not the specific production points they would choose. To know where A would like to operate on its PPF, we need to know A's preferences over X and Y, and likewise for B. For simplicity, assume A and B have identical preferences represented by an equal weight Cobb-Douglas (CD) utility function $U = XY$. A convenient property of a CD utility function wherein each good is equally important is that a utility maximizer operating in autarky will allocate an equal amount of resources to each good. Hence, given $R_A = 200$, player A will maximize utility in autarky by allocating 100 units of resources to produce good X and 100 units of resources to produce good Y. With unit resource requirements $a_X = 1$ and $a_Y = 2$, this results in 100 units of good X, denoted $\hat{X}_A = 100$, and 50 units of good Y, denoted $\hat{Y}_A = 50$. Similarly, for player B with $R_B = 200$, $b_X = 2$, and $b_Y = 1$, B will allocate 100 units of resources to the production of each good, leading to $\hat{X}_B = 50$ and $\hat{Y}_B = 100$. The determination of A and B's optimal production and consumption in autarky are shown in Figure 8.3, where each player's indifference curve is tangent to its PPF.

Gains from Specialization and Trade

Beginning from the autarky equilibrium in Figure 8.3, mutual gains are available to A and B from specialized production and trade. To demonstrate this we rely on a graphical device known as the Edgeworth box. Figure 8.4 shows the box for the autarky equilibrium of Figure 8.3. The dimensions of the box reflect the total quantities of X and Y produced by A and B in autarky. Since $\hat{X}_A = 100$ and $\hat{X}_B = 50$ in Figure 8.3, the width of the box in Figure 8.4 is 150 units of X. Similarly, since $\hat{Y}_A = 50$ and $\hat{Y}_B = 100$ in Figure 8.3, the height of the box in Figure 8.4 is 150 units of Y. We measure A's autarky production and consumption of $\hat{X}_A = 100$ and $\hat{Y}_A = 50$ in the usual manner from the lower-left origin 0_A, leading to point C in the Edgeworth box. For B's autarky production and consumption of $\hat{X}_B = 50$ and $\hat{Y}_B = 100$, however, we measure left and down from the upper-right origin 0_B. Due to the way the box is constructed, this places B's autarky point also at C. In summary, the dimensions of the Edgeworth box in Figure 8.4 reflect the aggregate production of the two goods under

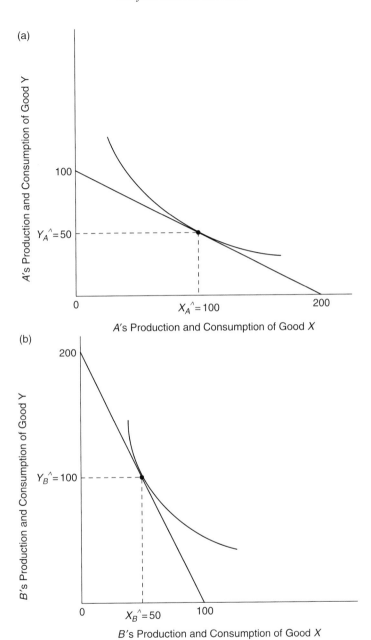

Figure 8.3 Optimal production and consumption in autarky.
(a) Player *A*
(b) Player *B*

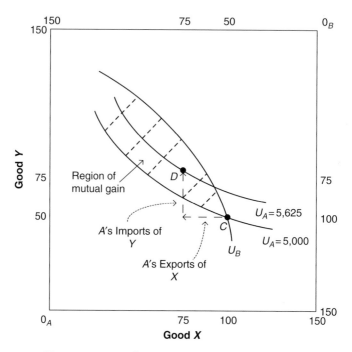

Figure 8.4 Gains from exchange in an Edgeworth box.

autarky, while point *C* reflects the distribution of this total production between *A* and *B*.

Now consider *A*'s and *B*'s indifference curves passing through the autarky point *C*. From Figure 8.4, *A*'s indifference curve at the optimum has a slope of $-\frac{1}{2}$ (equal to the slope of *A*'s PPF) while *B*'s has a slope of -2 (equal to the slope of *B*'s PPF). In Figure 8.4, these divergent slopes are shown by the intersection of *A*'s and *B*'s indifference curves at point *C*. Since the indifference curves cross at point *C*, a region of mutual gain arises to the northwest of *C*. Hence, both players have an incentive to work out a trade that moves them into this region. For example, beginning from point *C*, if *A* were to export 25 units of *X* to *B* in exchange for 25 units of *Y*, the players' consumption bundles would be at point *D*. Both players would gain from this exchange. Player *A*'s utility would rise from $U_A = X_A Y_A = 100 \cdot 50 = 5,000$ in autarky at point *C* to $U_A = X_A Y_A = 75 \cdot 75 = 5,625$ under trade at point *D*. Player *B* would experience the same increase in utility when moving its consumption bundle from *C* to *D*.

There are two sources of increased wealth from trade in the production possibilities model: (1) gains from exchange and (2) gains from productive

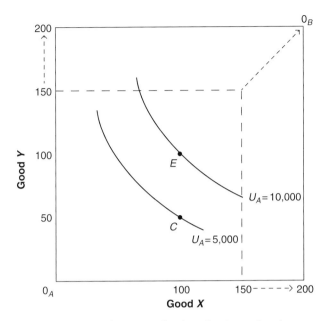

Figure 8.5 Gains from specialized production and exchange.

specialization. When moving from point C to point D in Figure 8.4, we only considered gains from exchange. Specifically, we allowed the players to use exchange to redistribute their existing stocks of goods at point C so that each was better off, but we did not allow them to alter production to take advantage of gains from specialization. Figure 8.5 shows what happens when we do. Since $a_X = 1$, $a_Y = 2$, $b_X = 2$ and $b_Y = 1$, A is comparatively better at producing good X, and B is comparatively better at producing good Y. Given $R_A = 200$ and $R_B = 200$, if each player completely specializes in producing the comparative advantage good, then 200 units of each good will be produced. Figure 8.5 shows the substantial increase in the dimensions of the Edgeworth box under completely specialized production. The Edgeworth box under autarky is shown by the dashed box with dimensions $150X$ and $150Y$. Complete productive specialization expands the Edgeworth box by 50 units along each dimension to $200X$ and $200Y$, as shown by the solid-lined box. Beginning from complete specialization at the lower right corner of the expanded box, suppose that A exports 100 units of X in exchange for 100 units of Y, with B the other side of the trade. The consumption bundles of A and B will now each be $X = 100$ and $Y = 100$, as shown by point E in Figure 8.5. Recall that A's autarky consumption bundle was $\hat{X}_A = 100$ and $\hat{Y}_A = 50$, as shown by point C. At point E, A's consumption of X remains at $X_A = 100$, but its consumption of Y increases by 50 units to $Y_A = 100$. Hence, A's gains from trade are equal to 50 units of Y. Similarly, B's gains from trade are 50 units of X. The total gains from trade of $50Y$ and $50X$ are also reflected in the expansion of the Edgeworth box by these same amounts when moving from autarky to specialized production and trade. Note also that A's utility rises from $U_A = 100 \cdot 50 = 5,000$ in autarky to $U_A = 100 \cdot 100 = 10,000$ under specialized production and trade. Player B experiences the same increase in utility.

Insecure Resources and Dissipation of the Production/Exchange Economy

We now consider how conflict radically changes the idealized production/exchange economy of Figure 8.5 by re-introducing the numerical example of resource conflict from Table 8.1. In the example, the amount of disputed resource is $\tilde{R} = 200$, A and B have respective secure resource holdings $R_A = R_B = 100$, the destructiveness of conflict is $\delta = 0.2$, and relative military effectiveness is $Z = 1$. Whether there is fighting or a split-the surplus settlement, each player diverts 40 units of secure resources to military goods. Under fighting, each player controls 140 units of resources, made up of the 60 units of secure resources not diverted to military goods plus 80 units of the remaining disputed resource claimed in the fight. Under settlement, each player controls 160 units of resources, consisting of 60 units of secure resources not diverted to military goods plus 100 units of the disputed resource acquired in the settlement. For simplicity, assume that potential gains from trade between A and B and war's diminution of such gains do not alter the parameters or equilibrium values of the resource conflict model in Table 8.1. This assumption allows us to illustrate, in the simplest way possible, how resource conflict undermines the idealized production/exchange economy.

Diversion

We repeat the idealized production/exchange economy as the large dashed Edgeworth box in Figure 8.6 with dimensions $200X$ and $200Y$. For reference purposes, we show again A's indifference curve through consumption point E with utility level $U_A = 100 \cdot 100 = 10,000$. From the resource conflict model, assume that the players reach a settlement so that the destructiveness of conflict is avoided. Under settlement, each player allocates 40 units of secure resources to military goods and controls 160 units of resources on net. Since violence is avoided, we assume the players are able to maintain

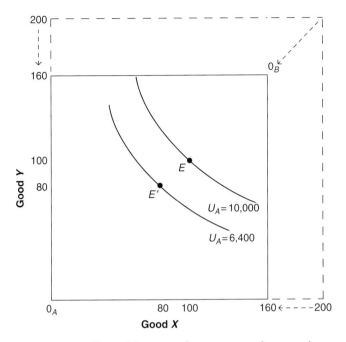

Figure 8.6 Effects of diversion of resources to military goods.

trade. The diversion of resources to military goods, however, shrinks the dimensions of the Edgeworth box as shown in Figure 8.6. Because specialized production and trade continue under settlement, A produces $160X$ and B produces $160Y$, causing the solid-lined box to emerge with A's origin remaining fixed but B's origin shifting inward. Suppose that A exports $80X$ in exchange for $80Y$ with B the other side of the trade. Thus, specialization and trade result in consumption bundles for both A and B at $X = 80$ and $Y = 80$, as shown by point E' in the reduced Edgeworth box. Note that diversion of resources to military goods causes the Edgeworth box to shrink by 40 units along each dimension, with the result that both players consume 20 fewer units of each good relative to what they would in the idealized economy with perfectly secure property. As shown in Figure 8.6, A's utility falls from $U_A = 10,000$ to $U_A = 80 \cdot 80 = 6,400$, and similarly for B.

Destruction, Displacement, and Disruption
Figure 8.7 now shows the effects of resource destruction, displacement, and trade disruption when violence erupts. We repeat the idealized

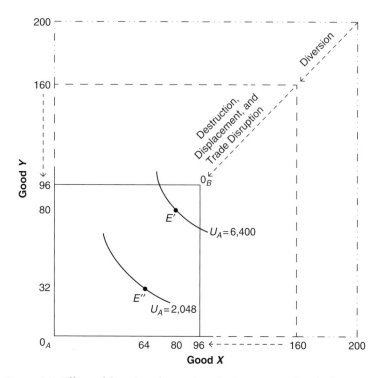

Figure 8.7 Effects of diversion, destruction, displacement, and trade disruption.

production/exchange economy as the large dashed-and-dotted Edgeworth box with dimensions 200X and 200Y. Within the large box is the dashed Edgeworth box with dimensions 160X and 160Y, which recall results when each player diverts 40 units of secure resources to military goods but reach a settlement. Suppose instead of settlement, the players fight over the disputed resource. We assume that the outbreak of violence not only destroys $\delta \tilde{R} = 40$ units of the disputed resource, it also leads to the displacement of people from the economy in the form of internally displaced persons and refugees. Assume that fleeing people from the two groups, A and B, each take the equivalent of 12 units of their secure resources out of the Edgeworth box economy. Consider also that conflict disrupts trade between A and B (Anderton and Carter 2003). For simplicity, assume that trade ceases altogether.

Under fighting, cessation of trade causes the players to operate in autarky, where each player in the end controls 128 units of resources. Given the equal weight Cobb-Douglas utility function $U = XY$, each player allocates half of its 128 resource units to the production of each good. Given $a_X = 1$, $a_Y = 2$, $b_X = 2$, and $b_Y = 1$, A produces $\hat{X}_A = 64$ and $\hat{Y}_A = 32$, while B produces $\hat{X}_B = 32$ and $\hat{Y}_B = 64$. Hence, under fighting the solid-lined Edgeworth box emerges with dimensions $96X$ and $96Y$. When moving from settlement to fighting, 64 units of each good are lost from the production/exchange economy: 20 units due to resource destruction, another 12 units owing to displacement, and an additional 32 units from the termination of specialized production. Since trade has ceased, consumption occurs at production point E''. Comparing points E' (with settlement) and E'' (with fighting) reveals that A's utility falls from $U_A = 80 \cdot 80 = 6,400$ to $U_A = 64 \cdot 32 = 2,048$. Note that the amount of goods available to the players in total under fighting ($96X$ and $96Y$) in Figure 8.7 is less than the amount of goods consumed by one player ($100X$ and $100Y$) in the idealized Edgeworth box economy in Figure 8.5.

Development Difficulties after Conflict

Polachek (1994, p. 12) characterizes violent conflict as "trade gone awry," and so it is in Figure 8.7. The standard Edgeworth box of Figure 8.5 can be found in virtually all principles and intermediate economics textbooks in microeconomics, but such idealized representations of the economy can be radically torn asunder by violent conflict. Furthermore, once the economy is so devastated it can be quite difficult to put it back together. Among the many challenges for moving the economy forward are the return of refugees and IDPs to their communities, homes, and businesses and their reintegration into productive activities; reconstitution of laws and institutions; reignition of markets including specialized production and trade; rebuilding and recapitalization of physical infrastructure, social capital, and educational opportunities (human capital); and restoration of basic security including individuals' safety and access to food, clothing, shelter, water, and healthcare.

Appropriation Possibilities and Equilibrium in a Production/Exchange Economy

Figure 8.7 suggests that the textbook model of peaceful economic activity is but a special case of a more general model wherein appropriation possibilities both shape and are shaped by the traditional economic activities of production and trade. At one extreme of this general model, appropriation possibilities are ignored and the full potential of specialized production and trade is realized. This is the approach taken in standard economics texts. At the other extreme, gains from trade are ignored under actual or

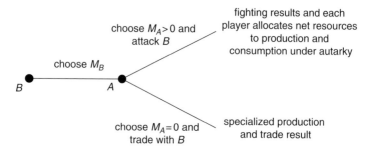

Figure 8.8 Predator/prey game.

threatened violent conflict. Many theoretical models of conflict ignore potential gains available from peace including the flourishing of specialized production and trade. Between these extremes lies a wide range of human behavior where specialized production and trade occur, but they are radically modified by appropriation possibilities. To show further the interdependence of appropriation, production, and trade, and to illustrate the emergence of equilibrium out of this interdependence, we conclude with a few numerical examples based on a model due originally to Anderton, Anderton, and Carter (1999).

A Predator/Prey Model of Appropriation, Production, and Exchange
We begin again with the resource conflict example, where the amount of the disputed resource is $\tilde{R}$ = 200, the secure resource holdings of A and B are $R_A = R_B = 100$, and the destructiveness of fighting is $\delta = 0.2$. Assume now that the disputed resource is split evenly between A and B such that $R_A = R_B = 200$. Unlike earlier, assume now that A's resource holding is secure but B's resource holding is vulnerable to attack by A. This assumption casts A in the role of attacker or predator and B as defender or prey. One possible outcome of the predator/prey relationship between A and B is that a fight will ensue over B's vulnerable resource holding. Another possibility is that A and B will avoid fighting and instead engage in specialized production and trade. For simplicity, assume that an attack by A against B's resources precludes the possibility of specialized production and trade. Moreover, suppose that a peaceful settlement of the predation is not possible, perhaps due to a commitment problem.

Figure 8.8 provides a schematic of the predator/prey game. Player B moves first, diverting some of its resources to produce military goods M_B with which it defends its remaining vulnerable resources. Player A moves second, taking as given B's stock of military goods M_B.

Player A either diverts some of its resources into military goods ($M_A >$ 0) and attacks B's remaining resources or produces no military goods ($M_A = 0$) and engages in specialized production and trade with B. The combined decisions of A and B result in either fighting or specialization and trade, as shown by the top and bottom branches of the game tree respectively.

As the first mover, B anticipates A's reaction and chooses a level of military goods that brings about the state of the world (fighting or specialization and trade) that yields B the higher utility. When profitable to do so, B chooses a level of military goods that defends its resources to the point that A prefers to trade rather than attack B. When it is not profitable to induce trade, B chooses a level of military goods that minimizes its loss from A's attack. If fighting occurs, the ratio CSF determines the proportion of B's surviving net resources $(R_B-M_B)(1-\delta)$ claimed by A and B respectively. Following the fight, the players use their respective net resource holdings in autarky to produce goods X and Y according to the unit resource requirements $a_X = 1$, $a_Y = 2$, $b_X = 2$, $b_Y = 1$. If trade occurs, A specializes in good X, B in good Y, and trade ensues.

Under these assumptions, which economy will emerge in equilibrium, and what will be its production, consumption, and utility characteristics? In the predator/prey game, the Z parameter in the CSF reflects the security of B's resource holdings. Figure 8.9 illustrates the equilibrium economies that emerge for $Z = \infty$, $Z = 1$ and $Z = 0.1$. For $Z = \infty$, B's resources are perfectly secure, so neither player has an incentive to produce military goods. This generates the idealized Edgeworth box economy with origins 0_A and 0_B, dimensions 200X and 200Y, consumption bundles for each player of X = 100 and Y = 100 at point E, and utility for each player of U = 100·100 = 10,000. For $Z = 1$, B's resources are moderately vulnerable to attack by A, and thus B has an incentive to defend them. It can be shown in the predator/prey game that the utility maximizing action by B when $Z = 1$ is to produce $M_B = 13.4$ units of military goods to induce A to trade rather than attack. This diversion of resources to defense alters the economy in numerous ways, as shown by the dashed Edgeworth box with origins 0_A and $0_B'$ in Figure 8.9. The new box has dimensions 200X and 186.6Y, consumption bundles for each player of X = 100 and Y = 93.3 at point E', and utility for each player of U = 100·93.3 = 9,330. The volume and terms of trade are also altered. In the idealized economy 100X is exchanged for 100Y at a terms of trade of one; for $Z = 1$, 100X is exchanged for 93.3Y at a terms of trade of 0.93.

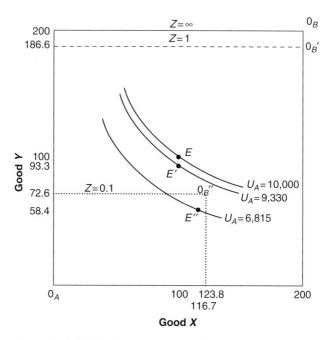

Figure 8.9 Equilibrium economies in the predator/prey game.

When Z falls to 0.1, B's resources are so vulnerable to attack by A that specialized production and trade are precluded altogether and fighting ensues. Specifically, when $Z = 0.1$, B is unable to profitably induce A to prefer to trade. The best that B can do is to defend itself with $M_B = 100$ units of military goods and fight it out with A. Player A's optimal allocation for military goods is $M_A = 18.3$. Following the fight, the players' net resource holdings are $NR_A = 233.4$ and $NR_B = 28.3$, which lead to autarky production and consumption bundles of $\hat{X}_A = 116.7$, $\hat{Y}_A = 58.4$, $\hat{X}_B = 7.1$, and $\hat{Y}_B = 14.2$. Hence, when $Z = 0.1$, the dotted Edgeworth box emerges in Figure 8.9, with origins 0_A and $0_B''$, dimensions 123.8X and 72.6Y, autarky consumption bundles shown at E'', and much reduced utilities of $U_A = 116.7 \cdot 58.4 = 6,815$ for the predator and $U_B = 7.1 \cdot 14.2 = 101$ for the prey.

Discussion: Toward a General Model of Conflict Economics

The broad lesson of Figure 8.9 is that appropriation, production, and trade are indeed deeply intertwined: appropriation possibilities determine the security of property upon which specialized production and trade depend, while at the same time, production and trade possibilities shape the incentives for appropriation. Modern physics provides an analogy to the interconnectedness of appropriation, production, and trade in the economic realm. In the physical universe, space, time, and matter are profoundly intertwined because matter alters space-time and space-time in turn alters the paths of matter. Hence, the fundamental categories of physical reality are understood integrally in the general theory of relativity. In a similar manner, the interdependence of appropriation, production, and trade requires that appropriation join production and trade as a fundamental dimension of economic activity, and that economic outcomes be understood as arising from this economic triad.

8.4 Bibliographic Notes

CSFs have been used in many areas of conflict analysis. See, for example, Garfinkel (1990) on arms racing, Garfinkel and Skaperdas (2000b) on conflict over the distribution of output, Konrad and Skaperdas (1998) on extortion, and Anderson and Marcouiller (2005) on piracy. For axiomatic foundations and generalizations of the CSF, see Skaperdas (1992, 1996), Garfinkel and Skaperdas (2007), Jia and Skaperdas (2012), and Vojnović (2016, ch. 4).

While previous chapters of this book use economics concepts and models to help understand conflict and peace, this chapter adds the theme that appropriation stands coequal with production and trade as a fundamental category of economic activity. This relatively new branch of conflict economics grows out of the seminal work of Bush (1972), Brito and Intriligator (1985), Hirshleifer (1988, 1991), Garfinkel (1990), Skaperdas (1992), and Grossman and Kim (1995), who developed models of appropriation and production. Further developments in the literature introduced appropriation into models of trade. See for example, Rider (1999); Anderton, Anderton, and Carter (1999); Skaperdas and Syropoulos (2002); Hausken (2004); Anderson and Marcouiller (2005); Garfinkel and Skaperdas (2007, pp. 682–90); Anderton and Carter (2008); Garfinkel and Syropoulos (2015); and Garfinkel, Skaperdas, and Syropoulos (2015). See Vahabi (2015) for models of appropriation and trade applied to a wide range of predatory activities including cannibalism, slavery, protection rackets, theft, terrorism, war, and corruption.

PART III

Economic Aspects of War, Terrorism, and Genocide

9

Geography and Technology of Conflict

Whereas traditional economics assumes that choices are from among peaceful alternatives, conflict economics, as we have seen, recognizes that some alternatives are violent or potentially violent. In this chapter we continue the move from traditional economics to conflict economics by presenting Boulding's (1962) classic model of intergroup rivalry over territory and O'Sullivan's (1991) three-dimensional extension of Boulding's model. The Boulding and O'Sullivan models highlight geographic and technological dimensions of conflict such as spheres of influence, offensive and defensive technologies, and strategic depth. We then turn to the Lanchester (1916) model of war attrition to illustrate how combinations of geography and weapons technologies create incentives for nations or groups to go on the offensive, or stay on the defensive, in violent encounters.

9.1 Boulding's Model of Spatial Conflict

Basic Model

In his classic work *Conflict and Defense: A General Theory*, Boulding (1962) modeled conflict over territory among states or nonstate groups by adapting prior economic theory on spatial competition. The basic model is shown in Figure 9.1, where two players A and B have home bases located at points A and B in a geographic space represented by line L_1 L_2. A player's home base might be its capital if the player is a state or a jungle or mountainous hideout if the player is a rebel or terrorist organization. In a battlefield context, the home base might be the location of a military's primary command center. In an all-out war, a home base

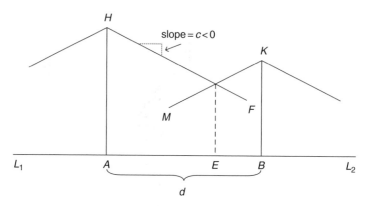

Figure 9.1 Boulding's basic model of spatial conflict
(with military strength measured vertically).

could be a player's networked command, control, communications, computers, collaboration, and intelligence (C^5I) infrastructure, which represents the central nervous system of its military organization. The parameter d measures the distance between the players' home bases. Measured vertically in the figure is the military strength that a player can project when it concentrates its power at a given point in geographic space. By assumption, each player's strength is at a maximum at the player's home base, from which it falls off in either direction. The relevant portions of A's and B's power projection curves are labeled HF and KM respectively in the figure. The negative slope of a power projection line c measures what Boulding called the loss-of-strength gradient, which is the rate at which a player's military strength decreases as it moves away from its home base. According to Boulding (1962, p. 231), "The law of diminishing strength . . . may be phrased as *the further, the weaker*; that is, the further from home any nation has to operate, the longer will be its lines of communication, and the less strength it can put in the field." In Figure 9.1, rivals A and B are equally strong at location E, which is called the boundary of equal strength. At points to the left of E, A is stronger and thus can defeat B, while to the right of E, B is stronger and can defeat A. Thus, A's sphere of influence lies to the left of E, and B's lies to the right.

   Boulding was particularly interested in the geographic and technological conditions under which one player could conquer another. In Figure 9.1, neither player can conquer the other because each is the stronger of the two at its own home base. Specifically, the height of A's power projection line is greater than the height of B's at location A, which implies that B cannot

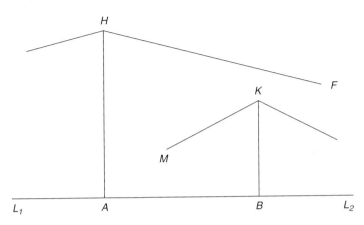

Figure 9.2 Conditional viability of player *B*.

conquer *A*. Likewise, *B*'s strength is greater than *A*'s at location *B*, indicating that *A* cannot conquer *B*. Because they are stronger at their home base than their rival, both players are said to be unconditionally viable. This is not true in Figure 9.2, where *B* is weaker at its home base than *A* is there. In this case, *B* can be conquered by *A* and thus is said to be conditionally viable, meaning that its survival is dependent on whether *A* chooses to attack its home base.

Assume that *A*'s and *B*'s power projection curves are linear with the same common slope *c*. Then the condition for unconditional viability of both players is:

$$\frac{AH - BK}{d} > c \text{ and } \frac{BK - AH}{d} > c, \tag{9.1}$$

where the first and second parts of the condition imply *A*'s and *B*'s unconditional viability respectively (Boulding 1962, p. 232). Note that *c* is negative because it measures the loss-of-strength gradient. Hence, (9.1) implies that at least one of the two players will be unconditionally viable, because if *AH-BK* is negative or zero, then *BK-AH* is positive or zero, and vice versa. More importantly, the condition shows that both players will tend to be unconditionally viable when military strength falls steeply with distance (so that *c* is highly negative), the players' home-base strengths are roughly equal (so that the difference between *AH* and *BK* is close to zero), and substantial distance separates the rivals (so that *d* is large).

Applications

Defensive and Offensive Military Innovations

Boulding (1962, pp. 258–9) used his model to distinguish between defensive and offensive weapons technologies. Defensive weapons held by A inhibit B's ability to attack A, without directly increasing A's ability to attack B. For example, concrete barriers around US embassies diminish the ability of terrorists to attack the embassies, but the barriers do not directly increase the USA's ability to attack terrorists. Offensive weapons held by A increase A's ability to attack B, but they do not directly inhibit B's ability to attack A. For example, Hezbollah can use missiles to attack Israel, but the missiles do little to thwart Israel's ability to attack Hezbollah in southern Lebanon. The distinction between defensive and offensive weapons is not precise because most weapons can be used for defensive or offensive purposes. Moreover, weapons may be used offensively in a particular battle, whereas the battle may be part of a broader strategy designed to achieve a strong defensive posture. Despite these difficulties, Boulding maintained that the distinction between defensive and offensive weapons is important for understanding the risk and nature of intergroup violence.

An example of a defensive weapons innovation was the use of soccer stadiums by UN peacekeeping forces to defend Tutsi civilians against Hutu extremists during the 1994 Rwandan genocide. As documented in Chapter 14, the Rwandan genocide claimed some 750,000 lives as the Hutu-led government sought to "cleanse" the country of Tutsis and moderate Hutus. Prior to the genocide, United Nations (UN) peacekeepers attempted to provide security to vulnerable civilians in the Rwandan capital of Kigali under the auspices of the United Nations Assistance Mission in Rwanda. The UN force had little capacity to control territory because it was significantly outnumbered by Hutu extremists.

Figure 9.3 depicts the strong position of the Hutus relative to the UN forces in Kigali. The initial Hutu and UN home strengths are AH and BK, and the respective power projection lines are HF and KM. The figure implies that UN forces were only conditionally viable, meaning that the Hutus could carry out ethnic cleansing virtually anywhere in Kigali. If more UN peacekeepers were brought to Kigali, UN strength might have risen to the point where UN forces would have been unconditionally viable over a relatively large area. This could have allowed the UN to sequester a significant amount of territory to serve as a safe haven for vulnerable Tutsi, possibly moving Hutu extremists to consider a negotiated settlement. Such troops, however, were never supplied (Dallaire 2004).

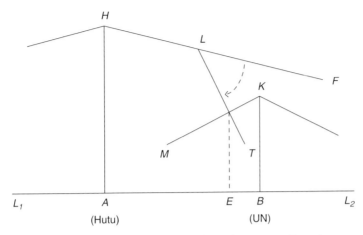

Figure 9.3 Protection of Tutsis in soccer stadiums during 1994 Rwandan genocide.

Given limited forces, UN Commander Roméo Dallaire developed a plan to protect civilians in soccer stadiums. At the Amahoro Stadium in Kigali, for example, Dallaire was able to defend about 10,000 civilians with just a few dozen UN troops. The stadium had high concrete walls and was surrounded by large open areas, making it highly defendable. Placement of UN troops on the walls of a soccer stadium did not enhance the UN's ability to attack the Hutus, but it did severely diminish Hutu ability to attack UN forces and Tutsis inside the stadium. In Figure 9.3, the defensive innovation is depicted by the redirection of the Hutu power projection line from *HF* to *HLT*. Near the stadium, Hutu ability to thwart UN troops and attack Tutsis was significantly diminished. In this way the UN was able to achieve a small niche of unconditional viability due to its defensive innovation.

In Boulding's model a defensive innovation by one player causes the power projection line of the other player to rotate downward in some fashion. In contrast, an offensive innovation by a player rotates its own power projection line upward as shown in Figure 9.4. Assume that *A* and *B* initially have a boundary of equal strength at *E* based on power projection lines *HF* and *KM*. Suppose that *A* implements improved supply lines, communications technologies, or tactics so that a given amount of military forces can be more effectively projected over distance. *A*'s power projection line rotates upward to *HF'*, pushing the boundary of equal strength to *E'* and increasing *A*'s sphere of influence. If *A*'s offensive innovations are large enough, *A*'s power projection line could reach *HF''*, thus jeopardizing *B*'s viability.

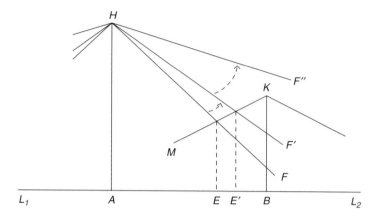

Figure 9.4 Offensive technological innovation by player *A*.

Figure 9.4 depicts, in a simplified way, Germany's (player *A*) deployment of blitzkrieg technologies and tactics against France (player *B*) in 1940. The German blitzkrieg encompassed improved military communications and weapons technologies such as decentralized command and maneuverable and speedy mechanized infantry, tanks, and artillery. Under the blitzkrieg, Germany was able to project power over distance with extraordinary effectiveness, thus rendering France and other European nations only conditionally viable.

Figures 9.3 and 9.4 suggest that armed rivals will be motivated to integrate new technologies into their military organizations, even if their intentions are not aggressive. Failure to do so could cause a player to lose control of territory or become vulnerable to conquest because of technological breakthroughs adopted by a rival. As Buzan (1987, p. 109) notes, "States … face the constant worry that their rivals will gain a military advantage by being the first to adopt a decisive technological breakthrough. Such conditions create relentless pressure on states to lead, or at least to keep up with, the pace of change by continuously modernizing their armed forces."

Military Bases

Figure 9.5 illustrates how a player can reverse its loss of strength in a particular area by utilizing a secondary center of home strength such as a military base (Boulding 1962, pp. 262–3). Assume that *A* and *B* initially have a boundary of equal strength at *E* based on power projection lines *HF* and *KM*. Suppose now that *A* establishes a military base at location *G*.

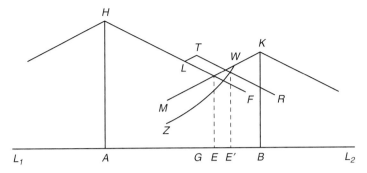

Figure 9.5 Installation of military base.

The base provides additional communications and logistics support for A, allowing it to partially offset the loss of strength over distance. Thus, A's power projection line becomes $HLTR$. A's base might also diminish B's ability to project power over space, because B must exert extra effort to navigate around or through that location. Assuming B's power projection line is now KWZ, a new boundary of equal strength emerges at E', constituting an increase in A's sphere of influence.

This illustrates the offensive and defensive nature of military bases (Boulding 1962, p. 263). On the one hand, A's base diminishes B's power projection line, suggesting that A will view the base as defensive. On the other hand, the increase in A's power projection line and the rightward movement of the boundary of equal strength suggest that B will view the base as offensive. During the 1962 Cuban Missile Crisis, for example, the USA viewed the Soviet attempt to place nuclear missiles on the island of Cuba as offensive, whereas Cuba and the Soviet Union viewed the base as defensive.

Figure 9.5 can also be used to highlight the strategic significance of high ground among armed rivals. In the 1967 Six-Day War, Israel captured the Golan Heights, a strategically important piece of geography in the border area between Israel and Syria. This action is easily translated in Figure 9.5, with Israel as player A, Syria as player B, and the Golan Heights as location G. Control of the Golan Heights elevates Israel's power projection line from HF to $HLTR$, while Syria's power projection line is diminished from KM to KWZ. The offensive/defensive nature of a prominent piece of geography is apparent in the Israel/Syria rivalry. Israel views control of the Golan Heights as defensive, because it diminishes the ability of Syria or other groups to launch attacks into agricultural and industrial locations in northern Israel. Syria views Israeli control of the Golan as offensive, due in part to the short distance (about 60 km) between the Golan and Syria's capital Damascus.

Base-like effects in strategic rivalries are not only land-based, but can be sea-based as well. For example, an aircraft carrier group deployed at sea represents a base at sea. China's recent island building program in the South China Sea also creates base effects. By piling sand and concrete blocks onto reefs, China has created seven new islets in the region since 2014 (South Front 2017). China's island building program seems oriented, in part, to strengthening its power projection and/or defensive abilities given its claims to territory in the region's Spratly Islands dispute. Among the assets constructed on the new islands are ports, military buildings, radar installations, and airstrips that can accommodate military aircraft (Watkins 2015).

Buffer Zones and Peacekeeping Forces

Boulding (1962, p. 263) also used his model to illustrate the theory of the buffer state. Assume in Figure 9.6 that state C's territory C_1C_2 lies between the home bases of A and B, where the latter are rivals to each other but not to C. The presence of C in between A and B causes the rivals' power projection lines to decline at a more rapid rate than otherwise, because the rivals must allocate extra effort to get around or through C's territory. As a consequence, notice that C's presence generates unconditional viability for B. Without C as a buffer, A's power projection line would decline at a constant rate, rendering B only conditionally viable.

Figure 9.6 provides a basic illustration of the role of peacekeeping operations (PKOs) in thwarting conflict between armed rivals. Although

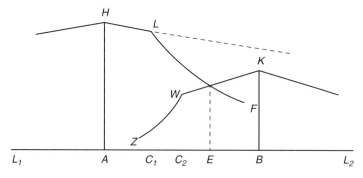

Figure 9.6 Effect of a buffer zone.

mandates vary widely among PKOs, many attempt to reduce the ability of rivals to project military force against one another, thus diminishing their power projection lines. For example, the United Nations Organization Mission in the Democratic Republic of the Congo (MONUC) was implemented in 1999 to diminish intrastate and interstate conflict associated with regime change and control of resources in the country. In 2010, the MONUC transitioned to the United Nations Organization Stabilization Mission in the DR Congo (MONUSCO). Despite deployment of about 22,000 personnel and an annual budget of about $1.1 billion in 2017, the ability of MONUSCO to induce stable peace in the DR Congo remains uncertain.

Strategic Depth

An oft-cited concept in the military history literature is strategic depth, which is a player's ability to absorb an attack while keeping its key information, industrial, agricultural, political, and security infrastructures unconditionally viable. Figure 9.7 illustrates the concept of strategic depth in the Boulding model. In panel (a), a boundary of equal strength initially exists at E. Assume that B increases its home strength from BK to BK' and attacks A. The attack pushes the boundary of equal strength to E', but A's key assets (for example, capital, industrial heartland, C^5I) remain unconditionally viable. Hence, A not only thwarts B's further advance but also retains the assets necessary to build up its home base strength, counter B's attack, and perhaps push the boundary of equal strength back toward E. In panel (a), A's robust strategic depth allows it to trade space for time, meaning that it initially loses territory but then gains time to mobilize its assets for a counterattack or a negotiated settlement. In panel (b), however, A's strategic depth is thin. Player B increases its home strength from BK to BK' and invades A, but in this case A's assets near E' are vulnerable. Their conquest erodes A's ability to provide strength over space, and in time its power projection line falls until A is ultimately rendered only conditionally viable (not shown).

An historical example of robust strategic depth was the Soviet Union's use of vast territory and forbidding climate to absorb Germany's attack in 1941. Although the Germans reached the suburbs of Moscow, it took them seven months to get there. This gave the Soviet's time to move key industrial assets east of the Ural Mountains. Moreover, consistent with the-further-the-weaker principle, German troops became extended over a great distance during the onset of a brutal Soviet winter, severely compromising their supply lines and communications. The Soviet's ability to

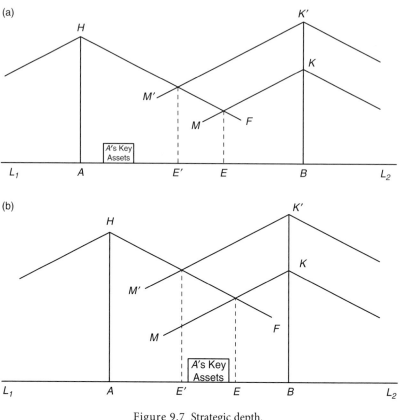

Figure 9.7 Strategic depth.
(a) Robust strategic depth
(b) Thin strategic depth

absorb an attack, resupply their defenders over a relatively short distance, and mount a robust counterattack rendered the German invasion a failure.

Contemporary examples of nations with thin strategic depth are Israel and its Arab neighbors. In the Israel-Syria rivalry, the Golan Heights is highly contentious because it borders key industrial and agricultural assets in northern Israel and is less than 60 kilometers from Damascus. To Israel's north, Beirut, Lebanon is less than 100 kilometers away, and to the west, Amman, Jordan is less than 40 kilometers away. To the south, Israel shares borders with Jordan and Egypt. Thin strategic depth in the Arab-Israeli arena can make each state feel highly vulnerable to a quick attack from a rival, causing militaries in the region to be poised to strike quickly in a crisis. In Kemp and Harkavy's (1997, p. 165) words, "distances are very short in the core Middle Eastern zone of conflict, producing fast-moving wars with quick outcomes." Contemporary examples of nations actively seeking to increase or preserve strategic depth through territorial acquisitions include Russia, with its 2014 annexation of Crimea and its military involvement in the civil conflict in the Ukraine following the 2013–4 Euromaidan Protests, and China, with its recent island building efforts in the South China Sea.

9.2 O'Sullivan's Three-Dimensional Model of Spatial Conflict

O'Sullivan (1991, pp. 80–5) provides an important extension of Boulding's spatial model of conflict, with applications to a rebel group's insurgency against a state. Implicit in Boulding's model is the assumption that a player's power projection line depicts the maximum military strength that the player can concentrate at a particular location, effectively leaving no military strength available at other locations. O'Sullivan, however, assumes that a player can spread its military power over geographic space to control multiple areas at the same time. As a result, whether a player concentrates its military power in a small area or spreads it over a large area affects its loss-of-strength gradient, whereas in Boulding's model the gradient is exogenously fixed. O'Sullivan develops his model of spatial conflict based on the geometry of a square pyramid, to which we now turn.

Pyramid Model of the Distribution of Military Power

Following O'Sullivan (1991, pp. 80–1), player A's total military power M_A is represented by the volume of a square pyramid, with the base of the pyramid called the coverage area. The pyramid's volume M_A, height h, and base length l are related by the equation:

$$M_A = \frac{l^2 h}{3}. \tag{9.2}$$

Figure 9.8 provides a graphical interpretation of the spatial distribution of A's military power based on equation (9.2). The coverage area is shown by the square base of the pyramid with length l and area l^2. The vertical distance from any geographic location in the base up to the surface of the pyramid measures A's military strength at that point. By assumption, this strength is at its maximum and equal to h at the center of the base, which

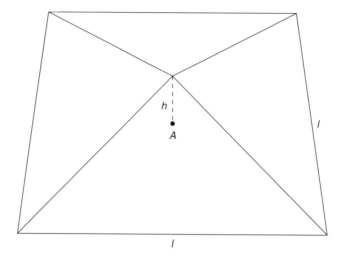

Figure 9.8 Pyramid model of spatial distribution of military power.
Source: Adapted from O'Sullivan (1991, p. 81).

might be a key city or C^5I location. The decline in military strength with movements away from the center reflects the-further-the-weaker principle, which as in Boulding's model is due to difficulties in transportation and communication.

Equation (9.2) is helpful in thinking about how military power can be spread over area. Assuming a fixed volume of military power, the equation reveals that if A increases its military strength h at the center, its coverage area l^2 will necessarily shrink. Going the other direction, if A increases its coverage area, its military strength at the center will necessarily decline. Thus, to increase its strength at the center without reducing its coverage area (or vice versa), A must increase its total military power M_A.

Territorial Conflict and the Concentration of Forces

Assume that a territorial conflict arises between government forces A and a rebel group B. Following O'Sullivan (1991, pp. 81–4), their respective military powers M_A and M_B can be visualized as two square pyramids. If the rebel group is comparatively weak, it nonetheless might be able to carve out an area in which it is unconditionally viable. Ordinarily it will do so by centering its power in the periphery of A's coverage area, where A's strength is more depleted, thus allowing B's pyramid to penetrate upward through A's. If the government spreads its military power in an attempt to

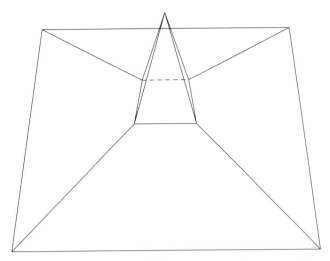

Figure 9.9 Rebel concentration of military power and conquest of the state.
Source: Adapted from O'Sullivan (1991, p. 84).

increase control in the periphery, it reduces its strength at the center. *B* might then be tempted to try to take control of the state by concentrating its rebel forces at key location *A*. If the rebel group is strong enough, the result will be like that pictured in Figure 9.9, in which *A*'s large pyramid is penetrated by *B*'s narrow but tall pyramid. With control of key assets at the center, the rebel group might then be able to hinder the government's ability to redeploy forces back at the center. This illustrates the dilemma of government forces when facing an insurgency. If the government concentrates its forces to protect a key location, it is vulnerable to the rebel group controlling some of the periphery of the state. If the government instead attempts to control a large area, it is vulnerable to a rebel group's concentration of forces at a key location.

Application: Taliban's Viability in Afghanistan

O'Sullivan's three-dimensional model is applicable to the Taliban's continued viability in Afghanistan. Following the September 11, 2001 terrorist attacks, the USA attacked Taliban forces in Afghanistan due to their support of al Qaeda. Although the Taliban was initially decimated in Afghanistan, they were able to establish new command centers in mountainous areas of central and eastern Afghanistan and tribal areas of northwestern Pakistan. The remoteness and difficult terrain of the mountainous areas has made it difficult for Afghanistan's and Pakistan's military forces to dislodge the Taliban. In 2016, the Taliban leveraged its viability in the remote areas to carry out 1,064 terrorist attacks in Afghanistan with estimated fatalities of 5,043, with most strikes occurring in the central and eastern portions of the country (Global Terrorism Database 2017).

9.3 Technology, Terrain, and Tactics: Schelling's Inherent Propensity toward Peace or War

According to Nobel-prize economist Thomas Schelling, certain configurations of weapons technologies, geography, and military organization can push adversaries toward peace or war, independent of the rivals' preferences, perceptions, and goals (Schelling 1960, chs. 9 and 10, 1966, ch. 6, Schelling and Halperin 1961, chs. 1 and 2).[1] In Schelling's (1966, p. 234) words, "There is, then, something that we might call the 'inherent propensity toward peace or war' embodied in the weaponry, the geography, and the military organization of the time." Here we develop Schelling's inherent propensity concepts using the Lanchester (1916) war model.

Basic Lanchester Model of War Attrition

Prior to war, suppose players A and B hold military stocks M_A^0 and M_B^0. The superscripts indicate that these are the players' initial or time-zero weapons holdings prior to the outbreak of war. Suppose now that A attacks B. The basic Lanchester model describes the attrition of the military stocks of the two sides with the following differential equations:

$$\dot{M}_A = -\beta_d M_B \tag{9.3}$$

$$\dot{M}_B = -\alpha_a M_A. \tag{9.4}$$

The $\dot{M}_A$ and $\dot{M}_B$ terms on the left side are the rates of change of the players' military stocks during the war. For example, if time is measured in months and $\dot{M}_A = -100$ at a point during the war, then A would be losing 100 weapons per month. The parameters α_a and β_d, sometimes called attrition coefficients, describe the effectiveness of each side's weapons in destroying the other's weapons when A is the attacker and B the defender.

---

[1] Parts of this section are adapted from Charles H. Anderton and John R. Carter's article, "A Survey of Peace Economics" published in *Handbook of Defense Economics, Volume 2* edited by Todd Sandler and Keith Hartley, pp. 1211–58, Copyright © Elsevier 2007. We gratefully acknowledge Elsevier's permission to republish material from the article.

Consistent with Schelling, we assume that the coefficients reflect the speed and accuracy of weapons, geographic impediments or enhancements to fighting ability, and effectiveness of military organization and training. The M_A and M_B terms represent the military stocks of the players at a point in time during the war. Because attrition causes these stocks to change over time, M_A and M_B are functions of time.

In the basic Lanchester model, the winner in a fight-to-the-finish war is determined when the rival's military stock is driven to zero. Given the pre-war stocks M_A^0 and M_B^0, this means that when A initiates war, equations (9.3) and (9.4) mathematically determine the winner in accordance with the Lanchester square law (Taylor 1983, v. 1, pp. 72–74):

$$\alpha_a(M_A^0)^2 > \beta_d(M_B^0)^2 \Rightarrow A \text{ wins}$$
$$\alpha_a(M_A^0)^2 < \beta_d(M_B^0)^2 \Rightarrow B \text{ wins.} \tag{9.5}$$

For example, suppose A has 2,000 soldiers with assault rifles with effectiveness $\alpha_a = 0.01$, and B has 1,000 soldiers with machine guns with effectiveness $\beta_d = 0.05$. Substituting the data into condition (9.5) yields $40,000 < 50,000$, implying that B will win the war even though B is outnumbered two-to-one. Condition (9.5) applies when A is the attacker and B the defender, which is indicated by the subscript a (for attacker) on A's weapons effectiveness coefficient α and by the subscript d (for defender) on B's weapons effectiveness coefficient β. If, instead B attacks A, the coefficients would be α_d and β_a in equations (9.3) and (9.4) and condition (9.5).

Lanchester Attack/Defend Model

We can use the Lanchester square law to formalize Schelling's notion of the inherent propensity for peace or war. Assuming that A is the attacker, solving the bottom half of (9.5) for M_B^0 defines the "B can defend" condition:

$$M_B^0 > (\alpha_a/\beta_d)^{0.5}M_A^0 \Rightarrow B \text{ can defend.} \tag{9.6}$$

For given attack and defense effectiveness coefficients α_a and β_d, condition (9.6) shows the amount of military stock M_B^0 that B must have prior to war in order to successfully defend itself should A attack with military stock M_A^0. As an example, suppose $M_A^0 = 2,000$ weapons, $\alpha_a = 0.01$, and $\beta_d = 0.05$. Substituting the data into condition (9.6) indicates that B needs at

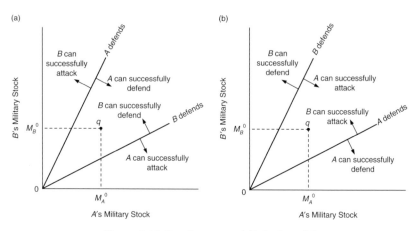

Figure 9.10 Lanchester attack/defend model.
(a) Inherent propensity toward peace
(b) Inherent propensity toward war

least $M_B^0 = 895$ weapons to thwart A's attack. When the defend condition in (9.6) is not satisfied, then A can attack and eventually defeat B. Assuming that B is the attacker, similar methods give the "A can defend" condition:

$$M_A^0 > (\beta_a/\alpha_d)^{0.5} M_B^0 \Rightarrow \quad A \text{ can defend.} \quad (9.7)$$

When (9.7) is not satisfied, B can attack and eventually defeat A. Conditions (9.6) and (9.7) highlight two elements that affect a player's ability to defend successfully in the event of war: first, own and rival military stocks prior to the war, and, second, weapons effectiveness, based on technology, geography, and military organization and training.

A graph of the defense and attack potentials of A and B is shown in Figure 9.10, where M_A is plotted on the horizontal axis and M_B on the vertical axis. Possible pre-war military stocks M_A^0 and M_B^0 are represented by points in the graph, such as point q in panels (a) and (b). Based on condition (9.6), B's defend condition is plotted as a straight line with slope equal to $(\alpha_a/\beta_d)^{0.5}$ and intercept equal to zero. At military stock points above and to the left of this line, B can successfully defend if A attacks; at points below and to the right, B cannot successfully defend and will eventually be defeated if A attacks. A's defend condition is plotted similarly from (9.7), with intercept equal to zero but with slope equal to $1/(\beta_a/\alpha_d)^{0.5}$.

Figure 9.10(a) is drawn under the condition that the B defends line has a smaller slope than does the A defends line, thereby creating a zone of mutual defense. The condition that determines the existence of a mutual defense zone is:

$$(\alpha_a/\beta_d)^{0.5} (\beta_a/\alpha_d)^{0.5} < 1. \tag{9.8a}$$

Condition (9.8a) tends to hold when geographic, technological, and military organization factors combine to cause low attack parameters α_a and β_a and high defense parameters α_d and β_d. Given an initial weapons stocks at point q in Figure 9.10(a), both sides can successfully defend, implying a relatively low risk of war. In Schelling's terminology, Figure 9.10(a) depicts an inherent propensity toward peace.

In Figure 9.10(b), the relative magnitudes of the parameters are reversed, creating a zone of mutual attack under the condition:

$$(\alpha_a/\beta_d)^{0.5} (\beta_a/\alpha_d)^{0.5} > 1. \tag{9.8b}$$

A problem arises at point q in Figure 9.10(b) due to the common knowledge that the first mover can successfully attack and eventually win. Even rivals that fundamentally wish to avoid war may nevertheless be compelled by a first mover advantage to attack before the rival does (Schelling 1966, ch. 6; Fischer 1984). In Schelling's terms, Figure 9.10(b) depicts an inherent propensity toward war.

Figure 9.10 highlights the importance of qualitative arms control. In Figure 9.10(b), reconfigurations of weapons technologies and military organization away from attack and toward defense, geographic repositioning of forces toward defensive postures, or placement of peacekeepers between the rivals could reduce relative attack effectiveness (lower β_a/α_d and α_a/β_d). Such efforts could change the rivalry from an inherent propensity toward war in Figure 9.10(b) to an inherent propensity toward peace in Figure 9.10(a).

Applications

Egypt-Israel 1967 War

In the two decades leading up to their 1967 war, Egypt and Israel acquired substantial weapons stocks through indigenous production and arms imports.[2] According to Mearsheimer (1985, p. 145), by the late spring of

---

[2] This application is adapted from Charles H. Anderton's article, "Toward a Mathematical Theory of the Offensive/Defensive Balance" published in *International Studies Quarterly*,

1967 "the opposing forces were approximately equal in size." This balance of forces could have implied an inherent propensity toward peace if the weapons technologies, geography, and military training of Egypt and Israel had given rise to a situation like Figure 9.10(a). A rough balance of forces at point q in Figure 9.10(a) would imply that both sides could successfully defend against an attack, thus enhancing the probability of peace, all else equal. Some observers at the time believed this was the case. For example, prior to the war O'Balance (1964, p. 210) wrote, "It has long been the aim of the Western powers to keep an even balance of military power in the Middle East so that neither Israel nor any one of the Arab countries develops a dangerous overwhelming preponderance. As long as a fairly even state of parity exists, prospects of peace in that region are better as no one country becomes strong enough to quickly gulp up another."

Missing from the analysis, however, is consideration of geography and weapons technology, which likely placed Egypt and Israel at a point like q in Figure 9.10(b), where despite the balance of forces the propensity toward war was high. Consider the post-war explanation of Fischer (1984, p. 19): "Both Israel and Egypt had vulnerable bomber fleets on open desert airfields. Each side knew that whoever initiated the first strike could easily bomb and destroy the hostile planes on the ground, thereby gaining air superiority." Fischer's analysis suggests that the attack effectiveness coefficients α_a and β_a were relatively large in the Egypt/Israel rivalry, because one plane in a surprise attack could destroy many vulnerable planes on the ground. Empirical evidence supports Fischer's contention. Epstein (1990, p. 45) reported that Israel's attack in 1967 caused Egypt to lose 20 aircraft for every Israeli aircraft lost. Also, the close proximity of the two countries enhanced the advantage of a surprise attack, further raising α_a and β_a. Prior to the outbreak of war, Aharon Yariv, head of Israeli intelligence, and General Yeshayahu Gavish, chief of Israeli Southern Command, "believed that if Israel did not strike soon, the Egyptians might strike first, gaining the attendant benefits of delivering the first blow" (Betts 1982, p. 150).

Militarization of Space

For centuries military strategists have emphasized the importance of controlling high ground in war. Geographically, space represents the ultimate high ground, creating enormous incentives for states to control regions of

volume 36, issue 1, pp. 75–100, 1992. Material is reprinted with the kind permission of Oxford University Press. Copyright © Oxford University Press 1992.

space. In the years ahead territorial disputes in space might prove to be even more dangerous than the now familiar earthly varieties. Growing reliance on military satellites and continuing research into anti-satellite weapons (ASATs) raise concerns about a possible arms race in space (Mutschler 2013, Johnson-Freese 2016). Particularly troublesome is the possibility that the technologies involved in the militarization of space will carry inherent propensities toward war.

Suppose in a future scenario that two equally armed foes are highly dependent upon satellites to conduct military operations. These satellites are highly vulnerable. The players have launched their own satellites, so presumably they also have the capability of launching space vehicles to destroy their rival's satellites. The development of laser technologies and legions of small killer satellites further increases the degree of vulnerability. Important here is the evident incentive to initiate a preemptive attack aimed at destroying a substantial portion of a rival's satellites before the rival attempts to do the same. As Hardesty (2005, p. 49) observes, "Space-based weapons . . . represent significant combat power if used before they are destroyed – leading to a strong incentive to use these weapons pre-emptively, to 'use them or lose them'." The scenario described might then be like point q in Figure 9.10(b), where despite a balance of forces, the propensity toward war is high, and the need for arms control is urgent.

Cyberwar

Cyber means of attack and defense are now being developed by many nations including the so-called cyber superpowers (USA, China, Russia, Israel, and the UK) and two major emerging cyber powers (Iran and North Korea) (Breene 2016). The Stuxnet virus that was used to attack Iran's nuclear research facilities in 2010 is considered by many security analysts as a new class of weaponry that has opened up a whole new domain of war (Public Broadcasting Service 2016) (see Appendix A). It also seems clear that the cyberwar genie is out of the bottle and that many states and nonstate groups are now pushing the technological edge of cyberattack and cyber defense research in what can be characterized as a cyber-arms race (Corera 2015).

Cyber weapons can be delivered virtually instantaneously. They also have the potential to achieve pinpoint accuracy against "security-sensitive" assets including communications networks, power grids, and command and control systems. In the long history of the ebb and flow between attack and defense advantage in military rivalries (see Boulding 1962, ch. 13), it is not clear whether cyber weapons might give rise to a first-strike advantage in war or whether mutual deterrence might prevail. The potential for cyber weapons to deliver a punishing first blow by seriously damaging the power supply or network-centric war capacities of a rival raises the possibility that, in a crisis, rivals would think: "I better launch my cyber weapons and gain the upper hand before they launch their cyber weapons and gain the upper hand." In the Lanchester attack/defense model, the growth of cyber weapons among rivals could elevate the risk of the scenario in Figure 9.10 (b) in which there is an inherent propensity toward war.

9.4 Bibliographic Notes

In addition to Boulding's (1962) seminal work, other early perspectives on the geography of conflict are available from Richardson (1960b), Wright (1942), and Schelling (1960, 1966) and in a special issue of *Journal of Conflict Resolution* (Singer 1960). A number of edited volumes consider the geography of conflict and peace from various disciplinary perspectives (for example, Kobayashi 2012; Megoran, McConnell, and Williams 2014). Meanwhile, recent books provide historical and contemporary perspectives on geographical aspects of war and peace (for example, Pickering 2017, Daly 2017).

During much of the twentieth century, the Lanchester model constituted the foundation of mathematical war modeling (Taylor 1983, MacKay and Price 2011). Although Lanchester theory has been criticized by war modelers (for example, Epstein 1985, Ancker 1995), it is still used in military service organizations to assess various dynamic aspects of war (Epstein 1985, p. 3) and in academic articles on war risk and duration (Anderton and Carter 2007, Langlois and Langlois 2009). Lanchester-type models have also been used to study, among other things, terrorist recruitment (Faria and Arce 2005), guerrilla warfare (Intriligator and Brito 1988), peacekeeping (Gaver and Jacobs 1997), so-called primitive warfare among people groups (Beckerman 1991), and historical battles (for example, Weiss 1966, MacKay and Price 2011, Sahni and Das 2015). For an extensive overview of quantitative methods of combat analysis, see Przemieniecki (2000).

10

Bargaining Theory of War and Peace

In conflict economics, the notion that war and peace emerge from bargaining processes traces back to Thomas Schelling, who noted in his classic book, *The Strategy of Conflict,* that to "study the strategy of conflict is to take the view that most conflict situations are essentially *bargaining* situations" (Schelling 1960, p. 5, his emphasis). The graphical model presented here is due originally to Hirshleifer (1995 pp. 172–5); a more formal version is available in Appendix B. Because the model is broadly consistent with what is known in political science as the bargaining or rationalist theory of war (Fearon 1995), we will offer in this chapter numerous so-called "rationalist" sources of war and peace. Although by no means complete, the model provides an effective framework for thinking systematically about elements of both war and peace, some of the prominent explanations for war, conditions necessary for peace, and possible effects of third-party intervention.

10.1 Two Propositions and a Key Question

The bargaining model of war and peace is built upon two basic propositions and a key question.*

Proposition 1: War Is Costly

We have already seen in this book that violent conflict can lead to serious costs including diversion of scarce resources to combat, destruction of

---

* Parts of this section are adapted from Charles H. Anderton's article, "The Bargaining Theory of War and Peace" published in *The Economics of Peace and Security Journal*, volume 12, issue 2, pp. 10–5, 2017. Material is reprinted with the kind permission of *The Economics of Peace and Security Journal.* Copyright © EPS Publishing 2017.

■ Resource Diversion ($121.1)   ▨ Property Destruction ($23.7)
■ Human Destruction ($99.0)   ■ Trade Disruption Costs ($177.0)

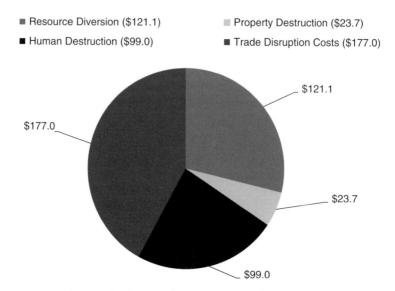

Figure 10.1 Estimated economic costs of World War I.
Note: Data in in billions of 1913 USA dollars.
Sources: Bogart (1920) for resource diversion and property destruction costs; Glick and
Taylor (2010) for human destruction and trade disruption costs.

people and property, disruption of economic and noneconomic activities,
and displacement of people in the form of refugees and internally displaced
persons. Such costs make the transition from a war economy to
a developing peace economy difficult. These five Ds as we called them
(Chapter 1) seem obvious, but let's put some real numbers to the costs
of war.

Figure 10.1 shows estimates of the economic costs of World War
I associated with diversion of resources, destruction of property, loss of
human life, and disruption of trade. Owing to methodological complex-
ities such as price changes over long periods of time and exchange rate
differences across countries, such costs should be viewed as rough estimates. The first two costs are based on figures provided by Bogart (1920).
We assume his estimates are denominated in 1918 dollars, which we
deflate to 1913 prices using the consumer price index. The resource diversion cost of $121.1 billion includes expenditures by belligerent and neutral
governments for military personnel and equipment in excess of what
would have been spent without the war. Property losses of $23.7 billion
include the costs of disabled factories, farms, and merchant ships and
cargo. The next two costs are from Glick and Taylor (2010). Their

human destruction cost of $99 billion in 1913 dollars includes both lost lives and the wounded, which are calculated according to labor market principles (pp. 117–8 and p. 124). Their cost of trade disruption for belligerent and neutral nations is $177 billion in 1913 dollars (p. 124).

When the estimated costs of World War I in Figure 10.1 are combined, they total $420.8 billion at 1913 prices. To appreciate the magnitude of such costs, consider that the world GDP in 1913 equalled $206.5 billion in 1913 dollars (this was calculated by taking Glick and Taylor's 2010 estimate of world 1913 GDP of $2,726,065 million in 1990 dollars and deflating the figure to 1913 dollars using the CPI). Thus, according to the estimates in Figure 10.1, the economic costs of World War I were about double the world's 1913 GDP, a truly staggering cost indeed!

Proposition 2: Peace Offers Potential Mutual Gains to the Combatants

When players go to war, they miss out on potential mutual gains that are available from avoiding the costs of war. In World War I, for example, if the nations avoided war, they could have, in theory, gained from divvying up the "avoidance of war costs pie" in Figure 10.1. About equal to twice the world's 1913 GDP, that's a big potential gain that was not realized. How could such a potential "bargain" be missed?

Key Question: Why Does War Occur?

Explaining why the potential mutual gains from peace are forfeited and war chosen instead is the main purpose of the bargaining theory of war and peace. Before we build the bargaining model and offer answers to the key question, notice the economic nature of the theory. It includes the costs of war and the potential mutual gains from peace. Economists are always thinking about costs, but even more so about mutual gains. Economists assiduously seek out opportunities for mutual gains. When mutual gains are not taken advantage of and are, in a sense, left on the table, we're baffled and we demand an explanation. But wars do occur, that is, the potential mutual gains from peace are sometimes left on the table and they are often left there as a result of the purposeful choices of decision makers. But sometimes (and actually quite often) the mutual gains from peace are chosen. Hence, the bargaining theory has at its center the notion that war and peace are chosen.

It is also important to note that in the bargaining theory, war and peace are not separate silos. The two-sided drama of whether disputes between parties turn violent or are managed non-violently is integrated in the bargaining theory of war and peace. This "integral-ness" of war and peace is quite clear, once again, in Schelling's (1960) *The Strategy of Conflict*: In the bargaining over war and peace, "the possibility of mutual accommodation is as important and dramatic as the element of conflict" (p. 5). This is a remarkable statement. Choosing peace is just as dramatic as choosing war! The potentials for war and peace are coupled in the bargaining theory (analogous to how space and time, space-time, are coupled in theoretical physics).

10.2 Elements of Conflict and Peace

Suppose a disputed resource is to be divided between two players A and B. The players might be nations disputing territory, a government and a rebel group clashing over natural resources, or a government and a terrorist organization competing for ideological control of a population. The players begin by diverting secure resources into arms, and then they divide the disputed resource either by fighting or by peaceful settlement. For simplicity, assume each player chooses a level of arms that is the same whether fighting or settlement is anticipated. If the players fight, a portion of the disputed resource is destroyed, with the surviving portion divided between them based on their comparative arms and military technologies. If they settle, the full amount of the disputed resource is divided by agreement, and the agreement is enforced by the threat embodied in the arms. Note here that the economic incentive to settle originates in the desire to avoid the resource destruction that accompanies fighting. On completion of either fighting or settlement, the players generate incomes from their final resources, which consist of their secure resources net of the diversion to arms plus their share of the disputed resource net of any destruction.

The choice between fighting and peaceful settlement rests on three elements: the expected income distributions based on fighting, the potential income distributions based on peaceful settlement, and the interpersonal preferences of the players. The attitudes of the players toward one another are reflected by their preferences over income distributions. These preferences may be benevolent, malevolent, or egoistic, depending on whether a player considers the other's income to be a good, a bad, or neither (called a neuter). Peaceful settlement occurs if there exists one or

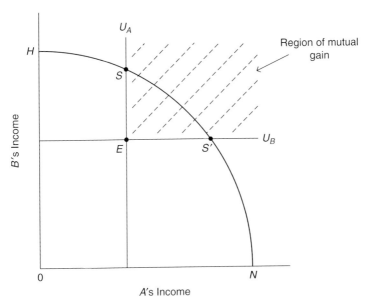

Figure 10.2 Bargaining model with peaceful settlement.

more distributions by settlement that would leave at least one player better off and neither player worse off than would be expected if they were to fight.

The elements of the model are shown in Figure 10.2 with a case of peaceful settlement. Assume the players have complete information about armaments, conflict technology, and productive capabilities. This means that each player holds the same expectation about the outcome of war and resulting income distribution, shown by the conflict (or disagreement) point E. If the resource is divided peacefully, then alternative income distributions are feasible. These potential distributions are shown by the settlement opportunities curve HN. The settlement curve could be linear (as in Figure 8.2), but we assume it bows out owing to complementarities in production that are available to the players when they cooperate rather than fight (Hirshleifer 1989). Both players are assumed to be strict egoists, as indicated by their respective indifference curves U_A and U_B passing through point E. Player A cares only about their own income; thus their indifference curves are vertical, and they prefer all distributions to the right of U_A. For the same reason, B's indifference curves are horizontal, and they prefer all distributions above U_B. The highlighted area above and to the right of E is thus the region of mutual gain and includes distributions that

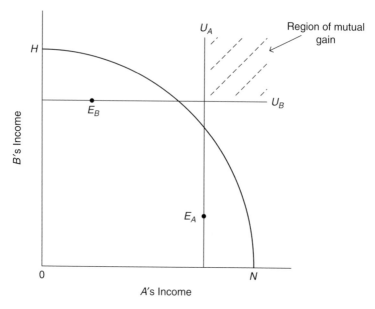

Figure 10.3 Inconsistent expectations with fighting.

are Pareto preferred to E, that is, distributions that make at least one player better off and neither player worse off relative to E. Because the settlement opportunities curve intersects the region of mutual gain, the model predicts peaceful settlement over violence, resulting in a final outcome somewhere between points S and S' along the settlement opportunities curve.

10.3 Rationalist Sources of Violent Conflict

Inconsistent Expectations

Various elements in Figure 10.2 combine to generate a peaceful settlement. To see how fighting might arise instead, assume now that the players' expectations are inconsistent. In particular, suppose in Figure 10.3 that A expects the outcome of fighting to be income distribution E_A located toward the lower right, while B expects it to be E_B toward the upper left. The region of mutual gain now lies entirely outside the settlement opportunities curve HN. Because of the players' divergent expectations, the settlement opportunities curve fails to intersect the region of mutual gain, and the predicted outcome is fighting.

Divergent expectations in this model imply that the players have incomplete information about factors that determine the outcome of fighting, such as the other's capabilities, costs, strategies, or tactics. Figures 10.2 and 10.3 together suggest that an exchange of relevant private information between the players could generate a peaceful settlement that would be preferred to fighting. However, because expected outcomes determine which settlements are acceptable, the players have an incentive to withhold, exaggerate, or misrepresent certain information in order to attain a settlement more to their own advantage. This means that private information, even if accurate, tends to lack credibility when it is provided by the players. In this way, the exchange of information that might close divergent expectations is problematic (Fearon 1995). Furthermore, the revelation of information that might close an expectations gap and lead to settlement can be frustrated by the presence of decentralized private information about violent capabilities (Wood 2018). Wood (2018), for example, shows that continual improvements in weapons capabilities by small groups of insurgents in Afghanistan and Iraq (for example, continual upgrades to improvised explosive devices or "roadside bombs") can drastically lengthen the amount of time for fighting to reveal enough information for the gap in war expectations to appreciably shrink.

Fearon (1995, pp. 398–400) maintains that the 1904–05 war between Japan and Russia was motivated in part by asymmetric information. The war was rooted in a disagreement over control of Manchuria and Korea as each state sought greater geographic buffer. According to Fearon, the Russians believed they would almost certainly win in the event of war, but the Japanese perceived they had a 50 percent chance of winning. Note that the expected probabilities of winning summed to more than one, which indicated that at least one player was incorrect. It turned out that Russia was incorrect. Specifically, the Japanese had private information about relative military capabilities, strategy, and tactics of which the Russians were unaware. Why would Japan not share this information in order to solicit a more favorable peaceful settlement from Russia? First, if the Japanese revealed their previously hidden strengths, the Russians would have taken countermeasures to diminish or even eliminate the Japanese advantages (Anderton and Carter 2011, p. 36). In this way, the strategic value of the information asymmetry could be lost to Japan. Second, Japan's claims about its abilities might cause the Russians to believe that the Japanese were simply manipulating information to extract a more favorable settlement leading the Russians to deem the information not credible

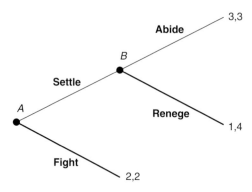

Figure 10.4 Two-person commitment problem.

(Anderton and Carter 2011, p. 36). Fearon concluded that the asymmetric information combined with the actors' incentives to manipulate information created a substantial risk of war between Russia and Japan in 1904.

Commitment Problems

A commitment problem exists when one player cannot trust the other because the latter has an incentive to renege after an agreement is reached. The essence of the problem is captured by the simplified game in Figure 10.4, which is part of a larger game wherein player B has proposed a settlement. Player A can either *Settle*, meaning agree to peaceful settlement, or *Fight*. If A selects *Settle*, B can either *Abide* or *Renege*. Payoffs appear at the ends of the game tree branches, with A's payoff listed first. As shown, both players are better off with peaceful settlement (3,3) than with fighting (2,2), but given A's choice of *Settle*, B is better off reneging than abiding (4>3). Knowing that B is better off reneging, A mistrusts B and so chooses *Fight*. The predicted outcome is fighting with payoffs (2,2), despite its Pareto inefficiency compared to the superior settlement with payoffs (3,3). To see how such commitment problems can lead to fighting, we look at three cases that are prominent in bargaining theory (Fearon 1995, Powell 2006).

Preemptive War

Preemptive war arises from a first-strike advantage available to each side. Assume the players have complete information and thus correctly

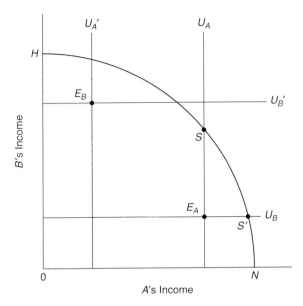

Figure 10.5 Commitment problem and preemptive war.

anticipate the offensive advantage. In Figure 10.5, both players expect fighting to result in income distribution E_A if A attacks first and in distribution E_B if B attacks first. Hence, the "E gap" in Figure 10.5 is not the result of incomplete information, but of weapons technologies and geography that give rise to a first-mover advantage in war. Suppose that the players bargain relative to E_A, the expected distribution if A attacks first. Any agreement by B to a settlement between S and S' is not credible, because B will have an incentive to renege, seize the first-strike advantage, and thereby shift the expected outcome to E_B in which utility U_B' can be achieved. Knowing that B's first strike would lower her utility to U_A', A will be inclined to launch her own preemptive strike. By the same argument, any agreement by A relative to E_B is not credible, thereby leading B to strike. Because neither player can credibly commit to a mutually advantageous settlement, fighting is the predicted outcome.

Preemptive military technology and geography seemed to be a source of violence in the Egypt/Israel war of 1967, which we covered in Chapter 9. Some scholars view World War I as a war with preemptive motives. For example, Van Evera (1999, p. 41) maintains that in 1914 Russian leaders ordered military mobilization because they feared that Germany might gain the upper hand in mobilizing for war first. Of course, observing the

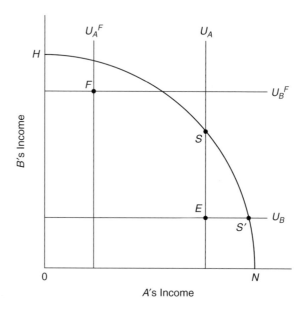

Figure 10.6 Commitment problem and preventive war.

Russian mobilization for war would cause the Germans to mobilize at a greater rate than otherwise, which would cause the Russians to hasten their mobilization, and so on in a spiral of mobilization. As Schelling (1966, p. 222) noted regarding the mobilization of troops and resources made possible by railroads at the onset of World War I: "This miracle of mobilization reflected an obsession with the need for haste—to have an army at the frontier as quickly as possible, to exploit the enemy's unreadiness if the enemy's mobilization was slower and to minimize the enemy's advantage if he got mobilized on the frontier first."

Preventive War

To understand preventive war, the bargaining model must be extended to allow for dynamic considerations across time. Suppose the model consists of two periods. In period 1, the players choose levels of arms that result in conflict point E and settlement opportunities curve HN. As seen in Figure 10.6, settlements between S and S' offer mutual gains relative to fighting. However, suppose it is known that a potential change in military technology exists that, if realized, would shift power toward B in period 2. Assume that the shift in power can be prevented by fighting in period 1 but not by settlement. If the potential shift in power is sufficiently large, then a commitment problem arises, and fighting in period 1 is predicted.

To see the commitment problem most simply, assume in Figure 10.6 that arms levels (but not arms productivities) remain fixed, so that the change in technology would shift the conflict point northwest to point *F* in period 2 but would leave the settlement opportunity curve unchanged. In this case, an agreement by *B* in period 1 to a settlement between *S* and *S'* would not be credible. This is because such an agreement would leave *B* with a clear incentive in period 2 to threaten a fight and thereby secure a more advantageous settlement somewhere to the northeast of conflict point *F*. Knowing this, *A* will weigh the prospective loss of income in period 2 against the cost of fighting in period 1. If the prospective shift in power is sufficiently large (as it is in Figure 10.6), *A* will refuse settlement in period 1 and instead lock in the distribution at point *E* by fighting.

A preventive war logic is often cited to explain Israel's 2007 airstrike against suspected Syrian nuclear assets in 2007 (Bass 2015). Known as Operation Orchard, the strike appeared to follow the dictates of the so-called Begin Doctrine, which was announced in June 1981 by Israeli Prime Minister Menachem Begin following an attack against Iraq's nuclear reactor near Baghdad. The doctrine stipulates Israel's intention to carry out preventive strikes against potential enemies' weapons of mass destruction assets.

Indivisibilities

Partial or complete indivisibility of a disputed issue can be an important source of violence in conflicts over territory or political control (Goddard 2006, Toft 2006, Skaperdas 2006, pp. 667–8). Suppose two players dispute control of a sacred site that both perceive to be completely indivisible. An example is shown in Figure 10.7, where each player is assumed to obtain income only when the site is completely held. If *A* controls the site, the outcome is at point *N*; if *B* controls the site, the outcome is at point *H*. Thus, the settlement opportunities frontier is represented entirely by the two points *H* and *N*. The expected outcome of fighting is shown by point *E*, which is determined by multiplying each player's probability of winning times its income from controlling that portion of the site not destroyed by fighting. Since the region of mutual gain includes neither settlement point *H* nor *N*, fighting is the predicted outcome.

Powell (2006) notes, however, that there are ways to peacefully distribute the disputed resource such that each player's expected payoff is greater under a settlement than under fighting. To see this, suppose each

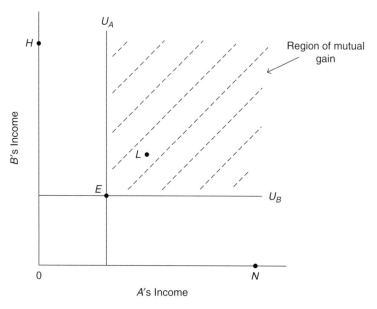

Figure 10.7 Commitment problem and indivisibilities.

player has a 50 percent chance of winning control of the site through fighting, but each would suffer costs because of destruction. A lottery (for example, a coin flip) that peacefully distributes the disputed item to each player with the same 50 percent probability would be preferred by both players because it avoids the costs of war. This is shown in Figure 10.7 by point L, which lies along a straight line (not shown) between H and N. Because costs of destruction are avoided under the lottery, point L lies within the region of mutual gain and is strictly preferred by each player to point E. Powell points out, however, that there is a commitment problem associated with the lottery. After the lottery, the disputed resource is distributed to the winning player, thus placing the outcome at either point H or N. But the loser has an incentive to renege on the lottery and initiate war, because the expected income from fighting at E is greater than the zero income assigned by the lottery.

The sacred site in Jerusalem, called the Temple Mount by Jews and Haram el-Sharif by Muslims, is an example of indivisibility as a potential source of hostilities (Anderton and Carter 2011, p. 39). According to Hassner (2003, p. 27), at the July 2000 Camp David negotiations, Palestinian Authority president Yasser Arafat indicated that his delegation should "not budge on this one thing: the Haram [el-Sharif] is more precious to me than anything else." Meanwhile, Israeli prime minister Ehud Barak stated: "The Temple Mount is the cradle of Jewish history and there is no way I will sign a document that transfers sovereignty over the Temple Mount to the Palestinians. For Israel that would constitute a betrayal of its holy of holies" (Hassner 2003, p. 29). According to Hassner (2003), the Camp David negotiations failed and violence resumed between Israelis and Palestinians due in part to the perceptions by the two sides of the indivisibility of the sacred site and the failure of mediators to fully understand the indivisibility.

According to Hassner (2013, p. 325), peacemaking is particularly challenging when disputes occur over indivisible territory because "sacred sites cannot be shared to the satisfaction of all parties involved." Consider also that "ideological territory" can be perceived as indivisible, thus making ideological conflict difficult to resolve. For example, ISIS leaders and leaders from liberal democracies face apparently indivisible differences over the nature of political systems and human rights for females and practitioners of a variety of religions. As such, ideological conflict between ISIS and liberal democracies seems intractable.

Political Bias

To this point we have assumed that A and B are unitary actors who distribute a disputed resource by costly fighting or peaceful settlement. It is clearly recognized, however, that a critical leader who substantially affects decisions to fight or settle can have different incentives relative to the group for whom the leader acts. Tarar (2006), for example, adapts Fearon's (1995) bargaining model of war to account for a critical leader's incentive to initiate war as a diversion from domestic problems (see also Tir 2010, Oakes 2012, and Blomdahl 2017). Fergusson, Robinson, Torvik, and Vargas' (2016) theoretical and empirical analyses find that political advantages can accrue to leaders who have enemies relative to those that do not. Also within a bargaining model, Jackson and Morelli (2007) consider a critical leader's "political bias," which encompasses anything that causes the leader to have different incentives for war or peace relative to the group as a whole.

Here we relax the unitary actor assumption to illustrate how incentives facing a critical leader can be a distinct source of violence within the model. For simplicity, suppose only one of the players, say B, is subject to political bias. Assume also that each player chooses a level of arms that is unchanged whether fighting or settlement is anticipated and any settlement achieved is enforced by those arms. Let b and $\hat{b}$ represent the proportion of B's income controlled by the critical leader under peaceful settlement and fighting, respectively. For example, if $b = 0.2$ and $\hat{b} = 0.3$, then B's critical leader controls 20 percent of B's income under peace but 30 percent of the income under fighting. Following Jackson and Morelli (2007, p. 1357), let $\hat{B} \equiv \hat{b}/b$ represent the political bias of B's critical leader. When $\hat{B} > 1$, the critical leader is biased in favor of fighting. For example, the critical leader might gain power or status with fighting that allows the leader to control a greater share of B's income than with settlement. Alternatively, a critical leader perpetrating atrocities during a war might expect retribution under settlement, causing the leader to control a smaller share (possibly zero) of B's income under peace relative to fighting. Political bias does not necessarily favor fighting. When $\hat{B} < 1$, the pivotal leader controls a smaller share of income under fighting than under settlement. This might arise, for example, when peace confers popularity on the critical leader. When $\hat{B} = 1$, the leader's incentives between fighting and settlement match those of the broader group.

The essential tradeoff for a critical leader with a political bias in favor of war is between controlling a larger share of less income by fighting versus a smaller share of more income by settling. To see how fighting might arise owing to political bias, begin by assuming in Figure 10.8 that $b = 0.2$ and $\hat{b} = 0.3$. Assume also that the critical leader controls the decision to fight or to settle. For A and B as unitary actors, the outcome of fighting at E returns an expected income of 100 to each player. By avoiding the destructiveness of fighting, peaceful settlement at (say) point $\hat{S}$ promises each player an income of 150. Clearly, settlement at $\hat{S}$ is better for each player relative to fighting. In this case, B's critical leader is indifferent between fighting and peaceful settlement at $\hat{S}$: as shown in the figure, the leader will achieve the same income of 30 at point C^1 under fighting (0.3*100 = 30) or peace (0.2*150 = 30). Starting from point C^1, however, suppose the proportion of B's income from fighting controlled by the critical leader rises from $\hat{b} = 0.3$ to $\hat{b} = 0.4$, all else equal. Now B's critical leader will expect to gain more at C^2 from fighting (0.4*100 = 40) than from settlement (0.2*150 = 30). Since the critical leader controls the decision to fight or to settle, fighting is the predicted outcome.

Player A could attempt to buy off B's critical leader by offering a more generous settlement, such as point S in Figure 10.8. As drawn, point S reflects the maximum that A would be willing to offer B's critical leader because A's expected income from fighting would just equal their income from settlement at S. Nevertheless, such a settlement offer would not be enough to prevent

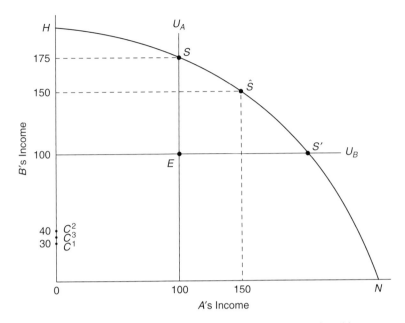

Figure 10.8 Possible fighting when player *B* is subject to political bias.

fighting. Under settlement at *S*, *B*'s critical leader would achieve income of $C^3 = 0.2*175 = 35$, which is less than the leader's expected income of 40 at C^2 from fighting. Hence, the critical leader would still have an incentive to fight. Anderton and Carter (2011, p. 46) note that "political bias is a potential explanation for why a war starts, but also for why a war endures." Consider, for example, a critical leader who initiated aggression or has been perpetrating atrocities. The leader may develop a strong political bias in favor of continuing the war because he is likely to be held accountable for his misdeeds after the war ends. Toward the end of World War II, for example, Hitler and his associates preferred to continue a war that was extremely costly for Germany. War continuation relative to termination was personally advantageous to Hitler because it delayed his virtually certain demise (Anderton and Carter 2011, p. 46).

Other Rationalist Sources of War

So far we have identified and modeled five distinct rationalist sources of war, three of which were commitment problems. Another rationalist source of war is concern for reputation (Schelling 1966, Walter 2009,

Sechser 2018). For example, a nation (player *A*) may perceive that it should fight a costly war against rebel group *B* in order to deter future uprisings by *B* or by other potential rebel groups. Incentive to eliminate a persistent rival is also a rationalist source of war. Garfinkel and Skaperdas (2000a, 2007) demonstrate in a formal model how a player (say, nation *A*) can gain from a war that eliminates a rival (nation or rebel group *B*). The rationale for such a war is that it is costly for *A* to continue building and maintaining arms year by year in its contest with *B*. If *B* ceases to exist, the cost savings for *A* could be substantial. Skaperdas (2006, p. 668) shows that increasing returns to production can be a rationalist source of war. Intuitively, when a production process is subject to increasing returns, concentrated use of resources for production by one player yields greater aggregate output than had the resources been divided and used for production by two or more players. If a potential attacker finds that the expected gains from increasing returns to production from the conquest of another player's resources outweigh the expected costs of war, war initiation can be rational. Sambanis, Skaperdas, and Wohlforth (2015) show that it can be rational for a critical leader to initiate an interstate war as a means of nation building. In this case, external war could cause groups within the state to identify nationally rather than along sectarian group lines, which in turn could reduce conflicts within the state and increase investments in state capacity.

10.4 Nonrational Sources of Violent Conflict

Perspectives from Behavioral Economics: Reference Dependence and Loss Aversion

Reference dependence in the political arena could be a critical leader's established holding of political, territorial, and/or ideological control relative to which gains and losses of control are valued. Loss aversion is the propensity for a decisionmaker to psychologically magnify the loss associated with falling short of the reference amount of control (see Chapter 6). Table 10.1 provides a numerical example of the effects of reference dependence and loss aversion for the case of preventive war. Assume that *A*'s critical leader (perhaps a state leader) holds substantially more power than *B* (perhaps a rebel group's critical leader). Suppose the power ratio in favor of *A* is 4 to 1, which is reflected in Table 10.1 as follows: If the players' reach a peaceful settlement in period 1, *A*'s leader receives income of 400 units and *B*'s leader receives 100 units as shown in the first column of row 1.

Table 10.1 *Reference dependence, loss aversion, and preventive war.*

Row	(1) Period 1 Incomes for A and B	(2) Period 2 Incomes for A and B	(3) Total Income	(4) Psychological Value for A's Leader (PV_A)
1	Peace $I_A=400$ $I_B=100$	Peace $I_A=375$ $I_B=125$	$I_A^{tot}=775$ $I_B^{tot}=225$	$PV_A=725$
2	War $I_A=350$ $I_B=50$	Peace $I_A=400$ $I_B=100$	$I_A^{tot}=750$ $I_B^{tot}=150$	$PV_A=750$

In the preventive war analysis in Figure 10.6 from earlier, we assumed two periods. If the players peacefully settle in period 1, a shift in power against A occurs in period 2. This is shown in the second column of row 1 of Table 10.1, where we assume that the power ratio in favor of A declines from 4 to 3 in period 2. As such, A's leader receives income of 375 units and B's leader receives 125 units (a ratio of 3 to 1). The third column of row 1 shows that the income of A's leader over the two periods is 400 + 375 = 775 units (for simplicity, we ignore discounting of future income).

In the preventive war analysis in Figure 10.6, we assumed the shift in power could be prevented by fighting in period 1 but not by settlement. This possibility is shown in the first column of row 2 of Table 10.1. Given the destructive costs of war, A's choice of war in period 1 leads to incomes of 350 and 50 units for the leaders in A and B, respectively. The war, however, prevents the shift in power and, as such, the peaceful settlement in period 2 leads to the outcome shown in the second column of row 2 in which A leader receives 400 units of income and B's leader receives 100 units. As shown in the third column of row 2, the income of A's leader over the two periods is 350 + 400 = 750 units. Unlike the outcome in Figure 10.6 from earlier, it is not in leader A's interest to initiate preventive war given the assumptions of Table 10.1. Note that A's leader gains more from peace in both periods (total income=775) relative to preventive war in period 1 followed by peace in period 2 (total income=750). If the power shift that follows peaceful settlement in period 1 is relatively small (in our case, the power ratio changes from 4 to 3), and the destructive costs of war are relatively large (in our case, 20 percent of income potential is destroyed by war in period 1), preventive war will not be beneficial on net and will not be chosen.

But what if A's leader is governed by reference dependence and loss aversion? Assume that A's leader has become accustomed to the 4-to-1 power advantage that it holds in period 1. That power holding would then be a reference point for A's leader from which a loss in power would be evaluated. Suppose A's leader is governed by the following psychological value function:

$$PV_A = \begin{array}{ll} I_A & if\,(R-4) \geq 0 \\ I_A + \lambda(R-4) & if\,(R-4) < 0, \lambda = 50. \end{array} \qquad (10.1)$$

In (10.1), I_A and PV_A are the income and the psychological value obtained by A's leader, respectively, R is A's power ratio, $\lambda = 50$ is the critical leader's degree of loss aversion when power falls short of the reference point, and the reference point power ratio is assumed to be 4. The final column of Table 10.1 shows the psychological values for A's leader for our two scenarios. In row 1 of the final column, the power ratio in favor of A declines from 4 to 3 in period 2 and thus lies below the reference point of 4. Based on equation (10.1), PV_A in period 1 is 400 units and PV_A in period 2 is 375 + 50(3–4) = 325 units. As shown in column 4 of row 1, PV_A over the two periods is 400 + 325 = 725 units. Meanwhile, in the second row there is no power shift in period 2. Hence, PV_A over the two periods is 350 + 400 = 750 units as shown in the final column. Table 10.1 shows that A's leader achieves higher psychological value by locking in its current power position with war in period 1 to achieve PV_A of 750 than to allow the power shift to occur, which would lead to PV_A of 725. The preventive motive for war alone is insufficient to cause war in Table 10.1, but that rationalist motive magnified by the psychological phenomena of reference dependence and loss aversion give A's critical leader an incentive to initiate war.

Perspectives from Identity Economics: Malevolent Preferences

In Chapter 6, we showed how manipulations of individuals' of identities within social contexts could lead to dramatic changes in individual's preferences and their resulting choices for violence and peace. In Figure 10.9 we offer a simple extension of the bargaining theory of war and peace into the realm of the economics of identity by considering the effects of preference manipulation on the risk of war. Assume the "E-gap" in Figure 10.9 is due to incomplete information, but suppose now (unlike Figure 10.3 from earlier) that the E-gap is too small to lead to war. Specifically, under *egoistic* indifference curves U_A and U_B, a set of acceptable peaceful settlements between S and S' implies that peace will occur.

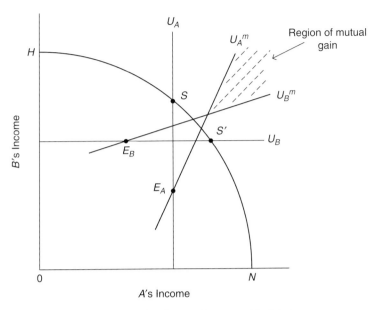

Figure 10.9 Malevolent preferences with fighting.

In this case, the degree of incomplete information is small relative to the costs of war, so peace prevails.

Or does it? What if each side, owing to past investments in identity solidarity within the group and identity enmity toward the other group, have developed malevolent preferences? In economic terms, malevolence is manifested by a group's willingness to sacrifice some of its own income to reduce the other's income. In Figure 10.9 the mutual malevolence of the players is shown by the darker positively sloped indifference curves U_A^m and U_B^m passing through the points E_A and E_B. Player A wants more income for herself and less for B; thus, A prefers income distributions down and to the right of U_A^m. Likewise, B wants more income for himself and less for A; thus, B prefers distributions up and to the left of U_B^m. In the figure, the combination of the E-gap and malevolent preferences causes the region of mutual gain to lie beyond the settlement opportunities curve, leading to war. The rationalist motive for war owing to incomplete information alone is insufficient to cause war in Figure 10.9, but that rationalist motive coupled with identity-based malevolence leads to war.

10.5 Sources of Peace in the Bargaining Model

We have employed the bargaining model to illuminate rationalist and nonrationalist sources of violence. The model can also be used to understand why peaceful settlement prevails rather than violent conflict. To fix ideas, assume you are the leader of a third-party intervention team. You see your objective as preventing the outbreak of war between A and B as distinct from intervening on behalf of one of the side's. Each potential war will have its own set of rationalist and nonrationalist elements pushing toward war. You will need to identify as many of the sources of violence as you can and minimize them as best you can give your limited resources. For example, if an E-gap exists you will need to determine whether it is the result of incomplete information, preemptive military technologies, or a combination of the two. You will then need policy options for reducing the E-gap such as information sharing, reconfiguration of weaponry to diminish preemptive incentives, and/or insertion of peacekeepers as a buffer force between the rivals. If nonrationalist sources of violence are in play, such as reference dependence or identity-based malevolence, you will need tools to minimize such elements. Two of the various possibilities are shown in Figures 10.10 and 10.11. Each figure assumes for simplicity that the players' arms levels are unchanged by third party intervention.

Consider first the possibility of economic intervention. In Figure 10.10, assume that a first-strike advantage exists such that the expected outcome is E_A if A attacks first and E_B if B attacks first. Consequently, the highlighted region of mutual gain lies outside of the settlement opportunities curve *HN*, setting up the likelihood of preemptive war. Suppose, however, that a third party offers economic inducements to the players' contingent on peaceful settlement. If the inducements are sufficiently large and are tied to suitable settlements, then distributions within the region of mutual gain are feasible and settlement is expected. For example, conditioned on settlement at point $\hat{S}$, the third party could offer subsidies to the players to push settlement opportunities to the bold curve *H'N'*. The new settlements curve would allow each player to gain from peace, for example, at a final distribution at point $\hat{S}'$.

As an alternative to economic subsidy, a third party might provide diplomatic mediation. In Figure 10.11, assume that A expects the outcome of fighting to be E_A while B expects it to be E_B. Suppose this E-gap is due to a combination of incomplete information and preemptive military technologies. Since the highlighted region of mutual gain lies outside the settlement opportunities curve *HN*, fighting is the predicted outcome.

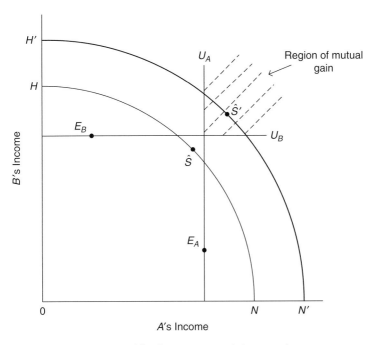

Figure 10.10 Third-party economic intervention.

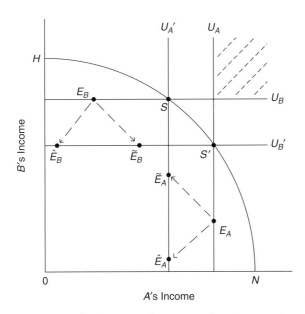

Figure 10.11 Third-party mediation or military intervention.

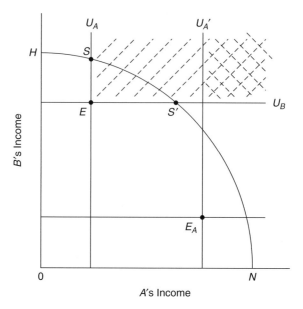

Figure 10.12 Third-party intervention favoring player *A*.

Suppose, however, that a third party facilitates the credible exchange of private information between the players and fosters the reconfiguration of the weaponry of the two sides to diminish first-strike advantage. If the expected outcomes of fighting are brought sufficiently close, then peaceful settlement becomes feasible. For example, if mediation shifts expectations to points $\tilde{E}_A$ and $\tilde{E}_B$, then peaceful settlement between points S and S' along the settlement opportunities curve is made possible.

Alternatively, suppose that a third party undertakes peace enforcement to terminate violence between the players. In particular, assume a third party deploys military forces against both A and B, thus eroding their expected returns from fighting. In this case, the expected outcomes from fighting shift southwest to $\hat{E}_A$ and $\hat{E}_B$ in Figure 10.11, and peaceful settlement between S and S' is again made possible.

Figures 10.10 and 10.11 show how third-party intervention can ameliorate violence. If an intervention favors one side, however, it can leave the prospect for peaceful settlement unchanged or even worsened. For example, in Figure 10.12 assume both players initially expect an outcome of fighting at E, thus forming a region of mutual gain intersected by the settlement opportunities curve between S and S'. Now suppose that a third party is privately available to the advantage of A, such that A expects the fighting outcome to be E_A while B continues to expect E. This means that the region of mutual gain, shown by the cross-hatched area, is reduced in size and now lies outside the settlement opportunities curve. Here, third-party intervention reduces the prospect for peaceful settlement and becomes a source of violent conflict.

10.6 Empirical Studies of Risk Factors for War

Inconsistent Expectations and War Onset

Absent commitment problems, incomplete information can generate inconsistent expectations and war initiation (Figure 10.3). Moreover, secret intervention by a third party on behalf of one side can be a source of war (Figure 10.12). The challenge presented to social scientists when statistically testing incomplete information as a mechanism for war is that expectations and the private information on which they rest are often not directly observable. As a result, empirical inquiries into inconsistent expectations and war often posit indirect measures of uncertainty between potential combatants (see, for example, Slantchev 2004). Bas and Schub (2016), however, offer a novel direct measure of one source of incomplete information in international relations, namely, secret alliances. Assume that nation A is in a territorial rivalry with nation B in which war or peaceful settlement are possible. Suppose A is in a secret alliance with nation C, that is, the A/C alliance is unknown to B. In the bargaining between A and B over the territory, it is reasonable to assume that A will make more strenuous settlement demands than otherwise because A believes that C will come to its aid in the event of war. Moreover, A may have little incentive to reveal the secret alliance to B to induce a more favorable bargain owing, for example, to the loss of tactical advantages to A that are available with war (for example, surprise). In this way, the availability of C's military capabilities to A in the event of war can cause the sum of the two sides' private estimates of the probabilities of winning the war to be greater than one. Bas and Schub (2016, p. 554) characterize this scenario as "mutual optimism," which holds "regardless of whether the private information is one- or two-sided."

The hypothesis that follows is that the greater the presence of mutual optimism between pairs of states, the more likely that conflict will occur between them, other things equal. According to Bas and Schub, there have been no secret alliances since 1956 and only one since 1923 (of which social scientists are aware). Hence, they test their hypothesis on a sample of politically relevant dyads between 1816 and 1923. A politically relevant dyad is a pair of states that share a border (contiguous) or in which at least one is a major power. Bas and Schub's dependent variable is the presence of a militarized interstate dispute (MID), which is the threat, display, or use of force between states (see Chapter 11 for data and further details on MIDs). With measures of mutual optimism based on secret alliances as their key explanatory variable, they include a number of control variables that affect the risk of a MID such as relative military capabilities and joint democracy. Bas and Schub's central finding is that there is a statistically significant and substantive effect of mutual optimism on the risk of interstate conflict. For example, when secret alliances "are more numerous or more powerful than anticipated, there is a roughly 60 percent relative increase in conflict likelihood," all else equal (Bas and Schub 2016, p. 559).

Offense/Defense Theory and Preemptive War

Offense-defense theory (ODT) maintains that war is more likely when offense has the advantage over defense in military operations (Van Evera 1999). An empirical test of ODT that aligns closely with bargaining theory's concern for preemptive military technologies as a source of war (Figure 10.5) is provided by Adams (2003/04). Adams distinguishes among offense, defense, and deterrence, where the latter occurs when a state prepares to use or shows an ability to use force against another state's nonmilitary assets in order to discourage that state from initiating or continuing an offensive operation. Based on a review of the best technologies available since 1800, Adams determines that offense was dominant during 1800–49 and 1934–45, defense was dominant during 1850–1933, and deterrence was dominant in the nuclear era beginning in 1946. Her central hypothesis is that attacks and conquests would be most frequent in offense-dominant eras, less frequent in the defense-dominant era, and rare in the deterrence-dominant era. To test the hypothesis, she constructs a dataset on attacks and conquests by great powers and nuclear states from 1800 to 1997. For each state and year, Adams codes three dependent variables, indicating whether the state's territory was conquered, whether the state attacked another great power, and whether it attacked a non-great power. The explanatory variable is the offense-defense-deterrence balance, which is coded 0 in the deterrence-dominant era, 1 in the defense-dominant era, and 2 in the offense-dominant eras. Control variables include relative military capability and number of years a state was a great power or a nuclear state.

Adams (2003/04, p. 76) finds strong support for her central hypothesis. She estimates that attacks on other great powers were 12 times more likely each year under offensive dominance (probability 0.156) than under defensive dominance (probability 0.013), and they were 13 times more likely each year under defensive dominance than under deterrence dominance (probability 0.001). She also finds smaller but significant effects with the predicted pattern for conquests and attacks on non-great powers.

Power Shifts and Preventive War

Bell and Johnson (2015) empirically study the risk of war between states based on the preventive war motive (see Figure 10.6). Empirical analysis of preventive war is challenging because it requires a "measure of leaders' *expectations about future shifts in power* rather than simply a measure of observed power" (Bell and Johnson 2015, p. 124; our emphasis). Bell and Johnson address the challenge by first developing a measure of leaders' expectations of future power of states based on regression analysis that incorporates various state characteristics including military spending and personnel, alliance commitments, and economic potential.

The second step of Bell and Johnson's analysis is to estimate the risk factors for war between states. For this step, the authors focus on what is known as the directed dyad year. Specifically, all possible pairs of states in the sample represent dyads and, for each dyad, the preventive war hypothesis predicts that the initiation of war (if any) would be directed by the state facing the prospect of a power shift against it. The dependent variable is coded one if the potential initiator launched war against the potential target in that year, otherwise it is coded zero. The key risk assessment variable is Bell and Johnson's measure of the expected change in military power in each dyad. Control variables include distance between the states, contiguity, and joint democracy. Statistical results support the preventive war hypothesis. Specifically, Bell and Johnson (2015, p. 131) report that their results "provide support for a prominent rationalist explanation for war: commitment problems caused by a shifting distribution of military power."

Indivisibilities and Ethnic War

Toft (2002, p. 84) maintains that understanding war between a state and an ethnic group within the state "requires understanding how two actors can view control over the same piece of ground as indivisible" (Figure 10.7). Toft's empirical test of indivisibility as a source of war also incorporates identity as a potential source of violent conflict. Toft hypothesizes that an ethnic group within a state will be more willing to fight for independence when the group is concentrated in a region of the state and the territory is a critical attribute of the group's identity. In Toft's theory, ethnic identity that is tied to territory (what she calls "homeland") gives rise to indivisibility of the territory from the ethnic group's perspective.

Toft's dependent variable is ethnic conflict within the state based on Minorities at Risk (MAR) Project data. The ethnic conflict score ranges from 0 (no conflict) to 7 (protracted civil war). Toft's key explanatory variables for ethnic group conflict against the state are whether the ethnic group is a majority of the population in a region of the state, whether the ethnic group views the region as its "homeland," and the length of time the group has occupied the region. Toft tests her hypotheses over the 1985–98 period. Her key result is that the risk of ethnic conflict is significantly greater when ethnic groups have majority status in a region of the state and have lived for a long time in what they perceive as their homeland, all else equal.

Political Bias and Protracted Conflict

Political bias (Figure 10.8) can explain why a war starts, but also why it endures. A critical leader who initiates war could be held accountable for various misdeeds once the war is over, thus causing the leader to prefer prolonging rather than ending the war. Prorok (2018) empirically tests this hypothesis for rebel and state leaders involved in civil conflicts from 1980 to 2011. To do so, she distinguishes between leaders who bear responsibility for the war ("responsible leaders") and those who are not initially responsible for the war ("nonresponsible leaders"). Prorok's main hypothesis is that a civil war is less likely to be terminated when at least one current leader (rebel and/or state) is responsible for the war.

Prorok's dependent variable is a dummy variable coded 1 in the month that a civil conflict ends based on civil conflict start and end dates available from the NonState Actor (NSA) dataset (Cunningham, Gleditsch, and Salehyan 2013). State leader data come from the ARCHIGOS dataset (Goemans, Gleditsch, and Chiozza 2009), while rebel leaders were identified by the author from original research. Prorok identified all leaders who held power when the first battle death occurred in civil conflicts identified by the Uppsala Conflict Data Program (UCDP). Control variables include state and rebel leadership changes, external military support for the state and rebels, and degree of territorial control by rebels. Prorok's key result is that when leaders who are responsible for war remain in power, civil conflict duration is significantly and substantively greater, all else equal. Prorok (2018, p. 1197) concludes that responsible leaders "will gamble for resurrection in the hope of achieving victory and avoiding punishment. This is particularly true for rebel leaders, whose baseline vulnerability to punishment is higher than that for the average state leader and for a subset of high-risk state leaders who also face an elevated risk of punishment."

10.7 Bibliographic Notes

The bargaining model sketched in this chapter is a modification of one first outlined by Hirshleifer (1985) and extended in Hirshleifer (1995) and Hirshleifer, Glazer, and Hirshleifer (2005). Early predecessors include Bush's (1972) model of anarchy and Wittman's (1979) model of war termination. Models that are both more complete and more formal include Fearon (1995), Powell (2006), Skaperdas (2006), Garfinkel and Skaperdas (2007), and Anderton and Carter (2011). Additional developments of the bargaining model allow for multiple periods and hence the possibility of intrawar bargaining and eventual war termination (see, for example, Ramsay 2008). For formal conflict-settlement protocols, see Isard and Smith (1982), Raiffa (2003), and Garfinkel and Skaperdas (2007, pp. 667–82).

In recent years, theoretical and empirical literature related to the bargaining theory of war and has grown rapidly with some contributions integrating two or more sources of war within one framework (see, for example, Powell 2006, Skaperdas 2006, Anderton and Carter 2011). Political scientists have long recognized that there can be many reasons why wars start (Vasquez 2012). Hence, several sources each operating at a moderate level could be enough for war to occur. Studies that focus on incomplete information and commitment problems include Wolford, Reiter, and Carrubba (2011) and Streich and Levy (2016), who theoretically integrate incomplete information and a preventive motive for war. Thyne (2012) combines incomplete information and commitment problems to understand why civil wars last so long. In a multiperiod model, Beard and Strayhorn (2018) analyze three sources of preemptive war advantage: tactical offensive advantages, mobilization advantages, and destructiveness of initial attack.

Additional contributions seek to refine understanding of particular sources of war in the bargaining theory. For example, McCormack and Pascoe (2017) show that sanctions can smooth shifts in relative power and thus serve to reduce the risk of preventive war. Amegashie (2014) shows that third-party intervention on behalf of one of the combatants, even when expected, can make conflict more severe than otherwise. Seschser (2018) provides recent research on reputation-building as a source of war, while Klein and Tokdemir (2016) and Machain and Rosenberg (2016) do the same for diversionary theories of war. In Krainin and Slinkman's (2017) model of political bias and war, a state or rebel group can have an incentive to select a leader that is biased toward war.

New rationalist and nonrationalist sources of war will be discovered and formally modeled in the years ahead. This may be especially true of work on war and peace occurring at the intersections of economics, psychology, sociology, and political science. For example, Bénabou and Tirole (2009) demonstrate in a model with complete information and no commitment problems that war can occur owing to "*belief distortions* endogenously generated by pride, dignity, or wishful thinking about future outcomes" (p. 465). This contribution falls within the literature on motivated reasoning and belief (see Chapter 6) and thus represents (along with loss aversion and identity) an additional nonrational source of war.

Literature reviews of the bargaining theory of war and peace include Powell (2002), Reiter (2003), and Jackson and Morelli (2011). More recently, Mitchell (2017) provides an insightful critique of the theory in the context of the field of peace science. Ramsay (2017) reviews literature on incomplete information and war and Sample (2017) does the same for power shifts and preventive war in the context of her own theoretical and empirical inquiry.

11

Conflict between States

For millennia, philosophers and sages have pondered the origins and horrors of war.* Despite this long history of inquiry, it is only in the last century that scholars from political science, economics, and other disciplines began to study the causes and effects of war with the quantitative methods of social science. Building on the early work of Lewis Richardson, Pitirim Sorokin, and Quincy Wright, the social scientific study of war was well established by the mid-1960s around a community of scholars associated with the Correlates of War Project, the Peace Science Society (originally Peace Research Society), the *Journal of Conflict Resolution*, and the like. Since then, a wealth of social scientific studies of interstate conflict has appeared in journals and books (Vasquez 2012; Mitchell and Vasquez 2013; Cashman 2014; Quackenbush 2014). In this chapter we focus on armed conflict between states before turning to civil war in Chapter 12.

11.1 Definitions

Interstate war is violent conflict between states that reaches a relatively high threshold of combatant or military-related (soldiers and civilians caught in the crossfire) fatalities. For some interstate conflict datasets, the threshold for war is 1,000 or more fatalities (see Appendix D.1). Subwar interstate conflict is threatened or actual violent conflict between states with comparatively few fatalities.

---

* The introductory paragraph and parts of Section 11.2 and Section 11.4 are adapted from Charles H. Anderton and John R. Carter's article, "A Survey of Peace Economics" published in *Handbook of Defense Economics, Volume 2* edited by Todd Sandler and Keith Hartley, pp. 1211–58, Copyright © Elsevier 2007. We gratefully acknowledge Elsevier's permission to republish material from the article.

11.2 Patterns of Armed Interstate Conflict

In what follows we use data from the Correlates of War (COW) Project on militarized interstate disputes (MIDs) and from COW and the Uppsala Conflict Data Program/International Peace Research Institute, Oslo (UCDP/PRIO) on interstate wars to highlight the frequency and other empirical aspects of interstate conflict associated with the upper portion of the conflict life cycle (see Appendix D.1). Before proceeding, we need to emphasize a key point about MIDs. According to COW, a MID is not a war. The threat, display, and use of military force represent three subwar categories in the MID definition. When a MID reaches a point where military combat is sufficiently sustained that it will lead to at least 1,000 military personnel deaths per 12-month period, then COW reclassifies the MID as an interstate war.

Figure 11.1 shows the number MID Onsets that occurred in the world during five-year periods from 1816 through 2010. Also shown are the number of MID onsets that involved the use of military force (labeled MIDs with Force) and the number that eventually rose to the level of interstate war (labeled MIDs to War). The horizontal axis indicates certain time periods identified as important by historians of international relations (Gochman and Maoz 1990, p. 198), to which we have added the post-9/11 era. Four facts stand out in the time series. First, the twentieth century witnessed considerably more MID onsets than the nineteenth century. There were 2,298 MID onsets between 1816 and 2000, of which 2,009 (87 percent) occurred in the

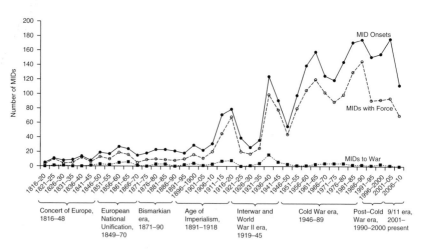

Figure 11.1 MID Onsets, MIDs-Use-Force, and MIDs-to-War, 1816–2010.
Sources: Palmer, D'Orazio, Kenwick, and Lane (2015) and Gochman and Maoz (1990).

Table 11.1 *Interstate war onsets, duration, severity, and intensity, 1816–2016.*

Historical Period	Interstate War Onsets	Average Duration (days per war)	Average Severity (deaths per war)	Average Intensity (deaths per day)
Concert of Europe (1816–48)	5	326.8	32,762	100.3
European National Unification (1849–70)	15	397.0	59,300	149.4
Bismarkian era (1871–90)	6	419.2	54,341	120.6
Age of Imperialism (1891–1918)	15	303.7	597,136	1,966.4
Interwar and WW II era (1919–45)	16	557.2	1,137,362	2,041.2
Cold War era (1946–89)	29	462.8	115,420	249.4
Post-Cold War era (1990–2000)	7	270.9	26,911	99.4
Post-9/11 era (2001–2016)	2	60.0	5,588	93.1
1816–2016	95	410.6	337,694	822.4

Note: The COW war data available in Sarkees and Wayman (2010) end in 2007, but no new interstate wars are reported by UCDP/PRIO from 2008 to 2016.
Source: Sarkees and Wayman (2010).

twentieth century (1901–2000). Second, a high percentage of MIDs involve military force, although this varies substantially by historical period. For the entire period 1816–2010, there were 2,586 MID onsets of which 1,809 (70 percent) involved military force. Third, in the first decade of the twenty-first century, the number of MID onsets appeared to reach a peak and then decline. Whether the downward trend will continue is still to be seen. Fourth, a small percentage of MIDs crossed COW's threshold into war. Of the 2,586 MIDs that arose in the period 1816–2010, only 107 (4.1 percent) intensified into war.

Table 11.1 presents various measures of the seriousness of interstate wars, as distinct from MIDS, from 1816 to 2016. The table reveals that the average duration, severity, and intensity of interstate war were highest during the Interwar and World War II era (1919–45). In the most recent period (Post-9/11 era), interstate wars have been rare with only two since 2001: the USA-led invasions of Afghanistan and Iraq in 2001 and 2003, respectively. Moreover, these wars were comparatively low on metrics of seriousness as shown in Table 11.1. It is important to note, however, that

COW reclassified the hostilities as extrastate wars after the Afghan and Iraqi regimes were toppled. Meanwhile, UCDP/PRIO classifies the ongoing hostilities between the Afghan and Iraqi governments and their respective resistance movements as intrastate wars.

11.3 Theories of Interstate War Risk and Prevention

Numerous theories of interstate war onset and prevention exist in the literature (Cashman 2014). Here we provide overviews of two major theoretical streams. The first is the bargaining theory of war and peace, which was covered in detail in Chapter 10. In that chapter we applied bargaining theory to the outbreak of violence between any parties (for example, states, a state and a rebel group, nonstate groups), but in this chapter, we focus specifically on conflict between states. The second is the theory of interstate rivalries.

Bargaining Theory

Recall in the bargaining model from Chapter 10 that a disputed item (for example, territory) is to be divided between two players A and B, here nations assumed to be unitary actors with egoistic preferences. Given complete information, the absence of commitment problems, and the minimization of other rationalist and nonrationalist sources of war, peaceful settlement rather than war is predicted. As noted in Chapter 10, the intuition favoring peace is straightforward: the avoidance of the costs of war provides a peace dividend that can be translated into mutual gains, thus leading the players to peacefully settle (see Figure 10.2).

There are numerous rationalist and nonrationalist elements in disputes between nations that can lead to war (see Chapter 10). In Figure 11.2 we consider one such element along with two economic conditions that can affect the choice of war. In the figure, assume the two sides are disputing territory and they have discrepant expectations, E_A and E_B, over the income distribution that would result from war. We assume the expectations gap (or E-gap) is due to incomplete information. Given the costs of war, a peaceful settlement is mutually advantageous between points S and S' in panel (a) of Figure 11.2 in which the settlement opportunities curve intersects the region of mutual gain. Notice in panel (a) that we have placed the war expectations points E_A and E_B far inside the settlement opportunities curve HN. The large distance of the E points from HN implies that the settlement opportunities available under peace are relatively high. This

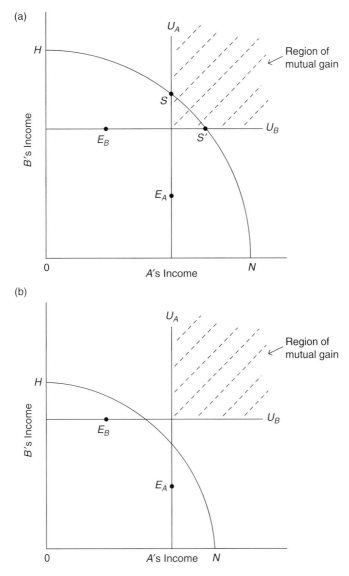

Figure 11.2 Incomplete information with outcome of peace or war dependent on economic conditions.
(a) Incomplete information with peace
(b) Incomplete information with war

would occur if the economies of the two sides were highly productive such that substantial economic well-being would be lost if war occurred. Hence, in Figure 11.2 (a) the E gap is not large enough to cause war.

Panel (b) of Figure 11.2, however, provides a decidedly different prediction. In panel (b), we assume the same gap between E_A and E_B as in panel (a). What's new in panel (b) is that the expected distribution from war points E_A and E_B are close to the settlement opportunities curve HN. This would occur if A and B had relatively unproductive economies such that the settlement opportunities curve is low (that is, squeezed down toward the origin). In Figure 11.2(b), the region of mutual gain fails to intersect the settlement opportunities curve, and war is the predicted outcome rather than peace.

Figure 11.2 shows how a given degree of incomplete information can lead to an acute risk of war under poor economic conditions. The principle generalizes to other rationalist and nonrationalist sources of war. For example, given preemptive military technologies, incentives for preventive war, political bias in favor of war, reference dependence and loss aversion, malevolent preferences, or combinations of such factors, relatively low costs of war and poor economic opportunities under peace will, all else equal, increase the risk of war between states. Regarding peace, bargaining theory suggests that economic linkages between states and vigorous development of physical, human, and social capital within states, undergirded by healthy political institutions, would make war quite costly relative to the robust opportunities available under peaceful settlement, all else equal.

Enduring and Strategic Interstate Rivalries

Theory building in social science often proceeds using a deductive approach in which the researcher conceptualizes the key actors, interests, constraints, and actor interrelationships for the topic being studied. Sometimes the researcher will build a formal model of the theory and mathematically derive key predictions. Whether mathematically derived or not, hypotheses generated by the theory can then be tested with data and case studies to determine whether they are supported or rejected. This deductive method is sometimes called a "top-down" approach to research. In contrast, the inductive method is a "bottom-up" approach in which the researcher studies data or cases related to a topic of interest and identifies patterns in the data or cases that a theory should explain. Such observations will lead the researcher to formulate hypotheses about what is being studied, leading eventually (and ideally) to a more general understanding of the topic (that is, a theory). Of course, social scientists often combine deductive and inductive methods in their work, but some approaches are more deductive and others more inductive. The empirical articles surveyed in Chapter 10 began with deductions from bargaining theory, which were then subjected to empirical testing. The theory of interstate rivalries and war, however, is comparatively more inductive, beginning with data regularities and then forming a theory based on such observations.

History and the contemporary scene are replete with cases of interstate rivalries. The Cold War rivalry between the USA and USSR (1946–89) dominated geopolitics for almost half a century. Today, rivalry between Russia and the USA persists, though it is less intense than during the Cold War. In the Middle East, rivalry between Israel and Iran is at a tense level today. There is also concern of growing tension between China and the USA and between North Korea and the USA.

Political scientists have developed two major conceptualizations of interstate rivalry: enduring rivalries and strategic rivalries. An enduring rivalry exists when a pair of states experience a certain number of militarized interstate disputes (MIDs) (say, at least six) over a certain time period (say, 20 years) (Cashman 2014, p. 252; see also Diehl and Goertz 2012). When states are in a short-lived rivalry with just one or two MIDs, they are isolated rivals. States in a long-lasting rivalry but with fewer MIDs (say, 3–5) are classified as proto-rivals (Cashman 2014, p. 252). For the period 1816–2001, Diehl and Goertz (2012, p. 87) identified 330 interstate rivalries of which 178 were proto-rivalries and 152 were enduring rivalries.

A strategic rivalry exists when a pair of states see each other as, first, competing over territory, influence (regional or global), or ideology; second, a potential source of one or more MIDs in the dyad; and, third, enemies (Cashman 2014, p. 252; see also Colaresi, Rasler, and Thompson 2007). Note that, unlike an enduring rivalry, a strategic rivalry does not require a certain number of MIDs or a certain time period. According to Colaresi, Rasler, and Thompson (2007, ch. 3), there were 173 strategic rivalries from 1816 to 1999.

Critical ideas have been generated about the risks of interstate war from research on enduring and strategic rivalries. For example, in research reported by Cashman (2014, pp. 254–5), 47 enduring rivalries that experienced at least 13 MIDs (so-called "heavy enduring rivals") accounted for 30 percent of all MIDs, enduring and proto-rivalries accounted for two-thirds of MIDs, the risk that enduring rivals will go to war at some point in the rivalry is 36 percent, and the risk that heavy enduring rivals will go to war is almost two-thirds. Regarding strategic rivalries, opponents were on opposite sides of 78.4 percent of interstate wars since 1816 and 91.3 percent of such wars since 1945 (Cashman 2014, p. 255). According to Diehl and Goertz (2000, p. 7), the presence of a shift in power coupled with enduring rivalry significantly elevates the risk of war; "loosely, both are necessary for war to occur." For Colaresi, Rasler, and Thompson (2007, p. 256), strategic rivalry along with contested territory and contiguity (shared border) between states is a particularly potent combination for dispute escalation to war.

11.4 Empirical Studies of Interstate Conflict Risk and Prevention

Risk Factors for Interstate Armed Conflict

A vast empirical literature on the determinants of interstate armed conflict has appeared over the past half century, pushed by advancements in data, computing power, and statistical methods. The objective of most studies is to estimate the likelihood of armed conflict by applying regression techniques to data for countries (called monads) or country-pairs (called dyads). Depending on the particular hypotheses, the studies typically focus on one or two explanatory variables, while including other possible factors for control purposes. Based on bargaining theory, factors that foster incomplete information and commitment problems such as power shifts can be expected to increase the risk of armed conflict. Also, unhealthy economic conditions should be relevant for understanding interstate conflict risk. Theories of interstate rivalries, meanwhile, can be expected to find that power shifts and issues related to territory elevate the risk of interstate conflict. Here we sample the risk factor literature by briefly surveying several studies that focus on territory, economic interdependence, and economic development. Along the way we make note of important political and military capability variables that are also considered.

Territory

Throughout history, issues of territory have played a prominent role in interstate conflict. Contemporary examples of interstate territorial disagreements include the Spratly Islands (involving China, the Philippines, Vietnam, Taiwan, Malaysia, and Brunei), the Golan Heights (Israel and Syria), Kashmir (India and Pakistan), and control of Crimea (Russia and

Ukraine). Disputes can be over land borders (for example, Ecuador and Peru in 1995), maritime boundaries (for example, Australia and East Timor), or access to resources such as oil or minerals (for example, disputed border areas between Sudan and South Sudan). Under the broad heading of territory we include not only issues of boundaries and natural resources but also geographic considerations of proximity and contiguity.

As noted by Fearon (1995), the control of territory often has high strategic and/or economic advantage which translates into future military power. For this reason, bargaining concessions involving territory can cause an anticipated shift in relative power, giving the recipient state an incentive to renege on an agreement at a future date by exploiting its strengthened position. Consequently a territorial dispute can generate a serious commitment problem, possibly leading to preventive war. Furthermore, as noted by Shelef (2016) and Goemans and Schultz (2017), national leaders can have incentives to cast some forms of territorial disputes as threatening to the country's "homeland" or "national identity," thus hardening the state's bargaining position and narrowing the range of peaceful settlement opportunities. Proximity and contiguity can likewise increase the risk of armed conflict. States that are closer to each other have an easier time projecting military power against each other. Thus, as we explored in Chapter 9, the closer are two countries, the lower is the cost of fighting, and hence the greater is the risk of armed conflict. Furthermore, proximity can increase the ability of a state to surprise its rival with a devastating first strike. Thus, states that are closer to one another, and especially those that are contiguous, are more likely to face the sort of commitment problem that favors preemptive war. As a practical matter, contiguous countries might be more apt to find themselves in disputes because of the frequency and multiplicity of their interactions (Bremer 2000). At the same time, proximity and contiguity can facilitate bilateral trade, which might reduce the risk of conflict, as suggested by the liberal peace hypothesis introduced in Chapter 2 and discussed further in the next subsection in this chapter.

According to Toft (2014, p. 185), "territory . . . will continue to be a core issue in explaining the escalation and onset of war." Wright and Diehl's (2016) study of the risks of interstate territorial disputes escalating to war provides a good example of empirical research related to Toft's point. Drawing upon perspectives from the bargaining theory of war and peace, enduring rivalry, and domestic politics, Wright and Diehl's main hypothesis is that territorial disputes between institutionally mixed pairs of states or dyads (that is, one democratic and the other authoritarian) will be more likely to escalate to war than for states that are institutionally similar (that is, both democratic or both authoritarian). The hypothesis rests upon the different incentives that democratic and autocratic leaders face when disputing territory. According to Wright and Diehl, democratic leaders will tend to frame a territorial dispute based on the public goods value of the land available to the country's citizens. In so doing, the leaders will tend to emphasize that the land is important to the "homeland" or "identity" of the country. Note that the incentive facing democratic leaders is not about the material value of the land that they will receive personally (in democracies, the leaders would generally not receive such personal material gains); rather, it is the gains in domestic political support that will come from framing the territorial dispute as a homeland or identity issue. Thus, Wright and Diehl (2016, p. 650) "anticipate, ceteris paribus, that a democratic state will bargain harder and longer, and be more willing to escalate a confrontation, and go to war over a territorial dispute." Meanwhile, autocratic leaders are more interested in the private gains that would accrue to them from territory, which would enhance their tough stands in a territorial dispute. Regarding democratic/democratic dyads, Wright and Diehl maintain that pairs of democracies generally settled their border disputes long ago, there are few democratic dyadic rivalries, and joint democracies rarely go to war. Regarding jointly autocratic dyads, the sides should be "more acceptant of stalemate outcomes" relative to mixed dyads because each side can gain from maintaining the current flow of private goods from the territory (Wright and Diehl 2016, p. 651).

To empirically test their main hypothesis, Wright and Diehl assemble data on MIDs in the world and MIDs within interstate rivalries from 1816 to 2001. There were 2,788 MIDs overall and 1,892 within interstate rivalries over this period. The dependent variable is whether a MID escalates to war. The key explanatory variables are whether the MID is over a territorial issue and whether the dyad is institutionally mixed. Control variables include the relative power in the dyad and whether the two states are jointly democratic. Empirical analysis reveals that institutionally mixed dyads with territorial MIDs are significantly more likely to escalate to war compared to institutionally mixed dyads with nonterritorial MIDs. Furthermore, territorial MIDs with institutionally mixed dyads are more prone to war than territorial MIDs with nonmixed dyads. According to Wright and Diehl (2016, p. 658), when institutionally mixed dyads fight over territory, as compared to fighting over nonterritorial issues, they "increase their chances of going to war within five years by roughly 257 percent, and by roughly 45 percent when compared to territorial MIDs fought between joint autocracies." (Note: No jointly democratic territorial MIDs escalated to war.)

Economic Interdependence

In Chapter 2 we introduced the liberal peace hypothesis, according to which trade partners are less likely to engage in armed conflict against one another, other things equal. One rationale for the hypothesis is that trading nations face higher opportunity costs of war because of the economic gains they stand to forgo when war disrupts trade between them. Other rationales have been proposed, including reduction in misinformation and promotion of shared values or trust between trading partners (Gartzke, Li, and Boehmer 2001, Reed 2003, Bearce and Omori 2005). Evidence relevant to the liberal peace hypothesis in the context of interstate conflict is provided by Martin, Mayer, and Thoenig (2008) and Kinne (2012). The studies are similar inasmuch as both find some evidence that trade reduces conflict. The studies differ, however, in their conceptualizations of multilateral trade openness and in their conclusions about the effect of trade openness on the risk of interstate conflict.

To test the pacific effect of trade, Martin, Mayer, and Thoenig (2008) (hereafter, MMT) begin with a bargaining model of war with asymmetric information. They then introduce a trade model that allows for differentiated products and multiple trade partners with varying distances between them. Based on the combined models, MMT hypothesize that, first, states with a high degree of bilateral trade dependence are less likely to fight one another due to the opportunity cost of forgone gains, and, second, states with greater multilateral trade openness will be at greater risk of conflict, all else equal. The intuition for the second hypothesis is that a country with high multilateral trade openness will have ample opportunity to offset forgone bilateral gains by trading elsewhere, thus lowering the opportunity cost of bilateral conflict. MMT test their hypotheses for a large sample of dyads spanning the years 1950 to 2000, where each observation is a dyad-year. Conflict is measured by a variable indicating whether the two countries in a dyad were involved in a MID during the given year that involved the display or use of force or crossed the threshold into war. For each dyad, bilateral trade dependence is measured by the arithmetic average of each country's bilateral imports relative to its GDP. To measure multilateral trade openness for each dyad, the authors use the arithmetic average of each country's total imports, excluding their bilateral imports, divided by its GDP. Control variables include contiguity, distance between the countries, and democracy.

MMT find that the risk of bilateral interstate conflict falls with greater bilateral trade dependence but rises with greater multilateral trade openness. For dyads with bilateral distance less than 1000 km, the average risk of interstate conflict is 0.045 in 2000. From this baseline, MMT find that if bilateral trade dependence declined to the level that prevailed in 1970, the risk of interstate conflict would rise to 0.048. For multilateral trade openness, a return to the lower level that prevailed in 1970 would reduce the risk of interstate conflict to 0.034. On net, MMT maintain that the increases in bilateral trade dependence and multilateral trade openness that occurred between 1970 and 2000 increased the risk of interstate conflict for proximate countries from 0.037 to 0.045.

Kinne (2012) argues that many empirical studies of interstate conflict and trade should refine their measurements of trade integration when testing the liberal peace hypothesis. Kinne (2012, p. 308) emphasizes two points: first, bilateral trade dependence, which focuses on trade between two states in a dyad, "provides little information about the integration of states into global markets" and, second, measures of multilateral trade openness that are common in the empirical literature "do not capture the complex interdependences that affect conflict behavior." For example, in 1955 Mongolia had only five trade partners, but the country's total trade relative to its GDP was 106 percent, "making it the second most 'trade open' state in the world that year (behind Bhutan)" (Kinne 2012, p. 310). One does not usually think of Mongolia as a leading example of a nation integrating into global trade markets. Similarly, Liberia was the most trade open nation in the world in 2000 even though it is rarely perceived as highly integrated in the global economy (Kinne 2012, p. 310). Kinne maintains that standard measures of multilateral trade openness fail to account for a state's connections to, or lack of connections to, every other state in the world. Mongolia in 1955, for example, had a high measure of multilateral trade openness conventionally defined (106 percent), but with only five trade partners, it was only minimally open to trade in regard to the breadth or number of its trade ties.

To refine measures of multilateral trade openness, Kinne (2012) draws on network theory and the concept of network centrality (see Chapter 7) to conceptualize trade integration. Kinne's approach incorporates three aspects of a state's multilateral trade networks: first, breadth of trade ties (that is, the number of the state's trade partners); second, depth of trade ties (that is, how strong the state's trade ties are to its trading partners);

and, third, closeness or commercial significance of indirect trade links (for example, the economic importance of state A's nontrading partners because those states trade with state B and A trades with B). Kinne's resulting trade centrality measure for states leads to quite different perspectives on trade integration relative to those based upon standard measures of trade openness. According to Kinne (2012, p. 315):

> The [traditional] openness index considers Liberia, Suriname, Djibouti, Congo, and Angola to be as economically integrated as South Korea, Ireland, Malaysia, and the Nordic states, while equating global economic actors like Brazil and India with autarkic states like North Korea and Afghanistan. Centrality, on the other hand, avoids overweighting economically troubled states like Liberia; gives greater weight to global economic actors like Brazil and India; and correctly recognizes the importance of small trading states like Malaysia, Singapore, South Korea, the Benelux countries, and the Nordic countries.

Kinne's main hypothesis is that multilateral trade integration, as measured by trade centrality, reduces a state's probability of initiating a MID, all else equal. To empirically test the hypothesis, Kinne constructs a sample of observations spanning the period 1950 to 2001, where each observation is a monad-year, meaning a single country in a single year. For each observation, Kinne records the count of MIDs initiated and whether or not any MID was initiated. Hence, there are two measures for the dependent variable: MID count and MID presence. The key explanatory variables are the measure of trade centrality and a standard measure of trade openness. Control variables include a state's political system (ranging from full autocracy to full democracy), GDP per capita, and power. Empirical analysis reveals that trade integration, as measured by trade centrality, has a significant and substantial effect in reducing the count and presence of MIDs initiated by states. Furthermore, Kinne generally finds that the standard measure of trade openness has no significant impact on MID risk.

Note that Martin, Mayer, and Thoenig (2008) and Kinne (2012) reach opposite conclusions on the effects of greater multilateral trade on interstate conflict. Discrepant results in social scientific studies of conflict are quite common. The two studies are, of course, different in regard to sample observations (dyads vs. monads), statistical techniques, and, perhaps most importantly, conceptualizations of multilateral trade. One of the benefits of cumulative social scientific inquiry is that both common and discrepant results emerge. The former tend to increase confidence in the results while the latter tend to spur new research designed to better understand phenomena. The use of network analysis in social scientific studies of war and peace is comparatively new; hence, Kinne (2012, p. 320) notes that his approach "shows how network analytics can be brought to bear on controversial and long-standing research questions in international relations."

Economic Development

In Book V, Chapter 1 of *Wealth of Nations*, Adam Smith (1776) provided a remarkable account of the effect of economic development on interstate conflict. Smith considered four levels of economic development: hunting, pastoral, agricultural, and manufacturing. According to Smith, the least developed (hunting) and most developed (manufacturing) societies would be unlikely to initiate war due to high opportunity costs. In hunter societies, armies would be limited in scale because if people spent time away from hunting and gathering, they would substantially reduce their means of livelihood. In developed societies, soldiers would have to be drawn away from manufacturing, leading to a significant loss in output. For moderately developed pastoral and agricultural societies, however, Smith believed that the opportunity cost of war was relatively low. Shepherds could bring their herds with them to war and maintain them during periods between battles. In agricultural societies, once the seeds were planted, younger men could participate in wars with little loss in output because crop maintenance could be left to women, children, and older men. Smith's ideas imply an inverted-U-shaped relationship between economic development and the risk of war.

Many statistical studies assume a linear or logarithmic relationship between development and interstate armed conflict. An exception is Boehmer and Sobek (2005, p. 5), who hypothesize an inverted-U relationship between development and armed conflict because the "changing orientation of economies from agricultural and extractive activities eventually to service-based economies alters the cost-benefit calculations concerning territorial acquisition." Less developed countries lack the wherewithal to project military power, and more advanced service-oriented countries have less to gain from territorial pursuits. In the middle are moderately developed countries that are most prone to armed conflict.

To test their hypothesis, Boehmer and Sobek construct a sample of over 5,000 observations spanning the period 1870 to 1992, where each observation is a monad-year. For each observation they record whether the country initiated a new MID, was involved in a new MID over territory, and participated in a new MID with fatalities. The first two of these dependent variables measure the onset of interstate conflict, while the third measures the seriousness of conflict. Energy consumption per capita is used to measure a state's level of economic development. To permit a nonlinear effect, both the log and the log-squared of per capita consumption are included in the regression analysis. Control variables include economic openness, democracy, and military capability.

Boehmer and Sobek's statistical results indicate that economic development affects all three measures of interstate conflict in an inverted-U fashion. For example, they find that as the level of development increases from its minimum to its maximum sample value, the estimated probability of MID onset in a given year rises from 0.0014 to 0.0275 before falling to 0.0088. Similarly, they estimate that the probability of a state's involvement in a new MID with fatalities is 0.0003 for less developed states and 0.0002 for highly developed states, but 0.0026 for moderately developed states. Based on their analysis, Boehmer and Sobek project that moderately developed countries will be most at risk for interstate armed conflict while in the future the risk will rise with continued development by poorer states.

More than a century after Adam Smith, Joseph Schumpeter ([1919] 1955) hypothesized that interstate wars would diminish in the world as a greater number of states became industrialized. Schumpeter's hypothesis is based upon a two-part theoretical rationale. The first is that industrialization creates material incentives to avoid war because of, first, the opportunity cost of reduced investments in industrialization as resources are diverted to war and, second, the greater destructiveness of war brought about by greater industrialization (Chatagnier and Castelli 2016, p. 854). Schumpeter also identifies a cultural resistance to war brought about by industrialization; as workers, managers, and political leaders become accustomed to profit-making and material gains from the economy, socioeconomic changes occur in the population leading to diminished interests in imperial power grabs in particular and wars in general (Chatagnier and Castelli 2016, p. 854). Schumpeter's ideas are rather remarkable given that he stated them right after the end of World War I (1918) in which interstate relations were tumultuous, and others, including Keynes (1919), predicted poor interstate relations in the post-World War I period.

Chatagnier and Castelli (2016) pick up on Schumpeter's ideas and subject them to empirical testing. Chatagnier and Castelli (2016, p. 852) argue that the decline in interstate wars over the last half century "is primarily due to the spread of economic modernization." They hypothesize that advances in a state's industrialization reduce its risk of participation in violent interstate conflict, all else equal. Chatagnier and Castelli test this hypothesis on samples of individual states (monads) and pairs of states (dyads) for the periods 1960 to 2007 and 1960 to 2002, respectively. Chatagnier and Castelli's dependent variable is whether an individual state or pair of states was involved in a new fatal MID in a given year. The key explanatory variable is a measure of a state's industrial sector as a proportion of its GDP. Chatagnier and Castelli emphasize that their key explanatory variable is not economic development, which is often measured by real GDP per capita, but industrialization. They also include a measure of the size of a state's service sector. Control variables include a state's political system score (ranging from full autocracy to full democracy), GDP per capita, military power, total trade, and, for dyads, whether the two states are contiguous, share an alliance, and the volume of dyadic trade.

Chatagnier and Castelli's empirical results show that industrialization has a significant effect in reducing the risk of fatal MIDs initiated by states. For example, in the baseline regression for the monadic sample, the risk of a fatal MID for a state with no industrial sector is about 0.11. This risk falls to about 0.02 for a highly industrialized state, all else equal. Results for the dyadic sample are less pronounced relative to the monadic sample, but industrialization nonetheless significantly reduces the risk of fatal MIDs. Chatagnier and Castelli conclude that their results seem broadly supportive of Schumpeter's thesis that greater industrialization will reduce the risks of interstate wars, but more time and further research are necessary to see if additional industrialization and development of knowledge-based economies can help reduce incentives for interstate war.

Interstate Conflict Prevention

Much like the literature on risk factors for war, empirical research on third-party intervention has grown enormously. The bargaining model in Chapter 10 shows that intervention can promote peace if third parties succeed in coordinating expectations or resolving commitment problems (see Figures 10.10 and 10.11 in Chapter 10). If an intervention favors one side, however, it can leave the prospect for peaceful settlement unchanged or even worsened (see Figure 10.12 in Chapter 10). Numerous questions then arise that can be addressed by empirical analysis. Most fundamentally, how successful are third-party interventions at resolving conflict? But also, where, when, how, and by whom is intervention most successful?

Frazier and Dixon (2006) illustrate how such questions can be addressed using large-sample regression analysis. To gauge the successfulness of intervention, they begin with a sample of more than 2,200 dyads involved in MIDs between 1946 and 2000. For each dyad they indicate whether or not the MID reached a negotiated settlement, thereby generating the dependent variable. At the same time, independent variables are constructed to indicate the presence or absence of various mediation methods (for example, diplomatic approaches, legal processes, or military involvement) and mediator identities (including states, coalitions, or intergovernmental organizations (IGOs)). Also included are control variables for dispute duration and the presence of a major power country in the dyad.

Frazier and Dixon's (2006, p. 398) fundamental result is that "the presence of a third-party intermediary's efforts tend to substantially improve the probability that disputes are settled by negotiated means." In particular, they estimate that the probability of negotiated settlement roughly quadruples from a baseline of 0.100 to a new level of 0.397 when an intermediary is present. In their more detailed analysis, they find that the likelihood of negotiated settlement is most responsive to intermediary military intervention and IGO involvement. Consistent with other research, they also find that negotiated settlement is less likely when the dispute is short-lived or the dyad includes a major power. (See also our review of Mishali-Ram's 2013 empirical analysis of third-party intervention in interstate conflicts in Chapter 17.)

11.5 Economic Consequences of Interstate Conflicts

In Chapter 1 we identified several economic costs of conflict including diversion of resources, destruction of people and property, disruption of economic activities, displacement of people (refugees and internal displaced persons (IDPs)), and development difficulties postconflict. In this section we focus upon how interstate wars disrupt trade, before turning our attention to the guns versus butter tradeoff that Austria-Hungary faced during World War I.

Impact of War on Trade

Glick and Taylor (2010) empirically estimate the effects of interstate wars on world trade over the period 1870–1997. Their study is distinctive because they use a gravity model to assess the determinants of international trade flows; this type of model is a standard empirical model used by international trade theorists to determine the various forces that pull states together to trade or that push them apart from trade. Moreover, Glick and Taylor's time period is long (128 years), which includes numerous inter-state wars including two massive ones: World Wars I and II.

To empirically estimate the effect of war on trade, Glick and Taylor assemble data on trade between pairs of states (dyads) for each year of the sample period. The dependent variable is measured by the amount of real (inflation-adjusted) trade in the dyad. The key explanatory variable is whether the two states in the dyad were involved in war. To account for the intertemporal effects of war on trade, Glick and Taylor include a measure of the presence or absence of current war as well as lagged measures of war going back up to ten years. Based on the gravity equation, Glick and Taylor include numerous control variables that are believed to affect the volume of dyadic trade including the size of countries (measured by real GDP, population, and area), and distance between countries.

Empirical results indicate that war has a statistically significant and substantial negative effect on trade between belligerents and between belligerent and neutral states. The negative impacts of war on trade are contemporaneous and lagged with significant negative impacts persisting for nine years for belligerents and for seven years for neutrals. Table 11.2 summarizes the average impact of war on trade for a given country pair based on Glick and Taylor's empirical model. Glick and Taylor note that trade between belligerents at war declines between 80 and 90 percent and trade between warring states and neutrals decline about 10 to 15 percent. They also find, as seen in the table, that the negative impacts of war on trade "decay slowly and persist for almost ten years" (Glick and Taylor 2010, p. 111). Further empirical analyses show that World Wars I and II were particularly disruptive to trade. Glick and Taylor (2010, p. 125) conclude that trade disruption from interstate wars is:

> [Q]uantitatively large, statistically significant, and highly persistent. Case studies of the two world wars show that these costs can be large – of the same order of magnitude as more traditional measures of the costs of conflict, such as loss of life. War is hell: the human toll suffered by belligerents as a result of war was immense. But on narrow economic grounds, the losses due to trade were also of a significant magnitude and are not as widely appreciated. Wars kill trade too ... The belligerents wrecked the world economy not just for themselves but also for everyone else.

Table 11.2 *Effects of interstate war on trade.*

Years Since the End of War	Trade between Adversaries	Trade between Belligerents and Neutrals
At War	−85%	−12%
1	−73%	−7%
2	−74%	−4%
3	−68%	−5%
4	−52%	−9%
5	−43%	−7%
6	−32%	−9%
7	−21%	−5%
8	−21%	+1%
9	−10%	+2%
10	−3%	+2%

Note: The table shows the average impact of interstate war on trade for a country pair based on Glick and Taylor's empirical model.
Source: Glick and Taylor (2010).

Austria-Hungary's "Guns Versus Butter" Tradeoff in World War I

As noted in Chapters 1 and 2, scarcity of resources and the resulting limits to the production of goods and services are fundamental starting points of economic analysis. A palpable example of the tradeoff between military goods ("guns") and food ("butter") can be seen in Austria-Hungary's economy during World War I. Austria-Hungary entered the war in July 1914 and signed an armistice in November 1918. Once a great power, Austria-Hungary collapsed in the autumn of 1918 and became two separate states.

Figure 11.3 shows Austria-Hungary's production of four types of agricultural goods in the year before the war (1913) and in the last full year of the war (1917). Also shown are four types of military goods produced in Austria-Hungary in the first (1914) or second (1915) year of the war and in the last full year of the war (1917). Note the downward-pointing trend lines for the agricultural goods and the upward-pointing trend lines for the military goods on the left and right sides of the figure, respectively.

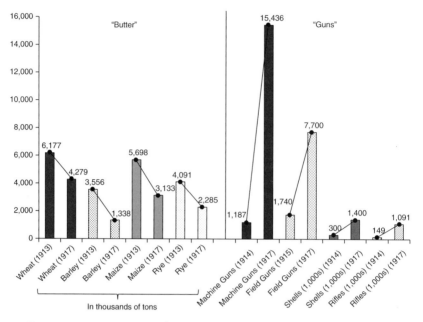

Figure 11.3 Austria-Hungary's guns vs. butter tradeoffs during World War I.
Source: Schulze (2005).

As Austria-Hungary was drawn deeper into the war it experienced substantial cutbacks in the production of "butter" and dramatic increases in the production of "guns." Consider, for example, that the production of wheat fell from 6.2 million to 4.3 million tons from 1913 to 1917, while Barley production fell over the same period from 3.6 million to 1.3 million tons. Meanwhile, production of shells increased from 300,000 units in 1914 to 1.4 million in 1917 and production of rifles went from 149,000 units to 1.1 million over the same period.

Schulze (2005) highlights the emergence of food riots and threats of starvation in Austria-Hungary during World War I. Food shortages began to emerge in the larger cities as early as the autumn of 1914 and food riots broke out in Vienna in the spring of 1915 (Schulze 2005, pp. 91, 94). By early 1918, "the Austrian authorities were no longer able to supply the urban population with as meagre a daily ration as 165 grams of poor-quality flour ... ; in Vienna even this was halved by June 1918" (p. 96). By the summer and fall of 1918, Austria-Hungary experienced escalating strikes, violence, and internal political hostilities over dwindling foodstuffs, all of which facilitated the country's incapacity to wage war (p. 97).

11.6 Bibliographic Notes

The scientific study of interstate armed conflict was inspired by Richardson (1960a, 1960b), Wright (1942), Sorokin (1937), and, according to Singer (2000, p. 5), the Polish economist de Bloch (1899). Singer (2000) and Isard (2000) describe the emergence of a critical mass of scholars devoted to the scientific study of war in the 1950s and 1960s, which led to the establishment of the Center for Research on Conflict Resolution at the University of Michigan in 1957 and the Peace Science Society (International) in the early 1960s. For reviews of the thought of early (pre-World War II) economists on war, see Silberner (1946), Goodwin (1991), Coulomb (1998), the special issue of *Defence and Peace Economics* (Brauer 2003), and Brauer (2017a).

Economic choice perspectives of war are significant in the early conflict economics literature. Schelling's (1960, 1966) classic works treated conflict initiation, management, and termination as processes of expectations formation among players within a mixed motive bargaining game. Isard and Smith (1982) utilized oligopoly principles to develop numerous theoretical procedures for preventing, shortening, or terminating conflict. Raiffa (1982) presented practical procedures for managing business conflicts, with obvious parallels to interstate conflicts. Boulding (1962) and Wittman (1979) explored how conflicts end, while Cross (1977) emphasized the role of learning in conflict bargaining. Each of these contributions by economists treated the onset, duration, and termination of conflict as the result of players' rational cost-benefit calculations in the context of changing circumstances and information.

Mitchell and Vasquez (2013), Cashman (2014), Quackenbush (2014), and Vasquez (2000, 2012) provide extensive surveys of what social scientists have learned about the determinants of interstate war and highlight important issues for future research. Diehl and Goertz (2000); Colaresi, Rasler, and Thompson (2007); and Rasler, Thompson, and Ganguly (2013) do the same, but with a focus on interstate rivalries. Hensel (2017) provides valuable coverage of theoretical and empirical literature on territoriality and interstate armed conflict. A special issue of *Conflict Management and Peace Science* (Prins and Wiegan 2017) focuses on the management of interstate territorial conflict. Vigorous research and debate continues on the effects of economic interdependence on interstate conflict. For theoretical and empirical perspectives, see Schneider, Barbieri, and Gleditsch (2003), Mansfield and Pollins (2003), Polachek and Seiglie (2007),

Polachek, Seiglie, and Xiang (2012), Goldsmith (2013), Gartzke and Westerwinter (2016), and Morelli and Sonno (2017).

Studies on the economic costs of interstate war include Keynes (1919), Seligman (1919) and Broadberry and Harrison (2005) on World War I, Harrison (2000) and Kesternich et al. (2014) on World War II, and Stiglitz and Bilmes (2012) on the Iraq and Afghanistan wars of the 2000s. For a study of the effects of interstate conflict on economic growth see Polachek and Sevastianova (2010), which also considers the growth effects of civil wars. Thies and Sobek (2010) empirically evaluate interdependencies between war, economic development, and political development.

12

Civil Wars

As documented in Chapter 1, wars within states have become far more numerous than wars between states in recent decades. Over the period 1990–2016, for example, the Uppsala Conflict Data Program/Peace Research Institute, Oslo, identified 23 war onsets within states compared to four between states. In this chapter we present theoretical and empirical perspectives on the onset, prevention, and economic consequences of civil wars.

12.1 Definitions

"Civil war" is violent conflict within a state between a government and one or more internal opposition groups, with sizeable combatant or battle-related (soldiers and civilians caught in the crossfire) fatalities (Marshall, Gurr, and Harff 2017, p. 5; Sambanis 2002, p. 218). "Sub-war civil conflict" is violence between a government and one or more internal opposition groups with relatively few fatalities. To distinguish it from a massacre, civil conflict must entail sizeable fatalities on both sides. The Correlates of War Project, for example, requires that the stronger side's fatalities be at least 5 percent of the weaker side's fatalities to qualify as a civil war (Henderson and Singer 2000, pp. 284–285).

An internal opposition group is usually identified by political, ethnic, or religious characteristics, and its objective might be to overthrow the government, seize power in a region, secede, or obtain major changes in its political, economic, or social status (Marshall, Gurr, and Harff 2017, p. 5). When an opposition group is significantly outnumbered, it often resorts to guerrilla warfare, whereby small bands of mobile forces attack larger government forces at times and locations advantageous to the rebels.

Guerrillas also typically control territory from which they cultivate support, recruit members, and coordinate operations. An armed uprising
against a government is referred to as an "insurgency," "insurrection," or
"rebellion," and the violent overthrow of a government is known as
a "revolution" (Sandler and Hartley 1995, pp. 306–307). When the opposition group in a revolution is itself part of the government, the conflict is
known as a "coup d'état." An "intercommunal war" within a state occurs
among opposing groups, none of which is the state.

12.2 Patterns of Armed Civil Conflict

We use data from the Uppsala Conflict Data Program/International Peace
Research Institute, Oslo (UCDP/PRIO) dataset to highlight various characteristics of civil wars and sub-wars (see Appendix D.2). We emphasize
two points about the UCDP/PRIO dataset. First, when battle-related
(military and civilian) deaths number between 25 and 999 per year, the
civil conflict is classified as a sub-war; when those deaths reach
1,000 per year, it is a civil war. Second, there can be more than one civil
conflict within a state in a given year. This occurs, for example, when
a state fights against one group over one incompatibility (for example,
territory) and against another group over another incompatibility (for
example, government control).

Figure 12.1 shows the number of armed civil conflicts present per year in
the world from 1946 to 2017. From the early 1950s to the early 1990s, the
number of civil wars and sub-wars increased substantially, although the
increases were by no means uniform. In 1950, for example, there were five
civil wars and six sub-wars; by 1991 these counts had risen to 12 and 38,
respectively. Collier et al. (2003, pp. 94–5) hypothesize that civil war risk in
many poor countries was suppressed by colonialism in the 1950s but then
rose with decolonization by Britain and France, particularly in Africa in
the early 1960s. Immediately after the end of the Cold War in 1989, there
was a noticeable increase in civil conflicts, followed by a substantial decline
in the mid-1990s. Collier et al. (2003, pp. 95–6) conjecture that Russian
decolonization in the early 1990s may have increased the risk of civil
conflict, but then unprecedented levels of peacekeeping operations became
possible in the post-Cold War era, leading to a surge of intrastate peace
settlements in the mid-1990s. But notice that since the early 2000s, civil
wars and sub-wars appear to be on the rise, although again the trends are
by no means uniform.

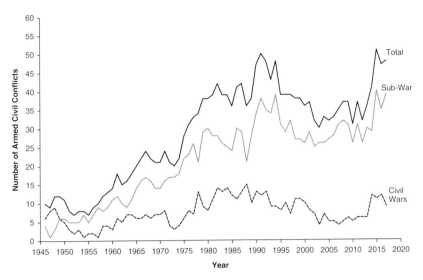

Figure 12.1 Stock of armed civil conflicts, 1946–2017.
Sources: Uppsala Conflict Data Program (UCDP) and International Peace Research
Institute, Oslo (PRIO) and Gleditsch et al. (2002).

The civil war data in Figure 12.1 does not provide information about intervention from other states on one or both sides. When one or more other states intervene, the conflict is classified by UCDP/PRIO as an "internationalized civil war." The internationalization of civil wars has grown dramatically in recent decades. Consider, for example, that there are 537 country years of civil war from 1946 to 2017 in the UCDP/PRIO dataset (this is the sum of all the years of all the countries that were in a state of civil war over the time period). Of these, there were 157 country years (29.2 percent) in which the civil wars were internationalized. For the period 2000–17, however, 66 of the 118 country years of civil war (55.9 percent) were internationalized. Most recently (2010–17), 47 of 67 country years of civil war (70.1 percent) were internationalized. The internationalization of civil wars has important implications, two of which we emphasize. First, civil wars often involve multiple internal opposition groups and factionalism within the groups, with shifting alliances and enmities across such groups. When secondary states intervene in these wars, the number of contesting parties and the dynamic realignments that occur make the conflicts particularly difficult to resolve. Second, even when such conflicts reach settlement, the many competing interest groups make it difficult for the conflict to stay resolved.

Table 12.1 *Geographic distribution of armed civil con-*
flicts, 1975–2015.

Region	1975	1985	1995	2005	2015
Europe	1	2	5	2	4
Middle East	4	5	6	5	10
Asia	13	14	15	16	14
Africa	7	10	10	7	21
Americas	3	5	3	2	2

Sources: Uppsala Conflict Data Program (UCDP) and International
Peace Research Institute, Oslo (PRIO) and Gleditsch et al. (2002).

Table 12.1 presents the geographic distribution of armed civil conflicts
from 1975 to 2015. As seen here, civil conflicts have been heavily concentrated in Asia and Africa. This may be due to the large number of countries
in these regions as well as to country and regional characteristics (for
example, poverty, political systems, colonial histories) that influence the
onset and termination of civil conflicts.

Table 12.2 highlights the persistence of civil violence in selected countries. The first column shows the country, while the second column shows
the number of years over the past 30 years (1987–2016) that each country
experienced violent civil conflict. For example, Afghanistan suffered 30
straight years of civil violence over the period. The same fate was experienced by Colombia, India, Myanmar, Philippines, and Sudan.
The remaining countries in the table also experienced an alarmingly high
number of years of civil conflict. It is indeed tragic that the norm for these
societies is not the absence, but rather the presence, of civil violence.
DeRouen and Bercovitch (2008) develop the concept of enduring internal
rivalry (EIR), which parallels Chapter 11's notion of an enduring interstate
rivalry. An EIR is not about the persistence of violent civil conflict generally (between the government and, potentially, multiple internal rivals)
but the dyadic violence between the government and a particular internal
opposition group. Examples of EIRs are indicated in the third column of
Table 12.2. The fourth column shows for each EIR the number of years
over the past 30 years that the government and the internal opposition
group experienced violent conflict. Colombia and Fuerzas Armadas
Revolucionarias de Colombia (FARC), for example, have fought in 29 of
the previous 30 years. Given that an EIR is dyadic, a state can experience

Table 12.2 *Persistence of civil conflict and enduring intrastate rivalries in selected countries, 1987–2016.*

Country	No. of Years of Civil Conflict in Past 30 Years	Enduring Intrastate Rivalry (EIR)	No. of Years of EIR in Past 30 Years
Afghanistan	30	Taliban	16
Algeria	26	Al Qaeda in the Islamic Maghreb	18
Colombia	30	Fuerzas Armadas Revolucionarias de Colombia (FARC)	29
Ethiopia	29	Oromo Liberation Front	26
India	30	Kashmir Insurgents	27
Iraq	23	Islamic State of Iraq and Syria (ISIS)	13
Israel	27	Hamas	14
Myanmar	30	Mong Tai Army/Restoration Council of Shan State	21
Philippines	30	Communist Party of the Philippines	28
Sudan	30	Sudan People's Liberation Movement/Army	18
Turkey	29	Kurdistan Workers' Party	29
Uganda	28	Lord's Resistance Army	22

Sources: Uppsala Conflict Data Program (UCDP) and International Peace Research Institute, Oslo (PRIO) and Gleditsch et al. (2002).

multiple EIRs. For example, Colombia has also been in an EIR with Ejército de Liberación Nacional (ELN) (25 of the previous 30 years; not shown) and India with the United Liberation Front of Assam (18 of the previous 30 years; not shown) and the Communist Party of India (Maoist) (12 of the previous 30 years; not shown).

DeRouen and Bercovitch maintain that EIRs are important for understanding civil violence because about three-quarters of civil war years worldwide since 1946 occurred in an EIR context. Moreover, the enduring nature of such conflicts can "promote a web of conflictual characteristics and hostile perceptions" and "psychological manifestations of enmity and deep feelings of fear and hatred" within states that make fertile ground for

Table 12.3 *Range of cumulative battle-related deaths from armed civil conflicts, 1989–2016.*

Range of Battle-Related Deaths	Number of Civil Conflicts
25–999	88
1,000–9,999	49
10,000–99,999	21
≥100,000	2

Sources: Uppsala Conflict Data Program (UCDP) and International Peace Research Institute, Oslo (PRIO) and Gleditsch et al. (2002).

the shortening of peace spells and the recurrence and persistence of civil conflict (DeRouen and Bercovitch 2008, p. 56).

Table 12.3 shows the range of cumulative battle-related deaths from armed civil conflicts over the period 1989–2016. More than 10 percent of these civil conflicts had cumulative battle-related deaths above 10,000, and two had fatalities above 100,000: Syria, 2011–6 (estimated fatalities of 222,732) and Afghanistan, 1989–2016 (162,001). The scale of civil war fatalities has reached even higher levels in the post-World War II period; for example, the civil war in China (1946–9) led to 1.2 million battle-related fatalities.

12.3 Theories of Civil War Risk and Prevention

Motives and Conditions for Civil Strife

Greed and Grievance Motives

Scholars often refer to greed and grievance motives for civil war. Some rebel leaders may be motivated by greed aimed at profits from control of natural resources (for example, oil, diamonds, precious metals, timber), illegal activities (for example, narcotics trafficking, protection rackets), or taxation. Other rebel leaders may be motivated by grievances stemming from the state's past or present mistreatment of a communal group. The notion that civil strife may be motivated by greed is associated with the research of economists Paul Collier and Anke Hoeffler, who maintain that a high level of natural resources within a state elevates the risk of civil war (Collier and Hoeffler 2004). Grievance explanations of civil strife are common in political science and sociology, where various in-group versus out-group behaviors are believed to control the risk of violence. For example, a group with sufficient power within a state may close off political, economic, or social opportunities to others for a variety of reasons, including ideological commitment, exploitation of power, or perceived threats. When structures of closure fall upon an identifiable ethnic, religious, or political group, and one or more catalytic events occur (for example, an extreme episode of deprivation), conditions are ripe for civil unrest (Gurr 1968; Tellis, Szayna, and Winnefeld 1997, pp. 86–96).

Weak State Conditions

For some scholars, a state's capacity to respond to a rebel movement is a crucial ingredient in the risk of civil violence. In "weak state" explanations of civil strife, the state lacks the ability to forestall rebellion with force or through accommodation of the rebel organization's demands. Ballentine and Sherman (2003, p. 9) note that the "defining condition of a weak or failing state is subject to competing definitions among scholars, [but] such states are minimally characterized by a loss of legitimacy and a loss of governing effectiveness in all or significant parts of their territory."

One important variable in weak state explanations of civil strife is the political system, often measured by a state's level of autocracy or democracy or by its transition from one political system to another. High levels of democracy are often found to correlate to a low risk of civil war, all else equal (Gleditsch and Ruggeri 2010). Democracies generally have institutional resources (for example, courts, elections, rights to protest) by which grievances can be addressed nonviolently. It is when political regimes are in transition that the risk of civil war can be elevated. Gleditsch, and Ruggeri (2010), for example, find that when leaders in transitioning regimes enter or exit irregularly, the risk of civil war is high. Irregular leadership transitions include coups, assassinations, and other forced removals in violation of existing rules. Cook and Savun (2016) find that even transitions to democratic regimes can elevate the risk of civil war, particularly if the transition is from a previous system of military rule.

A state's economic capacity for dealing with rebellion can also affect the risk of civil war. States that are relatively poor tend to be at greater risk of civil war onset and long duration (Collier, Hoeffler, and Söderbom 2004). One possible explanation for the correlation between poverty and civil war is that rebel recruitment is relatively easy when legal income-earning opportunities are paltry. Another possibility is that poverty generates grievances when it is concentrated on a particular communal group. The weak state explanation for the correlation between poverty and civil war, however, is that poor states do not have the economic means to gather intelligence about an incipient rebel movement, respond with financial incentives to rebel demands, or put down rebellion with force (Tellis, Szayna, and Winnefeld 1997, p. 104; Herbst 2004, p. 361).

Opportunistic Rebel Leaders and the Business of Rebellion

One or a few leaders are necessary to form a rebel group capable of engaging a state's military forces (Staniland 2014). A rebel leader's role in establishing a rebel group is similar in many respects to an entrepreneur starting a business. A rebel leader, like a business entrepreneur, typically has a high personal stake in the venture and is willing to accept significant personal risk to promote the organization's goals (Clapham 1988). The crucial difference between business and rebel entrepreneurs, of course, is that rebel activities are generally illegal and violent. Hence, the rebel leader and other rebel personnel face risk of incarceration or death.

For a rebel group to form and survive, it must overcome four significant hurdles. First, financial resources are needed to recruit and train members, purchase weapons and supplies, and conduct military operations. Second, a command and control infrastructure must be established to govern rebel military operations and interactions with the government, population, and other groups (for example, mediators, media, nongovernment organizations). This too requires financial resources but also geographic conditions conducive to rebel group viability, such as mountains or jungles that allow rebels to hide (Linke and Raleigh 2016). Third, rebel leaders must manage the cohesiveness of the rebel group to minimize the risk that disenchanted members will provide information to the government or form an opposing faction. Fourth, a rebel organization may have to overcome a free rider problem associated with recruitment. Even a person who is sympathetic to a rebel cause might abstain from joining a rebellion because of the risk of arrest or injury and the negligible impact of its individual participation. Collier (2000, p. 100) maintains, however, that when a rebellion is motivated by material gains to the rebels, the free rider problem can be eliminated if the gains are distributed exclusively to those who participate.

A Net Revenue Model of Rebellion

Here we draw upon several themes summarized in the previous subsections to construct a model of the optimal number of attacks chosen by a rebel organization against a state. Assume that the government's effort level against the rebel organization is fixed. This implies that our model amounts to partial equilibrium analysis because we focus only on one actor's optimizing behavior. Later in this chapter we cover bargaining theory perspectives on civil war, which incorporates strategic interdependence among the players and is thus in the vein of general equilibrium analysis.

We assume that the economic viability of a rebel organization is a necessary condition for sustained armed conflict. This is analogous to the economic principle that both for-profit and nonprofit enterprises must generate sufficient revenues to cover long run costs if they are to survive. Let the size of a rebellion be denoted by r, perhaps measured by the number of rebel attacks per year or the amount of territory controlled. Revenues for the rebel organization might include income from natural resources, voluntary or coerced material support from the surrounding population, and financial support from foreign governments, criminal syndicates, or diaspora. Costs to the rebel organization include labor and capital expenses, but also the opportunity cost of forgone political, economic, and social access once the rebellion is underway.

The revenues and costs of rebellion, R and C, are shown as functions of r in panel (a) of Figure 12.2. The positive vertical intercept on the cost curve allows for fixed costs, such as those associated with the startup of the rebel organization. As customary, we assume that revenues increase with r at a diminishing rate while costs increase at an increasing rate. For some intrastate conflicts, revenue and cost curves with alternative shapes might be applicable. In panel (b), net revenue or profit, $R-C$, is constructed by subtracting costs from revenues at each level of r in panel (a). In the case shown, there exists a range of rebel activities between r_0 and r_1 where the rebel group is economically viable (that is, $R \geq C$).

Implicit in Figure 12.2 is a fixed level of government resistance, meaning that the positions of the revenue, cost, and net revenue curves are dependent on government actions. For example, if the government exerts greater effort to cut off financial support to the rebel group, the revenue function would rotate downward, other things equal. Similarly, if the government improves legal employment prospects for potential rebels, it would be more costly for the rebel group to recruit labor, causing the cost curve to rotate upward, everything else the same.

To introduce preferences, assume that rebel utility is a function of net revenue and grievance, where grievance is satisfied by increases in rebel activity over a relevant range. If the rebel group desires both net revenue

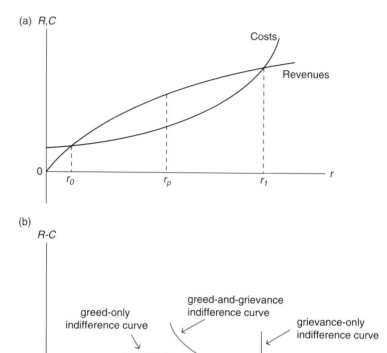

Figure 12.2 Net revenue model of rebellion.
(a) Revenues and costs
(b) Net revenues

and the satisfaction of grievances, then indifference curves will slope downward, yielding an optimal level of rebellion like r^* in panel (b). Alternatively, if the group is motivated purely by greed, the indifference curves will be horizontal, leading to a profit-maximizing level of rebellion at r_p. At the other extreme, if the group is motivated purely by grievance, then indifference curves will be vertical, leading to a maximum economically viable rebellion at r_1.

The net revenue model in Figure 12.2 lends itself to several comparative-static predictions. First, if grievance is weighted more heavily in the utility function relative to greed, the indifference curves will be steeper, and hence the optimal rebellion r^* will tend to increase. Second, if the revenue function rotates upward (thus raising marginal revenue), or the cost function rotates downward (thus lowering marginal cost), then the optimal rebellion will increase for both the pure greed and the pure grievance cases. Examples of increases in marginal revenue would be higher prices for opium harvested by rebels or easier market access for conflict diamonds. Examples of decreases in marginal cost would include higher unemployment among potential recruits, lower market wages, greater use of child soldiers, easier access to small arms and light weapons, and the incorporation of communications technologies (cell phones, YouTube videos, and social media) to increase recruitment and organizational cohesion. Third, if the cost curve is shifted upward sufficiently, then rebellion at any level will be economically unviable. An example would be political, economic, or social reforms that reduce closure against a previously disadvantaged group and thereby increase the fixed opportunity cost of rebellion.

Bargaining Theory

The rationalist and nonrationalist sources of violent conflict identified in the bargaining theory of war and peace (see Chapter 10) are applicable to understanding civil war risk. Particularly relevant are incomplete information, commitment problems, and concerns for reputation (Bussmann 2017, Hartzell 2017). Consider, for example, Figure 12.3 in which the income distributions available to the government and a rebel group challenger under peaceful settlement are shown by the settlement opportunities curve HN. The government's expected outcome from war is shown by point E_G, while the rebel group's is E_R. Assume the "E-gap" is due to incomplete information. Note that the "E-gap" is large in Figure 12.3 such that the region of mutual gain generated by indifference curves U_G and U_R lies outside the settlement curve. As a result, war is the predicted outcome. Assume that during the war the players' learn about each side's capabilities and the costs of war so that the expected outcomes from war converge to point $\tilde{E}$. Now a feasible settlement exists between S and S', say at $\hat{S}$, on the settlements curve.

For peace to be locked in, most governments will require that the rebel group lay down its arms. If the rebel group lays down its arms in Figure 12.3, however, it will become weaker and the government stronger, shifting the expected war outcome to, say, point F. What's to stop the government at point F from reneging on the peace deal at $\hat{S}$ and virtually wiping out the rebel opposition once and for all? Due to

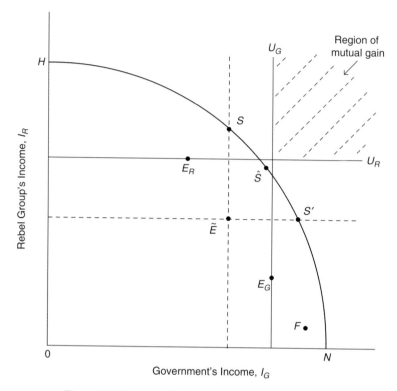

Figure 12.3 Sources of civil war in the bargaining model.

this threat, a commitment problem exists. The rebel group is unwilling to disarm; it thus maintains a form of resistance to counter the threat of being wiped out. Meanwhile, the government is unwilling to declare anything more than a fragile peace while a rebel group remains armed and capable of resistance. Under such circumstances, the risk of violence reemerging is high owing to new forms of incomplete information that could arise, the risk that the government takes a tough stand to enhance reputation, and/or the government's perception of threat becoming magnified by reference dependence and loss aversion. Figure 12.3 implies that there can be a variety of reasons why a civil war fails to really end, why a fragile peace can emerge, why the risk of war recurrence can be high, and why third-party help in the form of aid and/or security guarantees is often essential for a civil war to remain terminated.

12.4 Empirical Studies of Civil War Risk and Prevention

Risk Factors for Civil War

Greed, Grievance, and Weak States

Particularly influential early studies on civil war risk are by economists Collier and Hoeffler (2004) and political scientists Fearon and Laitin (2003). Both studies can be interpreted as testing two broad hypotheses of the net revenue model in Figure 12.2. Other things equal, the model predicts that rebel activity will increase, first, if grievance increases relative to greed, hence steepening the indifference curves, or, second, if marginal revenues increase or marginal costs decrease, thus shifting the net revenue curve to the right. While the two studies differ in method and detail, together they reach the same basic conclusion. Collier and Hoeffler (2004, pp. 587–8) find that "a model that focuses on the opportunities for rebellion performs well, whereas objective indicators of grievance add little explanatory power." Fearon and Laitin (2003, p. 76) elaborate, "Our data show that measures of cultural diversity and grievances fail to postdict civil war onset, while measures of conditions that favor insurgency do fairly well. Surely ethnic antagonisms, national sentiments, and grievances often motivate rebels and their supporters. But such broad factors are too common to distinguish the cases where civil war breaks out."

Both studies use regression analysis to estimate the probability of civil war onset based on samples encompassing 161 states. The samples differ, however, on the years covered and definitions of civil war. Collier and Hoeffler's dataset spans 1960–99 and includes 79 wars, which are counted as such if they caused at least 1,000 battle-related deaths per year. Fearon and Laitin's sample is larger, spanning 1945–99 and including 127 wars, which are required to have averaged at least 100 battle-related deaths per year and totaled at least 1,000 deaths during the conflict. Proxies for grievance, including measures of ethnic and religious diversity, political repression, and income inequality, are generally found to be statistically insignificant. In contrast, several variables gauging conditions favorable to rebellion are significant and substantively important. In particular, the risk of civil war is higher when income per capita and growth are lower, when exports of oil and other primary commodities are higher, and when terrain is more mountainous. Wars are also more likely when a state is new, has experienced recent instability or civil war, or is an inconsistent mix of autocracy and democracy.

While the two studies agree that civil war onset is determined primarily by nongrievance factors, they disagree on why particular factors operate as they do. For example, whereas Collier and Hoeffler see low per capita income as evidence of low opportunity costs for rebels, Fearon and Laitin treat it as an indicator of weak military and police capabilities of the state. Similarly, in Collier and Hoeffler exports of primary commodities represent sources of rebel revenues, but in Fearon and Laitin high oil exports are thought to matter because they correlate with weak state institutions. Differences like these motivate continued research on civil war onset, including both large-sample econometric tests and cases studies.

Poverty

Both Collier and Hoeffler (2004) and Fearon and Laitin (2003) find that low per capita income is correlated with greater risk of civil war, all else equal. Although we would expect low per capita income and poverty to be correlated, they are not the same thing; a person with low income may not be experiencing serious material deprivation. Hence, social scientists have probed deeper in recent years into possible connections between poverty and civil war risk. Braithwaite, Dasandi, and Hudson (2016) (hereafter BDH), for example, investigate whether there is a causal impact of poverty on civil conflict. In Chapter 1 we noted that poor countries can face conflict and poverty traps in which economic underdevelopment elevates the risk of violent conflict and conflict keeps states underdeveloped. If poverty can cause conflict and conflict can cause poverty, how does one untangle the particular effect of poverty on conflict? To address the challenge, BDH employ an instrumental variables methodology, which is designed to isolate the independent effect of poverty on conflict. The authors also integrate into their study the international context of countries experiencing poverty. Recall from Chapter 1 in our discussion of core/gap states that gap states tend to be disconnected (un-networked) from trade, technology, and intergovernmental organizations relative to core states. BDH believe that states that experience what we might call a poverty of such networks will tend to be poor and exploited in the international arena, which is an important context for understanding civil war risk.

The authors' dependent variable in the regression analysis is whether there was onset of civil conflict per country per year over the period 1980–2007. The key explanatory variable is the degree of poverty per country per year. Control variables include measures of economic growth, political system ranging from full autocracy to full democracy, and whether the state is a major oil exporter. Poverty can be measured in various ways such as the infant mortality rate (IMR) and real GDP per capita. Without getting too technical, the instrumental variables methodology requires that the authors find a measure of poverty that is a good substitute for IMR and real GDP per capita in order to isolate the independent effect of poverty on conflict. The authors' use the networked position of each country in the international trade system as their substitute measure for poverty. Countries with high trade networking can be considered core countries; those with low trade networking can be considered gap states. The authors' key result is that poverty, as instrumented by poor trade network position, significantly increases the risk of civil conflict. Specifically, when a country moves from the 10th percentile on poverty (that is, it is relatively well-positioned in the international network) to the 90th percentile, the risk of civil war onset increases almost sixfold, all else equal. BDH (2016, p. 60) thus conclude that "there is a causal arrow running from poverty to conflict."

Inequality

Recall that Collier and Hoeffler (2004) and Fearon and Laitin (2003) found little empirical effects of grievances on civil war risk. Those studies measured grievances by indices of ethnolinguistic fractionalization (ELF). Buhaug, Cederman, and Gleditsch (2014) (hereafter BCG) revisit empirical inquiry on potential correlations between grievances related to inequality and civil war risk. Particularly important in their study is the distinction between vertical inequality and horizontal inequality. Vertical inequality concerns the unequal distribution of income, wealth, and/or access to political goods across individuals in the society. Horizontal inequality has to do with inequality across groups.

BCG hypothesize that horizontal economic and political inequality will each increase the risk of civil war, even after controlling for vertical economic and political inequalities, all else equal. The authors' dependent variable in the regression analysis is whether there was occurrence of civil war per country per year over the 1960 to 2005 period. The key explanatory variables are the degrees of horizontal economic and political inequalities per country. The measure for horizontal economic inequality was developed from data on wealth distribution for all ethnic groups in each country. The measure for horizontal political inequality came from the Ethnic Power Relations dataset (Wimmer, Cederman, and Min 2009), which measures the political status (or lack thereof) of politically relevant ethnic groups worldwide. Control variables include measures of vertical economic inequality (Gini coefficient) and ethnic grievance (ELF), GDP per capita, and democracy. Key results indicate that "intergroup [horizontal] inequalities matter more for civil war risk than vertical disparities" (BCG 2014, p. 425). In extended analyses, the authors find that results vary depending on whether the civil wars are ethnic and over territory, ethnic and over control of the government, or nonethnic. For example, they find that the importance of horizontal political inequalities nearly triples for understanding the risk of ethnic civil wars over control of the government relative to the full sample of civil wars. Furthermore, the impact of horizontal economic inequality on the risk of separatist (territorial) civil wars is more than 50 percent greater relative to the full sample of civil wars.

Economic Interdependence

According to the liberal peace hypothesis, salient trade makes war less likely, all else equal. Evidence relevant to the hypothesis in the context of civil war is mixed. For example, Barbieri and Reuveny (2005) find that trade openness does not significantly affect the risk of civil war onset. In contrast, Bussmann and Schneider (2007, p. 94) report a negative effect that is both substantial and statistically significant, leading to the conclusion that "in the *long term* an open economy is related to less [civil] conflict" (our emphasis). It is important, however, to qualify Bussmann and Schneider's results because they also consider the short-term consequences of greater global economic integration on civil war risk. Specifically, they find that changes toward greater trade openness can increase civil conflict risk in the short run even while a greater level of trade openness reduces such risk in the long run.

Unlike most civil conflict risk studies in the literature, which focus on the correlates of violence, Karakaya (2018) explores whether greater interdependence is associated with nonviolent rather than violent resistance campaigns within states. The research is important for a variety of reasons, two of which we emphasize. First, as Karakaya notes, empirical evidence suggests that nonviolent campaigns are more effective than violent approaches for achieving political ends and for successfully transitioning to democracy. Second, globalization is multidimensional and subject to many interpretations and possible measures. Hence, it is important for ongoing research on civil conflict risk to continue to advance and refine measures of interdependence, which Karakaya does by using a multifaceted measure of globalization.

Karakaya explores a number of theories of how globalization might affect the ratio of nonviolent to violent protests against governments. On the one hand, globalization might increase grievances for those who lose from greater economic interdependence, which could promote violence through feelings of frustration and relative deprivation. On the other hand, greater interdependence might constrain political leaders from resorting to actions that would precipitate violence (from either side) owing to fears of forgone opportunities from global linkages, which could be disrupted by violence. Since theoretical arguments lead to ambiguity regarding the correlation between greater interdependence and the prevalence of nonviolent relative to violent protests, Karakaya turns to empirical inquiry.

Karakaya draws data from the Nonviolent and Violent Campaigns and Outcomes Data Project, in which a nonviolent campaign is "prosecuted by unarmed civilians who did not directly threaten or harm the physical well-being of their opponent" (Chenoweth and Lewis 2013, p. 418). The unit of analysis in the study is the country-year for all states from 1976 to 2006. Karakaya's dependent variable has three categories: no major campaign onset, violent campaign onset, and nonviolent campaign onset. The key explanatory variable is globalization, which is measured by the KOF index provided by the KOF Swiss Economic Institute (2018). The KOF index incorporates economic, social, and political dimensions of globalization. Control variables include GDP per capita growth, democracy, political instability, and education. Empirical results indicate that greater globalization "significantly increases the odds of nonviolent campaign onset, while decreasing the probability of violent campaigns" (Karakaya 2018, p. 325). Specifically, Karakaya finds that when globalization moves from its minimum to its maximum value, "the predicted probability of nonviolent campaign onset rises from 1.8 to 17%," all else equal (p. 15). Moreover, she finds under the same conditions that the probability of violent campaign onset falls from 6.6 percent to virtually zero.

Civil War Prevention

In Chapter 10 we used the bargaining model to show that third-party intervention can have a pacific effect if it coordinates expectations, reduces commitment problems, or ameliorates animosity. On the other hand, it can leave the prospect for peaceful settlement unchanged or even worsened if the intervention favors one side (see Figures 10.10–10.12 in Chapter 10). An empirical study focused on third-party efforts to reduce violence in civil wars is Hultman, Kathman, and Shannon (2014) (hereafter HKS), who note that the United Nations "is increasingly asked to halt active conflict" (p. 737).

HKS empirically test whether UN interventions reduce battle-related deaths in civil wars. Drawing upon perspectives from the bargaining theory of war and peace, HKS argue that UN peacekeeping operations can reduce battlefield violence by "providing security guarantees" that "assist the combatants in overcoming commitment problems that would make peaceful forms of resolution difficult to pursue" (p. 737). Furthermore, they note that such operations can increase the costs of continued warfare, thus increasing the incentives of the combatants to settle.

The authors' main hypothesis is that as the UN commits more military troops to a civil conflict, battlefield violence decreases, all else equal. The dependent variable in the regression analysis is the number of battle-related deaths (soldiers and civilians caught in the crossfire) per government-rebel group dyad in a month. The sample encompasses all intrastate armed conflicts in Africa from 1992 to 2011. The key explanatory variables are designed to measure UN mission capacity (amount of UN commitment) and constitution (composition of UN personnel). To do so, the authors develop three explanatory variable measures: first, number of UN armed military troops; second, number of UN police; and, third, number of UN observers. Control variables include the presence of a ceasefire agreement, relative strength of the rebel group, and whether there is biased third-party intervention. The authors report three key results. First, UN troops significantly reduce the amount of battlefield deaths, all else equal. Second, UN police units do not seem to increase or decrease the amount of battlefield deaths. Third, in some of the regressions, UN observers are associated with a significant increase in battlefield deaths. One possible explanation for this result is that increases in UN observers can signal a growing interest by the UN in the conflict in which more forceful UN actions may follow. Hence, the combatants may increase their hostilities in order to "improve their relative strength and gain bargaining leverage for future peace negotiations" (p. 747).

12.5 Economic Consequences of Civil Wars

Civil War and Economic Growth

As previously noted, economic costs of war include diversion of resources to conflict activities, which causes alternative production to be forgone;

destruction of resources, so that both current and future production are sacrificed; disruption of ordinary production and exchange, meaning that otherwise gainful activity is rendered uneconomical; and displacement of people in the form or refugees and internally displaced persons (IDPs), such that family economic activities are degraded. One way to gauge these costs at an aggregate level is to examine their impact on economic growth. Because of the multiplicity of intrastate conflicts, large-sample studies have yielded good estimates of the effect of civil war on growth.

Murdoch and Sandler's (2004) study is distinguished because it esti-mates the short- and long-run effects due not only to a country's own war but also to a war in a nearby country. Consider two countries A and B located close to one another. Nation A's growth can fall owing to the costs of conflict if a war occurs in its own territory. Nation A's growth can also suffer if a civil war in B disrupts economic activity between the two countries or heightens uncertainty in the region. To allow for both effects, Murdoch and Sandler add indicators of own civil war and nearby civil war to a standard model of country-level growth. They then estimate the model using regression analysis for a large sample of countries over the period 1961–95. Long-run growth is measured as the change in the logarithm of per-capita income over the full thirty-five year period; short-run growth is measured as the same over a five-year period. For the long-run case, Murdoch and Sandler estimate that own-country civil war will reduce thirty-five year growth from a sample mean of 0.55 to 0.39, or by about 30 percent, while nearby-country civil war will reduce it to 0.50, or by about 10 percent. Hence, the long-term impact of civil war is substantial, with the effect of a nearby civil war being about one-third that of a homeland war. For the short-run case, own-country civil war is estimated to reduce five-year growth from a sample mean of 0.06 to 0.01, or by about 85 percent, while nearby civil war will reduce it to 0.05, or by about 20 percent. Notice that the percentage reductions are greater in the short run than in the long run. Murdoch and Sandler interpret this as meaning that countries in the longer run are able to recover from past civil wars, both those at home and in neighbor countries.

Microlevel Costs

As in Murdoch and Sandler (2004), macrolevel studies use variation across countries to estimate the effects of conflict on aggregate measures of economic activity. In contrast, microlevel studies employ variation across individuals and communities to estimate more direct effects on variables like personal income, health, and education. An excellent example of microlevel research is Kibris' (2015) study of the effects of civil strife in Turkey on the educational achievements of high school students in the country. Recall from Table 12.2 that Turkey has been in an enduring intrastate rivalry with the Kurdistan Workers' Party or PKK (Partiya Karkerên Kurdistanêin). Kibris empirically analyzes the effects of Turkey/PKK civil strife on education using two country-specific datasets. The first consists of the 2005 Turkish university entrance test scores and other personal data for about 1.6 million high school students. The second is the date and location of Turkey security force casualties (SFCs) from the conflict from 1984 to 2012. Kibris' empirical work is finely grained (micro-oriented) in that her dependent variable is measured by the test score and county location of individual students. Her key explanatory variable is the number of SFCs that occurred per county over the 1990–2005 period. Note that students taking the 2005 university entrance test would generally have been in school in the 1990–2005 period. The research question is then: Did counties experiencing comparatively intense conflict as proxied by SFCs have diminished educational achievement, all else equal? Kibris' control variables include measures of student characteristics (gender, major, high school), county characteristics (ethnic composition, unemployment, share of agricultural employment), and the number of SFCs in neighboring counties. Kibris finds that SFCs have a significant and substantive negative effect on student test scores, all else equal. She also finds that conflict is more detrimental to females than to males for quantitative tests scores, which could reinforce "gender biases and roles in a society that already suffers severely from gender discrimination against women" (Kibris 2015, p. 660). Similarly, Silwal (2016) reports a greater negative impact of civil conflict on education for females relative to males from civil conflict in Nepal.

Education is characterized by economists as human capital formation. As an individual is educated, they develop knowledge and skills that build up over time. Human capital benefits the person individually but also the society at large as the individual exercises its abilities in the economy, civic life, and the family. Not only does education promote greater economic growth (Krueger and Lindahl 2001), it is associated with greater individual earnings, social equality, and democracy (Kibris 2015, p. 647). The adverse effects of civil strife on education can occur through multiple channels including school closings in conflict zones, reluctance of parents to send their children to school under dangerous conditions, reluctance of teachers to work in insecure environments, and psychological stresses that dampen learning even when students and teachers show up (Kibris 2015, pp. 648–9). Moreover, declines in human capital from conflict persist over time in the form of lower earning opportunities and greater risks of infant mortality; in the context of the conflict and poverty trap, such outcomes increase the risk of future conflict (Kibris 2015, pp. 648–9; Silwal 2016, p. 118).

Economic Effects of Syrian Civil War

So far in the twenty-first century, one could argue that no country has been torn asunder by civil war as much as Syria. In addition to deaths and injuries, another important aspect of civil conflicts is people on the run as refugees and IDPs. Recall from Table 1.6 that the number of refugees and IDPs for Syria is close to 12 million, which constitutes almost two-thirds of Syria's population. For Syrian individuals and families on the run, violent conflict is devastating socially and psychologically, but also economically. The economic costs alone to Syrian individuals and families (that is, the microeconomic costs) are immense. Families must sell assets and divert savings to attempt to achieve subsistence and security under the shadow of conflict; people are compelled to leave livelihoods behind such as small business activities; well-established social networks and access to local markets for meeting needs are no longer available; and human capital formation for children is seriously compromised through lost schooling, malnutrition, and stress.

The micro costs of conflict can also be intergenerational as weakened mothers and fathers are less able to care for children and elderly family members; children's stunted physical growth, lack of education, and psychological harm make them less productive and able to care for their own children later in life; and losses of businesses and homes disrupt opportunities for parents to pass assets onto their children, thus short-circuiting intergenerational wealth accumulation. Even if refugees and IDPs are able to return, their homes may be destroyed or occupied by others who refuse to leave, and the communities they once knew may have little hope of being reconstituted. Similar economic costs apply to individuals and families that choose to stay rather than flee from violence. Some of these "stayers" or "remainees," as they are called, can be even worse off than those on the run because they may be too poor to flee (Ibánez and Moya 2016; Lendorfer, Etang-Ndip, and Hoogeveen 2016).

The many microeconomic impacts of Syria's civil war add up and become reflected in the country's macroeconomy. Consider, for example,

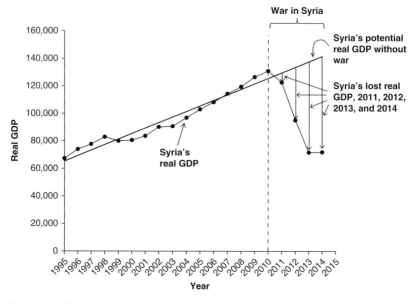

Figure 12.4 Syria's lost real GDP during civil war, 2011–14 (in millions of 2011 US$).
Sources: Penn World Tables (2017) and World Bank (2018).

the dramatic losses in Syria's GDP owing to civil war as shown in
Figure 12.4. Measured on the vertical axis and plotted by the times series
with the small circles is Syria's real GDP in millions of 2011 USA dollars
from 1995 to 2014 (real GDP means the monetary values have been
adjusted for inflation). Note how Syria's real GDP grows from a little
more than $65 billion in 1995 to about $130 billion by 2010. The civil
war in Syria began in 2011 and it became extremely severe. The straight
line in Figure 12.4 is a "best fit" line based on statistical analysis of Syria's
growth in real GDP from 1995 to 2010. Past 2010, if Syria's real GDP
continued to grow as it had from 1995 to 2010, the best fit line suggests that
Syria's real GDP would have risen to about $141 billion by 2014. Civil war
in Syria seriously disrupted the country's real GDP growth path as seen by
the actual GDP data points (the small circles) from 2011 to 2014.
The vertical arrows pointing down from the best fit line to the actual
GDP data points represent how much real GDP fell short from the best
fit prediction in each year from 2011 to 2014. The four downward arrows
sum to a loss of real GDP of about $176 billion, which is about 1.33 times
Syria's 2010 real GDP. It's as if the four years of war (2011–4) shown in
Figure 12.4 caused Syria's aggregate economy to shut down for a year-and

-a-third, a truly staggering economic blow. Moreover, as the war in Syria continues at present, the losses of real GDP to Syria continue to mount.

12.6 Bibliographic Notes

Research on aspects of civil war emphasized in this chapter continues apace including resources, greed, and grievances (Morelli and Rohner 2015; Berman, Coutenier, Rohner, and Thoenig 2017; Hunziker and Cederman 2017), poverty and inequality (Cederman, Gleditsch, and Buhaug 2013; Jazayeri 2015), economic interdependence (Schneider 2014), third-party intervention (Kim 2017), internationalization of civil wars (Gleditsch 2017, Jenne and Popovic 2017), economic growth (Minhas and Radford 2017), foreign direct investment (Li, Murshed, and Tanna 2017), financial development (Hasan and Murshed 2017), and education (Singh and Shemyakina 2016; Ullah, Khan, and Mahmood 2017).

In addition to civil war risk and economic consequences, numerous other facets of civil wars have been studied by social scientists including severity (Silwal 2013; Miranda, Perondi, and Gleditsch 2016), termination and recurrence (Ohmura 2011, Hartzell 2017), contagion across and within countries (Silwal 2013, Fisk 2014, Bara 2017), secession (Roeder 2017), child soldiers (Lasley and Thyne 2014, Haer and Böhmelt 2015), social and identity motives for participating in rebellion (Tezcür 2016), militias (Carey and Mitchell 2016), refugees and IDPs (Fisk 2014), effects of economic and military sanctions (Hultman and Peksen 2017), connections between social media and civil conflict (Zeitzoff 2017, 2018), roles of private military and security companies (Brauer 1999, Tkach 2017), gender (Johansson and Sarwari 2017; Kadera and Shair-Rosenfield 2017), networking (Hammond 2018), commodity price shocks (Dube and Vargas 2013, Gong and Sullivan 2017), and climate change (Jones, Mattiacci, and Braumoeller 2017; Witmer, Linke, O'Loughlin, et al. 2017).

Theoretical and empirical literature on civil conflicts is growing so rapidly that we recommend literature reviews, books, and journal special issues. See, for example, the literature reviews of Collier and Hoeffler (2007a), Blattman and Miguel (2010), Fiala and Skaperdas (2011), Hoeffler (2012), Murshed (2015), Cederman and Vogt (2017), and Florea (2017); edited books of Collier and Sambanis (2005, vols. 1 and 2), Newman and DeRouen (2014), Dixon and Sarkees (2015), and Mason and Mitchell (2016); and special journal issues of *Economics of*

Governance (Cusack, Glazer, and Konrad 2006), *Journal of International Development* (Addison and Murshed 2003), *Journal of Peace Research* (Hegre 2004; Brunborg and Urdal 2005; Verwimp, Justino, and Brück 2009), and *Journal of Conflict Resolution* (Ron 2005, Cederman and Gleditsch 2009; Jentzsch, Kalyvas, and Schubiger 2015).

13

Terrorism

In this chapter we present data on worldwide patterns of international and domestic terrorism.* We then apply principles from the rational choice model, game theory, and network economics to terrorists' resource allocation decisions and governments' counterterrorism efforts. Selected empirical studies of the risks, prevention, and economic effects of terrorism are also summarized.

13.1 Definition

There is disagreement among scholars and policymakers on distinctions between terrorism and other violent acts such as deadly criminality (for example, mass school shootings and gang killings), guerrilla war, and violence against civilians (Sandler 2015, pp. 3–4). In this chapter we adopt Enders and Sandler's (2012, p. 4) definition of *terrorism* as "the premeditated use or threat to use violence by individuals or subnational groups to obtain a political or social objective through the intimidation of a large audience beyond that of the immediate victims." By this definition, terrorism is political or social in the sense that terrorists desire to "change the system," something that is not a priority for criminals (Hoffman 2017, p. 37). The political or social goals of terrorists along with their desire to intimidate a large audience lead some terrorists to carry out shocking attacks such as beheadings and bombings in public places (Sandler 2015, p. 1; Hoffman 2017). Scholars also distinguish between domestic and

---

* Parts of Section 13.1 and Section 13.4 are adapted from Charles H. Anderton and John R. Carter's article, "Applying Intermediate Microeconomics to Terrorism" published in *Journal of Economic Education*, volume 37, issue 4, pp. 442–58, 2006. Material is reprinted with the kind permission of the Taylor & Francis Group. Copyright © Taylor & Francis Group 2006.

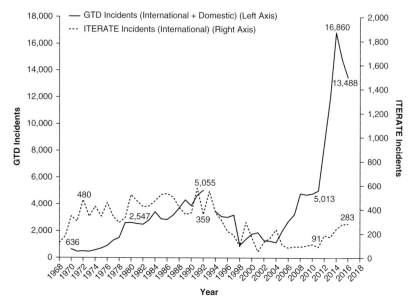

Figure 13.1 Terrorism incidents per year worldwide, 1970–2016.
Note: GTD data for 1993 are missing.
Sources: Global Terrorism Database (2017) and Mickolus et al. (2016).

international terrorism, where the former is "homegrown and home-directed," while the latter involves perpetrators or victims from a country different from the venue country (Sandler 2015, p. 5).

13.2 Patterns of Terrorism

Figure 13.1 shows the time paths for international and domestic terrorist incidents worldwide based on data from the Global Terrorism Database (GTD) and International Terrorism: Attributes of Terrorist Events (ITERATE) (see Appendix D.3). Numerical amounts for selected years are also shown. Three observations follow. First, there are major differences in the number of incidents reported by GTD and ITERATE, mainly because the former includes both international and domestic attacks, while the latter excludes domestic incidents. Second, although there are significant variations across GTD and ITERATE in definitions, coding rules, and incidents tracked, the large gap between the series suggest that domestic terrorism incidents worldwide are much more numerous than international incidents. Third, there is an enormous spike in GTD incidents in

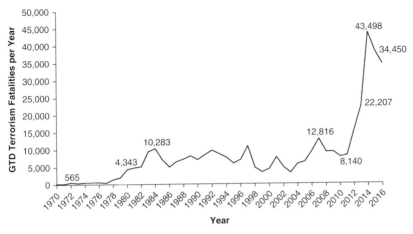

Figure 13.2 Terrorism fatalities per year worldwide 1970–2016.
Note: GTD data for 1993 are missing.
Sources: Global Terrorism Database (2017).

recent years from 5,013 in 2011 to 16,860 in 2014. Two countries that experienced dramatic increases in terrorist attacks over this period were Afghanistan (416 to 1,821 incidents) and Iraq (1,302 to 3,926). Although less noticeable given the graph's scale, ITERATE incidents also increased significantly in recent years (from 91 in 2011 to 283 in 2016).

Figure 13.2 shows yearly fatalities from international and domestic terrorism worldwide, with numerical amounts shown for selected years. Particularly noticeable are the higher fatality amounts in recent years, which increased from 8,140 in 2011 to 43,498 in 2014. The two countries that experienced dramatic increases in incidents from 2011 to 2014 also experienced severe increases in fatalities: Afghanistan (1,518 to 5,406) and Iraq (1,848 to 13,063).

Table 13.1 shifts attention to the geographic location of terrorist attacks by decade from 1980–9 to 2010–6. The table shows the emergence of terrorism in Eastern Europe, the substantial decline of terrorism in the Americas (especially South America), and the dramatic increases in incidents in Asia, the Middle East and North Africa, and Subsaharan Africa.

Table 13.2 focuses on terrorists' attack modes, which includes bombings, hostage incidents (hijackings plus kidnappings), facility/infrastructure attacks, assassinations, armed assaults, and "other" for unarmed assaults and incidents in which the attack mode is unknown. Bombings and armed assaults are the most frequent modes of attack, presumably

Table 13.1 *Terrorism by region, 1980–2016.*

Region	Number of Terrorism Attacks Per Time Period			
	1980–89	1990–99	2000–09	2010–16
Asia	4,066	7,233	10,962	31,720
Central America & Caribbean	7,490	1,847	59	26
North America	557	654	268	275
South America	9,698	5,763	1,149	1,156
Eastern Europe	43	1,062	1,324	2,577
Western Europe	4,768	3,978	1,401	1,489
Middle East & North Africa	2,883	5,426	8,086	29,043
Sub-Saharan Africa	1,576	2,690	1,720	9,268

Source: Global Terrorism Database (2017).

Table 13.2 *Terrorist attack modes, 1970–2016.*

Attack Mode	Number of Attacks
Bombings	83,559
Hostage Incidents (hijackings plus kidnappings)	12,309
Facility/Infrastructure attacks	11,136
Assassinations	18,567
Armed Assaults	43,372
Other	7,370

Source: Global Terrorism Database (2017).

because they are logistically simple and difficult to prevent. Islamic State of Iraq and Syria (ISIS)-sponsored attacks in Nice, France on July 14, 2016 (77 fatalities) and at the Westminster Bridge in London on March 22, 2015 (five fatalities) are examples of armed assaults, while the attacks in Brussels, Belgium on March 22, 2016 (32 fatalities) are examples of bombings.

Table 13.3 shows the number of international and domestic suicide attacks and associated fatalities worldwide from 1970 to 2016. Suicide attacks have grown from virtually zero per year in the 1970s and 1980s to close to 1,000 per year by the mid-2010s. Fatalities from suicide attacks have likewise dramatically increased from virtually zero per year in the

Table 13.3 *Number of suicide terrorist attacks and fatalities worldwide, 1970–2016.*

Year	Number of Suicide Attacks	Fatalities from Suicide Attacks
1970	0	0
1975	0	0
1980	0	0
1985	16	122
1990	2	8
1995	21	295
2000	39	286
2005	215	2,402
2010	174	2,500
2011	208	2,076
2012	402	2,793
2013	623	4,479
2014	742	5,931
2015	915	8,421
2016	982	10,313

Source: Global Terrorism Database (2017).

1970s and 1980s to more than 10,000 in 2016. According to GTD data, the total number of terrorist attacks from 2010 to 2016 was 75,494, of which 5.4 percent (4,046) were suicide attacks. If this percent seems low, it is because it contrasts sharply with the figure for related fatalities. From 2010 to 2016, the total number of persons killed from terrorism was 169,612, of which 21.5 percent (36,413) were due to suicide attacks. A good summary statistic, therefore, is that recently, suicide attacks worldwide account for about 1 in 20 terrorist attacks but they lead to about one in five fatalities caused by terrorism. Most recently, in 2016, suicide attacks accounted for 7.3 percent (982 of 13,488) of total terrorist attacks and 29.9 percent (10,313 of 34,450) of all terrorist fatalities. Hence, the dramatic increase in suicide terrorism does not appear to be leveling off; if anything, it may be increasing.

Table 13.4 shows the number of terrorist attacks and associated fatalities from 2012 to 2016 for five prominent terrorist organizations. ISIS is by far the most serious perpetrator of terrorism in recent years, accounting for

Table 13.4 *Terrorism attacks and fatalities by terrorist organization, 2012–16.*

Organization	No. of Attacks	Estimated Fatalities
al Qaeda	1,374	4,618
al-Shabaab	2,364	6,355
Boko Haram	1,938	19,409
Islamic State in Iraq and Syria (ISIS)	4,343	31,245
Kurdistan Workers' Party	941	1,422

Note: Data for al Qaeda includes data for al Qaeda and al Qaeda in Iraq, Lebanon, Saudi Arabia, the Indian Subcontinent, the Arabian Peninsula, the Islamic Maghreb, and Yemen.
Source: Global Terrorism Database (2017).

6.6 percent of terrorism incidents (4,343 of 65,696) and 20.3 percent of terrorism fatalities (31,245 of 153,806) worldwide over the period. The incidents and fatalities for al Qaeda include most (but not all) of the al Qaeda affiliated groups, which are summarized in the notes at the bottom of the table. Meanwhile, substantial terrorism activities are carried out by al-Shabaab (mostly in Somalia), Boko Haram (mostly in Nigeria), and the Kurdistan Workers' Party (almost all in Turkey).

13.3 Theories of Terrorism Risk and Prevention

Rational Choice Model of Terrorism

Basic Model
In Chapter 4 we applied the rational choice model to a terrorist organization's allocation of resources to attack political and civilian targets. The same model can be adapted to other choices faced by terrorists including those that pertain to levels of terrorist activity or to more specific targets of attack such as airlines or diplomats (Enders and Sandler 2012, Hausken 2018). Beginning from an initial optimum, various aspects of terrorism and counterterrorism can be explored by changing the parameters of the model, specifically income, prices, and preferences.

To understand decisions about levels of terrorism, Figure 13.3 assumes that a terrorist organization allocates income I between terrorist activity T and composite good Y, where T is measured in some standardized unit, and Y is real (inflation-adjusted) expenditures on all other goods such as food, clothing, and shelter. The terrorists' budget constraint HN satisfies

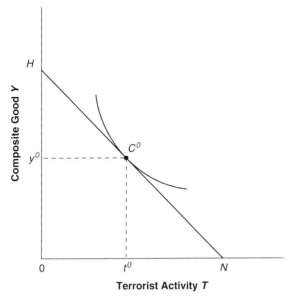

Figure 13.3 Terrorists' optimal choice of terrorist activity and composite good.

the equation $P_T T + P_Y Y = I$, where P_T is the price or per unit cost of carrying out terrorist activities and P_Y is the price of the composite good. Indifference curves represent preferences over T and Y in the usual manner. Negative-sloped indifference curves imply that terrorists are willing to give up some of the composite good to obtain more terrorist activity. Steeper indifference curves indicate a greater willingness to engage in terrorism, while more curvature implies a lower degree of substitutability between T and Y. The optimal choice occurs at point C^0, where the marginal rate of substitution between T and Y is just equal to the relative price of terrorism P_T/P_Y.

To understand decisions about targets, we could alternatively assume that terrorists allocate an exogenous amount of resources R between two targets T_1 and T_2, which for example might be civilian and political targets, as in Chapter 4. In this case the budget equation would become $P_1 T_1 + P_2 T_2 = R$, where P_1 and P_2 are the prices or per unit costs of carrying out the two missions. Indifference curves would show preferences over competing targets and hence the subjective value of one target in terms of another.

Terrorist Response to Price Changes

Governments try to thwart terrorism with price policies. For example, defense of potential targets, military strikes against training centers, and capture of terrorist leaders increase the unit cost of terrorism P_T. Following Frey and Luechinger (2003) we refer to actions that raise the cost of terrorism as deterrence, although Schelling (1966) uses the term more narrowly to mean threats of retaliation designed to alter preferences. In contrast to deterrence, Frey and Luechinger consider benevolence policy to reduce terrorism, which raises the opportunity cost of terrorism, not by increasing the price of terrorism directly, but by reducing the price of the composite good. Examples include subsidized consumption goods or, as suggested by Frey and Luechinger, increased access to normal political processes.

Figure 13.4 contrasts deterrence and benevolence price policies to reduce terrorism. Assume the initial budget constraint is HN, leading the terrorist group to choose terrorist activity equal to t^0. In panel (a), deterrence policy increases the price of terrorism P_T by raising the expected cost of terrorist activity, causing the budget constraint to rotate inward along the horizontal axis to HN'. The increased opportunity cost of terrorism is reflected in the steeper slope of the budget line. Consistent with the law of demand, terrorist activity falls to some lower level t^1. In panel (b), benevolence policy also raises the opportunity cost of terrorism, but it does so by increasing terrorist access to other goods by lowering P_Y, the price of the composite good. Beginning from HN, benevolence policy rotates the budget line upward along the vertical axis to $H'N$. Again, the steeper budget line reflects the higher opportunity cost of terrorism. Under the benevolence policy shown in panel (b), terrorists choose a reduced level of terrorism equal to t^1. However, as shown in panel (c), it is entirely possible for the decrease in P_Y instead to increase the level of terrorism. For the same benevolence policy but different preferences, terrorists in this case choose an increased level of terrorism equal to t^1.

The rational choice model thus shows an important contrast between deterrence and benevolence price policies. To the extent that deterrence raises the per unit cost of terrorism, terrorist activity can be expected to decrease based on the law of demand. On the other hand, if benevolence policy succeeds in lowering the price of the composite good, the effect on the level of terrorism is theoretically ambiguous (Anderton and Carter 2005).

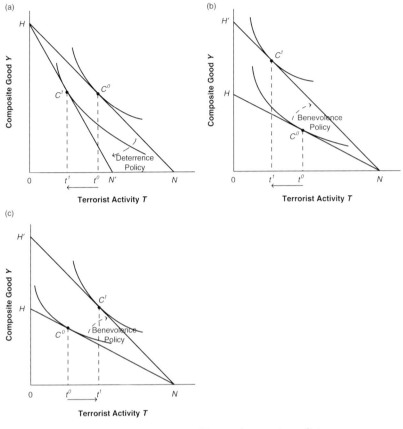

Figure 13.4 Deterrence and benevolence price policies.
(a) Deterrence with terrorism decrease
(b) Benevolence with terrorism decrease
(c) Benevolence with terrorism increase

Terrorist Substitution Possibilities

An important general issue raised by terrorism-thwarting price policies is the potential for terrorists to substitute into other activities. For example, the question raised by consideration of benevolence policy is whether terrorism will rise or fall in response to a lower price of the composite good. A similar question arose in Chapter 4 when we considered whether greater protection of political targets would cause terrorist attacks against civilians to rise or fall. The scope of terrorist substitution possibilities is extensive; terrorists can substitute between terrorism and ordinary goods,

Table 13.5 *International terrorist hijackings, 1968–77.*

Year	Total International Incidents	Hijackings	Hijackings as Percent of Total
1968	123	3	2.4
1969	179	12	6.7
1970	344	22	6.4
1971	301	10	3.3
1972	480	15	3.1
1973	340	6	1.8
1974	425	7	1.6
1975	342	2	0.6
1976	455	6	1.3
1977	340	6	1.8
Mean		8.9	2.9

Note: Metal detectors placed in airports in 1973.
Source: Mickolus (1980).

across target classes, across countries, among weapons technologies, and across time (Sandler 2003, pp. 794–6).

An excellent illustration of terrorist substitution involves the placement of metal detectors in airports around the world in 1973, which immediately raised the cost of hijackings to terrorists. Based on the law of demand, rational choice theory predicts that hijackings would fall, all else equal. This is just what is observed in data collected by Mickolus (1980) for the period 1968–77 and shown in Table 13.5. Beginning in 1973, hijackings declined both in number and as a percentage of international terrorist incidents. Subsequent research by Enders and Sandler (1993, 1995), however, showed that metal detectors had the unintended consequence of significantly increasing hostage incidents and assassinations. Figure 13.5 summarizes this result. On the X axis we plot the number of hijackings, while the Y axis shows the number of other high profile missions (that is, hostage missions and assassinations). Metal detectors raise the price of hijackings, causing the budget line to rotate in from HN to HN'. Since hijackings and other high-profile missions are roughly equal in their "theatrical effects" in creating fear in the public and fostering recruitment of radicals, terrorists' likely see such missions as highly substitutable.

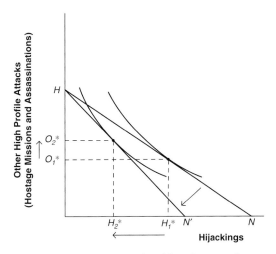

Figure 13.5 Metal detectors, reduced hijackings, and increases in other high-profile attacks.

The high substitutability is reflected in the low curvature of the indifference curves in Figure 13.5. As such, a higher price of hijackings creates a large cutback in hijackings from H_1^* to H_2^* and a substantial substitution into other forms of terrorism from O_1^* to O_2^*.

Numerous other terrorist substitutions across targets are reported in the literature. For example, Enders and Sandler (2012, p. 286) find that increases in homeland security in the USA and other countries coupled with changes in al Qaeda's leadership and finances have caused the organization to substitute away from logistically complex attacks such as hostage missions into simpler attacks such as bombings. Enders and Sandler (2012, p. 286) also provide evidence that fundamentalist terrorist organizations since 9/11 have substituted away from attacks in the Western Hemisphere and Europe, given the greater protection efforts there, to the Middle East and Asia where protections are not as strong and there are more population groups that might support the terrorists.

Terrorist Access to Income

Terrorist groups depend upon financial resources to carry out terrorism, so they obviously seek to maintain or increase their income. In Figure 13.3 from earlier, suppose a terrorist group secures new financing, perhaps as a response by sympathizers to a publicized attack. This would shift out the group's budget constraint *HN* (not shown), which would allow it to increase its terrorist activity and consume more of the composite good. As part of counterterrorism policy, governments attempt to reduce resources available to terrorists by disrupting their financing. For example, the USA Patriot Act of 2001 expanded the power of federal authorities to restrain money laundering through new regulations. Most of the provisions of the Patriot Act, including controversial protocols related to civil liberties, were renewed in the 2015 USA Freedom Act. Such counterterrorism income policies keep terrorists' budget constraints shifted in, thereby reducing the level of terrorist activity.

Terrorist Preference Formation, Preference Policies, and Social Media

Although economists typically take preferences as given, how terrorist preferences form and change are important for understanding terrorist actions and counterterrorism efforts. Social media can have important effects on terrorist preference formation including who becomes a terrorist and the strength of an individual's commitment to a terrorist cause. Two prominent terrorist organizations, ISIS and al Qaeda, have made extensive use of social media and other internet resources to recruit individuals, raise financing, and disseminate training materials and propaganda (Byman 2015). As former al Qaeda leader Osama Bin Laden said, "90% of the preparation for war is effective use of the media" (quoted in Byman 2015, p. 102).

We can think of a terrorist group's use of social media as a form of advertising, which is designed to alter the preferences of individuals whom the group seeks to influence. Building on the preferences and identity model from Chapter 6, the light indifference curves in Figure 13.6 show the initial preferences of four people over a composite good Y measured on the vertical axis and individual actions to support terrorism t plotted on the horizontal axis. For simplicity, assume the budget constraints of the four individuals are the same as given by HN. The absolute value of the slope of the budget constraint is P_t/P_Y where P_t is the average cost of terrorist actions and P_Y is the price of a unit of the composite good. Person A has upsloping indifference curves, meaning that she views terrorism as a "bad." A's optimal choice is represented by the corner solution, labeled a in the figure, in which all their income is allocated to the composite good. Person B has horizontal indifference curves, meaning that they receive utility from good Y and neither utility nor disutility from terrorism. B's optimal choice is also the corner solution, labeled b, in which all of their income is allocated to the composite good. Individual C has a moderate preference for both the composite good and terrorism as given by the modestly down-

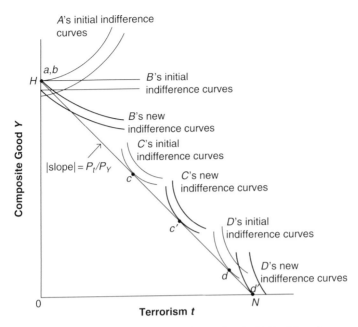

Figure 13.6 Terrorists' use of social media to alter individuals' preferences.

sloping indifference curves in the figure. Person *C*'s optimal choice includes both the composite good and terrorism as shown by point *c*. Finally, *D*'s indifference curves are steep indicating a high subjective valuation of terrorism relative to the composite good. Like *C*, *D*'s optimal choice includes both the composite good and terrorism, but *D* chooses more terrorism relative to *C* as shown by optimal choice point *d*.

Use of social media by a terrorist organization can have multiple effects within the rational choice model including increasing the organization's income or making it easier to conduct terrorist activities. Here we focus exclusively on social media as a means to alter preferences through modifications of people's identities and/or ideological commitments. To begin, assume the terrorist organization's advertising through social media has no impact on *A*. Hence, *A*'s optimal choice remains the corner solution labeled point *a* in the figure. The bold indifference curves of *B*, *C*, and *D* in Figure 13.6, however, indicate that the terrorist organization's social media campaigns affected how those individuals value terrorist actions. Person *B*'s indifference curves now slope down, indicating that he now values terrorism. Nevertheless, given the price or cost of terrorism, *B* still finds it optimal to allocate no income to terrorist actions; his optimal choice remains the corner solution at point *b*. Notice that the choices of *A* and *B* are the same even though *A* sees terrorism as a "bad" and *B* now sees it as a "good." What people do depends on what they subjectively value, but also on the prices or costs of various possible actions. Meanwhile, the terrorist organization's advertising has had a "salutatory" effect on *C* and *D*. As their indifference curves become steeper, the optimal choice point for each rolls down the budget line to the new optimum points c' and d', respectively. The new choice points reflect increases in the optimal amount of terrorism chosen by the two individuals. For *D*, a corner solution is reached in which he is no longer interested in choosing the composite good and allocates all resources to supporting terrorism. Such an extreme outcome in the model would apply to a suicide terrorist.

We can think of counterterrorist preference policies in broad terms as counter-advertising. In Figure 13.6, the goal of counter-advertising is to render the indifference curves less steep and, ideally, as horizontal or upsloping lines, so that heretofore terrorists would place no positive value on terrorism. Because terrorist preferences are formed within a complex web of social, historical, political, and economic factors, the advertising could take on many guises. For example, governments are aware of regions of the world where terrorists reside and where the potential for terrorist recruiting is high. Some of these regions face a relatively high risk of natural disasters such as earthquakes, hurricanes, and tsunamis. Extra-normal publicity of natural disaster relief in these regions by the USA and other countries at risk of terrorism might affect preference formation at the margin. For example, following the severe earthquake in Pakistan in October 2005, USA military personnel delivered tons of relief supplies to Pakistani victims. According to Pervez Hoodbhoy, a political commentator and professor of physics in Pakistan, "The [USA] Chinook helicopters are usually used to bomb al Qaeda but now they are being used to save people's lives so they have become birds of peace, and that ... so changes the view of America in Pakistan" (ABC News 2005).

Unfortunately, there are examples of what can be thought of as negative advertising from a counterterrorism perspective. Consider the abuse of Iraqi prisoners by USA military personnel in 2004. Images of abused prisoners were shown around the world in media outlets such as *CNN* and *Aljazeera* and they remain in social media platforms such as YouTube. The degrading images of Iraqi prisoners likely hardened the preferences of terrorists against the USA. They may have also created terrorist preferences among individuals who previously were at least neutral toward terrorist activities. Moreover, the persistence of images and videos of the scandal on Internet outlets represents a form of "capital stock" that terrorist organizations can repeatedly draw upon to enhance recruiting and fundraising and to keep recruits ideologically committed. In many parts of the world today, governments and terrorist organizations are engaged in an advertising game for the hearts and minds of people. In this advertising game, each side tries to gain market share by affecting what people know, or think they know, about themselves, governments, and terrorists. Such strategic interdependence between terrorists and governments, and among governments themselves as they attempt to counter terrorism, implies that game theory can be a useful supplement to the rational choice model in the study of terrorism.

Game Theory Models of Terrorism

Hostage Game between a Government and Terrorists

Here is a puzzle to be explained. Governments often pledge never to give in to terrorist demands when hostages are taken, yet governments sometimes deal with terrorists for the release of hostages. For example, in 1986 media reported that the Reagan Administration in the USA had broken from its non-negotiation policy by exchanging arms for hostages held in Lebanon (Lapan and Sandler 1988, p. 16). So why do governments often pledge, and why do they sometimes deal? We address this question using a simplified version of a hostage game due to Lapan and Sandler (1988).

In Figure 13.7, terrorists begin a one-shot sequential game by choosing whether to attack or not. If the terrorists do not attack, the status quo obtains with both players receiving a payoff of 0. If the terrorists attack, they either fail or succeed in capturing hostages, with the probability of logistical failure equal to θ. If they fail to capture hostages, both the terrorists and the government suffer losses with respective payoffs of $-L < 0$ and $-A < 0$. If the terrorists succeed in taking hostages, the government must decide whether to capitulate to terrorist demands. If the government gives in, the terrorists receive payoff $M > 0$ and the government suffers a loss of $-B < -A$. If the government does not give in, the terrorists obtain payoff $N < M$, where N can be negative or positive, and the government endures a loss of $-C < -B$.

The game is solved by backward induction under the assumption that the players maximize their expected payoffs. Working backwards, if the terrorists attack and achieve logistical success, the government will reluctantly but rationally capitulate, thereby suffering a loss of $-B$ rather than sacrificing the hostages at a greater loss of $-C$. Deducing that the

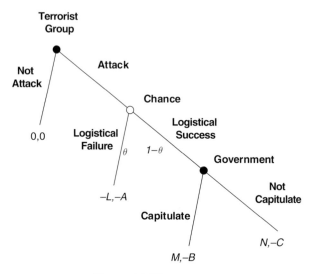

Figure 13.7 Hostage game.
Source: Adapted from Lapan and Sandler (1988).

government will capitulate, the terrorists infer that if they attack, their payoff will be $-L$ with probability θ or M with probability $1-\theta$. Thus, if they attack, their expected payoff Z will be $Z = \theta(-L) + (1 - \theta)M$, compared to a sure payoff of 0 if they do not attack. With a little algebra, it is shown that $Z > 0$ and hence they will attack if $\theta < M/(M + L)$. In words, knowing that the government will capitulate, the terrorists will attack as long as the probability of logistical failure is not too high given what they stand to gain from success.

It is obvious to both players that the terrorists' payoff to a successful attack is lower if the government refuses to give in to terrorist demands. Thus, it is understandable the government might hope to discourage attack by pledging beforehand that it will not negotiate with terrorists. But is the pledge credible? If the pledge is credible and hence believed by the terrorists, then it will lower the terrorists' expected payoff from attack. If the pledge is not credible and hence not believed, then there is no change in incentives, and the one-shot game predicts that the government will capitulate if hostages are taken. So what makes for a credible commitment to not capitulate? For a pledge to be credible, it must be coupled with some prior action that either eliminates the capitulation option or alters the payoffs so that capitulation is more costly to the government than noncapitulation. One example might be a reputation for noncapitulation earned in the past that would be damaged by capitulation in the present. Of course, this latter example suggests that the hostage game can be enriched if extended to a multiperiod framework, as found in Lapan and Sandler's (1988) more complete model.

We conclude by emphasizing that, from the government's perspective, solving the commitment problem is not equivalent to solving the hostage threat. Suppose the government achieves a credible prior commitment of no capitulation. Returning to Figure 13.7, the terrorists will anticipate that if they attack, the government will not capitulate, so their payoff will be $-L$ with probability θ or N with probability $1-\theta$. Thus, if they attack, their expected payoff Z will be $Z = \theta(-L) + (1 - \theta)N$, which again is compared to a sure payoff of 0 if they do not attack. If N is negative, meaning that the terrorists take a loss when the government stands firm, then obviously Z will be negative, and the terrorists will not attack. In this case the credible prior commitment has served the government's interest well. But suppose N is positive, as it might be if the terrorists gain notoriety from media coverage of their hostage taking. Then the same algebra shows that $Z > 0$ and the terrorists will attack if $\theta < N/(N + L)$. This means that if the likelihood of logistical failure is sufficiently low, the terrorists will still attack. If the attack succeeds in taking hostages, and if the commitment is truly credible as assumed, the government will not capitulate, and presumably the hostages will be lost. This result coupled with Brandt, George, and Sandler's (2016) empirical evidence that terrorist negotiation successes in hostage missions increases the risk of later kidnappings make clear why high profile hostage incidents are so difficult for governments.

Counterterrorism Games between Governments

The hostage game investigates strategic interdependence between a government and a terrorist organization. Here we consider strategic interdependence between governments themselves as they attempt to counter terrorism. Government counterterrorism efforts can be broadly classified as offensive or defensive. Offensive counterterrorism includes attacks against terrorist training centers, bases, resources, and leaders. Defensive counterterrorism includes screening devices in airports and buildings; risk-reducing protocols for diplomats, businesspeople, and military personnel; security alerts for private citizens and civil authorities; and disengagement and reintegration protocols designed to change the identities and ideological commitments of people who are terrorists or at risk of becoming so. Although counterterrorism actions cannot always be neatly classified as offensive or defensive, the distinction is useful because of the different incentives faced by nations as they attempt to counter terrorism.

Consider, for example, offensive counterterrorism efforts against a geographically dispersed organization like al Qaeda. The security benefits of degraded al Qaeda networks are nonrival, because they can be enjoyed by other nations at zero added cost, and nonexcludable, because they can be enjoyed by other nations even if they do not contribute to the efforts. Hence, a degraded al Qaeda organization is a public good for at-risk nations. According to public goods theory, these nations have an incentive to free ride on each other's efforts, which can lead to under-provision of offensive counterterrorism worldwide.

This naturally suggests modeling governments' offensive counterterrorism efforts as a prisoner's dilemma game (Sandler 2003). Assume in the effort to degrade a terrorist organization, nations A and B simultaneously choose between two levels of offensive effort, *High* and *Low*. To introduce numerical payoffs, suppose that security benefits and resource costs are calibrated such that the strategy pair (Low_A, Low_B) returns 0 to each nation. Suppose further that when either nation raises its effort to *High*, costs increase by 12 for that nation alone, and security benefits increase by 10 for each nation. The result is the prisoner's dilemma payoff matrix in Figure 13.8(a). To understand the payoffs, suppose B chooses *High*. If A also chooses *High*, then A enjoys an increased security benefit of $10 + 10 = 20$ but incurs an increased cost of 12, for a payoff of $20 - 12 = 8$; alternatively, if A free rides and chooses *Low*, then A receives an added benefit of 10 with 0 added cost, resulting in a higher payoff of 10; thus, A's best reply is *Low*. Suppose instead that B chooses *Low*. If A chooses *High*, then A receives an added benefit of 10 but an added cost of 12, for a payoff of -2; if A chooses *Low*, then A receives 0 added benefit and incurs 0 added cost, yielding a higher payoff of 0; thus, again A's best reply is *Low*. Hence, A's dominant strategy is a *Low* effort. The game is symmetric and the result is the unique but Pareto inefficient Nash equilibrium (Low_A, Low_B).

The prisoner's dilemma provides an explanation for low offensive counterterrorism prior to 9/11 (Cauley and Sandler 1988). However, the also familiar chicken game might be more useful in characterizing offensive counterterrorism since 9/11. Continue to assume that strategy pair (Low_A, Low_B) returns 0 to each nation and that when either nation increases its effort to *High*, an increased resource cost of 12 is incurred by that nation alone. Now assume there exist what might be thought of as diminishing marginal returns to security from offensive counterterrorism efforts. If one nation increases its effort to *High*, an added security benefit

(a) Prisoner's Dilemma

Player B

		High Offense	Low Offense
Player A	High Offense	8,8	−2,<u>10</u>
	Low Offense	<u>10</u>,−2	<u>0</u>,<u>0</u>

(b) Chicken

Player B

		High Offense	Low Offense
Player B	High Offense	8,8	4,<u>16</u>
	Low Offense	<u>16</u>,4	0,0

Figure 13.8 Offensive counterterrorism games between governments.
(a) Prisoner's dilemma
(b) Chicken

of 16 accrues to both nations, and if a second nation does the same, a further security benefit of 4 results.

The result is the chicken game of Figure 13.8(b), wherein a *High* effort is optimal for a nation only when the other nation chooses *Low*. To follow the payoffs, assume *B* chooses *High*. If *A* also chooses *High*, then *A* receives an increased security benefit of $16 + 4 = 20$ and incurs an increased cost of 12, for a payoff of 8; if *A* chooses *Low*, then *A* receives an increased benefit of 16 and incurs 0 added cost, for a higher payoff of 16; thus, *A*'s best reply is *Low*. Suppose instead that *B* chooses *Low*. If *A* chooses *High*, *A* receives an added security benefit of 16 and incurs an added cost of 12, for a payoff of 4; if *A* chooses *Low*, *A* has 0 added benefit and cost, for a lower payoff of 0; thus, *A*'s best reply is *High*. Two pure-strategy Nash equilibriums arise in Figure 13.8(b), $(Low_A, High_B)$ and $(High_A, Low_B)$, which are both Pareto efficient. Nation *A* prefers the first equilibrium, wherein *B* contributes the greater effort and *A* free rides, whereas *B* prefers the second. The essence of this game is that each nation believes "something serious must be done" to counter terrorism, but each prefers that the other take the lead.

The prisoner's dilemma and chicken games are distinguished by the size of security benefits relative to resource costs. Clearly, other games are plausible. For example, if security benefits are sufficiently high, then both nations can have a dominant strategy of *High* counterterrorism effort. To move away from symmetric games, if the security benefits vary between nations, one can have a dominant strategy of *High* while the other has a dominant strategy of *Low*.

In our offensive counterterrorism games, counterterrorism effort by one nation creates a positive security externality for other nations. In defensive counterterrorism games, however, counterterrorism effort by one nation can create a negative security externality for other nations. For example, greater homeland security efforts in the USA and other relatively wealthy states could cause terrorists to strike at less protected countries, as implied by the substitution principle. If nations ignore the negative security externalities of terrorism defense, the allocation of terrorism defense worldwide can be Pareto inefficient. Numerous defensive counterterrorism games are possible depending on how security externalities and resource costs are structured in the game (Arce and Sandler 2005).

Networking Perspectives on Terrorism

Linear Quadratic Model of Terrorist Group's Network

Figure 13.9 shows several ways that seven individuals might organize themselves into a terrorist network (similar analysis is done in Enders and Sandler 2012, pp. 250–1). The individuals are represented by the small circles or nodes in the diagram and the links between them are represented by lines. Panel (a) in Figure 13.9 shows a highly connected or dense network in which person 1 is connected to everybody and persons 2–7 are each directly connected to three other individuals. Panel (b) shows a star network in which person 1 is connected to everybody and persons 2–7 are each directly connected to person 1 only. Panel (c) shows a circle network (even though it is not shaped like a circle) in which each actor has two neighbors and one cycle exists across the network from any node back to itself (Jackson 2008, p. 28). A chain network is shown in panel (d), a combination of a star and chain in panel (e), and seven lone wolf terrorists in panel (f). Other network organizations are possible.

Of the networks in Figure 13.9, which would be most effective in promoting terrorism from the terrorists' point of view? One way to address the question is by using Chapter 7's linear quadratic model (LQM). Recall from Chapter 7 that each person i ($i = 1, 2, \ldots 7$ in our case here) obtains benefits from its own choice of action x_i based on the benefits function $B = ax_i$, where a is the benefit generated for each unit of

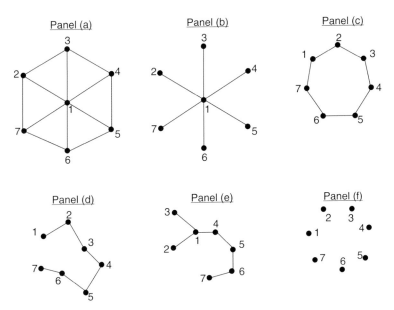

Figure 13.9 Terrorist network structures.

x_i chosen. Carrying out actions incurs costs, which for person i are determined by the cost function $C = (b/2)x_i^2$, where b is a cost parameter. Independent of the network, the benefit and cost functions imply that person i's optimal amount of action to maximize net benefits $B-C$ is $x_i^* = (a/b)$. For example, if $a = 2$ and $b = 1$, each disconnected individual in the network would choose 2 units of terrorism action (how the units are measured would depend on the application of the theory). We now have the aggregate amount of terrorism from the lone wolf structure (panel f in Figure 13.9); each individual chooses 2 units of terrorism action for a total of 14 units of terrorism activity.

Among the other networks in Figure 13.9, which would maximize terrorism output? To address the question, we now introduce influence weights w across the links of the network in Figure 13.9. An influence weight captures the ability of linked individuals to support one another through synergies such as sharing information and other resources (material and psychological). For example, if individuals 1 and 2 are linked, then 2's action of $x_2 = 2$ would, through a synergy effect, add to the benefits of 1 and vice versa. Assume that w_{12} is the benefit accruing to 1 from the synergy of the two individuals' actions. Person 1's benefit function would now be $B = ax_1 + w_{12}x_1x_2$.

Table 13.6 *Optimal terrorism network when secure and when vulnerable.*

(1) Network Structure from Figure 13.9	(2) Terrorism Output from Secure Network	(3) Number of Terrorists Destroyed	(4) Terrorist Output from Degraded Network
Highly Connected panel a in Fig. 13.9)	152.0	7	0.0
Star (panel b)	32.0	7	0.0
Circle (panel c)	28.0	3	13.1
Chain(panel d)	25.1	3	10.7
Star/Chain Combination (panel e)	25.7	3	9.1
Lone Wolves (panel f)	14.0	1	12.0

Notes: In columns 3 and 4, it is assumed that the government attacks the key individual in the network and that individual and those directly linked to him/her are destroyed.

The addition of $w_{12}x_1x_2$ to person 1's benefit function represents the strategic complementarity or synergy effect that occurs when 1 and 2 work together as terrorists. For simplicity, assume the weight parameter is $w = 0.25$ for all links in Figure 13.9. There are no links in panel (f), so there are no synergy effects. As noted, for $a = 2$ and $b = 1$, the lone wolf terrorism structure leads to a total of 14 units of terrorism activity. Column 2 of Table 13.6 shows the aggregate terrorism output for each network in Figure 13.9 assuming each is secure from attack. We now have an answer to our question regarding the optimal terrorism network. Of the six possibilities in Figure 13.9, the densest network, panel (a), generates the most amount of terrorism (152.0 units), all else equal.

Vulnerability of Terrorism Networks

But all else is not equal. Governments attack and disrupt terrorist networks. For example, suppose that a government attack against an individual in the network would destroy that person and the people directly linked to that person. Assume the government will attack the individual in the network that would degrade the terrorist organization's output the most. This can be seen as the "key player" in the network. Under these assumptions, the previously optimal dense network in panel (a) of Figure 13.9 would be completely destroyed by such an attack. Hence, the dense network is quite vulnerable. The lone wolf terrorism network (panel f in Figure 13.9) is not too effective in producing terrorism ("only" 14 units of terrorism output), but it is relatively secure. The government's ability to destroy one terrorist and others directly linked to the one would leave six lone wolves in play with aggregate terrorism activity of 12 units. Given that the terrorists expect the government to attack, would any of the other panels in Figure 13.9 outperform the lone wolf model? Columns 3 and 4 of Table 13.6 provide the answer. Column 3 shows the number of terrorists killed from the government's attack for each network, while column 4 shows the amount of terrorism output remaining for the remnant of each network. The circle network (panel c in Figure 13.9) is the "optimal" network in our stylized example in that it preserves terrorism output the most, conditional on government efforts to degrade the organization. Of course, the government's attack causes the circle network to cease to be a circle; the reformulated network following the attack is a chain with four remaining terrorists. Note also that when the terrorist network is coerced into a less dense structure, terrorism output falls substantially.

In an application of network concepts to terrorism, Kenney, Coulthart, and Wright (2017) analyze changes in the network structure of the extremist group al-Muhajiroun given efforts by British authorities to disrupt the organization. The authors found that al-Muhajiroun was initially a centralized network with a small number highly connected hubs each connected to many nodes. Following British disruption efforts, al-Muhajiroun's transitioned to a less centralized organization characterized by locally clustered nodes with various actors serving as "bridges" connecting different clusters. Although al-Muhajiroun lost some effectiveness over time, its network reorganization allowed it to become more resilient to British counterterrorism efforts while also achieving a moderate degree of terrorism capacity.

13.4 Empirical Studies of Terrorism Risk and Prevention

Risk Factors for Terrorism

Income and Terrorism Risk

Prominent explanations for terrorism include economic distress, political repression, and cultural and religious differences. A vast literature seeks to sort through the comparative importance of various explanations by means of systematic empirical observation. Empirical analysis of risk factors for terrorism faces serious conceptual and methodological challenges because terrorism is a tactic that can serve different strategic ends; hence, the motives for terrorism are likely to be diverse and complex. For example, a wide range of results have been reported in the literature on the empirical relationship between income (often measured by real GDP per capita) and terrorism outcomes (see Enders, Hoover, and Sandler 2016, pp. 196–202 and Danzell, Yeh, and Pfannenstiel 2016, pp. 2–4 for surveys). Here we briefly survey Enders, Hoover, and Sandler's (2016) (hereafter EHS) empirical investigation of the relationship between income and terrorism.

EHS note that the composition of terrorism has changed from attacks mostly perpetrated by issue-specific left-wing terrorist organizations in the 1970s and 1980s to attacks conducted primarily by fundamentalist religious groups since the 1990s. The left-wing attacks occurred mostly in relatively wealthy European countries. Despite the notoriety of the 9/11 attacks in the USA, most terrorist attacks by religious fundamentalists occur in poor countries, an outcome likely incentivized by the substantial defensive measures initiated by wealthy countries since 9/11 (EHS 2016, p. 196). These considerations suggest that any relationship between income and terrorism could have changed over time. Furthermore, EHS (2016, p. 200) hypothesize that different subsets of countries could experience different effects of income growth on terrorism risk. For example, poor countries would tend to experience more terrorism because they would not have enough resources to effectively counter terrorism and the opportunity cost to individuals who join a terrorist organization would be relatively low. For middle income countries, higher income could be associated with greater terrorism risk because more resources can lead to greater economic sustenance for terrorist organizations and middle income countries would still be relatively weak and unable to properly address grievances. Finally, after some threshold of income is reached, the opportunity cost of terrorism could be quite high and relatively rich states would be better able to address grievances, thus mitigating terrorism risk (EHS 2016, p. 201). These considerations lead EHS to deploy a nonlinear and flexible empirical model to assess the effects of income on terrorism risk (see also Ghatak and Gold 2017).

The authors' dependent variable is measured in multiple ways based on GTD and ITERATE data including the number of domestic terrorist incidents with casualties, number of transnational terrorist incidents with casualties, and attacks in pre- and post-1993 time periods (to reflect the rise of fundamentalist terrorism in the 1990s). The key explanatory variable is income as measured by real GDP per capita. Control variables include democracy, ethnic and religious tension, and unemployment. Among the authors' results, we highlight three: first, there is a nonlinear relationship between terrorism risk and income across multiple measures of the dependent variable; second, terrorism risk is generally highest for middle income countries, all else equal, and, third, the lack of a clear relationship between income and terrorism risk in previous empirical work may have resulted from an over-aggregation of terrorist incidents and periods, which "introduced too many confounding and opposing influences" (EHS 2016, p. 220).

Suicide Attacks

Iannaccone (2006) analyzes suicide terrorism using the supply and demand model. On the supply side of the market are the individuals who execute suicide missions. Iannaccone argues that, given appropriate incentives, a supply of would-be attackers will always exist. After all, many soldiers in wars past have undertaken missions despite knowing they faced near certain death. On the other side of the market are the terrorist organizations, whose demand for suicide attackers is derived from the demand for terrorist activity in general and for suicide missions in particular. In broad terms, the demand for suicide attackers depends on the value of the missions and the productivity of the attackers. For Iannaccone, demand is the crucial side of the market; since supply can be taken as given, it is the level of demand that will determine whether there exists an active market for suicide attackers. From an economic standpoint, it is also the more interesting side: terrorist organizations must somehow overcome free-rider problems as well as defections when they recruit and train suicide attackers.

Consistent with Iannaccone's approach, Berman and Laitin (2008) derive two demand-side hypotheses from a formal model of club goods. The first is that suicide bombing is more likely to be demanded by terrorist organizations that are part of a radical religious sect. The logic relies on Iannaccone's insight that terrorist organizations face a free-rider problem among those who support terrorism. It happens that religious sects are adept at overcoming free-rider problems among their members by providing spiritual and material goods that are excludable to nonmembers. Moreover, the sects are skilled at screening out those who are less committed and increasing the participation of the more committed (see also Iannaccone 1992 and Iannaccone and Berman 2006). Berman and Laitin's second hypothesis distinguishes between soft and hard targets. Hard targets are more heavily defended and therefore carry a higher risk of capture. Terrorist organizations are apt to be particularly sensitive to this risk because capture can result in information breaches that threaten the organization's survival. When a suicide bomb is successfully detonated, a high-quality operator is lost, but at the same time the risk of capture is eliminated. The hypothesis is then that suicide attacks are more likely to be demanded when targets are harder.

Drawing from multiple datasets on suicide terrorism from 1981 to 2003, Berman and Laitin provide empirical support for both hypotheses. Regarding the link between suicide attacks and religious sects, Berman and Laitin identify seven terrorist organizations that undertook at least one suicide attack in Israel or Lebanon. Three are radical Islamic organizations – Hamas, Hezbollah, and the Palestinian Islamic Jihad (PIJ). Of these, Hamas and Hezbollah are classified as strong religious organizations based on their provision of educational, medical, and welfare services. Because the social services are excludable, they can be used along with spiritual goods to support practices that screen out less committed people. The remaining four organizations are secular. The suicide data show that the religious organizations, particularly the two strong ones, were more effective in both the number and lethality of attacks. On average, the three religious organizations carried out 48.0 suicide attacks with 9.5 fatalities per attack, compared to 10.3 attacks and 2.6 fatalities per attack for the secular groups. Berman and Laitin also look at the proportion of terrorist attacks that involve suicide bombs. Consistent with their hypothesis, religious organizations are more likely to choose suicide bombing as a mode of attack. For two Islamic organizations (Hamas and PIJ, with Hezbollah unavailable), the proportion of attacks that were suicidal is 0.35, compared to 0.10 for the secular organizations.

On the hypothesis linking suicide attacks and target hardness, Berman and Laitin provide two supporting observations. First, suicide attacks are seldom directed at persons whose religion is the same as the bombers. In their full suicide dataset, Berman and Laitin find that only about one in eight victims has the same religion as the attacker. The explanation is that when targets are coreligionists, attackers tend to speak and appear much like the victims, making apprehension less likely. Thus coreligionists are softer targets against which other modes of attack are more effective. In contrast, when targets are of a different religion, the attackers are more easily profiled, making capture more probable. In this case the targets are harder, and suicide bombing is more likely to be the favored tactic. Berman and Laitin's second observation pertains to the comparatively greater incidence of suicide attacks on Israeli targets inside the 1949

Armistice line (also called the "Green Line") than in the West Bank and Gaza. For terrorist attacks inside the Green Line between September 2000 and July 2003, there were 511 fatalities, of which 78 percent were due to suicide attacks. In contrast, for similar attacks in the West Bank and Gaza, there were 341 fatalities, of which only 2 percent resulted from suicide attacks. Again, this pattern is consistent with the hard target hypothesis. Because of the large Palestinian population and the favorable terrain, Israeli targets in the West Bank and Gaza are softer and hence more suitable for shootings and bombs. Inside the Green Line the targets are more heavily defended and profiling is easier, so the targets are harder and thus favor suicide attacks. In a large sample empirical inquiry, Choi and Piazza (2017) also find evidence that suicide attacks are more likely to be used when targets are hardened.

Nuclear and Radiological Terrorism

Many governments fear that a terrorist group could create an explosion at a nuclear power reactor or disperse radioactive materials using a radiological dispersion device (RDD) known as a dirty bomb (National Council on Radiation Protection & Measurements 2014). Early, Fuhrmann, and Li (2013) (hereafter EFL) empirically assess the risk factors for nuclear and radiological (NR) terrorism. EFL compile a dataset of 40 incidents in which states were targeted with NR terrorism and 64 NR terrorism plots that did not become incidents over the period 1992–2006. The authors' dependent variable is coded 1 if a country experiences a NR terrorism incident in a given year, otherwise it is coded 0. Data on NR terrorism plots is used to test the robustness of the results. The key explanatory variable is the size of a state's nuclear program, measured by the number of nuclear power reactors per state per year. Control variables include a country's commitment to nuclear security, real GDP per capita, and presence of civil war. Based on a sample of 152 countries, EFL find that the nuclear program size of states has a significant and substantive effect on the risk of NR terrorism, all else equal. In particular, EFL find that an increase in nuclear program size from 0 to 0.79 (the sample mean) raises the risk of NR terrorism by 200 percent, all else equal.

Terrorism Prevention

In a world in which the number of terrorism incidents and fatalities have reached new heights (see Figures 13.1 and 13.2), it is critical to consider whether at least some terrorists can be disengaged from political violence. Terrorists who are truly committed to the terrorist cause are people who have "bought in" to the identities and ideologies of the violence-producing organizations. Such individuals have "hardened preferences" such as those with steep indifference curves in Figure 13.6. Moreover, individual terrorists are often deeply impacted by their peers in the social contexts of the terrorist group's network. Within such a network, individuals' preferences can become locked in and made even harder over time. How might such preferences become unlocked and turned toward peace? Clubb (2014) provides in-depth analysis of a case in which former Irish Republican Army (IRA) terrorists turned into peacekeepers. Clubb's study highlights the importance of cultivating preference changes among terrorists as well as the significance of understanding such changes in a network context.

Based on GTD data, the IRA conducted 2,607 terrorist attacks with 1,770 fatalities from 1970 to 1996. From 1997 to 2011, there were 50 terrorist attacks by the IRA with 10 fatalities. Since 2012, the IRA has conducted zero attacks (there are splinter groups from the IRA that carried out several attacks since 2012). What happened? In 1994, the IRA declared an end to its violent activities. When a violence-producing organization declares an end to violence, an opportunity arises to "lock in" its intention through disarmament, demobilization, and reintegration (DDR) (Clubb 2014, p. 845). DDR programs help former members of the organization to reintegrate into normal civilian life to reduce the risk of both recidivism and a return of the organization to violence. Clubb (2014, pp. 845–7) outlines the long and often arduous processes of the IRA's disengagement from violence through various DDR programs in the 2000s.

Based upon interview data of former IRA combatants and workers, Clubb discovered an important trigger for high-level terrorist attacks in Belfast, Northern Ireland. During the period of high tension in Northern Ireland (approximately pre-2000), the IRA and Loyalist militant groups were geographically separated in Belfast by "peace walls." While the peace walls kept the rival groups apart, they also reinforced notions of the "other" and "us versus them" identities (p. 849). Such identities could be readily exploited by radical leaders through each side's social networks. As such, relatively minor incidents could be escalated by motivated leaders into more severe forms of violence. Such escalations often occurred in the areas of the peace walls because these locations often drew parades, bonfires, and flag issues initiated by the two sides. Clubb characterizes the peace walls as locations of "interface violence" (p. 850).

To combat the outbreaks of violence at the peace walls, a mobile phone network of local peacekeeper citizens was begun in 1997. During periods in which the two sides would come close to each other through parades or other events, the citizen peacekeepers would use their phones to contact leaders on each side and encourage them to avoid violence. As part of its demobilization, former combatants of the IRA joined the mobile phone network in efforts to promote peace. What emerged in Belfast were a series of peace-keeping phone networks, some dominated by former combatants of the IRA and other violence-producing groups. The Police Service of Northern Ireland (PSNI) encouraged the development of the phone networks. For example, PSNI personnel formed phone links with former militants in which the police would call key leaders to encourage them to help keep the peace when activities seemed to be getting out of control. Despite challenges, the phone network "led to trust developing, which facilitated other militant groups to disengage, who could then work to contain the trigger causes of violence . . ." (p. 858). We view the attitudinal and trust changes described by Clubb as changes in preferences in Figure 13.6 toward indifference curves that are less steep in a downward way and perhaps even upsloping.

13.5 Economic Consequences of Terrorism

Terrorism and Economic Growth

Violent conflict can depress a country's economic growth by disrupting economic activity and destroying and diverting resources. Blomberg, Hess, and Orphanides (2004) provide a careful study of the growth effects of external conflict (including interstate war), internal conflict (including civil war and genocide), and international terrorist attacks, with emphasis on the latter. They base their analysis on a standard country-level growth model, wherein annual growth in per capita income is a function of lagged per capita income, investment as a share of GDP, and trade openness. To this baseline model the authors add explanatory variables that indicate the presence or absence of each of the three forms of violent conflict. Their sample involves 177 countries from 1968 to 2000, yielding approximately 4000 country-year observations.

The authors' central finding is that all three forms of conflict have a statistically significant negative impact on economic growth. For terrorism they estimate that the presence of an attack reduces growth by about 0.5 percentage points in that same year, with larger effects found for external and internal conflict. To better understand the mechanism by which terrorism affects growth, the authors consider how terrorism influences the composition of a country's economic activity. Interestingly, they find that a terrorist attack tends to decrease the investment rate by about 0.4 percentage points while increasing the government spending rate by the same amount. Notice this means that a terrorist event can have a further indirect effect by crowding out investment, which in turn impacts negatively on subsequent economic growth.

Terrorism and Microlevel Investment

Singh (2013) analyzes the impacts of terrorism in the Punjab region of the Indian subcontinent on farmers' investments in agricultural technology. Singh's empirical work is micro-oriented in that his dependent variable is measured by the investments of individual farmers in the Punjab from July 1978 to June 1990. The data include measures of each surveyed farmer's expenditures on wells including new purchases of electric motors, pipes, and water tanks, which Singh characterizes as long-term investments. Also included in the data are farmer expenditures on fertilizers and compost, which Singh classifies as short-term investments. Singh's key explanatory variable is the number of major terrorist events (at least three civilian fatalities) in the Punjab per district based on data from the South Asia Terrorism Portal. Control variables include district characteristics and year in which attacks occurred. Singh finds that major terrorism attacks significantly and substantively reduce the long-term investments of farmers in the districts where the attacks occur. Specifically, "a major terrorist attack in a district in a year ... causes a decline of more than 20 percent on average on investments in wells" (p. 154). In this way, the adverse effect of terrorism on farmers' long-term investments found by Singh represents one (micro) channel leading to terrorism's reduction in aggregate investment and growth found by Blomberg, Hess, and Orphanides (2004).

13.6 Bibliographic Notes

The literature on terrorism economics is so vast that we primarily highlight book-length treatments, special journal issues, and survey articles. Enders (2016) compiles an extensive volume of key articles on the economics of terrorism. Enders and Sandler (2012) and Caruso and Locatelli (2014) provide accessible and comprehensive books on the social scientific study of terrorism with emphasis on economic aspects. Studies on political economy aspects of terrorism can be found in special issues of *Journal of Monetary Economics* (King and Plosser 2004), *Journal of Conflict*

Resolution (Rosendorff and Sandler 2005), *Public Choice* (Rowley 2006, Sandler 2016a), *European Journal of Political Economy* (Brück and Schneider 2011), and *Oxford Economic Papers* (Sandler 2015).

Sandler (2014) surveys the literature on rational choice approaches to the study of terrorism, while Sandler and Arce (2007) and Enders (2007) do the same for game theoretic and empirical approaches, respectively. A survey of empirical literature on suicide terrorism and their own empirical inquiry are available in Santifort-Jordan and Sandler (2014). A rapidly growing literature analyzes terrorism and counterterrorism from the perspective of networks (Zech and Gabbay 2016, Scaife 2017). On lone wolf terrorism see Kaplan, Lööw, and Malkki (2015) and Hamm and Spaaij (2017).

14

Genocides and Other Mass Atrocities

Warfare is violent conflict involving the armed forces of states and/or nonstate groups. Civilians are often caught in the crossfire of wars and many are killed and injured. In World War II, for example, it is estimated that 45 million civilians were killed owing to the war (National WW II Museum 2018). Sometimes civilian destruction seems to be an inevitable outcome in war. For example, combatants may attack cities to degrade the enemy's warfighting industries and/or morale, and in the process many civilians are killed. But what are we to make of intentional, planned, and orchestrated destruction of thousands or even millions of civilians by states and nonstate actors? Destruction of people in war is troubling enough, but intentional killing of vast numbers of civilians might seem to be beyond comprehension. Following the Nazi Holocaust of the Jews and the destruction of other people-groups in Europe (1933–45), the field of "genocide studies" emerged as scholars sought to understand how such atrocities could occur and what might be done to prevent them. This chapter draws upon perspectives from genocide studies, as well as economics, to analyze the occurrence, consequences, and prevention of genocides and other forms of mass atrocity.

14.1 Definitions

In his path-breaking book on the Holocaust, *Axis Rule in Occupied Europe* (1944), Raphael Lemkin joined the Greek word *genos* (race, tribe) with the Latin *cide* (killing) to create a new word: *genocide*. At its most basic level, genocide means destruction of a people-group. Lemkin (1944, pp. xi–xii and 79) stressed that genocide is a "synchronized attack" and a "coordinated plan of different actions" that undermine one or more of eight "fields" that sustain a people's existence. Lemkin's eight fields are the political, social, cultural, economic, biological, physical, religious, and moral.

In December 1948, the United Nations (UN) Convention on the Prevention and Punishment of the Crime of Genocide established genocide as a crime under international law. Article II of the Convention defines genocide as "any of the following acts committed with intent to destroy, in whole or in part, a national, ethnical, racial or religious group, as such: (a) Killing members of the group; (b) Causing serious bodily or mental harm to members of the group; (c) Deliberately inflicting on the group conditions of life calculated to bring about its physical destruction in whole or in part; (d) Imposing measures intended to prevent births within the group; (e) Forcibly transferring children of the group to another group" (United Nations 2018). A substantial literature analyzes weaknesses of the Convention's conception of genocide including criticisms regarding groups left out (for example, political and gender groups), emphasis on physical destruction (parts a–c) to the exclusion of other fields of oppression noted by Lemkin, and difficulties with proving intent. As a result, many scholars have proposed their own definitions of genocide and other atrocities. To further complicate matters, there are other atrocities that are distinct from but often associated with genocide including war crimes, crimes against humanity, and ethnic cleansing.[1]

In this chapter we categorize genocide and other large-scale atrocity crimes under the broad category of mass atrocities. Following Anderton and Brauer (2018a), we define mass atrocity as "an episode of large-scale, intentional, and systematic violence committed against civilian populations." Large-scale suggests a violence against civilians (VAC) threshold, which is sometimes 1,000 civilian victims in the empirical literature. Intentional means an episode occurs by design as distinct from an accident. By systematic is meant planning and execution in addition to intent. Violence means threatened or actual physical or mental harm including

---

[1] According to Anderton and Brauer (2016b, p. 25), "*Crimes against humanity* are systematic attacks against civilians involving inhumane means such as extermination, forcible population transfer, torture, rape, and disappearances. *War crimes* are grave breaches of the Geneva Conventions including willful killing, willfully causing great suffering or serious injury, extensive destruction and appropriation of property, and torture. *Ethnic cleansing* is the removal of a particular group of people from a state or region using such means as forced migration and/or mass killing (Pégorier 2013). Ethnic cleansing is not, however, defined as an atrocity crime under the Rome Statute of the International Criminal Court."

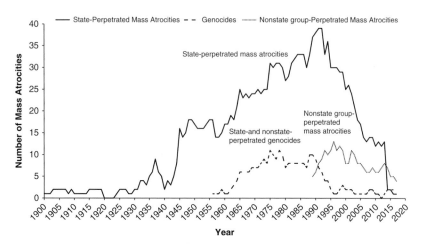

Figure 14.1 Mass atrocities perpetrated by states and nonstate groups over time.
Sources: Marshall, Gurr, and Harff (2017) for genocide data; Easterly, Gatti, and Kurlat
(2006), Ulfelder and Valentino (2008), and Ulfelder (2017) for state-perpetrated mass
atrocity data; and Eck and Hultman (2007) and Allansson and Croicu (2017) for state
and nonstate group mass atrocity data.

killing, forced relocation, torture, or rape. Finally, civilian means people
who are not part of combat, including prisoners of war.

14.2 Patterns of Mass Atrocity and Low-Level
Violence against Civilians

In this section we draw upon the following datasets to analyze trends in
atrocities against civilians: Political Instability Task Force Geno-Politicide
(PITF-G), Ulfelder and Valentino (2008) (UV), Ulfelder (2017) (ULF),
Easterly, Gatti, and Kurlat (2006) (EGK), Uppsala Conflict Data Program
One-sided Violence Dataset (UCDP-V), and Political Instability Task
Force Worldwide Atrocities (PITF-W) (see Appendix D.4). The top dark
line in Figure 14.1 shows the number of state-perpetrated mass atrocities
occurring per year in the world from 1900 to 2017. The dotted line shows
the same for nonstate groups from 1989 to 2017. The dashed line is the
number of genocides perpetrated by state and nonstate groups per year
from 1956 to 2016. Note that mass atrocities represent intentional destruction of civilians for any reason (for example, strategic killing of civilians in
war, destruction of a people-group per se (genocide)). Hence, we would
expect to see more state and nonstate (combined) mass atrocities than

genocides, which indeed is what the data show. Furthermore, although the dashed line in Figure 14.1 includes genocides perpetrated by both states and nonstate groups, almost all of the cases involve the state as the main perpetrator of genocide. Specifically, the PITF-G dataset from which the genocide data are drawn contains "only" four cases in which a nonstate group was a main architect of genocide: National Union for the Independence of Angola (UNITA) rebels (1975–94 and 1998–2002), Seleka and anti-Balaka militias in the Central African Republic (2013–16), and the Islamic State of Iraq and Syria (ISIS) (2014–16).

We highlight five implications of Figure 14.1. First, from 1900 to 2017, at least one state-perpetrated mass atrocity existed in the world every year except for 1920–3. Second, during the Cold War (1946–89) and immediate post-Cold War years (1990–2000), there were more than 10 state-perpetrated mass atrocities in the world per year and sometimes more than 30. Third, for the years shown by the dashed line (1956–2016), there was at least one genocide in the world each year except 2012. Fourth, state-perpetrated mass atrocities and genocides declined in frequency in recent years. Perhaps greater mass atrocity awareness and prevention policies from intergovernmental organizations (IGOs), nongovernment organizations (NGOs), governments, and businesses, along with new atrocity prevention norms (for example, the Responsibility to Protect or R2P) and legal institutions (for example, litigation by the International Criminal Court or ICC), have "raised the price" (cost) to states of perpetrating mass atrocities. Fifth, mass atrocities perpetrated by nonstate groups are a prominent aspect of the world's mass atrocity landscape. Specifically, there were at least four mass atrocities perpetrated by nonstate groups each year over the 1989–2017 period and, in some years, there were more than ten.

Table 14.1 shows estimated civilian fatalities for selected state and nonstate group mass atrocities. State-led mass atrocities are shown in the top half of the table, while nonstate actor cases are shown in the lower half. Note that two of the cases in the table report estimated fatalities of one million or more: the Holocaust and the India/Pakistan partition. Much research has gone into the Holocaust and rightly so, but comparatively little into the India/Pakistan partition event though it "is central to modern identity in the Indian subcontinent, as the Holocaust is to the Jews" (Dalrymple 2015, p. 2). Following the Holocaust, many adopted the phrase "never again." The data in Figure 14.1 and Table 14.1 reveal, however, that mass atrocities keep happening "again and again and again" (Totten 2004, p. 40).

Table 14.1 *Estimated civilian fatalities for selected state and nonstate-group mass atrocities.*

State/Nonstate Group	Time Period	Estimated Fatalities
State		
Angola	1998–2002	60,000
Democratic Republic of the Congo	1998–2017	101,684
Germany (Holocaust)	1933–45	9,939,850
India/Pakistan Partition	1947–48	1–2 million
Iraq	1991–2003	45,000
Rwanda	1994	750,000
South Sudan	2013–16	1,244
Sudan (Darfur)	2003–11	400,500
Syria	2011–13	3,867
Yugoslavia (Bosnia)	1992–95	228,000
Nonstate Group		
al Qaeda (9/11)	2001	2,753
Alliance of Democratic Forces for the Liberation of Congo-Zaire	1996–97	35,126
Boko Haram	2012–17	8,804
Islamic State of Iraq and Syria (ISIS)	2005–17	25,033
Kashmir Insurgents	1996–2006	2,812
Lord's Resistance Army	2002–11	5,722
National Patriotic Front of Liberia	1990–95	6,042
National Union for the Independence of Angola (UNITA)	1998–2002	60,000
Revolutionary United Front	1991–2000	5,963
Unknown Perpetrators in Syria	2012–16	128,710

Sources: Eck and Hultman (2007), Easterly, Gatti, and Kurlat (2006), Ulfelder and Valentino (2008), Dalrymple (2015), Schrodt and Ulfelder (2016), and Marshall, Gurr, and Harff (2017).

Table 14.2 shows the seriousness of mass atrocities relative to wars and terrorism. Since 1900, state-led mass atrocities have led to about three times more estimated fatalities and about 40 percent more fatalities per case than for interstate wars. Not surprisingly, World Wars I and II account for most of the interstate war fatalities. When these two wars are removed in row 4, estimated fatalities per case are about eight times greater for state-led mass atrocities than for interstate wars. State-led mass

Table 14.2 *Comparative measures of seriousness for mass atrocities, wars, and terrorism.*

Conflict Type	Number of Distinct Cases	Time Period	Seriousness	
			Total estimated fatalities	Estimated fatalities per case
State-Perpetrated Mass Atrocities	152	1900–2016	98,882,833	650,545
Nonstate group-Perpetrated Mass Atrocities	39	1989–2016	380,831	9,765
Interstate Wars	66	1900–2007	30,698,060	465,122
Interstate Wars Excluding WW I and WW II	64	1900–2007	5,485,122	85,705
Intrastate Wars	228	1900–2007	5,469,738	28,192[1]
Terrorism (Domestic and International)	170,350	1970–2016[2]	383,554	2.3

Notes:
[1] 32 intrastate war cases have no reported fatalities and two report only 550 and 9 fatalities, respectively. Hence, estimated fatalities per case is calculated as (total estimated fatalities minus 550 minus 9) divided by (228 minus 32 minus 2).
[2] Data for 1993 are missing.

Sources:
For Mass Atrocities:
Easterly et al. (2006), Eck and Hultman (2007), Ulfelder and Valentino (2008), Marshall et al. (2017), and Ulfelder (2017).
For Wars:
Sarkees and Wayman (2010) and the COW website at: www.correlatesofwar.org.
For Terrorism: Global Terrorism Database (2017).

atrocities relative to intrastate wars are about 18 times more severe in total estimated fatalities and about 23 times more serious on a per case basis. Consider also the seriousness of mass atrocities relative to terrorism. On average, an estimated 7,500 people were killed per day (over 100 days) during the 1994 Rwandan genocide. Hence, more were killed in 52 days of the Rwandan genocide (52 x 7,500 = 390,000) than were killed worldwide by domestic and international terrorists (383,554) over close to a half century (1970–2016).

Table 14.3 shifts attention from mass atrocities to intentional "low-level" civilian attacks by states, nonstate actors such as rebels and militia groups, and unknown perpetrators. Three critical messages

Table 14.3 *"Low-level" violence against civilians worldwide, various years.*

	Number of Attacks				Estimated Fatalities			
Year	States	Nonstate Groups	Unknown Groups	Total	States	Nonstate Groups	Unknown Groups	Total
1997	45	305	69	419	5,450	6,381	6,334	18,165
2002	50	202	42	294	3,208	5,523	400	9,131
2007	48	101	377	526	678	1,045	3,611	5,334
2012	228	260	300	788	4,400	3,334	20,931	28,665
2016	104	331	2,155	2,590	1,837	5,655	13,368	20,860

Source: Schrodt and Ulfelder (2016).

emerge from Table 14.3. First, is the dramatic increase in small-scale civilian attacks from 419 in 1997 to 2,590 in 2016. Second, a large majority of small-scale civilian attacks are *not* carried out by states; states carried out "only" 45 of 419 such attacks in 1997 and 104 of 2,590 in 2016. Third, small-scale civilian attacks are increasingly being committed by "who knows who"; that is, by unknown perpetrators. The number of civilian attacks by unknown groups was 69 of 419 in 1997, but 2,155 of 2,590 by 2016. Based on such data patterns, Anderton (2018) conjectures that the composition of intentional VAC worldwide may be undergoing a shift away from large and visible state-centric mass atrocities toward attacks that are smaller in scale and perpetrated by nonstate and unknown groups.

14.3 Key Actors in Mass Atrocities: Perspectives from Genocide Studies

The Triangle of Perpetrators, Victims, and Others

Figure 14.2 is a modification of the mass atrocity actors' triangle attributed to Ehrenreich and Cole (2005, p. 216). The right side of the triangle shows a spectrum of *perpetrator* behaviors ranging from those actively involved (that is, architects, bureaucrats, and on-the-ground "troops") to those who directly or indirectly aid atrocity such as businesses that supply atrocity-supporting goods (for example, IG Farben, which produced the Zyklon B gas used to exterminate Jews during the Holocaust). The lower portion of the triangle represents victims and their degree of vulnerability. The left

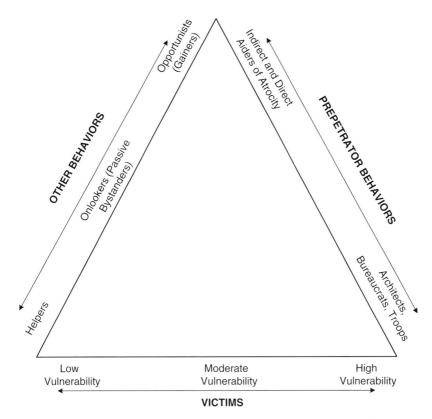

Figure 14.2 Mass atrocity actors' triangle.
Source: Adapted from Ehrenreich and Cole (2005, p. 216).

side shows a spectrum of other behaviors ranging from active forms of helping (for example, rescuing victims and resisting perpetrators), to merely observing (onlookers or passive bystanders), to not directly perpetrating atrocity but taking advantage of the abandoned wealth of the victims (opportunists or gainers).

We emphasize three points about Figure 14.2. First, owing to constantly changing circumstances before and during mass atrocities, actor identities are not necessarily fixed as perpetrator, bystander, and victim (Kalyvas 2006, pp. 21–2; Fujii 2011). The *behaviors* of atrocity actors can be fluid, for example, when one switches from bystander to perpetrator actions or vice versa. For example, Oscar Schindler initially joined the Nazi party and ran a confiscated factory in Poland in which he benefitted from Jewish slave labor (Staub 1993, p. 335). Later, Schindler risked his life to rescue Jews. Furthermore, actor behaviors in mass atrocities can be multiplex, that is, display more than one behavior at the same time. For example, during the 1994 Rwandan genocide, a Hutu who was killing Tutsi and thus behaving as a perpetrator acted (at the same time) to hide and thus rescue a Tutsi who was a former soccer teammate (Donà 2018, p. 12). Second, perpetrator and bystander behaviors reflect the actions of individuals, but also of organizations including states, IGOs, NGOs, and businesses. For example, when IGOs merely observe an ongoing mass atrocity, they would be classified as external bystanders who are onlookers. Third, people in mass atrocity contexts are situated in social networks that are often in flux (Donà 2018). Donà (2018) characterizes people acting as bystanders in mass atrocity contexts as "situated bystanders," which Anderton and Brauer (2018a) generalize to "situated perpetrators" and "situated victims."

Situational Paradigm in Genocide Studies

An early view of the Holocaust was that extraordinarily bad people perpetrated extraordinary evil, which Waller (2007, p. 59) labels the "Mad Nazi Thesis." One major problem with the Mad Nazi Thesis is that foundational laboratory experiments in social psychology revealed surprising degrees of human obedience to authority (Milgram 1963), conformity to erroneous social norms (Asch 1951), and extreme authoritarianism in hierarchical contexts (Zimbardo 1971). Such results emerged among ordinary human subjects and were seen to be applicable to mass atrocity contexts. The Mad Nazi Thesis was also undermined by research in the 1970s and 1980s that emphasized the "ordinary" origins of extraordinary evil (Waller 2007, chs. 5–8; Anderton 2015a, p. 156). In this research, perpetrators, gainers and onlookers in mass atrocities are "ordinary" people; they score within normal ranges on personality tests; their behaviors outside of atrocity contexts are normal and even admirable; and in social interactions with others they seem to be "fine people" (see perpetrator case histories in Waller 2007). The thrust of decades of research in genocide studies is that "ordinary" people get caught up in sociological and psychological situations leading into and during mass atrocities in which some end up supporting persecution of the out-group and others to do little to help the victims. These behaviors can be reinforced by economic situations in mass atrocities such as opportunities to grab the wealth of victims or advance one's career in the atrocity leader's bureaucracy (Breton and Wintrobe 1986).

Mass Atrocities: Why?

Empirical research suggests that mass atrocities are more likely to occur in societies with nondemocratic governments (Rummel 1995, Harff 2003). Some studies also find that ethnic, religious, and ideological differences between groups elevate mass atrocity risk, especially during wars or coup attempts (Kuper 1977, Robinson 2010, Fjelde and Hultman 2014). The first of Stanton's (2016) ten stages of genocide is the classification of people into "us and them" by race, religion, or nationality. During war or other crisis, government, rebel, and militia leaders may accentuate such group characteristics to achieve political and/or territorial control.

Nondemocratic regimes and ethnic/religious divisions can go part way in explaining mass atrocity risk, but a puzzle remains. Specifically, there are *many* areas around the world where nondemocratic polities and ethnic/religious divisions are entrenched, yet most do not experience mass atrocity (Valentino 2004). Hence, nondemocracy and ethnic/religious division may often be necessary for mass atrocity to arise, but they are hardly sufficient. Efforts to find a more encompassing explanation of mass atrocity are further complicated by the fact that motivations for intentionally attacking civilians can vary dramatically depending on whether the perpetrators are governments, rebels, or militia groups, whether such actors get caught up in retaliatory atrocities, and the evolving settings in which such actors operate.

For these reasons, some genocide scholars have approached the challenge of developing a more general explanation of mass atrocities by focusing less on political and social conditions and more on the "specific goals and strategies of high political and military leaders" (Valentino 2004, p. 2). This by no means implies that political and social conditions do not matter for understanding atrocity risk. Rather, leaders bent on conducting mass atrocity can often manipulate conditions to the point that society-wide support or indifference for mass atrocity is in place. As Valentino (2004, p. 2) notes, "the minimum level of social support necessary to carry out mass killing has been uncomfortably easy [for leaders] to achieve."

Given that leaders can often manipulate conditions to carry our mass atrocity, why would they do so? Genocide scholars largely agree that leaders strategically choose mass atrocity when they perceive that they are under severe threat during wars or other crises and other measures to overcome the threat have failed (Valentino 2004, Davenport 2007). States, but also rebel and militia groups, strategically resort to VAC when facing threats to their viability (Weinstein 2007; Wood 2010; Salehyan, Siroky, and Wood 2014; Wood and Kathman 2015). By destroying the opposing player and its civilian support structure the immediate threat is removed and the long-term threat is removed because the rival group no longer exists or is substantially weakened (Valentino 2004, p. 3). A second strategic reason for mass atrocity is ideology. According to Valentino (2004, p. 4), mass atrocity "can be an attractive strategy for regimes seeking to achieve the radical communization of their societies," which often leads to a "nearly complete material dispossession of vast populations." VAC can also arise as a tactical choice during wars or other crises. During civil war, for example, the economic strength of the government relative to that of the rebels can be important in determining the outcome of the war. A "non-natural" resource that is critical during war is people. If the government or the rebel group is comparatively strong in controlling populations, it is better positioned to acquire new recruits, deny recruits to the rival, and secure financing, information, and safe havens from civilians (Valentino, Huth, and Balch-Lindsay 2004; Kalyvas 2006, ch. 5; Weinstein 2007). The combatants sometimes resort to intimidation and VAC to compel civilians to support them or to deny such support to the enemy.

14.4 Rational Choice Models of Mass Atrocity Risk and Prevention

Risks of Mass Atrocity Onset

Following Anderton and Brauer (2016c), assume a key state leader (or core group of leaders) seeks to preserve or expand its political or territorial control Q (quantity of control). Suppose the leader perceives that its control is under severe threat from an armed out-group of a given size such as a rebel organization. Within the society-wide contest between the state and the rebel group are many civilians who might be supporting the rebel group or who may be perceived by the leader as a threat in their own right owing to their group identity. In this context, we can use the rational choice model to analyze why the state leader might choose to destroy civilians. Such analysis, unpleasant as it is, can help one discover risk factors for mass atrocities.

To understand a leader's decisions about securing control, assume in Figure 14.3 that the leader allocates income I between contesting rebels R and attacking civilians C. The leader's income constraint satisfies the equation $I = P_r R + P_c C$, where P_r is the average cost or "price" for each unit

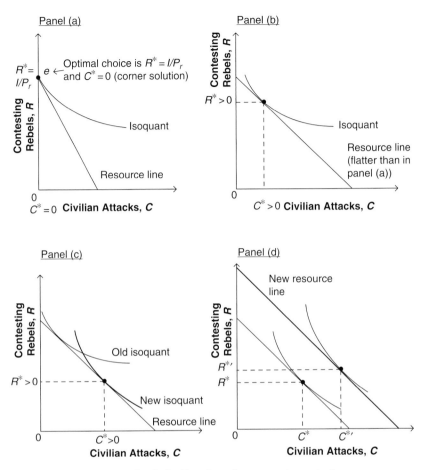

Figure 14.3 Leader's allocation of resources to contesting
rebels and attacking civilians.

of rebel attack and P_c is the "price" per unit of civilian attacks. Each panel
in Figure 14.3 shows the leader's straight line budget constraint. The curve
in each panel is the isoquant, which shows combinations of R and C that
achieve a given amount of control Q. The leader's optimal choice of R and
C in panel (a) occurs at corner solution e in which there are no civilian
attacks ($C^* = 0$) and all available income is used to contest rebels ($R^* = I/P_r$).
Panel (b) shows an interior solution in which the leader chooses to
intentionally kill civilians ($C^* > 0$) and to contest rebels ($R^* > 0$). Finally,
panels (c) and (d) show that the leader contests rebels, but attacks civilians
even more relative to panel (b).

Figure 14.3 illustrates several reasons why the state might attack civilians. The difference in moving from panel (a) to (b) is that the price of attacking civilians P_c has gone down, all else equal. This causes the budget line to be flatter in (b) than in (a). As disturbing as it is to contemplate, if attacking civilians is sufficiently inexpensive (that is, P_c is low), the leader finds it "cost effective" to intentionally attack civilians along with contesting the rebels when maximizing control. This is an example of the law of demand, which we have seen elsewhere in this book. In this context, the lower the price of attacking civilians, the greater the number of civilian attacks, all else equal. What would make the price of civilian attacks low? Suppose people associated with the leader's group believe it is "socially acceptable" (perhaps even "good" for the body politic or for one's own career advancement) to attack civilians from designated out-groups. This could occur, for example, if regime-inspired "advertising" (propaganda) gives license to citizens to attack and loot the assets of a designated out-group or "successful" perpetrators are promoted within the regime. Under such conditions, it would be relatively inexpensive for the leaders to recruit personnel into killing civilians and the price of such activities would be comparatively low.

The key difference in moving from panel (b) to (c) in Figure 14.3 is that the isoquant associated with inputs R and C has changed. Specifically, in panel (c) the isoquant has become steeper and "rolled down" the budget line such that even more civilians are attacked relative to panel (b). When the isoquants change, it implies that the underlying production function for control has changed. In our context, when the isoquant becomes steeper it implies that the marginal productivity of civilian attacks has gone up, the marginal productivity of rebel attacks has gone down, or some combination of the two. High marginal productivity of civilian attacks would occur, for example, if civilians were concentrated in villages with dense road networks, which government troops could easily exploit (Zhukov 2016). Civilian attacks would also become more productive when peacekeepers providing safe havens to civilians depart and leave civilians to their fate. Meanwhile, a decline in the marginal productivity of attacking rebels could occur, for example, if a third party sent in military forces to support the rebels. Finally, panel (d) relative to panel (c) shows what happens when the in-group has more resources I. In panel (d), the budget line shifts out in a parallel fashion, which leads to more civilian attacks assuming C is a normal input.

Mass Atrocity Prevention

Figure 14.3 can be "pointed in the other direction" to identify elements that could protect civilians. For example, panel (a) relative to panels (b), (c), and (d) has a relatively flat isoquant and a comparatively steep and low budget line, which create a "gravitational pull" into the corner solution *e* in panel (a) in which no civilian attacks occur. Policies that could help bring about outcome *e* include the creation of safe havens for vulnerable civilians, counterpropaganda and threats of litigation that offset the state's efforts to recruit perpetrators, and reduction of the regime's income by, for example, cutting off foreign aid.

Identity-Modified Preferences in Mass Atrocity Contexts

Chapter 6 emphasized individuals' identities and social contexts in understanding conflict and peace. The identities and social contexts of people lie at the core of genocides and other forms of mass atrocities. Specifically, an out-group is identified by an in-group as "other," usually based upon some ethnic, religious, and/or political identity. In Rwanda in 1994, for example, Hutu extremists used radio broadcasts, print media, and political rallies to label Tutsis as threatening, inferior, and accomplices of the rebel group, the Rwandan Patriotic Front (Straus 2006). Here we extend the identity-modified preferences model of Chapter 6 (Figure 6.5) to analyze how people can shift their behavior in atrocity contexts owing to identity manipulations by architects.

Assume Figure 14.4 applies to a range of individuals within a society. Political leaders would like such individuals to support mass atrocity against an out-group. The individuals are not from the out-group, but are potential recruits into mass atrocity work. Each person in Figure 14.4 has individualized preferences over acts of meanness *M* directed against the out-group and consumption goods *C*. If an individual finds identity association with the perpetrators to be repugnant, the person would obtain disutility from acts of meanness and thus view such acts as a "bad." If an individual has no identity association or disassociation with the perpetrators, it would obtain utility only from consumption and thus view acts of meanness as a "neuter." An individual with a positive identity association with the perpetrators, however, would obtain utility from acts of meanness and thus view such acts as a "good." We make two assumptions for analytical convenience. First, acts of kindness *K* are negative acts of meanness. This implies that one who views meanness toward the out-group as

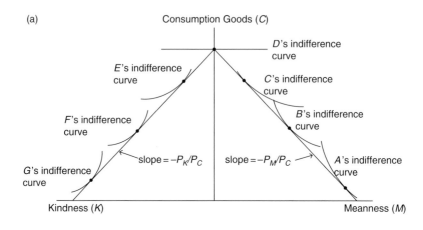

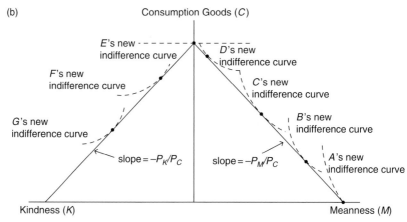

Figure 14.4 Effects of propaganda on individuals' preferences.
(a) Initial pattern of preferences
(b) Modification of preferences owing to propaganda

a good will view kindness toward the out-group as a bad and vice versa. Also, one who views meanness as a neuter will view acts of kindness as a neuter. Second, each individual in Figure 14.4 has the same income I, which is allocated to purchasing units of C at price P_c and to directing acts of meanness M or acts of kindness to the out-group at unit cost P_m or P_k, respectively.

The right side of panel (a) of Figure 14.4 shows the initial preferences of people who view meanness as a good. The left side of panel (a) shows people whose initial preferences reflect kindness directed toward other groups as a good. Given a large enough sample, the preferences of people in society range from those who are quite harsh toward outsiders (for example, individuals *A* and *B* in panel (a)), to those whose preference for meanness is less intense (individual *C*), to those who obtain no utility or disutility over *M* or *K* (individual *D*), to those who have various preference strengths to be kind to outsiders (individuals *E*, *F*, and *G*). The people in panel (a) can be influenced by the ideologies made available over the airwaves and through social media. For example, the Ministry of Propaganda and Public Enlightenment, led primarily by Joseph Goebbels, played a critical role in manipulating people within German society to support or not resist the outing of Jews and other people-groups during the Holocaust (United States Holocaust Memorial Museum 2017).

In panel (b) of Figure 14.4, extremist propaganda leads to steeper indifference curves for those with a predisposition to meanness on the right side of the figure. If enough such people "get the message" of extremism, they will direct greater meanness against outsiders. Meanwhile, those who waver with indifference or mild kindness to outsiders (for example, individuals *D* and *E* in panel (a)) may become indifferent or "convert" and adopt a preference for enmity against outsiders (see *D* and *E* in panel (b)). Finally, individuals *F* and *G* may still direct acts of kindness to outsiders, but less so than before as shown in the figure. Regarding mass atrocity prevention, governments, IGOs, and NGOs can devote resources to counter the atrocity architects' messages such that the preferences of people tilt toward kindness.

14.5 Game Theory Models of Mass Atrocity Risk and Prevention

The Race to the Bottom: VAC in Civil Wars

Figure 14.5 considers the strategic incentives facing a government (*G*) and a rebel group (*R*) to conduct VAC. Assume *G* is the row player, *R* is the column player, and each contests the other in a civil war. Since civilians can be sources of funding, information, logistical support, and recruits, the player who has an advantage in controlling them will have an advantage in the war, all else equal. By carrying out VAC, a player can compel civilian support and/or deny civilian support to the enemy. In Figure 14.5, the two strategies available to each player are to conduct or to abstain from VAC. In each cell of the matrix, the first number is the payoff to *G*, the second is the payoff to *R*, and the third is the payoff to civilians. Although civilians are not making choices in Figure 14.5, they face the consequences of the choices of *G* and *R*, so we track their fates with the third number in each

	R	
	No VAC	VAC
G No VAC	−1,−1,−1	−2,1, −2
VAC	1,−2, −2	−1,−1,−3 *

*Nash equilibrium

Figure 14.5 Strategic incentives for violence against civilians in civil war.

cell. We are not concerned with the unit of measure of the numbers (perhaps −1 is −1 billion US$) because it is the ordinal rank of each player's payoff that will determine its choices. Nevertheless, we put negative signs in front of most payoffs as a reminder that war is costly (recall the 5 Ds from Chapter 1), including for civilians. Moreover, VAC is especially costly (obviously) for civilians. Government and rebel leaders often do not care about civilians per se, but instead view them as an exploitable resource to achieve tactical and strategic goals in war (Kalyvas 1999, Slim 2007, Metelits 2010, Mitchell 2015).

In the upper left cell of Figure 14.5, both G and R abstain from VAC. Assume the fighting is stalemated in this case, that is, neither G nor R win the war, but neither loses. Since war is costly, we give each combatant a payoff of −1. Civilians also lose from war, but they are not being deliberately attacked, so they too get a payoff of −1, which leads to the payoff set −1, −1, −1 in the upper left cell. The upper right cell shows the outcome when G abstains from VAC, but R does. By exploiting a critical resource in war when the rival is not exploiting that resource, R achieves the upper hand in the war and we assume G loses. This leads to a payoff of −2 for G for experiencing costly war and losing and +1 for R for winning the war and taking over the government. Meanwhile, civilians face a double loss; they experience costly war and intentional attacks against them by R. Hence, we assign a payoff of −2 to the civilians, which leads to the payoff set −2, +1, −2 in the upper right cell of the matrix. The lower left cell is the obverse of the upper right cell. In the lower right cell, both G and R carry out VAC. In this case, the war is stalemated and G and R each receive a payoff of −1 owing to war's costliness. Civilians, meanwhile, face a triple loss. They not only suffer from the costs of war, they also face attacks from both G and R. Hence, we assign a payoff of −3 to civilians in the lower right cell.

The predicted outcome of the game is a "race to the bottom" in which both G and R choose to victimize civilians, leading to payoffs $-1, -1, -3$ in the lower right cell of Figure 14.5. Note that each player has a dominant strategy to carry out VAC. For example, if R abstains from VAC (putting the game in column 1 of the matrix), G's best reply is to carry out VAC ($+1 > -1$). If R instead carries out VAC (putting the game in column 2 of the matrix), G's best reply is once again to carry out VAC ($-1 > -2$). Similar logic implies that VAC is a dominant strategy for R also. The outcome in the lower right cell of the matrix is a Nash equilibrium, but it is Pareto inferior. Specifically, $-1, -1, -1$ in the upper left cell gives the same payoff to G and to R as the lower right cell, but a higher payoff for civilians ($-1 > -3$). Why does this better outcome not prevail? Assume the outcome is temporarily in the upper left cell in which there is no VAC. From there, G has an incentive to change its action and carry out VAC to gain the upper hand in the war and defeat R. Beginning from the upper left cell, R also has an incentive to change its action and carry out VAC to gain the upper hand in the war. Both players know the strategic setting they are in and each is lured by the precept, "if we don't play our dominant strategy, they will, and we will lose the war." The biggest losers in the game are civilians.

One way in which the outcome in Figure 14.5 can be changed is through third-party intervention. Suppose third parties are able to implement policies to induce R and G to end the war, such as peace missions and/or subsidies to peace. Since Figure 14.5 assumes the two sides are fighting, ending the war would achieve an outcome not shown in the matrix. Suppose such third-party efforts lead to a payoff set of $+1, +1, +1$ for our three actors. Not only would the war be over, so would strategic VAC which accompanies war. But even if third parties are not able to end the war, they can still attempt to manipulate incentives to protect civilians. Suppose, for example, that the international community is able to detect and punish VAC during war through peace enforcement, naming and shaming, or cutting off of aid and trade. Assume that third parties are able to impose in Figure 14.5 an added penalty of -2 to an actor that chooses VAC. G's payoffs in the second row would change from $+1$ to -1 and from -1 to -3. This would now make "No VAC" a weakly dominant strategy for G. Similar changes would also apply to R. The outcome of the game would then change to the upper left cell in which no VAC occurs.

Evolutionary Game Theory and the Social Evolution of Aggression and Peace

The games covered in Chapters 5 and 13 and so far in this chapter focus on a small number of players.[2] Suppose, instead, we have a large number of individuals in society – a "population" – and we would like to know what strategies might emerge and persist in that population. If we think of the strategies that emerge (or that disappear) as "traits," we can focus on the evolution of traits to see which emerge and which fall out of favor. Evolutionary game theory is designed to understand the emergence and falling away of traits in a population. Here we use selected elements from evolutionary game theory to analyze how people's social contexts and adoption of traits can change over time (sometimes dramatically) and how such elements can be manipulated by those promoting mass atrocity as well as those seeking to protect civilians.

Stage Game and Fitness Equations
Imagine a village of 10,000 people. Assume an authority group seeks to perpetrate atrocity against an out-group and would like the village to support its aggression. Assume the out-group encompasses people who are not part of the village. Suppose 1,000 of the villagers (10 percent) already have a latent desire for aggression against the out-group. Assume the other 9,000 (90 percent) would resist aggression against the out-group under current social conditions. As the village currently stands, it would not be particularly useful to atrocity architects in perpetrating aggression against the out-group because a relatively small proportion of the village's population supports such action. Under certain conditions, however, the authority group can engineer a social metamorphosis of the village such that many people come to support aggression.

Assume each person in the village has one of two dispositions toward people from the out-group: peaceful (*P*) and aggressive (*A*). The villagers are not genetically hardwired to a disposition; people have free will, so each can choose the trait that it prefers. Humans are social creatures, so there is a lot of interaction among people in the village at work, in the marketplace, and so on. Suppose Figure 14.6 represents the payoffs to any two individuals in the village, say Anne (row player) and Bob

---

[2] Parts of this section are adapted from Charles H. Anderton's article, "The Social Evolution of Genocide across Time and Geographic Space: Perspectives from Evolutionary Game Theory" published in *The Economics of Peace and Security Journal*, volume 10, issue 2, pp. 5–20, 2015. Material is reprinted with the kind permission of *The Economics of Peace and Security Journal*. Copyright © EPS Publishing 2015.

Bob

Peacefulness (*P*)   Aggression (*A*)

Figure 14.6 Stage game for the social evolution of peace and aggression.

(column player), when they socially interact. For example, Anne and Bob's interaction leads to a per person payoff of 6 when each chooses the peace trait (*P*). If both choose aggression (*A*), each receives 4 from their encounter. If Anne is peaceful and Bob aggressive, Anne receives −2 and Bob 2 as shown in the upper right cell of the matrix (the obverse interaction is shown in the lower left cell). In evolutionary game theory, Figure 14.6 is the "stage game." It governs the payoffs to individuals in all pairwise social interactions in the village. The payoffs reflect the village's institutions, history, and culture. Although simplified, Figure 14.6 is a type of "social genome" for the village.

In social contexts, the traits of people – peaceful (*P*) and aggressive (*A*) – can be thought of as strategies they choose in their social interactions. Assume for simplicity that people cannot play a mixed strategy in which they choose *P* or *A* with a random device. Imagine two people are randomly drawn from the village and paired with one another. The pairing represents a social encounter and the payoff to each person is governed by Figure 14.6. Many social encounters occur in the village throughout the day and we can construct the expected payoff for each strategy from an encounter. Let *N* represent the number of people in the village (here *N* = 10,000) and n_A the number who initially choose the aggressive trait (here n_A = 1,000). It follows that the number of people initially choosing peacefulness n_P is equal to *N*-n_A (n_P = 9,000). Define r_A as the ratio of the village's population that has actually adopted the aggressive trait at a point in time. Given our numbers, $r_A \equiv (n_A/N) = (1,000/10,000) = 0.1$. In other words, 10 percent of the population has adopted the aggressiveness trait. Note that if you were a member of the village's population, you would have a 10 percent chance of interacting with an aggressive type and a 90 percent chance of interacting with a peaceful type in a random pairwise encounter.

From Figure 14.6, the expected payoff F_P to a villager who adopts the peaceful strategy in a random pairwise encounter is:

$$F_P = -2(r_A) + 6(1 - r_A) = 6 - 8r_A. \qquad (14.1)$$

The expected payoff F_A to a villager adopting aggression in a random pairwise encounter is:

$$F_A = 4(r_A) + 2(1 - r_A) = 2 + 2r_A. \qquad (14.2)$$

F_P and F_A represent the "fitness" of the P and A traits in the village. If peace is highly valued, then P would be relatively fit. If aggression is rewarded, then the A trait would be relatively fit. Equations (14.1) and (14.2) show that each strategy's fitness depends on the ratio of the villagers playing each strategy and the payoffs generated from pairwise social encounters.

Selection Dynamics and Evolutionary Stable State

In social environments, humans look around and learn from the behavior of others. They observe which traits are rewarded and which are penalized and they tend to mimic successful traits. In violence contexts, people who refuse to support aggression toward an out-group can be subject to dire penalties including incarceration or execution. In this way, such people are "weeded out" of the population. Others may act "as if" they support aggression to save their lives or careers or their family and friends. In our model we treat such people as adopting aggression.

Selection dynamics in evolutionary game theory describe how fitter strategies are adopted and less fit strategies are rejected over time. We explain such dynamics intuitively in Figure 14.7 where we plot fitness equations (14.1) and (14.2) in panel (a). Along the X axis we measure the actual ratio of the village's population adopting aggressiveness r_A at a point in time which necessarily lies between 0 and 1. On the Y axis we plot the fitness of the peaceful and aggressive traits, F_P and F_A. The fitness equations cross at a critical value of 0.4, which we call $r_A^{critical}$. There are two important points to keep in mind about $r_A^{critical}$. First, the actual proportion of aggressive types in the village r_A can be greater than, less than, or equal to $r_A^{critical}$. Second, $r_A^{critical}$ is not an equilibrium in an evolutionary sense, as will be explained shortly, even though the two lines cross there.

To begin our analysis of social evolution in the village, suppose the actual ratio of villagers adopting aggression at this moment in time, which we call time 0, is $r_A^0 = 0.25$ as shown in panel (a) of Figure 14.7. At this value of r_A, peacefulness is more rewarding (fitter) than aggression in the village ($F_P > F_A$), which leads to a growing proportion of people choosing peace over time. Hence, r_A declines over time, as shown by the leftward-pointing arrows, until the village arrives at an evolutionary stable state in which all villagers adopt peace ($r_A^* = 0$),[3] Suppose from $r_A^0 = 0.25$ in panel (a), the atrocity architects insert aggressors from the outside to raise r_A^0 to 0.35. Such a policy is insufficient to turn the social evolution away from peace because $r_A^0 = 0.35$ is less than $r_A^{critical} = 0.4$; hence, peace is still fitter than aggression ($F_P > F_A$). But suppose the "invasion" is coupled with policies that increase payoffs in aggressive/aggressive encounters from 4,4 to 5,5 and reduce payoffs in peaceful/peaceful encounters from 6,6 to 5,5 in Figure 14.6. As shown in panel (b) of Figure 14.7, the small changes in payoffs cause $r_A^{critical}$ to fall to 0.3. Coupled with the increase in r_A^0 from the invasion, r_A^0 is now greater than $r_A^{critical}$. Hence, in panel (b), aggression is fitter than peace ($F_A > F_P$), leading more people to choose aggression. Over time, r_A increases as shown by the rightward-pointing arrows in panel (b) until arriving at an evolutionary stable state in which all villagers are aggressive types ($r_A^* = 1$).

Third-Party Intervention

Third parties can attempt to offset the social evolution of aggression. For example, insertion of a sufficiently large number of peacekeepers would reduce the initial proportion of aggressors r_A^0 below the critical value ($r_A^0 < r_A^{critical}$), thus tipping the village into a social evolution of peace. But suppose, owing to budget or political constraints, only a few peacemakers, or none at all, are inserted into the village. Another policy is to manipulate payoffs from the village's social encounters such that $r_A^{critical}$ rises so that $r_A^0 < r_A^{critical}$. For example, by reducing payoffs to aggressors in social encounters in the stage game, the F_A line in panel (b) of Figure 14.7 would shift down (not shown), implying lower expected payoff to

---

[3] According to Maynard Smith (1982, p. 204), a "population is said to be in an 'evolutionarily stable state' if its genetic composition is restored by selection after a disturbance, provided the disturbance is not too large." In our context, possible "genetic compositions" are aggression and peacefulness. In panel (a) of Figure 14.7, random generation of a small number of aggressive types (that is, a "small disturbance") would cause r_A to rise slightly above $r_A^* = 0$. Since peace would be fitter than aggression following this disturbance, ($F_P > F_A$ at small r_A), selection would reduce the ratio of aggressive types and restore $r_A^* = 0$.

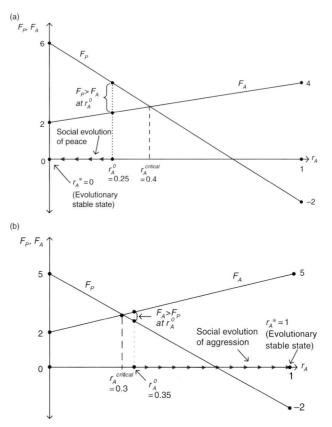

Figure 14.7 Fitness equations and the social evolution of peace and aggression.
(a) Social evolution of peace
(b) Social evolution of aggression

aggression for any given r_A. Furthermore, if the village's peaceful types achieve greater rewards in social encounters, the F_P line in panel (b) would shift up (not shown), implying greater expected payoff to peacefulness for any given r_A. Such line shifts would increase $r_A^{critical}$ which, if large enough, would achieve $r_A^0 < r_A^{critical}$ and thus a social evolution of peace. Numerous policies could alter interpersonal payoffs toward peace in the village. Examples include cell phone videos that expose aggressive actions, widespread presence of journalists, counterpropaganda through social media, embassy protection for peace proponents, and sanctions against aggressors.

Figure 14.7 also points to an important issue regarding civilian protection. If the social evolution of aggression in panel (b) has been going on for some time, the ratio of aggressors in the village will be relatively high and rising toward $r_A = 1$. At this point, bringing in peacemakers and/or implementing policies to alter the payoffs from social encounters will need to occur at significantly higher levels than otherwise to achieve $r_A < r_A^{critical}$ because r_A is so high. Once the growth of the social acceptance of aggressiveness is underway, delayed implementation of prevention policies will becoming increasingly unlikely to alter the aggressive dynamic.

Social Evolution of Aggression in Rwanda in 1994

During the 1994 Rwandan genocide, some 750,000 Tutsi and moderate Hutu civilians were killed by extremist Hutus (Table 14.1). Since 1994, numerous studies have probed the causes, consequences, and policy failures of the Rwandan genocide (among a vast literature see Power 2002; Straus 2006, 2008; Fujii 2009; and Friedman 2016). Our focus here is not a top-down or macro view of the 1994 Rwandan genocide, but analysis of the social evolutionary dynamics of genocide onset and spread at the local or micro level, specifically, for the rural commune of *Gafunzo*. At the time of the genocide, Rwanda was made up of 12 administrative areas known as prefectures. Each prefecture contained subprefectures or districts, which were further subdivided into communes of which there were 154 across the country (Rwanda's administrative organization is different today). In 1994, communes in Rwanda averaged 182 square km in size and more than 50,000 inhabitants (Straus 2006, p. 67). According to Straus (2006, p. 69), an estimated 6,000–6,800 Tutsi civilians were killed in Gafunzo during the genocide.

What emerged in Gafunzo in the early days of the genocide were "an initial gap in social authority, confusion, and fear – a short rupture" and a "space of opportunity" for mass murder to take root and spread (Straus 2006, p. 71). Among the social evolutionary factors that fostered genocide in Gafunzo, consider first the assassination of Rwanda's Hutu president, Juvénal Habyarimana, on April 6, 1994. This event, coming in the midst of civil war between the Hutu-led government and the Tutsi-led Rwandan Patriotic Front, catalyzed a sense of crisis in the country. Hutu extremists, who perceived an existential threat to their power and position in society, began to cajole moderate Hutu leaders to help exterminate Tutsi civilians. Those who refused were murdered or fled. Meanwhile, some ordinary Hutu civilians willingly joined the extremist cause, others joined with reluctance, and still others resisted and were killed or forced into hiding. In a stage game like Figure 14.6, the catalyzed crisis tilts the payoffs in intra-Hutu social encounters in favor of aggression and against peacefulness. Such changes shift up the aggression fitness line and shift down the peaceful fitness line in Figure 14.7a (not shown). If the line shifts are large enough, the actual ratio of aggressive types will lie above $r_A^{critical}$ leading to the social evolution of aggression within the Hutu in-group. In short, the magnification of threat and crisis (real or contrived) created a "space of opportunity" in the social evolutionary game model in which aggression became fitter than peace and the commune was overcome with genocidal violence.

Straus (2006, p. 71) documents another shock that occurred in Gafunzo early in the genocide. Specifically, Yusuf Munyankazi, an extremist Hutu militia leader, brought several busloads of killers to Gafunzo on April 27. In Figure 14.7b from earlier, such an action increases the initial ratio of aggressive types in the area. If this ratio increases enough (as it does in Figure 14.7b), it creates a "space of opportunity" for extremists to initiate and spread a growing acceptance of aggression (genocide) in the locale over time. According to Straus (2006, p. 71), the insertion of the armed militias from the outside "easily overwhelmed the resistance and decimated the Tutsi population."

14.6 Network Models of Genocide Propagation and Prevention

Mass atrocities involve the exploitation of existing political, social, and economic networks, and the creation of new ones, among architects, managers, and troops. Networks also form between helpers and victims and within resistance and victim groups. Some mass atrocity case studies recognize the importance of networks in the title of the work, for example, *Networks of Nazi Persecution* (Feldman and Seibel 2004). Despite extensive applications of networking models to terrorism and to other forms of criminality (see Chapter 7), there are few formal models of mass atrocity networks (an exception is Anderton and Brauer 2018b). In this section we present two stylized networking models of genocide propagation and prevention.

Tentacles of Nazi Persecution

On September 1, 1939, Nazi Germany invaded Poland. Browning (2004) provides a detailed account of the first few weeks of the invasion and the accompanying mass atrocities. On September 3, SS commander Heinrich Himmler ordered the Einsatzgruppen (mobile killing units) to "shoot all insurgents, defined loosely as anyone who endangered German life or property" and, also in September, "Waffen-SS units were involved in mass shootings" (Browning 2004, pp. 28–9). It is estimated that 12,137 people on Polish territory were executed in September 1939 (Browning 2004, p. 29). Meanwhile, on September 15, Nazi chief of police Reinhard Heydrich sought instructions from the armed forces so that the military police could participate in the executions. Browning also documents the forced deportations of Jews and Poles, which began in earnest in early October 1939 under the leadership of Adolf Eichmann. Of course, at the center of the decision-making for the atrocities unfolding in Poland was Adolph Hitler, "whose anti-Semitism was both obsessive and central to his political outlook" (Browning 2004, p. 10). Despite the strong impetus for mass atrocity in Poland emanating from key Nazi leaders, some German military personnel, for example, Major Rudolf Langhäuser, were adamantly opposed to Nazi brutalities against civilians (Browning 2004, p. 18).

Drawing on principles from Chapter 7, Figure 14.8 depicts a stylized network associated with the Nazi invasion of Poland. Hitler (player 1) is in the center of the star. Moving out from the center along three tentacles are key managers of atrocities in Poland: Himmler, Heydrich, and Eichmann (players 2, 5, and 8). At the end of each tentacle are two military commanders (players 3, 4, 6, 7, 9, and 10). Assume initially that odd-numbered commanders (3, 7, 9) support atrocity, but even-numbered commanders (4, 6, 10) are resistant. For simplicity, the analysis that follows focuses only upon the top tentacle involving actors 1–4. As such, we ignore the effects of 1's links with 5 and 8. Note that along the top tentacle there are three perpetrators (1, 2, and 3) and one resister (4).

Following Chapter 7's linear quadratic model (LQM), each perpetrator's utility U_i ($i = 1, 2, 3$) depends on the benefits ax_i and costs $(b/2)x_i^2$ from acts of harm x_i against "undesirables." Meanwhile, the lone resister along the top tentacle, actor 4, receives utility U_4 based on benefits $a\tilde{x}_4$ and costs $(b/2)\tilde{x}_4^2$ of resistance actions $\tilde{x}_4$. The scalars a and b are benefit and cost parameters, respectively, which we assume are the same for each actor. There are also spillover benefits w for linked perpetrators owing to their comradery and their ability to share information. Meanwhile, there are spillover costs $\tilde{w}$ associated with the link between 2 and 4 owing to their disagreement over atrocity policy. The objective functions for actors 1–4 are:

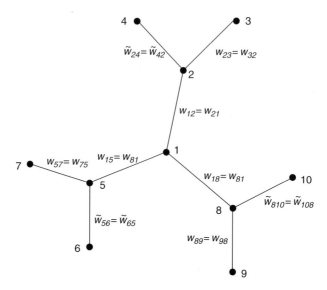

Figure 14.8 Stylized model of network tentacles of Nazi persecution.

$$U_1 = ax_1 - \left(\frac{b}{2}\right)x_1^2 + w_{12}x_1x_2 \tag{14.3a}$$

$$U_2 = ax_2 - \left(\frac{b}{2}\right)x_2^2 + w_{21}x_2x_1 + w_{23}x_2x_3 + \tilde{w}_{24}x_2\tilde{x}_4 \tag{14.3b}$$

$$U_3 = ax_3 - \left(\frac{b}{2}\right)x_3^2 + w_{32}x_3x_2 \tag{14.3c}$$

$$U_4 = a\tilde{x}_4 - \left(\frac{b}{2}\right)\tilde{x}_4 2 + \tilde{w}_{42}\tilde{x}_4x_2. \tag{14.3d}$$

Equations (14.3a)-(14.3d) imply the following reaction functions for each actor:

$$x_1 = \left(\frac{a}{b}\right) + \left(\frac{w_{12}}{b}\right)x_2 \tag{14.4a}$$

$$x_2 = \left(\frac{a}{b}\right) + \left(\frac{w_{21}}{b}\right)x_1 + \left(\frac{w_{23}}{b}\right)x_3 + \left(\frac{\tilde{w}_{24}}{b}\right)\tilde{x}_4 \tag{14.4b}$$

$$x_3 = \left(\frac{a}{b}\right) + \left(\frac{w_{32}}{b}\right)x_2 \tag{14.4c}$$

$$\tilde{x}_4 = \left(\frac{a}{b}\right) + \left(\frac{\tilde{w}_{42}}{b}\right)x_2. \tag{14.4d}$$

Assume the model's parameters are $a = 2$, $b = 1$, $w_{12} = w_{21} = w_{23} = w_{32} = 0.2$, and $\tilde{w}_{24} = \tilde{w}_{42} = -0.2$. Using the matrix algebra methods of Appendix C.2, total harm directed by the Nazi perpetrators along the top tentacle in Figure 14.8 is $X^{harm} = x_1^* + x_2^* + x_3^* = 2.55 + 2.73 + 2.55 = 7.82$. The unit of measure could be the number of attacks per week against outed groups. Meanwhile, the amount of resistance from 4 is $X^{resist} = \tilde{x}_4^* = 1.45$. Assuming for simplicity that we can add and subtract harming and resistance actions, the net harm generated against out-groups by the top tentacle in Figure 14.8 is $X^{net} = 7.82 - 1.45 = 6.37$.

During the Holocaust, Nazi leaders invoked bureaucratic tactics to induce those resisting atrocities to conform and become complicit in such actions (Lemkin 1944, Breton and Wintrobe 1986, Browning 2004). In some cases, military commanders who resisted were replaced. Other commanders weighed the potential gains from career advancement in the Nazi hierarchy against their conscience and, sadly, gave in to the former. Still others quickly became supporters of the Nazi extermination program. What happens to the net harm directed to out-groups in the networking model when the resistant military commander (actor 4) is replaced or conforms to Nazi ways? To answer the question, assume that commander 4 in Figure 14.8 is now like commander 3. This implies that 4's actions are acts of harm and the negative spillover parameter $\tilde{w}$ governing the link between 2 and 4 is now positive and equal to 0.2. Total harm against out-groups now becomes $X^{harm} = x_1^* + x_2^* + x_3^* + x_4^* = 2.73 + 3.64 + 2.73 + 2.73 = 11.83$. Once the one resister conforms or is replaced by a perpetrator, the top tentacle in Figure 14.8 becomes "fully dedicated" to exterminating out-groups. The positive synergies generated by the complementary actions of the perpetrators leads to a dramatic 86 percent increase in harm simply by converting one resister in the tentacle. Numerous mass atrocity case studies report dramatic increases in harm once struggles between perpetrators and resisters within the in-group tipped in favor of the perpetrators (see, for example, Straus (2006) on the Rwandan genocide and Browning (2004, pp. 15–24) on atrocities in Poland).

The networking model can also be used to analyze genocide prevention. For example, following Chapter 7's analysis of key player policy, suppose

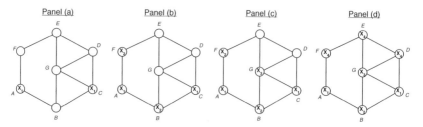

Figure 14.9 Genocide contagion in a networked neighborhood.

actor 2 is removed from the top tentacle in Figure 14.8. For our given parameter values, aggregate harm would fall among the perpetrators by almost half from 11.83 to 6.0. And as Chapter 7 noted, more forceful third-party interveners can bring their own network into direct contestation with a violence-producing organization's network to mitigate violence.

Genocide Contagion in a Neighborhood

Consider the seven actors *A-G* and their friendship links in a locale shown in panel (a) of Figure 14.9. Suppose the locale is located in a country that begins to experience genocide. Owing to cultural, historical, and idiosyncratic factors, some actors in Figure 14.9 may be predisposed to participating in genocide. Suppose this is true of *A* and *C* at time 1, which we indicate by putting an X_1 in the *A* and *C* nodes in panel (a). Now we invoke a key assumption: suppose owing to peer effects, kinship ties, etc., other actors in the neighborhood also become genocide supporters if at least half of their friends participate. Note in panel (b) that *B* has three friendship links (with *A, C,* and *G*), and at least half (two-thirds actually) are genocide supporters. As such, *B* becomes a perpetrator in period 2, which we label as X_2 in *B*'s node in panel (b). Similarly, *F* has two friendships (with *A* and *E*) and one of the two (half) is a genocide supporter. Hence, F supports genocide in period 2, which we label with an X_2 in *F*'s node in panel (b). The contagion has only just begun. Note in panel (b) that *G* has four friends (*B, C, D,* and *E*), two of which are genocide supporters (*B* and *C*). Hence, *G* joins the genocide in period 3, which we label as X_3 in *G*'s node in panel (c). In panel (c), *D* and *E* each has two of its three friends as perpetrators, so each becomes a perpetrator. We label in panel (d) an X_4 indicating that *D* and *E* have become part of the genocide network. Beginning with *A* and *C* as perpetrators and the social links in the locale, genocide acceptance spread like a disease through the neighborhood such that all actors became perpetrators.

But consider Figure 14.9 again. Suppose in panel (a) that *A* and *B* began as genocide perpetrators rather than *A* and *C* (imagine labeling X_1 at nodes *A* and *B*). Actor *F* would now join the network because one of its two friends joined (namely, *A*). We could label X_2 at node *F* to reflect *F*'s participation. But now the contagion stops. No other actors in the locale have at least half of their friends participating in the genocide, so they do not participate either. In arriving at this result we did not change the friendship links in the neighborhood, the number of actors, or the number of actors initially supporting genocide. The network structure remains the same, but the prospect of contagion has changed dramatically. The model shows how apparently trivial and even idiosyncratic factors at the micro level can lead to dramatically different outcomes at the macro level. Something as seemingly trivial as whether an out-group despiser who moved into the neighborhood happened to buy a house at location *C* rather than *B* can determine whether atrocity takes over the whole village once it breaks out or whether it is essentially contained. Once a mass atrocity begins, it can propagate unevenly across locales depending on political, social, and economic connections among individuals in neighborhoods (Verwimp 2005, Straus 2006, McDoom 2014). Furthermore, the same locale at different points in time can have quite different experiences with atrocity propagation depending on initial conditions (Ray 2017).

14.7 Empirical Studies of Mass Atrocity Risk and Prevention

Risk Factors for Mass Atrocity Onset

An early and major step forward in empirical research on genocide risks was provided by Harff (2003). According to Harff, many modern genocides occur in conjunction with or immediately after a civil conflict or regime collapse. The reverse is not true, however, in that many conflicts do not involve purposeful elimination of people-groups. Harff therefore frames the research question as follows: given the existence of internal conflict or regime change, what factors predispose authorities to resort to mass elimination? Her sample consists of 126 countries, all of which experienced internal war or regime change sometime during 1955–97, of which 35 involved genocide. Harff applies regression analysis to determine the risk of genocide based on factors culled from the political repression literature. She finds that six factors have important and statistically significant effects. Given internal conflict or regime change, the risk of genocide is higher when, first, the severity of political upheaval is greater, second, there is a history of prior mass killing, third, the ruling elite holds an exclusionary ideology, fourth, the regime is autocratic, fifth, the ruling elite is from an ethnic minority, and, sixth, a country is less open to economic trade. From a baseline probability of about 3 percent, Harff calculates that any one of these six factors increases the risk of genocide by somewhere between two and six percentage points. The cumulative effect of the factors is huge: if all six factors occur together, then the probability of genocide rises to 90 percent. Also interesting, Harff finds that other anticipated factors, including active discrimination against minorities, high infant mortality, and sparse international political linkages, do not have a significant impact on genocide risk, conditioned again on the presence of internal conflict.

Risk Factors for Genocide Propagation

Much of the empirical literature on mass atrocity risks has a macro or top-down orientation in that it considers risks that state and nonstate leaders choose mass atrocity for the societies that they control. McDoom (2014), however, empirically analyzes factors at the grass-roots or microlevel that drew individuals from the Tare sector of Butare prefecture in southeastern Rwanda into perpetration during the 1994 genocide. His theoretical analysis is strongly rooted in networking theory. Specifically, McDoom hypothesizes that an individual from Tare would be more likely to participate in genocide: first, the greater the number of its social connections; second, the greater the number of its social connections to other participants; and, third, the stronger its ties to other participants (pp. 871–2). He also notes that social connections are multivalent, that is, they involve multiple types of connections such as kinship, economic, social, and religious. Hence, McDoom also hypothesizes that the nature of an individual's ties to a participant affects its likelihood of becoming a participant.

McDoom's sample encompasses the survey responses of 116 males age 14 and older from Tare's 647 households who were present in Tare in April 1994. Within this sample there are 37 genocide participants and 79 nonparticipants. McDoom focuses on six types of ties between individuals: kinship, economic, social, neighbor, religious, and political. McDoom's dependent variable is dichotomous indicating participation or not in at least one act of violence during the genocide. McDoom's key explanatory variables include network-level characteristics (size of an individual's network, number of participants an individual was connected to) and connection types (kinship, neighbor, etc.). Control variables include the age, marital status, education, and wealth of individuals.

McDoom finds that the addition of one social connection to an individual elevates his risk of becoming a participant by 9 percent, all else equal. He also finds that for each added participant an individual is connected to, the individual's risk of participation rises between 15 and 24 percent, all else equal. Among the many types of ties, McDoom finds that kinship and neighbor ties have significant impacts on genocide participation. For each added family member who participates in genocide, the risk of individuals' participating rises between 51 and 75 percent, all else the same. Moreover, the greater the number of an individual's ties to neighbors, regardless whether the neighbors participated, the greater the risk the individual participated. McDoom's results seem consistent with the situational paradigm in genocide studies, which focuses on "the importance of *social structure* and *social interaction* for [understanding individual] participation in collective violence" (McDoom 2014, p. 865; our emphases).

Mass Atrocity Prevention

Hultman, Kathman and Shannon (2013) (hereafter HKS) note that civilian protection is now a major objective of United Nations (UN) peacekeeping operations (PKOs) in civil wars. HKS theorize that the UN's ability to protect civilians during civil war depends upon both the size and the composition of UN personnel deployments. All else equal, the greater the number of UN personnel committed to a PKO, the greater the protection of civilians. HKS note, however, that the UN deploys three types of personnel in PKOs: armed military troops, police units, and unarmed observers. Importantly, "different personnel components of PKOs send different signals to the combatant factions" (p. 876). HKS maintain that a relatively large presence of military troops and police in a PKO signals strong UN resolve to diminish hostilities and to protect civilians because such personnel can physically restrain violence. A high proportion of UN observers, however, signals relatively weak UN resolve.

HKS's sample encompasses intrastate conflicts in sub-Saharan Africa from 1991 to 2008. The unit of analysis is the conflict month. Three measures of the dependent variable are used in the empirical analysis; the number of civilians killed by: any combatant, rebel groups, and government forces. The three key explanatory variables are: number of UN troops, number of UN police forces, and number of UN observers. Control variables include prior period civilian killings, seriousness of intrastate conflict, and whether the conflict is over territorial or government control. Across all regressions HKS find that UN troops and police each have a significant negative effect on VAC severity. They also find that UN observers have a significant adverse effect on VAC severity.

There is debate in the genocide prevention community about the effects of third-party intervention on the risks and severity of mass atrocities. HKS's study provides important contextualization, at least regarding UN missions in sub-Saharan Africa. Among their key policy results, we emphasize two. First, "military observers are not adequate for civilian protection" and observers "may in fact create incentives for civilian targeting, without having the ability to offer protection" (p. 888). Second, given the right composition of UN intervention, specifically, a robust presence of troops and police, "peacekeeping operations are effective at stifling anti-civilian violence and saving innocent lives" (p. 888).

14.8 Economic Consequences of Mass Atrocity

Economic Growth

Soudis, Inklaar, and Maseland (2016) (hereafter, SIM) empirically estimate the impact of genocide on GDP per capita growth. SIM's theoretical analysis is rooted in Solow growth theory, particularly, the Solow growth accounting equation (Taylor and Weerapana 2012, p. 223):

$$\text{Growth of } Y/L = \alpha(\text{Growth of } K/L) + \text{Growth of } A, \qquad (14.5)$$

where Y/L is the economy's output per laborer, which is also called *productivity*; K/L is the economy's capital stock per laborer; α is a weight capturing the importance of K/L growth for productivity growth; and A is total factor productivity (TFP). Growth in TFP is often attributed to improvements in knowledge or technology in deploying inputs to create output.

SIM begin with three possible negative effects of genocide on productivity growth: first, temporary drop in productivity with eventual recovery to the economy's prior growth path; second, permanent drop in productivity with no change in the economy's subsequent growth rate, but the economy never recovers to its prior growth path; and, third, permanent drop in productivity with permanent decline in economy's growth rate. To determine which scenario seems consistent with the data, SIM collect data on productivity, capital per worker, and TFP for 167 countries from 1950 to 2011. SIM's empirical analyses lead to four key results. First, in the three years after the start of genocide, productivity declines by close to 10 percent and the result is statistically significant. Second, after the initial drop in productivity, the subsequent growth rate is not impaired, but the loss in productivity is not recovered in later years. Hence, SIM's empirical results line up with the second scenario previously noted. Third, SIM's long run analysis implies that the negative effect of genocide on an economy's productivity persists for ten years or more. Finally, almost the entire decline in productivity due to genocide comes from a decline in TFP rather than a decline in capital per worker in equation (14.5). Wars destroy capital (for example, roads, buildings, and bridges) and people; genocide's emphasis on people-destruction and not on capital destruction per se suggests that wars and genocides may not be alike in the nature and persistence of their economic consequences (Soudis, Inklaar, and Maseland 2016, p. 137).

Economic Impacts of the Holocaust in Russian Locales

Acemoglu, Hassan, and Robinson (2011) (hereafter, AHR) empirically analyze the long-run economic and political consequences of genocide against Jews in Russian cities and administrative districts (called oblasts) during World War II. The killings of Jews in Russia were conducted primarily by Nazis following the German invasion of Russia in June 1941. In our brief review of AHR's study, we focus upon the economic consequences of Nazi atrocities against Jews in Russian locales.

Based upon census information on Russian cities and oblasts for various years from 1939 to 1989, AHR construct data on total populations, Jewish shares of populations, and occupational status of Jews and nonJews for 278 cities (76 of which were occupied by the Nazis) and 48 oblasts (11 of which were occupied by the Nazis). Among AHR's dependent variables are four that we focus upon: first, city population for various years; second, city average wage in 2002; third, oblast GDP per capita for various years; and, fourth, oblast average wage for various years. AHR's key explanatory variables are a dummy variable indicating Nazi occupation of a city or oblast (1=yes, 0=no) and a "potential impact of the Holocaust" on a city or oblast. The potential impact measure involves the multiplication of the Nazi dummy variable by the share of Jews in the population of a city or oblast. Control variables include the number of defense industries per city and per oblast and oil and gas output per oblast.

AHR find that Russian cities that were comparatively more affected by the Holocaust had significantly lower population growth over the period 1939 to 1989. They note that "the Holocaust may have induced a *long-lasting*, divergent trend on the [populations] of the affected cities" (p. 921, our emphasis). AHR also find that cities that were comparatively more affected by the Holocaust were more likely to have lower wages in 2002, all else equal. For oblasts, AHR find that areas that were comparatively more affected by the Holocaust were significantly more likely to have shrunken middle classes in 1989. Jews constituted a much larger share of the middle class than nonJews in the cities and oblasts in which they lived. Hence, AHR note that the "disappearance of the largely Jewish middle class in certain oblasts may have changed the overall economic and social development of the area and led to an occupational structure that has many fewer middle-class occupations today" (p. 936). Finally, oblasts that were comparatively more affected by the Holocaust were significantly more likely to have lower wages and lower GDP per capita in 2002. AHR note that wars (even those with severe general declines in population) do not seem to show the same long-run negative impacts that one finds for the Holocaust, which targeted the social structures and the educated people from the out-groups. AHR's study thus suggests that mass atrocities may pose greater challenges for post-conflict economic recovery than for wars.

14.9 Bibliographic Notes

Wide-ranging coverage of the field of genocide studies is available in Bloxham and Moses (2010), Meierhenrich (2014), and Waller (2016). Extensive coverage of economic aspects of mass atrocities and their prevention are available in Anderton and Brauer's (2016a) edited volume.

Since Harff's (2003) early and influential empirical study of genocide risk, as well as those of Rummel (1995) and Krain (1997), follow-on empirical research has continued to find that conditions of war and state crisis and nondemocratic political systems elevate the risk of mass atrocities. Importantly, and consistent with their game theory model, Esteban, Morelli, and Rohner (2015) find empirical evidence that political regime transitions toward democracy elevate the risk of mass atrocities. Other studies have found in addition that low economic development, concentration of natural resources, and economic discrimination seem to increase mass atrocity risk. However, some of Harff's findings have not continued to receive strong empirical support as risk factors for mass atrocities including trade openness and prior mass atrocity. Meanwhile, other empirical work includes mass atrocity forecasting, analysis of the effects of third-party interventions on mass atrocity seriousness, risk factors for VAC by nonstate actors such as rebel and militia groups, the effects of individual and local conditions (situational characteristics) on the spread or severity of mass atrocity actions, and the political, social, and economic consequences of mass atrocities. For surveys of these streams of empirical research, see Hoeffler (2016), Waller (2016, pp. 147–94), and Anderton and Brauer (2018a).

PART IV

Security and Peace

15

Arms Rivalry, Proliferation, and Arms Control

Born in the tense early years of the Cold War, conflict economics has long been interested in arms rivalry, proliferation, and arms control.* This chapter summarizes principles and research results in this historically important branch of conflict economics. We begin with definitions followed by an overview of military spending, weapons of mass destruction, and arms control treaties. We then sketch the seminal arms race models of Richardson and Intriligator and Brito. To these we add a rational choice model that highlights the interdependence of economics and security in issues of arms rivalry and arms control. We also briefly survey selected empirical studies related to arms rivalry and the proliferation of weapons of mass destruction.

15.1 Definitions

There are four classes of weapons that states and nonstate groups might acquire: small arms and light weapons (SALW), such as machine guns, assault rifles, and improvised explosive devices; major conventional weapons (MCW), such as tanks, destroyers, fighter aircraft, and unmanned aerial vehicles; weapons of mass destruction (WMD), including nuclear, biological, chemical, and radiological weapons; and cyber weapons (see Appendix A). Furthermore, weapons can be applied in one or more of the five main domains of war – land, air, sea, outer space, and cyberspace – and may include significant interconnections of weapons types across domains

---

* Parts of sections 15.1, 15.3, and 15.4 are adapted from Charles H. Anderton and John R. Carter's article, "A Survey of Peace Economics" published in *Handbook of Defense Economics, Volume 2* edited by Todd Sandler and Keith Hartley, pp. 1211–58, Copyright © Elsevier 2007. We gratefully acknowledge Elsevier's permission to republish material from the article.

in network-centric warfare (Wilson 2007). Issues of arms rivalry, proliferation, and arms control can apply to any of the weapons classes and domains of war.

"Arms rivalry" is a competitive increase in the weapons quantities or qualities of two or more parties. Arms rivalries occur between states, but they can also occur between a government and a rebel group and between nonstate actors (for example, communal groups, drug cartels, and local gangs). Although the terms arms rivalry and arms race are often used interchangeably, an "arms race" is a special case of arms rivalry characterized by an unusually rapid rate of increase in weapons quantities or qualities.

"Proliferation" is an increase in the number of parties obtaining a certain class of weaponry and can grow out of an arms rivalry and can spawn new rivalries. Although the term proliferation usually refers to the spread of WMD to more parties, it can also refer to the spread of non-WMD weapons such as unmanned aerial vehicles and robotic weaponry.

Based upon Schelling and Halperin's (1961) classic text, "arms control" refers to all forms of military cooperation between potential adversaries (who could be states or nonstate groups) designed to reduce first, the risk of war, second, damage should war come, and, third, economic and political costs of military preparation. This conception of arms control asserts a common interest between enemies, with the possibility of reciprocation and cooperation over military postures. The forms of cooperation might include changes in political or military communications, modes of force deployment, quantity or quality of weapons, and rates of weapons accumulation. Note that Schelling and Halperin's three arms control goals are distinct, which raises the possibility of tradeoffs among them.

15.2 Patterns of Military Spending, Arms Rivalry, Proliferation, and Arms Control

We use data from the Stockholm International Peace Research Institute, Nuclear Threat Initiative, Arms Control Association, and other organizations to summarize worldwide and nation-specific trends in military spending, proliferation of WMD, SALW, and arms control agreements (see Appendix D.5).

Military Spending

Figure 15.1 summarizes the trend in worldwide real (inflation-adjusted) military spending from 1988 through 2017. The high spending seen during

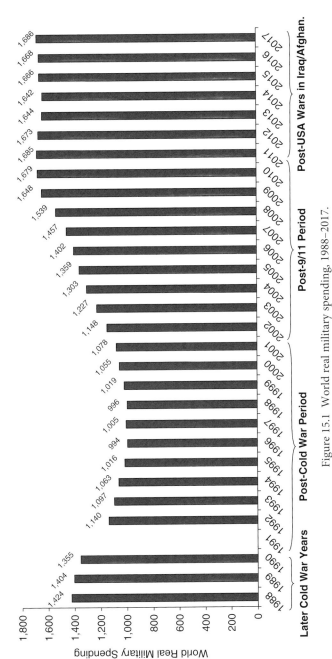

Figure 15.1 World real military spending, 1988–2017.

Note: Data in billions of USD at constant 2016 prices and exchange rates. Data unavailable for 1991.

Source: Stockholm International Peace Research Institute (2018).

the later Cold War years is not surprising given the pervasive geopolitical significance of the USA-Soviet rivalry at the time. The reductions in the 1990s reflected a hoped for "peace dividend" following the decline of the Cold War, while the increases since 2001 corresponded in part to new challenges of terrorism faced by many nations and the emergence (or renewal) of tensions within and between states. Notice in recent years that annual spending has been greater than $1.6 trillion (>$1,600 billion). To appreciate the economic enormity of such resource diversion, consider that world military spending of $1.67 trillion in 2016 was larger than the total gross domestic product ($1.52 trillion) for the 46 sub-Saharan African countries for that year (World Bank 2018).

Arms Rivalry

Figure 15.2 shows real military spending for selected years for four inter-state arms rivalries. We designate the first three panels as arms rivalries for three reasons. First, each shows a general increase in real military spending, a frequent proxy for armaments and soldiers, over the periods specified. Second, according to Thompson (2001, p. 560), the actors in each dyad were involved in a strategic rivalry, whereby each regarded the other as an enemy and a source of threats that could become militarized. Third, Gibler, Rider, and Hutchison's (2005) historical analyses indicated that each of the three pairs increased armaments or military personnel competitively for some of the years shown. We also classify the four nations in panel (d) as part of a multiactor arms rivalry in South Asia owing to Tan (2015).

But are the four cases in Figure 15.2 arms races? In our view, panels (a) and (b) suggest arms racing for the years shown, but panels (c) and (d) do not. In the first two panels, average annual growth rates in real military spending were 28.7 percent for Israel and 26.9 percent for Egypt, and 30.7 percent for Turkey and 20.8 percent for Greece. These growth rates represent unusually rapid increases in real military spending for the periods shown. The Soviet-USA case in panel (c) does not depict arms racing in our view, even over the more limited period 1980–5. From 1980 to 1985, real military spending by the USA rose at an average annual rate of 7.4 percent, which we would count as fairly rapid. For the Soviet Union, however, real military spending grew at an average annual rate of only 1.6 percent over the same period. Finally, panel (d) does not suggest intense arms racing in our view. The average annual growth rates in real

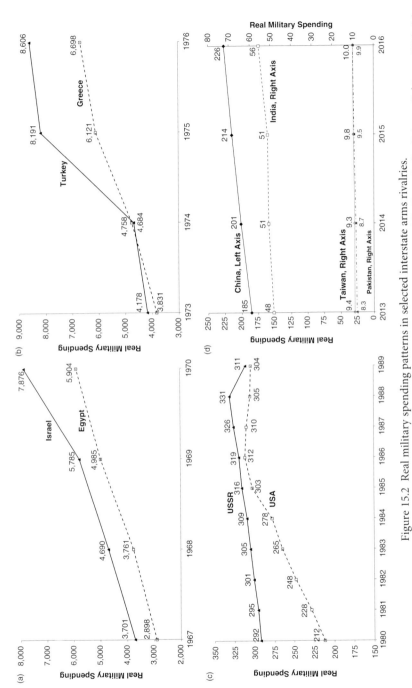

Figure 15.2 Real military spending patterns in selected interstate arms rivalries.

(a) Egypt and Israel, 1967–70 (b) Greece and Turkey, 1973–76 (c) USA and USSR, 1980–89 (d) China, India, Taiwan, Pakistan, 2013–16
Note: In millions of USD at constant 2015 prices and exchange rates for panels (a) and (b), in billions of 1989 USD for panel (c), and in billions of USD at constant 2015 prices and exchange rates for panel (d).
Sources: Stockholm International Peace Research Institute (2018) and World Military Expenditures and Arms Transfers (2017).

military spending over the periods shown are 6.8 percent for China, 4.8 percent for India, 6.1 percent for Pakistan, and 2.1 percent for Taiwan.

Proliferation

The term "proliferation" often refers to the spread of WMDs, which includes nuclear, biological, and chemical (NBC) weapons. Since the beginning of the Cold War, the spread of WMDs to states and nonstate groups has received much attention by scholars and policymakers. At the time of this writing, there is concern about the nuclear weapons program in Iran and increases in North Korea's nuclear weapons capabilities. There is also apprehension about Syria's and ISIS' willingness to use chemical weapons in their military operations (Hummel 2016, Smith-Spark and Perry 2017).

Nuclear weapons create enormous explosive yield through the fission of heavy atoms such as uranium or plutonium (for an atomic bomb) or the fusion of light atoms like hydrogen (for a hydrogen bomb). The explosive power of nuclear warheads is measured in kilotons (kt; one thousand tons of TNT equivalent) or megatons (mt; one million tons of TNT equivalent). The atomic bomb dropped on Hiroshima in 1945 had an explosive force of 15kt and resulted in approximately 140,000 deaths. Today, the maximum explosive yield among China's nuclear warheads is 5mt, while for Russia and the USA it is 800kt and 475kt, respectively (Stockholm International Peace Research Institute 2017, pp. 414, 422, 434). Biological weapons use microorganisms such as bacteria and viruses to kill or incapacitate humans, livestock, or crops. Diseases that might be unleashed by biological weapons include anthrax, cholera, plague, smallpox, botulism, and Ebola. Chemical weapons use nonliving toxic chemicals to kill or incapacitate humans, livestock, or crops. Chemical weapons can be based on nerve agents such as tabun, sarin, or VX; blister agents such as sulphur mustard, nitrogen mustard, or lewisite; protein synthesis inhibitors such as ricin; or choking agents such as phosgene or chlorine.

Table 15.1 summarizes the WMD status for selected states and one nonstate group (ISIS) as of 2017. The first column shows the nine states that possess nuclear weapons, while Iran is believed by many analysts to be researching nuclear weapons. The next column shows the number of nuclear warheads in each nuclear state's arsenal. The columns on biological and chemical weapons show the recent status of various nations programs in these areas. We qualify the data in Table 15.1 by acknowledging that there is disagreement about the classification of states' WMD

Table 15.1 *Weapons of mass destruction for selected nations and ISIS, 2017.*

Nation or Group	Nuclear	Estimated Number of Warheads	Biological Weapons (BW)	Chemical Weapons
USA	Known Weapons	6,800		Eliminating Weapons
Russia	Known Weapons	7,000	Suspected Research	Eliminating Weapons
UK	Known Weapons	215		
France	Known Weapons	300		
China	Known Weapons	270		
Israel	Known Weapons	80	Suspected Research	Suspected Research
India	Known Weapons	120–30		
Pakistan	Known Weapons	130–40		
North Korea	Known Weapons	10–20	Suspected Weapons	Known Weapons
Iran	Suspected Research			
Kazakhstan			Suspected BW materials	
Libya				Eliminating Weapons
Syria				Known Weapons
Uzbekistan			Suspected BW materials	
ISIS				Suspected Weapons

Note: Estimated number of warheads includes those that are deployed, stored, and awaiting dismantlement.
Sources: For nuclear warheads: Stockholm International Peace Research Institute (2017).
For biological and chemical weapons: Nuclear Threat Initiative (2017a).

stocks and programs, particularly for biological and chemical weapons. The table reflects our conservative interpretation of information available in the sources indicated.

Table 15.2 summarizes the estimated effects of large-scale WMD attacks on area and people based on hypothetical simulations reported in seven studies. The first four studies compare the effects of NBC attacks. Of particular concern are the biological line attacks summarized in the fifth and sixth studies, which show the potential for biological weapons to affect vast area and cause hundreds of thousands of casualties. In a line attack, a crop duster or ground vehicle sprays a biological agent along a line so that prevailing winds disperse the agent over a population center. The seventh study shows that a radiological dispersion device (RDD) or dirty bomb detonated in Washington, DC could eventually affect an area similar to that of a 12.5 kiloton nuclear detonation. In regard to estimated fatalities from a dirty bomb, the numbers are much less than for nuclear and biological weapons. Overall, the studies in Table 15.2 reveal that biological weapons have the same or even greater potential to affect area and cause casualties as nuclear weapons, while chemical weapons and RDD attacks are less devastating.

Arms Control

During and after the Cold War, Russia and the USA negotiated many arms control agreements to limit or reduce nuclear warheads, missiles, ballistic missile defenses, and conventional forces. Table 15.3 summarizes selected Russia/USA arms control treaties. Note that some agreements such as SALT I and SALT II limited nuclear delivery systems (for example, intercontinental ballistic missiles (ICBMs) and submarine-launched ballistic missiles (SLBMs)), but they put no brake on the number of nuclear warheads. Other treaties such as START I, SORT, and New START were designed to reduce warheads as well as delivery systems. The ABM Treaty limited each side's ability to defend itself in a nuclear attack, and SALT II and later strategic arms treaties reduced multiple independently targetable reentry vehicles (MIRVs), which allow one missile to carry multiple warheads.

Bilateral arms control was important during the Cold War and it will remain salient for Russia, USA, and other states in the years ahead. Nevertheless, it is likely that efforts to stem the proliferation of WMDs to new states and nonstate groups will dominate the arms control agenda in the near-term. Table 15.4 summarizes selected nonproliferation treaties and programs designed to limit the spread NBC weapons, missile delivery

Table 15.2 *Estimated effects of large-scale weapons of mass destruction attacks.*

Study	Weapon System	Area Affected (km^2)	Casualties
1. United Nations (1969)	1mt nuclear	300	90% killed
	10t biological	100k	50% ill; 25% killed
	15t nerve agent	60	50% killed
2. Robinson, Heden, and von Schreeb (1973) – bomber attack	10kt nuclear	30	
	biological agent	0–50	
	VX nerve gas	0.75	
	5t–6t high explosive	0.22	
3. Fetter (1991) – missile attack on sparsely populated city	20kt nuclear		40k killed; 40k injured
	30kg anthrax spores		20k–80k
	300kg sarin		200–3k killed
4. Office of Technology Assessment (1993) – missile attack on city with sparse to moderate population	12.5kt nuclear	7.8	23k–80k killed
	30kg anthrax spores	10	30k–100k killed
	300kg sarin	0.22	60–200 killed
5. United Nations (1969) – line attack	biological agent, 10^{10} per gm concentration along 100km line	5k	50% killed
6. Office of Technology Assessment (1993) – line attack	100kg anthrax spores	46 (clear day)	130k–460k killed
		140 (overcast)	420k–1.4m killed
		300 (clear night)	1m–3m killed
7. Medalia (2011) based on work by William Rhodes III	About 50 grams of cesium –137 chloride from an RDD	2.1 (first year)	233 all cancers (159 fatal)
		7.6 (any subsequent year)	278 all cancers (189 fatal)
		13.2 (50 years)	461 all cancers (314 fatal)

Note: Areas and counts for Medalia (2011) are cumulative.
Sources: Studies shown in first column are cited in Dando (1994), except for Medalia (2011).

systems, and conventional weapons. The first four treaties concern the nonproliferation of nuclear weapons, while the next two target biological and chemical weapons proliferation. Finally, the Outer Space Treaty limits WMDs in outer space, while the Arms Trade Treaty seeks to stem the proliferation of conventional weapons through the arms trade.

Table 15.3 *Selected USA/Russia (USSR) arms control treaties.*

Arms Control Treaty	Summary Description
Strategic Arms Limitation Talks I (SALT I) Entered into force: 1972	Limited number of ICBMs, SLBMs, and ballistic missile submarines. Included ABM Treaty.
Treaty on the Limitation of Anti-Ballistic Missile Systems (ABM Treaty) Entered into force: 1972 USA withdraws: 2002	Limited each side's ABMs to two sites (national capital and ICBM silos) with no more than 100 ABM interceptor missiles at each site.
Strategic Arms Limitation Talks II (SALT II) Signed: 1979 (never entered into force) USA announces nonabidance: 1986	Limited each side to 2,250 strategic nuclear delivery vehicles (ICBMs, SLBMs, and heavy bombers) and 1,320 multiple independently-targetable reentry vehicle (MIRVs).
Intermediate-Range Nuclear Forces Treaty (INF Treaty) Entered into force: 1988	Committed each side to eliminate medium-to-intermediate-range (1,000–5,500km) and short-range (500–1,000km) missiles.
Conventional Forces in Europe Treaty (CFE Treaty) Entered into force: 1992 Russia suspends participation: 2007	Limited NATO and Warsaw Pact conventional forces to 20,000 battle tanks, 30,000 armored combat vehicles, 20,000 artillery pieces, 6,800 combat aircraft, and 2,000 attack helicopters.
Strategic Arms Reduction Treaty I (START I) Entered into force: 1994	Committed each side to deploy no more than 6,000 nuclear warheads on no more than 1,600 delivery vehicles.
Strategic Offensive Reductions Treaty (SORT) (Moscow Treaty) Entered into force: 2003	Committed each side to reduce strategic nuclear warheads and agree that START I remain in force.
New Strategic Arms Reduction Treaty (New START) Entered into force: 2011	Limited each side to 1,550 deployed strategic warheads and 800 deployed and nondeployed ICBM launchers, SLBM launchers, and heavy bombers.

Key:
ICBM – Intercontinental ballistic missile
SLBM – Submarine-launched ballistic missile
ABM – Antiballistic missile
NATO – North Atlantic Treaty Organization
Sources: Arms Control Association (2017) and Nuclear Threat Initiative (2017b).

Table 15.4 *Selected nonproliferation treaties and programs.*

Nonproliferation Treaty or Program	Summary
Non-Proliferation Treaty (NPT) Entered into force: 1970 Membership: 191 states	The "five nuclear weapons states" (USA, Russia, UK, France, and China) agree not to transfer nuclear weapons technologies to other parties and to pursue disarmament. Non-nuclear weapons states agree not to receive or produce nuclear weapons.
Comprehensive Test Ban Treaty (CTBT) Opened for signature: 1996 Signatories: 183	Prohibits any nuclear weapon explosion for testing or peaceful purposes.
Treaty of Tlatelolco Entered into force: 1969 Signatories: 33 Latin American and Caribbean states	Prohibits testing, use, production, storage, or acquisition of nuclear weapons by the parties or on behalf of anyone else.
African Nuclear Weapons Free Zone Treaty (ANWFZ) Entered into force: 2009 Membership: 39 African states	Parties agree not to research, develop, or acquire nuclear weapons, and not to support others or to receive support in acquiring nuclear weapons.
Biological and Toxin Weapons Convention (BTWC) Entered into force: 1975 Signatories: 173 states	Parties agree not to develop, produce, stockpile, or acquire biological agents or toxins for hostile purposes or for armed conflict and not to assist others in acquiring such means.
Chemical Weapons Convention (CWC) Entered into force: 1997 Signatories: 193 states	Parties agree not to develop or acquire chemical weapons or to assist others in doing so; not to engage in military preparations for use of chemical weapons; and to destroy all chemical weapons and chemical weapons production facilities.
Outer Space Treaty (includes the Moon and Other Celestial Bodies Agreement) Entered into force: 1967 Signatories: 89 states	Parties agree not to place in earth orbit nuclear weapons or any other weapons of mass destruction and not to install such weapons on celestial bodies or station them in any other manner in outer space.
Arms Trade Treaty Entered into force: 2014 Signatories: 130 states	Parties agree not to authorize arms transfers which would violate United Nations Security Council Article VII, break international treaties or arms embargoes, or be used to attack civilians or in other crimes.

Sources: Arms Control Association (2017) and Nuclear Threat Initiative (2017b).

A major difficulty associated with efforts to control the spread of NBC weapons is their dual-use nature. Nuclear facilities for enriching uranium and reprocessing plutonium for nuclear energy purposes can be converted to

Table 15.5 *Selected SALW control organizations and protocols.*

Organization or Protocol	Summary Description
United Nations Conference on the Illicit Trade in Small Arms and Light Weapons Established: 2001	Involved representatives from states, international organizations, and NGOs. States agreed to a Programme of Action to control SALW trade.
Mine Ban Treaty (also known as Ottawa Convention) Entered into force: 1999 Parties: 164 states	Parties agree not to use, produce, acquire, stockpile, or transfer antipersonnel mines; to destroy all antipersonnel mines it possesses within four years; and to clear all laid landmines under its jurisdiction within 10 years.
Convention on Cluster Munitions Entered into force: 2010 Signatories: 108 states	Bans the use, production, transfer and stockpiling of cluster munitions, aids in clearance of contaminated areas, and provides risk reduction assistance for people in areas with cluster munitions.
International Action Network on Small Arms (IANSA) Established: 1998 Membership: Almost 300 full members and hundreds of other affiliates	A global network of civil society organizations working to stop the proliferation and misuse of SALW through national and local legislation, regional agreements, education, and research.

Sources: Arms Control Association (2017), International Action Network on Small Arms (2017), and United Nations Office for Disarmament Affairs (2017)

produce nuclear weapons-grade material. Virtually all of the technologies and many of the precursor materials necessary to produce biological and chemical weapons are used in the production of civilian goods. Hence, it is relatively easy for states to take steps toward nuclear weapons under the guise of peaceful nuclear energy development and to hide production of biological and chemical weapons within civilian infrastructure. This suggests that robust inspection regimes are necessary to control WMD developments.

Despite the emphasis of past and present arms control initiatives on WMD and MCW, most casualties in armed conflicts around the world are due to SALW such as assault rifles, machine guns, and improvised explosive devices. Stemming the production and trade of SALW can be difficult because of the large number of SALW producers and recyclers, the profitability available from such weapons, and the ability of suppliers to bypass government controls (see Chapter 3). Nevertheless, efforts to monitor and control the flow of SALW exist as shown in Table 15.5. The table implies that SALW control is being promoted by a mixture of governmental and nongovernmental organizations, whereas traditional arms control and nonproliferation regimes tend to be initiated by states.

Regarding cyber weapons and emerging military technologies, arms control and nonproliferation possibilities are being discussed. For example, scholars and policymakers are debating the feasibility of bilateral cyber arms control between China and the USA and multilateral control among current and rising cyber powers (Ford 2010, Litwak and King 2015, Nye 2015, Porter 2017). Furthermore, the International Committee for Robot Arms Control (2017) was formed in 2009 to control the development of military robots.

15.3 Richardson Arms Race Model

In the context of growing tension between the USA and the USSR in the 1950s, Richardson's (1939, 1960a) mathematical model of arms rivalry captured the imagination of a growing number of social scientists, particularly from political science. What was significant to this community of scholars was Richardson's conviction that arms rivalry, the risk of war, and other international relations phenomena could be fruitfully studied with mathematics and statistics. Some consider Richardson's arms race model and statistical methods to be crude by today's standards, but his (and Quincy Wright's) vision of applying scientific methods to the study of war and peace became the wellspring for numerous organizations and journals devoted to quantitative research on conflict including the Peace Science Society (International), Correlates of War Project, *Journal of Conflict Resolution, Journal of Peace Research*, and *Conflict Management and Peace Science.*

Richardson's Differential Equations

Let M_A and M_B be the military stocks of two rivals A and B, while $\dot{M}_A$ and $\dot{M}_B$ are the rates of change in military stock per unit time. Richardson hypothesized that three factors would affect a player's military buildup: first, insecurity created by the rival's military stock, second, fatigue or expense of the player's own military stock, and, third, grievances or ambitions of the player toward the rival. The three factors are embodied in the Richardson arms race model, which is characterized by the following differential equations:

$$\dot{M_A} = kM_B - \alpha M_A + g \qquad (15.1)$$

$$\dot{M_B} = rM_A - \beta M_B + h. \qquad (15.2)$$

In equations (15.1) and (15.2), k and r are reaction parameters that reflect how sensitive each player is to the military stock of its rival, while α and β are fatigue parameters representing the economic or political costs of a player's own military stock. Parameters g and h are grievance or ambition terms, representing sources of hostility between the players, such as past conflicts or territorial disputes.

Reaction Functions and Equilibrium

In the Richardson model, A adjusts its military stock until the elements on the right side of the equality in equation (15.1) are such that $\dot{M_A} = 0$. Intuitively, $\dot{M_A} = 0$ means that A's desired change in military stock is zero. By the same reasoning, $\dot{M_B} = 0$ signifies that B does not want to change its military stock. By setting $\dot{M_A}$ and $\dot{M_B}$ equal to zero in equations (15.1) and (15.2), the following reaction functions for A and B can be derived:

$$M_A = \left(\frac{k}{\alpha}\right)M_B + \left(\frac{g}{\alpha}\right) \qquad (15.3)$$

$$M_B = \left(\frac{r}{\beta}\right)M_A + \left(\frac{h}{\beta}\right). \qquad (15.4)$$

A reaction function shows the level of military stock that each player chooses in reaction to the level of military stock of its rival. Equilibrium military stocks (M_A^*, M_B^*) are then found by solving the two equations (15.3) and (15.4) simultaneously for M_A and M_B, yielding:

$$M_A^* = (kh + \beta g)/(\alpha\beta - kr) \qquad (15.5)$$

$$M_B^* = (rg + \alpha h)/(\alpha\beta - kr). \qquad (15.6)$$

Arms Race Stability

Richardson was particularly concerned about the risk of war associated with an unstable arms rivalry. Given an initial increase in military stocks above the equilibrium, a rivalry is unstable if the players react by further building up their stocks, and it is stable if they respond by reducing their stocks back toward equilibrium levels. In the Richardson model, the arms rivalry equilibrium is stable when $(k/\alpha)(r/\beta) < 1$. Note that the stability condition is governed by the slope terms, k/α and r/β, of the reaction functions in equations (15.3) and (15.4). If each player is sufficiently insecure and hence sensitive to its rival's armaments, so that k and r are large, relative to the cost of building weapons, shown by α and β, then (k/α) (r/β) will be greater than one, giving rise to an unstable arms rivalry. Under these conditions, an arms rivalry could become a true arms race, with accelerating armaments leading to growing fears and suspicions and an elevated risk of war (Richardson 1960a, p. 61). Hence, in Richardson's view, limiting weapons buildups in an unstable arms rivalry could contribute to all three of Schelling and Halperin's arms control objectives: reduced risk of war, less damage should war come, and lower costs of military preparations.

Numerical Examples

Assume the following symmetric values for the reaction, fatigue, and grievance parameters of the Richardson model: $k = r = 1$, $\alpha = \beta = 2$, and $g = h = 10$. Based upon equations (15.5) and (15.6), equilibrium military stocks are $(M_A^* = 10, M_B^* = 10)$. Figure 15.3(a) shows the determination of equilibrium graphically using the reaction functions of equations (15.3) and (15.4). Since $(k/\alpha)(r/\beta) = 1/4 < 1$, the players are not overly sensitive to rival military stocks, and the equilibrium at point e is stable. Hence, an upward shift in military stocks to a point above the equilibrium, like m, causes military stocks to move back toward the equilibrium, as governed by the reaction functions. At point m, player A prefers to move to point a, and player B prefers to move to point b. Both moves taken together imply that the military stocks arrive at point c. From there the process repeats itself, and eventually, military stocks arrive back at equilibrium point e.

Assume now that $k = r = 4$, with all other parameter values remaining the same. Mathematically, equilibrium military stocks become negative, which is not meaningful in an armaments context. What is meaningful, however, is that the relatively large reaction coefficients cause the slope terms on the reaction functions in equations (15.3) and (15.4) to become large. Now each player reacts more strongly to the military stock of its rival. In Figure 15.3(b), the reaction functions imply an escalation of military stocks. Beginning from the origin of zero military stock for each player, A prefers to move to point a, and B prefers to move to point b. Both moves

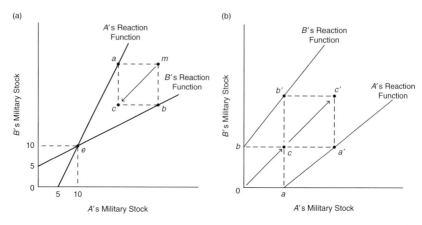

Figure 15.3 Richardson arms race model.
(a) Stable arms race
(b) Unstable arms race

taken together imply that military stocks arrive at point *c*. In the next round, *A* increases its military stock to *a'*, while *B* does the same to *b'*, bringing the joint weapons point to *c'*. Note that the increases in military armaments in the second round are greater than the first. Subsequent rounds will depict ever-increasing armaments for each side, reflecting a run-away arms race when $(k/\alpha)(r/\beta) > 1$.

15.4 Intriligator-Brito Model

Richardson focused on the accumulation of weapons in an arms rivalry assuming that the reaction, fatigue, and grievance parameters were constant. Hence, Richardson ignored strategic elements such as the deterrent or attack capability of accumulated weapons that might affect the degree of reactivity of each player to its rival. In an influential model developed in a Cold War context, Intriligator and Brito (I-B) focused on the deterrence and attack implications of two nations' missile stocks M_A and M_B. Here we present a simplified version of the I-B model drawing from Intriligator and Brito (1986) and Wolfson (1985).

Deterrence and Attack Conditions

Consider first how a nation can deter an attack by its rival. Suppose *A*'s military planners fear that rival nation *B* might launch an all-out attack to destroy some or all of A's missile forces. In an all-out counterforce (military against military) attack by B, assume that $f_B M_B$ of A's missiles would be destroyed, where the parameter f_B is the number of A's missiles destroyed per counterforce missile launched by B. With any surviving missiles, A could then launch a countervalue (military against civilian) strike against B. Assume A believes there exists for B an unacceptable level of casualties $\overline{C}_B$ such that if A credibly threatens that level of casualties in retaliation, then B will be deterred from initiating the attack. Let v_A be the number of casualties in B caused per countervalue missile fired by A in retaliation. Then the number of surviving missiles that A believes it needs to deter B is $\overline{C}_B/v_A$. Putting this together, if A's missile stock is at least equal to $f_B M_B$ (the number of its own missiles that would be destroyed by an attack) plus $\overline{C}_B/v_A$ (the number of missiles required to retaliate), then A believes it can successfully deter B from attacking. Applying similar logic to B's deterrence of A leads to the following deterrence conditions for nations A and B:

$$M_A \geq f_B M_B + \overline{C}_B/v_A \tag{15.7}$$

$$M_B \geq f_A M_A + \overline{C}_A/v_B. \tag{15.8}$$

Now consider how each nation can successfully attack its rival. Let $\hat{C}_A$ be the maximum casualties that A is willing to sustain if B retaliates to an attack by A, and let v_B be the number of casualties suffered by A per countervalue missile launched by B. In an all-out counterforce attack by A, $f_A M_A$ of B's missiles would be destroyed, leaving $M_B - f_A M_A$ missiles with which B could retaliate and thereby cause $(M_B - f_A M_A)v_B$ casualties in A. If such casualties are no more than $\hat{C}_A$, then A can successfully attack. Applying similar logic to B's attack potential leads to the following attack conditions for A and B:

$$(M_B - f_A M_A)v_B \leq \hat{C}_A \text{ or equivalently } M_A \geq (M_B/f_A) - (\hat{C}_A/f_A v_B) \tag{15.9}$$

$$(M_A - f_B M_B)v_A \leq \hat{C}_B \text{ or equivalently } M_B \geq (M_A/f_B) - (\hat{C}_B/f_B v_A). \tag{15.10}$$

Figure 15.4 shows graphically the deterrence and attack conditions (15.7)–(15.10) of the I-B model. In I-B's later writings, conditions (15.7)–(15.10) do not specify the number of weapons that A and B will choose to accumulate. Rather, the conditions reveal various strategic implications for alternative military stocks that A and B might accumulate. Combinations of M_A and M_B on or to the right of the "A deters" line (regions 1, 2A, and 4A) are missile holdings for which A believes it can deter B, while combinations on or above the "B deters" line (regions 1, 2B

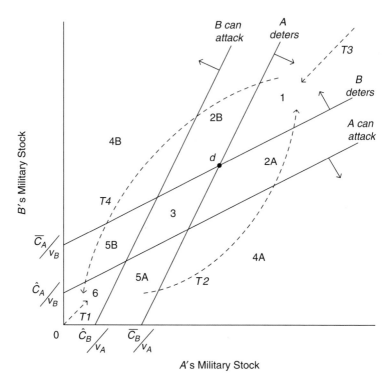

Figure 15.4　Intriligator-Brito model.
Source: Adapted from Intriligator (1975, p. 349).

and 4B) are those for which *B* believes it can deter *A*. Formed at the upper right is the cone of mutual deterrence (region 1), with *d* representing a point of minimum mutual deterrence. Combinations of M_A and M_B on or to the right of the "*A* can attack" line (regions 4A, 5A, and 6) imply that *A* can successfully attack *B*, while points on or above the "*B* can attack" line (regions 4B, 5B, and 6) imply that *B* can successfully attack *A*. In the region of jittery deterrence (region 3), *A* and *B* can neither attack nor deter. Areas 5A, 5B and 6 are regions of war initiation. In regions 5A and 5B one side can attack and neither can deter. Region 6 is particularly dangerous because it represents weapons holdings such that each side can attack and neither can deter.

The I-B model can be used to explore the effects of increases or decreases in weapons on the risk of war (Intriligator and Brito 1986). Beginning from the origin in Figure 15.4, trajectory *T1* is an arms rivalry that moves the nations' weapons holdings into region 6. Because each nation can successfully attack and neither believes it can deter, each has an incentive to attack before its rival does, and the likelihood of war is high. Trajectory *T1* aligns with Richardson's view that an arms rivalry increases the risk of war. But Richardson's view is not the only one implied by the I-B model. Suppose trajectory *T2* occurs, which Intriligator and Brito maintain is roughly descriptive of the first few decades of the Cold War rivalry between the USA and USSR. Trajectory *T2* pushes the weapons holdings into region 1, where each nation believes it can deter. Trajectory *T2* thus lowers the risk of war, contrary to Richardson's view. Nevertheless, damage should war come and the cost of military preparation are both higher along *T2*, suggesting that tradeoffs among the several goals of arms control exist for some trajectories.

The effects of arms reduction on the risk of war can also be considered in the I-B model. Trajectory *T3* moves the nations' weapons holdings further down in the cone of mutual deterrence, implying less damage should war come and lower costs of military preparation, but no increase in the risk of war. In this case, two of the three goals of arms control are promoted without attenuation of the third. A substantial reduction in weapons along trajectory *T4*, however, moves the nations' holdings into the dangerous region 6 where the risk of war is high. Note also that arms reduction trajectories *T3* and *T4* are implicitly assumed to be costless. In reality, destroying weapons and enforcing arms control treaties are costly, which tends to reduce the peace dividend available from arms control.

Applications

Nuclear Weapons Proliferation
Currently, there is uncertainty whether Iran will attempt to acquire nuclear weapons in the future. Furthermore, North Korea's nuclear warhead stocks and missile technologies appear to be increasing. Here we restrict our attention to the risk of war that can emerge when a state first acquires nuclear weapons or begins to build up its stock from a small level. In Figure 15.5, acquisition or growth of nuclear weapons is represented by an arms trajectory that emerges from or near the horizontal axis. Of the many possible proliferation trajectories that could occur, two are shown in the figure. Trajectory *T1* assumes that *A* is already well-stocked with nuclear weapons, the emergent nuclear state *B* begins to accumulate nuclear weapons, and a nuclear arms rivalry occurs between *A* and *B*. It is conceivable that such an arms rivalry could move into a cone of mutual deterrence (region 1), but not before passing through region 4A

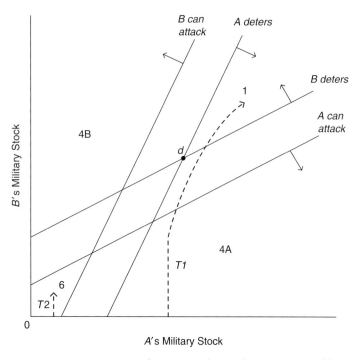

Figure 15.5 Emergent nuclear state in the Intriligator-Brito model.

where *A* can attack and perhaps prevent *B*'s emergence as a nuclear weapons state. Whereas trajectory *T1* is potentially dangerous, trajectory *T2* is particularly disconcerting. For this trajectory, the weapons holdings move into region 6, where each country can attack and each believes it cannot deter. The I-B model by itself cannot determine whether trajectory *T1, T2,* or some other trajectory might better reflect the strategic implications of nuclear proliferation in a particular context. It does indicate, however, that a move toward first deployment or growth of nuclear weapons has the potential to raise the risk of war.

Antiballistic Missile Defense

In 2016, the USA installed a new antiballistic system in Romania as part of its ongoing efforts to have a missile defense shield in Europe. Russia reacted negatively to action by the USA, claiming that an antimissile shield in Europe is a "threat" and an "attempt to destroy the strategic balance" in the region (Browne 2016). It seems reasonable that states would want greater defense, so why would Russia react so

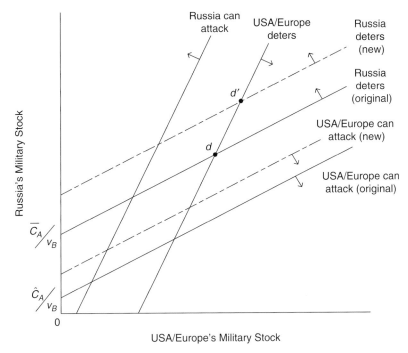

Figure 15.6 One-sided antiballistic missile defense in the Intriligator-Brito model.

negatively? Let's turn to the I-B model for some guidance on the question. In Figure 15.6, let nation A be the USA and its European allies and nation B be Russia. The deployment of an ABM system in Europe to protect cities from an accidental or purposeful missile strike from a third party also serves to lower the countervalue effectiveness v_B of Russia's missiles. This shifts the "Russia deters" and "USA/Europe can attack" lines upward in Figure 15.6. Note that the USA/Europe's attack capability is expanded at the same time that Russia's deterrent capability is undermined. This prospective change in relative capabilities in favor of the USA/Europe and against Russia helps explain Russia's strong opposition.

Inherent Propensity toward War
In Chapter 9 we explored Thomas Schelling's (1966, ch. 6) idea that certain configurations of military technology, geography, and military organization could imply a first-mover advantage in war. Such an "inherent propensity toward war," to use Schelling's phrase, is shown in the

I-B model by region 6 of Figure 15.4, where each side can attack the other and neither can deter. Nevertheless, a more pervasive form of mutual attack arises in the I-B model when the usual counterforce effectiveness assumptions are altered so that region 1, the cone of mutual deterrence, vanishes. To demonstrate this point, note that the cone exists only when the product of the counterforce effectiveness terms is less than one, that is, when $f_A f_B < 1$ (Wolfson 1987, p. 293). Suppose that f_A and f_B are both less than one. As indicated by equations (15.7) and (15.8), the slopes of the "A deters" and "B deters" lines in Figure 15.4 are $1/f_B$ and f_A respectively. This means that when $f_B < 1$ and $f_A < 1$, the "A deters" line is steeper than the "B deters" line, so that a cone of mutual deterrence arises, as depicted by region 1 in Figure 15.4. Intuitively, when one missile in a counterforce attack destroys less than one rival missile, then attack effectiveness is relatively low and mutual deterrence is possible.

Now assume that attack effectiveness for each player is high so that the condition for the cone is not satisfied, that is, $f_A f_B > 1$. For example, suppose f_A and f_B are each greater than one, such that one missile in a counterforce attack can destroy more than one rival missile. In this case the "A deters" line is flatter than the "B deters" line, and as a consequence no cone of mutual deterrence exists as shown in Figure 15.7. With the disappearance of the cone, notice that an area of mutual attack now occupies a substantial portion of the graph. Whereas the customary Figure 15.4 predicts that relatively high and roughly balanced missile stocks imply mutual deterrence and a low risk of war, Figure 15.7 suggests that such missile holdings can be associated with a dangerous risk of war.

The possibility of an inherent propensity toward war in the context of WMD cannot be precluded. We saw in Chapter 9 how fleets of fast and deep-strike military aircraft may have contributed to an inherent propensity toward war between Egypt and Israel in 1967. Imagine a future nuclear weapons rivalry between Israel and Iran wherein aircraft are a primary delivery platform and each aircraft contains multiple warheads. In such a scenario, the risk of nuclear war could be high because each attack plane could potentially destroy multiple enemy planes and warheads in a first strike (that is, the counterforce effectiveness terms could be greater than one). The militarization of space discussed in Chapter 9 also suggests the potential for "futuristic" technologies to generate an inherent propensity toward war. For example, suppose two nuclear rivals each deploy sophisticated satellites designed to detect and target enemy missile sites and to shoot down incoming missiles with satellite-based laser technologies. If such technologies could be made effective against fast-moving missiles,

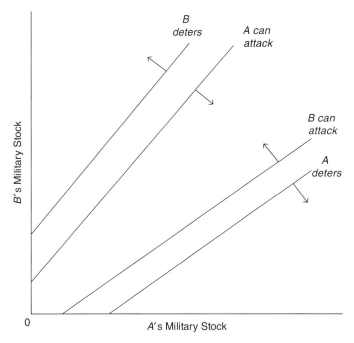

Figure 15.7 Inherent propensity toward war with high attack effectiveness.

the same technologies could be used to destroy the slow-moving satellites of a rival, thus conveying a first-mover advantage in war.

15.5 Economic Choice Model of Arms Rivalry

Optimal Allocation of Resources to Military and Civilian Goods

We turn now to a rational choice model of arms rivalry due to Anderton (1990). Assume there are two rivals A and B, who may be nations or nonstate groups. Player A's choice problem is to allocate its resources between military output M_A and a composite civilian good Y_A to maximize utility, where utility is a function of A's composite good and level of security S_A. Because the two players are rivals, A's security can be written generally as $S_A(M_A, M_B)$, with the assumption that its security increases with its own military output M_A but decreases with its rival's output M_B. Player B faces an analogous choice problem.

Figure 15.8 depicts A's choice problem in a 4-quadrant diagram, where all variables are measured positively as distances from the origin. Quadrant II, at the upper left, shows A's production possibilities frontier (PPF) for alternative combinations of military and civilian outputs M_A and Y_A. Quadrant III simply plots a 45-degree line, which serves to project A's military output from quadrant II into quadrant IV. Quadrant IV graphs A's security function, which shows A's level of security for alternative stocks of military output, holding B's military output M_B constant. These three quadrants systematically join various levels of civilian output Y_A with corresponding levels of security S_A, thereby generating in quadrant I a civilian-security possibilities frontier (CSPF). Included also in quadrant I are A's indifference curves, representing A's preferences over alternative combinations of civilian output and security. Geometrically, A's choice problem is to choose a feasible combination of civilian output and military output (and hence security) to reach the highest indifference curve along the CSPF, taking as given the military output of player B.

To understand Figure 15.8, assume initially that the military output of B is M_B^0, thus generating the higher security line $S_A(M_A, M_B^0)$ shown in quadrant IV. This security line and the PPF in quadrant II combine in quadrant I to generate the CSPF labeled HN. Given M_B^0, player A maximizes its utility at optimum C° by producing outputs M_A^0 and Y_A^0, thereby enjoying the security benefit S_A^0 of its military output and the consumption benefit of its composite good. Now suppose that player B increases its military output to M_B^1. Because B is a rival, A suffers a decrease in security, other things equal, causing its security function to rotate downward to $S_A(M_A, M_B^1)$. Due to the linkages in the model, the CSPF in turn rotates downward to HN'. As a consequence, A is motivated to reallocate its resources to achieve optimum C^1 with military output M_A^1, civilian goods Y_A^1, and security S_A^1. Notice that A reacts to B's increase in military output with an increase of its own, a point to which we return later.

Two broad themes emerge from Figure 15.8. First, economic and security variables are inextricably linked. The point at which a player operates on its production possibilities frontier in quadrant II is governed in part by security considerations. Moreover, the level of security a player is able to achieve is influenced by its economic capacity. Second, the figure reflects the multidisciplinary nature of a player's resource allocation decision. Quadrant II reflects the supply side of the model, a traditional domain of economics. Quadrant IV involves security issues, which are emphasized in international relations. The preferences of

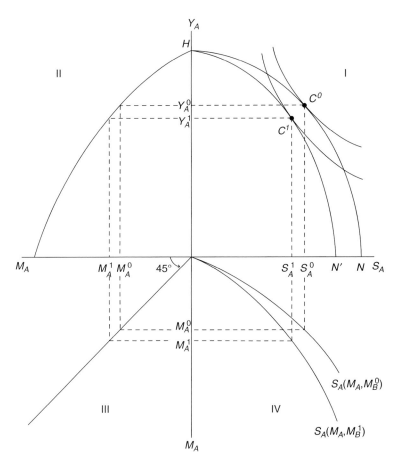

Figure 15.8 Player A's optimal allocation of resources to civilian and military goods.
Source: Adapted from Anderton (1990, p. 152).

a group over Y and S in quadrant I are shaped by various people within the group and by the institutions that govern the group's collective actions. Hence, preference formation belongs in the domains of economics (public choice and political economy), political science, psychology, and sociology.

Reaction Functions and Arms Rivalry Equilibrium

The rivalry between A and B induces A to respond to increases in B's military output with increases of its own. This principle is formally

Part IV Security and Peace

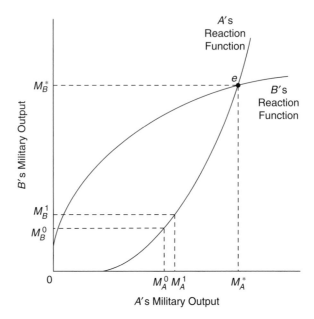

Figure 15.9 Arms rivalry equilibrium in the economic choice model.

represented in Figure 15.9 by A's reaction function, which shows A's optimal military output for any given military output by B. We have already derived two points on A's reaction function in Figure 15.8: if B produces M_B^0, A's best reply is M_A^0, and if B produces M_B^1, A's best reply is M_A^1. Additional points on A's reaction function are derived by repeating the exercise in Figure 15.8 for various other outputs by B. In an analogous manner, working again through a 4-quadrant analysis generates B's reaction function, also shown in Figure 15.9.

A Nash equilibrium exists when each rival's military output is a best reply to the other's. Geometrically, this means that an equilibrium is determined in Figure 15.9 at point e, where the two reaction functions intersect. In equilibrium, A chooses output M_A^*, which is a best reply to B's M_B^*, at the same time that B chooses M_B^*, which is a best reply to A's M_A^*. Because the reaction functions are generated from each player's 4-quadrant model, the equilibrium in Figure 15.9 is equivalent to the simultaneous solution of the players' economic choice problems.

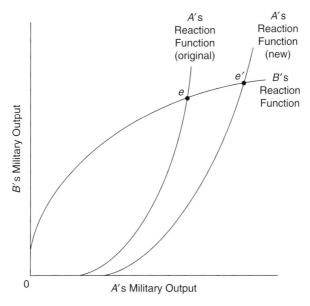

Figure 15.10 Effect of economic growth in *A* on arms rivalry equilibrium.

Applications

Economic Strength and Arms Rivalry Competitiveness

The position and curvature of a player's reaction function is determined by the components of the economic choice model from which it is derived. One of these components is the PPF, which reflects the economic capacity of a player to react to an arms rival by producing weapons of its own. In Figure 15.10 we show how the arms equilibrium moves from *e* to *e'* when *A* experiences economic growth but *B*'s economy is unchanged. In *A*'s 4-quadrant model, economic growth pushes outward the PPF in quadrant II, thus expanding *A*'s CSPF in quadrant I (not shown). Player *A* finds that economic growth allows it to expand its military and civilian production, holding *B*'s military output constant. Hence, *A*'s reaction function shifts outward, indicating an increased demand for military output. This shift sets off new rounds of action and reaction between *A* and *B* until a new equilibrium emerges at point *e'* in the figure. Note that *A*'s military output increases substantially more than *B*'s, which is plausible because *A*'s economic strength has expanded while *B*'s is unchanged. As an illustration of the process depicted in Figure 15.10, some scholars maintain that economic stagnation in the USSR during the 1980s made it increasingly difficult for it to maintain competitiveness in the Cold War rivalry with the USA (Wolfson 1985).

Arms Control

An arms rivalry generates a security dilemma, wherein each player's attempt to improve its security by increasing its own weapons causes the rival to respond by also increasing weapons, which in turn reduces the original player's security. This dilemma provides a basic rationale for arms control, namely that a mutual reduction in weapons can save resources without sacrificing security. We demonstrate this rationale for arms control with Figure 15.11, which is similar to Figure 15.9 but is more complete and thus more intricate. Recall that A's utility is a function of its civilian output Y_A and its security S_A. With a little work, this function can be translated mathematically into a utility function defined in terms of both players' military outputs M_A and M_B. Without getting formal, the key is to recognize that A's PPF implicitly defines Y_A as a function of M_A, and its security function explicitly defines S_A as a function of M_A and M_B. Consequently, A's PPF and security function can be substituted into its utility function, thereby resulting in a translated utility function written generally as $U_A(M_A,M_B)$. As usual, this utility function can be represented with indifference curves, but their behavior needs some explanation.

Of A's many indifference curves in Figure 15.11, we have drawn just one, that being the curve passing through the Nash equilibrium point e. Because e lies on A's reaction function, we know that A's military output at that point is A's best output, given the corresponding military output of B. Player A could be equally satisfied with less military output, but only if A was compensated for its lost security by an appropriately reduced level of military output by B. Thus, A's indifference curve must fall off to the left of e, as shown. Going the other direction, A could be equally satisfied with more military output, but only if A was compensated for its forgone civilian output, once again, by an appropriately reduced military output by B. Thus, A's indifference curve must also fall off to the right of e. Repeating the logic for other points along A's reaction function means that A's indifference curves are positively sloped to the left of A's reaction curve and negatively sloped to the right. Notice also that because unilateral reductions in B' military output M_B leave A better off, points on lower indifference curves are more preferred by A. Similar reasoning applies to B, whose original utility function can be translated into a function written generally as $U_B(M_B,M_A)$. The translated function can then be represented by indifference curves, one of which is drawn for B passing through point e.

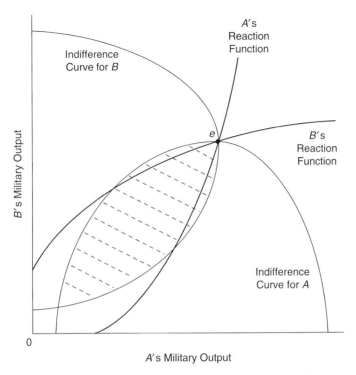

Figure 15.11 Arms control in the economic choice model.

As shown, *B*'s indifference curves are negatively sloped above *B*'s reaction function and positively sloped below it, and points on indifference curves to the left are more preferred by *B*.

With the properties of *A*'s and *B*'s indifference curves in mind, we can illustrate the basic rationale for arms control using Figure 15.11. Notice that the two indifference curves drawn through equilibrium point *e* form a highlighted lens-shaped area. Points within the lens lie below *A*'s indifference curve through *e* and hence are preferred to *e* by *A*; they also lie to the left of *B*'s indifference curve through *e* and hence are preferred to *e* by *B*. Therefore, the lens-shaped area forms the region of mutual gain, wherein at least one player is better off and neither is worse off relative to the equilibrium *e*. This means in principle that the players should be able to negotiate an arms control agreement whereby they both benefit by reducing their weapons levels to some specified point within the lens. The immediate qualification to this statement, however, is that each player will have an incentive to cheat on the agreed arms control point by unilaterally increasing its weapons output toward its reaction function, thereby increasing its utility. This incentive explains why many arms control agreements contain formal inspection and verification protocols to guard against cheating.

By jointly reducing weapons outputs from point *e* into the region of mutual gain in Figure 15.11, the players can keep their security levels roughly the same while freeing up resources to produce civilian goods, thus increasing overall utility. There are a number of important factors that might offset the resource savings generated by arms control. For example, inspection and verification procedures are not costless, and efforts to dismantle or destroy weapons can be costly. Moreover, the substitution principle reminds us that efforts to restrain one form of activity can lead to substitutions into other activities. If the weapons classes controlled in Figure 15.11 are, for example, missiles and warheads, the players might increase the quantity or technological sophistication of their conventional weapons. In intrastate arms rivalries, if rebel leaders lose access to landmines, they might recruit additional personnel and arm them with assault rifles (see Chapter 4). As Schelling and Halperin (1961, p. 120) note: "[I]t is by no means obvious that arms control, even rather comprehensive arms control, would entail rapid and substantial reductions in military outlays ... It is quite possible that arms control would increase them." There have been few empirical studies of the resource cost or effectiveness of arms control agreements. One exception is Craft (2000), who finds empirical evidence that the Washington Naval Agreements of the 1920s between Japan, USA, and UK provided resource savings for a limited time period, followed by greater expenditures to promote new naval technologies. Another exception is Fuhrmann and Lupu (2016) who find that the NPT has significantly curbed the spread of nuclear weapons.

15.6 Empirical Studies

Structure of Arms Rivalries

Many studies have attempted to estimate Richardson-type arms models, but they tend to yield reaction coefficients that are statistically insignificant or incorrectly signed. Reviewing the literature, Dunne and Smith (2007) argue that changing technologies and environments mean that action-reaction relationships among arms rivals are probably too unstable to support the usual time-series analysis. They express optimism, however, that studies employing panel or cross-section methods can yield useful estimates of average interaction effects.

An example of such a study is Collier and Hoeffler (2007a), who estimate a military expenditures model based on a data set spanning 161 countries over the period 1960–99. Observations are country averages computed over five-year periods 1960–4, 1965–9, ..., and 1995–9. The dependent variable is the logarithm of (average) defense burden, where defense burden is equal to military expenditure as a percent of GDP. The key explanatory variable for our purposes is the lagged logarithm of a measure of the defense burden of neighboring countries. Control variables include war, foreign aid, income, democracy, and post-Cold War period.

Collier and Hoeffler's (2007a) estimated coefficients on the control variables are as expected: war and the risk of war lower security and hence generate increased military spending; foreign aid increases military spending, reflecting the fungibility of foreign financial assistance (see Chapter 4); and defense burdens are lower in democracies and after the Cold War. On the issue of arms rivalry, Collier and Hoeffler estimate that the reaction coefficient for neighbors' military spending is 0.10. This means that if a country's neighbor increases military spending by 10 percent, then the country on average will react by increasing its own spending by 1 percent. This action and reaction between the country and its neighbor then sets up a multiplier effect that further increases spending in equilibrium. As one example, Collier and Hoeffler estimate that if the risk of civil war increases generally by 10 percentage points across a region, then each country within the region will increase military spending immediately by 7.3 percent and eventually by 8.1 percent after all actions and reactions are completed (p. 16).

Arms Rivalry and the Risk of War

Wallace (1979) found that arms rivalries between major powers had a positive effect on the escalation of militarized interstate disputes to war. Diehl (1983) and others questioned Wallace's results in subsequent studies. Since the 1980s, theoretical and empirical research of the effects of arms races on war has incorporated conditional and/or indirect effects such as power distribution, shifts in balance of power, and/or enduring interstate rivalry (Mitchell and Pickering 2017).

An example of an empirical study of the relationship between arms races and war in which results are conditional and indirect is Rider, Findley, and

Diehl (2011) (hereafter, RFD). Specifically, RFD consider how enduring rivalries between states can impact the arms race/war relationship. Recall from Chapter 11 that an enduring rivalry exists when a pair of states experience a certain number of militarized interstate disputes (MIDs) (say, at least six) over a certain time period (say, 20 years) (Cashman 2014, p. 252; see also Diehl and Goertz 2012). Given that enduring rivalries elevate the risk of war all else equal, what if enduring rivalries also elevate arms racing behavior? A study that ignores enduring rivalry and focuses only on the arms race/war connection might conclude that arms races elevate the risk of war, when, perhaps, there is no independent effect of arms races on war. In this case, the conclusion that arms races elevate war risk would be spurious. On the other hand, enduring rivalries might elevate the risk of both wars and arms races, but arms races might have a further (independent) effect on the risk of war. RFD's empirical methodology is sensitive to these conditional and indirect effects in assessing the arms race/war relationship.

RFD hypothesize that arms races are more likely to occur when rivalries have lasted for some time (middle or later in the rivalry cycle) because budget and political processes required to sustain military buildups take time to become institutionally locked in. Note here that RFD are hypothesizing that arms races are a consequence of rivalries. RFD also hypothesize that the arms race/war relationship is spurious to the underlying rivalry context, that is, arms races do not independently increase the risk of war. RFD compile a large dataset on pairs of states (dyads) for the period 1816–2000 to test these hypotheses. RFD assume that an arms race occurred in a dyad when each state increased its military spending or armed forces personnel by 8 percent or more over a three-year period. Based upon data on interstate rivalries, RFD find empirical support that arms races are more likely to occur in rivalries than in nonrivalries. They also find empirical support for the hypothesis that arms races are more likely to occur in the middle or later stages of rivalries. Turning to the issue of arms races and war and controlling for several variables that can affect the risk of war between states (for example, contiguity, joint democracy, military capability), RFD reject their hypothesis that arms races have no independent effect on the risk of war. Specifically, they find that "arms races, even when one accounts for the rivalry process, are still correlated with the outbreak of war" (RFD 2011, p. 96).

Proliferation of Weapons of Mass Destruction

Empirical studies of nuclear weapons proliferation find that states that face external security challenges, receive nuclear technology transfers, or receive certain forms of technical nuclear assistance from the International Atomic Energy Agency (IAEA) have a significantly greater risk of pursuing or acquiring nuclear weapons (Singh and Way 2004, Jo and Gartzke 2007, Kroenig 2010, Fuhrmann 2012, Brown and Kaplow 2014). Other studies find that nuclear security guarantees to non-nuclear states tend to reduce the proliferation of nuclear weapons to those states (Bleek and Lorber 2014). While most empirical studies of WMD proliferation focus on nuclear weapons, Horowitz and Narang (2014) consider how nuclear weapons proliferation is conditional on a state's broader interest in WMDs, which includes chemical and biological weapons (CBWs). In particular, Horowitz and Narang would like to know whether acquisition of CBWs reduces (substitutes for) or increases (complements) the demand for nuclear weapons and whether acquisition of nuclear weapons reduces (substitutes for) or increases (complements) the demand for CBWs.

Horowitz and Narang distinguish two stages of WMD proliferation: "pursuit" and "possession." Their dependent variable is measured variously as nuclear weapons pursuit, chemical weapons (CW) pursuit, and biological weapons (BW) pursuit for the period 1945–2000. They key explanatory variables are the pursuit or possession of the other two WMDs. Control variables include GDP per capita and membership in the Non-Proliferation Treaty (NPT), Chemical Weapons Convention (CWC), and Biological Weapons Convention (BWC). The authors find that pursuit of CWs has a significant positive impact on the pursuit of nuclear weapons. Specifically, "pursuing a chemical weapon increases the risk that a state will initiate pursuit of nuclear weapons nearly 20 times" (p. 524). The authors also find that possessing "a chemical weapon increases the ... risk that a state will initiate pursuit of nuclear weapons 38 times" and possession of nuclear weapons reduces BW pursuit (pp. 524 and 530). The authors conclude that BWs can be viewed as a "poor man's nuclear bomb" such that, once nuclear weapons are acquired, states have little interest in pursuing BWs (p. 528). Among the WMD nonproliferation treaties, the authors find that only NPT membership has a significant dampening effect on WMD (in particular, nuclear) proliferation.

15.7 Bibliographic Notes

Hammond (1993) provides historical analysis of interstate arms races from 1840 to 1991 while Mahnken, Maiolo, and Stevenson (2016) provide studies of pre-World War I, pre-World War II, Cold War, and post-

Cold War arms races. Data and policy articles on WMD proliferation, bilateral and multilateral arms control treaties, and nonproliferation are available from the Arms Control Association (www.armscontrol.org) and the Nuclear Threat Initiative (www.nti.org). For coverage of causes, consequences, policy implications, and research needs associated with nuclear weapons proliferation see Pilat and Busch (2017), Gartzke and Kroenig (2017), and the special issue of *Journal of Conflict Resolution* (Gartzke and Kroenig 2014). On biological weapons proliferation, see Johnson and Nolan (2016). On risks of terrorist use of biological and chemical weapons see Tu (2017). Martellini and Malizia (2017) cover threats and counter-measures associated with cyber, chemical, biological, radiological, and nuclear weapons proliferation. Dando (2015) provides extensive coverage of the potential development of novel biological and chemical neuro-weapons. The Norwegian Initiative on Small Arms Transfers (nisat.prio .org) and the Small Arms Survey (www.smallarmssurvey.org) offer data and policy articles on the production, trade, and control of small arms and light weapons (SALW). Brauer (2007) provides an excellent survey of data and models on the production and trade of MCW, SALW, and WMD.

Hess (1995) offers an insightful overview of Richardson's quantitative approach to war and peace. Boulding's (1962, ch. 2) extension of the Richardson model generalizes action-reaction processes to numerous forms of hostility and friendliness, not just arms rivalry, and includes applications to states, nonstate groups, and individuals. Isard (1988, ch. 2) and Sandler and Hartley (1995, pp. 82–9) review other extensions of the Richardson model. Wolfson (1985) combines the strategic components of the I-B model with resource scarcity inherent in an economic choice model, which he then applies to the USA's "arms race economic warfare" against the USSR during the Cold War. McGuire (1965) offers an early economic choice model of arms rivalry and explores Cournot/Nash and Stackelberg solutions and the effects of information (and secrecy) on arms rivalry and arms control. Reviews of theoretical arms race models include Isard (1988), Brito and Intriligator (1995), and Sandler and Hartley (1995).

Literature reviews on the structure of military buildups and the demand for military spending include Dunne and Smith (2007) and Brauer (2002). For a survey of literature on arms races and the risk of war see Mitchell and Pickering (2017). Stoll (2017) provides a broad survey on what we know about arms races from theoretical and empirical literature and offers several important questions about arms races that remain unresolved.

16

Security Alliances

Agreements wherein parties pledge various forms of security cooperation in military contexts are often prominent in conflict settings. In 1949, for example, the USA, Canada, and numerous West European states formed the North Atlantic Treaty Organization (NATO) to counter the threat of attack by the Soviet Union. In turn, the Soviet Union and various Central and East European nations formed the Warsaw Pact in 1955 to counter threats from NATO. Since the end of the Cold War (1990), the Warsaw Pact has dissolved while NATO has remained and expanded its membership. Article 5 of NATO specifies that an attack against any member state will be considered an attack against all member states. Following al Qaeda's attack against the USA on September 11, 2001, Article 5 was invoked for the first time. The USA and its NATO allies then cooperated in an invasion of Afghanistan to topple the Taliban who had supported al Qaeda.

In this chapter we focus primarily on economic aspects of military alliances. We begin with definitions and examples followed by an overview of data on interstate alliances. We then use the economic choice model from Chapter 15 to explore the seminal contributions of Olson and Zeckhauser (1966) and Sandler and his colleagues (Sandler and Cauley 1975, Sandler 1977, Murdoch and Sandler 1982) on the economic theory of alliances. Brief summaries of selected empirical studies pertaining to burden sharing within NATO and the effects of alliances on the risk of armed conflict then follow. The chapter concludes with brief coverage of the applicability of alliance theories and concepts to a broad array of global challenges.

16.1 Definitions and Examples

We define a military alliance as a formal cooperative arrangement between two or more parties that conditions their involvement in military conflict

Table 16.1 *Selected military alliances.*

Name	Type	Members	Time Frame	Brief Summary
North Atlantic Treaty Organization (NATO)	Interstate	USA, Canada, various European states	1949–present	Formed to counter Soviet threat during the Cold War. Carries out peacekeeping, counterterrorism, and other operations today.
Warsaw Pact	Interstate	Soviet Union and various Eastern European states	1955–91	Formed to counter NATO threat during the Cold War.
Triple Alliance	Interstate	Germany, Austria-Hungary, Italy	1882–1915 (periodic)	Formed to counter threat by France and others.
Triple Entente	Interstate	France, Russia, United Kingdom	1907–1917	Served as counterweight to Germany and the Triple Alliance.
Tripartite Axis Pact	Interstate	Germany, Italy, Japan (later other states became members)	1940–45 (Italy departs in 1943)	Opposed the Allies of WW II.
Allies of WW II	Interstate	Numerous states	1939–45	Opposed the Axis powers of WW II.
People Nation	Nonstate	Approximately two dozen USA gangs operating in Chicago and other cities	1978–present	Involved in violent crimes and turf wars against rival alliance Folk Nation.
al Qaeda Affiliates	Nonstate	More than a dozen affiliates including AQAP, AQIM, AQIS, and AQIY	Formed in 2000s	Goals are to drive Western influences out of Islamic lands and see Islamic law imposed in states.

Key:

AQAP – al Qaeda in the Arabian Peninsula

AQIS – al Qaeda in Somalia

AQIM – al Qaeda in the Islamic Maghreb

AQIY – al Qaeda in Yemen

Sources: Encyclopedia Britannica Online (www.britannica.com), Hubbard and Shoumali (2013), Habeck (2012), Florida Department of Corrections (2017), and Hoffman (2017).

or other security-related issues in which violent conflict is possible or underway. Such arrangements can pertain to offensive action, defensive action, neutrality, consultation, and/or nonaggression (Leeds 2003, p. 429). Although the alliance literature focuses on cooperative security arrangements between states, the definition allows for alliances among nonstate parties such as rebel groups, transnational terrorist organizations, or criminal syndicates. Table 16.1 provides summary information for a selection of historical and contemporary alliances. The top entries show that the Cold War and World Wars I and II all involved rivalries between alliances. As subsequent entries show, nonstate alliances exist. The USA, for example, faces major security challenges from within by gang alliances and from abroad by transnational alliances of terrorist organizations and criminal syndicates.

16.2 Patterns of Interstate Alliances

In what follows we use data from the Correlates of War (COW) Project and the Alliance Treaty Obligations and Provisions (ATOP) dataset to illustrate data patterns for interstate alliances (see Appendix D.6). Figure 16.1 shows the number of interstate alliances in force by year based on COW and ATOP. As indicated, many interstate alliances have existed over the past two centuries and particularly since World War I. The most striking aspect of the figure, however, is the close correspondence between COW and ATOP data on the number of alliances up to 1945, followed by a growing divergence since then. The divergence apparently is due to differences in criteria for membership of states in the international system and treatment of nonaggression and offense-only pacts (Gibler and Sarkees 2004, p. 217).

Figure 16.2 provides some sense of the composition of interstate alliances over time based on COW data. The figure shows by year the number of alliances that contained promises of active military support in the event that an ally is attacked (that is, defense pacts). The number of such alliances increased for most of the time period shown, but there was a sharp decline at the end of the Cold War followed by relatively small changes. Since the Cold War's end, agreements other than defense pacts have become increasingly significant. Specifically, of the 86 alliances in force worldwide in 1989 there were a total of 133 obligations (one alliance can have multiple obligations). Of the 133 obligations, 44 (33 percent) were defense, 6 neutrality, 47 nonaggression, and 36 entente (an entente requires members to consult in the event of a crisis). By 2012, total

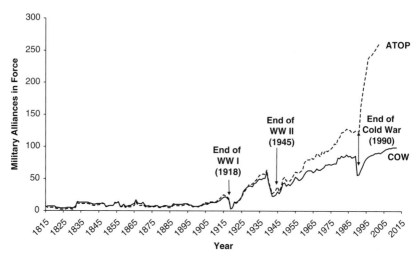

Figure 16.1 Number of interstate alliances as reported by ATOP and COW.
Sources: Leeds et al. (2002) for ATOP and Gibler (2009) for COW version 4.1.

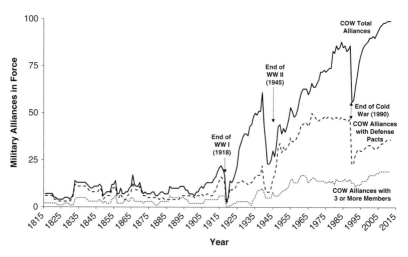

Figure 16.2 Number of interstate alliances with defense pacts and with three or more members.
Source: Gibler (2009) for COW version 4.1.

obligations for the 99 alliances was 174 of which 31 (18 percent) were defense, 37 neutrality, 58 nonaggression, and 48 entente. Figure 16.2 also reports by year the number of multilateral alliances, defined as those with three or more members. Since the end of World War II, multilateral alliances have generally increased in frequency but declined as a proportion of total alliances.

16.3 Pure Public Good Model of Alliances

Public Goods and Alliances

Recall from Chapter 3 the distinction between private and public goods. A good is private when its benefits are rival and excludable. For example, cereal is a private good because one person's consumption of cereal means that the same cereal cannot be consumed by others (rival); furthermore, the person possessing the cereal can withhold it from others (excludable). In contrast, consumption benefits of a public good are nonrival and nonexcludable. For example, mosquito control is a public good for neighborhood residents. One family's benefit of reduced risk of disease does not preclude another family's consumption of that same benefit (nonrival); nor can the other family be denied that benefit depending on whether it contributes to the cost of the mosquito control (nonexcludable).

Olson and Zeckhauser's (1966) seminal economic model of alliances builds on the basic insight that "above all alliances produce public goods" (p. 272). The premier example of a public benefit for alliance members is deterrence of a common enemy. Suppose alliance members credibly commit to retaliate against any attack on one of its members. If the retaliatory threat successfully deters the enemy, then all alliance members benefit from increased security in a manner that is both nonrival and nonexcludable. Similarly, as seen in Chapter 13, offensive counterterrorism efforts can provide a public good for alliance members. To the extent that a terrorist organization is a common threat, degradation of the organization benefits all alliance members, and no member can be excluded from the enhanced security.

A Diagrammatic Model

Optimization
In the model that follows, two players A and B form an alliance in the provision of a pure public good, which is a good that is perfectly nonrival and nonexcludable. For concreteness, the public good can be thought of as military strength aimed at deterring a common enemy C. The allies' respective military outputs M_A and M_B are equally effective against the enemy, and the deterrence produced by one ally spills over fully to the

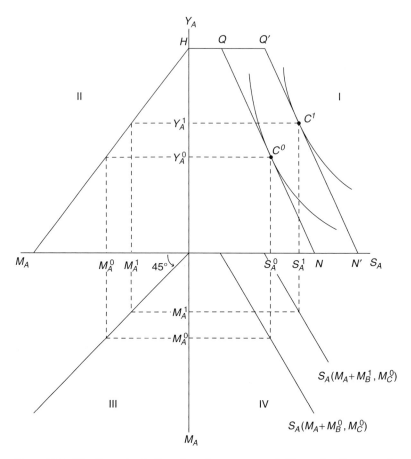

Figure 16.3 Ally A's optimal allocation of resources to civilian and military goods.

other. Hence, the allies share a common military strength M equal to the sum of their military outputs, or $M = M_A + M_B$. Security for each ally $i(i = A, B)$ is a function of the strengths of the alliance and the enemy and can be written $S_i(M_A + M_B, M_C)$. The choice problem for each ally is to allocate resources between military output M_i and a composite civilian good Y_i to maximize utility, where utility $U_i(S_i, Y_i)$ is a function of security and the civilian good.

Figure 16.3 depicts the choice problem for ally A using a linear version of the 4-quadrant model introduced in Chapter 15; a similar figure would apply for ally B. To review, quadrant II shows A's production possibilities frontier (PPF) for alternative combinations of military and civilian outputs M_A and Y_A. Quadrant III uses a 45-degree line to project A's military output into quadrant IV, which shows A's security function given the military outputs of ally B and enemy C. These three quadrants systematically link various civilian outputs Y_A with corresponding levels of security S_A, thus generating the civilian-security possibilities frontier (CSPF) in quadrant I. The diagram is completed by adding A's indifference map to quadrant I. In geometric terms, A's chooses a combination of civilian and military outputs (and hence security) to reach the highest indifference curve possible along the CSPF, taking as given the military outputs of B and C.

To see how the model works, suppose the initial military outputs of ally B and enemy C are respectively M_B^0 and M_C^0, thus generating the lower security line $S_A(M_A + M_B^0, M_C^0)$ shown in quadrant IV. Notice that the intercept of the security line is not at the graph's origin. This is because even if ally A chose zero military output, it would still enjoy some positive level of security due to the deterrence spillover from ally B's military output M_B^0. The security line together with the PPF in quadrant II combine in quadrant I to generate the CSPF labeled HQN, which is shown with an initial horizontal stretch, again due to the spillover from B's military output. Given M_B^0 and M_C^0, ally A maximizes utility at optimum C^0 by producing outputs Y_A^0 and M_A^0, thereby enabling A to enjoy the consumption benefit of the former and the security benefit S_A^0 of the latter.

Suppose now that ally B's military output increases to M_B^1, with the enemy's output held fixed at M_C^0. Because military strength in the alliance is a pure public good, ally A benefits from increased security, other things equal, causing A's security line to shift rightward to $S_A(M_A + M_B^1, M_C^0)$. Due to the linkages in the model, the CSPF in turn shifts rightward to HQ'N'. This allows ally A to reallocate resources to achieve optimum C^1 with civilian good Y_A^1, military output M_A^1, and security S_A^1. Notice carefully what has happened. Given the increased output of its ally, A has been able to reduce its own military output, while also enjoying more civilian goods and more security. The result is increased utility for A and thus a compelling incentive to free ride off the military output of ally B. This perhaps surprising result is quite general, relying only on the publicness of the alliance's military strength and the additional but reasonable assumption that the civilian good and security are both normal goods.

Reaction Functions and Alliance Equilibrium

The pure public good model is completed by bringing the optimal behavior of ally A together with the optimal behavior of B to determine

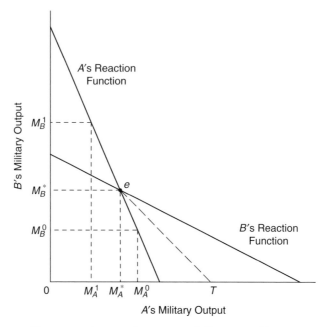

Figure 16.4 Reaction functions and alliance equilibrium.

the equilibrium military outputs of the two allies. Notice that the preceding analysis already sketches how Figure 16.3 can be used to derive
a reaction function for A. For example, if ally B chooses output M_B^0, A's
best reply in Figure 16.3 is M_A^0, and if B chooses M_B^1, A's best reply is M_A^1.
As seen in Figure 16.4, this generates two of the points along A's
reaction function, which shows A's best reply for any given output by
B. Similar analysis for ally B generates B's reaction function. Notice that
the reaction functions are negatively sloped, reflecting the incentive of
each ally to free ride off the military output of the other. A Nash
equilibrium exists when each ally's output is a best reply to the others.
Hence, the equilibrium for the alliance is determined in Figure 16.4 at
point e, where the two reaction functions intersect. In equilibrium,
A chooses output M_A^*, which is a best reply to B's M_B^*, while B chooses
M_B^*, which is a best reply to A's M_A^*. The total alliance strength
$M^* = M_A^* + M_B^*$ equals the distance OT, determined geometrically by
the dashed line drawn from the equilibrium to the horizontal axis with
slope -1 (Cornes and Sandler 1996).

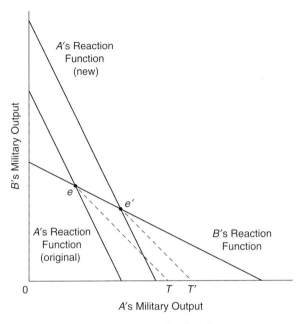

Figure 16.5 Free riding by ally *B*.

Implications

Free Riding

The incentive to free ride identified in the allies' reaction curves carries over to the comparative-statics of the full equilibrium model. Suppose, for example, that ally *A* perceives a new threat to its security, but *B* does not. *A* will tend to increase demand for military goods, as shown by the rightward shift of its reaction function in Figure 16.5. A new alliance equilibrium emerges at point *e'*, which entails increased military output by *A* but decreased output by *B*. Note that *B* clearly free rides on *A*'s increased output: despite *B*'s own decrease in military output, *B* nonetheless is able to enjoy an increase in total defense from *OT* to *OT'* and therefore an increase in its own security.

Alliance Suboptimality

Alliance formation can improve each player's well-being relative to "going it alone" but still be inefficient in the sense that additional gains are available to the allies relative to the alliance equilibrium. We demonstrate this implication by supplementing the allies' reaction curves with their associated

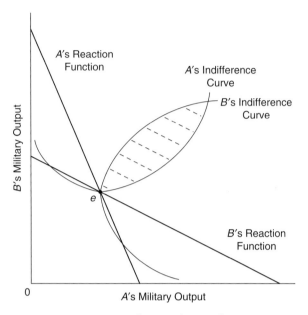

Figure 16.6 Alliance suboptimality.

indifference curves, as shown in Figure 16.6. The logic of adding indifference curves is similar to that used for the arms rivalry model in the preceding chapter. In brief, the PPFs and security functions are substituted into the respective allies' utility functions, resulting in translated utility functions defined in terms of both allies' military outputs M_A and M_B (along with the enemy's output M_C).

The translated utility functions are represented by indifference curves in the usual manner. Of A's many indifference curves, in Figure 16.6 we have drawn just one, that being the curve passing through equilibrium point e. Because e lies on A's reaction function, A's military output at that point is optimal given the corresponding military output of B. Thus, A would be content with an increase in its own output only if it was compensated for the added cost by a higher level of security emanating from an increase in B's output. This means that A's indifference curve must turn upward to the right of e, as shown. In the other direction, A would be indifferent to a decrease in its own output only if it was compensated for its forgone security by higher security generated by an increase in B's output. Thus, A's indifference curve likewise must turn upward to the left of e. Repeating the same reasoning for other points along A's reaction function means that A's indifference curves are U-shaped around its reaction function. Also, because unilateral increases in *B*'s military output leave *A* strictly better off, points on higher indifference curves are more preferred by *A*. For ally *B* we likewise show a single indifference curve passing through the equilibrium point *e*. Similar reasoning means that *B*'s indifference curves are U-shaped relative to the vertical axis, and points on indifference curves farther to the right are more preferred by *B*.

Notice that the two indifference curves drawn through equilibrium point *e* form a highlighted lens-shaped area in Figure 16.6. Points within the lens lie above *A*'s indifference curve and hence are preferred to *e* by *A*; they also lie to the right of *B*'s indifference curve and hence are preferred to *e* by *B*. Thus, the lens-shaped area forms a region of mutual gain and thereby demonstrates the equilibrium *e* to be Pareto inefficient. In the absence of unspecified transaction costs, this means that both allies can benefit if they coordinate their military outputs to reach some specified point within the lens.

The source of the alliance's inefficiency is subtle but important. In the pure public good model, the players enjoy the defense benefits that spill over from their ally's military goods. Nevertheless, in their own utility functions they place no value on the defense benefits created for their ally from their own military goods. Hence, the players may form an alliance and enjoy security benefits from each other's military goods, but they make autonomous allocation choices that ignore the spillover benefits to their ally. This leads to under-provision of military goods for the alliance as a whole, a result echoed in the government counterterrorism games of Chapter 13. Elimination of the under-provision requires an alliance agreement that goes well beyond the sharing of the public good to include some form of centralized coordination of the allocation choices (Sandler and Hartley 1999, ch. 8).

Disproportionate Burden Sharing

Under certain assumptions, the pure public good model predicts that the wealthier ally will bear a disproportionately large defense burden, as measured by the ratio of its military goods to its aggregate output (Olson and Zeckhauser 1966, pp. 269–70). We call this the disproportionality hypothesis; in the alliance literature it is also known as the exploitation hypothesis. Note that the hypothesis does not say simply that the wealthier ally will produce more military goods than the poorer ally, but that the wealthier ally will allocate a greater proportion of its aggregate output to defense than the poorer ally. Figure 16.7 offers a stylized example of the disproportionality hypothesis. Assume *A* and *B* are initially identical in

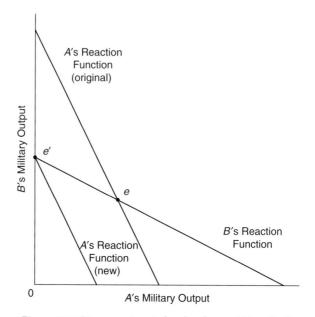

Figure 16.7 Disproportionate burden for wealthier ally *B*.

every respect, including the same PPFs, security functions, and preferences, thus generating a symmetric equilibrium at point *e*. Assume now
that *A*'s aggregate output, as modeled by the PPF in the 4-quadrant model,
falls until *A*'s reaction function just intersects the vertical intercept of *B*'s
reaction function. In this corner solution at point *e'*, *A* produces zero
military goods, while *B* produces all of the alliance's output. This then is
an extreme but clear example of the disproportionality hypothesis inasmuch as the wealthier ally *B* incurs a positive burden while *A* suffers no
burden at all.

Optimal Alliance Size
Suppose an additional player joins the *A/B* alliance arrayed against *C*,
and the transaction costs of assimilating the new ally are zero. In the
pure public good model, the military output of the new ally is a perfect
substitute for the outputs of *A* and *B*. Hence, the addition of the ally
enables *A* and *B* to reduce their respective demands for military goods,
increase civilian production, and enjoy greater security, all else equal.
Similar benefits would arise if even more players enter the alliance.
Consequently, there are no benefit/cost reasons to limit the number of
allies. In practical terms, when the security benefits generated by

military goods are purely public and the transaction costs of new allies are minimal, an alliance has the incentive to bring in as many new allies as possible. A contemporary example that may approximate a purely public defense good for many players is degradation of the al Qaeda terrorist organization. If al Qaeda is weakened, all potential targets of al Qaeda benefit at the same time, and they cannot be excluded from such benefits. The pure public good model suggests that states arrayed against al Qaeda should bring in as many allies as possible if the transaction costs of operating as an alliance are sufficiently low.

16.4 Joint Product Model of Alliances

Pure Public, Impure Public, and Private Goods

The key assumption in the previous model is that each ally's security is based exclusively on the sharing of a pure public good. The assumption is restrictive in at least two ways. First, it requires that security be derived from a pure public good, meaning a good that is both perfectly nonrival and perfectly nonexcludable. The prototypical example is deterrence of a common enemy based on strategic nuclear weapons. In practice, however, the public good shared by an alliance need not be pure; rather, it can be partially rival and/or partially excludable, in which case it is called an impure public good. An example of an impure public good is territorial defense based on conventional forces. Suppose A is attacked by C, leading ally B to send military forces to help counter C's advance against A. Notice that the defense provided is partially rival: the forces committed by B are not available at the same time to counter an attack by C on B's territory. Sandler and Hartley (1995, p. 31) describe this as force thinning, whereby forces are spread along a border or across an area. The defense provided by B is also partially excludable: ally B can choose to hold back some of its forces to defend its own territory. Second, the model's key assumption is restrictive in that it requires security to be based solely on a public good. Military activity, however, can generate security derived from goods that are wholly private to the providing ally (Olson and Zeckhauser 1966, p. 272). For example, many nations use military forces to protect coastlines or defend against domestic terrorists. All or most of the benefits of such activity do not spill over to the security of allies.

Technology of Public Supply and the Joint Product Model

In a series of formal extensions, Sandler and his colleagues relaxed the restrictive pure public good assumption and developed what is known as the joint product model of alliances (Sandler and Cauley 1975, Sandler 1977, Murdoch and Sandler 1982). In this model, allies' military goods generate a variety of defense products that range from purely public (for example, deterrence), to impurely public (for example, damage limitation), to private (for example, control of domestic terrorism). The extensions represent far more than minor adjustments to the pure public good model of alliances. Rather, they culminate in a general alliance model which includes the original pure public good model as a special case. In what follows, we highlight the main elements and key results of the joint product model. More formal and complete coverage is provided by Cornes and Sandler (1984) and Sandler and Hartley (2001).

Suppose the military outputs of allies A and B generate shared security benefits, which may be either pure or impure, and possibly also defense benefits that are strictly private. Assuming symmetry in the technology of public supply, the security functions for A and B can be written:

$$S_A = S_A(M_A + \theta M_B, \delta M_A, M_C), \qquad (16.1a)$$

$$S_B = S_B(\theta M_A + M_B, \delta M_B, M_C), \qquad (16.1b)$$

where $0 < \theta \leq 1$ and $\delta \geq 0$. The θ term in either equation is the degree to which a player benefits from a spillover from the ally's output. When θ equals one, the alliance's shared good is purely public; when θ is less than one, the shared good is impurely public. The δ term captures the extent to which a player's military output generates private benefits. If δ is zero at the same time that θ equals one, then the security functions are identical to those in the pure public good model.

Figure 16.8 shows reaction functions for two alternative technologies of public supply, assuming for simplicity that the allies have identical PPFs, security functions, and preferences. In both cases we stipulate no private benefits, so $\delta = 0$. For the first case we assume $\theta = 1$, meaning that the allies share a pure public good. The result is the set of solid-lined reaction functions, which yield equilibrium military outputs at point e. For the second case we assume $\theta < 1$, meaning that the spillover from each other's military output is less than complete, so that the allies share an impure public good. The result this time is the set of dashed reaction functions with equilibrium point f. Relative to the first case, the reaction

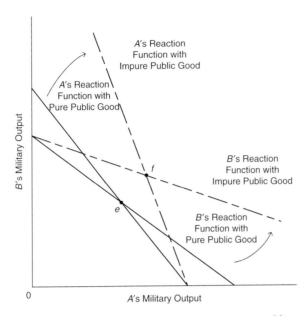

Figure 16.8 Reaction functions for a pure versus impure public good.

functions with an impure public good are rotated outward around a fixed intercept. Because the spillover benefit is reduced, the incentive to free ride on an ally's output is reduced, causing the steepness of A's reaction curve to increase and B's to decrease. If as a third case we were to introduce private benefits with $\delta > 0$, we would expect a more general outward shift in the reaction functions (not shown), with all intercepts changing relative to cases of pure or impure public goods.

Implications

The joint product model modifies the predictions of the original pure public good model in important ways (Cornes and Sandler 1984, Sandler and Hartley 2001). When military goods generate partially rival and/or partially excludable defense benefits among allies, then the allies must rely more on their own military outputs to achieve security. Under such conditions, one can expect that the extent of free riding, suboptimality, disproportionality, and optimal number of allies will all be reduced relative to what is implied in the pure public good model. Recall in Figure 16.8 that A's reaction function is steeper when the alliance's public good is impure rather than pure. Hence, a given increase in M_B will lead to a smaller decrease in M_A and hence less free riding. In the same way, diminished free riding is also implied by the flatter slope of B's reaction function. The presence of excludable private benefits further increases the allies' reliance on their own military outputs. With decreased incentives for free riding, disproportionate burdens on wealthier allies and under-provision of alliance defense are reduced. Moreover, the impurity of the public good that arises with force thinning causes the optimal alliance size to be finite. In the presence of force thinning, optimality requires that allies be added only to the point where the marginal security benefits created by additional military goods just equal the marginal costs due to additional thinning (Sandler and Hartley 1995, p. 34).

16.5 Empirical Studies

Burden Sharing within NATO

A key implication of the pure public good model is that larger allies bear a disproportionate share of the alliance burden due to free riding by smaller allies. In their seminal paper, Olson and Zeckhauser (1966) operationalized the hypothesis as follows: "In an alliance, there will be a significant positive correlation between the size of a member's national income and the percentage of its national income spent on defense" (p. 274). They tested their hypothesis using a cross section of 14 NATO allies in 1964. The test was based on the correlation between two rank orderings – one for income (measured by GNP), and another for defense burden (that is, defense budget as a percent of income). These rank orderings are replicated in the left side of Table 16.2. If the disproportionality hypothesis is correct, countries that rank higher in income should also tend to rank higher in defense burden. That is what the data show. Of the top six allies in income, four rank among the top in defense burden. As reported by Olson and Zeckhauser, across all 14 allies the correlation between the two rank orderings equals 0.490 and is statistically significant. Olson and Zeckhauser (1966, p. 265) concluded that "large nations in NATO bear a disproportionate share of the burden of the common defense," thus supporting the public good model of alliances.

Subsequent researchers, however, discovered that the rank correlation between income and defense burden diminished and ceased to be statistically significant after the mid-to-late 1960s (Sandler and Forbes 1980, Oneal and Elrod 1989, Khanna and Sandler 1996, Sandler and Murdoch 2000). This evidence suggests that the Olson/Zeckhauser

Table 16.2 *Burden sharing in NATO, 1964, 1971, and 2015.*

Country	1964 GNP Rank	1964 Defense Burden Rank	Country	1971 GNP Rank	1971 Defense Burden Rank	Country	2015 GDP Rank	2015 Defense Burden Rank
USA	1	1	USA	1	1	USA	1	1
Germany	2	6	Germany	2	10	Germany	2	15
UK	3	3	France	3	6	UK	3	7
France	4	4	UK	4	3	France	4	3
Italy	5	10	Italy	5	9	Italy	5	12
Canada	6	8	Canada	6	13	Canada	6	22
Netherlands	7	7	Netherlands	7	7 (tie)	Spain	7	14
Belgium	8	12	Belgium	8	12	Netherlands	8	16
Denmark	9	13	Denmark	9	11	Turkey	9	4
Turkey	10	5	Turkey	10	4 (tie)	Poland	10	5
Norway	11	11	Norway	11	7 (tie)	Belgium	11	26
Greece	12	9	Greece	12	4 (tie)	Norway	12	10
Portugal	13	2	Portugal	13	2	Denmark	13	19
Luxembourg	14	14	Luxembourg	14	14	Portugal	14	8
						Greece	15	2
						Czech Rep	16	23
						Romania	17	11
						Hungary	18	24
						Slovak Rep	19	20

Table 16.2 (cont.)

Country	1964 GNP Rank	1964 Defense Burden Rank	Country	1971 GNP Rank	1971 Defense Burden Rank	Country	2015 GDP Rank	2015 Defense Burden Rank
						Luxembourg	20	27
						Bulgaria	21	13
						Croatia	22	9
						Slovenia	23	25
						Lithuania	24	18
						Latvia	25	21
						Estonia	26	6
						Albania	27	17
Correlation		0.490*			0.165			0.364*
p-value (one-tailed)		0.038			0.286			0.031

Note: *Significant at the 5 percent level (one-tailed).
Sources: Olson and Zeckhauser (1966, p. 267), International Institute for Strategic Studies (1974, p. 78), and Stockholm International Peace Research Institute (2017).

disproportionality result for NATO seemed to vanish by the 1970s. As an illustration, in the middle of Table 16.2 we replicate Olson and Zeckhauser's methodology for 1971. Notice that of the top six allies in income, only three also ranked among the top in defense burden. Across all 14 countries, the rank correlation fell sharply to 0.165 and became statistically insignificant.

More recently, Sandler and Shimizu (2014) maintain that disproportionality might be reemerging in NATO. On the right side of Table 16.2, we once again replicate Olson and Zeckhauser's methodology but for the year 2015 based upon 27 NATO allies. As shown in the table, across the 27 allies the correlation between the two rank orderings equals 0.364 and is statistically significant. Hence, there is once again evidence of disproportionality in NATO.

How might we understand the "on" and then "off" and then "on again" nature of disproportionality in the NATO alliance? According to Sandler and Forbes (1980), the explanatory power of the pure public good model as it pertained to NATO in the early years of the alliance diminished owing to changes in weapons technologies, strategic arms control, and NATO strategy. In the late 1960s, NATO shifted from a doctrine of mutually assured destruction, with its objective of pure nuclear deterrence, to one of flexible response, with its increased emphasis on protection and damage limitation. As a consequence, NATO relied more on conventional and tactical nuclear weapons and hence produced more private and impure public defense goods. Based on the joint product model, Sandler and Forbes (1980, p. 426) hypothesized that as a result of the change in NATO doctrine, free riding would be reduced and defense burdens shared more in accordance with the distribution of alliance benefits. Across all 14 NATO allies, Sandler and Forbes found that the differences between relative defense burdens and those predicted based on benefit shares diminished in the 1970s, leading them to conclude that changes in NATO doctrine favored the applicability of the joint product model over the pure public good model. (For contrary views of disproportionality in the NATO alliance after the late 1960s, see Oneal and Diehl 1994 and Solomon 2004.)

More recently, Sandler and Shimizu (2014) maintain that disproportionality may be reemerging in NATO. Over the past quarter century, NATO has undergone significant transformations including expansion of alliance membership, increasing reliance on combat and nation-building missions far from home, changes in the composition of public and private benefits from counterterrorism, and substantial differences in tastes for country-specific and alliance-wide benefits (Sandler and Shimizu 2014, pp. 44–5). Based on their analysis of defense burdens and GDP for NATO allies since 1999, Sandler and Shimizu (2014, p. 45) indicate there is "clear evidence that the various average benefit shares of the allies no longer match their defense burdens. This means the cohesiveness of NATO falls following the war on terror, NATO expansion, and the growing importance of out-of-area missions ... leading to evidence of exploitation of the rich by the poor starting in 2004 ..."

Alliances and the Risk of Armed Conflict

A natural question to ask about interstate alliances is whether they increase or decrease the likelihood of armed conflict between states. As argued by Leeds (2003), however, the question is poorly posed because alliance agreements can give rise to different obligations and hence different effects. Leeds (2003) finds that defensive pacts decrease the likelihood of interstate armed conflict while offensive and neutrality pacts increase the likelihood. Furthermore, Senese and Vasquez (2008) maintain that the effects of alliances on the risk of war depend upon numerous conditions including the nature of alliance ties between states, the political relevance of the alliance in terms of states' capabilities and geographic regions, the stakes that nations dispute (for example, territory), and the time periods of the alliances.

An empirical study in which context affects the impact of alliances on the risk of interstate conflict is Fuhrmann and Sechser (2014), who hypothesize that when a state is allied with a nuclear power it is less likely to be attacked by other states. Fuhrman and Sechser note that pledges of military support by one state to another may not be deemed credible by other states because violent conflicts are costly. Fuhrmann and Sechser theorize, however, that when a state formally signs a public defense pact with an ally, it is sending a strong signal to other actors that it will help militarily if its ally is attacked because the state will bear significant reputation costs if it fails to do so. Fuhrmann and Sechser also emphasize that for nuclear states, "the construction of public alliances may be sufficient to accrue the extended deterrence benefits of nuclear weapons" (p. 922). The authors thus hypothesize that a state with a public defense pact with a nuclear weapons state will be less likely to be a target of a militarized interstate dispute (MID).

Fuhrmann and Sechser test their hypothesis based on the COW and ATOP alliance data. Besides being an important contribution to the alliance literature, Fuhrman and Sechser's article has the bonus benefit for our purposes of illustrating the use of directed dyads. Consider any two countries, say Japan and North Korea. This single dyad provides two directed dyads in empirical research. In the context of Fuhrmann and Sechser's article, one directed dyad treats North Korea as the potential attacker, that is, as the country that might initiate a MID against the potential target country, in this case Japan. The second directed dyad reverses the roles, with Japan as the potential attacker and North Korea as the potential target.

Drawing on all politically relevant directed dyads for each year between 1950 and 2000, Fuhrmann and Sechser construct a large sample of observations, where each observation is a directed dyad-year. The dependent variable is one if a fatal MID (involving at least one fatality) is initiated and zero otherwise. The key explanatory variables indicate whether a state that could be attacked has a defense pact with a nuclear state and whether it has a defense pact with a non-nuclear state. Control variables include contiguity, common foreign policies, and relative strength. Fuhrmann and Sechser find that potential targets of fatal MIDs are significantly less likely to be attacked when they are allied to a nuclear power. On the flip side "states lacking defense commitments from nuclear powers are more than three times as likely to be targeted in violent disputes than states with nuclear-armed allies" (p. 927). Defense pacts with non-nuclear powers had no significant effect on the risk of a state experiencing a fatal MID.

16.6 Applications of Alliance Theory to Global Challenges

Security is a broad concept, which can include security from military attack, natural disasters, unsafe climate change, degrading living conditions, diseases, and so on. Since states and other organizations formally cooperate with each other to address global and regional challenges, theories and concepts from the economics of alliances are applicable to a broad array of contexts beyond conflict and peace narrowly conceived. The applicability of alliance concepts to such challenges depends upon, first, the nonrivalry and nonexcludability of the benefits of a collective good (that is, whether the collective good is a pure or impure public good), second, how actor contributions aggregate to generate the collective good (that is, the technology of public supply), and, third, transactions costs (Sandler 2004, 2016; Peinhardt and Sandler 2015).

Consider, for example, money laundering. One might think that money laundering is only a problem for those countries that experience it within their borders, but this would be a misconception. If even just one or a few states experience money laundering, many states can be harmed. For example, terrorist groups and other criminal organizations would be able to exploit the money laundering "havens" available in just a few states even if money laundering was substantially reduced elsewhere in the world (Sandler 2016b). Hence, all states that can be harmed by those exploiting money laundering opportunities can gain from the degradation of money laundering havens. Even if each nation's contribution to the global good of reduced money laundering leads to spillover benefits to others that are impurely (rather than purely) public, there are still incentives for free-riding and suboptimal provision of the collective good as we saw in alliance theory. Moreover, Sandler (2016b) maintains that the aggregation of the efforts of nations to degrade money laundering (that is, the technology of public supply) faces a "weak-link" challenge. Specifically, the availability of money laundering to criminal organizations will only be as low as the nation (the weak link) in which laundering opportunities are the greatest. Other collective challenges that are similar to money laundering include threats to endangered species and monitoring the outbreak of contagious diseases (Sandler 2016b, p. 35).

A second collective challenge requires that a certain threshold of aggregate effort be achieved among the contributors before the harm can be overcome. For example, if three countries agree to contribute effort to reduce pollution, but dozens of other countries do not join the effort (hoping to free ride on the efforts of others), the threshold required to avoid environmental harm can be missed. Once again, key concepts from alliance theory (free riding, suboptimal alliance efforts, suboptimal alliance size) can be relevant in conceptualizing insecurities associated with environmental degradation. Other collective challenges that are similar to reaching a threshold to reduce environmental harm include inoculations against diseases (Sandler 2016b, p. 40).

A third collective challenge is known as "best shot," in which the largest contribution among the agents determines the amount of the public good available to all agents (Sandler 2016b, p. 35). Consider, for example, a serious disease that has broken out in nation A, but nowhere else (yet). The size of the "best effort" in A (by A and by other potential contributors) can have a significant effect on whether the disease is cured or a contagion breaks out and spreads to other countries. Again, insights from alliance theory can be applied to the problem to reduce free riding, identify the optimal number of contributors, and so on. Other collective challenges that are similar to a best shot effort to cure a disease include reducing the risk of conflagration in a country prone to forest fires and shoring up the financial weakness of a country that could be the source of a regional or global financial crisis (Sandler 2016b, p. 42).

16.7 Bibliographic Notes

Since the seminal contributions of Olson and Zeckhauser (1966, 1967), Sandler and Cauley (1975), Sandler (1977), and Murdoch and Sandler (1982), numerous extensions to the economic theory of alliances have appeared. These include models that incorporate action and reaction among allies and a rival (Niou and Tan 2005), alternative technologies of public supply (McGuire 1990; Conybeare, Murdoch, and Sandler 1994), and equilibrium concepts other than Nash (Sandler and Murdoch 1990). The theory is applied and/or tested in studies of the Warsaw Pact, Triple Alliance, and Triple Entente (Conybeare, Murdoch, and Sandler 1994), peacekeeping operations (Sandler 2017), global strategic defense (McGuire 2004), peace as an international public good (Brauer and Roux 2000), provision of security services (Brauer and van Tuyll 2008, pp. 308–12), arms trade control (Sandler 2000), protection against national emergencies (Ihori 1999), and counterinsurgency operations (Elias 2017).

The economic analysis of alliances includes the effects of economic factors on alliance behavior and the effects of alliances on economic outcomes. The former includes studies of the effects of trade (Jackson and Nei 2015) and financial constraints (Allen and Digiuseppe 2013) on alliances. The latter considers the effects of alliances on trade (Haim 2016), effectiveness of economic sanctions (Early 2012), defense industrial policy (Hartley 2006), economic growth (Macnair, Murdoch, Pi, and Sandler 1995), and exchange-rate regimes (Li 2003). Sandler and Hartley (2001) provide an extensive survey of theoretical and empirical literature on the economic theory of alliances.

Although we emphasize the economics of alliances in this chapter, political scientists have delved into many other aspects of alliance behavior including why alliances form (Horowitz, Poast, and Stam 2017; Quirk 2017), connections between alliances and interstate war (Vasquez and Rundlett 2016), the effects of internal alliances of nonstate actors on civil war (Zeigler 2016), and alliances among terrorist organizations and criminal syndicates (Mincheva and Gurr 2012, Hesterman 2013). Special issues of *International Interactions* (Krause and Sprecher 2004), *Journal of Peace Research* (Sprecher and Krause 2006), and *Conflict Management and Peace Science* (Millard 2016) offer excellent summaries of quantitative research on alliances.

17

Peace

Given the long history of violence in human relations, scholars and policy-makers have devoted substantial resources to analyzing and promoting peaceful approaches to conflicts. Over many decades, such work has coalesced into wide-ranging multidisciplinary fields including *peace and conflict studies, conflict resolution,* and *peace science* (Barash and Webel 2018; Ramsbotham, Woodhouse, and Miall 2011; Isard 1988, 1992; Peace Science Society 2018). It cannot be overstated how large such fields have become. A small sample of topics includes reasons for war and sources of peace; conflict prevention, management, and resolution; peacemaking, peacekeeping, and peacebuilding; the art and science of negotiation; and arms control, disarmament, and defense conversion. In this chapter we draw upon topics within the peace-focused fields to analyze economic aspects of peace. Given the wide-ranging nature of the peace-focused fields, our presentation is selective and can best be thought of as a gateway into economic aspects of peace.

17.1 Definitions

Barash and Webel (2018, p. 12 and pp. 7–12) note that "peace remains notoriously difficult to define," but that the concepts of "negative peace" and "positive peace" have achieved a reasonable degree of acceptance within the peace-related fields. At its most basic level, negative peace is the absence of threatened or actual violence in the processing of conflicts (Barash and Webel 2018, p. 7). Meanwhile, positive peace constitutes the absence of violence (and thus incorporates negative peace) and the absence of "structural violence," where the latter represents conditions in which the economic, political, social, and/or other rights of individuals are repressed

(Barash and Webel 2018, pp. 7–10). As seen in this book, conditions of structural violence such as suppression of political and economic rights can foster explicit violence. In other words, the lack of positive peace can foster the lack of negative peace. In turn, threatened or actual violence can damage economic, political, and social fabrics and thus cause patterns of structural violence to remain "locked in" or even become worse. Hence, the lack of negative peace can reinforce the lack of positive peace.

Another critical concept in the peace-related fields is "conflict," which is the pursuit of incompatible goals by contesting individuals or groups (Ramsbotham, Woodhouse, and Miall 2011, p. 30). The incompatibilities might be over control of the government, territory, or ideology, access to economic and political rights, and so on. Conflict in this sense is ubiquitous in human affairs and, in some cases, desirable. As Ramsbotham, Woodhouse, and Miall (2011, p. 124) note: "Conflicts pursued constructively are creative and form a necessary means of bringing about change." The key to those working in the peace-related fields is not to avoid conflicts but, whenever possible, to avoid the "violent" processing of conflicts.

Within the peace-related fields, particularly peace and conflict studies, a vast array of harms to people and to the environment are conceptualized as structural violence (Galtung 1996). In much of what follows, we focus more narrowly on selected concepts and topics from the field of conflict resolution. Ramsbotham, Woodhouse, and Miall (2011) characterize "conflict resolution" as the prevention of violent conflicts; the treatment of deep-rooted sources of violence so that behavior is no longer violent, attitudes cease to be hostile, and the structure of the conflict has changed; and transformation of the institutions and conflicting parties that spawn violence. Conflict resolution work is often "multitrack"; that is, it is conducted by intergovernmental organizations (IGOs), governments (via diplomats, aid agencies, etc.), international nongovernmental organizations (INGOs), domestic nongovernmental organizations (NGOs), private businesses, and individuals. Such work often involves an array of programs that draw upon best practices in negotiation, mediation, problem-solving, and reconciliation. Furthermore, for conflicts where violence is imminent, underway, or terminated, one will often find peace missions sponsored by governments and/or IGOs such as those that focus upon settlement of armed conflicts (peacemaking) or the consensual or nonconsensual insertion of international armed forces between belligerents to keep the peace (peacekeeping and peace enforcement, respectively). Also included is amelioration of longer-term structural issues that foster violence, especially after conflict, but also applicable throughout the conflict and peace life cycle (peacebuilding) (Ramsbotham, Woodhouse, and Miall 2011, p. 32).

But what of economics and peace? As seen throughout this book, economic incentives and conditions can affect the risk and intensity of violent conflict. But perhaps most important in what follows are two overarching principles on the economics of peace. First, economic variables and conditions provide opportunities for peace to prevail over violence (Wennmann 2011, p. 1). The vast majority of individuals around the world desire to provide economically for their families and to live lives that are relatively free of harm, especially threatened or actual physical violence (recall from Chapter 1 that security in this sense is one of the most important services that an economy can provide). In short, most people deeply desire peace; that is, their demand for peace is high. Second, peace is something that can be produced (created) and invested in (maintained and expanded) through the creative efforts (that is, resources) of individuals and organizations. In other words, peace can be supplied. Regardless of whether one believes that the sources of violent conflict are primarily rooted in human nature or in social systems, the high demand for peace that resonates throughout the world and the hoped-for growing supply of peaceful alternatives to violence hold the promise of substantial economic and noneconomic gains for many people across the globe.

17.2 Patterns of Peace

The Global Peace Index and the Positive Peace Index

We begin our analyses of global, regional, and nation-state trends in peace with the Global Peace Index (GPI) produced by the Institute for Economics and Peace (2018) (see Appendix D.7). The GPI measures the level of negative peace each year for 163 countries across three domains: first, the extent to which a country is involved in internal and external conflicts, second, the level of harmony or discord within a country, which is characterized as "societal safety and security," and, third, the country's level of militarization. The aggregate, regional, and country-specific GPI scores can range from 1 (most peaceful) to 5 (least peaceful).

From 2008 to 2018, the average GPI score for the world deteriorated by 2.4 percent (Institute for Economics and Peace 2018, p. 2). Table 17.1 shows the trend in the GPI by region from 2014 to 2018, where higher GPI scores represent less peacefulness. As the table shows, in recent years the least peaceful region has been the Middle East and North Africa followed

Table 17.1 *Regional global peace index (GPI) scores, 2014–18.*

Region	2014	2015	2016	2017	2018
Asia-Pacific	1.92	1.88	1.94	1.92	1.91
Central America & Caribbean	2.11	2.09	2.10	2.10	2.10
Europe	1.61	1.57	1.66	1.66	1.68
Middle East & North Africa	2.24	2.39	2.55	2.56	2.53
North America	1.72	1.66	1.77	1.80	1.84
Russia & Eurasia	2.29	2.25	2.36	2.33	2.34
South America	2.04	2.05	2.11	2.07	2.09
South Asia	2.40	2.35	2.41	2.40	2.40
Sub-Saharan Africa	2.27	2.20	2.23	2.24	2.24

Note: Higher GPI score represents lower peacefulness.
Source: Institute for Economics and Peace (2018).

by South Asia and Russia and Eurasia. GPI scores for the Middle East and North Africa have been poor owing to ongoing conflict in Syria and increased hostility on the Arabian Peninsula (Institute for Economics and Peace 2018, p. 15). The most peaceful region in recent years has been Europe followed by North America and Asia-Pacific. Nevertheless, Europe's GPI score has worsened (risen) owing to deteriorating political conditions in Poland, Spain, and Turkey (Institute for Economics and Peace 2018, p. 14). Table 17.2 shows the 10 least peaceful and most peaceful countries in the world in 2018 based upon their GPI scores.

The GPI focuses upon measures of threatened or actual violence such as wars, terrorism, and murder; as such, it indexes negative peace. In recent years, the Institute for Economics and Peace also developed a Positive Peace Index (PPI), which tracks trends in the world, across regions, and for countries of "the attitudes, institutions and structures that create and sustain peaceful societies" (Institute for Economics and Peace 2017, p. 6). The PPI measures the level of positive peace each year for 163 countries based upon such areas as good government, sound business environment, human rights, free flow of information, and good relations with neighboring countries (see Appendix D.7). From 2008 to 2017 the average PPI score for the world improved by 1.9 percent (Institute for Economics and Peace 2017, p. 6). Regional scores are not yet generally available in the Institute for Economics and Peace's Positive Peace Report, but PPI scores are

Table 17.2 *Ten most and least peaceful countries based on GPI, 2018.*

Most Peaceful (Low GPI)		Least Peaceful (High GPI)	
Country	GPI Score	Country	GPI Score
Iceland	1.10	Syria	3.60
New Zealand	1.19	Afghanistan	3.59
Austria	1.27	South Sudan	3.51
Portugal	1.32	Iraq	3.43
Denmark	1.35	Somalia	3.37
Canada	1.37	Yemen	3.31
Czech Republic	1.38	Libya	3.26
Singapore	1.38	Dem. Rep. Congo	3.25
Japan	1.39	Central Afr. Rep.	3.24
Ireland	1.39	Russia	3.16

Source: Institute for Economics and Peace (2018, pp. 8–9).

available for countries. Table 17.3 shows the 10 least peaceful and most peaceful countries in the world in 2017 based upon their PPI scores.

The negative and positive peace indices offered by the Institute for Economics and Peace have been criticized in the academic literature. For example, Ulfelder (2018) points out that countries' military expenditures worsen their GPI scores: "Most people would probably think of the avoidance of war as a peaceful outcome, but the GPI casts the preparations that sometimes help to produce that outcome as a diminution of peace. In an ideal world, disarmament and peace would always go together; in the real world, they don't …" We would also add that the high military spending level of a country that carries a disproportionate burden of an alliance's military spending would worsen that country's GPI score and improve the GPI scores of the free riding countries, all else equal. Such criticisms of datasets are a natural part of the progress of social science because datasets can always be improved through further research. In our view, the Institute for Economics and Peace has provided an important and even ground-breaking service to the academic and policy communities by beginning to track measures of negative and positive peace across the globe. Such data will be refined over the decades and, we predict, provide important insights into the sources of peace in human relations.

Table 17.3 *Ten most and least peaceful countries based on PPI, 2017.*

Most Peaceful (Low PPI)		Least Peaceful (High PPI)	
Country	PPI Score	Country	PPI Score
Sweden	1.26	Somalia	4.62
Switzerland	1.27	Central Afr. Rep.	4.39
Finland	1.27	Yemen	4.28
Norway	1.29	Eritrea	4.25
Denmark	1.34	North Korea	4.23
Ireland	1.34	Iraq	4.22
Netherlands	1.38	Afghanistan	4.21
New Zealand	1.43	South Sudan	4.20
Germany	1.44	Chad	4.19
Iceland	1.44	Dem. Rep. Congo	4.17

Source: Institute for Economics and Peace (2017, pp. 14–5).

Macro Multilateral Peace Operations

We already saw in Chapter 1 (Table 1.3) the ten-year trend in the number of worldwide multilateral peace operations conducted by IGOs and coalitions of states. Since the focus there was on peace missions by IGOs and states, we characterized them as "top-down" or "macro" peace operations. Table 17.4 presents a snapshot of data on such peace operations for 2016. As the table shows, a total of 62 macro peace missions were in operation across the world in 2016. Africa had the most missions (26) followed by Europe (18). Note that most peace missions were conducted, not by the United Nations (UN) (22), but by regional organizations or alliances (31). Nevertheless, the UN was by far the largest contributor of military troops (87,563 of 131,245), police (12,772 of 13,711), and civilian personnel (5,899 of 8,100) across the macro peace missions worldwide. Table 17.4 demonstrates substantial commitment of human resources to peace operations around the world by IGOs and coalitions of states. Nevertheless, the UN's peacekeeping budget for the 2017/2018 fiscal year is about $7 billion compared to worldwide military expenditures in 2017 of $1.7 trillion (Coleman 2017, Stockholm International Peace Research Institute 2018a).

Table 17.4 *Intergovernmental organization (IGO) peace missions worldwide, 2016.*

IGO	Region						Military Troops	Police	Civilian Personnel	Total
	Africa	Americas	Asia & Oceania	Europe	Middle East	Total				
United Nations	12	2	2	2	4	22	87,563	12,772	5,899	106,234
Regional Organizations or Alliances	12	1	2	14	2	31	40,865	856	1,925	43,646
Ad Hoc Coalitions of States	2	0	3	2	2	9	2,817	83	276	3,176
Totals	26	3	7	18	8	62	131,245	13,711	8,100	153,056

Source: Stockholm International Peace Research Institute (2017, p. 177 and pp. 205–6).

Micro Peace Operations by Nongovernment Organizations

The peace-focused fields devote substantial research efforts to understanding the effectiveness of macro multilateral peace missions on conflicts in the world, and rightly so. Nevertheless, comparatively little theoretical modeling and empirical research has been conducted on the peace efforts and effects of nongovernment organizations, specifically, INGOs, NGOs, and private businesses (for exceptions, see Murdie 2014 and Wilson, Davis, and Murdie 2016; the latter is reviewed later). Valuable case study approaches include Paffenholz 2010, Amutabi 2013, Christie 2013, Forrer and Seyle 2016, McMahon 2017, and Richmond and Carey 2017. We view the peace work of NGOs and INGOs as bottom-up or "micro" peace operations, occurring as they often do through communities and local leaders.

Table 17.5 shows the number of NGOs and INGOs fostering peace in selected conflict areas in 2018 based on data from Peace Direct (2018).

Table 17.5 *Number of peacebuilding organizations in selected conflict areas, 2018.*

Conflict Area	NGOs	INGOs	IGOs
Afghanistan	31	22	6
Colombia	25	24	5
Côte d'Ivoire	15	24	8
Democratic Republic of the Congo	35	27	6
Iraq	15	18	3
Israel and the Occupied Territories	25	25	3
Lebanon	41	22	6
Myanmar	10	14	7
Nigeria	53	18	7
Northern Ireland	32	3	1
Philippines	36	22	3
Syria	835*	31	5
Ukraine	20	22	6
Yemen	0	25	4
Zimbabwe	57	19	3

*As reported by the Citizens for Syria Database (2018).
Key:
   NGO – nongovernment organization
   INGO – international nongovernmental organization
   IGO – intergovernmental organization
Source: Peace Direct (2018).

For comparison, the number of IGOs working in the conflict zones are also shown in the table. The peace work by NGOs and INGOs include peacebuilding, conflict resolution, economic development assistance, refugee and IDP assistance, governance and rule of law training, and support for women's rights, civil rights, and childhood education. One can also add private businesses to the organizations operating in conflict zones. Obviously, there is great potential for business leaders to influence political leaders and other stakeholders to pursue nonviolent approaches to conflicts in the areas in which they operate (Forrer and Seyle 2016).

17.3 Economic Models and Peace Creation

In this section we apply two models featured in this book – networking and bargaining – to peace creation. By peace creation we mean intentional policies designed to transition a social system experiencing a high risk or actuality of war into a system experiencing what Boulding (1978) characterizes as stable peace. Stable peace exists between states or between a government and opposition groups when the institutions and norms for peace are sufficiently strong relative to strains between the actors that the system would never be carried over a boundary into war (Boulding 1978, p. xi). Peace creation policies can also keep a system of stable peace from transitioning into unstable peace or war.

Network Perspectives on Peace Creation

An organization working directly to promote peace is known as a conflict resolution organization (CRO) (Wilson, Davis, and Murdie 2016). CROs can do many things to promote peace. For example, CROs can provide information to actual or potential belligerents about the true costs of war; offer creative solutions to preemptive military technologies, indivisibilities, or threatening shifts in power that hinder conflict resolution; help reframe issues to diminish reference dependence and loss aversion; reduce malevolence through trust-building activities and education; and assist potential third-party interveners in overcoming free-rider incentives to do little to help. Furthermore, CROs can sometimes broker informal information flows between disputants' diplomats or other political elites when formal connections are not feasible (such work is often called Track 2 diplomacy in contrast to direct interactions between political elites, known as Track 1 diplomacy).

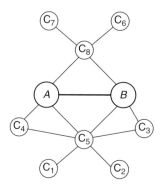

Figure 17.1 Network of conflict resolution organizations.

To analyze how networked CROs can foster peace, consider the stylized networking model in Figure 17.1. The CRO network encompasses the lower set of CROs (C_1 to C_5) and their links and the upper set of CROs (C_6 to C_8) and their links. The figure also shows two potential belligerents A and B, who could be states, nonstate actors, or one a state and the other a nonstate actor. Tied to the disputants and connected to each other are the eight CROs. C_5 and C_8 each have direct access to the disputants as shown by the links in the figure. Meanwhile, C_4 has direct access to A, and C_3 has direct access to B. The CROs conduct peace efforts to reduce the intensity of the dispute and to help resolve it without violence occurring. The actors and links in Figure 17.1 are for illustrative purposes. Many other CRO networks and disputants are possible.

Assume the benefits, costs, and network spillover benefits of peace efforts follow the linear quadratic model (LQM) detailed in Chapter 7. Here we present some of the formal aspects of the LQM, but leave most of the mathematical details to Appendix C.3 for the interested reader. Consider the LQM payoff function for the most networked CRO in Figure 17.1, C_5. The parameter a represents the marginal benefit and b is a cost parameter associated with C_5's peace efforts x_5. The parameter w captures the positive spillover benefits or peace synergies that accrue to C_5 from the CROs linked to it, namely C_1 through C_4. The positive synergies can arise from the sharing of information and resources between CROs. C_5's payoff π_5 from its peace efforts is:

$$\pi_5 = ax_5 - \frac{b}{2}x_5^2 + w_{51}x_5x_1 + w_{52}x_5x_2 + w_{53}x_5x_3 + w_{54}x_5x_4. \qquad (17.1)$$

It follows that C_5's best reply line or reaction function is:

$$x_5 = \frac{a}{b} + \left(\frac{1}{b}\right)(w_{51}x_1 + w_{52}x_2 + w_{53}x_3 + w_{54}x_4). \qquad (17.2)$$

Assume that the same parameter values for a, b, and w in equation (17.1) apply to the other seven CROs. These other CROs would have payoff functions that follow the structure of (17.1), but with the caveat that there would only be as many wx_ix_j synergy terms as a CRO has links with other CROs. For example, C_1's payoff function is:

$$\pi_1 = ax_1 - \frac{b}{2}x_1^2 + w_{15}x_1x_5, \qquad (17.3)$$

and its resulting reaction function is:.

$$x_1 = \frac{a}{b} + \left(\frac{1}{b}\right)(w_{15}x_5). \qquad (17.4)$$

As an example, assume $a = 2$, $b = 1$, and $w = 0.2$. Appendix C.3 shows that C_5 will produce 4.3 units of peace effort ($x_5^* = 4.3$) and C8 will produce 3.0 units ($x_8^* = 3.0$). (We are not concerned here with unit of measure; perhaps the measurement is number of peace overtures per week.) Assume that C_5 and C_8 each direct half their units (2.15 and 1.5, respectively) to A and the other half to B. Meanwhile, C_4's peace effort of $x_4^* = 2.9$ is directed to A, and C_3's peace effort of $x_3^* = 2.9$ is directed to B. The peace efforts of the other CROs in Figure 17.1 ($x_1^* = x_2^* = 2.9$ and $x_6^* = x_7^* = 2.6$) do not directly affect A or B but they do synergize the efforts of other CROs as shown in Figure 17.1. Given our numerical example, total units of peace effort directed to A is 6.55 (2.15 + 1.5 + 2.9), and the same number of units is directed to B.

To see how network structure affects the peace efforts directed to the disputants, consider one thing that can diminish the network's production of peace and one that can increase it. First, suppose C_5 goes out of business and vanishes from the network in Figure 17.1. Given C_5's significant brokerage role in the network, its loss would be a serious blow to peace efforts. C_5's absence leads to a loss of C_5's direct efforts on A and B, diminished synergies to C_4's and to C_3's efforts, and no channel for C_1's and C_2's efforts to affect A and B. Rerunning the model with C_5 absent shows a severe change. Specifically, the total units of peace effort directed to A and B fall from 6.55 to 3.5 each. Hence, the removal of just one CRO on the network (C_5) causes peace efforts directed to each disputant to fall by 47 percent.

Returning to the original scenario, assume now that a new synergy link is forged between C_5 and C_8 in Figure 17.1. Rerunning the model with the new link causes the total units of peace effort directed to A to rise from 6.55 to 7.85 (a 19.8 percent increase)) and the same result applies to B. The LQM model shows that the addition of just that one link between C_5 and C_8 in Figure 17.1 has a significant impact on the peace promotion efforts coming from the network.

Peace Creation in the Bargaining Model of War and Peace

Figure 17.2 depicts the promotion of negative peace by a third party. In panel (a), two players A and B, who could be states or nonstate actors, face the likelihood of violent conflict. The underlying dispute might be over political, territorial, or ideological control. Recall from Chapter 10 that the conflicting parties can jointly generate income according to the peaceful settlement opportunities curve HN, which can then be distributed under peace with I_A going to A and I_B to B. Alternatively, if the dispute is processed violently, A expects the income distribution to be E_A while B expects it to be E_B. The "E-gap" in panel (a) may be due to inconsistent expectations rooted in incomplete information or a commitment problem such as preemptive military technologies. Going through the E points are the malevolent (upsloping) indifference curves of each actor, which could be rooted in "us versus them" identities, perhaps fostered by historical harms that each side inflicted on the other. In panel (a) of Figure 17.2, the region of mutual gain lies outside the settlement opportunities curve, implying a high probability of violence. The sources of violence in the figure are low peaceful settlement opportunities, large E-gap, and malevolent preferences.

In panel (b) of Figure 17.2, a third party can attempt to alter the hostility in panel (a) by: first, increasing peaceful settlement opportunities, second, narrowing or completely closing the E-gap, and/or, third, fostering less malevolence in the actors' preferences. Peaceful settlements are increased in panel (b) from HN to $H'N'$, which could occur through policies that promote economic growth in the economies of A and B and/or an aid package available to the actors if they avoid violence. The narrowing of the E-gap in panel (b) could occur through third-party efforts to promote information flows (if the E-gap is due to incomplete information) or through a peace mission that reduces first-mover advantages (if the

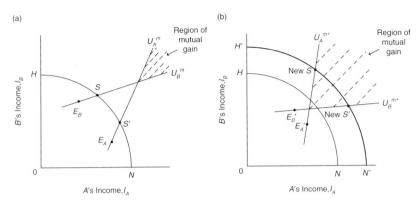

Figure 17.2 Third-party promotion of negative peace in the bargaining model.
(a) Likelihood of violent conflict
(b) Likelihood of peace owing to third-party policies

E-gap is due to preemptive technologies). Finally, panel (b) shows the tilting of preferences toward less malevolence, which could be accomplished through mediated dialogue or cultural exchanges between the conflicting parties. As shown in panel (b), if sufficient movements occur in *HN*, the E-gap, and preferences, the region of mutual gain will intersect the settlement opportunities curve, thus switching the predicted outcome from violence to peace.

Figure 17.2 focuses upon negative peace, that is, the prevention of violence. Preventing violence of course is a central topic in the peace-focused fields in general and the economic analysis of peace in particular. But the bargaining theory of war and peace can also be applied to positive peace. Imagine, for example, war between Canada and the USA. This (unlike during the 18th and 19th centuries) is unthinkable! Canada and the USA have been in a state of stable peace for more than a century (Boulding 1978, pp. 44–5). What does "war unthinkable" look like in the bargaining model of war and peace? Figure 17.3 provides an answer. In the figure, the settlement opportunities curve *HN* is robust (far from the origin) owing to healthy economic growth in the two countries and rich webs of intersections between them in trade, investments, tourism, diplomatic exchanges, and sports. Notice also in the figure that the E-gap is *negative*. Rather than the war expectations being overoptimistic (as in a "regular" E-gap) or even neutral (no E-gap), they are pessimistic. Furthermore, the *E* points are pushed far in and are close to the origin. This would occur if the costs of war are quite high. For example, suppose

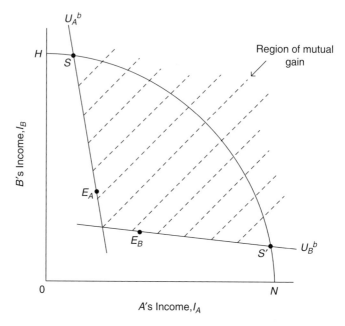

Figure 17.3 Positive peace in the bargaining model.

there are additional costs of war beyond the 5 Ds of Chapter 1, such as psychic costs from physically fighting a friend or alliance disruption costs given the importance of Canada and the USA in the North Atlantic Treaty Organization (NATO) alliance. In this case, the E points would be pushed even closer to the origin. Finally, Figure 17.3 displays benevolent (downward sloping) preferences, which reflect the rich goodwill built up between Canada and the USA over many decades. The region of mutual gain from peace is so large in Figure 17.3 that only the most extreme (and absurd) changes in the Canada/USA relationship could flip it from peace to war.

Transition to Stable Peace

Boulding (1978) analyzes dynamic transitions from peace to war and from war to peace using a phase diagram such as shown in Figure 17.4. To understand the figure, assume a government and an opposition group within a state are experiencing tension. If tensions rise, the opposition group might become a mobilized rebel group and civil war could break out. The horizontal axis measures the degree of strength for peace within the country S. Peace strength could include rule of law, democratic

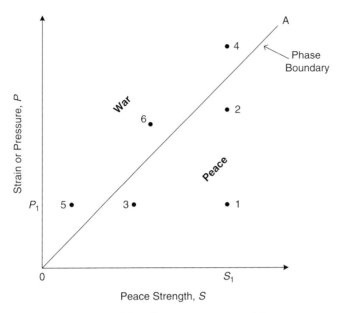

Figure 17.4 Dynamic transitions from peace to war and from war to peace.
Source: Adapted from Boulding (1978).

checks and balances on the abuse of political power, and a long history (or norm) for peaceful resolution of disputes. The vertical axis measures strain or pressure P in the country, perhaps in the form of political, economic, or social discrimination directed by current rulers to an "outed" group. We are not concerned here with how the dimensions of strength and strain might be measured or in interdependencies among them, but in the notion that a social system has within it a degree of strength for peace and a degree of strain pushing toward war (Boulding 1978, pp. 33–5). Boulding emphasizes that, for a given degree of peace strength, rising strain can "break" a social system and lead to war. Going the other way, growing costs of war and the emergence of strengths or movements for peace can "break" a war system and lead to peace. In Figure 17.4, the transitions from peace to war and from war to peace are demarcated by the phase boundary line 0A. When combinations of peace strength and strain on the system are to the right of the phase boundary, the system will be at peace. When such combinations put society to the left of the boundary, the system will be at war. The phase boundary need not be linear, but we assume it is for simplicity (Boulding 1978, p. 37).

To see how Figure 17.4 works, suppose society is initially operating at point 1 in which the strength for peace is relatively high and equal to S_1, and the strain or pressure on the system is relatively low at P_1. Beginning from point 1, even relatively substantial increases in strain (moving to point 2) or decreases in peace strength (moving to point 3) would not "break" the system and lead to war (both points 2 and 3 are to the right of the phase boundary 0A). Nevertheless, if beginning from point 1 the strain becomes large enough (for example, point 4), peace strength becomes too small (for example, point 5), or some combination of the two (for example, point 6), the system will transition to war.

Boulding uses phase diagrams to represent a society's peace or war condition at a point in time, but also to analyze transition from one state to another over time. Consider, for example, the two cycles in Figure 17.5. The cycle to the left of the boundary depicts "stable war" (Boulding 1978, pp. 39–40). Under stable war, society begins at, say, point 1 of low strength and moderate strain. As the war continues, peace strength diminishes, strain between the combatants grows, and war is reinforced (point 2). Eventually, peace movements emerge (peace strengthens) even as the strain between the combatants continues to grow (point 3). Tragically, even if peace continues to strengthen and strain dissipates (to point 4), the changes are too small to transition the system into peace. Stable war characterizes societies that experience ongoing violence over most of their years of existence (see enduring internal rivalries in Table 12.2). The cycle to the right of the phase boundary, however, depicts stable peace. Beginning from point 1′, diminishing peace strength and rising strain between groups (to point 2′) are not enough to "break" the system into war. Moreover, such a society may respond relatively quickly with peace movements in the face of rising strain (to point 3′) to insure that war is avoided. Over time, such efforts can lead to both growing peace strength and diminished strain (to point 4′).

One way to conceive of peace creation is to consider how policies can help the stable peace cycle in Figure 17.5 to remain to the right of the phase boundary. This requires policies that reduce strains between potential combatting groups and support institutions and norms that strengthen peace. A second way to conceive of peace creation is to consider how the stable war cycle in Figure 17.5 might cross over the phase boundary into stable peace. For example, suppose that timely interventions into the war cycle at point 3 substantially reduce strain between the combatants and significantly increase the institutions and norms (strength) of peace. If such changes are substantial, the system could break through the

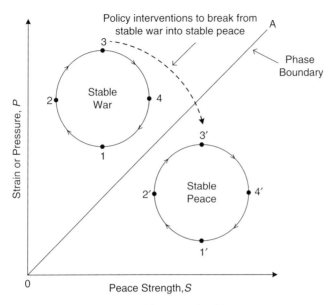

Figure 17.5 Stable war and stable peace.
Source: Adapted from Boulding (1978).

phase boundary from point 3 to point 3′, generating a dynamic in favor of peace in which strains between former combatants diminish and new laws and institutions strengthen peace (from 3′ to 4′).

The models highlighted in this section as well as the many other economic models presented in this book point to a wide range of potential peace creation policies that can bring about or insure stable peace. For example, networks of CROs can bring important information, financial resources, moral suasion, and creative solutions to potential and actual combatants. Notice how the works that CROs can do connect to the bargaining theory of war and peace and to the oft-seen failures of third parties to effectively nurture peace. Specifically, CROs can help close "E-gaps" between potential belligerents, push the E-gap points closer to the origin, emphasize the opportunities available from settlement, alter social norms and identity hardening into "us vs. them" so that malevolence diminishes, and help third parties overcome free rider incentives associated with peace efforts.

17.4 Economic Aspects of Postwar Reconstruction

The challenges of postwar reconstruction vary significantly from case to case because each war has its own idiosyncrasies. Nevertheless, there are common challenges that virtually all war-torn societies face during post-war reconstruction including how to restore economic normalcy, refurbish political systems and legal institutions, reconstitute community bonds and other forms of social relations, and renovate the hearts and minds (psyches) of war-ravaged people. Each of these areas, and the sequencing and coordination of them together, fall within the broad field of peacebuilding (Mac Ginty 2015, Joshi and Wallensteen 2018, Karbo and Virk 2018) as well as the more specialized field of peacebuilding and humanitarian economics (Dumas 2011, Carbonnier 2015). Our objective in this section is to highlight a selection of economic aspects of postwar peacebuilding.

Macroeconomic Challenges

We use the following equation as a platform to demonstrate why postwar economic reconstruction at the macro level can be quite challenging:

$$\text{Consumption (C)} = \text{Production (P)} - \text{Capital Investment (I)} - \text{Military Production (M)} - \text{Exports (EX)} + \text{Imports (IM)}, \qquad (17.5)$$

where C, P, I, M, EX, and IM are dollar values of goods and services. For example, assume a country produces $100 billion of goods this year (P=100), $15 billion of which are new capital goods such as roads, bridges, and factories (I=15), and another $10 billion is military goods such as tanks and naval vessels (M=10). Assume the country exports $20 billion and imports $10 billion of goods in trade with other countries (EX=20, IM=10). It follows from equation (17.5) that the country can consume $65 billion worth of goods this year in food, clothing, healthcare, and so on (C=65).

The normal functioning of equation (17.5) is anything but normal during and after war. Recall the costs of war in the form of the 5 Ds from Chapter 1. The first is diversion, which is war's elevation of M, which can stay ratcheted up in an insecure postwar environment. All else equal, higher M in equation (17.5) means less C available to the country's citizens. The second D is destruction of people and property including capital. This causes P in equation (17.5) to be lower than otherwise. Furthermore, the destruction of physical capital, social and community networks (social capital), and human capital-creating institutions (schools, hospitals) requires a high investment (I) in equation (17.5) to begin reconstructing the capital destroyed by war. The low P combined with the high I in equation (17.5) imply less C available to the country's citizens, all else equal. The third D is disruption of economic and other activities from war, which persist in the postwar period. Such disruptions can twist numerous markets and industries in the economy, which we detail in the next subsection. The fourth D is displacement of people in the form of refugees and internally displaced persons (IDPs). In addition to the psychological costs experienced by insecure people on the run, there are enormous macro- and microeconomic costs too. At the macro level in equation (17.5), the displacement of people implies that production (P) will be lower than otherwise and human and social capital formation (I) will need to be higher than otherwise. The fifth D is the difficulty of postwar development, which is manifest at the macro and micro levels.

Equation (17.5) implies then that citizens in a severe postwar environment will face acute consumption challenges. Severely war-torn economies usually face significant, sometimes desperate, needs for food, clothing, shelter, clean water, and healthcare. Furthermore, the country left to its own capacities will find it extremely difficult to reconstruct itself. To increase consumption, the country needs to increase production, but its war-diverted and war-torn people and capital may be unable to do so. When consumption goods are scarce, many people will be malnourished and thus not be well-positioned to participate in the society's increase in production. This in turn can lead to a poverty trap. As Boulding (1945, p. 8) notes: "Since the people are poor, they do not produce enough food and warmth to keep their bodies and minds active. Because their bodies and minds are not active, they do not have the energy to produce enough food and warmth."

To compound postwar economic difficulties, high capital investments (of all kinds) are needed to increase production possibilities in the future, but such investments drain away goods available for needed consumption today. As such, a war-torn economy can get caught in a stagnation trap. It is unable to free up resources for capital investment owing to pressing consumption needs. As a result the economy grows more slowly (if at all) over time. Consider also the perverse nature of corruption for a postwar economy in equation (17.5). Corruption is essentially the inappropriate draining of consumption goods from the economy for personal use by those with the power to do so. As such, corruption leaves less C for the already strapped population, which further elevates the challenges of promoting capital formation in the country.

Finally, consider the implications of equation (17.5) for a war-torn society forced to pay war reparations as Germany was required to do following World War I. Many nations fund their imports (IM) of goods from other countries through their exports (EX) of goods. War reparations often imply that a country must export more than it imports, which is a form of payment to the winner(s) of the war. As Taussig (1920, pp. 33–4) notes: "[E]xports from Germany will increase, being stimulated by lower prices; imports into Germany will decline, being checked by that same situation. The gap between merchandise imports and exports will steadily increase, until finally that stage is reached when the total spread between the two will be equal in money value to the sum total which the German Government needs annually to remit." But when EX>IM in equation (17.5), a further drain on the country's consumption of goods ensues, thus compounding the challenge of economic reconstitution.

Equation (17.5) reveals macroeconomic challenges faced by a war-torn economy, but it also points to ways to address such challenges, specifically, borrowing and/or aid. Boulding (1945, p. 9) notes: "Had the battlefields of World War I been cut off from the rest of the world, they would still be devastated areas. Their rapid recovery arose from the fact that they were able to import great quantities of food, materials, livestock, equipment, and labor without paying for these things by exports." In equation (17.5), if the war-torn country can increase IM without increasing EX it can increase consumption to overcome the malnourishment that many of its citizens might otherwise face. This allows such people to contribute to production of consumer and capital goods (of all kinds) and break out of a potential poverty trap. Moreover, if many of the goods being imported are capital goods, future production possibilities can be enhanced, thus helping the country break out of a potential stagnation trap. Finally, if aid, trade, and lending do not entrench vested interests nor foster corruption, the country will be better positioned to be a productive member of communities of nations rather than a broken state that contributes to future conflict. For a summary of such policies following World War II, known as the Marshall Plan, see Brauer and Dunne (2012, p. 50).

Microeconomic Challenges

A critically important aspect of economic reconstruction following war is the composition of reconstruction needs, which varies from case to case. Composition deals with the particular goods and capital resources that are needed at specific locales, when and in what sequence such items are needed, and how such efforts are coordinated with noneconomic aspects of reconstruction such as political and social reconstitution.

By way of example, suppose a war-torn country is facing a severe shortage of food. According to Boulding (1945, p. 10), "relief must always precede reconstruction." Before the reconstruction of the society's capital stock and long-term growth potential occur, the immediate needs of the population (the same population that will propel the country's long-term economic future) must be met. It is here that states, IGOs, INGOs, and NGOs can potentially bring much needed relief, subject of course to challenges of coordination and corruption avoidance. For example, not much good will come from delivering supplies of food and medical supplies to a country if the transportation routes upon which many in the population depend are badly degraded or insecure. Likewise, providing seed for the next cycle of agricultural production will not do much good if the tractors and harvesting machines have been destroyed by war (Boulding 1945, p. 10).

Beyond specific examples, the more general point relates to the deep embeddedness of economic activities in modern economies. Specifically, production and supply of most economic goods require vast networks of coordination across many actors. To produce a cotton shirt requires the planting and harvesting of cotton, the transportation of cotton to textile production facilities, the use of dyes and numerous other goods (also produced and transported) in the production of shirts, and the distribution of the final goods to wholesalers and then to stores (who utilize their own resources and expertise in managing supply chains and marketing). For a cotton shirt to be brought to market in a modern economy requires little bits and pieces of effort from thousands of people. This deep embeddedness is disrupted by war across thousands of goods and services that were formerly produced in the war-torn country. "War distorts this whole structure of relative proportions, and the decline in production which is observed as a result of war is perhaps even more due to the distortion of the relative structure of capital than to any absolute decline" (Boulding 1945, p. 11).

In the midst of the immense challenges related to the reconstitution of the relative structures of economic activities in a postwar environment, the sequencing of reconstruction efforts is critical. That said, there is no blueprint or "one size fits all" methodology for how to sequence reconstruction and, hence, debate inevitably arises among policymakers, violence-afflicted groups, and peace-promoting organizations over reconstruction priorities. Nevertheless, most scholars and policymakers agree that reconstructing subsistence industries is a high priority, which generally necessitates the reconstruction of the country's transportation system, agricultural production and/or imports, and production of clean water (Boulding 1945, p. 16). Another high priority for reconstruction is the country's home stocks (houses and rental units) and hospitals. Returning refugees and IDPs may find their homes and businesses destroyed by war or taken over by others without due process. Whether and how the relative imbalances in home occupancies are processed will have a major impact on the society's economic and social well-being going forward (Leckie and Huggins 2013). Still another high priority for reconstruction is the validity of the country's currency, which depends on its banking system and financial sector more generally. A stable currency is critical for renewing the vast array of markets, specialized productions, and trades that modern economies depend upon for economic well-being. In many postwar economies, governments sometimes try to meet the overwhelming economic, political, and social demands by printing more money, which tends to lead to severe inflation, unemployment problems, and economic crises. As such, mismanagement in the financial sector can lead to the eventual failure of postwar economic reconstruction, which tends to elevate the risk of violent conflict in the future (Brauer and Dunne 2012, ch. 3).

Institutional Economics and Reconstruction

Given the many economic, political, and social challenges of postwar reconstruction, Brauer and Dunne (2012, ch. 5) offer 12 principles related to the design of postwar peace in which economics and institutions are emphasized. They note that a major challenge of peace economics "is to understand both peace failures and peace successes from a design perspective – what in the field of industrial organization is referred to as the structure, conduct, and performance triplet, or rules, strategies, and outcomes – and to invent new mechanisms to arrive at stable peace within and between societies" (Brauer and Dunne 2012, p. 111). Table 17.6 summarizes Brauer and Dunne's principles of economic and institutional design to promote peace in postwar (and prewar) contexts.

17.5 Empirical Studies of Conflict Prevention and Peace

We have already seen in this book empirical evidence that mediation efforts by third parties in militarized interstate disputes increase the probability that the disputes will end in negotiated settlements (Frazier and Dixon 2006; see Chapter 11). For intrastate armed conflicts, we have seen empirical evidence that intervention in the form of UN troops reduces the

Table 17.6 *Brauer and Dunne's 12 principles for designing peace.*

Principles	Summary
1. Changing Payoffs	Agreement design must align incentives and payoffs toward cooperation.
2. Create Vested Interests and Leadership	Create vested interests among leaders and other actors in the prevention of violence.
3. Graduated Reciprocity and Clarity	Tit-for-tat reciprocity in negotiations is vulnerable to misperceptions (see Chapter 5). Limited responses to provocations are necessary to prevent negotiations from spiraling into growing antagonisms.
4. Repeated, Small Steps	It is usually easier to bring small rounds of negotiations to success than to bring an all-or-nothing proposal to success. Nevertheless, small approaches can sometimes be a ploy to stall negotiations.
5. Common Value Formation	Foster elements that bring conflicting parties together to work for common causes rather than highlighting what divides them.
6. Authentic Authority	All stakeholders should have authentic representation in negotiations.
7. Subsidiarity	Address problems at the most localized level in which they occur.
8. Conflict Resolution Mechanisms	Peacemaking and peacekeeping require mechanisms (for example, mediation, arbitration, courts) to keep disagreements from escalating.
9. Information and Monitoring	Incomplete information can create incentives for violence and give rise to mutual suspicions (see Chapter 10). Peacemaking and peacekeeping are enhanced when uncertainty is minimized.
10. Accountability	Negotiations require a continuation of accountable leaders who can make credible and binding commitments.
11. Self-Policing Enforcement	Self-policing of an agreement involves the design of incentives for the conflicting parties to cooperate rather than defect from the agreement without the need for external enforcement mechanisms.
12. Nesting and Networking	Economies of scale (disproportionally greater results produced from larger-scale efforts), learning economies, and economies of scope (peace efforts that generate multiple goods) in peacebuilding will be more likely to come from complementary and coordinated peacebuilding institutions and organizations.

Source: Brauer and Dunne (2102, ch. 5).

severity of battlefield violence (Hultman, Kathman, and Shannon 2014; see Chapter 12) and of violence against civilians (Hultman, Kathman and Shannon 2013; see Chapter 14). In this section we briefly summarize several additional studies of third-party intervention as well as empirical research on the correlates of peace.

Third-Party Intervention and the Termination of Interstate Conflicts

Mishali-Ram (2013) analyzes the effects of third-party intervention on interstate conflicts. She distinguishes between interstate crises that involve only states (what she calls "pure interstate crises") and those that are between states but also involve nonstate actors ("ethnic-interstate crises"). Mishali-Ram considers two types of third-party interveners in interstate crises: major powers, in particular the USA and USSR/Russia, and IGOs, specifically the UN and regional organizations.

To determine how third-party intervention affects interstate conflict, Mishali-Ram draws upon data from the International Crisis Behavior (ICB) Project, which leads to a sample of 349 interstate crises between 1945 and 2005. Her dependent variable measures whether interstate crisis endings are accommodative (that is, with formal, semiformal, or tacit agreements) or nonaccommodative (for example, imposed agreements or unilateral acts such as severing diplomatic ties). Mishali-Ram has three key explanatory variables: intervention by major powers (USA and/or USSR/Russia), which is either low (none or political/economic) or high (semimilitary or direct military); intervention by IGOs, which is either low (none or moderate diplomacy) or high (severe diplomatic/ economic or military force); and crisis type (whether pure interstate or ethnic-interstate). Control variables include relative power in the crisis dyad, crisis magnitude, and whether the crisis period was pre- or post-Cold War.

Among Mishali-Ram's results, we highlight four. First, greater intervention by the USA alone significantly reduces the likelihood of accommodative outcomes. Second, unilateral interventions by the USSR do not help, but greater interventions by the USA and the UN together significantly increase the prospect of accommodation. Third, IGO interventions significantly increase the chances that interstate crises will end with accommodation. Finally, ethnic-interstate crises are significantly less likely to end with accommodation relative to non-ethnic interstate crises, all else equal.

Comprehensive Peace Agreements and Civil War Termination

Empirical research suggests that when civil war negotiations reach a comprehensive peace agreement (CPA), postconflict peace lasts longer, all else equal (Joshi and Quinn 2017). Joshi, Lee, and Mac Ginty (2017) (hereafter JLM) hypothesize that building three safeguards into civil war negotiations – transitional power-sharing, dispute resolution protocols, and verification mechanisms – will increase the rate of CPA implementation in civil war negotiations. JLM test their hypotheses using data for 1989 to 2012 from the Peace Accords Matrix Implementation Dataset (see Appendix D.7). Their dependent variable is a peace implementation index (PII) for more than 300 negotiated civil war outcomes over the sample's time frame. The three key explanatory variables are transitional power-sharing, dispute resolution protocols, and verification mechanisms. Each is coded based on an ordinal scale which ranges from 0 (no implementation) to 3 (full implementation). Control variables include constraints on the executive, conflict type (over territory or government), and GDP per capita. JLM find strong empirical support for their hypotheses. Each of the three safeguards has a significant positive effect on the implementation of peace agreements and all three together increase peace accord implementation by over 47 percent. JLM conclude that their results underscore the importance of connections between the details of peace processes and peace accord resilience. They also offer an important caveat. Some peace agreements, though they foster negative peace, can nonetheless lock in or worsen power asymmetries, exclusion, and/or patriarchy (p. 996). Furthermore, JLM focus upon peace accord implementation, but what about peace accord duration? DeRouen and Chowdhury's (2018) empirical study finds that peace accords are significantly more likely to hold over time when they are facilitated by mediation and UN peacekeeping operations, all else equal.

Networks of Peace Organizations

Wilson, Davis, and Murdie (2016) (hereafter WDM) theoretically and empirically analyze the peace promotion effectiveness of INGO networks (see also Lupu and Greenhill 2017, who do the same for IGO networks). They focus upon INGOs that work directly on conflict resolution and thus are conflict resolution organizations (CROs). WDM maintain that one cannot properly assess the effects of CROs on peace simply by counting the number of CROs present in peace processes. Rather, one must account for the connections of CROs to other CROs in contexts in which violent conflict may break out or is occurring. In short, WDM are interested in how CRO networks can foster peace. WDM hypothesize that the greater the strength of a CRO network within and between states, the more likely that conflicts will be processed nonviolently, all else equal. The CRO network can make peace more likely via multiple channels such as increasing information flows, persuading elites to process conflicts nonviolently, and connecting key players for peace who might otherwise remain disconnected (pp. 444–8).

To test their hypothesis, WDM first use the *Yearbook of International Organizations* to identify INGOs that are CROs and to identify the connections of each CRO to other CROs. This leads to a sample of 1,191 CROs, which WDM use to create a matrix of ties among CROs present in each state (for monadic analysis) and across pairs of states (for dyadic analysis). Based upon networking theory, WDM then calculate measures of networked presence of CROs per state and per dyad for the years 1997 and 2001. For the monadic analysis, WDM's dependent variable is a state's level of belligerence directed to other states based on coding methods from the Integrated Data for Event Analysis (IDEA) project. WDM's key explanatory variable for the monadic analysis is a measure of each country's CRO network based on a weighted sum of the eigenvalue centrality (EC) scores of CROs within the state. Recall from Chapter 7 that EC not only accounts for the number of connections among actors, but also how well-connected actors are to others who are well-connected. A high network measure for a state would signify a strong and well-connected CRO network in that state. For the dyadic analyses, the dependent variable is the three year average of conflict events involving the states in the dyad. For the dyadic analyses, the key explanatory variable is the maximum number of CRO network ties among states in the dyad. Control variables for monadic and dyadic analyses include a country's regime type, human rights record, and major power status.

Empirical results support WDM's hypotheses. For the monadic analysis, counts of CROs do not significantly impact the belligerence of states in any of the regressions, but high CRO network scores significantly reduce belligerence in two of three regressions. For the dyadic analyses, the number of shared CROs significantly reduces belligerence in one of two regressions, but the maximum number of CRO network ties significantly reduces belligerence in four of four regressions. WDM conclude that it is not the count of CROs alone that promotes peace but the CRO network structure that does so.

When Third-Party Interventions Go Awry

Humanitarian Aid and Civil War Duration

Although numerous empirical studies find evidence that third-party intervention can reduce the risk and severity of violent conflicts, it is important for those who work for peace to understand how third-party efforts can potentially lead to negative consequences. Narang (2015) maintains that a major channel by which humanitarian aid might prolong civil wars has been under-theorized and under-researched. Building upon the bargaining theory of war and peace, Narang (2015, p. 185) maintains that "humanitarian assistance can inadvertently prolong fighting by slowing down the accrual of information, [which] ... prevents opponents from coordinating expectations about what each is prepared to accept in a settlement." Recall in the bargaining model in Chapter 10 that a large "E-gap" owing to incomplete information can lead to war rather than peaceful settlement. Such a theoretical perspective leads Narang to two hypotheses: First, the greater the level of humanitarian aid provided during a civil conflict, the longer the duration of the conflict. Second, the prolongation of civil conflict will be greater when humanitarian aid is more difficult to observe (thus increasing uncertainty). Narang's sample encompasses civil wars from 1945 to 2004 based on data from UCDP/PRIO's Armed Conflict Dataset (see Appendix D.2). His dependent variable is the duration of civil wars. Narang's key explanatory variable is the amount of humanitarian assistance disbursed in each conflict year based upon official development assistance data from the Organization for Economic Cooperation and Development. Control variables include the severity of civil war, political regime, and "lootable" resources.

For hypothesis 1, Narang finds that greater aid significantly increases the likelihood of war continuing even after controlling for the selection of aid into harder and easier cases. To test the second hypothesis, Narang creates an interaction variable in which the level of aid in a conflict is multiplied by a 1/0 variable indicating whether the civil war occurred on the outskirts of the state. The idea is that peripheral insurgencies would be associated with greater uncertainty for governments, and aid into such conflicts would increase uncertainty and make the wars last longer, all else equal. Narang finds empirical support for the hypothesis; humanitarian aid into civil wars with peripheral insurgencies makes civil wars 50 percent less likely to terminate in a given year.

Lootable Resources and Intervention by States

Empirical and case study literature on civil war suggests that third parties intervene to end the violence and/or improve their geopolitical influence in the region (Regan 1998, Gent 2007). Findley and Marineau (2015) (hereafter FM), however, maintain that interventions into civil wars can be governed by more nefarious intentions, specifically, incentives to tap into valuable natural resources. FM note that empirical "linkages between lootable resources and civil war intervention have scarcely been explored" and "there are compelling reasons to suspect that lootable resources frequently motivate intervention" (p. 467). Their main hypothesis is that states are more likely to intervene in a civil war if lootable resources are present in the country. They also hypothesize that states will be more likely to intervene in civil wars on the side of the opposition if the opposition has strong access to lootable resources.

FM begin with a dataset of 150 civil wars from 1944 to 1999, 101 of which experienced third-party intervention. The dependent variable in the regression analysis is the occurrence of third-party military or economic intervention in the civil war. The key explanatory variable is whether rebels have access to lootable resources. Control variables include contiguity between third party and civil war states, whether the intervener(s) is a major power, and alliance between the civil war state and intervener(s). Empirical results strongly support FM's hypotheses. They find, for example, that when diamonds and gems are present in a civil war country, the likelihood of third-party intervention is 83 percent greater, all else equal. They also find that that when rebels have access to or control of lootable resources, opposition-biased intervention is 89 percent more likely, all else equal.

Empirical Study of the Correlates of Peace

Theoretical and empirical research of the correlates (risk factors) for war and other forms of violence dominate the field of conflict economics and quantitative peace research more generally. Empirical studies that directly inquire into the correlates and causes of peace are rare (Gleditsch, Nordkavelle, and Strand 2014, Diehl 2016, Davenport, Melander, and Regan 2018). One study, however, that empirically investigates the correlates of peace is Kollias and Paleologou (2017) (hereafter KP). KP are particularly interested in the possible nexus between peace and globalization. We have already seen in this book theoretical and empirical inquiries into the effects of trade on violent conflict and the effects of violent conflict on trade (see, for example, Chapters 1, 11, 12, and 14). KP, however, are interested in how a broad measure of globalization might correlate to peace and how peace might correlate to globalization. Hence, they build their empirical analysis on a broad measure of globalization, the KOF Index, and a broad measure of peace, the Global Peace Index (GPI). The KOF Index provides a yearly composite measure of economic, social, and political dimensions of globalization for more than 200 countries (Gygli, Haelg, and Sturm 2018). Meanwhile, the GPI measures the level of negative peace each year for 163 countries based upon each country's external conflicts, internal harmony or discord, and level of militarization.

A knotty empirical challenge faced by KP is how to sort out the effect of globalization on peace given that peace affects globalization. For example, states that avoid wars and terrorist attacks may be more likely to receive foreign direct investments and tourists. Likewise, globalization may affect the risk of violent conflict as we have seen elsewhere in this book. KP address the empirical challenge by adopting a statistical methodology that is sensitive to the nexus between globalization and peace. Based upon a sample of 132 countries over the 2008–12 period, KP find in a majority of their regressions (2 of 3) that globalization positively and significantly affects peace. Going the other way, they find less evidence in their regressions (1 of 3) that peace positively and significantly affects globalization. KP conclude that there is some evidence that globalization broadly defined promotes peace broadly defined.

17.6 Economic Consequences of Peace

Agricultural Economic Impacts of UN Peacekeeping in South Sudan

Caruso, Khadka, Petrarca, and Ricciuti (2017) (hereafter CKPR) empirically analyze the effects of UN personnel deployments on agricultural production across counties in South Sudan. CKPR hypothesize that UN personnel deployments have a positive impact on agricultural production through two channels: first, a supply channel in which more UN personnel leads to greater security which in turn leads to greater agricultural production, and, second, a demand channel in which more UN personnel increases the demand for food, thus stimulating greater production of agricultural goods. CKPR indicate that the supply channel itself has two channels related to security. The first is an increase in microsecurity in which individual farmers are at lower risk of having their goods appropriated by militia groups and other roving bandits. The second is a macro channel by which UN troops might help a weak government to enforce contracts and improve governance.

CKPR test their hypothesis for the period 2008 to 2011. CKPR's dependent variable is the amount of cereal produced per county per year based on data from South Sudan's National Bureau of Statistics. The key explanatory variable is the number of UN troops physically stationed per county each year. County control variables include number of households, share of farming households, harvesting area, and ethnicity. Nation-state control variables include rainfall and number of conflict-related deaths per year. Empirical results strongly support the authors' hypothesis. Their baseline analysis shows that a ten percent increase in UN troops deployed per county leads to an increase in agricultural production by 600 metric tons, all else equal. CKPR's study is important because the "economic impact of peacekeeping ought to be ... the study of how war-torn economies can be restored to their capacity of stimulating economic development thanks to the security spillover generated after peacekeeping has taken place" (p. 253).

Benefits of Peace to Tourism in Colombia

When a country at civil war is able to resolve its conflicts and move into peace, it can experience many economic benefits including the release of resources from the military sector to produce more civilian goods, renewal of trade ties and market activities, and restoration of tourism. This latter channel of development seems promising for Colombia following the peace agreement that was signed in 2016 between the government and the Revolutionary Armed Forces of Colombia (FARC) rebel group. Maldonado, Moreno-Sánchez, Espinoza, et al. (2018) (hereafter MME) focus in particular on the bird-watching tourism benefits to Colombia available from peace.

MME note that Colombia has the greatest diversity of birds in the world with approximately 1,900 species, which makes up about 20 percent of all bird species in the world (p. 78). MME's research objective is to estimate the economic benefits of bird tourism in Colombia now that peace seems more promising there. To do so, they undertake a large survey of members of the USA-based National Audubon Society (NAS) to estimate their demand for bird tours in Colombia. The amount of bird tourism demanded would vary by price, so MME estimate the potential economic impact of greater NAS bird tourism in Colombia for prices ranging from

$250 to $500 per day. MME find that the number of additional NAS tourist visits to Colombia per year would range from about 9,000 to about 17,000 (depending on price). The annual expenditures from these additional tourists were estimated to be $42 to $48 million. Finally, MME estimated that the number of new jobs that would be created from such extra tourism ranged from about 4,400 to 8,500.

17.7 Bibliographic Notes

On a broad array of economic challenges in postwar settings see Boulding (1945) and Wennmann (2011). For valuable overviews of economic aspects of peacekeeping see Solomon (2007), Bove and Smith (2011), Sheehan (2011), and Dorussen (2014). Empirical studies of the economic impacts of peace (as distinct from war) are rare, but see Feyzabadi, Haghdoost, Mehrolhassani, and Aminian (2015) and Sarwar, Siddiqi, Nasir, and Ahmed (2016). For a survey of datasets in conflict and peace research, see Gleditsch, Metternich, and Ruggeri (2014). For a review of peacekeeping data, see Clayton (2017).

Large literatures exist on various postconflict economic challenges including how to manage disputes over natural resources like precious minerals, oil, and water (Wennmann 2011, Young and Goldman 2015, Keels 2017, Roy 2018); how to transform rich resource endowments into improved healthcare and education (Brière, Filmer, Ringold et al. 2017), how to design economic reconstruction in postconflict settings (Brauer and Dunne 2012, ch. 5, Myerson 2016, Joshi and Wallensteen 2018); the promises and pitfalls of postconflict development assistance and humanitarian aid, including the potential for aid to lock in dysfunctional leaders and institutions (Carbonnier 2015, Marriage 2016, Wennmann 2018, DiLorenzo 2018); reintegrating refugees and IDPs (Harild, Christensen, and Zetter 2015), how to rebuild education after war (Johnson and Hoba 2015, Silwal 2016), how businesses can promote peace and participate in postconflict reconstruction (Forrer and Seyle 2016, Fort 2016, Ganson and Wennmann 2016, Bartkus 2018); and how gender, social inclusion, and forgiveness (or their lack) can affect postwar development (Noor, Hewstone, and Branscombe 2015, Durbach, Chappell, and Williams 2017, Karim and Beardsley 2017, Kadera and Shair-Rosenfield 2017, Justino 2018).

Brief Primer on Weapons Technologies

Modern weapons categories include small arms and light weapons (SALW), major conventional weapons (MCW), weapons of mass destruction (WMD), and cyber weapons. Also important are emerging military technologies.

A.1 Small Arms and Light Weapons (SALW)

The United Nations (2016) defines small arms as "weapons designed for individual use [including] . . . revolvers and self-loading pistols, rifles and carbines, sub-machine guns, assault rifles and light machine guns," Light weapons are defined as "weapons designed for use by two or three persons serving as a crew [including] . . . heavy machine guns . . . grenade launchers, portable anti-aircraft guns, portable anti-tank guns, . . . and mortars of a caliber of less than 100 millimetres" (United Nations 2016). Table A.1 shows the Norwegian Initiative on Small Arms Transfers (2017) categorization system for tracking the trade in SALW.

Perhaps the most well-known small arm in the world is the AK-47 assault rifle, which was designed by Russia's Mikhail Kalashnikov and first produced in 1947. More than 30 varieties of the rifle have been produced worldwide based on the ideas of Kalashnikov's 1947 weapon (Small Arms Survey 2007, p. 260). Of the estimated 875 million firearms worldwide, about 50–100 million are Kalashnikov-style assault rifles (Small Arms Survey 2007, p. 258). Owing to their firepower, ease of use, durability, and relatively low cost, Kalashnikov-style weapons are present in most violent conflicts in the world today (Kahaner 2006, Solomon 2015). Another important SALW is the landmine, which is a munition placed under, on, or near the ground and is designed to explode based on the device's contact or proximity with combatants or vehicles (United

Table A.1 *Small arms and light weapons categories and subcategories.*

Categories	Subcategories
Small Arms	Pistols and Revolvers
	Rifles and Shotguns (Sport)
	Rifles and Shotguns (Military)
	Machine Guns (Sub and Light)
	Military Weapons
Light Weapons	Machine Guns (Heavy)
	Cannon
	Mortars < 100mm
	Man-Portable Missile and Rocket Launchers
	Grenade Launchers
Ammunition, Explosives, and Missiles	Ammunition – all categories
	Small Arms and Cannon Ammunition
	Small Arms Ammunition
	Grenades
	Missiles and Rockets
	Landmines
	Military Explosives
Parts and Accessories	

Source: Norwegian Initiative on Small Arms Transfers (2017, p. 6).

Nations Office at Geneva 2016). Landmines became prominent in twentieth and twenty-first century wars in which states and nonstate groups "reengineered terrain" to make it inhospitable to the enemy (Bolton 2015).

A.2 Major Conventional Weapons (MCW)

Most definitions of conventional weapons indicate that they are not nuclear, biological, or chemical (NBC) weapons. Such definitions include SALW. Here, however, we focus on major conventional weapons (MCW), which excludes NBC weapons but includes armaments that are generally larger and more technologically complicated than SALW. Table A.2 shows categories of MCW used by the United Nations Register on Conventional Arms (2016).

A prominent example of an MCW is the cruise missile (CM), which is an unmanned self-propelled vehicle that flies like an airplane (Federation of

Table A.2 *Major conventional weapons (MCW) categories.*

MCW Category	UN Register Description (Selected)
Battle Tanks (Category I)	Tracked or wheeled self-propelled armored fighting vehicles with high mobility and high self-protection. Caliber of main gun is at least 75mm.
Armored Combat Vehicles (ACVs) (Category II)	Tracked, semi-tracked, or wheeled self-propelled vehicles with armored protection. An ACV can transport a squad of four or more or is armed with at least a 12.5mm weapon or a missile launcher.
Large-caliber Artillery Systems (Category III)	Guns, howitzers, artillery pieces, mortars, or multiple-launch rocket systems with a caliber of at least 75mm.
Combat Aircraft (Category IV)	Manned and unmanned aircraft that employ guided missiles, unguided rockets, bombs, guns, cannons, other weapons, or electronic warfare technologies.
Attack Helicopters (Category V)	Manned rotary-wing aircraft that employ guided or unguided air-to-surface, air-to-subsurface, or air-to-air weapons, or electronic warfare technologies.
Warships (Category VI)	Military vessels or submarines that can launch missiles or torpedoes with a range of at least 25km.
Missiles and Missile Launchers (Category VII)	Guided or unguided rockets, ballistic, or cruise missiles that can deliver a weapon at least 25km. Category includes remotely piloted vehicles (RPVs, often called UAVs [unmanned aerial vehicles] or "drones") with the characteristics of missiles.

Source: United Nations Register of Conventional Arms (2016).

American Scientists 2016). CMs can gather intelligence and/or deliver ordnance to a target and can be launched from land, air, and sea (including from submarines). Owing to onboard computerized guidance systems, satellite guidance technologies, and terrain contour matching, a CM can strike within several meters of its target from a distance of hundreds of kilometers. Another important MCW is the unmanned aerial vehicle (UAV), sometimes called a "drone," which is a reusable aircraft without a human pilot onboard. UAV military applications include gathering intelligence and attacking enemy land and sea targets (Fuhrmann and Horowitz 2017). When UAVs are armed with ordnance, they are called unmanned combat aerial vehicles (UCAVs).

A.3 Weapons of Mass Destruction (WMD)

Nuclear Weapons

Nuclear weapons create enormous explosive yield through the fission of heavy atoms such as uranium or plutonium (for an atomic bomb) or the fusion of light atoms like hydrogen (for a hydrogen bomb). Currently, nine nations possess nuclear weapons: USA, Russia, UK, France, China, Israel, India, Pakistan, and North Korea. Chapter 15 provides information on these nations' stockpiles of nuclear warheads.

Biological Weapons

Biological weapons use microorganisms such as bacteria and viruses to kill or incapacitate humans, livestock, or crops. Diseases that might be unleashed by biological weapons include anthrax, cholera, smallpox, and botulism. Lethality of a biological attack can vary widely depending on dispersal methods, health responses, weather conditions, and contagiousness of the biological agent. In the early 1990s, the Aum Shinrikyo cult attempted biological attacks in Tokyo using anthrax. The attacks failed because the cult mistakenly weaponized a nonvirulent form of anthrax.

Chemical Weapons

Chemical weapons use nonliving toxic chemicals to kill or incapacitate humans, livestock, or crops. Chemical weapons can be based on nerve agents such as tabun, sarin, or VX; blister agents such as sulphur mustard or nitrogen mustard; protein synthesis inhibitors such as ricin; or choking agents such as phosgene or chlorine. According to Human Rights Watch (2018), the Syrian government has carried out dozens of chemical weapons attacks since August 2013.

Radiological Weapons

A radiological weapon, more commonly known as a radiological dispersion device (RDD) or dirty bomb, is any device other than a nuclear weapons detonation designed to spread radioactive material over an area to contaminate property and possibly cause radiation-related illnesses. To date, RDDs have not been used in war or in terrorist attacks, so there is debate over how effective they would be and how serious the technical hurdles are for conducting an RDD attack. For most people in the vicinity of an attack, radiation exposure would not be immediately life-threatening and, even over the longer term, increases in cancer risk would likely be small. Nevertheless, if sufficient radiological materials became ensconced within office buildings or other prime real estate areas, it could be more cost effective to seal off the infected property rather than undertake an expensive cleanup. In this way, an RDD could be an effective weapon of mass disruption (National Council on Radiation Protection & Measurements 2014).

A.4 Cyberwar Technologies

Stuxnet

In 2010, software engineers discovered a strange form of malware, which they concluded was a whole new kind of weapon. Stuxnet, as the malware was called, was designed to attack nuclear centrifuges at Iran's Natanz nuclear facility. Before being detected by Iran, it is estimated that about 20 percent of Iran's 4,592 nuclear centrifuges were disabled by Stuxnet (Zetter 2014). Regarding Stuxnet, Michael Hayden, former director of the USA's Central Intelligence Agency and National Security Agency, stated that somebody "has used an entirely new class of weapon to affect destruction" (Public Broadcasting Service 2016).

What Is Cyberwar?

General hacking of computer systems and cyber espionage (economic and political) are forms of cyber insecurity but not cyberwar. The US government defines cyberwar as the use of cyber weapons in a cyberattack that "proximately results[s] in death, injury or significant destruction" (Singer and Friedman 2014, p. 121). Recent cases seem close to fitting this definition. For example, Israel's aircraft strike against a Syrian nuclear research facility in 2007 included cyber means that disabled Syrian air defenses (Singer and Friedman 2014, pp. 126–8). In a 2008 war, Russia apparently carried out cyberattacks against Georgian government websites, which hampered Georgia's communications during the war (Singer and Friedman 2014, pp. 111, 125). Moreover, Stuxnet brought about physical destruction of a rival's potential weapons infrastructure, not with bombs or human infiltrators, but with computer code. Various nations and nonstate groups are developing cyberattack and cyber defense capabilities (Nance and Sampson 2017). According to Breene (2016), Iran and North Korea are emerging as cyber powers (the other cyber powers are China, Israel, Russia, UK, and USA).

A.5 Emerging Military Technologies

A transistor holds a bit of data or information (that is, either a 1 or a 0), switches or amplifies the data based on an electronic signal, and passes the information to other components (Wolchover 2012). In 1958, Texas Instruments produced an 11-millimeter-long integrated circuit or "chip" that held one transistor. By 1964, a chip could hold 30 transistors. By 2017, Advanced Micro Devices placed 19.2 billion transistors onto a single chip measuring about 1.2 square inches (Rahul 2017). Breakthroughs in computer and nanotechnologies, along with advances in materials and optical technologies, are having dramatic impacts on weapons technology developments.

An example of emerging military technology is bird- and insect-sized drones, known as micro air vehicles (MAVs), which can gather intelligence in tight spaces (for example, within buildings). Although the widespread use of MAVs could be years away, they have the potential to dramatically change the information that can be acquired and exploited in war, especially in urban environments. Another emergent military technology is robotic weaponry. A robot is a machine that can sense the environment, think and make decisions about how to respond, and carry out actions reflecting such decisions (Singer 2009, p. 67). For example, UAVs can be programmed to take off, carry out reconnaissance, surveillance, and target acquisition, and land by themselves. UAVs carrying ordnance, could, theoretically, be programmed to attack targets without a human making the attack decision (although this is not the current practice of states). Fully autonomous robotic weaponry seems like science fiction, but the robotics revolution is well underway and weapons that require no human interface to sense, think, and act are already possible. According to Singer (2009, p. 41): "Man's monopoly of warfare is being broken. We are entering the era of robots at war."

Formal Bargaining Model of War and Peace

Here we present a linear mathematical version of the bargaining model of war and peace introduced in Chapter 10. We derive a peaceful settlement equilibrium and then show how fighting can emerge based on inconsistent expectations and preemption incentives. Throughout this appendix we assume each player is risk neutral and that an interior solution holds.

B.1 Basic Model of Resource Conflict

We begin with the resource conflict model of Chapter 8, which is a variation of a model due to Skaperdas (2006). Assume players A and B have respective holdings of secure and undisputed resources R_A and R_B, but they dispute control of a fixed resource $\tilde{R}$. The players divert M_A and M_B units of their respective secure resources to produce military goods, which can be used to fight over the disputed resource. Each diverted unit generates one unit of military goods, and fighting destroys a fixed proportion δ of the disputed resource, where $0 < \delta < 1$.

Net Resource Functions under Fighting

Let p_A be A's conflict success in the dispute, with p_B the same for B. We assume conflict success is the proportion of the disputed resource controlled by a player, although it could be the probability that a player controls the entire resource in a winner-take-all contest. The technology relating the military inputs M_A and M_B and the conflict success proportions p_A and p_B is summarized by a ratio form conflict success function (CSF):

$$p_A = \frac{M_A}{M_A + ZM_B} \text{ and } p_B = \frac{ZM_B}{M_A + ZM_B}, \tag{B.1}$$

where the parameter $Z > 0$ represents the relative effectiveness of B's military goods. The net resources controlled by the players if fighting occurs, denoted as fighting net resources FNR_A and FNR_B, are:

$$FNR_A = R_A + \left(\frac{M_A}{M_A + ZM_B}\right)\tilde{R}(1 - \delta) - M_A \tag{B.2a}$$

$$FNR_B = R_B + \left(\frac{ZM_B}{M_A + ZM_B}\right)\tilde{R}(1 - \delta) - M_B. \tag{B.2b}$$

Reaction Functions and Fighting Equilibrium

Assume that players choose their respective military goods to maximize their net resource holdings under fighting, with their rival's military goods held fixed. For $i = A, B$ in (B.2), setting the derivative of FNR_i with respect to M_i to zero and solving for M_i gives the reaction functions for A and B:

$$M_A = \sqrt{ZM_B\tilde{R}(1 - \delta)} - ZM_B \tag{B.3a}$$

$$M_B = \frac{1}{Z}\left(\sqrt{ZM_A\tilde{R}(1 - \delta)} - M_A\right). \tag{B.3b}$$

Solving the reaction functions simultaneously yields equilibrium military goods M_A^* and M_B^*, where:

$$M_A^* = M_B^* = \frac{Z\tilde{R}(1 - \delta)}{(1 + Z)^2}. \tag{B.4}$$

Substituting M_A^* and M_B^* into (B.2a) and (B.2b) gives the equilibrium fighting net resources FNR_A^* and FNR_B^*, where:

$$FNR_A^* = R_A + \frac{\tilde{R}(1 - \delta)}{(1 + Z)^2} \tag{B.5a}$$

$$FNR_B^* = R_B + \frac{Z^2\tilde{R}(1 - \delta)}{(1 + Z)^2}. \tag{B.5b}$$

Net Resource Functions under Settlement

Given the destructiveness of conflict, both players can potentially gain from peaceful settlement. Let s_A be the proportion of the disputed resource received by A in the settlement, with s_B the same for B. Under settlement, assume that players divide the disputed resource according to a split-the-surplus division rule (Garfinkel and Skaperdas 2007, p. 674). According to this rule, the surplus from peaceful settlement $\delta \tilde{R}$ is split evenly, while the remaining disputed resource $(1 - \delta)\tilde{R}$ is divided according to the players' military goods and the CSF in (B.1). This leads to the following peaceful settlement proportions:

$$s_A = \delta\left(\frac{1}{2}\right) + (1 - \delta)\left(\frac{M_A}{M_A + ZM_B}\right) \text{ and}$$

$$s_B = \delta\left(\frac{1}{2}\right) + (1 - \delta)\left(\frac{ZM_B}{M_A + ZM_B}\right). \tag{B.6}$$

Net resources under settlement, denoted as settlement net resources SNR_A and SNR_B, are:

$$SNR_A = R_A + \left[\delta\left(\frac{1}{2}\right) + (1 - \delta)\left(\frac{M_A}{M_A + ZM_B}\right)\right]\tilde{R} - M_A \tag{B.7a}$$

$$SNR_B = R_B + \left[\delta\left(\frac{1}{2}\right) + (1 - \delta)\left(\frac{ZM_B}{M_A + ZM_B}\right)\right]\tilde{R} - M_B. \tag{B.7b}$$

Reaction Functions and Settlement Equilibrium

Assume that players choose their respective military goods to maximize their net resources under settlement, with their rival's military goods held fixed. Since their net resource functions under settlement in (B.7) differ from their respective net resource functions under fighting in (B.2) by a fixed amount $\delta\left(\frac{1}{2}\right)\tilde{R}$, the same reaction functions and equilibrium military goods in (B.3) and (B.4) obtain here. Substituting M_A^* and M_B^* from (B.4) into (B.7a) and (B.7b) yields the equilibrium settlement net resources SNR_A^* and SNR_B^*, where:

$$SNR_A^* = R_A + \frac{\tilde{R}(1 - \delta)}{(1 + Z)^2} + \delta\left(\frac{1}{2}\right)\tilde{R} \tag{B.8a}$$

$$SNR_B^* = R_B + \frac{Z^2 \tilde{R}(1 - \delta)}{(1 + Z)^2} + \delta\left(\frac{1}{2}\right)\tilde{R}. \tag{B.8b}$$

Since settlement avoids the destructiveness of war, net resources under settlement in (B.8) are greater than net resources under fighting in (B.5) for each player by $\delta\left(\frac{1}{2}\right)\tilde{R}$. Hence, peaceful settlement is the predicted outcome of the resource conflict model.

B.2 Selected Sources of Violence

Inconsistent Expectations

As shown in Chapter 10, there are various reasons why violence might occur even though it is destructive. One possibility is that the rivals have inconsistent expectations about how well they would do in a fight. For example, A might have private information about the tactical potential of its military stock that would convey an advantage to A during war. We assume that if A revealed this information to B prior to war, the advantage would disappear or the information would be deemed not credible by B. Let e represent A's advantage, which is perceived by A but not by B. We introduce e as an additive exogenous term in A's conflict success function, and we assume that e is not so large that A would perceive the proportion of conflict success to be greater than one. This leads to the following perceptions of conflict success under fighting:

$$p_A = \frac{M_A}{M_A + ZM_B} + e \text{ and } p_B = \frac{ZM_B}{M_A + ZM_B}. \tag{B.9}$$

The net resource function of A under fighting will now be:

$$FNR_A = R_A + \left(\frac{M_A}{M_A + ZM_B} + e\right)\tilde{R}(1 - \delta) - M_A, \tag{B.10}$$

while B's net resource function will continue to be given by (B.2b). Comparing the net resource functions in (B.10) and (B.2a) reveals that A's additional expectation of conflict success adds a fixed amount $e\tilde{R}(1 - \delta)$ to its net resource function. Hence, the same reaction function for A in (B.3a) and equilibrium military goods in (B.4) again hold. It follows that the equilibrium fighting net resources for A are:

$$FNR_A^* = R_A + \frac{\tilde{R}(1 - \delta)}{(1 + Z)^2} + e\tilde{R}(1 - \delta), \tag{B.11}$$

while B's equilibrium fighting net resources continue to be given by (B.5b).

If instead of fighting the players peacefully settle under the split-the-surplus division rule in (B.6), the equilibrium net resources under settlement are given by (B.8). Inspection of (B.8a) and (B.11) shows that A strictly prefers peaceful settlement to fighting when $\delta(\frac{1}{2})\tilde{R} > e\tilde{R}(1 - \delta)$. Hence, the following relationship arises between the destructiveness of conflict δ and the degree of A's additional conflict success e:

$$\delta \; \begin{matrix} > \\ < \end{matrix} \; \frac{e}{\frac{1}{2} + e} \quad \begin{matrix} \Rightarrow \textit{ settlement} \\ \Rightarrow \textit{ war} \end{matrix} . \tag{B.12}$$

Condition (B.12) implies that for a given degree of additional conflict success e, a sufficiently high degree of conflict destructiveness δ will lead to peaceful settlement rather than fighting. Alternatively, for a given degree of conflict destructiveness, a sufficiently high degree of additional conflict success will lead to fighting rather than settlement.

Preemption

Preemptive war can arise from the existence of a first-strike advantage. Assume that A and B have complete information and thus correctly anticipate the offensive advantage. Assume also that one of the players strikes first if fighting occurs. We introduce a first-strike advantage into the model by adding an exogenous term e to the first-mover's CSF while subtracting the same value e from the second-mover's CSF. We assume that e is not so large that the proportion of conflict success would be greater than one.

If A strikes first, the following conflict success proportions apply under fighting:

$$p_A = \frac{M_A}{M_A + ZM_B} + e \text{ and } p_B = \frac{ZM_B}{M_A + ZM_B} - e. \tag{B.13}$$

Alternatively, if B strikes first, the algebraic signs on e are reversed in (B.13). The net resource functions for A and B under fighting when A strikes first are:

$$FNR_A = R_A + \left(\frac{M_A}{M_A + ZM_B} + e \right) \tilde{R}(1 - \delta) - M_A \qquad \text{(B.14a)}$$

$$FNR_B = R_B + \left(\frac{ZM_B}{M_A + ZM_B} - e \right) \tilde{R}(1 - \delta) - M_B. \qquad \text{(B.14b)}$$

Alternatively, when B strikes first, the signs on e are reversed in (B.14a) and (B.14b). In either case, since a first-strike advantage adds or subtracts a fixed amount $e\tilde{R}(1 - \delta)$ to a player's net resource function, the same reaction functions and equilibrium military goods in (B.3) and (B.4) obtain. It follows that the equilibrium net resources after A initiates an attack are:

$$FNR_A^* = R_A + \frac{\tilde{R}(1 - \delta)}{(1 + Z)^2} + e\tilde{R}(1 - \delta) \qquad \text{(B.15a)}$$

$$FNR_B^* = R_B + \frac{Z^2 \tilde{R}(1 - \delta)}{(1 + Z)^2} - e\tilde{R}(1 - \delta). \qquad \text{(B.15b)}$$

Alternatively, if B initiates attack, the algebraic signs on e are reversed in (B.15a) and (B.15b).

When considering a first strike, players compare their settlement net resources in (B.8) with their net resources if they attack first. Each player prefers peaceful settlement to fighting when $\delta\left(\frac{1}{2}\right)\tilde{R} > e\tilde{R}(1 - \delta)$. Hence, the relationship between δ and e set forth in condition (B.12) holds here, with the proviso that e now represents the presence of a common first-strike advantage available to the first-mover rather than A's additional conflict success. Applying condition (B.12) to preemption implies that for a given degree of first-strike advantage e, a sufficiently high degree of conflict destructiveness δ will lead to peaceful settlement rather than fighting. Alternatively, for a given degree of conflict destructiveness, a sufficiently high degree of first-strike advantage will lead to fighting rather than settlement.

Matrix Algebra Methods for Solving Network Models

This appendix provides information on matrix algebra methods for solving for equilibrium actions of actors on a network assuming the actor reaction functions are linear.

C.1 Equilibrium Actions for Figure 7.5 Network

Figure 7.5 has seven actors, A–G. Each achieves marginal benefit $a = 2$ and faces a marginal cost parameter $b = 1$ for each unit of its action x_i ($i = A$, $B, \ldots, G$) according to the linear quadratic model (LQM) payoff function. The parameter values give rise to reaction function intercept values of $a/b = 2$. In Figure 7.5, A is linked to B, C, and D according to weight parameter $w = 0.2$. Links also exist between B and E, C and F, and D and G, each with $w = 0.2$. There is also a link between E and F with weight $\tilde{w} = 0.1$. These weight link parameter values are divided by $b = 1$ when they appear in each actor's reaction function. For example, A's reaction function from Figure 7.5 is:

$$x_A = \frac{a}{b} + \frac{w}{b}x_B + \frac{w}{b}x_c + \frac{w}{b}x_D = 2 + 0.2x_B + 0.2x_C + 0.2x_D. \quad \text{(C.1)}$$

Equation (C.1) can be written as follows:

$$x_A - 0.2x_B - 0.2x_C - 0.2x_D = 2. \quad \text{(C.2)}$$

The structure in (C.2) would apply to the reaction functions of the other actors in Figure 7.5, but with the caveat that the elements on the left side of the equals sign would reflect the linkages pertinent to each actor.

The system of reaction function equations written in matrix algebra form AX=B is

$$
\begin{bmatrix}
1 & -0.2 & -0.2 & -0.2 & 0 & 0 & 0 \\
-0.2 & 1 & 0 & 0 & -0.2 & 0 & 0 \\
-0.2 & 0 & 1 & 0 & 0 & -0.2 & 0 \\
-0.2 & 0 & 0 & 1 & 0 & 0 & -0.2 \\
0 & -0.2 & 0 & 0 & 1 & -0.1 & 0 \\
0 & 0 & -0.2 & 0 & -0.1 & 1 & 0 \\
0 & 0 & 0 & -0.2 & 0 & 0 & 1
\end{bmatrix}
\cdot
\begin{bmatrix}
x_A \\ x_B \\ x_C \\ x_D \\ x_E \\ x_F \\ x_G
\end{bmatrix}
=
\begin{bmatrix}
2 \\ 2 \\ 2 \\ 2 \\ 2 \\ 2 \\ 2
\end{bmatrix}.
$$

$$(C.3)$$

The numbers in the first row of the A matrix in (C.3) align with the numbers from A's reaction function in equation (C.2). The remaining numbers in the A matrix are based upon the reaction functions appropriate to the other six actors in Figure 7.5. The B column vector to the right of the equality in (C.3) encompasses the $a/b = 2$ intercept values from each actor's reaction function.

The solutions to the x variables in (C.3) are given by $X^* = A^{-1}B$ where A^{-1} is the inverse of the A matrix. The inverse of A can be found with Excel by using the MINVERSE command. Specifically, enter the numerical values of the A matrix in (C.3) into an Excel spreadsheet. Then select a 7x7 empty area elsewhere on that spreadsheet. Enter =MINVERSE, select the A matrix array of numerical values, and then simultaneously hit the Shift, Ctrl, Enter keys. Now that you have the A inverse matrix, enter seven 2s in a column in an empty area in the spreadsheet. This is your B column vector. Now select an empty area that encompasses one column and seven rows. This will be for your X* solution vector. To get that solution, enter =MMULT, which is the matrix multiplication formula. For the first array, select your 7x7 A inverse matrix. For your second array, select your 7x1 column vector of 2s. Then simultaneously hit the Shift, Ctrl, Enter keys. The result will be the X* solution vector:

$$
\begin{bmatrix}
x_A^* = 4.0 \\
x_B^* = 3.4 \\
x_C^* = 3.4 \\
x_D^* = 3.3 \\
x_E^* = 3.0 \\
x_F^* = 3.0 \\
x_G^* = 2.7
\end{bmatrix}.
$$

$$(C.4)$$

C.2 Equilibrium Actions for Top Tentacle of Figure 14.8 Network

Following the methods from C.1, the AX=B system of reaction functions for the top tentacle of Figure 14.8 is:

$$
\begin{bmatrix}
1 & -0.2 & 0 & 0 \\
-0.2 & 1 & -0.2 & 0.2 \\
0 & -0.2 & 1 & 0 \\
0 & 0.2 & 0 & 1
\end{bmatrix}
\cdot
\begin{bmatrix}
x_1 \\
x_2 \\
x_3 \\
\tilde{x}_4
\end{bmatrix}
=
\begin{bmatrix}
2 \\
2 \\
2 \\
2
\end{bmatrix}
\tag{C.5}
$$

Based upon the Excel methods of matrix inversion and matrix multiplication described in C.1, the $X^* = A^{-1}B$ solution for the top tentacle of Figure 14.8 is:

$$
\begin{bmatrix}
x_1^* = 2.55 \\
x_2^* = 2.73 \\
x_3^* = 2.55 \\
\tilde{x}_4^* = 1.45
\end{bmatrix}.
\tag{C.6}
$$

C.3 Equilibrium Actions for Figure 17.1 Network of Conflict Resolution Organizations

The reaction functions for the eight conflict resolution organizations (CROs) in Figure 17.1 with the numerical values for the parameters plugged in are:

$$x_1 = 2 + 0.2x_5 \text{ or } x_1 - 0.2x_5 = 2 \tag{C.7a}$$

$$x_2 = 2 + 0.2x_5 \text{ or } x_2 - 0.2x_5 = 2 \tag{C.7b}$$

$$x_3 = 2 + 0.2x_5 \text{ or } x_3 - 0.2x_5 = 2 \tag{C.7c}$$

$$x_4 = 2 + 0.2x_5 \text{ or } x_4 - 0.2x_5 = 2 \tag{C.7d}$$

$$x_5 = 2 + 0.2x_1 + 0.2x_2 + 0.2x_3 + 0.2x_4 \text{ or}$$
$$x_5 - 0.2x_1 - 0.2x_2 - 0.2x_3 - 0.2x_4 = 2 \tag{C.7e}$$

$$x_6 = 2 + 0.2x_8 \text{ or } x_6 - 0.2x_8 = 2 \tag{C.7f}$$

$$x_7 = 2 + 0.2x_8 \text{ or } x_7 - 0.2x_8 = 2 \tag{C.7g}$$

$$x_8 = 2 + 0.2x_6 + 0.2x_7 \text{ or } x_8 - 0.2x_6 - 0.2x_7 = 2. \tag{C.7h}$$

The AX=B system of reaction functions for Figure 17.1 is:

$$
\begin{bmatrix}
1 & 0 & 0 & 0 & -0.2 & 0 & 0 & 0 \\
0 & 1 & 0 & 0 & -0.2 & 0 & 0 & 0 \\
0 & 0 & 1 & 0 & -0.2 & 0 & 0 & 0 \\
0 & 0 & 0 & 1 & -0.2 & 0 & 0 & 0 \\
-0.2 & -0.2 & -0.2 & -0.2 & 1 & 0 & 0 & 0 \\
0 & 0 & 0 & 0 & 0 & 1 & 0 & -0.2 \\
0 & 0 & 0 & 0 & 0 & 0 & 1 & -0.2 \\
0 & 0 & 0 & 0 & 0 & -0.2 & -0.2 & 1
\end{bmatrix}
\cdot
\begin{bmatrix}
x_1 \\ x_2 \\ x_3 \\ x_4 \\ x_5 \\ x_6 \\ x_7 \\ x_8
\end{bmatrix}
=
\begin{bmatrix}
2 \\ 2 \\ 2 \\ 2 \\ 2 \\ 2 \\ 2 \\ 2
\end{bmatrix}.
\tag{C.8}
$$

Based upon the Excel methods of matrix inversion and matrix multiplication described in C.1, the $X^* = A^{-1}B$ solution for Figure 17.1 is:

$$
\begin{bmatrix}
x_1^* = 2.9 \\
x_2^* = 2.9 \\
x_3^* = 2.9 \\
x_4^* = 2.9 \\
x_5^* = 4.3 \\
x_6^* = 2.6 \\
x_7^* = 2.6 \\
x_8^* = 3.0
\end{bmatrix}.
\tag{C.9}
$$

In Chapter 17, the CRO network was rerun under two scenarios: removal of C_5 from the network and C_5 restored to the network with a new link forged between C_5 and C_8. To find the solution for the first scenario, C_5 must be removed from the model, which would then generate a 7x7 A matrix and a 7x1 B column vector. Rerunning the model with Excel generates the outcome described in Chapter 17. For the second scenario, the new link between C_5 and C_8 would require that –0.2 replace 0 in row 5 column 8 and in row 8 column 5 of the A matrix in (C.8). Rerunning the model with Excel generates the outcome described in Chapter 17.

Conflict and Peace Datasets

D.1 Interstate Conflicts (Chapter 11)

Correlates of War (COW) Wars

Interstate war – Combat between states involving a minimum of 1,000 battle deaths per 12-month period among all states involved. Battle deaths are military personnel only (Sarkees and Wayman 2010, p. 51). Coverage: 1816–2007, updated occasionally.

Uppsala Conflict Data Program/International Peace Research Institute, Oslo (UCDP/PRIO) Wars

Interstate war – Combat between states involving a minimum of 1,000 battle-related deaths (military and civilian) per year among all states involved (Gleditsch et al. 2002, Uppsala Conflict Data Program 2017). Coverage: 1946–present, updated annually.

Uppsala Conflict Data Program/International Peace Research Institute, Oslo (UCDP/PRIO) Subwars

Apply UCDP/PRIO's interstate war definition, but with battle-related deaths between 25 and 999 (Gleditsch et al. 2002, Uppsala Conflict Data Program 2017). Coverage: 1946–present, updated annually.

COW Militarized Interstate Disputes (MIDs)

Militarized interstate dispute – United historical case in which the "threat, display or use of military force short of war by one member

state is explicitly directed towards the government, official representatives, official forces, property, or territory of another state" (Jones
et al. 1996, p. 168). Coverage: 1816–2010, updated occasionally.

International Crisis Behavior (ICB) Crises

Interstate crisis – A state's leaders perceive a threat to basic values,
time pressure for response, and a heightened probability of military
hostilities (Brecher et al. 2016, p. 10). Coverage: 1918–2013, updated
occasionally.

D.2 Intrastate Conflicts (Chapter 12)

Uppsala Conflict Data Program/Peace Research Institute, Oslo (UCDP/PRIO) Armed Conflict Dataset – Civil Wars

Civil war – Combat between a state and one or more internal opposition groups leading to minimum of 1,000 battle-related deaths (military and civilian) per year among the parties involved (Gleditsch et al.
2002, Themnér 2017). Coverage: 1946–present, updated annually.

Uppsala Conflict Data Program/Peace Research Institute, Oslo (UCDP/PRIO) Armed Conflict Dataset – Subwar Civil Conflicts

Apply UCDP/PRIO's civil war definition, but with battle-related
deaths between 25 and 999 (Gleditsch et al. 2002, Themnér 2017).
Coverage: 1946–present, updated annually.

Correlates of War (COW) Intrastate Wars

Intrastate war – Combat "between or among organized armed forces
that takes place within the territorial boundaries of a state system
member and leads to 1,000 battle ... deaths [military personnel only]
per year" (Sarkees and Wayman 2010, p. 337; see also p. 50). Civil
war involves combat between a national government and one or
more internal opposition groups (Sarkees and Wayman 2010,
p. 338). Coverage: 1816–2007, updated occasionally.

Political Instability Task Force (PITF) Revolutionary/Ethnic Civil Wars

Civil war – Conflict between a government and a politically organized group or between a government and a national, ethnic, religious, or other communal minority leading to a minimum of 1,000 direct conflict-related deaths (military and civilian) for the whole war among the parties involved. In addition, each party mobilizes at least 1,000 people in the conflict and there must be at least one year when the annual conflict-related deaths exceed 100 (Marshall, Gurr, and Harff 2017, p. 5). Coverage: 1955–2016, updated occasionally.

Minorities at Risk (MAR) and All Minorities at Risk (AMAR) Intrastate Conflicts

Three types of intrastate conflict are considered: conflict within a communal group (factional or intracommunal), between communal groups (intercommunal), and between one or more communal groups and a regime (civil) (Minorities at Risk 2009). MAR covers 284 groups from 1945 to 2006. AMAR (forthcoming) will cover 1,202 groups. Update status unknown.

D.3 Terrorism (Chapter 13)

Global Terrorism Database (GTD)

A terrorist attack is "the threatened or actual use of illegal force and violence by a non-state actor to attain a political, economic, religious, or social goal through fear, coercion, or intimidation" (Global Terrorism Database 2017). Covers domestic and international incidents. Coverage: 1970–present, updated annually.

RAND Worldwide Terrorism Incident Database (RWTID)

"Terrorism is defined by the nature of the act, not by the identity of the perpetrators or the nature of the cause; key elements include: violence or the threat of violence, calculated to create fear and alarm, intended to coerce certain actions, motive must include a political objective, generally directed against civilian targets, can be a group or an individual" (RAND Worldwide Terrorism Incident Database 2017). Covers domestic and international incidents. Coverage: 1968–2008, not updated.

International Terrorism: Attributes of Terrorist Events (ITERATE)

International/transnational terrorism is "the use, or threat of use, of anxiety-inducing, extra-normal violence for political purposes by any individual or group, whether acting for or in opposition to established governmental authority, when such action is intended to influence the attitudes and behavior of a target group wider than the immediate victim and when, through the nationality or foreign ties of its perpetrators, its location, the nature of its institutional or human victims, or the mechanics of its resolution, its ramifications transcend national boundaries" (Mickolus, Sandler, Murdock, and Flemming 2016, p. 2). Covers international (perpetrators are controlled by a sovereign state) and transnational (perpetrators are nonstate actors) incidents. Coverage: 1970–present, updated annually.

Center for Systemic Peace, High Casualty Terrorist Bombings (HCTB)

High casualty terrorist bombings are "bomb attacks on non-combatant (civilian and political) targets by non-state actors resulting in 15 or more deaths" (Center for Systemic Peace 2017). Covers domestic and international HCTB. Coverage: 1989–present, updated annually.

Chicago Project on Security and Threats (CPOST) Suicide Attack Database

A suicide attack is as "an attack in which an attacker kills himself or herself in a deliberate attempt to kill others" (Chicago Project on Security and Threats 2017). Covers domestic and international suicide attacks. Coverage: 1974–2016, updated occasionally.

D.4 Mass Atrocities (Chapter 14)

Political Instability Task Force Geno-politicide (PITF-G) Database

"Genocide and politicide events involve the promotion, execution, and/or implied consent of sustained policies by governing elites or their agents – or in the case of civil war, either of the contending authorities – that result in the deaths of a substantial portion of a communal group or politicized non-communal group" (Marshall, Gurr, and Harff 2017, pp. 14–15). Coverage: 1955–2016, updated occasionally.

Ulfelder and Valentino Data (UV) Mass Killings Dataset

Mass killing is "any event in which the actions of state agents result in the intentional death of at least 1,000 noncombatants from a discrete group in a period of sustained violence" (Ulfelder and Valentino 2008, p. 2; emphasis removed). Coverage: 1945–2006, not updated.

Ulfelder (ULF) Mass Killings Dataset

Mass killing is "the deliberate actions of state agents, or other groups acting at their behest, [that] result in the deaths of at least 1,000 noncombatant civilians in a relatively short period of time" (Early Warning Project 2018, Ulfelder 2017). Coverage: 1945–2013, does not appear to be updated.

Easterly, Gatti, and Kurlat Data (EGK) Mass Killings Dataset

In defining mass killing, EGK use the broad definition of genocide from Charny (1999, p. 7): "Genocide ... is the mass killing of substantial numbers of human beings, when not in the course of military action against the military forces of an avowed enemy, under conditions of the essential defenselessness and helplessness of the victims" (Easterly, Gatti, and Kurlat 2006, p. 132). Coverage: 1820–1988, not updated.

Uppsala Conflict Data Program One-Sided Violence Dataset (UCDP-V)

"One-sided violence is the use of armed force by the government of a state or by a formally organized group against civilians which results in at least 25 deaths" (Allansson and Croicu 2017, p. 2). Coverage: 1989–present, updated annually.

Political Instability Task Force Worldwide Atrocities Dataset (PITF-W)

"We define an atrocity as implicitly or explicitly political, direct, and deliberate violent action resulting in the death of noncombatant civilians ... We have only coded incidents involving five or more non-combatant deaths" (Schrodt and Ulfelder 2016). Coverage: 1995–present, updated regularly.

Rummel Democide Dataset

Democide is the "murder of any person or people by a government, including genocide, politicide, and mass murder" (Rummel 1994). Coverage: twentieth and pre–twentieth centuries, not updated.

D.5 Military Spending, Armaments, and Armed Forces Personnel (Chapter 15)

Stockholm International Peace Research Institute (SIPRI) Military Expenditures Database

Provides military spending levels for countries and regions of the world. Coverage: 1949–present, updated annually.

Stockholm International Peace Research Institute (SIPRI) Arms Transfers Database

Provides data on major conventional weapons exports, imports, and transfers for countries and regions of the world. Coverage: 1950–present, updated annually.

World Military Expenditures and Arms Transfers (WMEAT) Database

Provides data on military spending, arms transfers, and armed forces personnel for countries and regions of the world. Coverage: 1964–2015, updated annually.

International Institute for Strategic Studies (IISS), *The Military Balance*

Provides data on armaments stocks and armed forces personnel for countries and regions of the world. Coverage: 1969–present, updated annually.

Correlates of War (COW) Project National Material Capabilities Dataset

Provides Composite Index of National Capability (CINC) measures for countries of the world based upon: Military Spending, Military Personnel, Energy Consumption, Iron/Steel Production, and Urban and Total Population. Coverage: 1816–2012, updated occasionally.

Nuclear Threat Initiative Portal on Arms Control Treaties

Details of bilateral and multilateral treaties on the control of weapons of mass destruction, conventional weapons, and the use of outer space for military purposes.

Arms Control Association Portal on Arms Control Treaties

Details of bilateral and multilateral treaties on the control of weapons of mass destruction, conventional weapons, and the use of outer space for military purposes.

D.6 Interstate Alliances (Chapter 16)

Correlates of War (COW) Formal Alliance Dataset

A formal interstate alliance meets each of three criteria: "first, the alliance must be signed by two qualified system members; second, the alliance treaty must contain language that would qualify it as a defense pact, neutrality or nonaggression pact, or an entente; and third, the effective dates of alliance have to be identifiable" (Gibler and Sarkees 2004, p. 214). Coverage: 1816–2012, updated occasionally.

Gibler's International Military Alliances

Gibler (2009, pp. li–lv) follows COW's three criteria, but with three caveats. First, written agreements that are not ratified are excluded. Second, alliances in which the treaties could not be found were included if two secondary sources could verify the existence and terms of the treaties. Third, neutrality and nonaggression pacts were treated as one type of alliance rather than two. Coverage: 1648–2008, not updated.

Alliance Treaty Obligations and Provisions (ATOP) Dataset

Interstate alliances are "written agreements, signed by official representatives of at least two independent states, that include promises to aid a partner in the event of military conflict, to remain neutral in the event of conflict, to refrain from military conflict with one another, or to consult/cooperate in the event of international crises that create a potential for military conflict" (Leeds, Ritter, Mitchell, and Long 2002, p. 238). Coverage: 1815–2003, does not appear to be updated.

D.7 Peace (Chapter 17)

Institute for Economics and Peace Global Peace Index (GPI) and Positive Peace Index (PPI)

Based upon 23 subindices, the GPI measures a country's level of negative peace based from three domains: ongoing domestic and international conflict, level of societal safety and security within a nation, and militarization of the country (Institute for Economics and Peace 2018). GPI scores for most nations and regions of the world are available annually since 2007. Based upon 24 subindices, the PPI measures a country's level of positive peace based upon eight domains: well-functioning government, equitable distribution of resources, free flow of information, good relations with neighbors, high levels of human capital, acceptance of the rights of others, low levels of corruption, and sound business environment (Institute for Economics and Peace 2017). PPI scores for most nations of the world are available annually since 2015. GPI and PPI scores updated annually.

The Georgetown Institute for Women, Peace and Security and the Peace Research Institute in Oslo Women, Peace, and Security (WPS) Index

The WPS index "incorporates three basic dimensions of well-being – inclusion (economic, social, political); justice (formal laws and informal discrimination); and security (at the family, community, and societal levels) – and captures and quantifies them through 11 indicators. It ranks 153 countries – covering more than 98 percent of the world's population – along these three dimensions in a way that focuses attention on key achievements and major shortcomings"

(Georgetown Institute for Women, Peace and Security 2018). Regular updates expected.

Peace Direct's Peace Insight Database

Data on the work of almost 1,700 peacebuilding organizations (IGOs, INGOs, NGOs) working in more than 40 conflict areas around the world. Regular updates expected.

Uppsala Conflict Data Program (UCDP) Conflict Termination Dataset

Data on the start and end dates for interstate, intrastate, and extra-state conflicts. Coverage: 1946–2014, occasional updates expected.

Uppsala Conflict Data Program (UCDP) Peace Agreements Dataset

Data on peace agreements signed between at least two opposing primary warring parties. Coverage: 1975–2011, does not appear to be updated.

UCDP Managing Intrastate Conflict (MIC) Dataset

Data on all third-party (states, IGOs, INGOs, NGOs, etc.) interventions in conflict dyads in Africa. Coverage: 1993–2007, does not appear to be updated.

UCDP Managing Intrastate Low-intensity Conflict (MILC) Dataset

Data on all measures taken by third parties (states, IGOs, INGOs, NGOs, etc.) in low-intensity conflict intrastate dyad-years. Coverage: 1993–2004, does not appear to be updated.

Peace Accords Matrix (PAM) Database

Data on 34 intrastate comprehensive peace agreements. Coverage: 1989–2012, does not appear to be updated.

Everyday Peace Indicators (EPI) Project

EPI personnel team up with local NGOs and community focus groups to generate indicators of conflict and peace at the local level. Indicators are based on information across four domains: security, development, social outcomes, and human rights (Firchow and Mac Ginty 2017). Regular updates expected.

Regression Methods

Social scientists understand the world as a complex web of relationships. These relationships are formalized by assuming that certain dependent variables of interest are functions of one or more independent variables. The primary method of estimating and testing these postulated relationships is called regression analysis. We illustrate regression analysis with an example.

Suppose for a sample of countries we are interested in the relationship between democracy and military spending. In particular, suppose we want to test the hypothesis that more democratic nations on average spend less on military activities. For our limited purposes, we postulate two linear regression models:

$$\text{E(Military Spending)} = \beta_1 + \beta_2 \text{Democracy} \tag{E.1}$$

and

$$\text{E(Military Spending)} = \beta_1 + \beta_2 \text{Democracy} + \beta_3 \text{Income}. \tag{E.2}$$

Equation (E.1) is called a simple regression because it specifies expected military spending as a function of a single explanatory variable, here democracy. Equation (E.2) is an example of multiple regression because it includes two or more explanatory variables, here democracy and income. In this case income is used as a control variable which, as explained later, allows for a better estimate of the effect of democracy, the variable of primary interest.

We estimate the two spending equations based on 2003 data for a sample of 40 European countries. Military spending and income are measured in millions of 2003 US$ and are derived from the Stockholm International Peace Research Institute (2005). Democracy is measured by an index ranging from −10 (strongly autocratic) to +10 (strongly

Table E.1 *Regression results for military spending as a function of democracy and income.*

	(E.1)	(E.2)
Intercept (β_1)	1481.05 (1456.30) [1.02]	813.61 (709.91) [1.15]
Democracy (β_2)	611.83 (253.10) [2.42]	−83.90 (86.73) [−0.97]
Income (β_3)		0.02 (0.00) [5.61]
No. of Observations	40	40

Notes: See text for variable definitions and sources. Robust standard errors are shown in parentheses and *t*-statistics in brackets.

democratic) and is taken from Marshall and Jaggers (2007). The equations are estimated by a regression technique called ordinary least squares (OLS). In brief, OLS fits a line through the data by choosing estimates of β_1, β_2, and (in equation (E.2)) β_3 to minimize the sum of the squared differences between the actual and the estimated expenditures of the sample countries.

The regression results are shown in Table E.1. Consider first the substantial difference between the estimated values for β_2 in equations (E.1) and (E.2). In the first equation, the coefficient on democracy is 611.8, meaning that an increase of one point in a country's democracy index is estimated to increase that country's military spending by approximately 612 million dollars. In the second equation, however, the same coefficient is −83.9, meaning that a one-point increase in democracy is estimated to decrease spending by about 84 million dollars. The contrast between the two estimates illustrates the critical importance of including relevant control variables that might be correlated with the primary variable of interest. In the case here, more democratic countries tend to be more developed with higher levels of income, and countries with higher incomes tend to spend more on the military. When income is omitted from equation (E.1), its positive effect on spending is inadvertently picked up by the estimated coefficient for democracy. As a consequence, the OLS estimator for β_2 is biased upward if income in omitted.

Focus now on the more appropriately specified equation (E.2). Recall that the hypothesis being tested is that more democratic countries on average less on the military, holding constant other relevant factors like income. Formally, the null hypothesis is that democracy has no effect (H_0: $\beta_2 = 0$), which is tested against the one-sided alternative that the effect is negative (H_1: $\beta_2 < 0$). As already noted for equation (E.2), the estimated marginal effect of democracy is −83.9, thus suggesting that the hypothesis is correct. But is the evidence sufficiently strong to reject the null hypothesis H_0 in favor of the hypothesis H_1? In regression analysis, the answer is determined by what is known as the t-statistic, whose probability distribution is widely available in statistical software.

The t-statistic is typically computed as the ratio of the estimated coefficient and its standard deviation, where the latter is commonly known as the standard error. For the democracy variable in equation (E.2), the estimated coefficient of −83.9 divided by its standard error of 86.7 (shown in parentheses) yields a t-statistic of −0.97 (shown in brackets). Suppose we choose for our standard of evidence a significance level of 0.05. Using the probability distribution of the t-statistic, it can be shown that the probability value (or p-value) associated with the observed statistic of −0.97 is approximately 0.17. Because the risk of incorrectly rejecting H_0 (equal to 17 percent) exceeds the risk we are willing to bear (equal to five percent), we cannot reject the null hypothesis. Thus, while the regression result in equation (E.2) is suggestive of a negative relationship between democracy and military spending, the evidence is not sufficiently strong to permit us with confidence to conclude in favor of the conjecture. Turning to the income variable, however, the t-statistic of 5.61 is quite large and yields a p-value of 0.00. As anticipated, therefore, income is shown to have a statistically significant positive effect on military spending.

References

ABC News (2005), "Will Aid Effort After Asia Quake Help U.S. Image?" (https://abcnews
.go.com/WNT/Weather/story?id=1227341&page=1. Accessed: November 9, 2005).

Acemoglu, Daron, Tarek A. Hassan, and James A. Robinson (2011), "Social Structure
and Development: A Legacy of the Holocaust in Russia," *Quarterly Journal of
Economics*, 126(2), 895–946.

Acemoglu, Daron, Azarakhsh Malekian, and Asu Ozdaglar (2016), "Network Security
and Contagion," *Journal of Economic Theory*, 166(November), 536–85.

Adamic, Lada A. (1999), "The Small World Web," in Serge Abiteboul and Anne-Marie
Vercoustre (eds.), *Research and Advanced Technology for Digital Libraries,* ECDL
1999, Lecture Notes in Computer Science, Volume 1696 (Berlin: Springer),
443–52.

Adams, Karen R. (2003/04), "Attack and Conquer? International Anarchy and the
Offense-Defense-Deterrence Balance," *International Security*, 28(3), 45–83.

Addison, Tony and S. Mansoob Murshed (eds.) (2003), "Special Issue: Explaining
Violent Conflict: Going beyond Greed versus Grievance," *Journal of
International Development*, 14(4), 391–524.

Akerlof, George A. and Rachel E. Kranton (2010), *Identity Economics: How Our
Identities Shape Our Work, Wages, and Well-Being* (Princeton: Princeton
University Press).

Albright, David (2017), "North Korea's Nuclear Capabilities: A Fresh Look," Washington:
Institute for Science and International Security (http://isis-online.org/isis-reports
/detail/north-koreas-nuclear-capabilities-a-fresh-look/. Accessed: May 5, 2017).

Ali , F. Menla and Ourania Dimitraki (2014), "Military Spending and Economic
Growth in China: A Regime-Switching Analysis," *Applied Economics*, 46(28),
3408–20.

Allansson, Marie and Mihai Croicu (2017), "UCDP One-sided Violence Codebook Version
18.1," (http://ucdp.uu.se/downloads/nsos/ucdp-onesided-181.pdf. Accessed: June 29,
2018).

Allansson, Marie, Erik Melander, and Lotta Themnér (2017), "Organized Violence,
1989–2017," *Journal of Peace Research*, 54(4), 574–87.

Allen, Michael A. and Matthew Digiuseppe (2013), "Tightening the Belt: Sovereign
Debt and Alliance Formation," *International Studies Quarterly*, 57(4), 647–59.

Amegashie, J. Atsu (2014), "Asymmetric Information and Third-Party Intervention in Civil Wars," *Defence and Peace Economics*, 25(4), 381–400.

Amutabi, Maurice N. (2013), *The NGO Factor in Africa: The Case of Arrested Development in Kenya* (New York: Routledge).

Ancker, C. J., Jr. (1995), "A Proposed Foundation for a Theory of Combat," in Jerome Bracken, Moshe Kress, and Richard E. Rosenthal (eds.), *Warfare Modeling* (Alexandria: Military Operations Research Society), 165–97.

Anderson, James E. and Douglas Marcouiller (2005), "Anarchy and Autarky: Endogenous Predation as a Barrier to Trade," *International Economic Review*, 46(1), 189–213.

Anderton, Charles H. (1990), "Teaching Arms-Race Concepts in Intermediate Microeconomics," *Journal of Economic Education*, 21(2), 148–66.

  (2014), "A Research Agenda for the Economic Study of Genocide: Signposts from the Field of Conflict Economics," *Journal of Genocide Research*, 16(1), 113–38.

  (2015a), "Genocide: Perspectives from the Social Sciences," *Sociologias Plurais*, 3(2), 155–85.

  (2015b), "The Social Evolution of Genocide across Time and Geographic Space: Perspectives from Evolutionary Game Theory," *The Economics of Peace and Security Journal*, 10(2), 5–20.

  (2018), "Subterranean Atrocities: A Twenty-First Century Challenge for Mass Atrocity Prevention," in Samuel Totten (ed.), *Last Lectures on the Prevention and Intervention of Genocide* (New York: Routledge), 163–70.

Anderton, Charles H., Roxane A. Anderton, and John R. Carter (1999), "Economic Activity in the Shadow of Conflict," *Economic Inquiry*, 37(1), 166–79.

Anderton, Charles H. and Jurgen Brauer (eds.) (2016a), *Economic Aspects of Genocides, Other Mass Atrocities, and Their Prevention* (New York: Oxford University Press).

  (2016b), "On the Economics of Genocides, Other Mass Atrocities, and Their Prevention," in Charles H. Anderton and Jurgen Brauer (eds.), *Economic Aspects of Genocides, Other Mass Atrocities, and Their Prevention* (New York: Oxford University Press), 3–27.

  (2016c), "Genocide and Mass Killing Risk and Prevention: Perspectives from Constrained Optimization Models," in Charles H. Anderton and Jurgen Brauer (eds.), *Economic Aspects of Genocides, Other Mass Atrocities, and Their Prevention* (New York: Oxford University Press), 143–71.

  (2018a), "Mass Atrocities and Their Prevention," Working Paper.

  (2018b), "Network Models of Genocide Contagion and Prevention," Working Paper.

Anderton, Charles H. and John R. Carter (2003), "Does War Disrupt Trade?" in Gerald Schneider, Katherine Barbieri, and Nils Petter Gleditsch (eds.), *Globalization and Armed Conflict* (Boulder: Rowman & Littlefield), 299–310.

  (2005), "On Rational Choice Theory and the Study of Terrorism," *Defence and Peace Economics*, 16(4), 275–82.

  (2006), "Applying Intermediate Microeconomics to Terrorism," *Journal of Economic Education*, 37(4), 442–58.

  (2007), "A Survey of Peace Economics," in Todd Sandler and Keith Hartley (eds.), *Handbook of Defense Economics, Volume 2* (New York: Elsevier), 1211–58.

  (2008), "Vulnerable Trade: The Dark Side of an Edgeworth Box," *Journal of Economic Behavior & Organization*, 68(2), 422–32.

(2011), "A Bargaining Theory Perspective on War," in Derek Braddon and Keith Hartley (eds.), *Handbook on the Economics of Conflict* (Cheltenham: Edward Elgar), 29–51.

Arce, Daniel G. and Todd Sandler (2005), "Counterterrorism: A Game-Theoretic Analysis," *Journal of Conflict Resolution*, 49(2), 183–200.

Arizona Public Media (2015), "'Programa Frontera Sur': US Intercedes in Southern Mexico," (www.azpm.org/p/featured-news/2016/6/7/89501-programa-frontera-sur-interceding-in-southern-mexico/. Accessed: September 30, 2016).

Arms Control Association (2017), "Treaties & Agreements," (www.armscontrol.org/treaties. Accessed: October 24, 2017).

Asch, Soloman E. (1951), "Effects of Group Pressure on the Modification and Distortion of Judgments," in H. Guetzkow (ed.) *Groups, Leadership and Men* (Pittsburgh: Carnegie Press), 177–90.

Augier, Mie, Robert McNab, Jerry Guo, and Phillip Karber (2017), "Defense Spending and Economic Growth: Evidence from China, 1952–2012," *Defence and Peace Economics*, 28(1), 65–90.

Axelrod, Robert (1984), *The Evolution of Cooperation* (New York: Basic Books).

Aziz, Nusrate and M. Niaz Asadullah (2017), "Military Spending, Armed Conflict and Economic Growth in Developing Countries in the Post-Cold War Era," *Journal of Economic Studies*, 44(1), 47–68.

Ballentine, Karen and Jake Sherman (2003), "Introduction," in Karen Ballentine and Jake Sherman (eds.), *The Political Economy of Armed Conflict* (Boulder: Lynne Rienner), 1–15.

Ballester, Coralio, Antoni Calvó-Armengol, and Yves Zenou (2006), "Who's Who in Networks. Wanted: The Key Player," *Econometrica*, 74(5), 1403–17.

Bara, Corinne (2017), "Legacies of Violence: Conflict-specific Capital and the Postconflict Diffusion of Civil War," *Journal of Conflict Resolution*, https://doi.org/10.1177/0022002717711501.

Barash, David P. and Charles P. Webel (2018), *Peace & Conflict Studies*, 4th edn. (London: Sage).

Barber, Victoria (2015), "The Evolution of Al Qaeda's Global Network and Al Qaeda Core's Position within It: A Network Analysis," *Perspectives on Terrorism*, 9 (6), 1–35.

Barbieri, Katherine and Rafael Reuveny (2005), "Economic Globalization and Civil War," *The Journal of Politics*, 67(4), 1228–47.

Barnett, Thomas P. M. (2004), *The Pentagon's New Map: War and Peace in the Twenty-First Century* (New York: G. P. Putnam's Sons).

Bartkus, Viva Ona (2018), "Business on the Frontlines," in Madhav Joshi and Peter Wallensteen (eds.), *Understanding Quality Peace: Peacebuilding after Civil War* (London: Routledge), chapter 6.

Bas, Muhammet, and Robert Schub (2016), "Mutual Optimism as a Cause of Conflict: Secret Alliances and Conflict Onset," *International Studies Quarterly*, 60(3), 552–64.

Bass, Warren (2015), *A Surprise Out of Zion? Case Studies in Israel's Decisions on Whether to Alert the United States to Preemptive and Preventive Strikes, from Suez to the Syrian Nuclear Reactor* (Santa Monica: Rand Corporation).

BBC News (1998), "World: America's Clinton Statement in Full," August 26, 1998. (http://news.bbc.co.uk/2/hi/americas/155412.stm. Accessed: May 12, 2017).

Bearce, David H. and Sawa Omori (2005), "How Do Commercial Institutions Promote Peace?" *Journal of Peace Research*, 42(6), 659–78.

Beard, Steven and Joshua A. Strayhorn (2018), "When Will States Strike First? Battlefield Advantages and Rationalist War," *International Studies Quarterly*, 62 (1), 42–53.

Beckerman, Stephen (1991), "The Equations of War," *Current Anthropology*, 32(5), 636–40.

Bell, Sam R. and Jesse C. Johnson (2015), "Shifting Power, Commitment Problems, and Preventive War," *International Studies Quarterly*, 59(1), 124–32.

Bénabou, Roland and Jean Tirole (2009), "Over My Dead Body: Bargaining and the Price of Dignity," *American Economic Review*, 99(2), 459–65.

(2011), "Identity, Morals, and Taboos: Beliefs as Assets." *Quarterly Journal of Economics*, 126(2), 805–55.

(2016), "Mindful Economics: The Production, Consumption, and Value of Beliefs," *Journal of Economic Perspectives*, 30(3), 141–64.

Benoit, Emile (1973), *Defense and Economic Growth in Developing Countries* (Boston: D. C. Heath).

Berman, Eli and David D. Laitin (2008), "Religion, Terrorism and Public Goods: Testing the Club Model," *Journal of Public Economics*, 92(10–11), 1942–67.

Berman, Nicolas, Mathieu Couttenier, Dominic Rohner, and Mathias Thoenig (2017), "This Mine Is Mine! How Minerals Fuel Conflicts in Africa," *American Economic Review*, 107(6), 1564–610.

Betts, Richard K. (1982), *Conventional Deterrence: Predictive Uncertainty and Policy Confidence; Compound Deterrence vs. No-First-Use: What's Wrong Is What's Right*. Brookings General Series Reprint 412 (Washington: Brookings Institution).

Binmore, Ken (2007), *Playing for Real: A Text on Game Theory* (New York: Oxford University Press).

Blanchard, Olivier (2016), *Macroeconomics*, 7th edn. (New York: Pearson).

Blattman, Christopher and Edward Miguel (2010), "Civil War," *Journal of Economic Literature*, 48(1), 3–57.

Bleek, Philipp C. and Eric B. Lorber (2014), "Security Guarantees and Allied Nuclear Proliferation," *Journal of Conflict Resolution*, 58(3), 429–54.

Bloch, Jean de [1899] (1903), *The Future of War* (Boston: Ginn).

Blomberg, S. Brock, Gregory D. Hess, and Athanasios Orphanides (2004), "The Macroeconomic Consequences of Terrorism," *Journal of Monetary Economics*, 51(5), 1007–32.

Blomdahl, Mikael (2017), "Diversionary Theory of War and the Case Study Design," *Armed Forces & Society*, 43(3), 545–65.

Bloxham, Donald and A. Dirk Moses (eds.) (2010), *The Oxford Handbook of Genocide Studies* (New York: Oxford University Press).

Boehmer, Charles R. and David Sobek (2005), "Violent Adolescence: State Development and the Propensity for Militarized Interstate Conflict," *Journal of Peace Research*, 42(1), 5–26.

Bogart, Ernest L. (1920), *Direct and Indirect Costs of the Great World War* (New York: Oxford University Press).

Bolton, Matthew (2015), "From Minefields to Minespace: An Archeology of the Changing Architecture of Autonomous Killing in US Army Field Manuals on Landmines, Booby Traps and IEDs," *Political Geography*, 44(May), 41–53.

Boulding, Kenneth (1945), *The Economics of Peace* (New York: Prentice-Hall).

Boulding, Kenneth E. (1962), *Conflict and Defense: A General Theory* (New York: Harper).

(1978), *Stable Peace* (Austin: University of Texas Press).

Bove, Vincenzo and Ron Smith (2011), "The Economics of Peacekeeping," in Derek L. Braddon and Keith Hartley (eds.), *Handbook on the Economics of Conflict* (Cheltenham: Edward Elgar), 237–64.

Bowen, John T. (2012), "A Spatial Analysis of Fedex and UPS: Hubs, Spokes, and Network Structure," *Journal of Transport Geography*, 24, 419–31.

Braddon, Derek L. and Keith Hartley (eds.) (2011), *Handbook on the Economics of Conflict* (Cheltenham: Edward Elgar).

Braithwaite, Alex, Niheer Dasandi, and David Hudson (2016), "Does Poverty Cause Conflict? Isolating the Causal Origins of the Conflict Trap," *Conflict Management and Peace Science*, 33(1), 45–66.

Bramoullé, Yann, Andrea Galeotti, and Brian Rogers (eds.) (2016), *The Oxford Handbook of the Economics of Networks* (New York: Oxford University Press).

Brandt, Patrick T., Justin George, and Todd Sandler (2016), "Why Concessions Should Not Be Made to Terrorist Kidnappers," *European Journal of Political Economy*, 44 (September), 41–52.

Brauer, Jurgen (1999), "An Economic Perspective on Mercenaries, Military Companies, and the Privatisation of Force," *Cambridge Review of International Affairs*, 13(1), 130–46.

(2002), "Survey and Review of the Defense Economics Literature on Greece and Turkey: What Have We Learned?" *Defence and Peace Economics*, 13(2), 85–107.

(ed.) (2003), "Special Issue: Economics of Conflict, War, and Peace in Historical Perspective," *Defence and Peace Economics*, 14(3), 151–236.

(2007), "Arms Industries, Arms Trade, and Developing Countries," in Todd Sandler and Keith Hartley (eds.), *Handbook of Defense Economics, Volume 2* (New York: Elsevier), 973–1015.

(2013), "Demand and Supply of Commercial Firearms in the United States," *The Economics of Peace and Security Journal*, 8(1), 23–28.

(2017a), "'Of the Expense of Defence': What Has Changed since Adam Smith?" *Peace Economics, Peace Science and Public Policy*, 23(2), Article 1.

(2017b), "Personal Correspondence," March 22, 2018.

Brauer, Jurgen and Raul Caruso (2013), "Economists and Peacebuilding," in Roger Mac Ginty (ed.), *Routledge Handbook of Peacebuilding* (London: Routledge), 147–58.

Brauer, Jurgen and J. Paul Dunne (2012), *Peace Economics: A Macroeconomics Primer for Violence-Afflicted States* (Washington: United States Institute of Peace).

Brauer, Jurgen and André Roux (2000), "Peace as an International Public Good: An Application to Southern Africa," *Defence and Peace Economics*, 11(6), 643–59.

Brauer, Jurgen and Herbert van Tuyll (2008), *Castles, Battles, and Bombs: How Economics Explains Military History* (Chicago: University of Chicago Press).

Brecher, Michael, Jonathan Wilkenfeld, Kyle Beardsley, Patrick James, and David Quinn (2016), "International Crisis Behavior Data Codebook, Version 11," (http://people .duke.edu/~kcb38/ICB/ICB1Codebook-v11.pdf. Accessed: August 1, 2017).

Breene, Keith (2016), "Who are the Cyberwar Superpowers?" (www.weforum.org /agenda/2016/05/who-are-the-cyberwar-superpowers/. Accessed: June 8, 2016).

Bremer, Stuart A. (2000), "Who Fights Whom, When, Where, and Why?" in John A. Vasquez (ed.), *What Do We Know about War?* (New York: Rowman & Littlefield), 23–36.

Breton, Albert and Ronald Wintrobe (1986), "The Bureaucracy of Murder Revisited," *Journal of Political Economy*, 94(5), 905–26.

Brito, Dagobert L. and Michael D. Intriligator (1985), "Conflict, War and Redistribution," *American Political Science Review*, 79(4), 943–57.

(1995), "Arms Race and Proliferation," in Keith Hartley and Todd Sandler (eds.), *Handbook of Defense Economics, Volume 1* (New York: Elsevier), 109–64.

Broadberry, Stephen and Mark Harrison (eds.) (2005), *The Economics of World War I* (New York: Cambridge University Press).

Brown, Michael E., Owen R. Cote, Jr., Sean M. Lynn-Jones, and Steven E. Miller (eds.) (2000), *Rational Choice and Security Studies: Stephen Walt and His Critics* (Cambridge: MIT Press).

Brown, Robert L. and Jeffrey M. Kaplow (2014), "Talking Peace, Making Weapons: IAEA Technical Cooperation and Nuclear Proliferation," *Journal of Conflict Resolution*, 58(3), 402–28.

Browne, Ryan (2016), "U.S. Launches Long-Awaited European Missile Defense Shield," (www.cnn.com/2016/05/11/politics/nato-missile-defense-romania -poland/index.html. Accessed: October 26, 2017).

Browning, Christopher R. (2004), *The Origins of the Final Solution: The Evolution of Nazi Jewish Policy, September 1939–March 1942* (Lincoln: University of Nebraska Press).

Brück, Tilman and Friedrich Schneider (eds.) (2011), "Special Issue: Terrorism," *European Journal of Political Economy*, 27(1), S1–S162.

Brunborg, Helge and Henrik Urdal (eds.) (2005), "Special Issue on the Demography of Conflict and Violence," *Journal of Peace Research*, 42(4), 371–519.

Buhaug, Halvard, Lars-Erik Cederman, and Kristian Skrede Gleditsch (2014), "Square Pegs in Round Holes: Inequalities, Grievances, and Civil War," *International Studies Quarterly*, 58(2), 418–31.

Buscone, Patrick (2017), "The Demilitarization of Costa Rica," College of the Holy Cross Honors Thesis. (crossworks.holycross.edu/cgi/viewcontent.cgi?refer er=&httpsredir=1&article=1011&context=honors. Accessed: June 26, 2018).

Bush, Winston C. (1972), "Individual Welfare in Anarchy," in Gordon Tullock (ed.), *Explorations in the Theory of Anarchy* (Blacksburg: Center for Study of Public Choice), 5–18.

Bussmann, Margit (2017), "Bargaining Models of War and the Stability of Peace in Post-Conflict Societies," *Oxford Research Encyclopedia of Politics*, DOI:10.1093/ acrefore/9780190228637.013.562.

Bussmann, Margit and Gerald Schneider (2007), "When Globalization Discontent Turns Violent: Foreign Economic Liberalization and Internal War," *International Studies Quarterly*, 51(1), 79–97.

Buzan, Barry (1987), *An Introduction to Strategic Studies: Military Technology and International Relations* (London: Macmillan).

Byman, Daniel (2015), *Al Qaeda, the Islamic State, and the Global Jihadist Movement: What Everyone Needs to Know* (New York: Oxford University Press).

(2017), "Review Essay: Explaining Al Qaeda's Decline," *The Journal of Politics*, 79(3), 1106–17.

Carbonnier, Gilles (2015), *Humanitarian Economics: War, Disaster and the Global Aid Market* (London: C. Hurst & Co).

Carey, Sabine C. and Neil J. Mitchell (2016), "Pro-Government Militias and Conflict," *Oxford Research Encyclopedia of Politics*, DOI: 10.1093/acrefore/9780190228637 .013.33.

Cartwright, Edward (2011), *Behavioral Economics* (New York: Routledge).

(2018), *Behavioral Economics*, 3rd edn. (New York: Routledge).

Caruso, Raul (2010), "On the Nature of Peace Economics," *Peace Economics, Peace Science and Public Policy*, 16(2), Article 2.

(2016), "Identity and Incentives: An Economic Interpretation of the Holocaust," in Charles H. Anderton and Jurgen Brauer (eds.), *Economic Aspects of Genocides, Other Mass Atrocities, and Their Prevention* (New York: Oxford University Press), 318–38.

Caruso, Raul and Andrea Locatelli (2014), *Understanding Terrorism: A Socio-Economic Perspective* (Bingley: Emerald Group Publishing).

Caruso, Raul, Prabin Khadka, Ilaria Petrarca, and Roberto Ricciuti (2017), "The Economic Impact of Peacekeeping: Evidence from South Sudan," *Defence and Peace Economics*, 28(2), 250–70.

Case, Karl E., Ray C. Fair, and Sharon E. Oster (2016), *Principles of Economics*, 12th edn. (New York: Pearson).

Cashman, Greg (2014), *What Causes War?: An Introduction to Theories of International Conflict*, 2nd edn. (Lanham: Rowman & Littlefield).

Cauley, Jon and Todd Sandler (1988), "Fighting World War III: A Suggested Strategy," *Terrorism: An International Journal*, 11(3), 181–95.

Cederman, Lars-Erik and Kristian Skrede Gleditsch (2009), "Special Issue on Disaggregating Civil War," *Journal of Conflict Resolution*, 53(4), 487–645.

Cederman, Lars-Erik and Manuel Vogt (2017), "Dynamics and Logics of Civil War," *Journal of Conflict Resolution*, 61(9), 1992–2016.

Cederman, Lars-Erik, Kristian Skrede Gleditsch, and Halvard Buhaug (2013), *Inequality, Grievances, and Civil War* (New York: Cambridge University Press).

Center for Systemic Peace (2017), "Integrated Network for Societal Conflict Research (INSCR) Data Page: High Casualty Terrorist Bombings," (www.systemicpeace.org /inscrdata.html. Accessed: September 12, 2017).

Central Intelligence Agency (2018), *The World Factbook* (www.cia.gov/library/publica tions/the-world-factbook/geos/us.html. Accessed: April 17, 2018).

Charny, Israel W. (ed.) (1999), *Encyclopedia of Genocide*, Volumes I and II (Santa Barbara: ABC-CLIO Incorporated).

Chatagnier, J.Tyson and Emanuele Castelli (2016), "A Modern Peace? Schumpeter, the Decline of Conflict, and the Investment-War Trade-Off," *Political Research Quarterly*, 69(4), 852–64.

Checkel, Jeffrey T. (ed.) (2017), "Special Issue on Socialization and Violence," *Journal of Peace Research*, 54(5), 591–730.

Chenoweth, Erica and Orion A. Lewis (2013), "Unpacking Nonviolent Campaigns: Introducing the NAVCO 2.0 Dataset," *Journal of Peace Research*, 50(3), 415–23.

Chicago Project on Security and Threats (2017), "Data Collection Methodology," (http://cpost.uchicago.edu/database/methodology. Accessed: September 12, 2017).

Choi, Seung-Whan and James A. Piazza (2017), "Foreign Military Interventions and Suicide Attacks," *Journal of Conflict Resolution*, 61(2), 271–97.

Christie, Ryerson (2013), *Peacebuilding and NGOs: Sate-Civil Society Interactions* (New York: Routledge).

Citizens for Syria Database (2018), "Citizens for Syria Database," (www.peaceinsight.org/conflicts/syria/peacebuilding-organisations/citizens-for-syria-database-draft/. Accessed: May 22, 2018).

Clapham, Christopher (ed.) (1988), *African Guerrillas* (Oxford: James Currey).

Clayton, Govinda (ed.) (2017), "The Knowns and Known Unknowns of Peacekeeping Data," *International Peacekeeping*, 24(1), 1–62.

Clubb, Gordon (2014), "'From Terrorists to Peacekeepers': The IRA's Disengagement and the Role of Community Networks," *Studies in Conflict & Terrorism*, 37(10), 842–61.

Colaresi, Michael P., Karen Rasler, and William R. Thompson (2007), *Strategic Rivalries in World Politics: Position, Space and Conflict Escalation* (New York: Cambridge University Press).

Coleman, Katharina P. (2017), "The Dynamics of Peacekeeping Budget Cuts: The Case of MONUSCO," *Global Observatory*, July 10 (https://theglobalobservatory.org/2017/07/monusco-drc-peacekeeping-budget-cuts/. Accessed: February 28, 2018).

Collier, Paul (2000), "Doing Well Out of War: An Economic Perspective," in Mats Berdal and David M. Malone (eds.), *Greed and Grievance: Economic Agendas in Civil Wars* (Boulder: Lynne Rienner), 91–111.

    (2007), *The Bottom Billion: Why the Poorest Countries Are Failing and What Can Be Done about It* (New York: Oxford University Press).

Collier, Paul and Alexander Betts (2017), *Refuge: Rethinking Refugee Policy in a Changing World* (New York: Oxford University Press).

Collier, Paul, Lani Elliott, Håvard Hegre, Anke Hoeffler, Marta Reynal-Querol, and Nicholas Sambanis (2003), *Breaking the Conflict Trap: Civil War and Development Policy* (Washington: The World Bank).

Collier, Paul and Anke Hoeffler (2004), "Greed and Grievance in Civil War," *Oxford Economic Papers*, 56(4), 563–95.

    (2007a), "Civil War," in Todd Sandler and Keith Hartley (eds.), *Handbook of Defense Economics, Volume 2* (New York: Elsevier), 711–39.

    (2007b), "Unintended Consequences: Does Aid Promote Arms Races?" *Oxford Bulletin of Economics and Statistics*, 69(1), 1–27.

Collier, Paul, Anke Hoeffler, and Måns Söderbom (2004), "On the Duration of Civil War," *Journal of Peace Research*, 41(3), 253–73.

Collier, Paul and Nicholas Sambanis (eds.) (2005), *Understanding Civil War: Evidence and Analysis*, Volumes 1 and 2 (Washington: The World Bank).

Conybeare, John A. C., James C. Murdoch, and Todd Sandler (1994), "Alternative Collective-Goods Models of Military Alliances: Theory and Empirics," *Economic Inquiry*, 32(4), 525–42.

Cook, Scott J. and Burcu Savun (2016), "New Democracies and the Risk of Civil Conflict: The Lasting Legacy of Military Rule," *Journal of Peace Research*, 53(6), 745–57.

Corera, Gordon (2015), "Rapid Escalation of the Cyber-arms Race," (www.bbc.com /news/uk-32493516. Accessed: June 8, 2017).

Cornes, Richard and Todd Sandler (1984), "Easy Riders, Joint Production, and Public Goods," *Economic Journal*, 94(3), 580–598.

   (1996), *The Theory of Externalities, Public Goods, and Club Goods*, 2nd edn. (New York: Cambridge University Press).

Coulomb, Fanny (1998), "Adam Smith: A Defence Economist," *Defence and Peace Economics*, 9(3), 299–316.

Coyne, Christopher J. and Rachel L. Mathers (eds.) (2011), *The Handbook on the Political Economy of War* (Cheltenham: Edward Elgar).

Craft, Cassady B. (2000), "An Analysis of the Washington Naval Agreements and the Economic Provisions of Arms Control Theory," *Defence and Peace Economics*, 11 (2), 127–48.

Cross, John G. (1977), "Negotiation as a Learning Process," *Journal of Conflict Resolution*, 21(4), 581–606.

Cunningham, Daniel, Sean Everton, and Philip Murphy (2016), *Understanding Dark Networks: A Strategic Framework for the Use of Social Network Analysis* (Lanham: Rowman & Littlefield Publishers).

Cunningham, David, Kristian Skrede Gleditsch, and Idean Salehyan (2013), "Non-state Actors in Civil Wars: A New Dataset," *Conflict Management and Peace Science*, 30 (5), 516–31.

Cusack, Thomas, Amihai Glazer, and Kai A. Konrad (eds.) (2006), "Special Issue on Social Conflict," *Economics of Governance*, 7(1), 1–107.

d'Agostino, Giorgio, J. Paul Dunne, and Luca Pieroni (2017), "Does Military Spending Matter for Long-run Growth?" *Defence and Peace Economics*, 28(4), 429–36.

Dallaire, Roméo (2004), *Shake Hands with the Devil: The Failure of Humanity in Rwanda* (New York: Carroll & Graf Publishers).

Dalrymple, William (2015), "The Great Divide: The Violent Legacy of the Indian Partition," *The New Yorker*, June 29. (www.newyorker.com/magazine/2015/06/ 29/the-great-divide-books-dalrymple. Accessed: June 29, 2018).

Daly, Sarah Zukerman (2017), *Organized Violence after Civil War: The Geography of Recruitment in Latin America* (New York: Cambridge University Press).

Dando, Malcolm (1994), *Biological Warfare in the 21st Century* (London: Brassey's).

   (2015), *Neuroscience and the Future of Chemical-Biological Weapons* (New York: Palgrave Macmillan).

Danzell, Orlandrew E., Yao-Yuan Yeh, and Melia Pfannenstiel (2016), "Determinants of Domestic Terrorism: An Examination of Ethnic Polarization and Economic Development," *Terrorism and Political Violence*, https://doi.org/10.1080 /09546553.2016.1258636.

Darley, John M. and Paget H. Gross (1983), "A Hypothesis-Confirming Bias in Labeling Effects," *Journal of Personality and Social Psychology*, 44(1), 20–33.

Davenport, Christian (2007), "State Repression and Political Order," *Annual Review of Political Science*, 10(June), 1–23.

Davenport, Christian, Erik Melander, and Patrick Regan (2018), *The Peace Continuum: What It Is and How to Study It* (New York: Oxford University Press).

Davis, John B. (2010), *Individuals and Identity in Economics* (New York: Cambridge University Press).

de la Brière, Bénédicte, Deon Filmer, Dena Ringold, Dominic Rohner, Karelle Samuda, and Anastasiya Denisova (2017), *From Mines and Wells to Well-Built Minds: Turning Sub-Saharan Africa's Natural Resource Wealth into Human Capital* (Washington: World Bank Group).

De Martino, Benedetto, Dharshan Kumaran, Ben Seymour, et al. (2006), "Frames, Biases, and Rational Decision-Making in the Human Brain," *Science*, 313(5787), 684–7.

DeRouen, Karl R. Jr. and Jacob Bercovitch (2008), "Enduring Internal Rivalries: A New Framework for the Study of Civil War," *Journal of Peace Research*, 45(1), 55–74.

DeRouen, Karl R. Jr. and Ishita Chowdhury (2018), "Mediation, Peacekeeping and Civil War Peace Agreements," *Defence and Peace Economics*, 29(2), 130–46.

Dhami, Sanjit (2017), *Foundations of Behavioral Economic Analysis* (New York: Oxford University Press).

Diehl, Paul F. (1983), "Arms Races and Escalation: A Closer Look," *Journal of Peace Research*, 20(3), 205–12.

(2016), "Exploring Peace: Looking beyond War and Negative Peace," *International Studies Quarterly*, 60(1), 1–10.

Diehl, Paul F. and Gary Goertz (2000), *War and Peace in International Rivalry* (Ann Arbor: University of Michigan Press).

(2012), "The Rivalry Process: How Rivalries Are Sustained and Terminated," in John A. Vasquez (ed.), *What Do We Know about War?* 2nd edn. (New York: Rowman and Littlefield), 83–109.

DiLorenzo, Matthew (2018), "Bypass Aid and Unrest in Autocracies," *International Studies Quarterly*, 62(1), 208–19.

Dixit, Avinash K. and Barry J. Nalebuff (1991), *Thinking Strategically: The Competitive Edge in Business, Politics, and Everyday Life* (New York: W. W. Norton & Company).

Dixit, Avinash K., Susan Skeath, and David H. Reiley Jr. (2015), *Games of Strategy*, 4th edn. (New York: W. W. Norton & Company).

Dixon, Jeffrey and Meredith Reid Sarkees (eds.) (2015), *Guide to Intrastate Wars: A Handbook on Civil Wars* (Thousand Oaks: Sage).

Donà, Giorgia (2018), "'Situated Bystandership' during and after the Rwandan Genocide," *Journal of Genocide Research*, 20(1), 1–19.

Dorussen, Han (2014), "Peacekeeping Works, or Does It?" *Peace Economics, Peace Science and Public Policy*, 20(4), 1–11.

Dorussen, Han, Erik Gartzke, and Oliver Westerwinter (eds.) (2016), "Special Issue on Networked International Politics," *Journal of Peace Research*, 53(3), 283–505.

Dube, Oeindrila, and Juan F. Vargas (2013), "Commodity Price Shocks and Civil Conflict: Evidence from Colombia," *The Review of Economic Studies*, 80(4), 1384–1421.

Dumas, Lloyd J. (2011), *The Peace-Keeping Economy: Using Economic Relationships to Build a More Peaceful, Prosperous, and Secure World* (New Haven, CT: Yale University Press).

Dunne, J. Paul and Ron P. Smith (2007), "The Econometrics of Military Arms Races," in Todd Sandler and Keith Hartley (eds.), *Handbook of Defense Economics, Volume 2* (New York: Elsevier), 913–40.

Dunne, J. Paul and Nan Tian (2015), "Military Expenditure, Economic Growth and Heterogeneity," *Defence and Peace Economics*, 26(1), 15–31.

Durbach, Andrea, Louise Chappell, and Sarah Williams (eds.) (2017), "Special Issue: Transformative Reparations for Sexual Violence Post-Conflict: Prospects and Problems," *The International Journal of Human Rights*, 21(9), 1185–350.

Dziubinski, Marcin, Sanjeev Goyal, and Adrien Vigier (2016), "Conflict and Networks," in Yann Bramoullé, Andrea Galeotti, and Brian Rogers (eds.), *The Oxford Handbook of the Economics of Networks* (New York: Oxford University Press), 215–43.

Early Warning Project (2018), "FAQ," (www.earlywarningproject.com/faq. Accessed: April 26, 2018).

Early, Bryan R. (2012), "Alliances and Trade with Sanctioned States: A Study of U.S. Economic Sanctions, 1950–2000," *Journal of Conflict Resolution*, 56(3), 547–72.

Early, Bryan R., Matthew Fuhrmann, and Quan Li (2013), "Atoms for Terror? Nuclear Programs and Non-Catastrophic Nuclear and Radiological Terrorism," *British Journal of Political Science*, 43(4), 915–36.

Easley, David and Jon Kleinberg (2010), *Networks, Crowds, and Markets: Reasoning about a Highly Connected World* (New York: Cambridge University Press).

Easterly, William, Roberta Gatti, and Sergio Kurlat (2006), "Development, Democracy, and Mass Killing," *Journal of Economic Growth*, 11(2), 129–56.

Eck, Kristine and Lisa Hultman (2007), "One-Sided Violence against Civilians in War: Insights from New Fatality Data," *Journal of Peace Research*, 44(2), 233–46.

Ehrenreich, Robert M. and Tim Cole (2005), "The Perpetrator-Bystander-Victim Constellation: Rethinking Genocidal Relationships," *Human Organization*, 64(3), 213–24.

Elias, Barbara (2017), "The Likelihood of Local Allies Free-Riding: Testing Economic Theories of Alliances in US Counterinsurgency Interventions," *Cooperation & Conflict*, 52(3), 309–31.

End Slavery Now (2017), "Slavery Today," (www.endslaverynow.org/learn/slavery-today?gclid=COCgksyCn9MCFRpWDQodkbELIg. Accessed: April 12, 2017).

Enders, Walter (2007), "Terrorism: An Empirical Analysis," in Todd Sandler and Keith Hartley (eds.), *Handbook of Defense Economics, Volume 2* (New York: Elsevier), 815–66.

(ed.) (2016), *The Economics of Terrorism* (Cheltenham: Edward Elgar).

Enders, Walter, Gary A. Hoover, and Todd Sandler (2016), "The Changing Nonlinear Relationship between Income and Terrorism," *Journal of Conflict Resolution*, 60 (2), 195–225.

Enders, Walter and Paan Jindapon (2009), "Network Externalities and the Structure of Terror Networks," *Journal of Conflict Resolution*, 54(2), 262–80.

Enders, Walter and Todd Sandler (1993), "The Effectiveness of Anti-Terrorism Policies: Vector-Autoregression-Intervention Analysis," *American Political Science Review*, 87(4), 829–44.

(1995), "Terrorism: Theory and Applications," in Keith Hartley and Todd Sandler (eds.), *Handbook of Defense Economics, Volume 1* (New York: Elsevier), 213–49.

(2000), "Is Transnational Terrorism Becoming More Threatening? A Times Series Investigation," *Journal of Conflict Resolution*, 44(3), 307–32.

(2012), *The Political Economy of Terrorism*, 2nd edn. (New York: Cambridge University Press).

Engel, Christoph (2011), "Dictator Games: A Meta Study," *Experimental Economics*, 14 (4), 583–610.

Epstein, Joshua M. (1985), *The Calculus of Conventional War: Dynamic Analysis without Lanchester Theory* (Washington: The Brookings Institution).

(1990), *Conventional Force Reductions: A Dynamic Assessment* (Washington: The Brookings Institution).

Esteban, Joan, Massimo Morelli, and Dominic Rohner (2015), "Strategic Mass Killings," *Journal of Political Economy*, 123(5), 1087–1132.

Faria, João Ricardo and Daniel G. Arce M. (2005), "Terror Support and Recruitment," *Defence and Peace Economics*, 16(4), 263–73.

Fearon, James D. (1995), "Rationalist Explanations for War," *International Organization*, 49(3), 379–414.

Fearon, James D. and David D. Laitin (2003), "Ethnicity, Insurgency, and Civil War," *American Political Science Review*, 97(1), 75–90.

Federal Bureau of Investigation (2017), "Gangs," (www.fbi.gov/investigate/violent -crime/gangs. Accessed: April 13, 2017).

Federation of American Scientists (2016), "Cruise Missiles," (http://fas.org/nuke/intro/ cm. Accessed: August 8, 2016).

Feldman, Gerald D. and Wolfgang Seibel (eds.) (2014), *Networks of Nazi Persecution: Bureaucracy, Business and the Organization of the Holocaust* (New York: Berghahn Books).

Fergusson, Leopoldo, James A. Robinson, Ragnar Torvik, and Juan F. Vargas (2014), "The Need for Enemies," *The Economic Journal*, 126(593), 1018–54.

Feridun, Mete (2014), "Foreign Aid Fungibility and Military Spending: The Case of North Cyprus," *Defence and Peace Economics*, 25(5), 499–508.

Fetherstonhaugh, David, Paul Slovic, Stephen M. Johnson, and James Friedrich (1997), "Insensitivity to the Value of Human Life: A Study of Psychophysical Numbing," *Journal of Risk and Uncertainty*, 14(3), 283–300.

Fetter, Steve (1991), "Ballistic Missiles and Weapons of Mass Destruction: What Is the Threat? What Should Be Done?" *International Security*, 16(1), 5–42.

Feyzabadi, Vahid Yazdi, Aliakbar Haghdoost, Mohammed Hossein Mehrolhassani, and Zahra Aminian (2015), "The Association between Peace and Life Expectancy: An Empirical Study of the World Countries," *Iran Journal of Public Health*, 44(3), 341–51.

Fiala, Nathan and Stergios Skaperdas (2011), "Economic Perspectives on Civil Wars," in Christopher J. Coyne and Rachel L. Mathers (eds.), *The Handbook on the Political Economy of War* (Cheltenham: Edward Elgar), 177–94.

Fiddian-Qasmiyeh, Elena, Gil Loescher, Katy Long, and Nando Sigona (eds.) (2014), *The Oxford Handbook of Refugee and Forced Migration Studies* (New York: Oxford University Press).

Findley, Michael G. and Josiah F. Marineau (2015), "Lootable Resources and Third-Party Intervention into Civil Wars," *Conflict Management and Peace Science*, 32(5), 465–86.

Firchow, Pamina and Roger Mac Ginty (2017), "Measuring Peace: Comparability, Commensurability, and Complementarity Using Bottom-Up Indicators," *International Studies Review*, 19(1), 6–27.

Fischer, Dietrich (1984), *Preventing War in the Nuclear Age* (Totowa: Rowman & Allanheld).

Fisk, Kerstin (2014), "Refugee Geography and the Diffusion of Armed Conflict in Africa," *Civil Wars*, 16(3), 255–75.

Fjelde, Hanne and Lisa Hultman (2014), "Weakening the Enemy: a Disaggregated Study of Violence against Civilians in Africa," *Journal of Conflict Resolution*, 58(7), 1230–57.

Fleming, Gerald (1993), "Engineers of Death," *New York Times*, July 18, sec. E.

Florea, Adrian (2017), "Theories of Civil War Onset: Promises and Pitfalls," *Oxford Research Encyclopedia of Politics*, DOI: 10.1093/acrefore/9780190228637.013.325.

Florida Department of Corrections (2017), "Street Gangs–Chicago Based or Influenced," (https://web.archive.org/web/20161214154126/www.dc.state.fl.us:80/pub/gangs/chicago.html. Accessed: November 9, 2017).

Ford, Christopher A. (2010), "The Trouble with Cyber Arms Control," *The New Atlantis*, 29(Fall), 52–67.

Forrer, John and Conor Seyle (eds.) (2016), *The Role of Business in the Responsibility to Protect* (New York: Cambridge University Press).

Fort, Tim (ed.) (2016), "Special Issue: The Business of Peace," *Business Horizons*, 59(5), 451–566.

Frazier, Derrick V. and William J. Dixon (2006), "Third-Party Intermediaries and Negotiated Settlements, 1946–2000," *International Interactions*, 32(4), 385–408.

Freedom United (2017), "One Voice to End Modern Slavery," (www.freedomunited.org/?gclid=CJySn5mDn9MCFUSBswodWUUKDQ. Accessed: April 12, 2017).

Frey, Bruno S. and Simon Luechinger (2003), "How to Fight Terrorism: Alternatives to Deterrence," *Defence and Peace Economics*, 14(4), 237–49.

Friedman, Willa (2016), "The Economics of Genocide in Rwanda," in Charles H. Anderton and Jurgen Brauer (eds.), *Economic Aspects of Genocides, Other Mass Atrocities, and Their Prevention* (New York: Oxford University Press), 339–55.

Fuhrmann, Matthew (2012), *Atomic Assistance: How "Atoms for Peace" Programs Cause Nuclear Insecurity* (Ithaca: Cornell University Press).

Fuhrmann, Matthew and Michael Horowitz (2017), "Droning On: Explaining the Proliferation of Unmanned Aerial Vehicles," *International Organization*, 71(2), 397–418.

Fuhrmann, Matthew and Todd S. Sechser (2014), "Signaling Alliance Commitments: Hand-Tying and Sunk Costs in Extended Nuclear Deterrence," *American Journal of Political Science*, 58(4), 919–35.

Fuhrmann, Matthew and Yonatan Lupu (2016), "Do Arms Control Treaties Work? Assessing the Effectiveness of the Nuclear Nonproliferation Treaty," *International Studies Quarterly*, 60(3), 530–39.

Fujii, Lee Ann (2009), *Killing Neighbors: Webs of Violence in Rwanda* (Ithaca: Cornell University Press).

   (2011), "Rescuers and Killer-Rescuers during the Rwandan Genocide: Rethinking Standard Categories of Analysis," in Jacques Semelin, Claire Andrieu, and Sarah Gensburger (eds.), *Resisting Genocide: The Multiple Forms of Rescue* (New York: Columbia University Press), 145–57.

Furuoka, Fumitaka, Mikio Oishi, and Mohd Aminul Karim (2016), "Military Expenditure and Economic Development in China: An Empirical Inquiry," *Defence and Peace Economics*, 27(1), 137–60.

Galtung, Johan (1996), *Peace by Peaceful Means: Peace and Conflict, Development and Civilization* (London: Sage Publications).

Ganson, Brian and Achim Wennmann (2016), *Business and Conflict in Fragile States: The Case for Pragmatic Solutions* (London: Routledge).

Garfinkel, Michelle R. (1990), "Arming as a Strategic Investment in a Cooperative Equilibrium," *American Economic Review*, 80(1), 50–68.

Garfinkel, Michelle R. and Stergios Skaperdas (2000a), "Conflict without Misperceptions or Incomplete Information: How the Future Matters," *Journal of Conflict Resolution*, 44(6), 793–807.

   (2000b), "Contract or War? On the Consequences of a Broader View of Self-Interest in Economics," *American Economist*, 44(1), 5–16.

   (2007), "Economics of Conflict: An Overview," in Todd Sandler and Keith Hartley (eds.), *Handbook of Defense Economics, Volume 2* (New York: Elsevier), 649–709.

   (eds.) (2012), *The Oxford Handbook of the Economics of Peace and Conflict* (New York: Oxford University Press).

Garfinkel, Michelle R., Stergios Skaperdas, and Constantinos Syropoulos (2015), "Trade and Insecure Resources," *Journal of International Economics*, 95(1), 98–114.

Garfinkel, Michelle R. and Constantinos Syropoulos (2015), "Trade Openness and the Settlement of Domestic Disputes in the Shadow of the Future," *Research in Economics*, 69(2), 191–213.

Gartzke, Erik and Matthew Kroenig (eds.) (2014), "Special Issue: Nuclear Posture, Nonproliferation Policy, and the Spread of Nuclear Weapons," *Journal of Conflict Resolution*, 58(3), 395–535.

   (2017), "Social Scientific Analysis of Nuclear Weapons: Past Scholarly Successes, Contemporary Challenges, and Future Research Opportunities," *Journal of Conflict Resolution*, 61(9), 1853–74.

Gartzke, Erik, Quan Li, and Charles Boehmer (2001), "Investing in the Peace: Economic Interdependence and International Conflict," *International Organization*, 55(2), 391–438.

Gartzke, Erik and Oliver Westerwinter (2016), "The Complex Structure of Commercial Peace Contrasting Trade Interdependence, Asymmetry, and Multipolarity," *Journal of Peace Research*, 53(3), 325–43.

Gaver, Donald P. and Patricia A. Jacobs (1997), "Attrition Modeling in the Presence of Decoys: An Operations-Other-Than-War Motivation," *Naval Research Logistics*, 44(5), 507–14.

Gent, Stephen E. (2007), "Strange Bedfellows: The Strategic Dynamics of Major Power Military Interventions," *The Journal of Politics*, 69(4), 1089–1102.

Georgetown Institute for Women, Peace and Security (2018), "Women, Peace and Security Index 2017–18," (https://giwps.georgetown.edu/the-index/chapters/. Accessed: May 23, 2018).

Gerdes, Luke M. (ed.) (2015), *Illuminating Dark Networks: The Study of Clandestine Groups and Organizations* (New York: Cambridge University Press).

Ghatak, Sambuddha and Aaron Gold (2017), "Development, Discrimination, and Domestic Terrorism: Looking Beyond a Linear Relationship," *Conflict Management and Peace Science*, 34(6), 618–39.

Gibler, Douglas M. (2009), *International Military Alliances, 1648–2008* (Washington: CQ Press).

Gibler, Douglas M., Toby J. Rider, and Marc L. Hutchison (2005), "Taking Arms against a Sea of Troubles: Interdependent Racing and the Likelihood of Conflict in Rival States," *Journal of Peace Research*, 42(2), 131–47.

Gibler, Douglas M. and Meredith Reid Sarkees (2004), "Measuring Alliances: The Correlates of War Formal Interstate Alliance Dataset, 1816–2000," *Journal of Peace Research*, 41(2), 211–22.

Gino, Francesca, Michael I. Norton, Roberto A. Weber (2016), "Motivated Bayesians: Feeling Moral While Acting Egoistically," *Journal of Economic Perspectives*, 30(3), 189–212.

Gintis, Herbert (2009), *The Bounds of Reason: Game Theory and the Unification of the Behavioral Sciences* (Princeton: Princeton University Press).

Gleditsch, Kristian Skrede (2017), "Civil War from a Transnational Perspective," *Oxford Research Encyclopedia of Politics*, DOI: 10.1093/acrefore/9780190228637.013.312.

Gleditsch, Kristian Skrede, Nils W. Metternich, and Andrea Ruggeri (2014), "Data and Progress in Peace and Conflict Research," *Journal of Peace Research*, 51(2), 301–14.

Gleditsch, Kristian Skrede and Andrea Ruggeri (2010), "Political Opportunity Structures, Democracy, and Civil War," *Journal of Peace Research*, 47(3), 299–310.

Gleditsch, Nils Petter, Jonas Nordkavelle, and Håvard Strand (2014), "Peace Research–Just the Study of War?" *Journal of Peace Research*, 51(2), 145–58.

Gleditsch, Nils Petter, Peter Wallensteen, Mikael Eriksson, Margareta Sollenberg, and Håvard Strand (2002), "Armed Conflict 1946–2001: A New Dataset," *Journal of Peace Research*, 39(5), 615–637.

Glick, Reuven and Alan M. Taylor (2010), "Collateral Damage: Trade Disruption and the Economic Impact of War," *The Review of Economics and Statistics*, 92(1), 102–27.

Global Terrorism Database (2017), "Codebook: Inclusion Criteria and Variables," (www.start.umd.edu/gtd/downloads/Codebook.pdf. Accessed: September 12, 2017).

Gochman, Charles S. and Zeev Maoz (1990), "Militarized Interstate Disputes, 1816–1976," in J. David Singer and Paul F. Diehl (eds.), *Measuring the Correlates of War* (Ann Arbor: University of Michigan Press), 193–221.

Goddard, Stacie E. (2006), "Uncommon Ground: Indivisible Territory and the Politics of Legitimacy," *International Organization*, 60(1), 35–68.

Goemans, Hein E. and Kenneth A. Schultz (2017), "The Politics of Territorial Claims: A Geospatial Approach Applied to Africa," *International Organization*, 71(1), 31–64.

Goemans, Hein E., Kristian Skrede Gleditsch, and Giacomo Chiozza (2009), "Introducing Archigos: A Dataset of Political Leaders," *Journal of Peace Research*, 46(2), 269–83.

Goldsmith, Benjamin E. (2013), "International Trade and the Onset and Escalation of Interstate Conflict: More to Fight About, or More Reasons Not to Fight?" *Defence and Peace Economics*, 24(6), 555–78.

Gong, Erick and Katherine A. Sullivan (2017), "Conflict and Coffee: Are Higher Coffee Prices Fuelling Rebellion in Uganda?" *Journal of African Economies*, 26(3), 322–41.

Goodwin, Craufurd D. (ed.) (1991), *Economics and National Security: A History of Their Interaction* (Durham: Duke University Press).

Granovetter, Mark (1973), "The Strength of Weak Ties," *American Journal of Sociology*, 78(6), 1360–80.

(1978), "Threshold Models of Collective Behavior," *American Journal of Sociology*, 83(6), 489–515.

(2005), "The Impact of Social Structure on Economic Outcomes," *Journal of Economic Perspectives*, 19(1), 33–50.

Griffiths, James (2016), "North Korea 'Continues to Invest' in Nazi-style Prison Camps," (www.cnn.com/2016/11/30/asia/north-korea-prison-camps-new-satellite-images/. Accessed: May 4, 2017).

Grossman, Herschel I. and Minseong Kim (1995), "Swords or Plowshares? A Theory of the Security of Claims to Property," *Journal of Political Economy*, 103(6), 1275–88.

Gurr, Ted Robert (1968), "A Causal Model of Civil Strife: Comparative Analyses Using New Indices," *American Political Science Review*, 62(4), 1104–24.

Gygli, Savina, Florian Haelg, and Jan-Egbert Sturm (2018), "The KOF Globalisation Index – Revisited," KOF Swiss Economic Institute, Working Paper 439, February (www.ethz .ch/content/dam/ethz/special-interest/dual/kof-dam/documents/Globalization/ 2018/KOF_Globalisation%20Index_Revisited.pdf. Accessed: March 12, 2018).

Habeck, Mary (2012), "What Does Al Qaeda Want?" *Foreign Policy* (http://foreign policy.com/2012/03/06/what-does-al-qaeda-want/. Accessed: November 9, 2017).

Haer, Roos and Tobias Böhmelt (2015), "The Impact of Child Soldiers on Rebel Groups' Fighting Capacities," *Conflict Management and Peace Science*, 33(2), 153–73.

Haim, Dotan A. (2016), "Alliance Networks and Trade," *Journal of Peace Research*, 53 (3), 472–90.

Hamm, Mark and Ramón Spaaij (2017), *The Age of Lone Wolf Terrorism* (New York: Columbia University Press).

Hamman, John R., George Loewenstein, and Roberto A. Weber (2010), "Self-Interest through Delegation: An Additional Rationale for the Principal-Agent Relationship," *American Economic Review*, 100(4), 1826–46.

Hammond, Grant T. (1993), *Plowshares into Swords: Arms Races in International Politics, 1840–1991* (Columbia: University of South Carolina Press).

Hammond, Jesse (2018), "Maps of Mayhem: Strategic Location and Deadly Violence in Civil War," *Journal of Peace Research*, 55(1), 32–46.

Hardesty, David C. (2005), "Space-Based Weapons: Long-Term Strategic Implications and Alternatives," *Naval War College Review*, 58(2), 45–68.

Harff, Barbara (2003), "No Lessons Learned from the Holocaust? Assessing Risks of Genocide and Political Mass Murder since 1955," *American Political Science Review*, 97(1), 57–73.

Harild, Niels, Asger Christensen, and Roger Zetter (2015), *Sustainable Refugee Return: Triggers, Constraints, and Lessons on Addressing the Development Challenges of Forced Displacement* (Washington: The World Bank Group).

Harrison, Mark (2000), "The Economics of World War II: An Overview," in Mark Harrison (ed.), *The Economics of World War II* (Cambridge: Cambridge University Press), 1–42

Hartley, Keith (2006), "Defence Industrial Policy in a Military Alliance," *Journal of Peace Research*, 43(4), 473–89.

Hartley, Keith and Todd Sandler (eds.) (1995), *Handbook of Defense Economics, Volume 1* (New York: Elsevier).

(eds.) (2001), *The Economics of Defense*, Volumes I–III (Cheltenham: Edward Elgar).

Hartzell, Caroline A. (2017), "Bargaining Theory, Civil War Outcomes, and War Recurrence: Assessing the Results of Empirical Tests of the Theory," *Oxford Research Encyclopedia of Politics*. DOI:http://dx.doi.org/10.1093/acrefore/9780190228637.013.569.

Hasan, M. Rashel and Syed Mansoob Murshed (2017), "Does Civil War Hamper Financial Development?" *Defence and Peace Economics*, 28(2), 187–207.

Hassner, Ron (2003), "'To Halve and to Hold': Conflicts Over Sacred Space and the Problem of Indivisibility," *Security Studies*, 12(4), 1–33.

(2013), "Conflicts over Sacred Ground," in Margot Kitts, Mark Juergensmeyer and Michael Jerryson (eds.), *Oxford Handbook of Religion and Violence* (New York: Oxford University Press), 324–31.

Hausken, Kjell (2004), "Mutual Raiding of Production and the Emergence of Exchange," *Economic Inquiry*, 42(4), 572–86.

(2018), "A Cost-Benefit Analysis of Terrorist Attacks," *Defence and Peace Economics*, 29(2), 111–29.

Hausken, Kjell and Mthuli Ncube (2017), "Incumbent Policy, Benefits Provision, and the Triggering and Spread of Revolutionary Uprisings," *The Economics of Peace and Security Journal*, 12(1), 54–63.

Hazen, Jennifer M. and Dennis Rodgers (eds.) (2014), *Global Gangs: Street Violence across the World* (Minneapolis: University of Minneapolis Press).

Hegre, Håvard (ed.) (2004), "Special Issue on the Duration and Termination of Civil War," *Journal of Peace Research*, 41(3), 243–348.

Henderson, Errol A. and J. David Singer (2000), "Civil War in the Post-Colonial World," *Journal of Peace Research*, 37(3), 275–99.

Hensel, Paul R. (2017), "Territory and Contentious Issues," in William Thompson (ed.), *The Oxford Encyclopedia of Empirical International Relations Theory* (New York: Oxford University Press) (http://politics.oxfordre.com/view/10.1093/acrefore/9780190228637.001.0001/acrefore-9780190228637-e-565. Accessed: August 1, 2017).

Herbst, Jeffrey (2004), "African Militaries and Rebellion: The Political Economy of Threat and Combat Effectiveness," *Journal of Peace Research*, 41(3), 357–69.

Hess, Gregory D. (1995), "An Introduction to Lewis Fry Richardson and His Mathematical Theory of War and Peace," *Conflict Management and Peace Science*, 14(1), 77–113.

Hesterman, Jennifer L. (2013), *The Terrorist-Criminal Nexus: An Alliance of International Drug Cartels, Organized Crime, and Terror Groups* (Boca Raton: CRC Press).

Hirshleifer, Jack (1985), "The Expanding Domain of Economics," *American Economic Review*, 75(6), 53–68.

(1988), "The Analytics of Continuing Conflict," *Synthese*, 76(2), 201–33.

(1989), "Conflict and Settlement," in John Eatwell, Murray Milgate, and Peter Newman (eds.), *Game Theory* (London: Palgrave Macmillan), 86–94.

(1991), "The Paradox of Power," *Economics and Politics*, 3(3), 177–200.

(1994), "The Dark Side of the Force," *Economic Inquiry*, 32(January), 1–10.

(1995), "Theorizing about Conflict," in Keith Hartley and Todd Sandler (eds.), *Handbook of Defense Economics, Volume 1* (New York: Elsevier), 165–89.

Hirshleifer, Jack, Amihai Glazer, and David Hirshleifer (2005), *Price Theory and Applications: Decisions, Markets and Information*, 7th edn. (Cambridge: Cambridge University Press).

Hitch, Charles J. and Roland N. McKean (1960), *The Economics of Defense in the Nuclear Age* (Cambridge: Harvard University Press).

Hoeffler, Anke (2012), "On the Causes of Civil War," in Michelle R. Garfinkel and Stergios Skaperdas (eds.), *Oxford Handbook of the Economics of Peace and Conflict* (New York: Oxford University Press), 179–204.

(2016), "Development and the Risk of Mass Atrocities: An Assessment of the Empirical Literature," in Charles H. Anderton and Jurgen Brauer (eds.), *Economic Aspects of Genocides, Other Mass Atrocities, and Their Prevention* (New York: Oxford University Press), 230–50.

Hoffman, Bruce (2017), *Inside Terrorism*, 3rd edn. (New York: Columbia University Press).

Horowitz, Michael C. and Neil Narang (2014), "Poor Man's Atomic Bomb? Exploring the Relationship between 'Weapons of Mass Destruction,'" *Journal of Conflict Resolution*, 58(3), 509–35.

Horowitz, Michael C., Paul Poast, and Allan Stam (2017), "Domestic Signaling of Commitment Credibility: Military Recruitment and Alliance Formation," *Journal of Conflict Resolution*, 61(8), 1682–710.

Hubbard, Ben and Karam Shoumali (2013), "Powerful Rebel Groups in Syria Announce Creation of Umbrella Alliance," *New York Times*, November 22 (www.nytimes.com/2013/11/23/world/middleeast/syria.html. Accessed: November 8, 2017).

Huettel, Scott A. and Rachel E. Kranton (2012), "Identity Economics and the Brain: Uncovering the Mechanisms of Social Conflict," *Philosophical Transactions of the Royal Society B*, 367, 680–91.

Hultman, Lisa and Dursun Peksen (2017), "Successful or Counterproductive Coercion? The Effect of International Sanctions on Conflict Intensity," *Journal of Conflict Resolution*, 61(6), 1315–39.

Hultman, Lisa, Jacob Kathman, and Megan Shannon (2013), "United Nations Peacekeeping and Civilian Protection in Civil War," *American Journal of Political Science*, 57(4), 875–91.

(2014), "Beyond Keeping Peace: United Nations Effectiveness in the Midst of Fighting," *American Political Science Review*, 108(4), 737–53.

Human Rights Watch (2018), "Syria: A Year On, Chemical Weapons Attacks Persist," (www.hrw.org/news/2018/04/04/syria-year-chemical-weapons-attacks-persist. Accessed: June 12, 2018).

Hummel, Stephen (2016), *The Islamic State and WMD: Assessing the Future Threat* (https://ctc.usma.edu/posts/the-islamic-state-and-wmd-assessing-the-future-threat. Accessed: October 26, 2017).

Hunziker, Philipp and Lars-Erik Cederman (2017), "No Extraction without Representation: The Ethno-Regional Oil Curse and Secessionist Conflict," *Journal of Peace Research*, 54(3), 365–81.

Iannaccone, Laurence R. (1992), "Sacrifice and Stigma: Reducing Free-Riding in Cults, Communes, and Other Collectives," *Journal of Political Economy*, 100 (2), 271–92.

(2006), "The Market for Martyrs," *Interdisciplinary Journal of Research on Religion*, 2 (article 4), 1–29.

Iannaccone, Laurence R. and Eli Berman (2006), "Religious Extremism: The Good, the Bad, and the Deadly," *Public Choice*, 128(1–2), 109–29.

Ibáñez, Ana María and Andrés Moya (2016), "Who Stays and Who Leaves during Mass Atrocities?" in Charles H. Anderton and Jurgen Brauer (eds.), *Economic Aspects of Genocides, Other Mass Atrocities, and Their Prevention* (New York: Oxford University Press), 251–73.

Ihori, Toshihiro (1999), "Protection against National Emergency: International Public Goods and Insurance," *Defense and Peace Economics*, 10(2), 117–37.

Ikeda, Yukihiro and Annalisa Rosselli (eds.) (2017), *War in the History of Economic Thought: Economists and the Question of War* (New York: Routledge).

Insight Crime (2017), "MS13," (www.insightcrime.org/el-salvador-organized-crime-news/mara-salvatrucha-ms-13-profile/. Accessed: June 27, 2018).

Institute for Economics and Peace (2017), "Positive Peace Report 2017," (http://economicsandpeace.org/research/#positive-peace. Accessed: June 28, 2018).

(2018), "Global Peace Index 2018," (http://visionofhumanity.org/indexes/global-peace-index/. Accessed: June 28, 2018).

International Action Network on Small Arms (2017), "Members," (www.iansa.org/members. Accessed: October 25, 2017).

International Committee for Robot Arms Control (2017), "Who We Are," (https://icrac.net/who/. Accessed: October 25, 2017).

International Institute for Strategic Studies (1974), *The Military Balance 1974–1975* (London: The International Institute of Strategic Studies).

(2017), *The Military Balance 2017* (London: The International Institute of Strategic Studies).

Intriligator, Michael D. (1975), "Strategic Consideration in the Richardson Model of Arms Races," *Journal of Political Economy*, 83(2), 339–53.

Intriligator, Michael D. and Dagobert L. Brito (1986), "Arms Races and Instability," *Journal of Strategic Studies*, 9(4), 113–31.

(1988), "A Predator-Prey Model of Guerrilla Warfare," *Synthese*, 76(2), 235–44.

Isard, Walter (1969), *General Theory: Social, Political, Economic, and Regional with Particular Reference to Decision-Making Analysis* (Cambridge: MIT Press).

(1988), *Arms Races, Arms Control, and Conflict Analysis* (New York: Cambridge University Press).

(1992), *Understanding Conflict and the Science of Peace* (Oxford: Blackwell).

(2000), "Formative and Early Years of the Peace Science Society (International)," *Conflict Management and Peace Science*, 18(1), 1–48.

Isard, Walter and Christine Smith (1982), *Conflict Analysis and Practical Conflict Management Procedures* (Cambridge: Ballinger).

Jackson, Matthew O. (2008), *Social and Economic Networks* (Princeton: Princeton University Press).

Jackson, Matthew O. and Massimo Morelli (2007), "Political Bias and War," *American Economic Review*, 97(4), 1353–73.

(2011), "The Reasons for Wars: An Updated Survey," in Christopher J. Coyne and Rachael L. Mathers (eds.), *The Handbook on the Political Economy of War* (Cheltenham: Edward Elgar), 34–56.

Jackson, Matthew O. and Stephen Nei (2015), "Networks of Military Alliances, Wars, and International Trade," *Proceedings of the National Academy of Sciences of the United States of America*, 112(5), 15277–284.

Jackson, Matthew O. and Yves Zenou (eds.) (2013), *Economic Analyses of Social Networks* (Cheltenham: Edward Elgar).

(2015), "Games on Networks," in Peyton Young and Shmuel Zamir (eds.), *Handbook of Game Theory, Volume 4* (New York: Elsevier), 95–163.

Jacobs, Frank (2012), "The First Google Maps War," *The New York Times*, February 28 (https://opinionator.blogs.nytimes.com/2012/02/28/the-first-google-maps-war/?_r=0. Accessed: May 5, 2017).

Javelin Strategy & Research (2018), "Identity Fraud Hits All Time High with 16.7 Million U.S. Victims in 2017, According to New Javelin Strategy & Research Study," (www.javelinstrategy.com/press-release/identity-fraud-hits-all-time-high-167-million-us-victims-2017-according-new-javelin. Accessed: April 11, 2018).

Jazayeri, Karen Bodnaruk (2015), "Identity-Based Political Inequality and Protest: The Dynamic Relationship between Political Power and Protest in the Middle East and North Africa," *Conflict Management and Peace Science*, 33(4), 400–22.

Jenne, Erin K. and Milos Popovic (2017), "Managing Internationalized Civil Wars," *Oxford Research Encyclopedia of Politics*, DOI: 10.1093/acrefore/9780190228637.013.573.

Jentzsch, Corinna, Stathis N. Kalyvas, and Livia Isabella Schubiger (eds.) (2015), "Special Issue: Militias in Civil Wars," *Journal of Conflict Resolution*, 59(5), 755–946.

Jia, Hao and Stergios Skaperdas (2012), "Technologies of Conflict," in Michelle R. Garfinkel and Stergios Skaperdas (eds.), *Oxford Handbook of the Economics of Peace and Conflict* (New York: Oxford University Press), 449–72.

Jo, Dong-Joon and Erik Gartzke (2007), "The Determinants of Nuclear Weapons Proliferation," *Journal of Conflict Resolution*, 51(1), 167–94.

Johansson, Karin and Mehwish Sarwari (2017), " Sexual Violence and Biased Military Interventions in Civil Conflict," *Conflict Management and Peace Science*, https://doi.org/10.1177/0738894216689814.

Johnson, Ane Turner and Pascal Hoba (2015), "Rebuilding Higher Education Institutions in Post-conflict Contexts: Policy Networks, Process, Perceptions, & Patterns," *International Journal of Educational Development*, 43(July), 118–25.

Johnson, Kristy Young and Paul Matthew Nolan (2016), *Biological Weapons: Recognizing, Understanding, and Responding to the Threat* (Hoboken: Wiley).

Johnson-Freese, Joan (2016), *Space Warfare in the 21st Century: Arming the Heavens* (New York: Routledge).

Jones, Benjamin T., Eleonora Mattiacci, and Bear F. Braumoeller (2017), "Food Scarcity and State Vulnerability: Unpacking the Link between Climate Variability and Violent Unrest," *Journal of Peace Research*, 54(3), 335–50.

Jones, Daniel M., Stuart A. Bremer, and J. David Singer (1996), "Militarized Interstate Disputes, 1816–1992: Rationale, Coding Rules, and Empirical Patterns," *Conflict Management and Peace Science*, 15(2), 163–212.

Joshi, Madhav, Sung Yong Lee, and Roger Mac Ginty (2017), "Built-in Safeguards and the Implementation of Civil War Peace Accords," *International Interactions*, 43 (6), 994–1018.

Joshi, Madhav and Jason Michael Quinn (2017), "Implementing the Peace: The Aggregate Implementation of Comprehensive Peace Agreements and Peace Duration after Intrastate Armed Conflict," *British Journal of Political Science*, 47 (4), 869–92.

Joshi, Madhav and Peter Wallensteen (eds.) (2018), *Understanding Quality Peace: Peacebuilding after Civil War* (London: Routledge).

Justino, Patricia (2018), "Violent Conflict and Changes in Gender Economic Roles: Implications for Post-Conflict Economic Recovery," in Fionnuala Ní Aoláin, Naomi Cahn, Dina Francesca Haynes, and Nahla Valji (eds.), *The Oxford Handbook of Gender and Conflict* (New York: Oxford University Press), 75–84.

Justino, Patricia, Tilman Brück, and Philip Verwimp (eds.) (2013), *A Micro-Level Perspective on the Dynamics of Conflict, Violence, and Development* (New York: Oxford University Press).

Kadera, Kelly M. and Sarah Shair-Rosenfield (eds.) (2017), "Special Issue: Gendered Participation, Well-being, and Representations in Political Violence," *Conflict Management and Peace Science*, http://journals.sagepub.com/doi/abs/10.1177/0738894217693618.

Kadushin, Charles (2012), *Understanding Social Networks: Theories, Concepts, and Findings* (New York: Oxford University Press).

Kahaner, Larry (2006), *AK-47: The Weapon that Changed the Face of War* (Hoboken: Wiley).

Kahneman, Daniel (2003), "Maps of Bounded Rationality: Psychology for Behavioral Economics," *American Economic Review*, 93(5), 1449–75.

 (2011), *Thinking, Fast and Slow* (New York: Farrar, Straus and Giroux).

Kalyvas, Stathis (1999), "Wanton and Senseless? The Logic of Massacres in Algeria," *Rationality and Society*, 11(3), 243–63.

 (2006), *The Logic of Violence in Civil War* (New York: Cambridge University Press).

Kaplan, Jeffrey, Heléne Lööw, and Leena Malkki (eds.) (2015), *Lone Wolf and Autonomous Cell Terrorism* (New York: Routledge).

Karakaya, Süveyda (2018), "Globalization and Contentious Politics: A Comparative Analysis of Nonviolent and Violent Campaigns," *Conflict Management and Peace Science*, 35(4), 315–35.

Karbo, Tony and Kudrat Virk (eds.) (2018), *The Palgrave Handbook of Peacebuilding in Africa* (New York: Palgrave Macmillan).

Karim, Sabrina and Kyle Beardsley (2017), *Equal Opportunity Peacekeeping: Women, Peace, and Security in Post-Conflict States* (New York: Oxford University Press).

Kaufman, Chaim (2005), "Rational Choice and Progress in the Study of Ethnic Conflict: A Review Essay," *Security Studies*, 14(1), 178–207.

Keels, Eric (2017), "Oil Wealth, Post-conflict Elections, and Postwar Peace Failure," *Journal of Conflict Resolution*, 61(5), 1021–45.

Kemp, Geoffrey and Robert E. Harkavy (1997), *Strategic Geography and the Changing Middle East* (Washington: Carnegie Endowment for International Peace in cooperation with Bookings Institution Press).

Kenney, Michael, Stephen Coulthart, and Dominick Wright (2017), "Structure and Performance in a Violent Extremist Network: The Small-world Solution," *Journal of Conflict Resolution*, 61(10), 2208–34.

Kesternich, Iris, Bettina Siflinger, James P. Smith, and Joachim K. Winter (2014), "The Effects of World War II on Economic and Health Outcomes across Europe," *Review of Economics and Statistics*, 96(1), 103–18.

Keynes, John Maynard (1919), *The Economic Consequences of the Peace* (London: Macmillan & Company Limited).

Khanna, Jyoti and Todd Sandler (1996), "NATO Burden Sharing: 1960–1992," *Defence and Peace Economics*, 7(2), 115–33.

Kibris, Arzu (2015), "The Conflict Trap Revisited: Civil Conflict and Educational Achievement," *Journal of Conflict Resolution*, 59(4), 645–70.

Kim, Sang Ki (2017), "Third-party Intervention in Civil Wars and the Prospects for Postwar Development," *Journal of Conflict Resolution*, 61(3), 615–42.

(2003), *North Korea at a Crossroads* (London: McFarland & Company, Inc.).

Kim, Sung Chull and Michael D. Cohen (eds.) (2017), *North Korea and Nuclear Weapons: Entering the New Era of Deterrence* (Washington: Georgetown University Press).

King, Robert G. and Charles I. Plosser (eds.) (2004), "Special Issue on Economic Consequences of Terrorism," *Journal of Monetary Economics*, 51(5), 861–1075.

Kinne, Brandon J. (2012), "Multilateral Trade and Militarized Conflict: Centrality, Openness, and Asymmetry in the Global Trade Network," *The Journal of Politics*, 74(1), 308–22.

Klein, Graig R. and Efe Tokdemir (2016), "Domestic Diversion: Selective Targeting of Minority Out-Groups," *Conflict Management and Peace Science*, https://doi.org /10.1177/0738894216658675.

Kobayashi, Audrey (2012), *Geographies of Peace and Armed Conflict* (New York: Routledge).

KOF Swiss Economic Institute (2018), "KOF Globalisation Index," (www.kof.ethz.ch /en/forecasts-and-indicators/indicators/kof-globalisation-index.html. Accessed: May 21, 2018).

Kollias, Christos and Suzanna-Maria Paleologou (2017), "The Globalization and Peace Nexus: Findings Using Two Composite Indices," *Social Indicators Research*, 131 (3), 871–85.

König, Michael D., Dominic Rohner, Matthias Thoenig, and Fabrizio Zilibotti (2017), "Networks in Conflict: Theory and Evidence from the Great War of Africa," *Econometrica*, 85(4), 1093–132.

Kono, Daniel Yuichi and Gabriella R. Montinola (2013), "The Uses and Abuses of Foreign Aid: Development Aid and Military Spending," *Political Research Quarterly*, 66(3), 615–29.

Konrad, Kai A. and Stergios Skaperdas (1998), "Extortion," *Economica*, 65(260), 461–77.

Krain, Matthew (1997), "State-Sponsored Mass Murder: The Onset and Severity of Genocides and Politicides," *Journal of Conflict Resolution*, 41(3), 331–60.

Krainin, Colin and John Slinkman (2017), "Bargaining with a Biased Autocrat," *Journal of Theoretical Politics*, 29(2), 273–98.

Krause, Volker and Christopher Sprecher (eds.) (2004), "Special Issue on Alliances," *International Interactions*, 30(4), 281–397.

Krebs, Valdis E. (2002), "Mapping Networks of Terrorist Cells," *Connections*, 24(3), 43–52.

Kroenig, Matthew (2010), *Exporting the Bomb: Technology Transfer and the Spread of Nuclear Weapons* (Ithaca: Cornell University Press).

Krueger, Alan B., and Mikael Lindahl (2001), "Education for Growth: Why and for Whom?" *Journal of Economic Literature*, 39(4), 1101–36.

Krugman, Paul R., Maurice Obstfeld, and Marc Melitz (2018), *International Economics: Theory and Policy*, 11th edn. (New York: Pearson).

Kuper, Leo (1977), *The Pity of It All: Polarisation of Racial and Ethnic Relations* (London: Duckworth).

Kydd, Andrew H. (2015), *International Relations Theory: The Game-Theoretic Approach* (New York: Cambridge University Press).

LaFree, Gary, Laura Dugan, Heather V. Fogg, and Jeffrey Scott (2006), "Building a Global Terrorism Database," NCJ 214260, United States Department of Justice, National Institute of Justice, Apr 27, 2006.

Lanchester, Frederick W. (1916), *Aircraft in Warfare, the Dawn of the Fourth Arm* (London: Constable).

Langlois, Catherine C. and Jean-Pierre P. Langlois (2009), "Does Attrition Behavior Help Explain the Duration of Interstate Wars? A Game Theoretic and Empirical Analysis," *International Studies Quarterly*, 53(4), 1051–73.

Lapan, Harvey E. and Todd Sandler (1988), "To Bargain or Not to Bargain? That Is the Question," *American Economic Review*, 78(2), 16–21.

Lasley, Trace and Clayton Thyne (2014), "Secession, Legitimacy and The Use of Child Soldiers," *Conflict Management and Peace Science*, 32(3), 289–308.

Leckie, Scott and Chris Huggins (2013), *Conflict and Housing, Land and Property Rights: A Handbook on Issues, Frameworks and Solutions* (New York: Cambridge University Press).

Leeds, Brett Ashley (2003), "Do Alliances Deter Aggression? The Influence of Military Alliances on the Initiation of Militarized Interstate Disputes," *American Journal of Political Science*, 47(3), 427–39.

Leeds, Brett Ashley, Jeffrey M. Ritter, Sara McLaughlin Mitchell, and Andrew G. Long (2002), "Alliance Treaty Obligations and Provisions, 1815–1944," *International Interactions*, 28(3), 237–60.

Lemkin, Raphael (1944), *Axis Rule in Occupied Europe: Laws of Occupation, Analysis of Government, Proposals for Redress* (Washington: Carnegie Endowment for International Peace).

Lendorfer, Julia, Alvin Etang-Ndip, and Johannes Hoogeveen (2016), "Socio-Economic Impact of the Crisis in Northern Mali on Displaced People," *Journal of Refugee Studies*, 29(3), 315–40.

Levy, Jack S. (1997), "Prospect Theory, Rational Choice, and International Relations," *International Studies Quarterly*, 41(1), 87–112

Li, Chengchun, Syed Mansoob Murshed, and Sailesh Tanna (2017), "The Impact of Civil War on Foreign Direct Investment Flows to Developing Countries," *The Journal of International Trade & Economic Development*, 26(4), 488–507.

Li, Quan (2003), "The Effect of Security Alliances on the Exchange-Rate Regime Choices," *International Interactions*, 29(2), 159–93.

Linke, Andrew M. and Clionadh Raleigh (2016), "The Geography of Civil War," *Oxford Research Encyclopedia of Politics*, DOI: 10.1093/acrefore/9780190228637.013.22.

Litwak, Robert and Meg King (2015), "Arms Control in Cyberspace?" (www.scribd .com/document/288212833/Arms-Control-in-Cyberspace. Accessed: October 26, 2017).

Lund, Michael S. (1996), "Early Warning and Preventive Diplomacy," in Charles A. Crocker, Fen Olser Hampson, and Pamella Aall (eds.), *Managing Global Chaos: Sources of and Responses to International Conflict* (Washington: U.S. Institute of Peace), 379–402.

Lupu, Noam and Leonid Peisakhin (2017), "The Legacy of Political Violence across Generations," *American Journal of Political Science*, 61(4), 836–51.

Lupu, Yonatan and Brian Greenhill (2017), "The Networked Peace: Intergovernmental Organizations and International Conflict," *Journal of Peace Research*, 54(6), 833–48.

Mabon, Simon (2016), "How to Understand Syria's 'Proxy War' – and Who's Fighting for Whom," The Conversation, September 29 (https://theconversation.com/how -to-understand-syrias-proxy-war-and-whos-fighting-for-whom-65685. Accessed: October 3, 2016).

Mac Ginty, Roger (ed.) (2015), *Routledge Handbook of Peacebuilding* (London: Routledge).

Machain, Carla Martinez and Leo Rosenberg (2016), "Domestic Diversion and Strategic Behavior by Minority Groups," *Conflict Management and Peace Science*, https://doi.org/10.1177/0738894216655461.

MacKay, Niall and Christopher Price (2011), "Safety in Numbers: Ideas of Concentration in Royal Air Force Fighter Defence from Lanchester to the Battle of Britain," *History*, 96(323), 304–25.

Macnair, Elizabeth S., James C. Murdoch, Chung-Ron Pi, and Todd Sandler (1995), "Growth and Defense: Pooled Estimates for the NATO Alliance, 1951–1988," *Southern Economic Journal*, 61(3), 846–60.

Mahnken, Thomas, Joseph Maiolo, and David Stevenson (eds.) (2016), *Arms Races in International Politics: From the Nineteenth to the Twenty-First Century* (Oxford: Oxford University Press).

Maldonado, Jorge H., Rocío del Pilar Moreno-Sánchez, Sophía Espinoza, Aaron Bruner, Natalia Garzón, and John Myers (2018), "Peace Is Much More Than Doves: The Economic Benefits of Bird-based Tourism as a Result of the Peace Treaty in Colombia," *World Development*, 106(June), 78–86.

Mankiw, N. Gregory (2018), *Principles of Economics*, 8th edn. (Independence: Cengage).

Mansfield, Edward D. and Brian M. Pollins (eds.) (2003), *Economic Interdependence and International Conflict: New Perspectives on an Enduring Debate* (Ann Arbor: The University of Michigan Press).

Maoz, Zeev (2011), *Networks of Nations: The Evolution, Structure, and Impact of Internationalized Networks, 1816–2011* (New York: Cambridge University Press).

   (ed.) (2012), "Special Issue: Networked Perspectives of International Relations," *Conflict Management and Peace Science*, 29(3), 247–369.

Marriage, Zoë (2016), "Peace and the Killing: Compatible Logics in the Democratic Republic of the Congo," in Charles H. Anderton and Jurgen Brauer (eds.), *Economic Aspects of Genocides, Other Mass Atrocities, and Their Prevention* (New York: Oxford University Press), 356–77.

Marshall, Monty G. and Keith Jaggers (2007), *Polity IV Project: Political Regime Characteristics and Transitions: 1800–2006*," (www.systemicpeace.org/polity/polity4.htm. Accessed: March 28, 2008).

Marshall, Monty G., Ted Robert Gurr, and Barbara Harff (2017), "PITF – State Failure Problem Set: Internal Wars and Failures of Governance, 1955–2016," (www.systemicpeace.org/inscr/PITFProbSetCodebook2016.pdf. Accessed: August 25, 2017).

Martellini, Maurizio and Andrea Malizia (eds.) (2017), *Cyber and Chemical, Biological, Radiological, Nuclear, Explosives Challenges: Threats and Counter Efforts* (New York: Springer).

Martin, Philippe, Thierry Mayer, and Mathias Thoenig (2008), "Make Trade Not War?" *The Review of Economic Studies*, 75(3), 865–900.

Mason, T. David and Sara McLaughlin Mitchell (eds.) (2016), *What Do We Know about Civil Wars?* (New York: Rowman & Littlefield).

Maynard Smith, John (1982), *Evolution and the Theory of Games* (New York: Cambridge University Press).

McCormack, Daniel and Henry Pascoe (2017), "Sanctions and Preventive War," *Journal of Conflict Resolution*, 61(8), 1711–39.

McDoom, Omar Shahabudin (2014), "Antisocial Capital: A Profile of Rwandan Genocide Perpetrators' Social Networks," *Journal of Conflict Resolution*, 58(5), 865–93.

McGuire, Martin C. (1965), *Secrecy and the Arms Race* (Cambridge: Harvard University Press).

   (1990), "Mixed Public-Private Benefit and Public-Good Supply with Application to the NATO Alliance," *Defence Economics*, 1(1), 17–35.

   (2004), "Economics of Strategic Defense and the Global Public Good," *Defence and Peace Economics*, 15(1), 1–25.

McMahon, Patrice C. (2017), *The NGO Game: Post-Conflict Peacebuilding in the Balkans and Beyond* (Ithaca: Cornell University Press).

Mearsheimer, John J. (1985), *Conventional Deterrence* (Ithaca: Cornell University Press).

Medalia, Jonathan (2011), "'Dirty Bombs': Background in Brief," *Congressional Research Service*, No. 7–5700.

Megoran, Nick, Fiona McConnell, and Philippa Williams (2014), *The Geographies of Peace: New Approaches to Boundaries, Diplomacy and Conflict Resolution* (London: I. B. Tauris).

Meierhenrich, Jens (ed.) (2014), *Genocide: A Reader* (New York: Oxford University Press).

Merrouche, Ouarda (2008), "Landmines and Poverty: IV Evidence from Mozambique," *Peace Economics, Peace Science and Public Policy*, 14(1), Article 2.

Metelits, Claire (2010), *Inside Insurgency: Violence, Civilians and Revolutionary Group Behavior* (New York: New York University Press).

Mickolus, Edward F. (1980), *Transnational Terrorism: A Chronology of Events, 1968–1979* (Westport: Greenwood Press).

Mickolus, Edward F., Todd Sandler, Jean M. Murdock, and Peter A. Flemming (2016), "International Terrorism: Attributes of Terrorist Events (ITERATE) Data Codebook, 1968–2016." Vinyard Software, Inc. (http://vinyardsoftware.com).

Midlarsky, Manus I. (2005), *The Killing Trap: Genocide in the Twentieth Century* (New York: Cambridge University Press).

Milgram, Stanley (1963), "Behavioral Study of Obedience," *Journal of Abnormal and Social Psychology*, 67(4), 371–78.

Millard, Matt (ed.) (2016), "Special Issue: Re-examining the Alliance Literature," *Conflict Management and Peace Science* (http://journals.sagepub.com/page/cmp/collections/virtual-special-issue/alliance-literature-reexamined. Accessed: March 22, 2018).

Mincheva, Lyubov Grigorova and Ted Robert Gurr (2012), *Crime-Terror Alliances and the State: Ethnonationalist and Islamist Challenges to Regional Security* (New York: Routledge).

Minhas, Shahryar and Benjamin J. Radford (2017), "Enemy at the Gates Variation in Economic Growth from Civil Conflict," *Journal of Conflict Resolution*, 61(10), 2105–29.

Minorities at Risk (2009), "Minorities at Risk (MAR) Codebook Version 2/2009," (www.mar.umd.edu/data/mar_codebook_Feb09.pdf. Accessed: August 25, 2017).

Miranda, Luiz C.M., Leonel F. Perondi, and Kristian Skrede Gleditsch (2016), "The Evolution of Civil War Severity, 1816–2005," *Peace Economics, Peace Science and Public Policy*, 22(3), 247–76.

Mishali-Ram, Meirav (2013), "The Role of Intervention in Multi-Actor International Crises," *International Journal of Peace Studies*, 18(1), 55–82.

Mitchell, David F. and Jeffrey Pickering (2017), "Arms Buildups and the Use of Military Force," *Oxford Research Encyclopedia of Politics* (http://politics.oxfordre.com/view/10.1093/acrefore/9780190228637.001.0001/acrefore-9780190228637-e-390. Accessed: October 30, 2017).

Mitchell, Jeni (2015), "Civilian Victimization during the Tajik Civil war: A Typology and Strategic Assessment," *Central Asian Survey*, 34(3), 357–72.

Mitchell, Sara McLaughlin (2017), "Dangerous Bargains with the Devil? Incorporating New Approaches in Peace Science for the Study of War," *Conflict Management and Peace Science*, 34(1), 98–116.

Mitchell, Sara McLaughlin and John A. Vasquez (eds.) (2013), *Conflict, War, and Peace: An Introduction to Scientific Research* (Washington: CQ Press).

Morelli, Massimo and Dominic Rohner (2015), "Resource Concentration and Civil Wars," *Journal of Development Economics*, 117(November), 32–47.

Morelli, Massimo, and Tommaso Sonno (2017), "On Economic Interdependence and War," *Journal of Economic Literature*, 55(3), 1084–97.

Muggy, Luke and Jessica L. Heier Stamm (2014), "Game Theory Applications in Humanitarian Operations: A Review," *Journal of Humanitarian Logistics and Supply Chain Management*, 4(1), 4–23.

Murdie, Amanda (2014), *Help or Harm: The Human Security Effects of International NGOs* (Stanford: Stanford University Press).

Murdoch, James C. and Todd Sandler (1982), "A Theoretical and Empirical Analysis of NATO," *Journal of Conflict Resolution*, 26(2), 237–63.

(2004), "Civil Wars and Economic Growth: Spatial Dispersion," *American Journal of Political Science*, 48(1), 138–51.

Murshed, S. Mansob (2015), "On the Nature of Disagreements Regarding the Causes of Civil War," in Paul Jackson (ed.), *Handbook of International Security and Development* (Cheltenham: Edward Elgar), 19–31.

Murshed, S. Mansoob and Mohammad Zulfan Tadjoeddin (2016), "Long-Term Economic Development in the Presence of an Episode of Mass Killing: The Case of Indonesia, 1965–1966," in Charles H. Anderton and Jurgen Brauer (eds.), *Economic Aspects of Genocides, Other Mass Atrocities, and Their Prevention* (New York: Oxford University Press), 481–509.

Mutschler, Max M. (2013), *Arms Control in Space: Exploring Conditions for Preventive Arms Control* (New York: Palgrave Macmillan).

Myerson, Roger (2016), "Local and National Democracy in Political Reconstruction," in Charles H. Anderton and Jurgen Brauer (eds.), *Economic Aspects of Genocides, Other Mass Atrocities, and Their Prevention* (New York: Oxford University Press), 663–74.

Nance, Malcolm and Christopher Sampson (2017), *Hacking ISIS: How to Destroy the Cyber Jihad* (New York: Skyhorse Publishing).

Narang, Neil (2015), "Assisting Uncertainty: How Humanitarian Aid can Inadvertently Prolong Civil War," *International Studies Quarterly*, 59(1), 184–95.

National Council on Radiation Protection & Measurements (2014), *Decision Making for Late-Phase Recovery from Major Nuclear or Radiological Incidents, NCRP Report No. 175* (Bethesda: National Council on Radiation Protection & Measurements).

National Gang Intelligence Center (2015), *National Gang Report 2015* (www.fbi.gov /file-repository/stats-services-publications-national-gang-report-2015.Rpdf /view. Accessed: April 13, 2017).

National WW II Museum (2018), "Research Starters: Worldwide Deaths in World War II," (www.nationalww2museum.org/students-teachers/student-resources/research -starters/research-starters-worldwide-deaths-world-war. Accessed: January 24, 2018).

Natsios, Andrew S. (2001), *The Great North Korean Famine* (Washington: U.S. Institute of Peace).

Newman, Edward and Karl DeRouen Jr (eds.) (2014), *Routledge Handbook of Civil Wars* (New York: Routledge).

Newman, Mark (2010), *Networks: An Introduction* (New York: Oxford University Press).

Nicholson, Walter and Christopher M. Snyder (2016), *Microeconomic Theory: Basic Principles and Extensions*, 12th edn. (Independence: Cengage).

Niou, Emerson M. S. and Guofu Tan (2005), "External Threat and Collective Action," *Economic Inquiry*, 43(3), 519–30.

Noor, Masi, Miles Hewstone, and Nyla R. Branscombe (2015), "Special Issue: Antecedents and Consequences of Intergroup Forgiveness," *Group Processes & Intergroup Relations*, 18(5), 577–739.

Norwegian Initiative on Small Arms Transfers (2017), "NISAT Database Public User Manual" (http://file.prio.no/Publication_files/NISAT/NISAT%20database% 20public%20user%20manual.pdf. Accessed: August 3, 2017).

Nuclear Threat Initiative (2017a), "Country Profiles," (www.nti.org/learn/countries. Accessed: October 24, 2017).

(2017b), "Treaties and Regimes," (www.nti.org/learn/treaties-and-regimes/treaties/. Accessed: October 24, 2017).

Nye, Joseph S. (2015), "The World Needs an Arms-control Treaty for Cybersecurity," (www.belfercenter.org/publication/world-needs-arms-control-treaty-cybersecurity. Accessed: October 26, 2017).

O'Balance, Edgar (1964), "Middle East Arms Race," *The Army Quarterly and Defence Journal*, 88, 210–14.

O'Sullivan, Patrick (1991), *Terrain and Tactics* (New York: Greenwood Press).

Oakes, Amy (2012), *Diversionary War: Domestic Unrest and International Conflict* (Stanford: Stanford Security Studies).

Office of Technology Assessment (1993), *Proliferation of Weapons of Mass Destruction: Assessing the Risk* (Washington: U.S. Government Printing Office).

Ohmura, Hirotaka (2011), "Termination and Recurrence of Civil War: Which Outcomes Lead to Durable Peace after Civil War?" *Japanese Journal of Political Science*, 12(3), 375–98.

Olson, Eric L. (2011), Testimony Before the Senate Committee on Foreign Relations Subcommittee on Western Hemisphere, Peace Corps, and Narcotics Affairs, "A Shared Responsibility: Counternarcotics and Citizen Security in the Americas," March 31 (www.foreign.senate.gov/imo/media/doc/REVISED% 20Olson%20Testimony.pdf. Accessed: September 30, 2016).

Olson, Mancur and Richard Zeckhauser (1966), "An Economic Theory of Alliances," *Review of Economics and Statistics*, 48(3), 266–79.

(1967), "Collective Goods, Comparative Advantage, and Alliance Efficiency," in Roland Mckean (ed.), *Issues of Defense Economics* (New York: National Bureau of Economic Research), 25–48.

Oneal, John R. and Mark A. Elrod (1989), "NATO Burden Sharing and the Forces of Change," *International Studies Quarterly*, 33(4), 435–56.

Oneal, John R. and Paul F. Diehl (1994), "The Theory of Collective Action and NATO Defense Burdens: New Empirical Tests," *Political Research Quarterly*, 47(2), 373–96.

Oppenheimer, Joe (2012), *Principles of Politics: A Rational Choice Theory Guide to Politics and Social Justice* (New York: Cambridge University Press).

Ouellet, Marie, Martin Bouchard, and Mackenzie Hart (2017), "Criminal Collaboration and Risk: The Drivers of Al Qaeda's Network Structure Before and After 9/11," *Social Networks*, 51(October), 171–7.

Paffenholz, Thania (ed.) (2010), *Civil Society & Peacebuilding: A Critical Assessment* (Boulder: Lynne Rienner Publishers).

Palmer, Glenn, Vito D'Orazio, Michael Kenwick, and Matthew Lane (2015), "The MID4 dataset, 2002–2010: Procedures, Coding Rules and Description," *Conflict Management and Peace* Science, 32(2), 222–42.

Peace Direct (2017a), "Insight on Conflict: Conflict Areas," (www.insightonconflict .org/. Accessed: April 19, 2017).

(2017b), "Peace Insight: Syria," (www.peaceinsight.org/conflicts/syria/. Accessed: September 22, 2017).

(2018), "Peace Insight," (www.peaceinsight.org/about/. Accessed: February 20, 2018).

Peace Science Society (2018), "Peace Science Society (International)," (http://sites.psu .edu/pssi/. Accessed: March 28, 2018).

Peck, Merton J. and Frederick M. Scherer (1962), *The Weapons Acquisition Process: An Economic Analysis* (Boston: Harvard University Press).

Pégorier, Clotilde (2013), *Ethnic Cleansing: A Legal Qualification* (New York: Routledge).

Peinhardt, Clint and Todd Sandler (2015), *Transnational Cooperation: An Issue-Based Approach* (New York: Oxford University Press).

Penn World Tables (2017), "The Database: Penn World Table Version 9.0," (www.rug .nl/ggdc/productivity/pwt/. Accessed: May 1, 2017).

Pickering, Steve (2017), *Understanding Geography and War: Misperceptions, Foundations, and Prospects* (New York: Palgrave Macmillan).

Pilat, Joseph F. and Nathan E. Busch (eds.) (2017), *Routledge Handbook of Nuclear Proliferation and Policy* (New York: Routledge).

Polachek, Solomon W. (1994), "Peace Economics: A Trade Theory Perspective," *Peace Economics, Peace Science and Public Policy*, 1(2), 12–5.

Polachek, Solomon W. and Carlos Seiglie (2007), "Trade, Peace and Democracy: An Analysis of Dyadic Dispute," in Todd Sandler and Keith Hartley (eds.), *Handbook of Defense Economics, Volume 2* (New York: Elsevier), 1017–73.

Polachek, Solomon W., Carlos Seiglie, and Jun Xiang (2012), "Globalization and International Conflict: Can Foreign Direct Investment Increase Cooperation Among Nations?" in Michelle R. Garfinkel and Stergios Skaperdas (eds.), *The Oxford Handbook of the Economics of Peace and Conflict* (New York: Oxford University Press), 733–62.

Polachek, Solomon W. and Daria Sevastianova (2010), "Does Conflict Disrupt Growth? Evidence of the Relationship between Political Instability and National Economic Performance," Institute for the Study of Labor Discussion Paper IZA DP No. 4762 (http://ftp.iza.org/dp4762.pdf. Accessed: August 1, 2017).

Porter, Christopher (2017), "Private Sector Cyber Intelligence Could Be Key to Workable Cyber Arms Control Treaties," (www.lawfareblog.com/private-sector-cyber-intelligence-could-be-key-workable-cyber-arms-control-treaties. Accessed: October 26, 2017).

Powell, Robert (2002), "Bargaining Theory and International Conflict," *Annual Review of Political Science*, 5(June), 1–30.

(2006), "War as a Commitment Problem," *International Organization*, 60(1), 169–203.

Power, Samantha (2002), *"A Problem from Hell": America and the Age of Genocide* (New York: Basic Books).

Prins, Brandon C. and Krista E. Wiegand (eds.) (2017), "Special Issue: Managing Territorial Conflict," *Conflict Management and Peace Science*, 34(2), 121–211.

Prorok, Alyssa K. (2018), "Led Astray: Leaders and the Duration of Civil War," *Journal of Conflict Resolution*, 62(6), 1179–204.

Proskurnikov, Anton V. and Roberto Tempo (2017), "A Tutorial on Modeling and Analysis of Dynamic Social Networks. Part I," *Annual Reviews in Control*, 43, 65–79.

Przemieniecki, John S. (2000), *Mathematical Methods in Defense Analyses*, 3rd edn. (Reston: American Institute of Aeronautics and Astronautics, Inc.).

Public Broadcasting Service (2016), "CyberWar Threat," (www.pbs.org/wgbh/nova/military/cyberwar-threat.html. Accessed: August 19, 2016).

(2017a), "Crips and Bloods: Made in America," (www.pbs.org/independentlens/cripsandbloods/film.html. Accessed: April 19, 2017).

(2017b), "The Staggering Death Toll of Mexico's Drug War," (www.pbs.org/wgbh/frontline/article/the-staggering-death-toll-of-mexicos-drug-war/. Accessed: April 19, 2017).

Quackenbush, Stephen L. (2014), *International Conflict: Logic and Evidence* (Washington: CQ Press).

Quirk, Patrick W. (2017), *Great Powers, Weak States, and Insurgency: Explaining Internal Threat Alliances* (Basingstoke: Palgrave Macmillan).

Rahul, Kumar (2017), "AMD's 'Naples' The New 32-Core CPU To Challenge Intel," (www.sciencetimes.com/articles/9953/20170308/amds-naples-new-32-core-cpu-challenge-intel.htm. Accessed: June 12, 2018).

Raiffa, Howard (1982), *The Art and Science of Negotiation* (Cambridge: Harvard University Press).

(2003), *Negotiation Analysis: The Science and Art of Collaborative Decision Making* (Cambridge: Harvard University Press).

Ramsay, Kristopher W. (2008), "Settling It on the Field: Battlefield Events and War Termination," *Journal of Conflict Resolution*, 52(6), 850–79.

(2017), "Information, Uncertainty, and War," *Annual Review of Political Science* 20 (May), 505–27.

Ramsbotham, Oliver, Tom Woodhouse, and Hugh Miall (2011), *Contemporary Conflict Resolution*, 3rd edn. (Cambridge: Polity).

RAND Worldwide Terrorism Incident Database (2017), "Database Scope," (www.rand.org/nsrd/projects/terrorism-incidents/about/definitions.html. Accessed: September 12, 2017).

Rasler, Karen, William R. Thompson, and Sumit Ganguly (2013), *How Rivalries End* (Philadelphia: University of Pennsylvania Press).

Ray, Subhasish (2017), "Intra-group Interactions and Inter-group Violence: Sikh Mobilization During the Partition of India in a Comparative Perspective," *Journal of Genocide Research*, 19(3), 382–403.

Reed, William (2003), "Information and Economic Interdependence," *Journal of Conflict Resolution*, 47(1), 54–71.

Regan, Patrick M. (1998), "Choosing to Intervene: Outside Interventions in Internal Conflicts," *The Journal of Politics*, 60(3), 754–79.

Reiter, Dan (2003), "Exploring the Bargaining Model of War," *Perspectives on Politics*, 1 (1), 27–43.

Richardson, Lewis F. (1939), *Generalized Foreign Politics* (London: Cambridge University Press).

(1960a), *Arms and Insecurity: A Mathematical Study of the Causes and Origins of War* (Pittsburgh: Homewood).

(1960b), *Statistics of Deadly Quarrels* (Pacific Grove: Boxwood Press).

Richmond, Oliver P. and Henry F. Carey (eds.) (2017), *Subcontracting Peace: The Challenges of NGO Peacebuilding* (New York: Routledge).

Rider, Robert (1999), "Conflict, the Sire of Exchange," *Journal of Economic Behavior & Organization*, 40(3), 217–32.

Rider, Toby J., Michael G. Findley, and Paul F. Diehl (2011), "Just Part of the Game? Arms Races, Rivalry, and War," *Journal of Peace Research*, 48(1), 85–100.

Roberts, Elizabeth (2017),"Report: Mexico Was Second Deadliest Country in 2016," (www.cnn.com/2017/05/09/americas/mexico-second-deadliest-conflict-2016/index.html. Accessed: June 26, 2018).

Robinson, Geoffrey (2010), "State-sponsored Violence and Secessionist Rebellions in Asia," in Donald Bloxham and A. Dirk Moses (eds.), *The Oxford Handbook of Genocide Studies* (New York: Oxford University Press), 466–88.

Robinson, Julian Perry, Carl-Göran Hedén, and Hans von Schreeb (1973), *The Problem of Chemical and Biological Warfare, CB Weapons Today Volume II* (Stockholm: Almqvist & Wiksell).

Roeder, Philip G. (2017), "National Secession," *Oxford Research Encyclopedia of Politics*, DOI: 10.1093/acrefore/9780190228637.013.530.

Ron, James (ed.) (2005), "Special Issue: Paradigm in Distress? Primary Commodities and Civil War," *Journal of Conflict Resolution*, 49(4), 441–633.

Rosendorff, B. Peter and Todd Sandler (eds.) (2005), "Special Issue: The Political Economy of Transnational Terrorism," *Journal of Conflict Resolution*, 49(2), 171–314.

Rowley, Charles K. (ed.) (2006), "Special Issue: The Political Economy of Terrorism," *Public Choice*, 128(1–2), 1–356.

Roy, Vita (2018), "Managing Resource-related Conflict: A Framework of Lootable Resource Management and Postconflict Stabilization," *Journal of Conflict Resolution*, 62(5), 1044–71.

Rummel, Rudolph J. (1994), "Death By Government, Chapter 2: Definition of Democide." (www.hawaii.edu/powerkills/DBG.CHAP2.HTM. Accessed: December 11, 2017).

(1995), "Democracy, Power, Genocide, and Mass Murder," *Journal of Conflict Resolution*, 39(1), 3–26.

Russett, Bruce M. and John R. Oneal (2001), *Triangulating Peace: Democracy, Interdependence, and International Organization* (New York: W. W. Norton & Company).

Sahni, Manvi and Sumanta Kumar Das (2015), "Performance of Maximum Likelihood Estimator for Fitting Lanchester Equations on Kursk Battle Data," *Journal of Battlefield Technology*, 18(2), 23–30.

Salehyan, Idean, David Siroky, and Reed M. Wood (2014), "External Rebel Sponsorship and Civilian Abuse: A Principal-agent Analysis of War Time Atrocities," *International Organization*, 68(3), 633–61.

Sambanis, Nicholas (2002), "A Review of Recent Advances and Future Directions in the Quantitative Literature on Civil War," *Defense and Peace Economics*, 13(3), 215–43.

Sambanis, Nicholas, Stergios Skaperdas, and William C. Wohlforth (2015), "Nation-Building through War," *American Political Science Review*, 109(2), 279–96.

Sample, Susan G. (2017), "Power, Wealth, and Satisfaction: When Do Power Transitions Lead to Conflict?" *Journal of Conflict Resolution*, https://doi.org/10.1177/0022002717707238.

Sandler, Todd (1977), "Impurity of Defense: An Application to the Economics of Alliances," *Kyklos*, 30(3), 443–60.

(2000), "Arms Trade, Arms Control and Security: Collective Action Issues," *Defence and Peace Economics*, 11(5), 533–48.

(2003), "Collective Action and Transnational Terrorism," *The World Economy*, 26 (6), 779–802.

(2004), *Global Collective Action* (New York: Cambridge University Press).

(2014), "The Analytical Study of Terrorism: Taking Stock," *Journal of Peace Research*, 51(2), 257–71.

(ed.) (2015), "Special Issue: The Economics of Terrorism and Counterterrorism," *Oxford Economic Papers*, 67(1), 1–183.

(ed.) (2016a), "Special Issue: Political Violence," *Public Choice*, 169(3–4), 161–393.

(2016b), "Strategic Aspects of Difficult Global Challenges," *Global Policy*, 7(S1), 33–44.

(2017), "International Peacekeeping Operations: Burden Sharing and Effectiveness," *Journal of Conflict Resolution*, 61(9), 1875–97.

Sandler, Todd and Daniel G. Arce (2007), "Terrorism: A Game-Theoretic Approach," in Todd Sandler and Keith Hartley (eds.), *Handbook of Defense Economics, Volume 2* (New York: Elsevier), 775–813.

Sandler, Todd and Jon Cauley (1975), "On the Economic Theory of Alliances," *Journal of Conflict Resolution*, 19(2), 330–48.

Sandler, Todd and John Forbes (1980), "Burden Sharing, Strategy, and the Design of NATO," *Economic Inquiry*, 18(3), 425–44.

Sandler, Todd and Keith Hartley (1995), *The Economics of Defense* (Cambridge: Cambridge University Press).

(1999), *The Political Economy of NATO* (Cambridge: Cambridge University Press).

(2001), "Economics of Alliances: The Lessons of Collective Action," *Journal of Economic Literature*, 39(3), 869–96.

(eds.) (2003), *The Economics of Conflict, Volume I–III* (Cheltenham: Edward Elgar).

(eds.) (2007), *Handbook of Defense Economics, Volume 2* (New York: Elsevier).

Sandler, Todd and James C. Murdoch (1990), "Nash-Cournot or Lindahl Behavior? An Empirical Test for the NATO Allies," *Quarterly Journal of Economics*, 105(4), 875–94.

(2000), "On Sharing NATO Defense Burdens in the 1990s and Beyond," *Fiscal Studies*, 21(3), 297–327.

Sandler, Todd and Hirofumi Shimizu (2014), "NATO Burden Sharing 1999–2010: An Altered Alliance," *Foreign Policy Analysis*, 10(1), 43–60.

Santifort-Jordan, Charlinda and Todd Sandler (2014), "An Empirical Study of Suicide Terrorism: A Global Analysis," *Southern Economic Journal*, 80(4), 981–1001.

Sarkees, Meredith Reid and Frank Wayman (2010), *Resort to War: 1816–2007* (Washington: CQ Press).

Sarwar, Saima, Muhammad Wasif Siddiqi, Abdul Nasir, and Zahoor Ahmed (2016), "New Direction to Evaluate the Economic Impact of Peace for Bilateral Trade among World Economies," *The Pakistan Development Review*, 55(4) (Part II), 725–40.

Savage, David A. (2016), "Surviving the Storm: Behavioural Economics in the Conflict Environment," *Peace Economics, Peace Science and Public Policy*, 22(2), 105–29.

Scaife, Laura (2017), *Social Networks as the New Frontier of Terrorism: #Terror* (New York: Routledge).

Schelling, Thomas C. (1960), *The Strategy of Conflict* (Cambridge: Harvard University Press).

(1966), *Arms and Influence* (New Haven: Yale University Press).

Schelling, Thomas C. and Morton H. Halperin (1961), *Strategy and Arms Control* (London: Pergamon-Brassey's).

Schneider, Gerald (2014), "Globalization and Social Transition," in Edward Newman and Karl DeRouen Jr (eds.), *Routledge Handbook of Civil Wars* (New York: Routledge), 186–96.

Schneider, Gerald, Katherine Barbieri, and Nils Petter Gleditsch (2003), "Does Globalization Contribute to Peace? A Critical Survey of the Literature," in Gerald Schneider, Katherine Barbieri, and Nils Petter Gleditsch (eds.), *Globalization and Armed Conflict* (Lanham: Roman & Littlefield Publishers), 3–29.

Schrodt, Philip A. and Jay Ulfelder (2016), "Political Instability Task Force Atrocities Event Data Collection Codebook Version 1.1B1," (http://eventdata.parusanalytics .com/data.dir/PITF_Atrocities.codebook.1.1B1.pdf. Accessed: December 12, 2017).

Schulze, Max-Stephan (2005), "Austria-Hungary's Economy in World War I," in Stephen Broadberry and Mark Harrison (eds.), *The Economics of World War I* (New York: Cambridge University Press), 77–111.

Schumpeter, Joseph A. ([1919] 1955), "The Sociology of Imperialisms," in Joseph Schumpeter *Imperialism & Social Classes* (Cleveland: World Publishing), 3–98.

Schweller, Randall, L. (1996), "Neorealism's Status Quo Bias: What Security Dilemma?" *Security Studies*, 5(Spring), 90–121.

Scott, John (2017), *Social Network Analysis*, 4th edn. (Thousand Oaks: Sage Publications Ltd).

Sechser, Todd S. (2018), "Reputations and Signaling in Coercive Bargaining," *Journal of Conflict Resolution*, 62(2), 318–45.

Seligman, Edwin R. A. (1919), "The Cost of the War and How It Was Met," *American Economic Review*, 9(4), 739–770.

Senese, Paul D. and John A. Vasquez (2008), *The Steps to War: An Empirical Study* (Princeton: Princeton University Press).

Senior, Nassau W. ([1836] 1965), *An Outline of the Science of Political Economy* (New York: Augustus M. Kelley, Bookseller).

Sheehan, Nadège (2011), *The Economics of UN Peacekeeping* (New York: Routledge).

Shelef, Nadav G. (2016), "Unequal Ground: Homelands and Conflict," *International Organization*, 70(1), 33–63.

Sherif, Muzafer, O. J. Harvey, William R. Hood, et al. (1988), *The Robbers Cave Experiment: Intergroup Conflict and Cooperation* (Middletown: Wesleyan University Press).

Silberner, Edmund (1946), *The Problem of War in Nineteenth Century Economic Thought* (Princeton: Princeton University Press).

Silwal, Shikha (2013), "A Spatial-Temporal Analysis of Civil War: The Case of Nepal," *The Economics of Peace and Security Journal*, 8(2), 20–5.

(2016), "Resilience Amidst Conflict?: Impact of Exposure to Violence on Secondary Education," *The International Journal of Conflict and Development*, 6(2), 97–120.

Singer, J. David (ed.) (1960), "Special Issue: The Geography of Conflict," *Journal of Conflict Resolution*, 4(1), 1–162.

(2000), "The Etiology of Interstate War: A Natural History Approach," in John A. Vasquez (ed.), *What Do We Know about War?* (New York: Rowman & Littlefield), 3–21.

Singer, Peter W. (2009), *Wired for War: The Robotics Revolution and Conflict in the 21st Century* (New York: Penguin Press).

Singer, Peter W. and Allan Friedman (2014), *Cybersecurity and Cyberwar: What Everyone Needs to Know* (New York: Oxford University Press).

Singh, Prakarsh (2013), "Impact of Terrorism on Investment Decisions of Farmers: Evidence from the Punjab Insurgency," *Journal of Conflict Resolution*, 57(1), 143–68.

Singh, Prakarsh and Olga N. Shemyakina (2016), "Gender-Differential Effects of Terrorism on Education: The Case of the 1981–1993 Punjab Insurgency," *Economics of Education Review*, 54(October), 185–210.

Singh, Sonali and Christopher R. Way (2004), "The Correlates of Nuclear Proliferation," *Journal of Conflict Resolution*, 48(6), 859–85.

Skaperdas, Stergios (1992), "Cooperation, Conflict, and Power in the Absence of Property Rights," *American Economic Review*, 82(4), 720–39.

(1996), "Contest Success Functions," *Economic Theory*, 7(2), 283–90.

(2006), "Bargaining versus Fighting," *Defence and Peace Economics*, 17(6), 657–76.

Skaperdas, Stergios and Constantinos Syropoulos (2002), "Insecure Property and the Efficiency of Exchange," *Economic Journal*, 112(476), 133–46.

Slantchev, Branislav L. (2004), "How Initiators End Their Wars: The Duration of Warfare and the Terms of Peace," *American Journal of Political Science*, 48(4), 813–29.

Slim, Hugo (2007), *Killing Civilians: Method, Madness and Morality in War* (London: Hurst & Company).

Slovic, Paul, Daniel Västfjäll, Robin Gregory, and Kimberly G. Olson (2016), "Valuing Lives You Might Save: Understanding Psychic Numbing in the Face of Genocide," in Charles H. Anderton and Jurgen Brauer (eds.), *Economic Aspects of Genocides, Other Mass Atrocities, and Their Prevention* (New York: Oxford University Press), 613–38.

Small Arms Survey (2007), *Guns and the City* (Cambridge: Cambridge University Press).

(2013), "Captured and Counted: Illicit Weapons in Mexico and the Philippines," (www.smallarmssurvey.org/fileadmin/docs/A-Yearbook/2013/en/Small-Arms-Survey-2013-Chapter-12-EN.pdf. Accessed: May 10, 2017).

(2017), "Producers," (www.smallarmssurvey.org/weapons-and-markets/producers.html. Accessed: May 10, 2017).

Small, Deborah A., George Loewenstein, and Paul Slovic (2007), "Sympathy and Callousness: The Impact of Deliberative Thought on Donations to Identifiable and Statistical Victims," *Organizational Behavior and Human Decision Processes*, 102(2), 143–53.

Smith, Adam [1776] (1976), *The Wealth of Nations* (Chicago: University of Chicago Press).

Smith, Carter F., Jeff Rush, and Catherine E. Burton (2013), "Street Gangs, Organized Crime Groups, and Terrorists: Differentiating Criminal Organizations," *Investigative Sciences Journal*, 5(1), 1–18.

Smith-Spark, Laura and Juliet Perry (2017), "What We Know about Syria's Chemical Weapons," (www.cnn.com/2017/04/05/middleeast/syria-sarin-chemical-weapons-explainer/index.html. Accessed: October 26, 2017).

Solomon, Binyam (2004), "NATO Burden Sharing Revisited," *Defence and Peace Economics*, 15(3), 251–58.

(2007), "Political Economy of Peacekeeping," in Todd Sandler and Keith Hartley (eds.), *Handbook of Defense Economics, Volume 2* (New York: Elsevier), 741–74.

Solomon, Chris (2015), "Economics of the AK-47," *Global Risk Insights*, 27 October (https://intpolicydigest.org/2015/10/27/economics-of-the-ak-47. Accessed: August 4, 2017).

Sorokin, Pitirim (1937), *Social and Cultural Dynamics* (New York: American Book Company).

Soudis, Dimitrios, Robert Inklaar, and Robbert Maseland (2016), "The Macroeconomic Toll of Genocide and the Sources of Economic Development," in Charles H. Anderton and Jurgen Brauer (eds.), *Economic Aspects of Genocides, Other Mass Atrocities, and Their Prevention* (New York: Oxford University Press), 125–39.

South Front (2017), "Island Building in South China Sea," (https://southfront.org/chinas-artificial-islands-south-china-sea-review/. Accessed: June 8, 2017).

Spencer, Jamie (2017), "60+ Social Networking Sites You Need to Know about in 2017," (https://makeawebsitehub.com/social-media-sites/. Accessed: September 22, 2017).

Sprecher, Christopher and Volker Krause (eds.) (2006), "Special Issue on Alliances," *Journal of Peace Research*, 43(4), 363–502.

Staniland, Paul (2014), *Networks of Rebellion: Explaining Insurgent Cohesion and Collapse* (Ithaca: Cornell University Press).

Stanton, Gregory H. (2016), "The Ten Stages of Genocide," (http://genocidewatch.net /genocide-2/8-stages-of-genocide/. Accessed: January 8, 2017).

Staub, Ervin (1993), "The Psychology of Bystanders, Perpetrators, and Heroic Helpers," *International Journal of Intercultural Relations*, 17(3), 315–41.

Stiglitz, Joseph E. and Linda J. Bilmes (2012), "Estimating the Costs of War: Methodological Issues, with Applications to Iraq and Afghanistan," in Michelle R. Garfinkel and Stergios Skaperdas (eds.), *The Oxford Handbook of the Economics of Peace and Conflict* (New York: Oxford University Press), 275–317.

Stockholm International Peace Research Institute (various years), *SIPRI Yearbook* (New York: Oxford University Press).

Stockholm International Peace Research Institute (2018), "SIPRI Military Expenditure Database," (www.sipri.org/databases/milex. Accessed: May 7, 2018).

Stoll, Richard J. (2017), "To Arms, To Arms: What Do We Know about Arms Races?" *Oxford Research Encyclopedia of Politics* (http://politics.oxfordre.com/view/10 .1093/acrefore/9780190228637.001.0001/acrefore-9780190228637-e-350. Accessed: November 1, 2017).

Straus, Scott (2006), *The Order of Genocide* (Ithaca: Cornell University Press).
  (2008), "The Historiography of the Rwandan Genocide," in Dan Stone (ed.) *The Historiography of Genocide* (New York: Palgrave Macmillan), 517–542.

Streich, Philip and Jack S. Levy (2016), "Information, Commitment, and the Russo-Japanese War of 1904–1905," *Foreign Policy Analysis*, 12(4), 489–511.

Tan, Andrew T. H. (2015), *The Arms Race in Asia: Trends, Causes and Implications* (New York: Routledge).

Tarar, Ahmer (2006), "Diversionary Incentives and the Bargaining Approach to War," *International Studies Quarterly*, 50(1), 169–88.

Taussig, F. W. (1920), "Germany's Reparation Payments," *American Economic Review: Papers and Proceedings*, 10(1), 33–49

Taylor, James G. (1983), *Lanchester Models of Warfare*, Volumes 1 and 2 (Arlington: Operations Research Society of America).

Taylor, John B. and Akila Weerapana (2012), *Principles of Macroeconomics*, 7th edn. (Boston: Houghton Mifflin).

Tellis, Ashley J., Thomas S. Szayna, and James A. Winnefeld (1997), *Anticipating Ethnic Conflict* (Santa Monica: Rand).

Tezcür, Güneş M. (2016), "Ordinary People, Extraordinary Risks: Participation in an Ethnic Rebellion," *American Political Science Review*, 110(2), 247–64.

Themnér, Lotta (2017), "UCDP/PRIO Armed Conflict Dataset Codebook, Version 17.1," (http://ucdp.uu.se/downloads/ucdpprio/ucdp-prio-acd-171.pdf. Accessed: August 25, 2017).

Thies, Cameron G. and David Sobek (2010), "War, Economic Development, and Political Development in the Contemporary International System," *International Studies Quarterly*, 54(1), 267–87.

Thompson, William R. (2001), "Identifying Rivals and Rivalries in World Politics," *International Studies Quarterly*, 45(4), 557–86.

Thyne, Clayton (2012), "Information, Commitment, and Intra-War Bargaining: The Effect of Governmental Constraints on Civil War Duration," *International Studies Quarterly*, 56(2), 307–21.

Tir, Jaroslav (2010), "Territorial Diversion: Diversionary Theory of War and Territorial Conflict," *Journal of Politics*, 72(2), 413–25.

Tkach, Benjamin (2017), "Private Military and Security Companies, Contract Structure, Market Competition, and Violence In Iraq," *Conflict Management and Peace Science*, https://doi.org/10.1177/0738894217702516.

Toft, Monica Duffy (2002), "Indivisible Territory, Geographic Concentration, and Ethnic War," *Security Studies*, 12(2), 82–119.

(2006), "Issue Indivisibility and Time Horizons as Rationalist Explanations for War," *Security Studies*, 15(1), 34–69.

(2014), "Territory and War," *Journal of Peace Research*, 51(2), 185–98.

Töngür, Ünal and Adem Yavuz Elveren (2016), "The Impact of Military Spending and Income Inequality on Economic Growth in Turkey, *Defence and Peace Economics*, 27(3), 433–52.

Totten, Samuel (ed.) (2004), *Teaching about Genocide: Issues, Approaches, and Resources* (Greenwich: Information Age Publishing).

Triandafyllidou, Anna (ed.) (2015), *Routledge Handbook of Immigration and Refugee Studies* (New York: Routledge).

Tu, Anthony (2017), *Chemical and Biological Weapons and Terrorism* (Boca Raton: CRC Press).

Ulfelder, Jay (2017), "ulfelder/earlywarningproject-statrisk-replication," (https://github .com/ulfelder/earlywarningproject-statrisk-replication. Accessed: December 11, 2017).

(2018), "The Trouble with Combining, or Why I'm Not Touting the Global Peace Index," (https://dartthrowingchimp.wordpress.com/2012/06/12/the-trouble-with-combining-or-why-im-not-touting-the-global-peace-index/. Accessed: February 19, 2018).

Ulfelder, Jay and Benjamin Valentino (2008), "Assessing Risks of State-Sponsored Mass Killing," Working Paper (http://papers.ssrn.com/sol3/papers.cfm?abstract_id=1703426. Accessed: February 1, 2018).

Ullah, Anayat, Karim Khan, and Hamid Mahmood (2017), "Understanding the Nexus between Conflict, Displacement, and Schooling: A Case Study of IDPs in Pakistan," *Asian Journal of Peacebuilding*, 5(1), 155–68.

United Nations (1969), *Chemical and Bacteriological (Biological) Weapons and the Effects of Their Possible Use* (New York: United Nations).

(2016), "United Nations Small Arms Review Conference," (www.un.org/events/smallarms2006/faq.html. Accessed: July 18, 2016).

(2018), "Definitions: Genocide," (www.un.org/en/genocideprevention/genocide .html. Accessed: February 1, 2018).

United Nations High Commissioner for Refugees (2006a), *Helping Refugees: An Introduction to UNHCR* (Geneva: UNHCR Media Relations and Public Information Service).

(2006b), *Internally Displaced People: Questions & Answers* (Geneva: UNHCR Media Relations and Public Information Service).

(2017), "UNHCR Statistical Yearbook 2016," (www.unhcr.org/en-us/statistics/country/5a8ee0387/unhcr-statistical-yearbook-2016-16th-edition.html. Accessed: April 11, 2018).

(2018), "Stories," (http://stories.unhcr.org/refugees. Accessed: May 9, 2018).

United Nations Office for Disarmament Affairs (2017), "Programme of Action on Small Arms and Its International Tracing Instrument," (www.un.org/disarmament/convarms/salw/programme-of-action/. Accessed: October 25, 2017).

United Nations Office at Geneva (2016), "Anti-Personnel Landmines Convention," (www.unog.ch/80256EE600585943/(httpPages)/CA826818C8330D2BC12571800 04B1B2E?OpenDocument. Accessed: July 25, 2016).

United Nations Register on Conventional Arms (2016), "The Global Reported Arms Trade: The UN Register of Conventional Arms," (www.un-register.org /Background/Index.aspx. Accessed: July 26, 2016).

United States Department of Homeland Security (2017), "What Is Human Trafficking?," (www.dhs.gov/blue-campaign/what-human-trafficking. Accessed: April 12, 2017).

United States Government Accountability Office (2006), "Human Trafficking: Better Data, Strategy, and Reporting Needed to Enhance U.S. Antitrafficking Efforts Abroad," GAO-06–825, US Government Accountability Office, Washington, DC.

United States Holocaust Memorial Museum (2017), "Ministry of Propaganda and Public Enlightenment, " (www.ushmm.org/wlc/en/article.php?ModuleId= 10008224. Accessed: December 28, 2017).

Uppsala Conflict Data Program (2016), "UCDP Non-State Conflict Dataset," (http:// ucdp.uu.se/downloads/. Accessed: May 10, 2017).

  (2017), "Definitions," (www.pcr.uu.se/research/ucdp/definitions/#Battle-related _deaths. Accessed: August 1, 2017).

Ureste, Manu (2015), "A Journey Through Corrupt Military Checkpoints in Mexico," (www.insightcrime.org/news/analysis/military-checkpoints-corruption-mexico/. Accessed: June 26, 2018).

Vahabi, Mehrdad (2015), *The Political Economy of Predation: Manhunting and the Economics of Escape* (New York: Cambridge University Press).

Valentino, Benjamin (2004), *Final Solutions: Mass Killing and Genocide in the 20th Century* (Ithaca: Cornell University Press).

Valentino, Benjamin, Paul Huth, and Dylan Balch-Lindsay (2004), "'Draining the Sea': Mass Killing and Guerrilla Warfare," *International Organization*, 58(2), 375–407.

Van Evera, Stephen (1999), *Causes of War: Power and the Roots of Conflict* (Ithaca: Cornell University Press).

Vanian, Jonathan (2016), "GM Is Using the Cloud to Connect Its Factory Robots," (http:// fortune.com/2016/01/30/gm-cloud-factory-robots-fanuc/. Accessed: October 4, 2017).

Vasquez, John A. (ed.) (2000), *What Do We Know about War?* (New York: Rowman & Littlefield).

  (ed.) (2012), *What Do We Know about War?* 2nd edn. (New York: Rowman & Littlefield).

Vasquez, John A. and Ashlea Rundlett (2016), "Alliances as a Necessary Condition of Multiparty Wars," *Journal of Conflict Resolution*, 60(8), 1395–418.

Verwimp, Philip (2005), "An Economic Profile of Peasant Perpetrators of Genocide: Micro-level Evidence from Rwanda," *Journal of Development Economics*, 77(2), 297–323.

Verwimp, Philip, Patricia Justino, and Tilman Brück (eds.) (2009), "Special Issue: The Analysis of Conflict: A Micro-Level Perspective," *Journal of Peace Research*, 46(3), 307–460.

Vojnović, Milan (2016), *Contest Theory: Incentive Mechanisms and Ranking Methods* (New York: Cambridge University Press).

Wallace, Michael D. (1979), "Arms Races and Escalation: Some New Evidence," *Journal of Conflict Resolution*, 23(1), 3–16.

Waller, James (2007), *Becoming Evil: How Ordinary People Commit Genocide and Mass Killing*, 2nd edn. (New York: Oxford University Press).

  (2016), *Confronting Evil: Engaging Our Responsibility to Prevent Genocide* (New York: Oxford University Press).

Walter, Barbara F. (2009), *Reputation and Civil War: Why Separatist Conflicts Are So Violent* (New York: Cambridge University Press).

Watkins, Derek (2015), "What China Has Been Building in the South China Sea," *The New York Times* (www.nytimes.com/interactive/2015/07/30/world/asia/what-china-has-been-building-in-the-south-china-sea.html?_r=0. Accessed: December 27, 2016).

Weinstein, Jeremy M. (2007), *Inside Rebellion: The Politics of Insurgent Violence* (New York: Cambridge University Press).

Weiss, Herbert K. (1966), "Combat Models and Historical Data: The U.S. Civil War," *Operations Research*, 14(5), 759–90.

Wennmann, Achim (2011), *The Political Economy of Peacemaking* (London: Routledge).

  (2018), "Peace Processes, Economic Recovery and Development Agencies," in Madhav Joshi and Peter Wallensteen (eds.), *Understanding Quality Peace: Peacebuilding after Civil War* (London: Routledge), chapter 7.

Wikipedia (2017), "Six Degrees of Separation," (https://en.wikipedia.org/wiki/Six_Degrees_of_Separation_(play). Accessed: October 30, 2017).

Wilson, Clay (2007), *Network Centric Operations: Background and Oversight Issues for Congress* (www.dtic.mil/dtic/tr/fulltext/u2/a466624.pdf. Accessed: October 3, 2017).

Wilson, Maya, David R. Davis, and Amanda Murdie (2016), "The View from the Bottom: Networks of Conflict Resolution Organizations and International Peace," *Journal of Peace Research*, 53(3), 442–58.

Wimmer, Andreas, Lars-Erik Cederman, and Brian Min (2009), "Ethnic Politics and Armed Conflict: A Configurational Analysis of a New Global Data Set," *American Sociological Review*, 74(2), 316–37.

Witmer, Frank D. W., Andrew M. Linke, John O'Loughlin, Andrew Gettelman, and Arlene Laing (2017), "Subnational Violent Conflict Forecasts for Sub-Saharan Africa, 2015–65, Using Climate-Sensitive Models," *Journal of Peace Research*, 54 (2), 175–92.

Wittman, Donald (1979), "How a War Ends: A Rational Model Approach," *Journal of Conflict Resolution*, 23(4), 743–63.

Wolchover, Natalie (2012), "What Is the Future of Computers?" *LiveScience*, September 10, (www.livescience.com/23074-future-computers.html. Accessed: August 24, 2016).

Wolford, Scott, Dan Reiter, and Clifford J. Carrubba (2011), "Information, Commitment, and War," *Journal of Conflict Resolution*, 55(4), 556–79.

Wolfson, Murray (1985), "Notes on Economic Warfare," *Conflict Management and Peace Science*, 8(2), 1–20.

(1987), "A Theorem on the Existence of Zones of Initiation and Deterrence in Intriligator-Brito Arms Race Models," *Public Choice*, 54(3), 291–97.

Wood, Garrett (2018), "The Enemy Votes: Weapons Improvisation and Bargaining Failure," *The Economics of Peace and Security Journal*, 13(1), 35–42.

Wood, Reed M. (2010), "Rebel Capability and Strategic Violence against Civilians," *Journal of Peace Research*, 47(5), 601–14.

Wood, Reed M. and Jacob D. Kathman (2015), "Competing for the Crown: Inter-rebel Competition and Civilian Targeting in Civil War," *Political Research Quarterly*, 68 (1), 167–79.

World Bank (2018), "World Development Indicators," (http://databank.worldbank .org/data/home.aspx. Accessed: May 7, 2018).

World Military Expenditures and Arms Transfers (2017), "World Military Expenditures and Arms Transfers 2017," (www.state.gov/t/avc/rls/rpt/wmeat/ 2017/index.htm. Accessed: April 17, 2018).

Wright, Quincy (1942), *A Study of War*, Volumes 1 and 2 (Chicago: University of Chicago Press).

Wright, Thorin M. and Paul F. Diehl (2016), "Unpacking Territorial Disputes: Domestic Political Influences and War," *Journal of Conflict Resolution*, 60(4), 645–69.

Yilgör, Metehan, Erdal Tanas Karagöl, and Çiğdem Ateş Saygili (2014), "Panel Causality Analysis Between Defence Expenditure and Economic Growth in Developed Countries," *Defence and Peace Economics*, 25(2), 193–203.

Young, Helen and Lisa Goldman (eds.) (2015), *Livelihoods, Natural Resources, and Post-Conflict Peacebuilding* (New York: Routledge).

Zech, Steven T. and Michael Gabbay (2016), "Social Network Analysis in the Study of Terrorism and Insurgency: From Organization to Politics," *International Studies Review*, 18(2), 214–43.

Zeigler, Sean M. (2016), "Competitive Alliances and Civil War Recurrence," *International Studies Quarterly*, 60(1), 24–37.

Zeitzoff, Thomas (2017), "How Social Media Is Changing Conflict," *Journal of Conflict Resolution*, 61(9), 1970–91.

Zeitzoff, Thomas (2018), "Does Social Media Influence Conflict? Evidence from the 2012 Gaza Conflict," *Journal of Conflict Resolution*, 62(1), 29–63.

Zenou, Yves (2016), "Key Players," in Yann Bramoullé, Andrea Galeotti, and Brian Rogers (eds.), *The Oxford Handbook of the Economics of Networks* (New York: Oxford University Press), 244–74.

Zetter, Kim (2014), *Countdown to Zero Day: Stuxnet and the Launch of the World's First Digital Weapon* (New York: Crown).

Zhukov, Yuri M. (2016), "On the Logistics of Violence: Evidence from Stalin's Great Terror, Nazi-Occupied Belarus, and Modern African Civil Wars," in Charles H. Anderton and Jurgen Brauer (eds.), *Economic Aspects of Genocides, Other Mass Atrocities, and Their Prevention* (New York: Oxford University Press), 399–424.

Zimbardo, Philip G. (1971), "The Power and Pathology of Imprisonment," Congressional Record, Serial No. 15, 1971-10-25. Hearings before Subcommittee No. 3, of the Committee on the Judiciary, House of Representatives, Ninety-Second Congress, First Session on Corrections, Part II, Prisons, Prison Reform and Prisoner's Rights: California (Washington: U.S. Government Printing Office).

Author Index

Subject Index